S0-BFB-343

One Way Up
Wall Street

THE FRED ALGER STORY

One Way Up
Wall Street

The Fred Alger Story

by
Dilip K. Mirchandani

FRED ALGER MANAGEMENT, INC.

Copyright © 1999 by Fred Alger Management, Inc.
All rights reserved
Printed and bound in Canada

ISBN 0-9670128-0-5

Produced by James Charlton Associates
Photo research by Joan Scafarello
Designed by Virginia Wells Blaker

Photo Credits:
Courtesy of Fred Alger: pp. 19, 34, 46, 52, 53, 62, 151, 164, 187, 311, 441
Courtesy of David Alger: pp. 49, 50, 56, 59, 228, 233, 241
Courtesy of Nicole Alger: pp. 23, 115
Courtesy of Fred Alger Management, Inc.: pp. 16, 124, 138, 144, 158, 210, 221, 259, 264, 275, 334, 347, 352, 366, 373, 388, 398, 405, 419, 431, 449, 452
Courtesy of Fred Alger Management, Inc./Photo by ©Steve Skoll, 1995: pp. 206, 410, 434
Courtesy of Fred Alger Management, Inc./Photo by Henry Wolf: pp. 154, 171
Courtesy of Fred Alger Management, Inc. and Rosemary Kiernan: p. 236
Courtesy of Fred Alger Management, Inc. and the Luring Augustine Gallery: p. 316
Courtesy of Fred Alger Management, Inc./BBC: pp. 129, 146
Courtesy of Fred Alger Management, Inc./CNBC: p. 293
Courtesy of Fred Alger Management, Inc. and Das Wertpapier: p. 325
Courtesy of Fred Alger Management, Inc./The White House: p. 301
MTU Archives and Copper County Historical Collections, Michigan Technological University: p. 81
Courtesy of the Burton Historical Collection, Detroit Public Library: pp. 54, 55, 72, 88, 97, 98, 103, 106
Frances Boyer Mead: p. 60
Reprinted from the August 18, 1986, issue of *BusinessWeek* by special permission. ©1986 by McGraw Hill Companies: p. 28
Reprinted courtesy of *The Boston Globe:* p. 178
By permission of *Dow Jones Investment Advisor:* p. 452
Copyrighted material is reprinted with permission from: *Institutional Investor*, 488 Madison Avenue, New York, NY 10022: pp. 39, 255
Ernest Sisto/*New York Times Pictures,* The New York Times Company, 229 West 43rd Street, 9th Fl, NYC 10036: p. 197

Acknowledgments

For this work I must give thanks to all those who contributed through interviews to the process of recalling the history of the Alger family and company.

Chief among them were Alger employees, past and present, who spoke with candor and attention to detail, notably Rosemary Kiernan, Lisa Gregg, Jim Connelly, and Isabella Coari. Other current employees who belong on this list are Ginger Risco, Jeanette Borras, Jim Barbi, Joe Maida, Joe Pakenham, John Messina, John Raspitha, Mike DiMeglio, Monica Smith, Morty Frankel, Ray Pfeister, Ron Curtis, Ron Reel, Ron Tartaro, and Seilai Khoo.

Special gratitude goes to former partners George Boggio, Irwin Schwartz, and Bill Scheerer for digging deep into their memories and providing an accurate picture of the firm's early years.

Former Alger analysts and managers gave life to the company's progress through their anecdotes: Bob Emerson, Bob Rescoe, Bruce Levine, Chris Schmeisser, Lavaun Vawter, Rob Lyon, Robert Friedlander, Shelton Swei, Tom Weil, and Will Stewart. Alger Fund board members Arthur Dubow, John Sargent, Nathan St. Amand, Ray Merritt, and Steve O'Neil also contributed valuable recollections.

Through intimate reflection on their relationship with Fred over the years, his friends and associates were especially helpful in enabling me to reach what I hope is a nuanced understanding of his character and philosophy: Chat Hickox, Jerry Tsai, Harry Bruce Levine, Jan Bailey, Joe Reich, John Cleland, John Howard, John Jennings, Lester Colbert, Leszek James, Martica Clapp, Frank Hunnewell, Michael Pochna, Ray Dirks, Richard Thompson, and Sam Clapp. I'm grateful also to Fred's sister Suzy and daughter Hilary for their insights.

Within the firm, two people deserve special recognition: Greg Duch, for his diligent involvement in helping me get the straight facts about the workings of the company, and Fred's secretary, Dolores Costa, for her liaison work during the course of the project.

Kathryn McGrath must be thanked for discussing her part in the SEC's case against Alger. And Manjeet Kripalani of BusinessWeek should be noted for introducing me to Fred Alger.

Outside the firm, information was provided by Joni Hamilton and Michelle Gamiao of the Investment Company Institute in Washington, D.C.; William Spiers at the BBC's News & Current Affairs Department in London; Scott MacDonald of Crain Communications Inc. in Chicago; David Koeppel of Koeppel &

Koeppel, 26 Broadway; Lewis J. Cowan of Silverstein Properties, 120 Broadway; Margaret Towers of Alan Towers Associates, Inc.; and Mark D. Tomasko from the Investment Counsel Association of America, Inc. in New York.

In uncovering the Alger family history, invaluable research assistance and access to primary source materials were provided by David L. Poremba, assistant manager of the Burton Historical Collection at the Detroit Public Library, and Robert S. Cox, curator of manuscripts, and John Harriman of the William L. Clements Library at the University of Michigan. A great deal of Russell A. Alger's story was derived from *The Life of Russell Alexander Alger, 1836–1907* by Rodney Ellis Bell, his 1975 doctoral dissertation at the University of Michigan.

I owe a large debt to Hudson Mead, whose infectious enthusiasm about the Alger forebears helped me to cast the proper historical light on their stories. I thank him also for carefully reviewing and correcting my manuscript in those sections.

Of course, my greatest appreciation belongs to the Alger brothers, Fred and David, who commissioned this work. Fred Alger, for his courage in entrusting me with his story and for his patience while I developed the manuscript, and David, for his thoughtful and incisive articulation of key situations. Through their opening up and giving me complete access to private papers and company documents, I was able gain a unique awareness of their business world and deliver a more faithful rendering of the events in their lives.

Finally, credit must be given to this book's editor, Kitty Ross, whose polish and insight contributed greatly in transforming the sprawling original manuscript into a more focused and improved composition.

—DILIP K. MIRCHANDANI

CONTENTS

Foreword

FRED ALGER is an original thinker. Not simply a man who draws unusual conclusions from other people's data, he is, rather, an individual who confronts the world with no preconceptions, as if newly born. Fred sees the commonplace with a sense of wonder and, from the resulting freshness of view, comes up with truly original insights.

This book reflects Fred Alger in numerous ways. The firm that he built has gotten to where it is by following its own unique path. It has not been a copier but an originator. In securities analysis, for instance, it has combined the technical with the fundamental in unusual ways to achieve early and acute insight on trends and values. It has been a maverick in relying only on that research and building its own execution capability, thereby freeing it from Street "wisdom" and commission sharing. And finally, amidst all of this originality, it has adhered to a military-like discipline that enables these systems to function smoothly and produce superior investment results.

Of course, as in the case with all originals, Fred has had his share of mistakes. While the tried and true may not produce spectacular results, it often avoids the pitfalls attendant on experiment. This book also reflects those aspects, frankly discussing some of the episodes and events that have made Fred controversial.

I have been a friend of Fred's and been associated with him as a director of Alger company funds for over twenty-five years. I have shared with him many of the ups and downs of his long and illustrious career on Wall Street. This book brilliantly illuminates that career—one might say that odyssey—and the factors, both personal and professional, that have gone into it. It is must reading for anyone interested in the workings of the investment business and the methods created by an original mind to deal with its pressures and opportunities.

—STEPHEN E. O'NEIL

INTRODUCTION

SEVERAL YEARS AGO a veteran financial journalist stopped me at a social event and inquired, "Is Fred Alger one of the good guys?" He had heard I was writing a book about him and was mindful of Fred's and the firm's consistently negative press. I replied that I couldn't answer the question yet but hoped that through my research I would arrive at the truth.

After three years of examining and writing about Fred's life and the rise of his company, I am confident in my conclusion that Fred Alger deserves to be observed as one of the most challenging and memorable personalities ever to work on Wall Street. The evidence shows that the Alger company, which evolved around the strength of Fred's character, has delivered one of the most enviable and enduring records in the financial world. Moreover, it has, over the course of 35 years, significantly contributed to the ideas and events that have shaped the U.S. investment business.

By itself, the story of how Fred Alger built his company makes a compelling tale, involving innovative commercial ventures, brilliant financial management, bold investment strategies, and financial titans. But Fred's saga is also an authentic American success story, rooted in the competitive spirit, about surviving difficulties through determination, persistence and intelligence, and overcoming obstacles through mostly nonconformist solutions.

In the 1960s Fred pioneered the approach to aggressive money management that led to his celebrity. Observing his rare and daring financial instincts in those days, a respected colleague described him as "one of the truly brilliant investment minds of our time."

During the seventies and eighties Fred gathered some of the brightest analytical minds in the country and laid the foundation for a financial enterprise, based on corporate integration, which advanced by stubborn adherence to a unique brand of investment research and growth-stock investing.

When Fred decided to offer mutual funds in the eighties, he did so in a way that shook up the industry and nearly undid the company. Before he retired in the nineties the company consolidated its market position by developing novel business strategies and reinvigorating its message of patient, long-term investing.

An important though little-known aspect of the Alger story is the profound contribution of his family to American political and financial history dating back to the Civil War. This background provides the context for Fred's development as a financial entrepreneur.

And so this book, though conceived as a way to chronicle the firm's deeds through three decades, was never intended to be just a promotional work to pump up more business on Wall Street. It is not a one-sided or uncritical examination of the Alger heritage, and has not been abridged to evade the truth or spare the feelings of its participants. By describing key management decisions and investment deals, I've tried to reveal the unique traits that set Fred's company apart from thousands of other money management firms. I've made an effort to be forthright and unsentimental in describing the encounters between Fred and the people he worked with.

My purpose has been simply to right the record. In giving Fred's account of controversial situations, much has been left to speculation. The reader can determine for him- or herself whether Fred is one of the good guys. Viewed either as hero or anti-hero, Fred Alger has always confounded his critics and damned his detractors. Yet he must be admired and respected for his personal and professional accomplishments, for artfully directing his company's course against the backdrop of a burgeoning information culture with rapidly changing financial values and social goals.

As intrinsic to the company's success as Fred's investment philosophy and drive have been the partners and employees who helped make his vision a reality. Their stories are threads in the weave of Alger's corporate fabric and essential to its tapestry.

In attempting to capture the exuberant spirit of working in the financial markets, I have sifted through countless company documents, personal files, press clippings, and oral recording. I believe that many of the curious and colorful episodes uncovered in the process deserve to be inscribed in any authoritative account of American business history, and I am grateful to have culled them before they were pushed too far back into distant memory.

It is rare for any company, especially a private one, to allow access to its innermost reaches in the way that Fred Alger has done. I see this not only as further proof (if one was needed) of the firm's uniqueness, but as a sign of the firm's essential self-confidence and growing influence.

In my mind the Alger story is relevant and meaningful because Fred and his firm have made an important difference in America's financial life. As this book becomes part of Fred's legacy on Wall Street, my hope is that it proves to be instructive, informative, and ultimately enjoyable.

1 🙰

New York Farewell

F RED ALGER is saying good-bye to Wall Street. Tonight, at his firm's traditional Christmas dinner, he is closing a circle around three exuberant and accomplished decades as head of one of America's most unique and successful investment firms by ceding power to his younger brother, David.

It is December 9, 1994. Inside the Lotos Club, employees of Fred Alger & Company and their spouses are clustered at the foot of the rounded staircase leading to the elegant dining hall. One by one they are drawn up the receiving line for friendly handshakes and holiday greetings from the troika of Fred, who founded the company, David, now the firm's president, and Greg Duch, its chief financial officer.

David is joined by his wife, Josie. Greg's wife, Eileen, stands beside him. Fred, however, is solitary. Absent from the tableau is Eleanor, his wife for over 30 years, whom he's battling in a divorce.

Fred is bent on knowing his people by their first names. So much that he practices the names of new employees from a phonetic list sent to his office before the affair. Tonight, Jeanette Borras, a vice president and account administrator, has been conscripted to coach Fred if he forgets a name or fails to recognize a face.

As always, Fred is charming and thoughtful, his gaze, penetrating. David is routinely friendly and high-spirited. Greg is very much in his role as the firm's top officer who is not a family member.

Name tags offering the evening's seating arrangements rest on the Steinway at the top of the stairs. These are quietly dispensed by Dolores Costa, Fred's secretary for eight years.

As the procession reaches its end, Fred throws a knowing nod at Clarina Notz, a new research associate in the company and niece of a former Swiss business connection.

The Christmas dinners have always been Fred's pleasure. He labored over them like a boy before a prom date, doting on every detail, including the seating chart. New employees normally sit with either Fred or David or one of the company's senior officers. Formal invitations are sent to all employees. Attendance is de rigueur. Dates are not welcome. Only one employee ever successfully challenged the mandatory rule of attendance. "Barbara Glazier never came to these things because she wasn't allowed to bring her boyfriend, Bobby," confided old-timer Isabella Coari. Usually the dinners are held on the first Friday in December.

Dolores is quick to correct new employees: "This is a Christmas dinner, not a Christmas party." For the last few years she's been the one who drew up the seating chart, then submitted it for Fred's approval.

This old-fashioned receiving line would be out of character at any other financial powerhouse. But it clearly has a significant place at Fred Alger. Sober formalism may not hold sway in today's relaxed social atmosphere, but then Fred Alger and his company have never followed the herd or succumbed to trends. If anything, the dinners symbolize how Fred has done things differently on Wall Street.

Fred Alger charged Wall Street in the sixties as an early champion of aggressive money management and one of the first apostles of growth-stock investing. As a brash young analyst, his spectacular mutual-fund performance brought him quick stardom. The company he started from a threadbare one-man office on Pine Street in Lower Manhattan, with discarded furniture and a capital foundation of merely $3,000, has since swelled in value greater than $100 million and earned him a large personal fortune.

The core of Alger's investment philosophy, which has remained unchanged from the start, is that rapidly growing companies provide the best stock price appreciation. Fred's favored firms exhibit high unit-volume growth—that is, the capacity to produce more products or services, not simply higher sales, in an expanding marketplace—or deliver new and improved services or products in response to increasing demand. They also exhibit a positive life-cycle change, such as a corporate restructuring or new management.

The search for vital, creative companies that match these criteria is conducted in an intense, pure-research environment that is fiercely challenging, peculiarly combative and genuinely idiosyncratic—just like Fred.

At seven, it's cocktails and canapés in the club's library with its famous sculpted marble fireplace. While winter's bluster bangs hard against the French Renaissance building on East 66th and Fifth—home to one of America's oldest literary clubs since 1947—inside excitement mixes with anxiety. Tonight is special not only as the thirtieth anniversary of the company but because the firm's three original partners are attending as chief guests. Yet the buzz is all about Fred leaving his company—for good.

For many employees the prospect of Fred's possible retirement is viewed with disbelief. How could he ever let go of the firm which bears his name, was built in his image, and operates as an extension of his personality? He'll never do it.

For those who have grown up with the firm, there is a sense of abandonment and nervousness about the future. How will the company thrive without his personal leadership qualities—upright character, intense focus and headstrong perseverance? Others anticipate a fresh spirit from David, who will finally be stepping out of his elder brother's long shadow and taking center stage. Truth be told, David was already in charge. On the investment side, he has been dictating the portfolio decisions for years.

The rumor is that the only promises Fred extracted from David when he handed over custody of the firm were that his office remain untouched and that his chauffeur, Jerry DeVito, and his secretary, Dolores, would not be terminated.

For Fred, as for his company, self-reliance is the operative paradigm. The Alger firm doesn't count on Wall Street's sell-side brokerage houses for its research but has constructed its own proprietary intelligence system for uncovering stocks. It trades from its own brokerage firm, retaining commissions for funding its research arm. For the sake of improved efficiency, the expenses of stock clearing and transfer are also managed in-house. Costs are further controlled by maintaining the back room and sales offices in New Jersey and owning its own building in New York's financial district. Even when it needs to recruit new analysts, the firm relies on itself. Analysts Resources, a premier Wall Street headhunting firm, is owned by Fred Alger. Virtually all of the details and requirements of producing and delivering its investment products, be it research, pension, insurance, trust or mutual fund account management, are kept in its control.

The success of Fred Alger Management, or any one of several tightly integrated firms controlled by Fred, is unmistakably a consequence of his far-reaching strategic outlook and his ability to implement that vision. As Fred explains it, "The dream was to build a company that would last forever, that is not locked to a particular capital asset, that can invest its own assets in a very well-diversified, conservative way so that it can continue to grow and be in a position to educate and take care of generations of Algers in the future."

"Wall Street Big Eyes Swiss Bliss," screeched the headline on page six of the New York Post. The article about Fred sent the entire office aflutter. That was in October 1994. The gossip column needled Fred for a plan to surrender his American citizenship and move to Switzerland to avoid taxes and, worse, push through a settlement in his divorce. It dished about his wealth and personal life, guessing wrong on both.

Soon after that Fred gathered his people around him in the office and assured

Fred Alger's investment philosophy and entrepreneurial spirit built one of the best-performing investment firms on Wall Street.

that any move he made would be best for the firm. The company was poised for its next big move. It was time for the next generation to carry the Alger banner. In this regard Jim Connelly, in charge of the firm's mutual funds, recalled Fred's departing notice: "I built the helicopter. Now it's up to you guys to fly it."

It was at the September Alger Fund board meeting a month earlier when Fred first unveiled his plan for leaving the country. To explain it, he traced the progress of his family's rich history. How his great-grandfather built an immense lumbering fortune, how his grandfather extended those investments to banking and the Packard Motor Car Company, and how his parents misspent their inheritance to the point that one day his mother told him that all the money was gone.

With the preservation of capital and his native conservatism at the base of his dynastic impulse, avoiding inheritance taxes and handing over to his children as much of his fortune as possible were simply the logical extensions of his original design to restore the family wealth. Living in Europe would certainly put him closer to the firm's mutual-fund operation in Germany, which started in 1993, and set the stage for a larger role in worldwide financial markets.

Fred's leaving was no great shock to Arthur Dubow, a longtime friend and

Alger Fund board member. "This is a planned transition," he said. "Fred's presence here is fading. David has really been managing the firm for the last several years. Fred had confidence that this move would not put the firm in jeopardy."

Former partner Irwin Schwartz observed that years earlier Fred was beginning to lose interest in parts of the business and tiring of its daily grind. "Fred never really got into the nitty-gritty of managing accounts. I think it bored him," he revealed. "Investment research was also beginning to tire him. Most of his time was spent in bringing his forward thinking to bear on the company."

Fred readily admitted that he turned over the research and portfolio-management authority to David because he was losing fortitude for those tasks. David and Fred had already paved the way for this transition and stifled any fallout from clients and investors.

Promptly at eight, gentle chimes sound for the guests to sit down to dinner. The table is set for a meal of Long Island duckling in a port-wine sauce served with wild rice; for dessert, chocolate truffle cake with raspberry and champagne sauces.

As much as Fred's leavetaking, what made this evening so memorable was the reunion with partners Bill Scheerer, George Boggio and Irwin Schwartz, who, with Fred as principal architect, built the firm from the ground up.

"Bill is the best thing that happened to me," Fred said emphatically. In sharp contrast to Fred's acerbic nature, Bill's genial, avuncular demeanor had a nourishing effect on the firm from the very beginning. As Fred's first employee in 1966, then his first partner, he brought stability and credibility to the firm at a time when Fred was unknown in the financial community. Bill was well liked on the Street and highly regarded as its premier oil analyst. He helped see the firm through tough markets in the mid-1970s resulting from the Arab oil embargo.

 Bill also had an extraordinary memory and judgment about stocks. As a diversion, Fred frequently ran down the names of stocks in the paper and tested Bill's knowledge of them. He always knew something important about each one.

"We had very complementary personalities. Bill was very steady, and I was forceful and high-strung. We were a great team together," Fred stressed.

George Boggio, the young CPA who did the firm's taxes, was Fred's next recruit, in January 1967. Although Fred needed him badly and they had come to terms months earlier, George was held up from joining the firm until Fred was satisfied that there was sufficient income to warrant the expense. That was Fred's way. He never assumed a cost which couldn't be supported by revenue. From the beginning the business was sustained by internal growth. No outside source ever added any capital to the firm.

George anchored the firm. He presided over the development of the clearing operation, the opening of the New Jersey office, and the purchase and renovation of its Wall Street headquarters at 75 Maiden Lane. He was the sergeant major for Fred's storm troopers. "George built up the business and ran it with an iron hand," said Fred. "To his credit, we hired an awfully good group of people, and he was a terrific role model for the firm's employees.

"I could turn over the entire administration of the company to him without a sleepless night. I always had a lot of things to worry about, but because of George, running the firm wasn't one of them."

For 20 years, starting in 1969, the unflappable, affable Irwin Schwartz was the soul of the firm. His chief contribution was setting up its highly efficient trading system and its network of $2 brokers which gave the firm an edge in executing stock transactions. That, in turn, served as a marketing hook which swung clients to the company's door.

Irwin was notorious for his contrarian plays and impeccable instincts for picking stocks. Buying and selling was never work for Irwin. Wall Street was just one big casino, and he was happiest at its table. In fact, it was this fondness for gambling that was responsible for the Christmas dinner tradition at Fred Alger.

Devotees of *Beat the Dealer*, Irwin and his wife, Geri, practiced card counting in their basement and regularly went on junkets to Las Vegas. Around Thanksgiving in 1972, as a lark, Fred gave him $500 dollars to play before one of those jaunts. Irwin doubled the money. The problem then became accounting for the winnings. George had no category for gambling loot. So why not throw a Christmas party?

Because Irwin won at 21, the first of these annual events, and many of the early parties, took place at the 21 Club. "We had a private room upstairs," said Irwin. "It was very casual." How this extremely informal event turned into a proper Christmas dinner was an outgrowth of Fred's thinking. "During the steep stock market declines of the mid-seventies, I wanted the parties to have a steadying effect, so they became more dignified," said Fred.

David Alger is the final plank in the stout pentagram that shaped the foundation of the company. As its director of research, he trained its energetic corps of analysts and led its investment teams. It was he who brought the firm into fluency with computers in the process of picking winning stocks. While David is intensely cerebral, like his brother, he also has a flair for dramatic prose and is often characterized by his volatile temper.

The mood of the dinner guests was celebratory for Fred and his former partners, as if relieved at the end of a long march or hard-won campaign.

As dinner progressed, memories of large and small events in the company's life swirled around the room. Many of the guests were caught up in reflection, each reveler topping the next with his or her favorite story.

Fred recalled that the night before Bill joined the firm a burglar had attempted

A playful moment with his miniature schnauzer, Luc, outside his home in Geneva.

a break-in, so when Bill turned up for work the next morning, the door to the office was still off its hinges. That same door was later a bane for Bill. Since the office was so small, whenever it opened, it banged into his desk.

It was lucky for Fred that Irwin hated to fight rush-hour traffic to get home to Bayonne, New Jersey, and so he often stayed late in the office. One night a researcher for an investment publication called up for answers to its annual survey. Since Irwin was alone in the office, he fielded the questions, one of which pertained to the size of its assets. "About $100 million," he replied, even though he knew the correct figure was closer to $80 to $90 million. With this quick thinking and evasive reply, Irwin subdued a major objection of potential investors that the company's assets had fallen beneath the century threshold. Said Irwin, "What I gave them is what they printed in the directory. After we got on that list, things started to roll. It was as simple as that."

Just before dessert Fred stood up to speak. He talked dryly about the firm and its accomplishments during the past year. If he had any doubts about his plans to move on, it was masked by his calm, reassuring delivery and the optimism served up with his message.

"Nineteen ninety-four was another good year," he started. Never mind that the markets were sloppy and the firm's performance was lackluster. Things had moved according to plan. In 1986, when he created the Alger mutual funds as a hedge against the vagaries of the tax-exempt pension business, they represented just 4% of the firm's assets under management. Today that percentage was hovering around 49%, and Fred projected it to rise to 66% within three years.

Even more promising was the expansion of the firm's distribution base to include 11 insurance companies, the addition of 5 financial planners, and the selling of Alger mutual funds in Germany. Gross operating revenues had jumped nearly 15% during the year. Fee income, management, and promotional assessments were at a record, and up 20%. Operating earnings before taxes climbed by a healthy 36.5%.

Approaching age 60, Fred wears his years lightly. Those who work with him are often awed by his intense intellectual curiosity and gravity-defying leaps of imagination in solving problems. By his own design, it seems, his run up Wall Street has often been provocative and controversial. His independent streak, often mistaken for arrogance, hasn't endeared him to the financial community, and he is often regarded with jealousy and suspicion. Though his desire for winning and enjoyment of success have been highly publicized, few realize how little those traits are connected with the desire to amass money.

It's far easier to respect Fred from a distance than to know him up close. His employees have learned that. For most of its years Fred guided his firm with a strong hand, following a management style embraced during his training in the Marine Reserves. One of the analysts explained the treatment like this: "He pays well, but you earn it." Daughter Hilary, who worked for him briefly, said, "He was hard on everybody. He wouldn't spare people when he was displeased. On the other hand, if he felt you did a great job, he would praise you to the stars. He had everyone's respect for that."

According to company legend, there was a two-year period when Fred used up a dozen or so secretaries. "You had to have just the right temperament for him," said Coari. Boggio was reminded of Wendy Furtado, one of three secretaries in the early days at the old Standard Oil building at 26 Broadway. She left for lunch and just never came back. He guessed she just had enough of Fred. She left a note pinned to her typewriter simply saying, "I hate long good-byes."

Despite his remoteness, Fred has the utmost confidence of his troops. Whether it was the company's uncertain shift into becoming a registered investment adviser, his strict methods of stock analysis or the difficult deadlines in setting up the back-office operations, Fred's people always upheld his leadership. Those who have survived his boot camp have gained immensely from the experience.

Fred dislikes interruptions. Some years back one of the waiters at the club persisted in serving coffee while Fred addressed the company. This upset him so that he ordered the server to leave the room. No Lotos waiter has since made that same mistake.

"Capital increased to nearly eighty-four million dollars, more than one million dollars per employee," Fred continued in his speech. "We are very strong financially."

Like the *Fantasticks* off-Broadway, Fred Alger's company is one of the longest-running successes on Wall Street. It has survived through seven presidential administrations, five recessions, two wars and eight bear markets. It's one of Fred's familiar refrains, and he's uniquely proud of this longevity.

Many of the firms on Wall Street, before and after him, have been forced into mergers or sold out entirely. He's watched some competitors overspend themselves into oblivion and others stumble over their poor investment performance. A few have been roiled by scandals or rocked by risky investments. Many more have played into the fads of junk bonds and derivative financial instruments. And there were those who just couldn't survive the crashes, bear markets and steep market declines.

The securities industry, while highly profitable, is also complex, volatile and demanding. It requires real intestinal fortitude from those who are drawn to it. Fred's achievement is all the more significant because for many years he ran everything by himself: training the analysts, picking the stocks, running the portfolios, managing the company, and providing the economic strategies for the market. Furthermore, this took place during a 30-year span that saw numerous transformations in the character of financial markets.

Fred had several chances to sell the firm, but he always held on—even in difficult periods. When all is told, the story of Fred Alger's company is one of survival through willpower and careful business management, its financial strength resting firmly on the bedrock of capital formation.

"The outlook for investment performance is excellent," Fred predicted in his speech. "The famous California charts are signaling a major market bottom. If history repeats itself, the stock market should advance thirty percent during the next eighteen months." This was one of his many prescient market calls. If anything, he was too circumspect. November 1994 marked the beginning of a huge bull run. The stock market ran up 37% in 1995 and over 20% in both 1996 and 1997. None of the other analysts saw the appreciation so clearly. Fred continued, "The world is on the threshold of the first post-Cold War boom, which will be led by American companies."

At the end of his speech, Fred introduced the 16 people who had joined the firm during the previous year. Among them, his new son-in-law, Daniel Chung, who gave up a promising legal career to become a research associate at Fred Alger Management. Fred acknowledged all the other employees and thanked them for a job well done. Next he saluted his three old partners and praised them for their part in building the business.

The evening's treat was the screening of a 10-minute promotional film, originally shot on Super 8 film in 1971 to court potential clients in the pension business. The film and bulky projector had been carted around to meetings all over the city. It was surely an early infomercial, probably the first in the financial-services sector.

The film is a sequence of talking heads—Fred, Irwin, Bill, George, and David each discuss a relevant investment or money-management strategy and give a flavor of the intense, brainy work that takes place in the company. The themes which are articulated in the brittle soundtrack still resonate in the firm today. Fred's core strategy for money management remains intact. He's stayed faithful to the analytical concepts, investment style and business precepts which, decades earlier, were used to launch the firm.

"Most satisfying to our clients is the assurance that we have never changed our investment philosophy and have continued to produce superior rates of return." It's a chorus that's often repeated. Yes, Fred's ideas have held up over the years.

While the film is running, Fred pauses to reflect about David and the changes he will inevitably impose on the firm. Predictably, he's apprehensive about the prospects of diminishing quality. "If I worry about the firm," Fred said later, "I worry if we will have people in place who will maintain high standards."

But his doubts are transient. He would later say, "What we've seen repeatedly in this firm is that when senior people leave, the people who take their place somehow do a better job. That may come as a surprise to George and Irwin. Nonetheless, that's what happens. The same will be true with me. David will do a better job."

As always the focus of attention is on Fred. Most of the comments at the table are about Fred's youthfulness and good looks in the film. The biggest laughs are saved for Bill Scheerer, who at the 1994 Christmas dinner was wearing the same tie he had put on for the promotional film shot in 1971.

Finally, in a ceremonial changing of the guard, Fred offers a good-luck toast to David. As he turns over the firm to his brother, the spotlight literally shifts away from Fred. David's intent is not to follow in Fred's footsteps but to direct the company in his own way. He has already planned to drive it forward into the Wall Street mainstream. Highly pragmatic and less original than Fred, David aims to take the firm on a more direct route to continued prosperity.

In closing, Fred reflected that the firm would have to forge ahead without the security provided by the brothers' combined presence and complementary personalities. With the new year approaching, Fred Alger & Company was in its best position ever to achieve huge gains from the strength and character which he had built into its foundation. The mutual funds were expanding their distribution, new initiatives were planned for marketing and customer service, and the company's costs and capabilities were more tightly controlled than

Fred is beaming as he's surrounded by family and friends on his sixtieth birthday. Daughter Hilary and sister Suzy are to his immediate left and right. Daughter Alexandra is standing second from camera left. David's wife Josie and Fred's daughter Nicole are seated second and third from left.

ever by the integration of its operations. Although Fred was stepping down, he appeared not like a man who has reached the pinnacle and has nowhere else to go, but rather like a commander who, resting at a plateau, is preparing another assault on the top.

Fred Alger's 1994 Christmas dinner was over. As the last guests were leaving the Lotos Club, Fred observed Rosemary Kiernan waiting by herself, using the adjacent building as a shield from the cold, pelting rain which had just begun to fall.

He joined her, saying, "I'll wait with you."

The dinner had ended earlier than expected, and it would be awhile before her daughter arrived to fetch her from New York's outer borough of Staten Island.

"No," Rosemary protested, "I can go back inside and wait." Fred insisted on standing. "No, I'll wait with you," he affirmed.

"I feel terrible. It's my fault. I should have called my daughter earlier."

The two stayed together for some time, shrugging off the winter and taking modest refuge from the building where America's eighteenth president, Ulysses S. Grant, lived between 1881 and 1885 and completed his final months by writing his personal memoirs. They chatted about Fred's twin daughters. Rosemary is a twin and Fred wondered if she needed to speak with her sister daily. Fred told Rosemary that his twins are lost if they don't communicate at least once a day.

Rosemary perfectly fits the Alger mold. Smart, efficient and industrious, she has been loyal to Fred for 28 years. Rosemary joined the company as a secretary when she was 21, left for a spell to raise her young children, then returned as George Boggio's assistant. She's even survived a bout as Fred's secretary. One quality they share is a rejection of computer technology. She won't give up her typewriter, and he still uses a slide rule for calculations.

Eventually Rosemary convinced Fred that she could wait for her daughter on her own. Fred departed, walking with his habitually purposeful, swift gait. Rosemary watched him disappear in the icy haze, his gray mohair overcoat hanging loosely over his slender frame. Soon, the once notorious gunslinger of Wall Street was out of sight. Alone with her thoughts, Rosemary resumed her evening's speculation about the company's prospects.

If the experience of the next several years is anything like the adventure of the last three decades, she thought, Rosemary and her Alger compatriots should come into a bold and abundant future.

2

The Alger Way

"I WOULD RATHER be down sixty percent in a year and be number one than be up sixty percent and be number ten."

As much as anything Fred Alger has ever said about himself, this battle cry, which he raised to storm the money-management business in the early sixties, fixed the order of his company. Fred's bluster was roundly reported in the press, and he was portrayed as a paladin of the investment world. That imperfect characterization would hound him for all his years on Wall Street.

"The essence of this business is to be first," Fred explained. "We are in a race, and the race is to the best. It's perfectly all right to win by a nose."

With his edgy bravado, a touch too prodigal for the entrenched generals of Wall Street, Fred easily struck at the heart of the money-management business. It's about beating the benchmarks—specifically, outperforming the Dow Jones Industrial or Standard & Poor averages.

More important for Fred, it's about being the best at his game.

Trumping the stock indexes is something which Fred and his firm have done with great consistency and acclaim for over 30 years. Fred Alger & Co. is in the top rung of money managers and practically peerless in its long-term performance in its pension, private and mutual-fund accounts.

In 1965, his rookie year on Wall Street, Fred ran Security Equity, the top-performing mutual fund in America, scoring a gain of 77.5%. Thirty years later, with brother David at the helm, the Alger Capital Appreciation fund was the number-one mutual fund in the country, scoring a spectacular 78.6% rise that eclipsed the 1995 average growth-fund gain of 31%. The 1995 gain was particularly noteworthy because it was one of the best years ever for the stock market, and most funds ended in the plus column. The competition was also fiercer, not only because more funds were available but because money managers were more active and aggressive than they had been in previous years. But in 1995, even when it was easy to find winning stocks, barely 30% of the mutual funds and only 15% of investment-newsletter portfolios managed to beat the popular averages. Most investment advisers and money managers didn't fare any better.

For Fred, it's never enough to be good. One has to strive to be the best. "In anything that I do, I want to compete at the very highest level within my ability," he explained. "I am competing with everybody all the time. Sometimes it is so intense, I can feel the competition rising in me." If aggressive competition drives the investment industry, then Fred Alger's intense desire to finish first was the engine that propelled his rise on Wall Street.

Consider the Alger track record. During the 25-odd years that Fred personally managed the stock portfolios, he left the S&P 500 in the dust. The extended performance of all portfolios in the current Alger Fund is far ahead of the averages in their respective categories. They are ranked with the best by the mutual-fund rating services and industry pundits. "Great investment results over time has always been at the heart of what Fred is all about," according to John Cleland, chief investment officer of Security Benefit Life, whose Security Equity Fund was built by Fred Alger's performance in the sixties.

When Fred Alger arrived on Wall Street in 1963, the dominant investment model for mutual funds was the buy-and-hold strategy. Mutual funds were a staid, uninspired product, bound up by an investment approach whose time was drawing to a close. The day still belonged to the Prudent Man, drawn in the image of bankers and so-called Boston Brahmins, who treated investing in terms of capital conservatorship, a philosophy which was conceived right after the Civil War.

By definition, the Prudent Man rule—to "act with discretion and intelligence, seek reasonable income, preserve capital and, in general, avoid speculative investments"—was a standard adopted by some states as a guide for those managing the financial welfare of others. The traditional role for financial institutions was passive, mainly to protect and preserve assets. The active striving for capital appreciation, so prevalent today, was frowned on.

Enter Fred Alger, whose advent sounded a bright note in a monotonous market. Wall Street was just recovering from the Kennedy Crash brought on by a reckless missile confrontation with Cuba. Slide rules were used to figure stock values, since portable mechanical calculators did not yet exist. Though the industry was 40 years old—it was born on March 21, 1924, when closed-end Massachusetts Investors Trust offered shares to the public—mutual funds were still in their nascent form. It was a golden time for this free-thinking, irreverent 28-year old, with his spirit of competitive enterprise, to invade Wall Street.

Mutual funds, where Fred Alger first made his name, are investment vehicles that pool money from individuals and small investors for professional management and diversification once available only to wealthy and institutional investors.

In 1963 the country's total assets in mutual funds were just $25 billion. The following year the amount jumped to $29 billion, and the Dreyfus Fund, then the largest of the aggressive growth funds, managed $800 million. By 1965, when Fred scored the year's best mutual-fund performance for Security Equity Fund, three million shareholders kept $35 billion in a total of only 107 mutual funds. Security Equity, for one, started the year with a paltry $375,000.

By comparison, in 1995 there were 131.8 million shareholder accounts in 5,761 mutual funds with over $2 trillion in assets. The largest equity fund, Fidelity Magellan, had nearly $54 billion under management. The industry's growth accelerated even faster in 1996. For instance, investors threw a record $29.4 billion into mutual funds in the month of January alone, and the number of open-end mutual funds in all categories climbed by an average of 44 per month to a year-end total of 6,293.

Armed with smart new insights about the market and an indefatigable will to win, Fred was in the vanguard of the growth-stock investing movement, which eventually discredited and displaced the Prudent Man rule and helped to redefine how Wall Street would ultimately be driven—purely by performance and the expectation of performance. Fred's aggressive approach set a new tone for the financial industry. Money managers, both new and old, heeded the clarion call of his success, and Wall Street was changed forever.

In the tug of war between value and growth styles of investing, Fred sides exclusively with growth stocks.

Value investing, as championed by Benjamin Graham and David Dodd, who are its "fathers," defines the pursuit of stocks whose intrinsic or private market value, as measured by assets, book value or low price-earnings multiples, is computed as greater than their offered price on the stock exchanges. The belief is that the stock price will eventually rise to its correct, higher level to reflect the underlying liquidation value of the company. Value investors seek stocks that are cheap or depressed relative to the market and other companies. Graham and Dodd first framed this approach in their milestone book, *Securities Analysis*, which appeared in the thirties.

Growth-stock investors, on the other hand, concentrate on rapidly growing companies with accelerating revenues and earnings, in the belief that those stocks will see the greatest price appreciation in terms of their growth rate and relative to the price-earnings multiples. Growth stocks are likely to sell at premiums over book value, pay no dividends, and possess higher price-earnings multiples even within their industries.

In today's parlance, Fred would have been called a momentum player, an intrepid variant of the growth-stock investor who is unafraid to bid up the price of a stock despite its expanding multiples. Fred was always willing to pay more for growth. He would build on his winners, especially those which exhibited his

Early model for Fred, Jerry Tsai was the first mutual fund manager who engaged in active, intensive money management.

favored scenario of undergoing a life-cycle change. "The big money comes from buying creative and exciting companies without worrying about prices. You can go broke buying cheap stocks," Fred once warned.

"Initially Fred did not care about volatility. He would take whatever risks he needed to make his fund or his performance better than anybody else's," according to Ron Tartaro, a current portfolio manager of the Alger Fund.

The new-frontier, high-growth companies in the sixties had names like Polaroid, Hewlett Packard, Avon, Gulf and Western, and Xerox, which today are considered mature and established, just as Standard Oil, U.S. Steel and Penn Central Railroad were thirty years ago. Consistent with the Alger investment style, today's high-growth glamour stocks, particularly technology and biotech firms, are the staples of Alger portfolios.

The Wall Street establishment was completely unprepared for the intensity with which Fred and his ilk challenged the stock market's status quo. For his sixties exploits Fred was branded one of the "go-go" boys, whose roaring, freewheeling ways electrified the investment landscape.

This hectic time was once pegged as the final bull market, in view of the precipitous and prolonged decline of stocks that followed it, from the late sixties to the early seventies and the general weakness of the stock market until the Reagan presidency. Though Fred's success and influence stretch beyond those years, he is still identified almost exclusively with that period. The era is best chronicled in John Brooks's *The Go-Go Years* and Robert Sobel's *The Last Bull Market,* and Fred is amply featured in both books.

As trading by committee gave way to celebrity money managers, Fred was certainly one of the brightest stars. But perhaps the first luminary in the industry was Gerald Tsai Jr. "My only hero was Jerry Tsai, the first really glamorous money manager who personified this intensive management of money," revealed Fred some years later.

He was taken by Tsai's active style, which shook the industry out of its moribund stupor and focused attention on mutual funds as a worthy and lucrative investment vehicle. The stubby, moon-faced Tsai was among the first to disprove the buy-and-hold strategy. He also argued that one might make more money with less diversification, since a concentration on fewer stocks produced greater understanding of each issue, which led to quicker and better responses.

Fred patterned himself after Tsai. Like him, Fred went against the grain. "Beginning in 1958, I had a tendency to buy aggressive growth stocks," said Tsai recently. "Not too many people were doing that. Fred was sort of like me in the old days. Maybe some people would consider us mavericks."

Four years older than Fred, Jerry Tsai was born in Shanghai in 1930, where his father, who had studied at the University of Michigan, was a district manager for the Ford Motor Company. In 1947 he was sent to America to study at Wesleyan. Two years later he transferred to Boston University, where he majored in economics.

Tsai acknowledged that he "fell into the industry at the right time" in 1952. He was working in the research department at Bache & Co. when he was hired by Fidelity Management & Research Co., now the nation's largest mutual-fund company. A friend at Scudder, Stevens and Clark, another Boston-based investment firm, recommended him for the job. He quickly became a protégé of Fidelity's owner, Edward Johnson II, who was impressed by Tsai's Eastern glamour. Johnson, a serious Orientalist, "treated me like a son," Tsai admitted.

Just 29 years old in 1957, Tsai convinced Johnson to let him start up and run Fidelity Capital, an aggressive growth-stock fund with a speculative character unlike other Fidelity funds. Through it Tsai would showcase his distinctive, bold approach to stock investing that would become the reference point of the day and set the pace for those who came after him. His heady performance would lure more and more money managers and financial institutions into the growth-stock camp and, finally, alter the investing habits of the mutual-fund industry.

Fidelity Capital started slowly, with only $12.3 million under management in 1959, but its assets boomed following some favorable publicity, and it took in $118 million in 1961 alone. Tsai was made an assistant vice president and purchased his first 10,000 shares of non-voting stock in Fidelity Management. By 1964 the fund's assets totaled $223 million.

Tsai was different because he did his own research and favored "high-flying" stocks. An advocate of technical analysis, he used market timing to get in and out of securities, taking profits as soon as they failed his momentum indicators. Unlike their "fundamental" brethren, technical analysts apply mathematical formulas based on factors such as trading volume and pricing to identify and project stock trends. They are generally unconcerned with fundamental financial indicators of a company, such as its balance sheet, and focus predominantly on the cycles and patterns of a stock's movement.

While the official line at Fidelity was to eschew this approach, Tsai had free rein to operate in his mercurial manner. He traded in and out of stocks at a pace that far exceeded what the industry had ever seen before. Turnover in Capital Fund, the number of times its equities were replaced during an accounting period, was typically 100% to 120%. For the traditionalists, this was nothing short of gambling.

In a nervy move and with the accord of E. John Rosenwald Jr., a young Bear Sterns & Co. broker, Tsai also innovated the block trade of stocks. This practice greatly benefited trading institutions and pushed the pedal on stock volatility. Block trades are transactions of 10,000 or more shares, where the broker acts as buyer or seller instead of as a middleman. Previously such trades were obtained only for bonds.

Tsai always credited his mother for his trading skills, which he developed while watching her bargain for provisions in the Shanghai markets. On the short side, he never fared well as a Dow predictor. Tsai once promised it would rise above 1,000 in 1965. The Dow briefly touched 1001.11 on February 9, 1966, but it never again closed above 1,000 until November 14, 1972.

Tsai bolted from Fidelity in December 1965, when he sensed he would be skipped as Johnson's successor in favor of Ed's son, Ned Johnson, who was making his own name in the fund business as portfolio manager of the less speculative Fidelity Trend fund. Tsai sold his 20% stake in Fidelity Management & Research for $2.2 million and planned to launch his own mutual fund, Manhattan Fund, Inc. He figured to raise anywhere from $25 million to $50 million, but when his new venture opened up on February 15, 1966, he was overwhelmed with $247 million (some reported $270 million) in investment assets to toss at the market. At the standard management fee of a half percent, the amount yielded $1.25 million for Tsai Management & Research and its 38-year-old chief. Assets in Manhattan Fund quickly zoomed to $400 million. Tsai liked to keep the fund's offices at 650 Fifth Avenue a chilly 55 degrees "to keep his head clear."

Fred is largely reverential when he speaks of Tsai. "Jerry Tsai had more influence than any money manager before or since," Fred would tell in 1986. "If there was a hall of fame in this business, he'd be the first one in."

When Fred first met Tsai, it was at a party hosted by stockbroker and industry gadfly Bobby Brimberg, known to his pals as Scarsdale Fats, who held court with elite money managers at raucous lunchtime round tables at the Harmonie

Club. Fred offered himself for a benediction. "Mr. Tsai, you are my hero. I couldn't be more excited to meet you," he said. "Well, if I'm your hero," Tsai prodded, "you must know how to spell my name." "Well, that's easy," Fred replied, earnestly misspelling his name, "it's S-I-G-H-E."

Fred deduced correctly that Tsai would seed Manhattan Fund with the same kind of stocks he had owned at Fidelity Capital and that his new quarter-billion war chest would rapidly inflate the prices of these stocks. Fred tracked his portfolio. He explained in Martin Mayer's *New Breed on Wall Street:* "We assumed Gerry would buy pretty much what he'd had at Fidelity Capital and that he'd concentrate in about fifty stocks. Now, if you assume an average price of fifty dollars, that made an imputed short interest of a hundred thousand shares in each of the stocks Gerry was going to buy. So that's what we bought.

"A couple of months later, we read in the paper that Manhattan Fund was more than eighty percent invested, and that day we went forty percent into cash. But the edge we got in those months while Tsai was buying the portfolio of his new fund gave us the second best performance record in the country for the whole year."

From this Fred realized, "We have the best sense of timing in the market. Our stock selection is no good. I can't think why—but our timing is superb." This knack for timing is something he would prove over and over: sensing the market bottom in 1982, predicting the Crash of '87, and betting high just in advance of the latest, incredible bull run starting in 1995.

Jerry Tsai was useful to Fred Alger because he gave him the shortcut to build his first-year track record. Fred had so much affection for Tsai that he even shoplifted his stock ideas. This is commonplace now, when money managers imitate the positions of superstar investors like Warren E. Buffett and even mirror their portfolios in copycat funds; for example, Buffett biographer Robert G. Hagstrom Jr. went on to establish Focus First Fund, a mutual fund patterned after his subject's investment style. While today's imitators rarely beat their models, Fred, in this early instance, managed to surpass Tsai.

In 1968, when Manhattan Fund rose 2% versus a Dow decline of 12%, Tsai unloaded his money-management firm, with about $500 million in assets, to C.N.A. Financial Assets for a reported $27–35 million in C.N.A. stock and a senior executive position. In this his timing was superb. In 1969, more than half the 45 stocks Manhattan Fund held at year end either went bankrupt or lost up to 90% of their value.

Tsai left C.N.A. and acquired a brokerage firm in February 1973 and Associated Madison Companies, an insurance holding company, in 1978. He sold the latter in 1982 to American Can, where he was made executive vice president. Tsai rose to be the company's chairman and CEO and presided over its name change to Primerica Corp. in 1987 and its merger with Sanford Weill's Commercial Credit in 1988. He remained on its board for several years before acquiring a controlling interest in Delta Life and Annuity in 1992 and becoming the chairman and CEO of this Memphis-based company in February 1993.

"In the sixties we were considered aggressive investors, but today, in terms of selection and style we would be considered old fuddy-duddies," said Tsai. "Half the stocks I see going up and down like crazy, I don't know what they do. Certainly Polaroid and Xerox are not viewed today with the same kind of speculative risk. Perhaps the old-line managers, when they were looking at what we were buying, had the same reaction."

One comical anecdote from this period involves an elderly Chinese broker at either Dean Witter or Reynolds who took a fancy to Fred and envisioned turning him into another Jerry Tsai. She proposed raising millions from Chinese flight capital for him to manage. A big meeting between them was planned in an elegant East Side restaurant. It was bad timing, for Fred was stricken by the flu just around dinnertime. When she arrived at the restaurant, Fred was retching in the bathroom. The meal—and the deal—was off, and the lady kindly drove Fred home to recover.

Today Fred Alger, like his hero, Jerry Tsai, is seemingly an anachronism on Wall Street: not one to be identified with the solemn and sluggish old-money investment types and a world away from the hustling, hardhearted Gordon Gekkos of the bull-led eighties and nineties. In the current universe of some 10,000 U.S. money managers and investment advisers, focused mostly on quick profits and motivated by power and greed, Fred is decidedly out of character.

He is often described as a classy guy with a driven personality and a fierce sense of purpose. Frequently contradictory, he is disarmingly unprepossessing and distinctively charming. At the same time, he is quick and crafty, personable and soft-spoken, a formidable competitor and a dangerous adversary.

In his best moments Fred is ready with a broad, unsparing, high-toned laugh. A pensive mood finds him fingering his trusty slide rule. When he's contemplative, his hands are loosely folded on his lap. Asked what he enjoys, his eyes light up with a mischievous twinkle, and an incandescent smile warms his face. "Making money," he replies without a second's hesitation. What does he value in himself? "The ability to stand alone and take a long-term view of things. "Even as a child," Fred acknowledges, "it helped to be a loner, not needing people, encouragement or reinforcement."

"Throughout his life Fred has had a clear plan about what to do. He never responded to situations the way others might have, by selling out or surrendering some of his values. He's kept his standards, and that's knowing yourself, " said Steve O'Neil, a longtime member of the Alger Fund board.

This certainty of purpose is seen as the deciding feature of Fred's success. He never veered from his chosen route. When he encountered roadblocks or came under criticism for his actions, he remained steadfast on his course. In time, he believed, his actions would be vindicated and his strategies would prevail. "An innate sense of leadership gives you the confidence to know that you have the right way," said Fred. "I certainly always believe that I have the right way."

Another quality that distinguishes Fred is the ability to pay complete attention to the business at hand. "What was so inspirational about Fred was how focused he is," said ex-partner George Boggio. "Fred has tremendous single-mindedness when he sets himself out to doing anything," seconded brother David. "He devotes one hundred percent to that one thing. The world could be disintegrating around him, but he'll do that one thing, in most cases extremely well."

Around Memorial Day 1978, Fred took a beating in tennis from players he had beaten handily in the past. In defeat he realized he was terribly out of shape. This rankled him down to his competitive bones, so much that he determined to take up running to rebuild his stamina.

"That weekend I decided to start getting in shape," he said. "I tried to run from my house in East Hampton to the beach, only one mile, yet I had to stop once or twice, perhaps three times. Later when I trained, my legs would hurt, particularly after running on concrete. They got very, very sore," Fred said. "It took a long time to get my legs in shape to run long distances."

Once he started running, his competitive nature kicked in and he was off to the races. Spurred by close friend and long-distance runner Lew Lehrman, the one-time Republican candidate for governor of New York, Fred made up his mind to enter the 1979 New York City Marathon. To complete the race, a distance of 26 miles, he committed himself to a rigorous training program. In the office he worked out on a stationary bike, taking business calls while he pedaled. A daily run was about 10 miles, six times around the Central Park reservoir. His weekly program exceeded 50 miles. "I would keep a little log and note my times," he said. "It was quite an organized effort."

Fred added, "I wanted to run the marathon in three hours and thirty minutes. That was my goal. Unfortunately, the day of the race was very hot and humid. In those days, people didn't know enough about the importance of taking water to combat humidity. Today, on humid days, you're told to take water at every water stop. No one told me that." Around mile 21 or 22, Fred was overcome by dehydration, but he pressed on, collapsing after he crossed the finish line. They kept him in the first-aid tent for over an hour, wrapped in blankets and flushed with water. "It was quite nerve-racking for my family," he said. "It was kind of a scary moment, but I was too exhausted to think too much about it."

Fred finished 4,822nd in the 1979 New York City Marathon out of some 12,000 runners. His time was 3:49:40, about 20 minutes longer than he had planned. A

In training for the marathon, Fred ran 10 miles a day; six times around the Central Park reservoir.

plaque in his office commemorates that effort. He was 45 years old then and had no previous running experience. Such is the determination of Fred Alger.

Fred Alger was odd man out on Wall Street, almost at his own insistence.

"Fred never had a desire to be well known or acquainted with other members of the community," according to first partner Bill Scheerer. "Here was his thinking. One, we don't trust them. Two, what can we learn from them? We do our own research." Fred never accompanied Bill to the coffee shop at 26 Broadway, a favorite hangout of renowned corporate raider Carl Icahn. Nor did he take a seat at Bobby Brimberg's round tables at the Harmonie Club, though Bill would go there on occasion.

Fred Alger never felt it was important, necessary or even desirable to blend in with other money men. Unlike David Alger today, he didn't feel that fitting in had much to do with running his business. Just as Fred's investment style initially found opposition from the Street, his personality got in the way of his acceptance by the rest of the investing community.

"Fred was never out to win friends and influence people," remembered Lavaun Vawter, his former secretary. "He was always strongly independent." One Alger detractor observed, "It seemed that Fred made it a practice to alienate everyone on the Street. He didn't need them. He was on his own, all by himself."

A case in point was his approach to his first large pension account, a leading airline, which balked at dealing him brokerage commissions on top of the customary management fees. "At that time we had no big accounts," explained David. "It was really important for many of us to get that account under our belt. But Fred said he was going to have the account on his terms or not at all. We were going to hold out and do it our way. Some of us felt that Fred was being a little too stubborn."

For Irwin Schwartz, this had to be a watershed event in the company. "We were desperate for the business. But Fred said, 'Once you cut a fee for one, you have to for everyone. It is all public information,'" Irwin recounted. "The rest of us felt even if we broke even with the account, it would have been fine."

"But he was right," David conceded. "A year later, the airline eventually caved in and accepted our structure. The account was fifty or sixty million dollars. It was huge for us at the time. Little did we know when we got the account that it would stipulate we couldn't disclose we were managing the money. Nobody would have known if we had cut a deal."

More than 25 years later the airline, which has three plans with Alger, is still the company's largest pension account.

Those who have bargained with Fred found that he could be infuriatingly obstinate. Ray Merritt at the law firm of Willkie Farr & Gallagher, who managed Fred's legal affairs from that time forward, offered this opinion: "His greatest virtue is also his greatest fault. To question basic tenets is a good idea and can be ennobling. On the other hand, to constantly question them and then to fight when there seems to be no possibility of success, then it becomes a flaw. He's often chased principle beyond what's pragmatic—and nobody can stop him."

Fred responds: "I would much rather create something myself than interpret what someone else has created."

For instance, not until 1993 did the firm grudgingly agree to accept First Call earnings estimates, as other investment firms had done for years. As the firm counts increasingly on over-the-counter or NASDAQ investments, it has only recently become more amenable to the supplementary-research contribution of sell-side brokerage firms which make a market in these stocks.

Fred Alger's company occupies roughly 25,000 square feet on the top three floors and penthouse of 75 Maiden Lane, an undistinguished 12-story brick structure wedged in an odd triangle overlooking Legion Memorial Square, close to the hive of Wall Street and about a furlong from the brackish waters of New York's East River. The square, a crudely spaced vein of the financial district, also goes by the name Louise Nevelson Plaza, after the famed American sculptor (1900–1988).

Fred Alger Management, where Fred has his office, is one of several companies starting with his name. After getting off an express elevator, past a comfortable, unpretentious reception area, one slips into a cozy foyer, flashing with a crowded display of consecutive first-place trophies won by the Alger Bulls in the Staten Island slow pitch softball tourney. Fred had a mantel built specially for those victories, which are to him are a matter of great pride.

The way to Fred's office is right off an open, circular bullpen, the trading area over which Joseph R. Maida rides herd. Computers rumble and monitors face off with their operatives for the heart-stopping action that is stock market trading. Ticker symbols and numbers scroll and beat with numbing speed. This is where carefully weighed investment decisions are transformed into orders to buy or sell, where quick thinking and response can result in gains or losses of hundreds of thousands of dollars at a pop.

Fred arrives at work early, about 8:15 A.M., chauffeured in a company-owned gray Lincoln Town Car. After reading the business press, *Financial Times*, *The Wall Street Journal*, *Investor's Business Daily*, *Barron's* and *The Economist.*, Dolores gets him his tea. He spends most of the day at his desk, usually in deep study or reflection about the markets, but every hour or so he hits the trading desk to catch the mood of the market. Sometimes he quizzes the traders and coaches their plays. Often he hovers over Dolores's desk, just outside his office, fully absorbed in some document or report. An egghead with a flinty gaze, like some mad professor by cartoonist R. Crumb, his thinning silver hair charges wayward, electrified by some shock of mental energy.

Fred's office, comfortable enough for two sofas and coffee tables and a large executive desk, is barely adorned except for a tall ficus tree and a life-size Chinese sculpture of a scarlet dog to ward off evil sprits, a gift from the office's decorator, Jim Wagnon. A certificate appointing his father as ambassador of Belgium from President Dwight D. Eisenhower on May 26, 1953, dominates the room from its vantage point on the ledge of the windows that gaze down on Maiden Lane.

Cast away and nearly hidden behind one of the couches is a framed reprint of a double-page magazine ad from Fred's infamous 1986 advertising campaign that preceded the launch of his mutual funds. The headline asks: What does it take to produce annual compound growth of 21% for 21 years? Answer: A Genius for Making Money. The promotion touts Fred's outperformance of the S&P stock index by a factor of 10 during the years 1965 to 1986.

The most revealing artifact on Fred's desk is a single piece of clear Plexiglas with the engraved message "No Surprises." Chief trader Joe Maida explained its special meaning to him. "When Fred is out at a client meeting, he'll call from the car to ask what the market is doing before he comes in. He doesn't want to walk into disaster. He doesn't want to be caught off guard. He wants to be able to control how he reacts in all situations."

Fred likes his offices to be spare and serviceable, an extension of the business-driven side of his personality. "In the early days, perhaps to a fault, Fred insisted on having very spartan offices," explained George Boggio. His rationale was that his frugality would have a positive effect on potential clients. This chary attitude was precisely what won over publishing giant George Delacorte, who turned over his sizable investment to Fred in the seventies after a meeting at the offices in 26 Broadway. "If you are as careful with our money as you are with yours, we'll do very well," Delacorte was reported to have said.

When Greg Duch, now the firm's chief financial officer, linked up with Fred Alger in 1981, he had this initial impression: "The 26 Broadway offices were very unpretentious. The furniture was a mishmash and not very good. It was a nothing office, not very well maintained, but this didn't turn me off." As a senior manager in the accounting firm Arthur Andersen, Greg had seen a worse setting in another prominent financial institution and imagined that, despite appearances, Alger could be a hidden gem.

"Lazard Freres had about the most dilapidated offices I had ever seen," he said. "While its name conjures up visions of megabucks, an office manager would turn off lights during the day to conserve electricity. The partners' offices were very small, and they would do silly things to save money.

"This is typical of a style of investment people who aren't trying to show off how much money they have, but rather demonstrate that they're going to be conscientious about managing your money. 'I'm charging you a fee, but that fee is not going into marble walls and Oriental rugs. It's being turned around and invested in services for you.'"

The office next to Fred's is occupied by executive vice president Ray Pfeister. At the opposite end of the floor, the other corner office belongs to David Alger.

Fred vaulted into the financial limelight from a cover story in one of the first issues of *Institutional Investor* magazine, dated February 1968. A crude head-and-shoulders close-up sketch of Fred stares directly at the reader and peers intently through owlish glasses with a half smile. The cover caption telegraphed his importance to the world. *Name: Fred Alger. Age: 32. Occupation: Portfolio Manager. 1967 Income: $1,100,000.*

The four-page article, "Portrait of a Star" by Chris Welles, once a business editor at *Life* magazine, baptized Fred as the reigning enfant terrible of the mutual-fund industry and crowned him with celebrity status. The feature reported that Fred managed $200 million, and that $1 million of his seven-figure income was derived from performance fees, which were obtained, ironically enough, because he resisted signing up as a registered investment adviser.

"In the early days most people thought of Fred as a very bright, aggressive money manager, but this article finally recognized that he was a force in the industry," said George Boggio.

The *Institutional Investor* article was not, however, the first time that Fred was lionized by the press. A *Business Week* story in its December 30, 1967 issue named him among "The Young Millionaires of Finance."

Twelve years later, in a largely critical *Institutional Investor* feature, Fred issued an erratum on the magazine's behalf about his 1967 earnings. "You got it wrong. It was $1.2 million." He didn't make that issue's cover, but the story gave him even greater coverage, keying on his shift into the pension business, his unique management ideas, and his impressive performance. The story was illustrated with a picture of a relaxed and broadly smiling Fred, seated cross-legged on top of the world.

Fred's secret was out. Great fortune and fame could be had by managing money. But it did little to help him professionally. "We found that something like that never produces any revenue," said Fred about the 1968 piece. "It was good for your ego, but in fact bad for business.

"The reason was, we had the field to ourselves. I could, using outside research, pick the brains of anybody almost, because there were so few people doing what I was doing. But late into the sixties every bank and insurance company was suddenly into the intensive money-management business. Everyone was using the same raw material for ideas, but the competition could outpay us."

Fred met this challenge with his own resolve to establish a brand identity for his firm, based on superior research that was independent from the Street, which he would finance with commissions from the brokerage business.

"The trouble with the mutual-fund business is there are too many Freds," stock-market veteran David L. Babson loudly proclaimed to an *Institutional Investor* conference in 1968. In addition to Fred Alger, he had in mind two other shoot-em-up managers, Fred Carr and Fred Mates. The quote was widely reported in an industry that at the time was in the throes of an immense lifestyle change.

"The three of us were the vanguard of change that occurred in the industry," Fred Alger explained, "the high-energy, intensive management of money that swept the industry starting in the late fifties and into the early sixties. We represented a change from the buy-and-hold style. We kept the money moving around on the leading edge of the market, wherever that market was. Babson, whose father was famous for warning about the 1929 crash, represented the old school. He felt, with a certain justification, that we had brought a lot of speculation to the market which hadn't existed before."

Like Fred Alger, Fred Carr was one of the mutual-fund stars who gained a following after reports about him in the financial press. In 1965 the 33-year-old Carr was managing Convertible Securities & Growth Stock Fund, later called Enterprise Fund, for Douglas Fletcher's Shareholder Management Co. During the seven-year period between 1965 and 1971, it was ranked number one in the country, followed by the Alger–run Security Equity Fund.

The**Institut**ï**onal**   February 1968
Investor   The journal for professional investment managers

NAME:
FRED ALGER
AGE:
32
OCCUPATION:
PORTFOLIO MANAGER
1967 INCOME:
$1,100,000

Fred's spectacular mutual fund performance brought him early stardom.

Fred Mates ran the best fund in America in 1968 when his Mates Investment Fund returned 153%. Its assets rose so quickly, from $1.7 in January to $17 million in June, that it was closed to new investors, which then initiated a brisk secondary market for its shares, usually at a 10% premium.

"The impression on the Street was that the three Freds and Jerry Tsai were meeting at Delmonicos and deciding how to manipulate the market," observed

Chat Hickox, Fred's first high-net-worth individual client. "The idea was preposterous. Nothing could have been further from the truth."

But the image stuck.

Ironically Babson's lament had the unintended result of propagating more Freds. Following their performance, wannabes were sprouting all over the financial map. Babson's time had passed. The old-line money managers would finally capitulate and make way for a new, aggressive, performance-driven investment season.

A second broadside was flung at Fred during another *Institutional Investor* meeting three years later. The term gunslinger, as a negative label for Fred, was shot by George J. W. Goodman, one-time editor of the publication who is now widely known as author, financial commentator and television personality Adam Smith. His seminal work, *The Money Game* exposed the sixties public to the first insider view of Wall Street. In a 1971 panel hosted by the magazine, Smith used the tag to shoot down aggressive money managers who played "fast and loose with speculation." Fred Alger was recognized as chief among them. Goodman's strident attack triggered intense animosity from the investing community. And decades after the Babson and Goodman fusillades, his reputation as a gunslinger still pursues Fred almost as stubbornly as the *Federales* chased the Sundance Kid. Press reports still cannot resist branding him as a renegade and tantalizing readers with hints of a shady past.

He suffered intense scrutiny and mostly unfair criticism. "I was often surprised by the vehemence of opposition to Fred as a money manager," said Bill Scheerer. "Fred had an image problem early on," he added, "so the firm somehow developed an image on the negative side, which was unwarranted in light of our success and generally salutary investment results."

"In the sixties there were five or six highly visible portfolio managers, Fred among them," said attorney Ray Merritt. "The 'go-go' boys were brash, outspoken and hot in terms of performance, and everyone was waiting for them to have a bad year, because it is normal for money managers go through cycles. Those who like certain types of industries get hot when those industries get hot; those that sell short get hot when the stock market goes down. Trends change, so those doing well one year wouldn't do so well the next. Except Fred, who had a resiliency about him that managed to live out these fads."

As is often the case with exceptional individuals, all that is said to be true about Fred is seldom more than a surface reflection of reality. Contrary to his public image, Fred is grimly conservative in the management of the firm's money. "Even though the image was that of a gunslinger, Fred doesn't throw money around. He doesn't take outrageous chances. The public persona and the real person are different, in the business sense," affirmed Bill Scheerer, the person who knew him best during his early years of business building. "Fred's philosophy was to invest the money very conservatively while the firm was growing."

The firm's chief financial officer, Greg Duch, explained, "Our firm is managed not so much to get the highest leverage on its capital, but to retain capital and to put the firm on a stable footing so that it can go forward for a long period of time.

"The clients' money is in growth stocks, which are the most volatile and have the greatest upside potential. Our own funds were invested, in effect, in money-market accounts or treasury bonds, which are extremely safe. It was not until 1986 or '87 that we took a substantial portion of the firm's money and actually invested in the same stocks we put our clients' money into. Fred, David, and George may have personally owned stocks, but not the firm."

Why such a conservative approach from an avowed evangelist of growth stock investing? "It's very simple," Fred pointed out. "If the market is doing well, we'll be doing well. The business will be doing well. We'll be getting assets under management. Fees will be going up. Conversely, if the business is doing badly, I don't want to worry about my own money."

"For the same reason I don't own stocks personally," said David. "I have at various times, but I haven't for some time."

In its March 1977 tenth-anniversary retrospective of the "100 Most Influential Individuals of the Decade," *Institutional Investor* put Fred Alger's name first in the alphabetic listing. Sharing the page with him was investing icon Warren Buffett, who, in a commonsense way, is opposed to Fred. "Warren Buffett buys companies off their balance sheet. We buy companies because of their products or their service, units of which are growing rapidly and that would translate to earnings," said Fred. "We're linked to earnings. He's linked to balance sheet or value." In contrast to Fred, Buffett believes that "severe change and exceptional returns usually don't mix," and is also "remarkably unconcerned about the price performance of his common stocks compared to a stock market index."

About the only thing Fred has in common with this famous investor and, after Microsoft founder Bill Gates, the second-richest man in America, is a passion for bridge. Buffett now even logs onto the Internet to compete with friends at a distance. Bridge was elemental for Fred. Every day he retired to the Regency Club on 67th Street and Fifth Avenue to indulge in the pastime. Another mutual-fund titan, Jack Dreyfus, is known as a high-stakes bridge player. It is not peculiar that these money masters should gravitate to bridge since, just like the stock market, its scoring stresses skillful bidding.

There is no equivalent to Fred Alger on Wall Street. The firm is totally independent and retains complete authority over every aspect of the investment management process: recruiting, training, stock analysis, the buying and selling of stocks, all back-office functions, which involves the flow of securities between brokerage firms and the balancing of assets in the firm's accounts for its clients, routine accounting operations, including the pricing and valuation of mutual funds and client portfolios, as well as marketing and customer service.

The only aspect of the business which Fred Alger relinquishes to an outside agent is the custodial activity, the physical warehousing of the securities in its accounts, because securities firms are proscribed from doing so by law. "If we can do it in-house, we don't have to rely on others," explains Greg Duch. "Anything we can control in-house makes it a better world for us."

The Alger firm manifests pure vertical integration at its best.

Alger Associates, Inc., is the parent holding company which is controlled by Fred and David.

Under this broad umbrella is Fred Alger Management, the registered investment advisory based in New York. It is an active money manager of private accounts, mutual funds, variable annuities and life insurance, and retirement plans of corporations, state and local governments, charitable foundations and trusts. Its income is derived from mutual-fund management fees and expenses ranging from .75% to 2%, and the firm's published institutional rates are 1% for the first $5 million, .5% for the subsequent $195 million, and .35% for amounts over $200 million in its equity accounts, with the minimum account size of $2 million. Fred Alger Management belongs to the Investment Company Institute, the Washington, D.C.–based national trade association for the investment industry and related businesses.

Fred Alger Asset Management is the investment advisory unit that manages assets derived from marketing efforts by the firm's West Coast office in La Jolla, California.

Fred Alger & Co., which is the security broker dealer, is the parent of Fred Alger Management and is registered in all states plus Puerto Rico.

Alger Shareholder Services, Inc., is the transfer agency domiciled in New Jersey.

Alger Properties, Inc., is a separate entity that has a 52% stake in Maidgold partnership, which owned 75 Maiden Lane.

Analysts Resources is a recruiting firm specializing in investment analysts.

Alger Life Insurance Agency was established to serve any needs arising from the firm's insurance relationships.

Integration fulfills the qualities of independence and self-reliance championed by Fred. "Most other firms in our business are built on a completely different economic model than ours," said David Alger. "We have a lot more analysts. We have fewer portfolio managers. And most other firms don't keep their own brokerage business. They give it out. They use Street research exclusively and rely on a lot more marketing people."

David admitted, however, that there is "nothing that we do that other people couldn't do if they had half a mind to."

While numerous Wall Street firms now fancy the aggressive style of managing money that distinguishes Fred Alger and have developed their own models for growth investing, none approaches vertical integration as a strategy for controlling profits. No other firm has built such an operationally efficient and sustained model for delivering performance leadership. Few are so committed to intense research and in-depth analysis.

In an era of megafirms, Fred Alger & Company thrives as a compact, sporty, rapidly accelerating investment enterprise with the technological horsepower to help its clients—mutual funds, insurance companies, retirement funds of large corporations, state and local governments, wealthy individuals, churches and trusts—reach their investment goals.

The company is a singular product of Fred Alger's creative imagination: a lean, focused organization, giving evidence of its founder's intellectual curiosity about the way money is made. Relationships are informal but impersonal. Operations do not favor bureaucracy. "There's not much in the way of hierarchies and no constructed chain of command," said senior bond analyst Lisa Gregg. "Nothing has to go through the line. You can walk directly into Fred's office."

"Decision making is very quick," expanded Greg Duch. "There's none of this hashing back and forth which detracts from the way a company can do things. If you're small and can make a fast decision, you're so much further ahead of your competitors."

Recently the word *way* has became an overused term for conferring credibility to business and political personalities. But the Alger way was a pragmatic reality long before the word became popular.

Joe Pakenham, in charge of the purchase-and-sales component of the back office, describes it as "simply doing the job you have, and doing whatever it takes to do it right." It proceeds from Fred's example and is forged by his personality. It is the practice of attacking life and playing the game on a higher scale.

Fred's whatever-it-takes attitude is rarely inelastic and is highly adaptive. "Fred Alger is willing to change to make it work," Greg declared. "The bottom line is making it work, and it doesn't necessarily matter how."

Fred's firm was his private dominion. He set the tone of the place and energized it around his point. It is a sober environment which aspires to be fiercely competitive, creatively independent, totally focused, supremely optimistic, and ultimately courageous. In short, a dynamic, forward-looking world that is rare even for keen business settings.

"People will, more or less, respond to what you expect of them," Fred believes. "If you're hard and difficult, in many respects it works out better and they're happier than if you're soft and easy." Success counts for a lot here, but more than that, hard work. Lightweights need not apply.

For Fred, "appearances do matter. I like to see people move fast, not walk slowly but nearly run from one thing to another," he explained. "The slothful ones just don't advance here. "

There's a story of an applicant who was on the verge of being offered a job, until she blew her chances by calling David while he was on holiday to discuss the company's vacation policy. Focusing on one's benefits first over one's responsibilities is not characteristic of the Alger way. The firm's informal style and open access does not equate to an absence of limits.

Greg was quick to observe that, despite Fred's trenchant style, or perhaps because of it, employees gave back to Fred much more than they took. Everyone was improved by his expectations.

"This company works by the dedication of its employees," he said. "This can be such an easy in-and-out business. Turnover can be huge. Your only real asset is people. Yet we've always been able to attract very intelligent people and people who might have been able to make even more money elsewhere, but who come to work for us because they are rewarded psychologically.

"Fred ran the company. He was never absent. Everything proceeded from his belief about how things should be run, and he's fashioned the firm in his image. Our performance is good because Fred has been able to continuously attract people who can contribute to that."

The Alger company's article of faith might well be the following passage by his great grandfather, Russell A. Alger, who rose from penniless orphan to be a Civil War hero, lawyer-statesman and lumber millionaire. "Hard work is as essential to happiness as exercise is to physical growth. It is the boy who goes ahead, who never knows when he is whipped, who never loses confidence in himself, who succeeds. Success is the result of hard work and sticking to it."

The character of Fred's firm is now changing to observe David Alger's personality and objectives. His approach is clearly more pragmatic. For the first time ever, the company is engaged in strategic planning, formalizing responsibilities, and preparing budgets in a structured way.

David highlights the difference: "There will be less innovation and more execution and more organization. We'll just go at it hammer and tong."

Soon after Fred decamped for Switzerland in April 1995, David began imprinting his own decorative influences on the Alger offices. The first impression is now elegant and softly inviting, conjuring up the power and aura of old money. The furniture is classic and comfortable, the carpeting richly patterned. A rich oak bookcase stands sentry in the reception area. A glass doorway which once allowed a sneak peek into the working area is now closed off by solid mahogany doors.

More interesting than the exterior scene, however, are the changes taking place inside the firm. With David's direction the firm is finally in its best position ever to capitalize on its strong underpinnings and to surge forward with massive gains. In 1995 it grew assets by 20%, over $1 billion, to levels for the first time above the firm's glorious period in the eighties. The next year investment assets swelled even more, topping $7 billion while the firm's net worth punched through the $120 million mark. By the close of 1997 assets had bumped up to $9 billion, and the firm had its most profitable year ever. Behind the strength were increased market penetration via distribution, a dramatic extension of the product line, the implementation of targeted marketing strategies, renewed attention to customer service and, of course, a fierce bull market.

The question is not whether David will succeed, but how fast he will make his mark and how high will he go.

Although Fred has always stood apart from the Street, he has been one of the leading players in its history and instrumental in shaping its commercial ideas. Almost greater than his astute investment analysis and decades of strong portfolio performance, Fred's business efforts serve up a success story which clearly merits study and reflection. Certainly he was the only one of the master money managers from the sixties to survive the bear market shoot-outs of the early seventies. Among the terrible Freds, only Alger was still standing when the dust had settled. By 1974 Mates's fund was busted by heavy liquidation, and he died eight years later at the age of 50. Carr has long since shifted away from money management. On April 2, 1990, *Forbes* extolled that, unlike the other Freds, "hosannas are falling at Fred Alger's feet." Assuredly he belongs in the Wall Street pantheon.

It is for the future, however, to settle if he left behind a long and enduring legacy on Wall Street or whether his influence should be consigned to a brief, spirited season in the sixties. Current evidence favors the former. The smart money is on Fred.

3

Born a Prince

F REDERICK MOULTON ALGER III was born on December 20, 1934, in Detroit, scion of a family that was prominent in business and politics.

He grew up wealthy and comfortable in Grosse Pointe, an affluent Detroit suburb and hereditary preserve of Michigan's Old Guard, which extends along a scenic six-mile stretch of Lake St. Clair. The Algers, along with the McMillans, the Joys, and the Newberrys, were considered the big four "old" Detroit families, even though the Buhls and the Fords had a higher profile in Grosse Pointe society. Grosse Pointe fortunes were made in shipping, banking, real estate, timber, chemicals and, of course, automobiles.

The mansion on the lake where Fred grew up resembled a rambling English manor house and was completed by prominent architects William B. Stratton and Frank C. Baldwin for his grandfather in 1908, the year after Fred's father was born. This long house is cited in *The Buildings of Detroit* as follows: "One of the most admirable characteristics of the cottage style was its dedication to the enjoyment of living. Nowhere could this be more apparent than on the lake side of the Alger house. Here a continuous series of rooms savored the delights of the waterfront through banks of windows

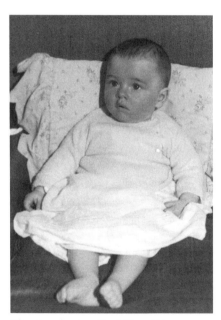

The story begins. Fred Alger III.

and French doors that opened upon a terrace extending the full length of the house." It was at least 30,000 square feet and required four or five live-in servants to manage. The property provided ample space for Fred's imagination.

The earliest story about Fred is one of the most revealing.

When Fred was in nursery school or kindergarten, he was administered a basic intelligence test which involved matching the cutout heads of animal figures with their appropriate trunks. When the headmaster saw Fred's configurations, he became so concerned that he immediately summoned Fred's mother to the school. All 20 of his pairings were incorrect. The head of a lion was pasted on the body of a dog, a sheep's face over a cow's frame, and so on.

His mother was perplexed. "Frederick, certainly you must know that these are wrong." One version has Fred replying, "Of course I know they're wrong. I just wanted to see if God was right." Another has Fred insisting, "Oh, yes, but it would have been better if God had done it my way."

Either way, that was Fred Alger.

As a child Fred was mostly given to solitary pursuits. He lived in a world by himself, "entertaining myself endlessly by inventing things." By age eight he was already designing and erecting meticulous and intricate models of swept-back winged airplanes from rice paper and balsa wood. He would then "fly" these aircraft with three- and four-foot wingspans, sans engines, from the top of the toboggan slide on the property.

Fred was mischievous and sometimes unruly. He enjoyed making land mines out of firecrackers and tried to kill rabbits with them. He also relished playing with matches, and this appetite once turned him into a minor celebrity. When he was seven, he and his six-year-old first cousin, Alger Boyer, lodged some tar paper in a large tree on the property and lit it, supposedly to keep them warm during an early winter outing. When the tree caught fire, the boys ran into the house and summoned the fire department. For this they were hailed as heroes by the local *Grosse Pointe News*. The next day during lunch at Grandmother's house, the family heaped praise on them for their bravery, even though Fred suspects the adults knew better.

Another time he broke his older sister's heart by strapping a pillowcase full of her collection of porcelain animals on the back of the family poodle. Then he played Pony Express with it, and all the figures were destroyed. "I could have killed him," said Suzy, four years older than Fred and named after their beautiful mother, the former Suzette de Marigny Dewey. "He knew what he was doing; but I don't think he imagined all the animals were going to break."

She remembers young Fred as a spoiled child who threw tantrums if he was not satisfied immediately. Once he sank his bicycle in the lake to force his parents to buy him a new one. "He was competitive to the point of being a bad sport," she said. "He became a spiteful little boy if he lost."

All three of Frederick M. Alger Jr.'s offspring—Suzette, Fred III and David— inherited an abundance of the competitive gene, the distinguishing trait of this generation of the Alger family. This ferocious quality would surface regularly in their personal relationships. Yet while they delighted in sparring with one another, the children always drew together when an outside force threatened one of them.

Attended by the family physician, Dr. Charles Jennings, Fred's father was born on August 3, 1907, and was one of the first incubator babies, "essentially a shoe box in a stove oven," as he described it. He was put on his first horse at three and grew up to be a great rider and avid polo player. After prepping at Phillips Academy in Andover, Massachusetts, he entered Harvard.

In his freshman year, however, Fred Jr. cut his exams to go on a ride at the Maryland Hunt Club. For this and other such self-willed antics, he was booted out of college. As a punishment his father, the first Frederick M. Alger, exiled him to Poland under assignment to Charles S. Dewey, the special U.S. financial adviser to the Polish government. There Fred's father instantly fell in love with his boss's daughter, "a dark beauty with a quick smile" a year older than him, who was unconvincingly engaged to another man at the time. He won her heart and married her in Warsaw in the spring of 1929. "When I was shown the Detroit stories of my wedding, I couldn't find my name. Everything was Freddie Alger!" said the new Mrs. Alger. The wedding, conducted in French in an Anglican church, was an international social event. Fred Jr. thought it was an omen that he and his bride came home to America on the day before the 1929 stock market crash.

Fred Alger Jr. was a tall, debonair sportsman who mainly indulged in social pursuits. "Father was never brought up to be a working person," said Fred. "My parents knew no one who had a job except for my uncle. The joke went that they had one friend who was employed for a day. When asked why he stopped, he replied that he couldn't work during the day and be charming at night. "

Thirsty Knob was the Alger lodge at Metamora, 50 miles outside Grosse Pointe, where the family stayed during the hunting season. At 27, Fred Jr. became vice president of the Detroit Racing Association, and for a while he ran an "immensely successful" racing stable. When Fred III was born, he asked Alfred Vanderbilt, regarded as "one of the best-known horsemen in the country, if not the world," to be his godfather.

That birth was a lucky portent, a precursor to his greatest racing success. Nearly two months later, on Saturday, February 23, 1935, Fred Jr.'s Irish–bred gelding, Azucar, raced to victory and a $108,480 prize in the first Santa Anita Handicap. This was extraordinary not only for the size of the winnings, but because the

Springtime in Warsaw, 1929. Fred Alger Jr. marries Suzette Dewey, daughter of the special U.S. financial adviser to the Polish government.

thoroughbred, acquired for between $6,000 and $8,000, had been tested only in steeplechase jumping and was raced over Alger Sr.'s objections. From this event Fred Jr. rose to prominence throughout the horse racing world.

He gave the trainer and the winning jockey, George Woolff, $10,000, and when he returned home, he threw an all-night bash at the Yondotega Club, Detroit's most exclusive social organization. And what a party it was. A souvenir program-invitation was issued to all members, citing "grateful and affectionate appreciation to Azucar, who has made it financially possible." The celebration started at four in the afternoon and lasted till dawn the following day. When the Club's manager for 40 years, Edward S. Thompson, retired in 1955, he recalled the event as the most memorable in all his years.

The Yondotega Club, conceived in 1891 at the home of its first chairman, William C. McMillan, has always been shrouded in secrecy. At one point in its charter, members were obliged to leave the room whenever the club's name was mentioned in the presence of a non-member. Membership in the club, whose

Fred's father was a great rider and avid polo player, a debonair sportsman who mainly engaged in social pursuits.

insignia is a rose and vine and whose name derives from the Algonquin word meaning "peaceful and happy spot," is restricted to men who live in the Detroit area. No woman has ever entered. Guests are permitted only if they reside out-side a radius of 50 miles. Fred III and his brother David could not carry on their father's and grandfather's membership since they moved away from Detroit.

In 1936, in the footsteps of his father and grandfather before him, Fred Alger Jr. entered the political arena, running for Congress from the 14th District. "I was anti-Roosevelt. I was tired of listening to people complain and then do nothing about it," he said. "I figured if I did have a good family name, this was the time to trade on it." In the end, he was beaten.

Fred Jr.'s prize-winning horse Azucar died in 1941, the same year World War II surprised America. As a lieutenant in the Naval Reserves, Fred was called to active duty, serving as an intelligence officer with the rank of commander. The family moved cross-country to Coronado, California, outside San Diego. That's where David Dewey Alger was born on December 15, 1943.

The way Fred, age eight, and Suzy, age twelve, were packed off separately to their new home overlooking the Pacific characterizes their upbringing by essentially absentee parents. During wartime they made the three-day rail trip from Detroit to San Diego without any supervision. "We were not undone by it," said Suzy. Deposited in a stateroom and handed $25, they explored the train and used the money to buy chocolates. In 1945, when the war had ended, Fred and Suzy were sent back to Michigan in the same manner. "I have no idea why they did that," she said. "I never questioned my family. We did what we were told. Fred too."

Back home from Coronado, California, Fred was enrolled in sixth grade at private Detroit University School. In the summer he was sent to Camp Kieve in Nobleboro, Maine. There he learned how to shoot a .22-caliber rifle and, starting as a tenderfoot, went up seven notches to win the junior championship. He also beat out John Tunney, son of world heavyweight champion Gene Tunney, in the camp's boxing finals.

The years from 1947 to 1949 were spent at Eaglebrook School in Deerfield, Massachusetts, 55 miles north of Hartford, Connecticut, on the side of Mount Pocumtuck. When the chauffeur first put Fred on the train bound for the school, he had no idea where he was headed. He discovered it only after he arrived. Established in 1922, the 630-acre boarding school has the motto *Lumen Fides Labor Facta*, which translates as "Light, Loyalty, Work, and Deeds." "I was just a skinny kid with wire-rimmed glasses," said Fred. "I was a year ahead of my class. I looked like I was eight and was as immature as a six-year-old."

It was at Eaglebrook, for boys from the sixth to ninth grades, where, as a way of easing the bother of making his bed every day, Fred invented the contour bed sheet, which he tried, unsuccessfully, to get the dorm housemother to sew for him. Although he never applied for a patent, he developed it long before such sheets were commercially available. Also at Eaglebrook, Fred devised a gadget which would automatically shut a window when it rained. Once, as manager of the ski team, he strung radio wire from the bottom to the top of the school's mountain in order to communicate to the crew at the base when the racer started. One year he received an award for being the most helpful boy.

After Eaglebrook, it was on to Milton Academy, like his father before him. Located in the sleepy town of Milton, Massachusetts, 10 miles outside Boston, population 26,000, Milton was originally established as a coeducational day

school under the Massachusetts land-grant policy in
1798. Along with Andover,
Exeter, and Groton, it is a
major springboard for Harvard, Yale and other Ivy
League colleges. The school's
motto is *Dare to Be True*. The
Milton yearbook for 1952,
when Fred graduated from the
school, contains the first mention of Fred Alger as "Fearless
Fred."

Before he entered Eagle-
brook, when he was 11, he
aspired to be the world's greatest golfer. This marked a key
developmental episode in his
life, which he frequently uses
to point out the value of a disciplined focus. "He tells it
every time the family gets

*Fred at age seven. As a child he was mostly
given to solitary endeavors.*

together, as if he's never said it before," said daughter Hilary. "He loves it."

The scene for his training was the elite Country Club of Detroit in Grosse
Pointe. Every day of summer vacation Fred would wake before dawn to catch a
bus that would take him to the club. When he reached his destination, he would
trek the long road to the clubhouse and submit himself to an inflexible routine,
which he determined would take him to his goal.

Dawn to dusk, day in and day out, the young southpaw hit golf balls, over a
thousand a day. He applied himself to his goal with utter dedication and passion.
He subscribed to all the golf magazines and did "everything one should do to be
a pro." Nothing else mattered to him but being number one at golf.

Seeing him in the same gray flannel outfit every day, most club members
thought he was just another poor kid who turned up to caddie. Certainly not
one of the mighty Algers of Grosse Pointe, for whom a street is named in Detroit
and a county in northern Michigan, where Fred's great-grandfather secured the
family's logging fortune.

Although Fred won Michigan district champion for his age group—he could
drive a ball 170 yards and score in the 90s when he was 12—he peaked at 14 and
abandoned his quest when he read magazine stories about kids his age in Texas

who could hit balls 250 yards and shoot in the high 60s and low 70s. "I realized I'd never be a great golfer," Fred admitted. "I gave it a three-year shot, played endlessly, and took my game as far as it would go. When I knew that I would never be great, I quit." Since then he's picked up his clubs perhaps only a dozen times in over four and a half decades. Now living in Switzerland, he's taken up the sport again for leisure.

"It isn't being number one as much as attempting to be your best that ignites Fred," said an admiring associate. Ever enthusiastic about sports, Fred quickly replaced golf with tennis, and though he mastered it, he had no extreme ambitions for the game. It wasn't something he would ever target in the same way as he had golf. Nothing would ever occupy that place for Fred—except the stock market.

Meanwhile, at the country club Fred first started a lunching habit which he would continue through all his career on Wall Street. He would order the same lunch every day. "They called it a chicken sandwich," said Fred, "but they always served turkey, which was cheaper than chicken in those days. And I think I had a chocolate sundae to go with it."

According to his secretaries, Fred would eat the same thing for lunch for months on end. In the early days it was a BLT on white bread, chocolate pud-

Young Fred with sister Suzy. They were sent without supervision on a three-day rail trip from Detroit to San Diego.

Campaign literature from Fred Alger Jr.'s 1952 bid to be Governor of Michigan.

ding, black coffee, and a pint container of milk. Then he switched to a hamburger, coke, and chocolate ice cream. During another stretch it was always cottage cheese. He also insisted on eating his lunch at the same time every day, exactly at noon. Asked for the meaning of his rarely changing bill of fare, Fred replied simply, "It saves thinking."

After the war and four and a half years of service in the Navy, Fred Alger Jr. was returned to inactive status, and when he returned to Grosse Pointe, he immediately reentered local politics. In 1946 he was elected to his first of three consecutive two-year terms as Michigan's secretary of state, a post he held until he launched a turbulent, anti-establishment bid for the governor's mansion in 1952.

In that race, proclaiming himself a watchdog for the public interest against the excesses and waste in government and the dishonesty of political bosses, he posed for the press with the family boxer, which had a sign around its neck that said "Alger." Another theme of his campaign was the distressingly "slim relationship that exists between political practices and business methods." In political advertising, he appeared side by side with Eisenhower and Nixon, decrying high taxes, the high cost of living and corruption. It was an intense, hard-fought political battle, and Fred Alger Jr. used up a lot of his own money trying to get elected governor against the Democratic incumbent who had been his boss for two terms.

The Alger children were very much in the public eye during the campaign. David recalled that on election night, November 3, 1952, "everyone was in the library of the big house" well into the next morning listening to the radio. The first returns were promising. With 1,210 precincts out of 4,480 reporting, Alger led G. Mennen "Soapy" Williams 370,002 to 363,307 votes. Sadly Alger's lead would not last. In the final tally he lost by 8,618 votes, or less than $^{1}/_{3}$ of 1% of total votes cast in the heaviest voter turnout to that point in Michigan history. Another two votes per precinct and he might have won. The Grosse Pointe vote was 5,364 for Alger and 1,125 for Williams.

Fred Alger Jr. would not concede until a recount.

As reward for his loyalty to the party, President Eisenhower appointed Fred Alger Jr. to succeed Myron Cowan as ambassador of Belgium in the spring of 1953,

In his campaign to be Michigan's governor, Fred Alger Jr. promoted himself as a public-interest watchdog.

At the court of King Baudoin of Belgium, Suzette Alger was a stylish trend-setter.

beating out Charles S. Dewey, his father-in-law, who was also in the running for the same diplomatic post. Fred, who was in college, did not accompany his parents to Belgium; nor did Suzy, who was already married and the mother of two children. But it was here, in the residence behind the embassy, that David grew up and became fluent in French and Flemish.

The ambassador and his wife moved easily in the company of European aristocracy. The U.S. embassy in Brussels was "more brilliant than ever" after they presented themselves at the court of King Baudoin. Suzette de Marigny Alger had the perfect social pedigree. The papers described her as a "stickler for protocol" and a "stylish trendsetter of fashion, food, wine and flower arrangement." Alternately she was called a "warm, colorful person, unpredictable and a bundle of energy." As an accomplished equestrian, bridge enthusiast and skilled golfer, she had all the social and athletic skills to appeal to the upper crust. *Detroit Times* society editor Jean Whiteshead reported, "From the day they arrived in Belgium until they left four years later, Suzy's life was 'all whipped cream' and she loved every spoonful."

However, it cost Fred Alger Jr. more to keep the job than it paid. His salary was just $20,000 a year plus a $3,500 annual-expense allowance. The family's travel bills alone exceeded that amount.

Fred Alger Jr. relinquished his diplomatic post after a political flap over too many absent days from work. The charge was blown up in the national headlines and embroiled several other Eisenhower appointees as well, including Clare Booth Luce, then ambassador in Rome. Ambassador Alger defended himself vigorously at first, then reluctantly quit his post in protest, just in advance of the Brussels World Fair, for which he had worked tirelessly on America's behalf.

Political insiders noted, however, that Alger's ouster was actually engineered by Postmaster General Arthur Summerfield, who was unimpressed by his modest financial gifts to the party and was urging Eisenhower to dispense his patronage to the more generous party faithful in his second term. Alger left the Belgian kingdom without a successor on March 27, 1957. The following day he and his family set sail from Le Havre, France, for the United States on board SS *America*.

When the Algers returned to Grosse Pointe, they moved into a more modest residence on 294 Lincoln Road. The home where Fred had grown up had been sold for $250,000 to William Clay Ford, who demolished the structure and developed the property into 12 smaller houses. Today there's a road that runs right through the spot where Fred Alger's house once stood.

According to Fred, on his return from Belgium, Ambassador Alger "got into his pajamas and started drinking." Much to his son's displeasure, that's about all he did for the rest of his life. Like his wife, he persisted in chain smoking, preferring a brand called Brennig's Own, which was specially ordered for him, as for his father, from a New York City tobacconist.

But he undertook one last political struggle before receding into obscurity. It was a vain effort, bravely fought, for a minor post in the second precinct of the 14th Congressional District. "It's just as low as you can go," he said, "but really it's the basis of our political system." His rival in this "slugfest," Republican District Vice Chairman Richard M. Durant, controlled the ultra-conservative Republican Voters Association, while Fred Alger Jr. stood for the opposing United Republican Council, which aimed to combat reactionary principles and preserve traditional Republican politics in Wayne County.

It was to be the first step in a comeback that had as its goal the U.S. Senate seat being vacated by Senator Pat McNamara. Alger was a great fan of Richard Nixon and hoped to be part of the team on his 1960 ticket.

About that period Whiteshead reported, "Mrs. Alger, with that intriguing Tallulah Bankhead voice, says they've lived their lives backward, playing when young, working hard in their 'old age.'"

Though his political ambitions remained unrealized, in his last gasp at public service Alger was offered the job of Secretary of the Navy in the Eisenhower administration, but by then he was too ill to accept the position. "Daddy was drinking very badly, Mummy was dying," said Suzy Alger Howard.

When they were young, Suzy, Fred and David led lives that were quite independent of one another, and each has a vastly different set of memories about childhood. They seem to be alike only in their competitive drive and in the fierce loyalty they have for each other.

David was the baby among them and the darling of the family. He was only four when Suzy got married and didn't share his formative years either with her or Fred III. Suzy recalled her frustration at David, who after his return from Belgium would tease her by speaking only in French. "He knew I couldn't understand it, and it was very aggravating," she said.

Suzy was pampered. She had her ponies and country beaus. Smart and engaging like her brothers, she also inherited her mother's beauty and relished her days at the Metamora Hunt Club. Suzy adored her father. Like him, her passion for horses won her professional distinction in the world equestrian community. Her prize steed, Warrior, in 1977 and 1978 "won both Badminton and Burley, which only two other horses have ever done," she said proudly.

Today Suzy Howard resides in Aiken, South Carolina, and spends her summers in Far Hills, in New Jersey's horse country, where she once lived.

Fred was undersized for his age and "not terribly coordinated." Even at 15 he was just five foot one. He was never popular in school and freely admitted, "I was very immature, very unaware of the world." He knew he didn't fit and was quite content doing things on his own and in his own way. "I was never part of the gang," Fred revealed about struggling through puberty. "I wasn't alienated, but I felt ill at ease, despite the fact that we were one of the leading families in the state."

Although Fred was playful, he was never a fun-loving child, according to his sister. After all, he grew up during the war. "When we went to California, life was very different," Suzy said. "There wasn't much fun for Fred." David's childhood memories of Fred were that he was always in trouble with the folks. "He was somewhat the black sheep," said David without flinching. "Father didn't like him very much."

Fred acknowledges that he had cold and distant relationships with both parents and still smarts from the fact that his parents never appreciated him as a son. "Perhaps they were disappointed to have a skinny little kid who wasn't a great athlete." He often muses about what it might have been like to have a son like himself. When he thinks of himself as a boy, he concentrates on "those outstanding characteristics about myself, especially my studiousness and the ability to focus and concentrate so completely." Fred suggested, "I think I would have been an interesting kid to have."

Said Fred, "I pretty much raised myself, only because my parents weren't around and were preoccupied with society and politics."

Today Fred Alger would be described as a prototypical Type A personality. He

Fred, with his mother and sister. "He wanted to prove himself to his mother," said Fred's daughter Hilary.

is obsessed with performance and achievement, always pushing harder. While it may be overly simplistic and imprecise to understand Fred's behavior as a way of winning his father's approval, his relentless drive to revive the family's fortunes falls squarely within this paradigm.

The insatiable need to succeed is what makes him tick. "My theory is that he wanted to prove himself to his mother," said daughter Hilary. "I remember writing that to him once and getting no reply." Despite his silent objection, the emotional scars that are the legacy of his difficult relationship with his mother are undeniable. We did not get along very well," he later admitted. "I was more like her than my father. She had a strong competitive side to her and a yearning for more. She was the one, after all, who told me when I was sixteen or seventeen that after she and my father were gone, there would be no money left." Since life was so easy and they were so comfortable, it came as a real shock for Fred to learn that his inheritance was being dissipated. That prompted the first stirrings of his dynastic impulse.

Fred's friend Arthur M. Dubow said, "I happen to agree with the theory that a vast majority of people who go on to great success in life are those who haven't had tremendously successful childhoods. In Fred's case it was compounded by the fact that the family had once been very wealthy, but his father died almost indebted." Putting it kindly, Fred described his father as "not an inventive man" when it came to business.

Suzy Alger defended her father saying "He was very patriotic, an accomplished rider and much beloved. He never squandered the money. He just never made any money, while he spent like he always did. Because they came from a certain era, I don't think my parents ever thought about cutting back." While their assets dwindled, Fred's paternal grandmother, Mary Eldridge Swift Alger Murphy, known as "Michigan's Great Lady" and a key supporter of the Prohibition movement, often stepped in to help.

Fred's mother died of inoperable cancer at the age of 56, in Palm Beach, Florida, on March 7, 1963. Fred III was starting his career in San Francisco. David was studying in Boston. Suzy was raising her family in New Jersey. In her obituary Jane Schermerhorn, a Detroit society writer recalled one of Suzette Alger's first press outings at a Junior League luncheon. "She was sparkling-eyed, dark hair

The Algers arriving in Brussels in 1953. Fred's father was the U.S. Ambassador to Belgium until 1957.

always worn short and softly curled. We still recall her slim, graceful figure in a navy and white printed frock, her tiny white straw hat with upturned brim. And, of course, there was another surprise at that first meeting—that was a definite quality—this time a deep red manicure, new and daring in the early thirties." It ended, "And so into memory, too, go the lessons of her loyalty, her devotion to family, her swift and amusing wit, her unconquerable courage."

Six months after she died, in September 1963, Fred's father took Katharine Sutton as his bride. She was a friend and neighbor in Palm Beach who traveled in the Algers' social set. She had thrown the farewell dinner before they left for Brussels and was later a frequent guest at the embassy. Fred believes they first met in Hawaii during the war.

Kay, as she was called, was born in Beverly Hills and was a contract player for RKO Pictures from 1930 to 1938. She starred in B westerns opposite cowboys like Richard Dix, George O'Brien and Richard Arlen before forsaking Hollywood for the brighter lights of Broadway. Before she quit show business altogether in 1940, she appeared in the chorus of a number of musicals, most notably *DuBarry Was a Lady*. Fred Alger Jr. was her fourth husband after Dan Topping, the millionaire sportsman and co-owner of the New York Yankees, whom she married in 1953.

"I didn't get along with my stepmother. She was a difficult woman," Fred admitted. "Among other things, Father got sick after he married Kay and never got around to distributing my mother's jewelry, which my mother specifically left to us. When he died, Kay inherited all his personal effects, which included the jewelry, which she promptly sold or gave away. This did not cement relationships with us."

Katharine Sutton Alger died at Grosse Pointe's Bon Secours Hospital in 1988.

Frederick Alger Jr. had died twenty one years earlier, at the age of 59, on January 5, 1967, in his home on Lincoln Road. The cause of death was given as a serious liver ailment. His obituary in *The New York Times* ends with a partial list of his clubs: Country Club of Detroit, Yondotega, Racquet, and Scarab of Detroit; the Grosse Pointe Club and Grosse Pointe Hunt Club; the Bloomfield Open Hunt and the Metamora Hunt Club; the Racquet and Tennis and the Turf and Field in New York; the Chevy Chase Club outside Washington, D.C.; and the Everglades and Seminole Golf Club of Palm Beach.

He was laid to rest in the family mausoleum at Detroit's Elmwood Cemetery, where Suzette's ashes had been interred. A friend observed, "It's unfortunate that both his parents died before they could see Fred's tremendous success."

Breaking with his past, Fred made sure that his children were raised in a close-knit family environment very different from the way he grew up, one that was both supportive and demanding. "Dad was always telling us to study hard and focus," said Hilary. "We felt the pressure. We were under the gun to perform."

Fred at age 16.

Fred entered Yale in the fall of 1952. He studied his subjects without much direction, gaining a degree in American studies in 1956. On campus he developed a fondness for movies and breezed through his first two years of college without any thought of a career or profession. "I had no plans for the future, had no job interviews, had no ambition to go to grad school," Fred admitted.

Fred spent the summers in Belgium, where he played the role of a wealthy young American and made full use of his diplomatic status. He drove fast cars, dated flashy women, and lived the high life. "It's very hard to see that in him now," said Hilary Alger. "But he's always been such a person of extremes. He's always one thing or the other."

After his junior year Fred's father insisted that he take a job at First of Michigan Corp., a regional brokerage firm where he was a director. There, he apprenticed and became attached to its head of research, Dr. Sidney Borden. "He made the whole business of investing so interesting, like a mystery story which, if you could figure it out, would make you a lot of money," said Fred. "I really wanted to pattern my life after him."

First of Michigan was started in 1933 and capitalized with $50,000 by some of Michigan's most influential families. Among its initial investors and first major clients were the Joys of Grosse Pointe, who, along with Fred's grandfather and great-grandfather, shared a stake in the now defunct Packard Motor Car Co.

Inspired by Borden, Fred entered business school at the University of Michigan and received his MBA in 1958. At Michigan Fred discovered his strength in finance. "I could see things that others just couldn't see" was his explanation. This became clearer to him after a midyear exam just before Christmas break. Fred was in an advanced finance class with a number of Ph.D. candidates. After the test they began complaining about the test's difficulty and discussing the answers they had given. Fred realized that his answers were radically different from the others. "As it turns out, I was right and they were all wrong," said Fred. Ever since then he has been separating himself from the pack.

Fred married Mary Lesly Stockard in New York's Lady Chapel of St. Thomas More Roman Catholic Church at noon on Saturday, October 11, 1958. Four months later, Lesly sought to annul the marriage, charging that Fred had "promised in writing to conduct marriage relations in accordance with the church doctrines." She complained that Fred had violated that promise by demanding birth control.

Fred never told his children about this first marriage; they discovered it on their own after they were grown.

If the child is father to the man, there's ample proof of it in Fred Alger. Many of the qualities he expresses in business were evident in him as a child or as a young man, when he was essentially raising himself.

His steady tinkering and curiosity about how things work would presage his development of proprietary investment models and his use of seemingly disparate financial and cultural data to identify movements in the economy and trends in market psychology. His creative approaches to problem solving as a young inventor would be recast as the original ideas that powered his business expansion. That experience of attempting to become the world's greatest golfer would show up later in his disciplined work ethic and attempt to be the first and best in the business. Fred's childhood character, so totally individualistic, lonely and self-reliant, would be reflected in his independence from the financial community and his company's organizational self-sufficiency.

4 🐾

Family Ties

"YOU KNOW, after your father and I are dead, there will be nothing left for you children," Fred's mother casually remarked the day he turned 18. She was referring to their share of the substantial fortune left by his great-grandfather, nearly $2.5 million dollars at his death in 1907, which had been dissipated in the intervening 45 years. Such a startling declaration might have melted down another young man of similar upbringing. Instead it steeled Fred's character, anchored his personal philosophy and steadied him on the course of rebuilding the family fortune and reviving the former glory of its name.

Fred Alger III is descended from one of eight Algers who were reported to have landed on the shores of New England in the middle of the seventeenth century. The name itself is derived from Teutonic words meaning "noble spear," and the ancestry is of mixed Scottish and English extraction.

His direct lineage is traced back to Matthew Alger, a fighting patriot during the Revolutionary War who lived in Connecticut and begat eight children. The most enterprising of his sons, John, married Sarah Baker in 1798 and migrated to central New York in 1809, after the birth of their third son, Russell. Several years later he uprooted the family once more and headed into the untamed Western Reserve, finally settling in Richfield, Ohio. Succumbing after a harsh and dangerous life as a pioneer farmer, John Alger died in 1818 at the age of 42.

In July 1832, when Russell Alger was 23, he married Caroline Moulton, a descendant of British-born Robert Moulton, who landed in Salem, Massachusetts, in 1627. Like Matthew Alger, Caroline's grandfather Freeborn Moulton distinguished himself in the War of Independence, fighting in Captain Danielson's regiment at Lexington Arms. The newlyweds soon moved to Lafayette, in northern Ohio's Medina County, to obtain one of the newly cleared farming tracts for settlers. A year later, the first of four children, a baby girl, was born.

Russell Alger had misfortune as a lifelong companion. Nothing ever prospered by his hand. He became bitter, ill-tempered, even cruel as a result. The property he picked turned out to be unproductive and forced him into debt. In 1840, after losing the farm by defaulting on its mortgage, he labored at a nearby woollen mill until it too failed. Next he joined his brother John in a shingle-making venture. Despite all the indications that success would be theirs—timber was abundant and construction demand was growing—the business flopped. Russell's family's financial condition deteriorated with every business failure and the birth of each new child.

Into this life of relentless penury was born Russell Alexander Alger on February 27, 1836, the date the current Alger saga begins in earnest. Young Russell's development was marked by physical hardship and emotional abuse by his father. Battered by feelings of inadequacy and defeat, Russell released his frustrations on his family, especially on the elder son who bore his name. He was so mean to the boy that once he watched him struggle and nearly drown in a millrace in order to teach him a lesson. As a result of his abusiveness Caroline left him for a time, returning to her father's home in nearby Canaan Township with the two youngest children.

In this negative environment Russell Alger suffered in silence and turned into a "shy, delicate, quiet and industrious lad." From an early age he was put in charge of numerous chores around the farm and consequently grew wise in the agrarian skills of plowing, planting, harvesting, milling, and the factory craft of shingle production. After his father lost the farm, home was a simple frontier log cabin with a single pitched roof—"not being dignified by a peak and ridge-pole, but sloped one way"—which signified the occupants' lowly station.

Russell's capacity for coping with adversity was tested early when both his parents fell ill, leaving him to manage the household. "At times, in 1847, we had little to eat and I remember one dreary period when both father and mother were sick for months in the same bed. Soon after this, mother died, and it was not long before father followed her to the grave," Russell later recalled.

The deaths of his parents, Russell at 39 and Caroline at 35, pushed Russell, just 12, into manhood. He met calamity with fortitude. He bartered his services with a neighbor for three teacups of flour a day. Mixed with milk from the cow that was their entire inheritance, this provided the only food his siblings—Ann Maria, 15, Sybil, 6, and Charles, 3; had. Russell and Ann Maria shelled all the leftover corn in the storage bin, and he carried it nine miles to sell at the mill. Though his first instinct was to keep the family together, their bare-bones existence made that goal unfeasible. Russell found homes for his brother and sisters, and he himself showed up at the door of his uncle, David Bruce Alger, a shrewd and prosperous businessman in Richfield.

The grand patriarch of this Alger line, Russell Alexander Alger became a man of immense stature—a rare breed of soldier, businessman and statesman whose triumph over fate and adversity was a model for his age and a unique example of the promise of America. Starting as a penniless farm boy, then an orphan, he advanced to be first a lawyer, then a Civil War hero, next a millionaire business-man with vast financial interests in lumber, mining, railroads, banking and real estate, and finally a statesman who served as governor of Michigan, secretary of war during the Spanish-American conflict, and U.S. senator.

Because he played significant roles in war, commerce, and politics, Alger's influence helped to shape American history. His life was emblematic of both the industrial development and territorial expansion that characterized this country during the second half of the nineteenth century, and it is his spirit that provides the impulse for Fred Alger's achievement. Any narrative of the Alger business would be hollow without reflecting on the roots that make it strong.

Russell's rough start in life and eventual triumph in business and politics is a story that might have been lifted from the pages of another more famous Alger, Horatio Alger Jr., the most prolific and widely read author of his day and a con-temporary of Russell Alger. There is no evidence of a direct familial relationship between the two Algers, who apparently did meet twice. It was said about Rus-sell that "he was self-taught and, making excellent use of his scant opportunities rose to prominence . . . providing proof of the rewards which await the poorest man if he possesses courage, character, patience, health and intelligence." The same was true for Horatio's fictional characters, like Ragged Dick and Phil the Fid-dler, who by hard work, virtue and thrifty habits overcame their poverty to real-ize wealth and honor.

The loss of his parents turned out to be a blessing in disguise for Russell Alger. Through their deaths he was freed at a young age from the constraints of poverty and family conflict. Thrust into situations that called for his survival, he was able to build himself up with the positive qualities of strength, self-reliance, initia-tive, enterprise and personal responsibility that might have been suppressed had he matured under the heavy hand of his father.

The older Russell was considered a "hostile, vindictive, alienated individual who could not function effectively in his efforts to rise above his station in life." His brother David, on the other hand, was a frugal and disciplined businessman-farmer whose personal success showed young Russell the possibilities in his own life. In him Russell found his mentor and role model.

But Uncle David was not easy on his young ward. For two years Russell never received any pay and worked just for room and board. It was hard labor. He plowed the fields with oxen, planted corn, and put in time at David's shingle mill. Tir-ing of this indentured condition and having proved his worth, in 1850 14-year-old Russell finally demanded and started receiving wages, which he needed for his faraway brother and sisters.

David Alger kept a strict accounting of any hours Russell lost from work and surely docked his meager pay accordingly. Following his rigid example, Russell religiously maintained a notebook of his income and expenses, assets and liabilities, at least during the early part of his life, and this slim volume has become one of the treasured keepsakes of the Alger legacy. Russell believed that his father's bad luck was due to his poor character and inadequate effort, and he was equally certain that acting in an opposite manner would attract good fortune. Russell worked furiously, as much for survival as to obliterate his father's negative example.

For seven years, eight months of the year, Russell was employed by his uncle. His wages rose steadily, by an average of $2 a month every year—from $3 a month in 1850 to $15 a month in 1855, which was the highest salary paid to farm workers in the region at the time. All his physical exertion had bulked up his body as well as his personality. At 19 he had grown to an impressive five-eleven and weighed 160 pounds. An exceptional worker, he could move a ton of hay in less than five minutes and boasted that he could cut 30 acres of hay with a scythe in two weeks. He was also reputedly a champion weight lifter.

From December to April in the years 1850 to 1856, Russell attended Richfield Academy in Summit, Ohio, to attain the knowledge required for his upward mobility. "I got the idea when I was very young that I must have an education if I expected to do anything in the world," he said. He worked for his board in the mornings and evenings and sawed wood at lunchtime to supplement his income. He was also a blacksmith's helper and cared for the livestock of the local physician.

At the age of 20 Russell finally left his uncle for better pay but held him in great esteem and affection for all his life. He took a job as a teacher in the district school near Akron. His first year's salary was $18 a month. The following year it was raised to $25.

But Russell had his sights on bigger things.

In May 1857 he began studying law under the sponsorship of the law firm of Wolcott & Upson in Akron, Ohio. Already he had figured out the importance of courting friends and associates in high places. Christopher P. Wolcott was the attorney general of Ohio, and William H. Upson was a prosecuting attorney in Summit.

After being admitted to the Ohio bar in March 1859, he began practicing law in the firm of Otis, Coffinberry & Wyman in Cleveland. It was mostly clerical work, record keeping and collections, and he soon grew weary of the office confinement, which was adversely affecting his health. As his temperament was better suited for an occupation outdoors and he saw opportunities farther north in the timber forests of Michigan, he made plans to abandon his legal career. Russell hooked up with Calvin Goddard, a Cleveland acquaintance, and together they took aim for Grand Rapids with $2,000 in seed capital borrowed from a New York contact.

Russell Alger may have had a few regrets in leaving Cleveland. For one, he had become quite a ladies' man. His "tall, lean good looks and his frank, friendly manner made him appealing" to the young daughters of the city's prominent families. Still, Grand Rapids was every bit the boomtown Russell imagined it to be when he, Goddard, and two friends reached it January 9, 1860, after a two-day journey. There was construction everywhere and brisk demand for, of all things, shingles, something which Alger knew a lot about. He and Goddard started purchasing modest consignments of shingles from independent producers and trading them on the open market for higher prices. It was backbreaking work and profits were slow in coming, but gradually their business grew. Eventually the pair ventured into lumber, acting as middlemen for logs which were bound for Chicago.

In Grand Rapids he was attracted to the preaching of Congregationalist minister Stephen S. N. Greeley and attended his Bible class regularly. At the same time he began to take an interest in the Republican Party, whose "great moral ideas . . . gave political expression to his core religious beliefs."

With his pocketbook swelling, Alger achieved a "measured degree of affluence" for that place and time. But he remained dissatisfied. On his birthday in 1860, Russell's diary entry conveys an impatient ambition. "Today I am 24 years old and what has my life amounted to. I fear not a great deal," he wrote. Russell Alger had high expectations for himself, and with great effort and skill, he meant to fulfill them.

First, though, he fell in love and married Annette Huldana "Nettie" Squier Henry, an accomplished young woman who shared his spiritual outlook. Born in New Haven, Vermont, on July 29, 1840, Nettie was the eldest daughter of leading Grand Rapids citizens, the Honorable William Gelman Henry and his cousin M. Huldana Squier. With their union Russell gained a family which gave him the emotional security he never experienced as a child and the social footing necessary to achieve his aims. Over the years William Henry turned into a close friend and business associate.

Russell and Nettie were married on April 2, 1861, in a double wedding with friends Carrie Burr and Eben Smith. Both couples boarded a train to New York for a honeymoon, which was bankrolled by Alger in anticipation of profits from a lumber shipment to a company in Chicago. Returning to Grand Rapids, Russell learned that the Chicago firm had failed, putting the finances of Alger & Goddard in grave jeopardy. War was in the air, and its uncertainty dampened all business activity. To secure his company's credit, Russell offered his most valuable possession, a gold watch, as collateral to his banker.

The following day, the bank, Daniel Ball and Company Exchange Bank, went bust. The town paper published a list of its assets, which included a draft on Russell's company secured by a gold watch and chain. The publicity devastated Russell. "This announced my failure to the people of Grand Rapids," he wrote in his diary. "I cannot tell you how badly I felt that day." More than money, Russell Alger was concerned about preserving his good name and character. But he had also ordered two rooms of furniture from Cleveland to begin his life with Nettie. It would soon be arriving, and he had no money to pay for it.

Although Alger & Goddard survived this crisis, its business faltered along with many others in the panic before the Civil War. In the following months, it became mired in debt. Alger would eventually satisfy all his creditors, but they would have to wait until after the war.

When the alarm bell rang for volunteers to fight the Civil War, Russell Alger enlisted. The Michigan quota was set at 21,337 out of 500,000 hoped-for recruits by the North. Though he had no training or previous military experience, he was unwilling to accept the status of private. So he made a deal: In exchange for signing up a regiment for battle he was commissioned Captain of Company C, Second Regiment, Michigan Volunteer Cavalry, which was mustered on September 2, 1861. Since he was an excellent horseman, the cavalry was his preference.

With resilience, fortitude, and bravery Alger managed a brilliant command and was twice wounded. At least four of the 66 battles and skirmishes he fought in affected the outcome of the Civil War and were recorded with high praise by chroniclers of that period.

His first heroic action was a 36-hour ride from Corinth to Pittsburgh Landing in May 1862 to petition Michigan Governor Austin Blair for a new regimental commander. Although the governor offered him the position—he had been the acting field officer—Captain Alger demurred for his lack of experience and endorsed Captain Philip H. Sheridan instead. Accepting Alger's recommendation, the governor ordered him to deliver this news to Sheridan, who was encamped 60 miles away. Without delay, the saddle-weary Alger jumped on his horse and rode to give "Little Phil" Sheridan his first independent command as colonel of the Second Regiment. From that point on, they were steadfast friends.

It was Sheridan who directed Captain Alger on a dangerous maneuver against the tail of the 5,000-strong force of Confederate General James Ronald Chalmers at Booneville, Mississippi, on July 1, 1862. With only 92 men, Alger occupied and confused Chalmers's rear guard, enabling Sheridan to rout the Confederates. Alger lost half his men in the operation and was himself seriously wounded and captured, although he escaped the very same day. He called this mission "the best thing I ever did in the service." Sheridan wrote that he "reckons it as one of the finest exploits of the war."

An intimate view of the fight was sent in a letter from the front to Uncle David, with whom he frequently communicated from the field of battle. It reveals that Russell had the touch of a poet, or may have been tinged with shell-shocked delirium. Written in flourishing long hand, it cries out about his personal privations and takes one intimately to the trenches of that bloody conflict.

> Head Quarters, Army of the Miss.
> Cavalry Division, 17 July 1862

Dear old uncle,

I once had a happy home in old Richfield where many happy homes were swept away by wide old time, and life danced along over the bounding billows of future homes and fond anticipation . . . . I found a home and all then that could make man happy in another state, but this too seemed only given as a silver lining to dark and looming clouds which hung beyond, and in my happiness I thought I heard my country call me to the field to defend her dishonor'd flag, . . . I bid fare well to all loved ones at home and rushed to the field where this 17th day of July finds me.

Occasionally a dark cloud sweeps and I think all at my former happy home have forgotten me and count me with the past. Is it not so! Do you not look upon me as something in the past but nothing present or for the future. If so let me assure you I am worth a single hope yet.

But why I write this, it is a fair conclusion to draw from the entire neglect I have received in hearing from home, and which not for Nettie and Grand Rapids friends, I should be entirely neglected. Nettie writes about two letters each week, which helps amazingly.

Have done no duty since July 1st. Am suffering very much from an injury rec'd in being thrown from my horse after the bloody battle of that day. Probably you saw an account of our fight (2d Mich and 2d Iowa under Col. Sheridan) at Boonville on that day, did you not! It was in all the papers.

Did you see an account of a battalion (4 companies) being sent to the rear and charging upon them with sabers! I commanded the battalion and was the first one in. I only had *90* men. Most of our men were on picket duty and this is all I could raise out of 4 companies. We killed and wounded over one hundred. I lost in killed, wounded and missing *one* officer and *34* men. I had 40 horses killed or ruined by wounding. We found ourselves . . . twice surrounded (the County is woody) and cut our way through. There were *4,700* of the rebels around us according to their own report. The rebel Col. Lee, who was there told our Col. who visited the Enemy's Camp a few days since that he was sure there was two or three thousand of our men in their rear. The effect was the whole rebel force (all Cavalry) stampeded and abandoned their position, thinking they were going to be cut off. We yelled loud enough for 4000 at least.

It was a bloody time and although I had my hat shot off and a hole shot through my coat I did not get wounded but was in the thickest of the fight. I was thrown from my horse and my stomach somewhat injured by sticking against a tree and shall not probably be able to do any thing for a month when I shall again be in the saddle. Have been since promoted and night before last I rec'd my commission from Gov Blair as Major with my complimentary letter. It is a fine position saying nothing about pay which is $197 per month.

Am waiting now expecting a furlough from Washington in a few days, which if I get I shall go home . . .

Love to all. Write Soon.

    "Major R. A. Alger
    2d Mich Cavalry
    Army of the Miss.
    Via Cairo
        Ills."

Alger was furloughed and convalesced in Grand Rapids throughout August 1862. Two months later he was promoted to lieutenant colonel, Sixth Regiment, Michigan Volunteer Cavalry. After that he was stationed in Washington, where he met President Lincoln for the first time in an introduction at the White House arranged by Michigan Congressman F. W. Kellogg. Alger found life at the capital to be dull and vacant. To get out of this tour, he applied for a post in the all-Negro regiment which was being organized at the turn of the year. To dissuade him from that course and satisfy his desire to return to the front, Governor Blair upgraded him to full colonel in the Fifth Regiment, Michigan Volunteer Cavalry, on February 28, 1863.

That summer, under the command of 23-year-old Brigadier General George Armstrong Custer, the youngest ever in the Union Army, Colonel Alger's troops pursued the retreating forces of General Robert E. Lee and blunted their escape with six major engagements in five days.

During the famous and bloody Battle of Gettysburg, Alger and his 5th Cavalry were greatly responsible for obtaining the military standoff. On July 3, 1863, they "repelled the repeated advance of a greatly superior force" with an intensity that left even the enemy in awe. In his memoirs Colonel Vincent Witcher of the 34th Virginia Cavalry wrote, "Alger at the head of the 5th Mich. Cavalry, most gallantly charged my line of dismounted Confederate Cavalry. By making the

Alger's exploits as a daring young cavalry officer were the stuff of legend.

charge that he did, Alger saved a Federal battery of artillery, which we would have captured, had he not prevented it."

The following night, July 4, 1863, Vicksburg fell and Lee's battered army drove toward the Potomac over mountain roads to meet up with General James Ewell Brown "Jeb" Stuart's wagon train of reinforcements and supplies, which was itself gathering speed for a position at Lee's rear.

Alger's 5th arrived near mountaintop Monterey House at midnight, when the 6th, under orders from General Judson Kilpatrick, rode down toward Stuart's wagon train. "There was much firing down where they were for some time, when General Kilpatrick ordered me with the 5th Michigan Cavalry to dismount and go and reinforce them," Alger wrote about the attack.

"Coming to the bridge, which I did not know existed until we arrived, I ordered my command, being under a very heavy fire, to lie down, and in the meantime sent word back to General Kilpatrick or General Custer—I don't remember which, informing him as to the situation and asking him to send down a mounted force.

"Meanwhile, a man close by me was shot and I seized his gun and ordered the regiment to follow me across the bridge, which they did with great cheer, and we immediately filed in on the left hand side of the road and formed a line—imperfectly, of course—under the flashes of our guns."

By four in the morning, when the fighting subsided, most of Stuart's train had either been captured or was burned by Alger's initiative. Praising his men's success, Alger said, "The dash of that Cavalry was the most creditable and very gallant. The 5th Michigan Cavalry was never driven back one inch. I would not detract one iota from the gallantry of the mounted force that came down, nor could I submit to anything that would cast reflection on my own command which never flinched in battle, and, as I said, did not recede a single inch, but pressed forward as rapidly as it could, dismounted, and after crossing the bridge, formed an imperfect line, not the entire regiment but of sufficient force to attack the enemy and capture a large number of prisoners."

About his performance that night, Custer stated in his cavalry report that he "always regarded Alger's charge as one of the most gallant in the war." In their attack on Stuart's train, Alger and his men kept Lee from receiving badly needed reinforcements and the chance of rebounding. Had his contingent not blocked Stuart's overwhelming force, how different might have been the outcome of the war? How altered American history?

Alger and the 5th's final pursuit of General Lee in that series was known as the second battle of Boonesborough, Maryland, on July 8, 1863. In it Alger took a gunshot wound in his left thigh and had to be carried off the field. After less than six weeks of medical treatment he was back with his men and ready to fight.

Alger cut a dashing figure in his uniform, as wartime photographs attest. A few solo poses have survived as well as group pictures with other Union commanders. A "slender man of erect, soldierly bearing," he wore an flowing mustache that rounded into a goatee, and his long, wavy hair was parted on the right. Russell's dark eyes were frank and intense whenever he faced a camera.

Custer, who commanded the 1st, 5th, 6th and 7th Michigan Volunteer Cavalry along with their artillery units, frequently sang Alger's praises. There was the famous charge of the Michigan Brigade at James City, Virginia, when Alger's 5th and the 1st "with sabers drawn and bands playing cut their way through Lee's army." Later that night Alger, with a small battalion, led another attack which Custer described as "daring in the extreme." About the Battle of Buckland Mills he reported, "the brunt of the attack fell on the 5th Michigan Cavalry, cutting it off from the main force, and which Colonel Alger met with his usual intrepidity and skill." Custer's view of his wartime performance would later prove significant to Alger's political aspirations, but not in the way his words of acclaim might suggest.

Meanwhile, Custer recommended in October 1863 that Alger, who by "meritorious conduct through discipline has proved himself worthy," be raised to the rank of brigadier general. Major General George Meade rejected the petition because he had "no use for cavalry or one of Sheridan's boys."

In February 1864, Colonel Alger was given a special role by the War Department to organize the mass distribution of handbills containing President Lincoln's amnesty proclamation behind enemy lines. Using scouts and cavalry expeditions, Alger traveled from Washington to Louisiana and spread over a million leaflets. The objective was to weaken Confederate resolve by offering a blanket pardon to any Confederate soldier who swore the oath of allegiance. In executing this job, Alger visited nearly every field position and reported directly to the president.

Another major blow to the South, leveled by Alger, occurred on May 11, 1864, at the battle of Yellow Tavern, six miles north of Richmond, Virginia. In this the conclusion of Sheridan's drive to disrupt Lee's road and rail links, one of Alger's men shot and mortally wounded General Jeb Stuart.

The following retelling of Stuart's demise is contained in a paper by Hudson Mead to the Prismatic Club, an old Detroit literary fraternity, in February 1996. Married to Fred Alger's first cousin, Frances A. Boyer, Mead is a retired Detroit lawyer and an enthusiastic scholar of Michigan and Alger history.

> Stuart brought his forces together and occupied a position across Sheridan's line of march at Yellow Tavern. The 5th Cavalry halted several hundred yards from the enemy position, and a moment later a Confederate general, accompanied by his staff with flags flying, rode up a small hill directly opposite where Alger was standing. Alger and the men around him all recognized the officer as General Stuart. "The order had been passed to cease firing for a moment," wrote Alger, "but one of my men standing close by me drew his gun and fired. An old sharpshooter named John A. Huff, of my regiment, Co. E I think, said to him, 'Tom, you fired too low and to the left,' and turning to me said, 'Colonel, I can bring that man down,' and I replied 'Try him'" The rest is history. Jeb Stuart died the next day.

Russell Alger suffered enough guilt over his involvement in Stuart's death that he tried to remedy it by helping out his son, as recorded in a letter dated February 15, 1901, to Elihu Root, his successor as secretary of war.

After the war, riding up Jefferson Avenue, this city, a gentleman with me said, "there comes Mrs. General Cook, [wife of General P. St. John Cook] and the lady accompanying her is her daughter, Mrs. J.E.B. Stuart." I had not known that Mrs. Stuart was their daughter and a queer feeling came over me, which I cannot describe. I always avoided meeting her, and one day just before leaving for Washington, a friend and neighbor who was in mourning called at my home accompanied by a lady in mourning; I met them at my front door and she introduced Mrs. Stuart. I do not think I even looked at her, and I do not believe she knows the history that I have just related to you, although it was made a record by the order of President Lincoln.

During the War with Spain she asked for an appointment for her son, which the president was kind enough to grant. He made a very good record. She now writes and requests me to ask that he be appointed again in the Army, and it is a matter that if I were to beg but one request, I would ask.

In June 1864, Custer would again try to push for Alger's promotion to brigadier general. This time the request made it all the way to Secretary of War Edwin Stanton, but it languished with him.

Alger's next major encounter took place at Trevilian Station, Virginia, on June 11 and 12, 1864, when he joined Major General Sheridan in the historic charge down Gordonsville Road, which ensnared 800 prisoners, 1,500 horses, one stand of colors, six caissons, 40 ambulances, and 50 army wagons. Their conquest was short-lived, however, as Alger and his men, having pushed too far into enemy lines, were themselves surrounded and forced to relinquish their spoils and fight their way back to safety. Alger's body count was 21, and 131 of his men were taken prisoner. In this, one of bloodiest cavalry battles of the war, the Confederates eventually beat back Sheridan, who took heavy casualties in the four-mile rout, but not before destroying six miles of the Virginia Central Railroad.

Afterward, Alger accompanied Sheridan and Custer into the Shenandoah Valley, where he was made to execute their scorched-earth policy, which he found extremely distasteful.

Weary of war, weakened by poor health, and disillusioned by his recent duties, Alger applied for an honorable discharge from the Army, which was sanctioned on September 20, 1864. Twenty-four years later, the events surrounding his release from military duty would be riddled with controversy resulting from a revelation that Custer, with the consent of Alger's good friend Sheridan, had tried to get him booted out of the Army.

Nevertheless, after Robert E. Lee's surrender at Appomattox, Russell Alger finally got his wish and was brevetted Brigadier General, United States Volunteers, by Ulysses S. Grant on the recommendation of General Custer, "for gallant and meritorious services" in the battle of Trevilian Station. Two years later he received his final military commission, the rank of major general. Brevetting is the promotion to a higher rank without a corresponding increase in pay.

In the smoke-cleared aftermath of the Civil War, Russell Alger turned his attention to business with the same courage, devotion, and discipline he applied to military duty.

The war hadn't left him poor. In fact, thanks to Nettie's clever management of savings from his salary, his assets grew during the war into a modest nest egg of real estate, bonds and cash. At least Alger was wealthy enough to refuse his $30-a-month pension as a gesture of patriotism.

Over the next 20 years Russell Alger built up a network of businesses and investments which prospered steadily as he became one of the wealthiest and most influential leaders in the country.

His first business venture after leaving the military, in partnership with an Army acquaintance, was a service agency based in Washington, D.C., to assist discharged veterans in making the transition back to civilian life.

Next, he shifted his attention to buying and selling oil leases on the East Coast, a trade which proved to be so lucrative he even considered moving to New York in 1865. One of his most profitable transactions was flipping 700 acres of Canadian oil fields in 1866. Alert to the uses of timber in oil production, he acquired a sawmill in Ohio and sold it to a Pennsylvania oil company. While he traveled up and down the coast, making deals and panning for business ideas, Nettie held down the fort in Grand Rapids.

But he quickly tired of his itinerant lifestyle, and he eventually brought his family to settle permanently in Detroit in May 1867. The Algers bought a home in the city's affluent Second Ward and kept a stable of fine horses and carriages. In Detroit, Alger made an investment in the Detroit Improved Brick Company, which turned out to be a losing proposition. Then he started buying scows to haul industrial cargo over the Detroit River and entirely owned or had a piece of nine vessels used in river transport.

In the fertile ground of the post–Civil War economy, Alger found his spot in the timber forests of upper Michigan. There it was known that choice pine forests, wrongly categorized as swampland, were frequently sold at auction by the state for as little as $1.25 an acre. Alger struck a partnership in 1867 with brothers Franklin and Stephen Moore, two Detroit lumbermen of Scottish and Irish descent, which enabled him to exploit that opportunity. Together they formed Moore, Alger & Co., with the brothers providing the capital and he the sweat equity for a third of the business.

After carefully surveying the region, Alger made a cautious $26,000 bid for several choice tracts of "swampland" in Iosco County on Au Sable River. From 1867 to 1870, the period of the first Alger-Moore partnership, Michigan white pine was selling for an average price of $12 per thousand board feet. Production, which commenced at 1.25 million feet a year, quickly surged to 70 million feet a year.

In typical fashion, Alger immersed himself totally in the lumber business. He took Nettie and his daughter Caroline to live in the logging camp for the entire winter of 1867 with the first 35 lumberjacks. They traveled there by sleigh, since the site was 100 miles from the nearest road. In this manner did he achieve success, with "the thorough knowledge of everything he touched . . . lumber, railroad, construction . . . no detail escaped him."

Logs from that camp initially were transported over land and sold to Brooks & Adams in Detroit. Once production increased, Alger was able to utilize his fleet of scows and rafts to open up additional markets in Toledo and Cleveland. The pride of the Alger armada were the mammoth tugs *Vulcan* and *Torrent*. In one trip to Toledo in 1871, *Vulcan* was able to tow 2,270 logs or the equivalent of 1.3 million board feet.

In mid-1873, just before a financial depression that would batter America, Alger expanded his lumber business by acquiring 9,000 acres of barely accessible pristine forests along the Black River in Alcona County, Michigan. Although financial conditions forced the Lake Huron plant to reduce its output and it would also have been prudent to trim expenses at Black River, Alger took the contrarian gamble of building up his new enterprise. He purchased an additional 30,000 acres from the main camp in Harrisville to the Black River and continued to invest in new and improved equipment and facilities. More important, it was here in 1876 that Alger first used rail transportation for shipping timber—an innovation that gradually transformed logging from an uncertain seasonal operation to a continuous, year-round business. In so doing, Alger irrevocably changed the lumber industry.

Franklin Moore, meanwhile, died in 1874, and his equity in the firm was acquired by Alger, George W. Bissell and an affluent jeweler named Martin S. Smith. When Franklin's brother Stephen Moore retired, the firm was rechristened R.A. Alger & Co. Large as it had grown, the Alger lumber cavalcade was just beginning to roll.

Rail traffic out of the camps was primitive at first. The cars were drawn by horses to start the trip, then attached to locomotives to complete the journey. Alger constructed a short railroad, about 3.5 miles, out of the pineries, at a cost of $3,000 a mile. He soon tacked on another six miles. After that, there was no turning back.

By 1879 there were 400 men working in 10 Alger lumber camps along the trail from the Black River to Harrisville. The firm had commitments from buyers for 60 million feet of timber. Alger's efforts during the down-turned economy were paying off, and R.A. Alger became the biggest source of timber along the Huron.

In April that year, Reverend D. Hawley of Baltimore, who owned the Cleveland Sawmill and Lumber Co. which specialized in the manufacture of long spars, bought out Bissell's stock. As a result the firm was recapitalized at $1 million, with Alger owning 20,400 shares valued at $510,000 and Smith and Hawley each with 9,800 shares equivalent to $245,000.

Two years later, the firm's growth called for another restructuring. The capital was raised to $1.5 million, and it was renamed as Alger, Smith & Co. Incorporated. As majority shareholder, Russell Alger became president. Joining treasurer Smith and vice president Hawley as its officers were secretary J. C. McCaul and John Millen, the valued and trusted superintendent of the Black River operation.

Over the next twelve years Alger, Smith positioned itself as the premier producer and wholesaler of long pine timber required for spars, masts and heavy construction. In its prime, the firm's vast pine lands totaled about 100 square miles, produced nearly 150 million feet of timber annually, and employed over 1,000 men. In 1896 its investments in timber properties were valued at over $1.7 million.

Russell Alger proved to be as formidable in business as he was valiant in war. He credited his success to a gritty and difficult childhood, as it "provided the formation of the habits of perseverance and industry which have been a great benefit in my business life." It was all "steady growth and constant hard work. I never made a dollar out of speculation," he counseled.

"When you come to look into the lives of the wealthy men of the country you will find that most of them started with little or nothing, only the determination to win. The successful business men of to-day are men who have adhered to a certain line of policy of business; they have made their money by legitimate means. Money that comes quick, however, seldom stays with a man, and the only way that men ever succeed is to fight the battle without reference to whether they suffer defeat occasionally or not. The business man who wins success never gets discouraged; reverses only sharpen and strengthen him for new encounters."

And so he survived the economic slump in 1883–84 and another devastating depression in 1893.

While most of his wealth was created via Alger, Smith, Russell Alger operated numerous other commercial interests throughout the land which, taken in their aggregate, surely qualified him as a one-man financial and industrial conglomerate.

Chief among his other concerns and investments was the Manistique Lumber Co., owning 62,000 acres of white pine and norway spruce in the Pacific Northwest, which yielded up to 140 million feet of lumber a year. Alger was president and Millen the vice president of this timber enterprise, capitalized with $3 million, which was established in 1882 in Seney, Michigan, with the participation of his Smith partners and 13 other lumber barons.

In 1882 Alger joined other lumber tycoons, who had followed his lead by building rail links to their own timber supplies, in splicing all the short lines into a central rail network, which eased transportation costs and reduced overhead. Then with fellow Detroiter John S. Newberry, he created the Tawas and Bay County Railroad, primarily to serve the timber industry, which was later renamed Detroit, Bay City and Alpena Railroad.

During his most prolific and profitable business cycle, 1887 to 1897, the railroads provided the central connection between Alger's business and political interests. When he visited his far-flung empire, he traveled in style. One newspaper account described the *Michigan,* a private railroad car he acquired in 1884, as "opulent, magnificent, handsome, incredible." It was considered a "palace on wheels" and slept 12 people comfortably. He used it judiciously for entertaining his political friends. A second private car, the famous *Grand Marais,* was used as the office car of the Manistique Railway, the principal rail operation of the Alger, Smith Lumber Co., which opened its line in 1887.

Alger's push into railroads was enhanced by a brief partnership with Allan Shelden and James F. Joy in Peninsula Car Works. Shelden had married Alger's daughter Caroline, and Joy's son Henry would develop the Packard Motor Car Company with his sons, Russell Jr. and Frederick.

Eighteen eighty-six was another spectacular year for Alger's timber investments. He gobbled up 10,000 acres along Louisiana's Red River, a large area near Washington's Puget Sound, and two redwood companies in Medocino, California, one of which had the sawmill concession at Fort Bragg. Alger's estates were scattered as far away as Mexico and all through Quebec, where he owned several mining operations. Through Alger, Smith he acquired forests and operations in Minnesota, Florida and Alabama. He also made other real estate investments, notably in Kansas and Tennessee.

Alger was president of the Detroit & Rio Grande Livestock Co. in New Mexico and the principal shareholder of the Volunteer Iron Mine, which worked the rich Palmer reserves in Marquette County. Closer to home, Russell Alger put his capital to work in the banking industry by starting two large banks, the Detroit National Bank and State Savings Bank, in which he remained a stockholder and director.

On the domestic front, Alger sold his original Detroit home on Lafayette Street to Frank Hecher in 1883 and constructed a spacious and opulent three-story brownstone on Fort Street West and First at a cost of $150,000 including furnishings. He had come a long way from that lowly log cabin of his destitute youth.

With their wealth Russell and Nettie Alger became avid acquirers of contemporary European art. Their much admired collection included portraits by Fernand Cormon, landscapes by Jean Baptiste Camille Corot and Narciso Virgilio Diaz de la Peña, and battle scenes by Alphonse (Marie) de Neuville. There were equestrian scenes by Adolf Shreyer and paintings of animals by Rosa Bonheur, who was considered the most important woman artist of the day.

The jewel of the group was Mihaly Munkácsy's *Last Moments of Mozart,* which depicts the dying composer, surrounded by his wife, eldest son and several principals of Vienna's opera aristocracy, as he drafts his own requiem. The purchase of the painting in 1888 was fussed over by the papers because of its cost—reportedly $100,000—and the renown of the artist, who had just brought an exhibition to New York.

The Algers' taste for finer things extended to a gallery of rare antiques, exquisite furniture and fine rugs. A *Detroit News* reporter found the Queen Anne decor of the Russell A. Alger house, designed by Gordon W. Lloyd, to be "as beautiful as money, refined taste and care and thought can make it . . . filled with treasures of art and bric-a-brac gathered from the four quarters of the globe."

To be sure, Alger had his detractors. His financial success was envied by some, and the liberal-socialist view was that "the northern county he helped wreck," Kingston Plains in Michigan's Upper Peninsula, is the one that "bears his name." Alger County was created on March 17, 1885, about the same time the Alger house was being built.

But most people simply marveled at the extent of his empire. Certainly, his partners and fellow investors had only gratitude and applause for Alger. James Joy once said, "He is an honorable and upright and public-spirited man. One of those by whose efforts and vigor the world is moved forward in its progress and is greatly benefited." Alger's partner John Newberry was so impressed with his character and personality that he arranged for his son to be apprenticed to him. He was also much beloved by his workers. Among the woodsmen of Michigan, the popular feeling was that one should "work for Alger; don't take anything else if you can hire with him." His operations provided benefits and amenities unheard of at other lumber camps. There was, for example, a convenience store at Black River, superior food in its mess halls, and his workers could redeem their wages at any time during the month. He provided the same kind of compassionate leadership for his laborers as he had given his troops during the war. Esprit de corps was high; production was up.

By many accounts, it is for his Christian kindness that Russell Alger was "remembered best and loved deeply." And rightly so, since it was reported that he distributed as much as a fifth of his income to the poor and needy.

In the deep freeze of January 1887 he, anonymously and at a personal cost of $5,000, arranged for relief in the form of a barrel of flour and a ton of coal or a cord of wood to be delivered to 500 indigent Detroit families who otherwise

In Houghton, Russell Alger founded the Michigan College of Mines, now known as Michigan Technological University.

might have perished in the winter. The myth surrounding this philanthropy was later enlarged to 1,000 tons of coal, 1,000 barrels of flour and 1,500 cords of wood to 1,200 families, but it is, regardless, just a glimpse of his philanthropy which aided thousands of people over the years.

The most colorful recipients of Alger's patronage were the Newsboys of Detroit, a ragged army of 2,000 impoverished youngsters who were licensed to sell the *Detroit Evening News*. Considered "generally a good class of toilers," perhaps he saw in their condition a trace of his own early plight. Around Christmas time every year he outfitted each one of them with a complete set of clothes: a shirt, trousers, socks and overcoat. For this and more, they called Russell Alger the "father of all the newsboys" and held him up affectionately as their patron saint.

During the Chicago World's Fair in 1893, he chartered a special train with 14 coaches from Michigan Central Railroad to take 700 newsboys as his personal guests to the Columbian Exposition. Alger went through every car, giving a short pep talk to the lads, aged seven to fifteen. In gratitude for his gifts, the newsboys heartily carried the Alger standard. It was they who first raised the chant, "What's the matter with Alger! He's all right!", which became the rallying slogan in all his political contests.

One of newsboys who eventually achieved success, Jim Brady, reminisced, "I can remember the first night he decided the boys could use a little help. He sent out word that he was giving quarters away. In less than an hour he had every newsboy in town in his offices in the old Telegraph Building . . . . He talked with us, and the boys who needed clothes got them. To the end of his life, he could point to dozens of successful men he had helped and he was proud."

As his commercial ventures continued to gain momentum, Alger turned his gaze to politics, which he looked on as a natural extension of his philanthropic and humanistic inclinations. He never imagined that the battles he would undertake in the political realm would be more fiery and strenuous than his Civil War engagements.

In 1884 Alger, running on the Republican ticket, wrested the job as Michigan's twentieth governor from incumbent Greenback-Democrat Josiah "Uncle Josiah" W. Begole by a slim plurality of 3,953 votes.

Alger's single term as governor, from 1885 to 1887, had the imprint of his upright and open management style. He made it understood that one of his principal strategies was getting government to work more like business. He demonstrated a "great capacity for work" while discharging his duties, and was known to be patient, careful and a genuine listener.

While he was in Lansing, he presided over the founding of the Soldiers' Home near Grand Rapids, the Michigan College of Mines in Houghton, the transfer of the Superior Ship Canal to the federal government, and the formation of the counties of Iron and Alger. An advocate of prison reform, he instituted the state Board of Pardons in 1885. As defender of poor children, he promoted leniency in Michigan's reform schools.

Because Michigan had prospered during Alger's administration, it was called the "Alger Boom." Another catch phrase for his public service was "Alger Means Business."

The only stain on his conduct was his handling of the brief but violent strike by sawmill workers in the Saginaw Valley, which occurred in the summer of 1885. The chief demand in this 56-day strike was for a 10-hour workday, down from 11 hours. The mill owners had been using private security forces, like Pinkerton's, to put down the labor uprising. Alger called out armed state troopers to keep both sides at bay. Many condemned his action as an unfair concession to fellow mill owners, which they believed was motivated by his interest in keeping the strike from spreading to his own operations in the Huron. In the end, enactment of the Barry Law on September 18 gave laborers the shortened day they were seeking.

Russell Alger's political ambition didn't stop at Michigan's borders. For his next prize, he was eyeing the U.S. presidency. So the Alger Club of Detroit was formed in February 1888 in order "to exert all honorable and worthy effort" to securing his nomination. A loyal Republican, he was reluctant at first to throw his hat into the ring, believing that James G. Blaine, the party's standard bearer in the previous presidential election, might again seek the office. They made a pact, which Blaine later reneged on, that finally freed him to pursue the Oval Office.

In his lengthy farewell address as Michigan's governor, Russell Alger promoted his pet issues, such as caring for the insane, the abuse of prison labor, and a constitutional amendment prohibiting the sale of liquor. He also exposed his strong nativist sentiments, which urged a tough, exclusionary, even racist immigration policy. Alger was against "undesirables, the dregs of creation," whom he counted as the insane and infirm, criminals, nihilists, anarchists and Chinese, being "dumped on our shores."

In the opening salvo of his drive to be the Republican presidential candidate, Alger made this unpopular group a target of his campaign. "They fill our prisons, poorhouses, and asylums, and we are taxed to support them; while in this fair land of the setting sun there has been poured a class of people who from their very nature cannot become citizens and must not be made slaves," he said, speaking at a San Francisco banquet in his honor on March 19, 1888. "They degrade labor; they live like animals and thrive and grow rich upon what would starve a white man. No one of either class named ever shouldered a musket or helped save this country, and therefore ought not to be here."

Sentiment ran high toward Alger. His political support grew from his popularity on the Pacific coast, favor among Irish Americans, endorsement from public figures, and strength with business leaders in New York. He could even count on the Negro vote. The influential Frederick Douglass stood behind him, and wrote that if Alger was nominated he would "put off his coat and go to work for him."

Russell Alger was clearly presidential timber, at least in the eyes of his beloved Michigan. With shameless adulation the *Detroit Sunday News* on May 27, 1888, made this presidential pitch for its favorite son:

> He is a gentleman of the broadest gauge and the highest principles. Pleasing in his address, genial in his disposition, active in the discharge of his duties, unbounded in his resources, faithful to his

friends, charitable to his enemies, unlimited in his capacity for work, staunch to his party, firm in his enlightened convictions, generous as he is brave, munificent in his charities, profound in his judgment, unrivaled in his grasp of great affairs, cool in an emergency, just at all time, vigorous in his mind and body, honest, industrious, sensible, unostentatious and happy in his domestic relations, he exemplifies the peculiar advantages of that government over which he now aspires to preside as chief executive.

And so Russell A. Alger's name was placed in nomination on July 19, 1888, at the Republican National Convention in Chicago. In his nominating speech, Robert B. Fraser, of Detroit, said:

General Alger will supply to you strength from all quarters of the Union. The rich men will trust him, for he is a man of business, and his honor among them has been unquestioned. If you think he is not a friend of the poor man, come with me to the city of Detroit, where he lives, enter with me into the poor man's home—aye, into the very abode of misery—and mention the name of our favorite, and you will find that, next to their God among the poor the name of General Russell A. Alger is held sacred.

His advocates believed that if Alger sailed through the balloting process, he would surely reach the White House. Alger was confident that his campaign would be aided by a clean record in business, government and military service. While he marched into the convention to the sound of "The Alger Grand Refrain," played to the tune of "Marching Through Georgia," plots were being hatched to crack his support by debasing his character. Alger's campaign was soon ambushed by a string of allegations that ultimately kept him from reaching the president's office.

One of the first, lesser slanders was that he had wrongly absconded with Franklin Moore's share of the lumber business. There were complaints about his role in dispatching the state militia to crush the Saginaw strike. He was charged with plotting to buy the election: $250,000 to win the nomination, with a similar figure earmarked to gain the presidency.

He was accused of buying Negro delegates. In a carefully worded statement that avoided direct accusation, prominent senator and presidential hopeful John Sherman released a statement that "friends of General Alger substantially purchased the votes of many of the delegates from the Southern States." Alger responded gently to the last charge with a letter to Sherman "hoping that the unfounded charges would not interrupt the existing friendship" between their families.

The most hurtful scandal, and the one that ultimately foiled his presidential bid, was the surfacing of a betrayal that had occurred nearly 25 years earlier. A story was leaked to Charles A. Dana of the *New York Sun*, following persistent rumors, that Russell Alger had abandoned his battle post in 1864 and was facing a dishonorable discharge at the time he resigned his commission. Worse for Alger, it was alleged that the order for his ouster had been signed by his old comrade General Custer and endorsed by his "warm personal friend" General Sheridan, along with Generals Torbert and Merritt.

This was all news to Alger. But sure enough, once his war files were unsealed, they gave up the smoking letter and subsequent recommendation:

> Headquarters, 1st Brigade,
> 1st Div., Cavalry, Mid.
> Mil. Div., Sept. 16, 1864

Captain A. E. Dana
A.A.G., 1st Division, Cavalry

In compliance with instructions of the General commanding the division I have the honor to submit the following "Report in the case of Colonel R.A. Alger, 5th Michigan Cavalry, stating the time at which he left the command, for what purpose, by what authority and his present whereabouts.

Colonel Alger left this command the morning of August 28, as it marched through Harpers Ferry to rejoin the Division near Halltown; he has been absent since that date. I was not aware of his absence until this brigade halted to feed near Halltown, when Assistant Surgeon St. Clair of the 1st Michigan Cavalry informed me that Colonel Alger, owing to some indisposition, had remained at a house in Harpers Ferry. At the same time Assistant Surgeon St. Clair presented, for my approval, an application from Colonel Alger for a leave of absence for 20 days. As Colonel Alger had, two or three times previous to this, applied for a similar leave of absence when, in my opinion, he was fit for duty, and which opinion subsequently proved to be correct as it has in the case now referred to, I returned Colonel Alger's application without my approval.

He failed to join his command. I first heard of him again as stopping at the Eutaw House, in Baltimore Maryland. I now have authentic and reliable information that he is staying at one of the hotels in Washington, D.C., and that he has been placed on duty, in the latter city, as a member of a General Court Martial. How he came to be detailed I cannot say. He left this command without authority and after having been refused leave of absence from these headquarters.

And I have directed that he be reported "Absent without leave" on the muster rolls of his regiment.

> Respectfully submitted,
> G.A. Custer,
> Brig. General Com. Brig.

> Headquarters, 1st Cavalry Div.
> Sept. 17, 1864

Respectfully forwarded for the action of the Chief of Cavalry. The case mentioned within is the third in which Colonel Alger absented himself from the command without proper authority since the commencement of the present year's campaign—Severe measures should be taken to prevent a recurrence of this evil.

> W. Merritt
> Brig. General Commanding

Alger was stunned. He was completely ignorant of the document. "I never knew or suspected there was the slightest question about my being properly sent with the large number of sick and wounded men to Annapolis, on General Custer's recommendation," he said in his defense. "If he knew the facts it was one of the most cruel outrages that was ever perpetrated upon a soldier." Alger was right. There was nothing on the muster rolls or regimental records to show that he had ever been A.W.O.L. He was legitimately absent from the war for only eight days during his three years of service. His acclaimed war exploits aside, the fact that he was subsequently released from the Army by no less than President Lincoln and then promptly promoted on Custer's insistence added to the mystery. But since both Custer and Sheridan were in their graves, neither man could rise up either to defend or accuse him.

Alger fought off his critics with an affidavit from Samuel R. Wooster, the acting brigade surgeon on General Custer's staff at the time, who confirmed that Custer was aware that Alger was hospitalized and not, as Custer had charged in the letter, reposing in a Washington hotel. As rumors about Alger's desertion persisted, Wooster wrote the following refutation in February 1892 to the Army's adjutant general,

> During this campaign General Alger's health was very much impaired, and the night after our crossing into Maryland from Shepherdstown he was very ill. The following morning, as we were gathering the sick and wounded together to send to hospital, I informed Colonel Alger that he was not able to march and must go to hospi-

tal. This was customary for Surgeons in the field to do when the command was on the move, and I accordingly directed Col. Alger sent to Annapolis with others, and I distinctly remember that I told him I would forward the proper papers to him there, as we wished to get the sick and wounded away at once.

I made application for his leave to General Custer, reporting the facts and supposed it was granted, and never heard to the contrary until yesterday. In my opinion there never was a more unjust act committed against a soldier than that which is reported to have been by General Custer in his reporting him as absent without leave, and recommending his dismissal.

According to Army records, Alger resigned on September 16, 1864, the same day that Custer wrote his recommendation for a dishonorable discharge. His resignation was accepted the following day by the secretary of war and approved by the adjutant general on September 20, 1864. The desertion charge was received just after the signing of the papers for his honorable release, but since Alger had already left the service, it was decided that no action would be taken against him. It was this freak of timing that kept Alger ignorant of the charge of desertion against him.

What could have prompted Custer to raise such an unfounded charge against the unknowing Alger, when only weeks earlier he was sending out letters of praise and commendation to secure his advancement? In his recommendation for raising Alger to the rank of major general, Custer wrote, "Too much praise cannot be given Col. Alger for the gallantry he displayed." Custer carried that dirty secret to his death, and we will never know for sure. But there was likely a personal motive behind his vendetta.

Several times in June and July 1864, Custer had entreated Alger to promote his brother Thomas, then a sergeant in the 21st Ohio Infantry, to second lieutenant in the Michigan 5th Cavalry so that he might serve on Custer's personal staff. Alger recoiled at his proposals. "I would rather resign than promote an outsider when there were deserving insiders," he told Custer. Failing to win him over, even after dangling a quid pro quo leading to Alger's coveted rank of brigadier general, Custer warned that Alger "would regret it one day." Indeed, it may have cost him the presidency. According to Alger, Custer was "very angry and from that day we were no longer friends." For a while his antagonism toward Alger was so deep it exceeded the bounds of fairness. Even though he knew that Alger and his men were instrumental in capturing prisoners in the Battle of Fort Royal on August 16, Custer gave official credit for their deeds to another regiment.

After the war they must have patched up their differences, since they exchanged letters for many years. Custer regularly sought Alger's business advice and was a frequent guest at his home. When Custer died in 1876, Alger organized the Michigan Brigade in his tribute.

Alger's relationship with another general and friend provided fodder for a different election scandal. Again, Charles Dana and the *New York Sun* were behind the exposé, which alleged that in 1886 Alger had given $10,000 to General Sheridan to scotch Custer's accusation and avoid a dishonorable discharge. Nothing was further from the truth, but it made good copy.

Sheridan had fallen on hard times while waiting for a veterans' pension bill

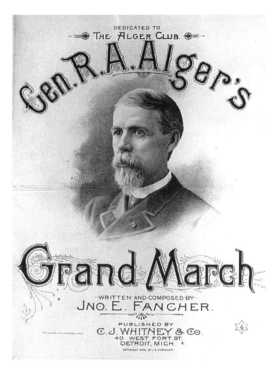

Songbook for the theme that raised Russell Alger's nomination for the U.S. presidency during the 1888 Republican convention.

to come through. Alger, a rich man, wanted to help out a beloved friend and former corps commander. He gave Sheridan $10,000 in 1886, on the condition that he invest it in Washington real estate and buy a $15,000 life insurance policy with the 6% interest. That's how, when he died in 1888, his wife, Irene Rucker Sheridan, was able to survive. The only money she had consisted of $10,000 from the original gift and $15,000 of life insurance.

Eventually Dana admitted that his printed libels lacked veracity and couldn't be substantiated. By then it was too late to resuscitate Alger's political reputation.

In the 1888 nomination balloting, Alger received 84 votes in the first count, far behind the leader, John Sherman, who had 229 votes. In the second ballot, Alger's support grew to 116 votes, but Sherman's also rose, to 249. When the third vote was counted, Alger's support was up to 122, while Sherman's strength stabilized at 244. Neither vote was enough to ensure victory, and there were three other contenders.

By the fifth count, with Alger receiving his highest tally of 143 votes, the process was still hopelessly deadlocked and taken to the party's back rooms to be resolved. New coalitions were formed. For one, there was talk of a McKinley-Alger ticket. But the final word belonged to James Blaine, the kingmaker who owned the caucuses, and Alger was unable to win him over.

When the seventh and final balloting was recorded, General Benjamin Harrison, U.S. senator from Indiana, who took only 94 votes in the third ballot, was able to overtake both Alger and Sherman and become the Republican Party's candidate.

With Levi P. Morton as his running mate, Harrison beat his Democratic opponent, Grover Cleveland, gaining a 233 to 168 victory in the electoral college, even though Cleveland had 100,000 more votes in the popular count.

Even in defeat Russell Alger was a good soldier for the Republican Party. He contributed up to $100,000 in the election. A gifted orator, he made speeches for the cause, which reflected his concern about tariff protection for American goods and controlling the Supreme Court.

Moving away from the Harrison, Sherman, Blaine wing of the party, Russell Alger drifted toward the camp of William McKinley and used that alliance to advance his place in politics. McKinley, then a U.S. congressman from Ohio, was, like him, an Ohio lawyer with protectionist sentiments for American industry. He would eventually gain prominence as the author of the McKinley Tariff Act of 1890 and use it to win the Ohio governor's race in 1892.

Alger's political camp derived its strength from veterans, especially the Grand Army of the Republic, a powerful society of nearly 400,000 Civil War heroes. He energized that base when he was elected its commander-in-chief in its twenty-fourth National Encampment in Milwaukee in 1889. During his year as its leader, he redoubled his lobbying for pension legislation. Alger was also a member of the Military Order of the Loyal Legion in New York, a Son of the American Revolution, the Society of the Army of the Potomac, Union League Club and Ohio Society, all of which influenced his decision to make another bid for the presidency in 1892.

Before the nomination the *New York Sun* was again at his heels. It reissued the slurs that he had deserted his post and was recommended for a dishonorable discharge by Custer. Around the same time his opponent in the previous race, John Sherman, published a second volume of his recollections, which reiterated that "the friends of Gen. Alger substantially purchased the votes of many of the delegates from the Southern States who had been instructed by their convention to vote for me." These haunting allegations were among the reasons that Alger declined to pursue his nomination with any real conviction. There was also a personal reason behind his lack of resolve: the sudden death of his nine-year-old son Allan on February 10, 1891, which devastated him emotionally.

In the 1896 elections Alger took another brief shot at running for president, but that quickly gave way to overwhelming support for his ally William McKinley. Shortly after Grover Cleveland took office in 1893, a severe financial depression struck America, in part due to the Democrats' repeal of the McKinley legislation for tariff protection and their support for a monetary standard backed by silver. Within a year 15,000 businesses had failed, 158 national banks had been liquidated, and four million Americans were out of work. It was easy to blame the Democrats and regain the White House.

McKinley's political survival was aided greatly by Alger's support. Alger used his own popularity to organize a major campaign effort called the "Generals' Tour," a frenetic 12-state, whistle-stop stump of Civil War luminaries, which left Detroit on September 20 and wound up in Philadelphia on October 24. The tour covered 8,448 miles, stopped at 255 locations and held 276 meetings—with as many as eight speeches a day—which was crucial in carrying McKinley to victory against the Democratic challenger, William Jennings Bryan. Led by the *Michigan*, Alger's caravan rolled into Minnesota in September. "Duluth gave Alger a stupendous welcome," reported the city's *Pioneer Press*, "as throngs of Civil War veterans and several marching bands carried Alger on their shoulders from the Depot to a rally where he gave his standard speech on patriotism, sound money and the gold standard."

McKinley repaid Alger's support by appointing him secretary of war, just in time to manage the Spanish-American War.

Lucky for America that this conflict occurred on Russell Alger's watch. By his deft leadership the military was able to marshal the forces necessary for an early victory. The political consequences were such that America gained the confidence and the inspiration to roll into the next century on the road of expansionism as a military superpower.

There had been sounds of war from the direction of Spain since 1895, but these were generally unheeded by the U.S. government. So America was desperately unprepared for any fighting when Alger arrived in Washington in March 1897 to take up his appointment. The branches of the military were divided and rife with jealousy, their staffs deeply entrenched in bureaucratic routines. The officer corps was tired and aging; the cabinet vacillated irrationally over how to respond to an armed conflict whose certainty was growing every day. On the table was the fortification of Key West and several other southern ports, for which Congress was reluctant to authorize $50 million in emergency appropriations. Alger shamed the government into action when he announced, "If Congress refuses to pay for such an emergency, then I'll pay for it myself." Soon after his dare, Congress signed off on the $50 million.

The sinking of the U.S. battleship *Maine* on February 15, 1898 provided the pretext for escalating the hostilities beyond a war of words and testing both Spain's resolve to challenge America and this country's willingness to respond with force.

The ship had been routed to Havana to protect U.S. citizens and property. The press fired up public opinion against the explosion and death of 260 crewmen, reporting it as a sneak attack by the enemy. Ostensibly succumbing to popular will and in the guise of liberating Cuba from Spanish oppression, the American government finally declared war against Spain on April 23, 1898.

But a War Department telegram dated February 16, 1898, and signed by Alger's secretary, Victor L. Mason, proposed that the ship's sinking was "accidental in the forward magazine"—something which many in the government came to believe. Later, the cause of the *Maine's* destruction was determined to be a defective boiler.

America's brisk victory obscured the truth of how ill prepared it was to face any kind of military conflict, much less subtropical jungle warfare on three separate fronts—Cuba and Porto Rico (as it was then called) in the Caribbean, and the Philippines, thousands of miles across the Pacific Ocean.

History records that, "In order to mount an adequate offensive, Alger was obliged to mobilize, train, equip and convey into battle a force of 275,000 men, mostly volunteers, from every corner of the land in a very short time. There were no army transports. Military storehouses were empty. Firearms and ammunition were in short supply." Yet within sixty days after war was declared, the first American armed flotilla was speeding to Cuba. And on board the USS *Yale,* which sailed for Santiago de Cuba on June 23, was Secretary Alger's son Frederick.

Across the Pacific, on May 1 a squadron of six ships under Commodore George Dewey obliterated the mighty Spanish fleet anchored in Manila Bay, and did so without the loss of a single American life and only eight wounded.

Cuba fell in 64 days, and it took only 113 days for total victory. Under terms of the peace treaty signed in Paris on December 10, 1898, Spain abandoned Cuba and ceded the Philippines, Puerto Rico and Guam to the United States in exchange for $20 million. With that, three centuries of Spanish imperialism, made possible by its dominion of the seas, came to an abrupt end.

Considering how much was achieved in preparing for and winning this disagreeable war, one might expect that Alger was honored for his masterful administration. Quite the opposite. What should have been the high point of his public life—a source of personal gratification and public admiration—became a politically motivated debacle ending in public censure over the troops' welfare.

Alger's troubles started after the war ended when homeward soldiers began voicing complaints about difficult wartime conditions. Their discontent cried out for satisfaction, and Russell Alger was a convenient scapegoat. It was easy to foist on him everything else that went wrong during the war. An Alger chronicler wrote, "After the war, he was criticized . . . for things over which he had no control: rains and muddy roads, failure of officers to observe sanitary conditions, fevers, promotion of friends, personal financial gain and unparalleled corruption."

In response to the allegations, the government enpaneled the Dodge Commission in September 1898 to evaluate the War Department's performance in the conflict. Out of this investigation erupted a juicy scandal that shook the department and embroiled Alger as its head.

The meat of the scandal was the shipment from Swift & Co. of Chicago to U.S. servicemen in Cuba of 337 tons of refrigerated beef and 198,000 pounds of canned fresh beef that turned out to be tainted. The embalmed beef was described as having a "chemical preservative which gave the meat an unnatural mawkish, sickening odor, like the odor of a human cadaver after the undertaker had injected the body with preservatives. After cooking, it had the flavor of decomposed boric acid."

Alger's principal adversary was Chief of Staff Major General Nelson A. Miles. Though he was aware that canned beef had been served in Army rations without incident since before the Civil War, he assumed a pose of being scandalized. Just like Custer, he had a personal motive for attacking Alger: The secretary of war had passed him over for the glamorous Cuban command in favor of General William R. Shafter, a landsman from Kalamazoo, Michigan.

The Dodge proceedings consumed 109 hearings and 495 witness. Although Commissary General Charles P. Eagan faced the brunt of the attack for procuring the tainted meat, Alger, as his boss, also had his feet held to the fire. After all was said, both men were found blameless. A separate military court, convened on February 9, 1899, similarly cleared both Eagan and Alger of responsibility for what was determined to be no more than a purchasing accident turned rancid.

Alger's exoneration in the beef inquiries did not bring an end to his troubles. Like a pit bull who wouldn't let go, Miles continued to incite the press and stir the public's distaste for Alger's alleged misdeeds. This "yellow journalism" even spread to London. Alger's swift resolution of the war faded quickly in people's minds. The fever of disapproval reached such a pitch that the term "Algerism" became the slang for dereliction of duty and administrative incompetence.

How trying must all this have been for Russell Alger, who as a young man in Grand Rapids had become perturbed that a newspaper announcement might cheapen his reputation? It didn't help that reporters followed him like flies, pressing for his resignation. Yet while Alger bore the pain, he kept his faith in the goodness of people and trusted in a favorable outcome. The president would defend him. After all, the two men were more than political allies. They were old and loyal friends. No one had spent as much time as Alger, smoking on the verandah of the White House with McKinley. "Well, take it all through," said Alger. "I have done pretty well by trusting people. Guess I'll take the chance." But he spoke too soon.

At first President McKinley refused their urgings and remained publicly steadfast with Secretary Alger, twice refusing to accept his resignation. McKinley replied, on one occasion, "Mr. Secretary, after your magnificent work in the War Department, rather than cast any reflection upon you by accepting your resignation, I would resign my office."

In the end, however, McKinley yielded to the insistent chorus of Alger detractors and made it known to Alger that he was "no longer welcome in the Cabinet." More distressing than his abandonment by McKinley, what Alger found "bitterly disappointing" was that the President didn't possess the moral courage to face him with his doubts. Instead he sent his ailing Vice President Garret A. Hobart to convey the message. Sparing the president further turmoil, which one editorial called "a kindness shown to the president," Secretary Alger turned in his handwritten resignation on July 19, 1899, and dejectedly prepared to leave for home.

The constant struggle to clear his name began to overwhelm him and left him dispirited. "His agitations began to affect his health. He could not eat well, he lost his sleep, and when he tried to divert his mind, he found always that he was confronted by a horrible specter, mocking his rest. He knew the truth, but could not vindicate himself." So reported a secret informant, close to General Alger who wished to keep his identity hidden, in a July 30, 1899 article in the *Detroit News-Tribune*. "The terrible exhaustions of his life are beginning to tell. He is growing grayer every day. He has aged immensely since he became secretary. I am glad that the strain is over at last."

"He Suffered Agonies, But Asked No Man's Pity" was the story's headline. "Confiding by Disposition, His Faith in Human Nature is Sadly Shaken—Gross Cartoons, Maliciously Sent to His Wife, Tortured Him Beyond Measure—He Was Plunged Into Dejection by the Calamities That Befell Him" read the subhead. Yes, there was even a sinister scheme to poison his home life by sending Nettie packages containing the most vicious cartoons and vitriolic harangues, which were usually kept hidden from Alger by his secretary.

The source went on, "Had McKinley come out and said strongly: 'Whatever mistakes were made were my mistakes; no man is responsible for the errors of the war.' Had he done this, Alger would be vindicated. Why did the president not do this? Why did he permit Alger to be crucified day after day, week after week?

"Alger's keenest sufferings were caused by his supposed friend's treachery."

Russell Alger left Washington quietly. Through all his troubles he refused to retaliate against his president. The closest he came to expressing his anger appeared in the account of his resignation which he gave to *The Milwaukee Journal* on March 4, 1900. McKinley "has many lovable qualities," he explained, "but he lacks backbone, and nothing can make up for the lack of backbone."

Russell Alger's lifetime of toil for the Republican Party was being dismantled as he watched. "All the good will he had so carefully fostered, all the credits he had arranged on the good will of the people at large he saw quickly vanish."

After all that he had been through, one commentator judged him to be "one of the most bitterly assailed figures in American history." Perhaps this is why his name is absent from standard desk references and histories of this country. While Russell remains virtually unknown, the other Alger, Horatio's name is found even in dictionaries.

In the waning days of his administration, when Alger's persecution was at its peak, both relief and distraction came by sitting before Detroit artist Percy Ives for his official War Department portrait. For three weeks the pair kept company in a secluded top-floor studio in Alger's Washington residence in a dash to complete the assignment before Alger left the capital.

"Do not paint the look of trouble, the sad, burdened expression," Nettie Alger begged Ives. "He is not always so. It is not natural. I do not want it perpetuated in a portrait." But it was impossible for the artist to brush over the strain that had settled so completely over his features. His steely eyes were blunted in a soulful gaze. Alger's pear-shaped face had narrowed with age; his eyebrows had grown bushy. Thinning silver hair, still combed to the right, met his sculpted goatee and overflowing mustache in proper fashion. It was a distinguished portrait—some even called it a masterpiece—but his careworn aspect couldn't have pleased Nettie even if it was true to his and the country's fin de siècle weariness.

"He is a picturesque man to paint," observed Ives. "His wonderfully bright penetrating eyes, that give one the impression of being dark brown, are a dark, graying blue. His beard has whitened much in the past year, and the contrast that it makes against the bronze of his face is striking."

If official Washington was eager to get Russell Alger out of the way, public Michigan couldn't wait for him to come back. On August 2, 1899, the Alger train from Washington was intercepted in Toledo, Ohio, by a welcome party of over 300 who filled eight coaches in a special train from Detroit. Banners were stretched along the cars announcing, "Michigan welcomes her honored son, Gen. Alger" and "There is only one Alger." Alger walked through the welcome train during the final leg of his journey home and pressed hands with everyone in the greeting party.

When Alger arrived at the Michigan Central station, his first sight was an army of his beloved newsboys chanting, "What's the matter with Alger? He's all right!" Welcoming Alger, Governor Hazen S. Pingree "tucked Secretary Alger's arm under his own," and they were whisked away on waiting carriages for a ceremony in front of city hall.

Detroit dressed up for Russell Alger's arrival. The buildings were draped with patriotic decorations. A large electric sign read, "Welcome Home." Alger and Pingree followed 300 bicyclists, a 100-piece band and an escort of 1,000 uniformed marchers past jubilant crowds to the dais. Awaiting them was a crush of 50,000 people, including groups of veterans, firemen, policemen and letter carriers who shouted praises for Michigan's hero.

Detroit Mayor William C. Maybury, the chairman of Alger Day, took the microphone at 9:00 p.m. and gave the first laudatory speech. Referring to Alger's trials in Washington, he said, "It will go forth to the world as a due notice that the standard of high character, built by patience and perseverance, honesty and uprightness, cannot be thrown down by slander."

Governor Pingree added his voice of support. "Your withdrawal from the cabinet was forced as an insult to the state," and pointing to the sympathetic throng, he proclaimed, "They are here today to rebuke the cupidity of politicians . . . and show their contempt for the cowardly attacks of a venal press."

When Alger finally took his turn at the podium, the crowd cheered wildly. He opened up to the faithful: "Since I went away two and a half years ago, the country has been through a terrific struggle. The office of which I was the head was taxed to the utmost of every man's strength who occupied any position in it. I gave it my best thought and honest effort, and did everything I could to carry out my part of that great work . . . . I come home without grievance. I can truthfully say that I had from the President all the support that he could give."

Nettie Alger, who traveled to Detroit with him, and members of Alger's family looked on admiringly from a canopied platform. After the speeches a grand reception took place inside city hall for 5,000 invited guests.

Russell Alger consumed the next two years of his life in writing a book about the Spanish-American War, which stressed his positive achievements and warned about the consequences of military unpreparedness.

Before the book was released, McKinley was assassinated by an anarchist named Leon Czolgosz and succeeded by Vice President Theodore Roosevelt. Because Russell Alger's book severely criticized the man who was now president for his "contemptible wartime behavior," the publisher, Harper & Brothers, destroyed the original printing and reedited the manuscript for passages which attacked Roosevelt or might have been taken as offensive. With a print run of 2,500 copies, this expurgated version was the one finally issued on October 10, 1901.

Among the book's most memorable passages is this tribute to public-spiritedness. "Should war ever again come upon this country and find it so totally unprepared as it was in 1898, I hope that those who have been so profuse in their criticisms and eager to discover faults may have the patriotism and pride of country to rise above personalities and, instead of striving to bear down, may endeavor to strengthen the hands of those upon whom the burden may fall and whose only hope of reward is that satisfaction which comes from the consciousness of having labored honestly and unremittingly to serve a government whose flag has never yet known defeat."

After leaving Washington, Alger focused his energy on running his wide-ranging enterprises, but he was not through serving his country. The U.S. Senate would be his last great challenge.

Though he had decided not to challenge the incumbent Senator James McMillan in the 1901 Senate race, as he was unwilling to split the party, fate stepped in and rewrote the book of life. McMillan won the election but died in August 1902, and Michigan Governor Aaron T. Bliss exercised his authority to appoint Alger to take McMillan's place. The Michigan legislature soon elected him to the U.S. Senate, for a four-year term ending March 3, 1907. In that era state lawmakers decided who represented Americans in the Senate, not as is done today, by popular vote.

The Algers returned to Washington and soon became prominent in the social scene. Their opulent home was a lively center of the city's political culture. Mrs. Alger was an "ideal hostess." Years earlier she had been described as "one of the charming ornaments of Mr. McKinley's cabinet." Now she assumed the same role for President Roosevelt. "Her lovely daughters were social favorites at dinner parties, receptions, lunches and afternoon teas," reported one paper.

Predictably, Russell Alger threw himself into his duties. He served on the committees of Coast Defenses and Pacific Railroads during the fifty-ninth Congress. He worked for passage of a veterans pension bill. He galvanized swift congressional relief for victims of the San Francisco earthquake and fire. He voted for meat-inspection and food-standards laws. He challenged Michigan's efforts to restore capital punishment.

About America's persistent armed conflict in the Philippines, he was steadfastly isolationist and lobbied for its quick independence, a view shared by fellow industrialist and philanthropist Andrew Carnegie, who publicly praised Alger for his stance. Alger promoted Philippine sovereignty even though he was in a great position to exploit its rich southern forests and had received many proposals to start lumber operations there during and after the war.

Closer to home, he quarreled with a proposal to unify the territories of New Mexico and Arizona into a single state on the grounds that the federal government had previously pledged never to do so. In this debate he went head to head with no less than President Roosevelt, who backed the single-state motion. Alger should also be remembered for volunteering to finance a relief expedition to the gold fields in the Yukon, where miners were trapped by grim winter weather.

As Russell Alger's term progressed, his health, which had been poor for several years, began to deteriorate. On March 1, 1905, he collapsed in the Senate chamber. Returning to Detroit from Arizona a month later, he was found unconscious in his rail car. Oppressed by physical ailments that kept him from his duties, he announced in July that he wouldn't seek renomination to the Senate. "I have filled many public offices, but there is none I relinquish with more regret than the office of United States Senator," he lamented to a reporter. "I really am in love with the position."

Russell Alger never saw the end of his term. In December 1906, he suffered a

Though Russell Alger was responsible for commissioning the Rough Riders, he was never on the best terms with Teddy Roosevelt.

mild heart attack, which was attributed to overworking, and he was bedridden during the holidays. His condition improved, and he was looking forward to hosting a party on February 5 to celebrate his retirement. The invitations were addressed and ready for mailing.

In the afternoon of Tuesday, January 22, Alger was seen relaxing with longtime friend and Secretary of the Navy Truman Newberry in the Senate cloakroom, happily engaged in a "favorite pastime" of retelling Civil War stories. Later that evening he was scheduled to appear at a dinner for his replacement, incoming Michigan Senator William Alden Smith, but he arrived home exhausted and was forced to miss the party.

The next day he completed his duties in the Senate and the War Department and, as usual, reached home late. Marion Alger, the wife of his eldest son, Rus-

All of Michigan mourns the passing of the state's favorite son. Thousands stood in the bitter cold to pay their last respects.

sell "Rusty" Alger Jr. wrote in her diary that she kept him company "talking of many things and he sings 'Nearer My God to Thee.'"

The next morning he awakened around seven-thirty. Nettie fed him a "spoonful of whiskey," and they made plans for the day. She then left the bedroom briefly, and when she returned, he was complaining of chest pains and gasping for breath. The family doctor was summoned immediately, but Russell Alger fell unconscious before his arrival. Death followed quickly, at 8:30 A.M. on January 24, 1907. Russell Alger was 71 years old.

His doctor gave the official cause of death as "chronic valvular disease of the heart and acute edema of the lungs." He wrote further, "Death was quiet and apparently painless." His wife and son Frederick were at his bedside.

On January 26, after a brief memorial service, attended by President Roosevelt and Vice President Charles W. Fairbanks, at Alger's residence, Russell Alger's body was taken by military escort to a waiting train for his final journey home to Michigan. The six-car burial train was met in Detroit the next morning by Mayor William B. Thomson and a host of state dignitaries.

On Monday, January 28, 1907, while flags all over the country were lowered at half mast, Detroit said farewell to Michigan's hero with the highest honors. The funeral cortege moved slowly past the multitude which lined the route from the Alger home at 150 Fort Street to city hall, where the bier was transferred for obsequies and public viewing.

An estimated 27,000 people "shivered and stamped" in the bitter cold as they waited to pay their last respects. General Alger's casket rested under a canopy of American flags and was arrayed with floral cornucopia—"banks of palms and walls of roses, violets, fleur de lis, lilacs, hyacinths, lilies, orchids, lilies of the valley, wreaths of laurel, fern and cypress leaves and victory palms. Roses, his favorites, in massive sprays and wreaths concealed the walls and to their heavy perfume, innumerable violets lent a milder fragrance."

Following the mournful notes from a solitary coronet, Alger's casket, now wrapped in an American flag, was carried down Jefferson Avenue to Elmwood Cemetery, where the Alger family mausoleum awaited its first occupant. Before Russell Alger's grave was closed, Nettie placed upon his coffin a bouquet of pink carnations. The card was inscribed, "The general was my friend. Please lay this small token on his coffin. From the son of a Confederate soldier," and signed "J. E. B. Stuart, Jr. 1907."

Thus ended a wondrous American life, of great honor and achievement. Not only is it worthy of remembrance for the obvious political, military and financial deeds, but, as was entered in the Congressional Record on February 23, 1907, by Speaker Pro Tempore Denby, for "kindness, generosity, tact and sweetness of disposition; the great human attributes that charm and attract and make the world akin."

Annette Alger lived to be 79 and died on August 24, 1919. Of the nine children born to Russell Alger, only five survived his death. Two sons: Russell Alger, Jr., and Frederick Moulton Alger, and three daughters: Caroline, who married Allan Shelden of Detroit; Frances, who married Charles B. Pike of Lake Forest, Illinois; and Fay, who married William F. Bailey of Harrisburg, Pennsylvania.

Unlike his father, who left behind nothing, Russell Alger gave his children a sumptuous inheritance. Though his wealth at times had ranged as high as four or five million dollars, his estate was valued at just under two and a half million dollars when he died. A million of this consisted of stock in Alger, Smith & Co.

Adjusting Alger's wealth for inflation hardly gives a true picture of how rich he was in terms of money's buying power today. Blue serge suits were on sale at Wm. Vogel & Son on Broadway and Houston in New York City for $13.75. Straw hats sold for $2. Fine shirts cost between $1.50 and $2.50 and made-to-order trousers, from $2.50 to $3 a pair. An elegantly furnished apartment with private bath, including meals, at the Alabama Hotel, 15 East 11th Street, could be had for $12.50 a week. Newspapers sold for one cent.

In investment terms, the Dow Jones industrial average ended 1906 at 129.80. Ninety years later, it closed out 1996 at 6448.27. If one applied the same growth to Alger's net worth, it should have risen above $122 million, and that's without reinvesting the dividends. But Wall Street suffered through several depressing periods in the intervening years, and real estate, which made up the bulk of his assets, often appreciated far greater than the stock market.

Fifteen years after his stirring send-off, the Russell A. Alger Memorial Monument was unveiled in Detroit's Grand Circus Park. Created by Daniel Chester French, it has a bronze portrait medallion, surrounded by a wreath, burnished in a five-foot red granite cylindrical base with the inscription, "Russell A. Alger, soldier, statesman, citizen 1836–1907." Rising ten feet from the pedestal is a bronze maiden carrying a sword and a shield with the coat of arms of the state.

Unlike Russell Alger's impoverished upbringing, an exceedingly bountiful childhood experience was given to Russell Alger's second son, Frederick Moulton Alger.

Like his father, he was born on the twenty-seventh day—not February but June—1876. Originally christened Frederick Charles Alger, he and his sister Frances decided that their mother's name Moulton "should be perpetuated among my father's children," and his name was accordingly modified in the register at Detroit's Fort Street Presbyterian Church in 1892.

Frederick and Frances were close throughout their lives. His letters to her often began, "Frances Dear, Sis" or "Frances my dear one." She was the one who taught him how to ride—on the family coach horse Curly. The family made semiannual trips on the *Michigan* to California. On one of these journeys in 1892, first Frances, then Frederick was laid down with the mumps. After the illness he suddenly put away the Horatio Alger books for boys in favor of grown-up stories. The author had given them to his father when he learned about Russell's work with the Detroit newsboys.

Frederick attended Phillips Academy in Andover, Massachusetts, and then entered Harvard in 1895, where he joined the Hasty Pudding Club, Phi Delta Psi, and the staff of the *Harvard Advocate*. He withdrew from college in May 1898 to serve his country in the Spanish-American War. He was sworn into the U.S. Army and rushed through basic training at Camp Alger, named for his father, in Virginia. By month's end he was ordered to duty in Tampa, Florida. And the following month he sailed with the First Infantry under General Joseph C. Breckenridge as part of America's first landing force in Cuba.

A short time later, though just 22, he attained the rank of Captain, U.S. Volunteers and was delegated to the staff of General Henry M. Duffield. Captain Alger also saw action in Puerto Rico and played a role in the clash that finally captured Santiago.

After the war he resumed his studies at Harvard and graduated in the Class of 1899. At that point he left the States in September for a year-long world tour.

On February 22, 1901, Frederick presided over the Michigan Club banquet, "much to father's delight," because the Michigan Club symbolized Republican leadership in the state. Every year the club held a gala affair on Washington's birthday, which often served as a rite of passage for its younger members.

On May 3, the same year, he married Mary Eldridge Swift, who was called Mignon, a pet name given by her French maid, and the second daughter of Detroit lawyer Edward Young Swift. The noon wedding took place at the Fort Street Presbyterian Church. "A combination of wild smilax and lilac foliage formed a bower from the street to the church, under which the guests passed." Brother Rusty was Frederick's best man. In the afternoon the newlyweds boarded General Alger's private rail car for New York to sail on the steamship *Werra* for Europe, where they traveled until the fall.

The couple met grief when they first tried to start a family. On February 12 the following year, Mary had a miscarriage, and their firstborn, Edward Swift Alger, died at the age of four. Finally, joy on Christmas Eve 1904, when Frances Alger was born. Four years later came Frederick M. Alger Jr.

In business, one could say Frederick Sr. was a chip off the old block. After the death of his father, he became the vice president and treasurer of Alger, Smith & Co. and a director of the Manistique Lumber Co. and the Manistique and Duluth & Northern Minnesota railways. But he also hit the mark on his own, especially in banking after World War I, as a director or major stockholder of no less than seven banks.

In 1912 he tried unsuccessfully to win the Republican nomination for governor. He was pitched as a "young man with progressive ideas" but didn't have the political backing to unseat the party's conservative standard bearers.

Even before America entered World War I, Frederick Alger sensed the coming crisis. In 1915 he reported to Fort Sheridan for a refresher on military operations. The following year he put himself through additional training at the Plattsburg Training Camp. So when America entered the war in 1918, he was ready for action and commissioned at once. As a major in the cavalry reserves, he was attached to 310th Ammunition Train of the 85th Division at Fort Sheridan. After his stint in field artillery, he finally shipped out to fight in France, where his conduct earned him a promotion to lieutenant colonel. His last posting was with the general staff at Tours, and he was sent home in February 1919.

Frederick Alger's tour of duty in France might have been brief, but his gallantry in action was remembered and appreciated by its government, which after his return home made him a *Chevalier* of the French Legion of Honor. In 1921 he was commissioned a full colonel in the Cavalry Officers' Reserve Corps.

Throughout his life Colonel Alger maintained an abiding fascination and regard for military organization. As Russell Alger had his Grand Army of the Republic, Frederick loved the American Legion. He was one of its founders, present at the St. Louis caucus that conceived it and a charter member of its Charles A. Learned post. Unlike the GAR, which restricted its membership to soldiers up to the Civil War, the Legion is an association for all honorably discharged veterans of any American war. He was president of the thirteenth American Legion Convention, held in Detroit in 1931, and was responsible for housing, feeding and entertaining about 100,000 men. When the corporation ran out of money, he paid the difference out of his pocket. That's why some called him Mr. American Legion.

As a private man Frederick Alger liked to set up his portable movie projector and watch the talkies after dinner. "Personally I could sit up all night looking at foolish cartoons," he said. Tall, handsome and cutting a dashing figure like Leslie Howard or a young Rex Harrison, he had a winning smile. He played hard: racquets, shooting, hunting and yachting, and kept Airedales and bulldogs as pets.

In the twenties, he became a vigorous opponent of Prohibition, even refusing nomination for another run at the Michigan governorship in 1931 because he was too caught up in campaigning for its repeal. "I consider Prohibition the greatest curse that has descended on this nation since slavery," he said, "and for the rest of my life I shall devote myself to the cause of repeal."

It may have been his wife's starring role in the temperance movement that led him to such a determined stand. Appointed by Governor William A. Comstock to the state's first Liquor Control Commission and as its only woman, Mary Alger was Michigan's loudest voice and strongest defender against the wet cause.

In opposing her, Frederick Alger took to drink as if to better make his point. "Mignon is busy controlling liquor and I am busy consuming it. I don't know which of us is the more successful," he wrote in a letter to his sister Frances on July 18, 1933. He even went as far as promoting the political heresy that "good wet Democrats where they are opposed to dry Republicans should be supported." Among Grosse Pointe's elite, Truman Newberry sided with him, while James Joy supported Mignon's position.

In business, Frederick Alger emerged as a tycoon in his own right. His days were crowded with activity, but his manner was more casual and with little of the intensity that characterized his father. Writer Walter Boynton said about him, "Fred Alger is a born leader. Goes to the point direct, puts his finger on the important things to be done, arranges for their doing and stays with them until they are accomplished. When he talks, he talks to the point, too. He can be very persuasive and he can be very firm when firmness is the essential."

Detroit newsboys idolized Frederick Alger as they adored his father, for he carried on Russell's generosity with the Goodfellows, which they renamed themselves. He kept up the tradition of giving them a new outfit every Christmas. In gratitude one paper reported, "Every year the Goodfellows band would stop under his window in the Penobscot Building to salute him and pay a tribute to his father. He knew most of the boys by name."

Motor City kids, Russell Alger's boys had their own run in the auto industry as major shareholders of an overhauled Packard Motor Car Co. They were part of the plan of Henry Bourne Joy, the son of James F. Joy, who ran the Michigan Central Railroad, to wrest control of the Ohio Automobile Co. in Warren, Ohio, from the Packard brothers, James Ward and Warren, move its operations to Detroit, and reinvigorate its finances by selling 2,500 additional shares to his friends and neighbors.

Caricature of Frederick Alger in "Our Michigan Friends As We see 'Em," 1905.

The Alger brothers located some venture capital of their own and rolled in with Joy, along with other financiers bearing the familiar Grosse Pointe money names: Truman Newberry, Philip McMillan and Joseph H. Boyer. Altogether $250,000 in new money was invested, while a matching amount was raised by mortgaging Packard's Ohio factory. The blueprint for turning Packard into a major car manufacturer was initialed on October 13, 1902, at a board meeting of its eight directors, including Frederick Alger and Russell Alger Jr., who had been made the firm's vice president a month earlier. Both Alger brothers remained as owners and directors of the company for the rest of their lives. In 1916 Packard's earnings were $6 million; its assets stood at $34 million, and the firm's undivided surplus was almost $11 million. Joy, who had presided over the firm's growth phase, resigned as president that year.

America's post-war zeitgeist served up the ideal track for Packard to run. Packard cars epitomized luxury and beauty and catered to snob appeal with the advertising slogan, "Ask the Man Who Owns One." Its Twin-Six model glorified the lifestyle offered up by the "moneyed, eccentric, conservative and flamboyant." Owning one meant you had arrived.

When Warren G. Harding became the first president to ride a car to his inauguration in 1921, he chose to be driven in a Packard Twin-Six. America's aristocrats, like Charles Lindbergh and Thomas Edison, owned custom-built models. Even Henry Ford rode in one. While Ford Model T's ambled between 20 and 30 mph, Packard, in June 1923, started volume production of the first eight-cylinder vehicles, which had a top speed of 80 mph. Packard dominated its niche during the firm's peak in the Roaring Twenties. Its dealers grew from 200 in 1920 to 1,000 by 1932. In the nine-year period from 1919 to 1928, sales swelled from fewer than 3,600 cars to nearly 50,000.

But things soured for Packard after the 1929 stock market crash. Even though the company shifted its production to more popularly priced lines, it never fully recovered. As unemployment exploded from five million people in 1930 to thirteen million in 1932, demand for all industrial production, especially cars, had stalled.

While the Dow stumbled from 381 in September 1929 to 41 in July 1932, Packard shares crashed from a high of $129 in early 1929 to a five-for-one split-adjusted $2 in 1933. In 1934, the year following Frederick Alger's death, the company closed its books with a loss of $7.3 million.

The company skidded downhill from that point forward. Packard's ride came to an end in its 1954 merger, on the advice of Lehman Brothers, with another ailing car manufacturer named Studebaker. By 1957 Studebaker stopped building cars with the Packard name.

Russell Jr. and Frederick had always been close, "inseparable in manhood,"; it was said, "they shared an affection that was of a Damon and Pythias type."

Each saw the other as his hero. After their father died, they bound themselves in a business called Alger Bros.

Between the two, Rusty, "a bit florid of face and stockily built . . . with a physique that a boxer might envy," was the more adventurous. He jumped at every chance to go ballooning, and one winter on a dare, he drove his car across Lake St. Clair from the Country Club of Detroit to the Old Club. Even his investments were high flyers. He backed the Wright Brothers in their first company to build flying machines, Wright Co. of New York, which was capitalized at $1 million and counted Cornelius Vanderbilt among its investors. At home in the clouds, he owned the first private airplane in Detroit.

When he died of pneumonia on Sunday morning, January 27, 1930, Frederick was totally crestfallen and "inconsolable" even though his passing, due to a stroke he suffered while yachting off Havana in December 1928, had been expected for some time.

Frederick Alger didn't wait long before joining his beloved brother. His own death came four years later in a most ironic way. Alighting from a car at the American Legion Convention in Chicago, he injured his leg in a freak accident. It caused such a slight bruise that he ignored it; a month later the leg went numb and had to be amputated below the knee. Complications after the operation sent him into shock and brought on heart failure, which led to his untimely death on December 31, 1933.

Frederick Alger's funeral, though not on the grand scale of his father's, was still an immense affair. He lay in state, wearing his Legion uniform, at the Grosse Pointe Memorial Church from noon to two on January 2, 1934. A large wreath stood sentry, adorned with the numbers 40 and 8 and the emblem of the Crusaders, in which he had been active. The flag draped over his casket was the same one that had covered his father's coffin.

After the services a military procession, with an honor guard of 50 commanders from various Legion posts, led him to his final rest at Elmwood Cemetery. He was posthumously awarded the Voiture medal of the Forty and Eight Club of the American Legion.

Frederick Alger died at the nadir of the Depression, prior to the enactment of the Glass-Steagall law, which requires banks to have deposit insurance. As a result his estate was depleted by claims resulting from his legal obligation, as the director of several banks, to cover depositors' withdrawals. To satisfy this personal liability, he was forced to sell off stock holdings and other assets at unfavorable prices.

Despite the losses, Frederick Alger still managed to leave behind a small fortune in an estate that was valued at $2.2 million. Almost all of it went to his wife and two children. Fred Jr.'s portion ended up being $1.6 million.

The S&P 500 was 10.10 at the end of 1933. Sixty years later it closed at 466.45.

For his gallantry in action during World War I, Colonel Frederick Alger was made a Chevalier in the French Legion of Honor.

If Frederick Alger's estate had merely grown as much as the S&P, it would have amounted to $101.6 million in December 1993.

The physical remnants of the Alger heritage on the shores of Lake St. Clair can be found in the 27-room Italian Renaissance villa that had been built in 1910 as Rusty Alger's home. Converted into the Grosse Pointe War Memorial in 1949, it has a 450-seat auditorium and is used for conferences, art exhibits, dance and music classes, and welcomes more than 200,000 people to about 5,000 annual events, the most popular of which is its Summer Music Festival.

General Alger's old home at 17620 East Jefferson Street was consumed by a three-alarm, seven-hour conflagration on September 12, 1960. It had been abandoned for some time and known as the Haunted House of Grosse Pointe. The fire was likely started by children who would to sneak into the house to play.

With her husband gone, Mary Eldridge Alger assumed the role of matriarchal head of the Alger family. Her contemporaries saw her as colorful, flamboyant and a lively conversationalist, who felt equally at home at a ballpark or in the symphony. She "entertained almost continuously and with elegance" and was a "familiar and powerful presence in Detroit society." An independent woman ahead of her time, she was called Michigan's Great Lady, not only for her significant charitable and cultural work, quite apart from her efforts on behalf of Prohibition, but because she displayed an "indomitable spirit" in old age.

She was born in Norfolk, Connecticut, where her grandfather was the pastor of the Congregational church. After attending Dobbs Ferry School in Westchester, New York, she studied music in New York City and Paris before marrying Frederick Alger.

Mary Alger's undertakings were almost as numerous as her days.

She was a board member of the Women's Hospital in Detroit beginning in 1908 and chairman of the American Red Cross' Nursing Activities and Canteen throughout World War I. She was the vice chairman of the Open Heart fund, which raised funds for building a home for young women that was run by the Salvation Army.

She was a founding member and director of the Detroit Women's Council of the Navy League and a life member of the Ladies Auxiliary of the General Russell A. and Colonel Frederick M. Alger Post, Veterans of Foreign Wars. For her humanitarian and financial contributions to the Polish war effort, she received two decorations from Polish veterans organizations in 1934: the Cross of the Order of Merit and the General Haller Sword Medal, named for the Polish Army commander in the western front at the end of World War I.

She was instrumental in constructing the Detroit Historical Museum, was on the board of the Friends of the Grosse Pointe Public Library, and was a charter member of the Detroit Symphony Society, where she raised funds for free concerts to school children.

In January 1947 an honorary Doctor of Laws from Wayne University was conferred on her. And in 1951, as chairman of the Women's Committee for Detroit's 250th Birthday Festival, she was honored in the celebration of the city's half century of automotive history.

And the above is only a partial list of her numerous awards, commendations and charitable activities.

In 1937, four years after Frederick Alger's death, Mary married Dr. Fred Towsley Murphy, a trusted family friend and neighbor, who had purchased and was living in Russell Alger's Grosse Pointe home—the one that eventually burned to the ground. The two had been brought together by mutual charities and social concerns, including Prohibition, the Red Cross and the Detroit Symphony, where Dr. Murphy succeeded Mrs. John Newberry as its president and director.

A graduate of Yale College and Yale Medical School, Dr. Murphy went on to Harvard for postgraduate medical studies, and briefly taught anatomy there before turning to private practice. Later in life he took up banking and was a director in some of the same banks where Frederick Alger was involved. He was also a builder and, like any respectable Detroiter, had an automobile connection, as director of the Maxwell Motor Corp. when it was reorganized by Walter P. Chrysler.

When Frederick and Mary Alger's son Frederick Jr. married, he chose a wife whose lineage was as distinguished as his own. Through the family of Suzette Dewey a similar rich vein of commercial success, personal enterprise, dignified public service, strong individual character and high achievement runs its vibrant course.

The first of the Deweys to reach the New World was Thomas, who landed in Dorchester, Massachusetts, in 1630 on the good ship *Mary & John*. Suzette's great-great-grandfather, Chauncey, was born 1821 in Cadiz, Ohio, named in imitation of Cadiz, Spain, which shared its principal industry of raising merino wool. He was a law partner of Abraham Lincoln's secretary of war, Edwin M. Stanton, and a principal in one of the first national banks to receive a charter in Ohio. By the time he died on February 15, 1880, at the age of 84, he had acquired thousands of acres of undeveloped farmland in northwest Kansas and southwest Nebraska. Suzette's grandfather, Albert Bromfield Dewey, was a first cousin of Commodore George Dewey, the hero of Manila Bay during the Spanish-American War.

Charles Schuveldt Dewey, Fred Jr.'s future father-in-law, was born on November 10, 1880, and graduated from the Yale class of 1904. He knew ju-jitsu, wrestled for sport, enjoyed painting, and was attracted to the arts. He also studied French and was proficient in languages.

He was commissioned lieutenant colonel at the age of 27 and received the American Legion of Merit with Palms, two oak leaf clusters and a Silver Star. He believed deeply that "service to one's government transcends all else in importance and vital interest" and guided his life accordingly.

During the administration of President Calvin Coolidge, he demonstrated uncommon financial skill as fiscal assistant to Secretary of the Treasury Andrew Mellon. This led to a special posting as financial adviser to the Polish government, which was forced to accept Dewey's authority over its local elected officials as a condition for getting American financial aid for its battered economy.

From November 1927 to November 1930, Dewey designed and administered a stabilization plan that returned Poland to fiscal propriety. Under his stewardship and with deft manipulation of sensitive alliances "the state of Poland had balanced her budget, had a favorable balance of trade and was paying service on her debt of all nature." A hunting triumph which earned him favor among Polish aristocrats was the felling of a wild boar with a single shot. This was apparently rare enough to qualify him as a Knight of St. Hubert.

Dewey's Poland adventure cost twice what the U.S. government had budgeted for his assignment, but he gladly paid the excess from his own pocket.

A staunch conservative and passionate Republican, Dewey, in the political realm, upheld the values of fiscal responsibility and opposed the concentration of power in the executive branch. Whenever he could, he decried U.S. military support for foreign countries that didn't accord freedom and opportunity to all its citizens.

Dubbed as "Silver Dollar" Dewey and "Nickel" Dewey, he was allied with a plan to reduce the size of paper currency. He opposed the devaluation of the dollar and printing more money to address public debt, the consequences of the Gold Reserve Act of 1934.

Dewey ran for Congress in 1938, representing the ninth District of Illinois, but was defeated by 4,000 votes. In 1940 he tried again, this time winning by 6,000 votes. He was reelected to Congress in 1942, where he proposed House Resolution 143, creating the Committee of Post War Economic Reconstruction and currency stabilization, and organized the Bank of International Cooperation to resettle refugees and take on non-commercial risks. "Stabilization is possible only after reconstruction has been successful," he believed. He surrendered his congressional seat in 1944.

In 1946 Dewey was a vice president of Chase National Bank. After that he spent four years as vice president and finance committee chairman of Colgate-Palmolive Peet Co. Next, as the chairman of the Northwestern Trust & Savings Bank, he directed its reorganization into the Milwaukee Avenue National Bank. In his retirement he was president of the Washington Hospital Corp. and the 800-bed Garfield General Hospital in Washington, D.C.

Charles Dewey's wife, Marie Suzette de Marigny Hall, came from an "extremely interesting and active line of ancestors." Her great-grandfather, Bernard de Marigny, fled to New Orleans during the French Revolution; she was also a direct descendant of William C. Claiborne, the first governor of Louisiana.

Their daughter Suzette, Fred's mother, was schooled at Mademoiselle Boissier's in Neuilly, France. A classmate and friend was the daughter of Lord George Curzon, governor-general of India. She was a Washington debutante and presented at the Court of St. James.

Following family tradition and observing their father's dogma of public service, both of Charles Dewey's sons served with glory in World War II. Charles Jr. received the Medal of Freedom for his brave deeds. Peter, the youngest child and a Yale graduate, was even more honored. He was awarded the Medal of Merit for parachuting into France and working with the underground for the success of the Normandy invasion. More than that, Peter has a place in U.S. military history as the first American casualty of its military conflict in Indochina. He was ambushed and killed at the age of 27 by the Viet Minh on the morning of September 26, 1945.

Fred and David Alger are the meeting points for both these exceptional family tributaries—the confluence of patriotism and public service, commerce and entrepreneurship. And it is not surprising that both excel in qualities conferred by these bloodlines. Devotion to fiscal responsibility is congenital. Political conservatism is ingrained. There is a genealogical predisposition for hard work and service. Even the allure of military models is consistent and highly appropriate. They were groomed to be comfortable with big money and high finance.

Fred Alger's personal odyssey strikes inevitable comparison with his great-grandfather's pioneering exploits. Though, like Russell, he achieved substantial wealth, it is in his work ethic, self-discipline and the puritanical way he sustained his company and its resources that Fred Alger most resembles his illustrious forebear.

5 ಌ

Making His Way

F RED'S DEBUT as an analyst for First of Michigan in 1957 was impressive. His first research reports on American Photocopy and Haloid Corp. originated the Alger approach of identifying companies on the cusp of a major life-cycle change through creative, comprehensive research.

In the 1950s, carbon paper was still the preferred medium for making copies of documents and correspondence. Duplicating technology in that day involved mimeographs, Photostats and other wet systems. American Photocopy and another small firm, Haloid Corp., had introduced the first dry-system photocopiers. 3M was also in the field with Thermofax. All this "looked interesting" to Fred.

He went to work by investigating various kinds of copiers and speaking with secretaries. He calculated what it cost—in terms of time and money—to make a photocopy and figured out that the new machines saved money. What's more, they were easier to use and provided a superior image. Although American Photocopy had the better sales force and was quite profitable, Fred saw lurking problems in the ownership of its patents. Haloid had the solid licenses for plain paper copying, so Fred placed his bets on Haloid.

Today Haloid is known as Xerox Corp.

"Haloid made one aware of what to look for when you buy a stock to make a lot of money," said Fred. "It represented change. You can't say that enough. That's what you're looking for. Big change is when the big money is made."

In 1957 Haloid, with revenues under $26 million, was viewed mainly as a manufacturer of "interesting toys" by the investment community. Not even Fred ever imagined how ubiquitous the photocopier would become, or how dramatically it would alter the copying, printing and document-handling habits of companies worldwide.

Before Fred Alger launched his assault on Wall Street, he spent an intense creative period in San Francisco, a less competitive place than New York City, where

"I could learn my trade." He landed his first job as a junior analyst at Wells Fargo Bank the same day he reached the city. His instant acceptance arose from two factors: The bank maintained a large research department, which encouraged an easy in flow and quick out flow of young researchers, and Fred came armed with the research reports that had been his key accomplishments at First of Michigan.

Fred worked at Wells Fargo from November 1958 until July 1959, when the Marine Corps summoned him to active duty in its Reserve program.

Fred had tried to enlist in the Marine Reserves in Michigan but was deemed ineligible because of a trick knee, which was inoperable at the time, and poor eyesight. Not one to accept rejection, Fred sought a waiver for his condition. "I wanted to be with the best, and that was the Marine Corps," he said. Barely eight months into his job at Wells Fargo, he received the waiver. Since the Marine delayed-entry program has an outside deadline of one year, Fred had to quick-step it to boot camp in San Diego even though it meant withdrawing from the firm.

Fred describes his encampment in San Diego and training with the Marines as one of the "most important periods" of his life. First, it was a maturing period which strengthened him physically and mentally. Second and more important, it introduced him to the personnel management style which he would follow for all of his business life.

"I always admired the leadership training and attitude of the Marine Corps officers," Fred said. "The style was that the officers were removed from the men. You didn't see officers around that much, and when they came by, they didn't say very much, which enhanced the overall effect. I thought this was a very good lesson in management."

In his company, Fred Alger was always separate and removed. "I don't mingle with the troops," he admitted. Using his relationship with the firm's second-in-command and former senior partner George Boggio as an example, Fred said, "George and I never had dinner together socially. I've never been to his house, nor was he ever to mine; nor did it cross my mind. My brother and I don't see each other very much, almost for the same reason. "

"Fred views the Marine Corps as his first brush with hypermasculinity, the place where he was made a man," according to David Alger. "He was small of stature and wore thick glasses and never saw himself as a rough-and-tough type. The Marines convinced him that he was. He will speak with tremendous pride about being in the Marines."

After eleven and a half weeks of basic training, Fred enrolled in advanced boot camp, one month with the Infantry Training Regiment at Camp Pendleton in Oceanside, California, to extend his pursuit of self-development. Then he remained in the Marines' active reserves for six more years, which meant reporting for duty one weekend a month and two weeks every summer. He was committed to the Marines Reserves for an additional two years in an inactive capacity.

Wells Fargo didn't have a spot for Fred when he finished with the Marines, so it recommended him to North American Securities Co., a mutual-fund management firm, perhaps the largest in the San Francisco Bay Area at the time, with assets of about $150 million.

Ralph Gish, who headed its investment division, remembers Fred, one of five or six securities analysts on his team, as "an industrious, intelligent and self-assured young man, obviously a desirable employee."

Gish ran the shop in the manner of a guild. The atmosphere was both supportive and protective—an incubator of new ideas. New analysts were given the latitude to commit mistakes and grow from their experiences. Fred would implement some of the more encouraging aspects of this approach later on in the Alger research associate program.

At North American Securities, Fred had the time and freedom to apply his intuition about complex research ideas and explore those factors which affected the movement of stock prices. One brainchild was a way of timing the market based on the inventory levels of steel.

Fred described his thought process:

"What I discovered was that cyclical or economically sensitive stocks tended to hit their highs and lows in the same week—many in the same day— regardless of what business they were in.

"Reviewing statistics from 1958 to 1961 and even going back a ways, I discovered that the principal moving factor in the economy was the inventory buildup and inventory runoff of steel. This, in turn, was tied to labor contract negotiations in the steel industry. The effect of the buildup and the runoff was evident when I correlated steel shipments with the Federal Reserve Board index of production, with the effect of steel pulled out. The buildup would start some months before the labor contract was to be terminated; then the runoff would last several months after the contract was settled.

"What was interesting is that since steel was a major influence in the economy, this same pattern would also be the driving pattern in the stock market, and not just for cyclical stocks.

"With this you could determine points to enter and exit the market. You could say, we will own stocks until November next year, then we'll sell and raise cash and buy them back again in October of the following year. Then you could say, 'Here are the better cyclicals for the following reasons.'

"That was the end of the job. Nothing else was required. To put forward and make this very convincing case with full research was so startling and new and had never been done before—and the kind of thing that is not even done today."

Over time Fred made adjustments to this investment model, as steel's role in economic output began to diminish. He shifted his focus to aluminum, which was experiencing greater acceptance as a result of improvements in processing, and wrote the definitive report about following aluminum companies based on the metal's supply and demand. While Fred was fired up by this new achievement, which radically simplified market timing, Gish, with his characteristic reserve, called Fred's aluminum study "something which demonstrated initial promise."

Fred's unique ability to take seemingly unrelated economic trends, financial statistics and social ideas and devise a complete, predictive model of the direction of the market and stock prices would be a mainstay of the Alger investment methodology. Those who followed the approach would gain immensely. "There's this incredible brilliance and originality of thinking that Fred applies to everything," explained David Alger. "In its best form, we can run circles around our competitors because Fred can seize things so quickly and go two or three steps ahead of the next player."

Fred exercised his great insight and leaps of understanding in numerous business projects, including an innovative, immensely productive cable-industry tax shelter and a complex charitable-giving program that also preserved the assets of high-net-worth investors. His creative gifts found their clearest voice in problem solving, just as they had when he was growing up. "I have a very limited curiosity about things around me," Fred admitted. "But I do have an imaginative ability that allows me to reason very deeply into a problem, and I have a sense of urgency that allows me to concentrate everything on something until I solve it,"

In his early days in San Francisco, Fred was intent on setting up a solid foundation for his professional interests.

Lester Colbert Jr., a lifelong friend—"perhaps his best," according to Fred—whom he met in San Francisco, had this to say about Fred as a young adult in the business world: "Fred always worked terribly hard—harder and smarter than the average person. His work habits gave evidence of his taking life very seriously and, beyond that, of his emotional concern for doing things well and right. He was very curious, inquisitive, and intensely ambitious."

Lester worked as a lab technician for Reichold Chemicals and became friends with Fred after boot camp in the fall of 1959. His father, Lester Lum "Tex" Colbert, was president of Chrysler Corporation in 1956 and its chairman in 1960. Fred and Lester shared an efficiency apartment above a converted bar in North Beach at 418 Union Street, which they rented for a pricey $90 a month.

It was on a triple date in the summer of 1960, with Colbert and a lawyer friend, Robert Buxton, that Fred went on his first date with Eleanor Calhoun Miller, who would soon become his wife.

Vacationing with his daughters in British Columbia, Canada, 1977. Fred always had time for his daughters.

They married in November 1960. She was barely 21, but had already earned a degree from Hollins College. A year and three days later, twin daughters, Alexandra and Hilary, were born to the delighted couple.

With a wife and two infants, Fred felt the pressure to make more money. So in 1962 he left North American Securities for Winfield & Co., a mutual-fund company which strongly focused on growth stocks.

However, unknown to Fred was the fact that Winfield was in decline and nearing its end when he joined the firm. Then the brief but spectacular stock market tumble in 1962 spooked the company and nudged it over the precipice. The market break was precipitated by fears of Attorney General Robert Kennedy's apparent anti-business outlook, which took the form of an antitrust challenge to the steel industry. Fully $107 billion of equity assets—or almost 20% of the gross national product—evaporated from the American economy between April 24 and June 26 that year. The stock which Fred had discovered, Xerox, dropped from $171 to $88.

It was the stock market's worst decline since 1937, according to Charles Partridge Jr., who ran Winfield. Thankfully, it didn't last long. After June stock prices resumed their ascent, and the Dow closed out the year at 652.10, down only 40 points from its April high.

At the start of 1963, Winfield promoted Fred to portfolio manager of one of its three mutual funds, Quarterly Distribution Shares. Around the same time, another of its funds, Blue Ridge Fund, with assets of $30 million and controlled by the crusty Milan Papovich in New York, was making noises about leaving Winfield.

Fred seized on the opportunity and persuaded Winfield to move him to Wall Street. "By then I felt ready for New York," he explained. He would establish a research outpost for the firm in the East and attempt to stabilize the situation at Blue Ridge as well as continue to handle the QDS investment decisions.

In the spring of 1963, Fred Alger packed up his wife and the twins in a beat-up black Volvo and drove cross country to start up Winfield's New York operation. The car was in such bad shape, Fred recalled, that he had to continually yank on a rod to keep its ventilators from closing. On the way he made a fortuitous stop in Denver for a discussion with John Jennings, whose family had started Quarterly Distribution Shares in 1944 and who was also on its board. They talked shop in his room at the Brown Palace Hotel and had a couple of beers together. "That's when I found out Fred was actually in charge of managing all the QDS money," Jennings explained. "Partridge was a pretty talented man, but he wasn't much of an analyst. Fred was. He knew more than the rest of us."

Despite the fund's improving performance, the directors of QDS became concerned—in sales and administrative matters—about the consultancy relationship with Winfield, which had already been reduced from a full management of the fund. They began thinking about delegating the stock picking back to the fund's investment manager, Security Management Company, Inc.

Security Management, operated by QDS board member Everett Gille, was a wholly owned subsidiary of Security Benefit Life Insurance Company of Topeka, Kansas—an early player in the mutual-fund industry when "most insurance companies wouldn't think of mentioning mutual funds and life insurance in the same breath."

It was only because Fred was on board at Winfield and had been "doing such a great job" of managing the fund that Jennings was able to persuade Security Management Co. to retain Winfield as the investment adviser for QDS.

After three days on the road, the Algers reached New York. They soon moved into a comfortable apartment on Riverside Drive and 86th Street. But first they bunked in the East Side home of one Chat Hickox, an acquaintance of the couple who would later give Fred his inheritance to manage. Hickox rarely used this apartment, since his job was running the airport in Burlington, Vermont. Eventually Hickox would follow Fred into the investment-advisory business after selling his stake in a charter carrier, Overseas National Airways. His firm, Ashland Management, was for a time a guaranteed subsidiary of Fred Alger Management.

Fred set up Winfield's office in New York on Broad Street, a couple of blocks south of Wall Street toward the Battery, and involved himself fully in picking stocks for the mutual funds managed by the firm. From QDS, Winfield earned one quarter of the standard management fee of a half percent of assets. A $7 million fund, it produced fees of around $8,750.

Meanwhile, weighed down by dual responsibilities of marketing and portfolio-managing Security Benefit's fledgling fund, Security Equity—which was started in September 1962 and was having a hard time growing—"Everett hit upon the idea of hiring Fred. He had come to respect him as an excellent stock picker, and believed he could boost the fund's performance record," said John Cleland, who is currently the chief investment strategist of the Security Benefit Group of mutual funds.

Since Fred was doing all the work anyway, why not pay him directly and cut out the middle man? And so, Fred Alger, not yet 29, was offered the job of running the Security Equity Fund and Quarterly Distribution shares, on his own and on the same basis as Winfield. Having its own research arm in New York would also add prestige to Security Management. "At some point I realized that I was more important for this account, as far as Security Benefit was concerned, than Winfield was," said Fred. Winfield barely put up a fight for the business, and it flowed right into Fred's hands.

That Gille should turn to Fred was inevitable considering his recent performance. Running Quarterly Distribution Shares for Winfield, "he got the best years in that fund that we ever had before or since," according to John Jennings. Quarterly Distribution Shares, with a comparatively large $10 million in assets, was renamed Security Investment Fund in the fall of 1964.

Like Winfield, as a research consultant Fred's take was just one-eighth of 1% of assets under management, a quarter of the standard fee for a fund management contract, which was half of 1%. Unlike Winfield, that's all the income he had. Still, this was the spark that Fred needed to strike out on his own. Cleland recalled that Fred's first check from Security Management was the princely sum of $34.57.

It didn't take Fred long to make his mark. In his rookie year at its helm, Security Equity Fund was the top performing mutual fund in the country. In 1965 it scored a stratospheric 77.5% compared to the Dow's advance of just 10.9%. Ned Johnson's Fidelity Trend was fourth in 1965, with a 53% gain. Jerry Tsai's Fidelity Capital Fund was sixth, up 48%.

With its strong appreciation, the fund attracted national attention throughout the year. From $375,000 nine months earlier, assets grew to $1 million by September 30, 1965; at year's end, they stood at $2.3 million. The fund's high performance was attributed to its small size, which kept it nimble when responding to price fluctuations, and the ability to take relatively large positions of small, rapidly growing companies. Huge gains came from Fairchild Camera, purchased at $38 and bid near $150 at the close of the year. Another winning stock, Iowa Beef Packers, was bought at $30 and ran up to $65.

In 1966, sporting a 9% gain, Security Equity was the number-two fund in the country. Its 67.8% rise in 1967 placed it among the top 15 funds in America and far outpaced the Dow's 19.2% performance.

Security Investment Fund didn't fare quite as well. Its 1965 gain was a respectable 17%, followed by a modest decline of 5.9% in 1966 and a healthy rise of 27.5% in 1967. In 1968, however, when the Dow rose only 8%, its 26.2% gain vaulted it to the top of mutual fund rankings.

On June 29, 1967, Fred Alger was elected to the board of directors of Security Management Company. By 1968, Security Equity Fund had swelled to $70 million in assets. It declared a four-for-one share split and an 11 cent dividend on October 30, 1968. By comparison, the Security Investment Fund had increased only modestly to $12 million.

In 1966 Fred Alger was "considered one of the sharpest research outfits on the street." Publications like *Fundscope,* the oracle of the mutual-fund industry, began to tout his performance, leading to his emergence as a luminary among money managers.

Despite his spectacular performance, Fred never negotiated a raise in compensation. He didn't have to. His plan was working, and very soon he shed his total reliance on Security Management. Fred's performance had pulled in a number of higher-fee accounts, including Bernie Cornfeld's Investors Overseas Services (IOS) and several private investors.

In 1969 Security Management Co. caught the evil eye of Abraham L. Pomerantz, who made a career of bringing class action suits against mutual-fund management companies. His Park Avenue law firm of Pomerantz, Levy, Hoodek and Block was the big daddy of the shareholder derivative action or Strike Suit—by its nature a nuisance case and a cause célèbre from the mid-'60s right into the seventies. The U.S. Supreme Court earlier had ruled that plaintiffs could demand a jury trial in shareholder derivative actions whose stated goal was a reduction of management fees or brokerage commissions. This made it desirable for management companies to reach out-of-court settlements to resolve litigation. The ground was set for suing lawyers to come away with money easily, regardless of the merits of the complaint, and mutual fund companies with assets over $100 million were targeted in these strike suits.

The nub of Pomerantz's case against Security Management was this: Since Alger was doing all the investment research in New York and Security Management merely followed his lead, they didn't deserve to keep most of the money, three-quarters of the management fee, in Topeka. Therefore its fees were excessive.

Fred's role with Security Management was always advisory. Security Management retained discretionary authority over the funds, even though it almost never exercised the prerogative to overrule him. As evidence, only once in 1965 was an Alger recommendation turned down, and that was for political reasons. Fred was de facto manager of the portfolios, even though Security Management always retained final control. A five-man committee met once a week to review, and mostly rubber-stamp, Fred's stock advice.

The lawsuit, which was eventually settled for a "relatively insignificant amount of money," irrevocably inverted the equation between Fred and Security Management. The spotlight forced the managing company to take a greater part in investment decisions, to earn its keep, so to speak, for receiving its fees. This didn't square well with Fred; nor did it have a positive effect on the funds' performance. "The company's business response was to hire a research staff internally and start thinking about replacing me," said Fred. "We had to start writing reports for them and getting prior approval. We knew that the end was coming as they were becoming progressively more demanding."

George Boggio added, "As Security Management took over more and more of the funds, it tainted our performance. That hurt our reputation."

Fred was ready for the change that was coming. After a down year in 1969—Security Equity lost 20.3%, its worst under Alger—he turned his gaze on the pension-fund business. Meanwhile, in September 1969 Security Benefit Life converted its wholly owned closed-end investment trust, with $3 million, into an aggressive-growth public mutual fund called Security Ultra Fund. It was also given to Fred Alger to manage.

In 1970 Fred upgraded the firm from a unregistered to a registered investment adviser, which put him under the aegis of the SEC and enabled him to promote himself as an investment adviser and increase the number of his clients, but prevented him from taking performance-based compensation.

Fred felt he needed to terminate the Security Management relationship and even drafted a letter of resignation, which he kept, unfinished and unsent, in his desk drawer. "Like a child, he couldn't let go," Boggio revealed .

On September 30, 1971, Security Equity Fund held $129,772,781. At the end of the year, the money in Security Investment Fund was up to $25 million. Security Ultra Fund, with a gain of 47.7% versus the Dow's rise of 8.3% in 1971, had built up $15 million.

"We had grown to the point that we had significant assets coming in the door in a variable-annuity product from Security Benefit Life," explained Cleland. "By then we had started a bond and a small-cap fund and had the resources to build our own investment advisory and management team."

In 1972 Fred finally received the phone call from Security Management telling him it was releasing him from his advisory duties.

According to Cleland, "his relationship with Security Management was becoming a nuisance to Fred in a lot of respects; he didn't have control over the process, and he didn't like that. Fred likes to have total control over everything he does." Nonetheless, actually losing the Security funds created a serious revenue shortfall for Fred Alger. When they let him go, he had resigned the IOS account and was in the "gruesome position of having no assets to manage except for a small sliver of private money."

"Fred was really upset about it," said Alger partner and confidant Irwin Schwartz.

After Fred, Security Equity fell 23.5% in 1973 and lost another 21.7% in 1974.

Despite dropping him, the plain-spoken Cleland was unrestrained in his praise: "Fred is the best stock picker I've been associated with in my 40 years in the business. He has a brilliant investment mind. He has a rare ability in the world of money management to look beyond what is apparent to us mere mortals, to identify trends in place and predict how that will impact individual stocks and groups of stocks and to structure portfolios to take advantage of that. He's not swayed by conventional wisdom and is willing to go against that grain to make his investment decisions."

In 1985, perhaps on a wave of nostalgia, but certainly with a plan in mind, Fred offered to purchase the management contract for the Security Benefit Group of mutual funds for $12 million. Security Benefit Life rejected his bid outright. The same year Fred also tried a leveraged buyout of Ford Motor Co.

6 ᎙

Romance of Wall Street

IN OCTOBER 1964, Fred Alger opened his business in a one-room office at 56 Pine Street. Fred Alger & Co. was capitalized with $3,000 and launched with the prospect of minimal research advisory fees—one-eighth of 1% of assets—from the Security Management account.

Sixteen stories tall, 56 Pine is on a short alley pitched off William Street and diagonally across from the Wall Street Atrium. The building's backside can be spied from Alger's current offices on Maiden Lane.

Fred made his first trade with $5 in exchange for junked furniture—"a black, ugly, marked-up desk and a red leather chair, well worn with indentations"—from the building's superintendent. It was the kind of desk designed for secretaries, with a pop-up typewriter tray on one side. The desk was so busted up it had lost the covering door, and even the typewriter leaf was blown out. It didn't matter to Fred. He used the gaping square hole to hold his paperwork.

From his twins' bedroom Fred borrowed a rickety rocking chair for visitor seating. In keeping with this utilitarian scrap-heap chic, cardboard transfer cartons served as filing cabinets. The finishing touch was a wicker wastepaper basket, also from his daughters' room at home. Fred had a habit of tossing his partially filled coffee containers, brought into the office every morning, into the unlined trash basket. The seeping liquid left a deepening brown stain on the already shabby linoleum floor.

In its first fiscal year, Fred Alger earned just $800 in management fees—hardly enough to support a family of four—while business expenses totaled $2,230. A large part of the initial investment went for legal fees and incorporation. As a business pragmatist, Fred was willing to improvise to get by. The address mattered more than the decor, which could wait until he made some money. What was essential was a presence in the financial district.

Fred's hardscrabble start in business, so far removed from his lush youth in Grosse Pointe and Europe, seemed improbable considering his family background.

But if his great-grandfather, who also had started from scratch, is to be believed, it shouldn't have mattered. "The best capital that a young man can have starting in life is energy and integrity," said Russell Alger. "A man whose word can be relied on at all times establishes a credit and wins a place in the business world that money cannot purchase."

It is a source of great pride for Fred that he started his firm from a lowly position, building it up to a great success using purely his own capital. That is not to say he had no outside support. Friends and business acquaintances helped him get through materially.

Fred's first friend in New York was Joseph H. Reich, whom he had met in San Francisco while working at Winfield. During the early sixties in New York, Reich was a rising analyst for the upstart Donaldson, Lufkin & Jenrette, which had yet to gain its reputation as one of the most influential institutional brokerages on Wall Street. At an early point of managing the IOS money and before the firm did its own research, Fred Alger was DLJ's second- or third-largest customer. Fred and Reich became friends as well as business associates. In addition, they were bridge partners at the Regency Club, where Fred sponsored Reich as a member.

When Fred was starting out, Reich helped him many times and in many ways. Fred had no secretary to do his correspondence, so Reich loaned him his own. And once, when Fred fell ill, Reich sent his staff to pick up his mail and cover for him. Reich confirmed the popular opinion of Fred as "one of the most imaginative and creative people" in the business at that time. He added, "Fred had an incredible knack for picking good investments. He could visualize what would happen in the future, which other people couldn't see." Fred was always certain of his own success. The only fear he showed to Reich in those days was the possibility of "losing it—his gift—that gut feel that made him successful."

Typical with Fred's close business relationships, there was an eventual falling out between the two.

The first rift came when Fred wanted to break stride from other money managers by veering into the brokerage business.

The big unknown about combining brokerage with money management was how it would be perceived by industry regulators. No one had ever tried it. A few brokers had developed money-management activities but, never before Fred, the other way around. Fred's first partner, Bill Scheerer, was especially concerned about the appearance of a conflict of interest and its potential harm to the business. So Fred Alger sought out Reich's insight and support before setting off into the uncharted territory. By then Reich had struck out on his own and co-founded the investment management firm of Reich & Tang with Oscar Tang. "We met with Reich and Tang at the Princeton Club and spelled out our plans," said Scheerer.

"As it turned out, what we wanted to do wasn't a problem at all. Meanwhile they stole the idea and we got nothing out of it. We even paid for dinner."

The second cleft came from discussions about joining forces in business. Fred was not always so certain that the independent route was the best way to proceed. At one time he entertained a merger with Reich & Tang. "We had a couple of discussions," Reich verified, "then we broke it off. After that we didn't see much of each other." It's unlikely that the combination of three strong personalities would have worked, as a clash of wills would likely have overwhelmed the operation.

The final break was "some unpleasantness" from Reich's participation in Fred's pioneering cable industry tax shelter, CI Associates. "Fred is not a person who takes well to criticism," explained Reich. "We felt that he wasn't doing a good enough job riding herd on TelePrompTer."

In February 1965, down to his last $300 in the bank, Fred Alger was a breath away from shutting down his business when he was rescued by Dan Lufkin of Donaldson, Lufkin & Jenrette. Like Fred, Lufkin had served in the Marine Corps and was a Yale alumnus. On Lufkin's recommendation, Fred received a modest assignment, paying $100 a week, to run a dummy portfolio for the leading hedge fund firm A. W. Jones and Company. No stocks were actually bought or sold by Fred. The transactions were made on paper, primarily for comparison against Jones's own performance. "That five thousand dollars a year was the difference between going bankrupt and making it," Fred admitted.

Hedge funds employ riskier, speculative investment techniques such as operating on margin, program trading, short sales, swaps and arbitrage. For example, in selling short, one anticipates a stock's decline and borrows shares which are then disposed of at the current market price. If the stock price declines, the trader profits from buying back those same shares at a lower price and returning them to the lender.

For the first 14 months of his company Fred toiled alone in his one-man office, doing everything by himself. His resources were so limited, he didn't even have his own stock ticker. The quotes came gratis, courtesy of Red Carley, the head trader at Shaskin & Co., whose offices were in the Broad Street building where Fred had set up Winfield's shop on Wall Street. In return for that accommodation, Fred gave much of his brokerage business to Shaskin.

Even when finances improved and Fred moved up, he kept the stock machine out of the office. "He felt that they would waste the entire day looking at the Quotron instead of working," explained David Alger.

At the end of its second year Fred Alger had earned $26,293 in management fees from a total income of $36,590. But this was already more than his expenses of $24,075 and enough to get by.

"In anything that I do, I want to compete at the very highest level within my ability."

Fred needed just that first year to make an impression on Wall Street. When Security Equity Fund was crowned winner of the mutual-fund performance derby in 1965, he came to the attention of Bernie Cornfeld, the phenomenal "king of mutual fund operators." The funds he gave Fred to manage were happily bound to lucrative performance fees on top of the standard management contract. This was how Fred started making his money.

The exploits of Bernard Cornfeld merit a fairly complete exposition in the Alger financial history for several reasons. One, he gave Fred his first real leg up on the ladder of financial success. Two, his character dominates a key progressive juncture in mutual-fund history and perhaps also its most tawdry and illicit chapters. Three, the people associated with him intersect with many future events in the Fred Alger story. Finally, his epic struggle with the SEC eerily prefigured Fred's own difficulties with the regulatory body.

The wild ride and final toppling of this go-getter from Brooklyn, who captivated the financial world and was for a time its most potent force, provided much of the drama during the freewheeling '60s when Fred first rose to public acclaim and personal fortune.

Seven years older than Fred, Cornfeld was born into a show-business family from central Europe that had fled to America after the rise of communism. As a student at New York City's Brooklyn College he gravitated toward socialism and initially pursued a career in social work before finding his place in the investment business. Seeing mutual funds as capitalism for the common man and an agent for achieving social equality, Cornfeld began selling mutual funds in 1954 for Investors Planning Corporation.

A year later he convinced Jack J. Dreyfus Jr. to let him pitch his hot Dreyfus Fund in Europe to U.S. servicemen and American expatriates—by contractual plan, as a saver program for investments to be made on an installment basis. In such a scheme, high commissions were first creamed off the top for salesmen and brokers before the investors' money was put to work.

Cornfeld's talent for showmanship made him as a superb marketer. He set up shop in Paris and placed an ad in the English-language *New York Herald Tribune* for "people with a sense of humor" to sell the fund. The sales force he assembled was a group of disparate, non-financial types, mostly foreigners on the make in Europe. Already the pudgy, balding, mouthy Cornfeld was displaying his penchant for a flashy, lavish lifestyle and an impossible talent for surrounding himself with beautiful women. Eventually he gathered this motley crew in a company called Investors Overseas Services and moved it to Geneva in 1958.

Faced with poor growth from IOS's own mutual fund, International Investment Trust, which was registered in Luxembourg in December 1960, Cornfeld hit on an idea that placed him center stage in mutual funds: the fund of funds concept, a subspecies of mutual funds that bought up shares in other mutual funds.

Cornfeld's Fund of Funds Ltd. was organized in October 1962 with an investment of $2 million dollars, including a stake from international mutual-fund legend Sir John Templeton's Lexington Research & Management Corp. By September 1963, assets in the fund had ballooned to $16.65 million, and at the end of 1964, Fund of Funds had a whopping $100 million invested in U.S. mutual funds.

According to the Investment Company Act of 1940, section 12(d)I, which governs mutual funds, no American registered investment company could own more than 3% of the shares in any other investment company. What permitted Americans to buy the fund was that it was constituted offshore and registered in

Ontario, Canada, and therefore nominally beyond the reach of U.S. securities regulations.

IOS's growth was less an outcome of superior investment performance than its ability to aggressively market its funds through contractual selling. At its worst, the IOS Investor Program took from investors up to 50% of their first year's installment through fees and high front-end charges, even though its paperwork established an upside limit of 12%. On top of this, once every quarter IOS garnished 10% of all gains in the value of the investment, regardless of whether these were realized or just on paper. Fund sales were helped by a pyramid of increasing compensation for salespersons as they made it up the ranks through performance. Sales were also artificially propped by a network of schemes involving captive offshore, tax-sheltered insurance companies and banks which provided policies and loans ancillary to or co-dependent with the mutual-fund investment. Meanwhile IOS enlarged its target of investors from the quarter-million U.S. servicemen and executives in Europe to local populations in countries all the way to the Middle East and Asia. Heading into 1966, IOS was managing close to $1 billion in U.S. securities for non-American investors and had an army of 8,000 salespersons.

Ever the shrewd businessman, Cornfeld figured out a way to avoid paying management fees to independent mutual funds and pile profit on profit by coursing Fund of Fund investments into his own proprietary funds, controlled by IOS as their sole investor. In doing so, he could earn two management fees and gain a share of brokerage commissions. That's how Fred Alger entered the picture. As the brains behind the top mutual fund in 1965, Fred was drafted in the first round by IOS's Fund of Funds Proprietary Funds Ltd. of Geneva.

The initial call to Fred came from C. Henry Buhl III, who was investment director at IOS. Of course Fred jumped at the opportunity. A meeting with Cornfeld was set for 8:00 A.M. one day in December 1965, at the house of a mutual friend, Bobby Freedman. A nervous and apprehensive Fred Alger showed up early, but was kept "waiting and waiting" in the living room. When Cornfeld finally appeared, wearing khaki pants and an open-neck shirt, he was quite apologetic for the delay. He explained to Fred that he "was upstairs balling a girl in the shower." "I had never heard that phrase, nor have I heard it since, nor does it make any sense to me," Fred observed about that moment. He had just gotten his first, close-up glimpse at Cornfeld's Playboy persona, and it was an eye-opener.

When they came to terms, Cornfeld said, "We'll call it the Alger Fund, so we'll know the schmuck to blame if it goes wrong." Although it has the same name as Fred Alger's current mutual-fund offering, the two investment products are entirely different and should not be confused. Cornfeld's performance-based compensation deal with Alger, and the 26 other money managers picked to run

IOS's proprietary funds, was 1% of assets, or 5% of the total realized and unrealized appreciation, whichever was greater. This was half of what IOS was billing its investors.

True to Fred's calling, the Alger Fund was the best performer among the proprietary funds for two or three years. Once, when an IOS pamphlet misprinted Alger Fund as number two instead of number one, Fred was so troubled he immediately flew to Geneva to correct the monthly ranking.

According to Bill Scheerer, who joined Fred as a result of the Cornfeld opportunity, Fred sensed early on that there was "an inherent instability about Bernie Cornfeld and his operation, that someday the account would disappear," so he set up a separate firm, Falcon Associates, to manage the Cornfeld money and so shielded his core company during their alliance. "That turned out to be a fortuitous move," Scheerer added.

In 1967 Fred's business was on a tear. Alger Fund income alone accounted for a blistering $500,000; but that was only 40% of the company's total revenue, which had exploded over 1,000% from the previous year. About the Cornfeld experience, Fred considers his best work was putting aside those earnings. "It did work out. We were always IOS's best manager and earned some substantial performance fees, which helped out later on," he said, "but what was important—and this was a key decision—was that we never spent these performance fees but stuck them in the bank in very conservative investments." In 1968, Cornfeld gave Fred a second fund to manage, Canadian Venture Fund.

While it may have stuck to the letter of the law in the jurisdictions where it operated, from its inception IOS was involved in financial misconduct for the benefit of the company and the ultimate detriment of its investors. The scope of these shenanigans is amply exposed in the definitive work on the Cornfeld era, *Do You Sincerely Want to Be Rich?*—whose title came from Cornfeld's pitch line when recruiting salesmen—written by Britain's *Sunday Times Insight* investigative team.

One of those accused of bringing about IOS's head-first decline was Edward M. Cowett, Cornfeld's number-one henchman, who ironically co-authored, in the year after obtaining his Harvard Law degree, the Blue Sky Law, a set of regulations intended to protect American investors from deception by unscrupulous promoters, which today is still considered the final word on the subject. Cowett virtually controlled IOS, while Cornfeld gave the business its glitzy, showbiz front.

In 1964, even before it socked its shareholders' money away in its proprietary funds, the Fund of Funds owned greater than 20% of at least three U.S. mutual funds, way above the 3% limit for regulated firms. Rightfully fearful of the concentration of assets in the Fund of Funds, an entity outside its jurisdiction, the SEC began to hunt for a way to curtail IOS's ability to evade governance by the

Securities Exchange Act of 1934, the second pillar of law that regulates mutual funds. The way came through Investors Continental Services, or ICS, a U.S. brokerage firm IOS had acquired in November 1958.

By requiring IOS to force open its customer files in compliance with SEC and NASD (National Association of Securities Dealers) rules of fair practice, the SEC was able to lower the boom. In February 1966 IOS was charged with a number of securities-law infractions including, by a technicality, illegally selling the Fund of Funds in the United States.

For his defense against the SEC, Cornfeld hired three former SEC operatives, chief among them Alan Conwill, director of its Division of Corporate Regulation until 1964, when he was hired as a partner in Willkie Farr, Gallagher, Walton & Fitzgibbon. Conwill, who also became a director of the Fund of Funds, was not unique in his defection. To this day, prosecutors at the SEC use their jobs as a springboard for higher paying positions in investment companies or law firms of the financial institutions they formerly regulated.

"All the SEC was seeking to do was extend its jurisdiction to foreign activities," said Sam Clapp, the Boston lawyer and tax consultant who was IOS's man in the Bahamas. "Their hounding of Bernie Cornfeld was totally unjustified." Clapp himself was behind the invention of one of the schemes for circumventing SEC rules involving the recapture of brokerage commissions for IOS. This was done by setting up his wife, Gloria Martica Clapp, a Cuban citizen from Bermuda, as a registered representative of a U.S. broker domiciled in the tax haven of the Bahamas. Complicit in this action was Jesup & Lamont, the reputable New York institutional brokerage which had been in business since 1877 and was identified with John D. Rockefeller.

At the time it was a standard practice for mutual funds to receive rebates from brokerage firms which executed their stock transactions. That custom was enabled by fixed, high-rate commissions. Rather than receiving the sums directly, these were typically assigned as "customer-directed give ups" to reward independent broker-dealers and their sales organizations which sold the fund shares. With its own managed funds, IOS exercised a great deal of clout in this area but was prohibited from receiving a share of this reciprocal business—a situation which Clapp remedied.

Acting on its belief that such commissions made their way back to IOS through its arrangement with Jesup & Lamont, the SEC made its case by targeting $750,000 out of $1.5 million in IOS brokerage commissions to the firm between July 1963 and May 1965. This money, it claimed, found its way via Martica Clapp to Fiduciary Trust Co., a private bank in Nassau controlled by Sam Clapp and which, not coincidentally, elected Ed Cowett to its board in January 1966. The SEC, however, was never able to prove its assertion that the sums were ultimately amassed by IOS.

Fred ate the same lunch every day for months on end. He also insisted on eating exactly at noon. "It saves thinking," Fred explained.

In its settlement with the SEC on May 23, 1967, IOS was forced into terms which included the liquidation or sale of all its U.S. operations, such as the proprietary funds, abiding by the U.S. law that prohibited the Fund of Funds from owning more than 3% of any public mutual fund or company and desisting from sales to Americans anywhere in the world. One of the companies it lopped off was Investors Planning Corp., the mutual-fund sales company which had given both Cowett and Cornfeld their start and in which IOS had taken an 80% position in 1965 for $1.9 million.

On December 5, 1968, customer-directed give ups were abolished by the SEC, and the brokerage industry started offering volume discounts of up to 30%. This was the death of mutual-fund dealers who lived off the reciprocal business while paying their salesmen with front-end load commissions.

Fred would briefly have a hand in steering Clapp's Fiduciary Growth Fund, a mutual fund that was an offshoot of Fiduciary Trust and marketed in Sterling territories. He was also party to a rich investment with Sam Clapp in Mary Carter Paint, which was about to become Resorts International and develop a casino on Paradise Island in the Bahamas.

During its peak, by the end of 1969, less than 5% of Fund of Funds investments were placed in independent, SEC-registered U.S. mutual funds. Most of it was harbored in the proprietary accounts, in risky real estate in places like Gabon and Liberia and speculative oil rights in Canada.

Fred Alger was a marquee player in the Fund of Funds. But despite its glowing performance during the first two years, the Alger Fund hit a sinkhole that coincided with the flow of events leading to the unraveling of Bernie Cornfeld's IOS. After its quick start, Fund of Funds bumped up its $5 million opening stake in Alger to $20 million. In less than two years, by December 1967, Fred had grown its assets to $82 million. A year later the Alger Fund stood at $95.9 million. That was before the fund caved. In December 1969 the account had been bloodied down to just $40.3 million.

To be fair, that plunge mirrored the rest of the market. The Dow Jones industrial average cratered at 631 in May 1970, down 36% from its December 1968 crest of 985. Fred's favored stocks—conglomerates, computer and other technology companies—fared even worse. Those groups were down 86%, 80% and 77% respectively. Despite this, Fred had a good hand in three issues, Milgo Electronics, Telex and TelePrompTer, which lifted the Alger Fund to a portfolio of $60 million dollars, when, by mutual agreement, he and Cornfeld parted ways in March 1970.

Several accounts from that period proclaim that Cornfeld, facing the double whammy of poor performance and Fund of Fund redemptions, sacked Fred. George Boggio, who was Fred Alger's administrator at the time, maintains, however, that it was Fred who initiated the split up. Fred's own recollection of the issue was; "IOS wanted to pay fees based on performance only, and we were changing our basic business from buying research to doing it all on our own—changing from being an unregistered investment adviser to being registered. In those days you couldn't be registered and charge a fee based on performance. We were going to be members of the NYSE, so we had to quit IOS."

Several Wall Street stories blamed the abrupt liquidation of the Alger portfolio for the serious down draft in the Dow, then hovering around 750, and setting off the "worst Wall Street panic since World War II." The Canadian Venture Fund, which was given into Fred's care at its inception in December 1968, suffered a 5.4% decline in 1969. In 1970, after Fred left, it had a precipitous 26.6% fall.

Gloria Martica Clapp, who in her time with Cornfeld from 1963 to 1968 was presumed to be the "richest broker in the world" from her take of IOS–diverted commissions, gave this generous assessment of why his empire finally disintegrated. She believes IOS sank from too much money. "I watched in Switzerland, on the tote board; what was coming in per day was at a rate that was frightening," she recalled in a phone interview from the Bahamas. "One hundred million dollars a month alone was coming from Germany. There was no way they could find places to put that money that would be safe."

In explaining IOS's collapse, Fred remarked, "Cornfeld was a man who was tremendously surprised by his success. I liken him to a rock star who hits it so big at age twenty-five that it consumes him. Bernie got so out of touch with the business, and he let lesser people make a lot of bad decisions."

Certainly Cornfeld's brash public image and opulent lifestyle made him an inviting target, especially as his company began to falter. His involvement with a conspicuous covey of sexy models and fancy affairs in a string of company-owned villas and condominiums across Europe was well publicized. He dressed in sixties pop fashion rather than business attire. IOS's headquarters at 119 rue de Lausanne in Geneva had the aura of an entertainment company rather than a financial services firm. Christmas parties would typically last till dawn and cost upward of $500,000. The last one, in 1970, served up 4,000 bottles of Château Pelly de Cornfeld, named for his twelfth century mansion in France.

The first evidence of IOS's demise was the sale, at the zenith of its power in September 1969, of a total of 11 million shares, or about 20% of the company, to the public in three separate stock offerings in Geneva, Toronto and Luxembourg. By then IOS had one million customers, served by 20,000 sales and support personnel, and commanded assets valued at $2.5 billion through 55 subsidiaries and hundreds of sales outfits worldwide. In its prospectus the IOS hydra was painted to include 11 banks and financial service firms, 12 mutual funds, five insurance and four real estate companies, two publishers, one construction firm and a computer-services company. There seemed to be no end in sight to its promise.

The Geneva stock offering involved 5.6 million shares, whose initial price of $10 a share escalated to an asking price of $19.50. A second batch of 1.45 million shares was sold to Canadian investors through the Toronto broker, J.H. Craig & Co. Most of the proceeds from the 3.92 million-share Luxembourg offering were used to cash out IOS's original financiers and those in its upper echelons.

Both by greed and necessity, about $20 million of the proceeds of the stock sale wound its way back to the market to create a false demand for the shares. The greed came first from foreknowledge of an impending $10 million paper gain. Then it became necessary to buy the stock owing to the realization that IOS profits, instead of the projected $25 to $30 million, were at best $17.9 million and perhaps closer to $10.3 million. One reporter found it "baffling how IOS was supporting itself into a state of collapse." The IOS sales organization was brilliant at mounting commissions for itself, but that had long been decoupled from assets and earnings. The cash flow from fund sales was just a small percentage of the contractual amounts, while commissions and overrides were being paid on the full value.

The next culprit, and the most openly scandalous of the IOS schemes, was attributed to the mendacity of John McCandish King, a larger-than-life Denver oil man who first appeared to be giving IOS a hand by showing it a way to invest its mad rush of money outside stocks but who ultimately suckered the company and made a play for its control.

King beguiled IOS into taking a 50% interest in about 22.4 million of "mostly undrillable" acreage in the Canadian Arctic at a substantially marked-up priced. The investment promised a paper profit from the contingent Canadian government-backed permits for developing the property. IOS Growth Fund Ltd. and Fund of Funds Ltd. then sold their 10% share of the gas-exploration deal, which artificially boosted the net asset value of those funds. In truth, IOS put down only a token cash payment in the deal and mortgaged the balance as future obligations. The hollow gain played its part in brightening IOS's stock at the end of 1969, as the company collected $9.7 million in performance fees on the projected gain from the entire deal.

The final ruination of IOS was the result of several elegant tax-avoidance schemes for its suddenly wealthy managers and salesmen. These were engineered by a New York lawyer Joel Mallin, who would later help design Fred Alger's groundbreaking cable-industry tax shelter and make another appearance in his Lansdowne European banking venture.

In essence, IOS was cannibalizing itself with the expectation that it could forever be regenerated by its perpetual money machine. When the stock market declined as 1970 rolled around, the pyramiding power of the sales organization began to vanish. One observer recalled, these were "just a series of deals in the minds of Ed Cowett and Bernie. They lost touch with even the fictional legalities of the offshore game."

How derelict was IOS? Let us recount the ways. The panoply of misdeeds is bountifully studded with overstated income and misleading claims of performance in issuing IOS stock, controversial loans, manipulative trades, illegal currency transactions, unsanctioned investments and undisclosed speculation, misrepresentation of investments and misappropriation of clients' investments for personal gain. The brutal karmic retribution for these acts left the company in financial shambles.

IOS staggered on in the months after Fred Alger ceased to have any part in it. Ostensibly humbled by the firm's weakened economics, Cowett and Cornfeld tried to salve the liquidity crunch with Band-Aids of cost-cutting measures including the shedding of some 6,000 employees. But that was barely enough to keep it going. By April 1970 redemptions were running at $3 million a day, on top of shrinkage in the value of investments.

In a rescue attempt negotiated by Cowett, John King was offered as a savior for the company in May 1970. His offer of $4 a share, however, was contingent on the departure of Bernie Cornfeld. Eight days after forcing Cornfeld's resignation, King aborted his bid for IOS by hiding behind the 1967 SEC prohibition of IOS sales to Americans. Ironically IOS's financial health might have been restored, if only momentarily, had King instead repaid the $10 million he owed the company.

What followed was an acrimonious and intrigue-filled, cross-Atlantic legal and boardroom drama which starred the belligerent Cornfeld valiantly clinging to his company by virtue of his voting stock. The denouement culminated in a shareholder meeting at the Royal York Hotel in Toronto on June 30, 1970, where, duped into pledging his preferred shares to the wrong side, he finally lost control of his mutual-fund complex.

Meanwhile, to save itself, the Fund of Funds on September 3, 1970, took the unprecedented and drastic step of defaulting on its shares. This was a gross violation of the basic covenant of mutual-fund liquidity, which guarantees the repurchase of mutual-fund shares on demand. By suspending redemptions on three-fifths of its assets, the fund's value dropped from $18.47 to $7.47 a share in one day.

Eventually a black knight named Robert L. Vesco, the 35-year-old chairman of Fairfield, New Jersey–based International Controls Corp., charged on the scene to bail out the company—with a merciless bargain of a $5 million loan for between six to seven million of its 44 million preferred shares. Vesco, who was hailed as IOS's messiah, was a villain far worse than any in the company's past. He subsequently looted nearly a quarter billion dollars from four of its mutual funds and, after his indictment in 1971, went on the lam from U.S. authorities. To this day he is America's most dazzling white-collar fugitive.

IOS eventually went bankrupt. A block of its preferred stock traded for one cent a share in June 1972.

Dispirited and discredited, Cornfeld embarked on a rollicking worldwide odyssey to recapture his faded financial glory. First, he left Geneva and repaired to France. Most of his time was occupied in fending off lawsuits. Following his November 1973 arrest and conviction for conning IOS's Swiss employees into buying stock in a faltering company, Cornfeld spent 11 months in St. Antoine prison. However, he voluntarily paid back every one of his disgruntled ex-employees the full $10 face value of each share, which cost him $1 million. After jail he moved to Beverly Hills. Once estimated to have a personal wealth of $150 million, Cornfeld was down to his last $5 million. His name had become synonymous with excessive financial speculation, and a full comeback was never in the cards.

By taking off when he did, Fred avoided the Waterloo that befell all IOS operations and escaped the taint of associating with Cornfeld that splattered over the financial community. While Fred maintained an arm's-length relationship with Cornfeld afterward, there was mutual fondness and honest respect between the two. Flash forward to the late seventies and one of the last times Fred Alger would meet Bernie Cornfeld. Alger Fund board member and friend of Fred, Arthur Dubow, recounted what transpired.

"Over the years Bernie would solicit Fred with business deals from time to time. Fred called up late one Sunday and asked me to come into New York for a breakfast meeting the next day with Bernie. 'He has a venture deal he wants to talk about,' said Fred. 'I'd like to help him with it.' I replied, 'I don't do venture capital.' Fred's answer was, 'I'd really appreciate it if you did.'"

So Dubow came in from Long Island, and they met early Monday at the Regency Hotel. Cornfeld entered with a man in tow who was introduced as Elizabeth Taylor's diet doctor. "Bernie's concept was to sell a diet drink house to house in New York, and he was going to reactivate his old IOS sales staff for that," continued Dubow. "I was very skeptical.

"The breakfast went on, and when Bernie could see I wasn't interested in the diet doctor, he did the one thing you should never do to salvage a sales call—he pulled out several other deals from his briefcase. It was very sad. He had become a pathetic figure. Breakfast over, Fred thanked me for coming. He had the same general reaction to Bernie."

After collapsing from a stroke, Bernie Cornfeld died of pneumonia at the Chelsea and Westminster Hospital in London on February 27, 1995. He was 67 years old.

In Cornfeld's *New York Times* obituary, only Fred Alger, among the many prominent financial professionals influenced by him, went on record with a positive word. Tipping his hat to a former colleague in the capitalism of mutual funds, Fred announced, "He was a brilliant, absolutely brilliant innovator in the field." Dubow confirmed, "The others declined comment and didn't want to refresh people's memories of their past association with him."

Chat Hickox, who knew Fred well during the Cornfeld period, said, "Fred believed that Bernie was the greatest entrepreneur of all time, and he was very vocal about it." Cornfeld, for his part, once paid Fred a precious compliment when he told the press, "Money management is an art form, and Fred Alger is a fine artist."

Fred Alger emerged from the Cornfeld experience a wiser and sturdier businessman. Deciding to give up the immediate gain of performance fees, he was prepared to alter his business model to establish his company more soundly and enduringly as a registered investment adviser.

When Bill Scheerer joined Fred Alger in 1965, two months after Fred's meeting with Cornfeld, he got a rude shock. "The office was only as big as a large closet," he recalled. "The venetian blinds were askew and broken. There were two or three desks and a wicker wastebasket with great big, gaping holes. The remains of Fred's lunch every day—that time consisting of chocolate ice cream and a hamburger— would often be spilling out of the basket. On the walls, old Christmas cards were still hanging by Scotch tape. Every time the door of the office would open, it would bang into my desk." To top it off, it had a view into a dingy airshaft.

Its physical space would not hinder 1966 performance or earnings. Prophetically Fred had moved 30% of the Security Equity portfolio into cash before the market decline and also successfully timed its upward stanza. This counter maneuver yielded a 9% gain for the year, which was second only to T. Rowe Price's New Horizon Fund and far exceeded the Dow, which had dropped by 15.7%. The best groups were the airlines and television. "We made a lot of money in color televisions, at that time a brand new consumer product which provided superior value, lower unit costs and higher unit volume," explained Scheerer. The firm's earnings from management fees rose to $115,000, and the performance income had yet to kick in. Fred Alger was on the move.

In 1967 Fred took in George Boggio as his second key man and, coincident with a 40% advance in the firm's composite performance, the firm shifted to the Equitable Building at 120 Broadway. The original seven-story Equitable Building, built in 1870 with the first passenger elevators, had been demolished by fire. When this 40-story edifice was raised from the ashes of the old one in 1915, it was the tallest skyscraper of the day and renowned for its soaring, block-through Beaux Arts lobby and terra-cotta molding.

But the threadbare look of the office remained. To the old furniture from 56 Pine, Fred added folding tables, a blackboard and some filing cabinets. Fred's old desk, with one missing leg, was propped up with a soup can. One large office was shared by Bill, George, Fred and the next hire, Will Stewart. Rosemary Kiernan was assisted by another secretary with a fancy name, Suzanne Salisbury Cartier.

Fred Alger was managing $200 million in investments, which included the IOS account, the Security Management mutual funds and an Alger-directed Mississippi hedging partnership called Southland. Fred was known for getting some of the highest incentive fees in the business. Although the Security Equity Fund was up a startling 67.8% in 1967, it had slipped to tenth place in the mutual-fund rankings. Despite his disappointment at this, he graciously accepted praise by the media for his continuing good performance. "It is not that we're any smarter," he said. "We just work at it, minute by minute, all day long."

Fred was obviously more brilliant than most in his field, and he was utterly jazzed by the investment business. "His whole life was stocks and bonds," observed Lavaun Vawter, who became Fred's secretary in 1968. That attitude remained unchanged 20 years later. Rob Lyon, a top Alger analyst in the eighties, confirmed, "Fred lived and breathed the stock market from the time he got up to the time he went to bed. He was very involved in it, both intellectually, emotionally." Ron Tartaro, currently a portfolio manager at the firm, added, "He is so in love with the stock market that it permeates his life. Everything else is secondary. He can totally focus so incredibly on the stock market and tune out everything else with incredible ease."

Fred confirms this, and loves to tell this story that took place when his third daughter, Nicole, was born in March 1966. "I was walking down the street and thinking about a stock called McLain Industries, which I bought very low and sold at the top of the market. In my mind I was trying to re-create why or how I was able to sell the stock at that high point; selling is really the hardest part of any stock decision. I ran into a friend who offered his congratulations. I wondered how he read my mind and knew of my success with McLain. 'How did you know?' I asked. 'Everybody knows,' he replied. Well, he was wishing me well about the birth of my child. I was thinking about McLain Industries."

In the late sixties, a whorl of intense activity set the pace for the firm. Turbocharged by the mutual-fund performance, Fred was able to build up his enterprise, in double time, and rapidly reached the point of financial security for the firm. "In the beginning, you'd come in the morning and they'd have a new company started," offered Rosemary Kiernan. Lavaun Vawter embellished. "Some were shell companies, some were companies to buy management companies and others to channel managed accounts."

Fred also realized that he needed to bring attention to himself in order to earn his fortune on Wall Street. Like everything else he did, he played the publicity game aggressively and well. By courting the print media, he kept his name in the financial pages and pumped up demand for his personal brand of investing. By design Fred pinned his public image on a pose that was repeated for all his media encounters. He always appeared with the same look: an intense, thoughtful, even defiant young man with tousled hair wearing a white dress-shirt and red suspenders. It was his visual refrain, as memorable as an advertising jingle. Vogueing for the press, he would usually lean back on his chair and have one foot bracing his desk with the clearly worn soles of his shoes facing the camera. Fred presented himself with this familiar imprint through the turbulent sixties and struck that pose at least through the seventies. It helped, of course, that he was the favorite manager of scapegrace international mutual-fund operator Bernie Cornfeld.

On the home front, Fred also moved up in 1967, from the Upper West Side into a nine-room apartment on Park Avenue.

Fred's personal network expanded to the smart set in the Hamptons, which was also good for business. His partner Bill Scheerer had a place there. So did Gilbert Kaplan, publisher and founder of *Institutional Investor* magazine, who put Fred on one of its first covers. Another friend from Long Island was Arthur Dubow, a venture capitalist and international investor, whose college roommate at Harvard was Fidelity's Ned Johnson and who produced the 1969 cult film on advertising *Putney Swope*.

Even in the relaxed atmosphere of the Hamptons Fred was "always very competitive," Dubow recalled. "Whenever we went over to dinner, he would bring out a puzzle or a word game or mathematical game. It wasn't always chitchat. His competitiveness is what I felt particularly at the outset. Whenever he did anything, he took it seriously. Especially tennis."

This sentiment is echoed by John Sargent, another Alger Fund board member and former head of Doubleday Books, who first met Fred when he moved to Bridgehampton. "Fred and I used to play tennis together at the Maidstone Club. He was very aggressive, very hard-playing, very enthusiastic. I was struck by his energy and enthusiasm. We got on pretty well right away."

Fred readily confesses to this trait. "I am as competitive as anyone I have run across," he admitted. "It's hard for me to be in a situation where I'm not competing, sometimes to my detriment. If I'm on a board of directors, I'll want to run it. It's just in my nature."

It was at dignified Maidstone, on Old Beach Lane at East Hampton, where one day Fred's Chevy station wagon was set upon by two valets in the parking lot. Fred observed this while standing by the pool about twenty yards away and rushed screaming to save his vehicle. It turned out that the kids were not up to any mischief. They were told to break into the car and move it because it didn't look like it belonged. Maidstone reserves parking spaces only for its members. "They couldn't believe that anyone with such a terrible car could be a member of the club," said Fred.

Fred revealed this about himself: "I've never been someone who is much interested in things. In contrast with my brother; he just loves beautiful things . . . cars, boats. I don't like any of that stuff. I had a car which was so beat up and so old, you could actually see through the floorboards—which was fine as far as I was concerned."

Another tale from his early years on Long Island, provided by Chat Hickox, is again both amusing and revealing.

"Around his house in the Hamptons were a lot of undeveloped potato fields. It was Saturday morning, and Fred, who had just bought a dirt bike, wanted to jump on it and take his first practice ride. His wife, Eleanor, said no. It was not yet registered. He had no license to drive and no helmet. 'Fred, if you get into an accident, the world would come to an end. You'd have nothing to stand on. They'd eat you up like raw meat, so don't take the risk. Wait until Monday.'

"Fred was in one of his more godlike moments and said, 'We're out in the country. Nothing will happen.'

"The house was not far from the main road, off a gravel path. We were sitting on the porch having breakfast when Fred drove out. In barely ten seconds, a siren went off and a police car came screaming by. It was an unlikely circumstance, a really shitty break. He got twelve points. They wiped him out and took his license

The company had its offices at 26 Broadway for twelve years.

away. If he'd go to driver's ed, they'd give him back his license. But he kept arguing with them. His sole thing in life became getting his license back without going to driving school. For years Eleanor had to drive him around because of this."

In 1970 Fred Alger & Co. migrated south to 26 Broadway, the prestigious curving office tower which rose up as world headquarters of Standard Oil Trust after it grew out of Cleveland. It was a premier site and another step up for the firm. North of Beaver and overlooking Bowling Green, the teardrop-shaped rotunda that softens the tip of the financial district, 26 Broadway was reconstructed in 1919 by Thomas Hastings, one of the architects of the New York Public Library.

Its exterior is imposing and stamped by an arching bay entrance that is adorned, even now, long after Rockefeller moved his company to New York's Midtown, by a large emblem with the proud letters S and O. In the grand lobby the walls are Kasota stone, and the pilasters of Italian rosato are inscribed with the names of the Standard Oil pantheon. Adjoining a sister building which houses Standard & Poor's, a separate entrance to 26 Broadway opens to the Museum of American Financial History.

Here Fred Alger made its home for a total of 12 years, including the entire decade of the seventies. First it took up space on the seventh floor but quickly ran out of room. So the firm expanded two floors down, which is when it finally got a new look. "He changed suddenly," recalled secretary Lavaun Vawter. "There was new furniture, a complete redecoration and a new paint job. The colors that he chose were startling. In the conference room it was green and white stripes in a zigzag that looked like lightning. I asked him why. It was so awful you didn't want to stay there. He said that was his purpose, so you wouldn't dilly-dally."

There were no airshaft views here. The high windows in Fred's office looked past Battery Park and the Hudson River to the Statue of Liberty.

Due to the great influx of business, Alger always fell short of space, and finding more room was a constant struggle. "Twenty-six Broadway was a disaster," Rosemary Kiernan remembered. "We were inundated with paper and research. There was so much of it, you couldn't pull the file cabinet drawers out. Every time we hired another analyst, that was four more tons of paper and more legal pads for research."

"I started in a cubbyhole at 26 Broadway. It was so cramped, people were on top of people," said Marine Corps veteran John R. Raspitha, who picked a job at Alger over an offer from prestigious Salomon Brothers in January 1977 and wound up controller of the firm.

On the sixth floor, right above Fred's office, was Ashland Management, which was run by Chat Hickox, at the time his main friend and business associate.

In November 1966 Hickox had become Fred's first high-net-worth individual client. The money in Hickox's private account came from a $1 million inheritance he received when he turned 21. Hickox's account was idling in the hands of Smith Barney, where his brother, a Yale graduate, was working. "Frankly," said Hickox, "I was underwhelmed by their results.

"I liked Fred's investment concepts," he continued. "I thought his analysis of Wall Street and other money managers was accurate. Fred, in the early days, was probably someone most people felt comfortable giving only fifteen percent of their money to, and they accepted that they might lose it all. In my case, I gave him everything."

Hickox's faith in Fred was seemingly balanced by his other business ventures. As manager of the airport in Burlington, Vermont, he and his partners had a monopoly on fuel sales and maintenance contracts in return for fees based on the gross revenue of the airport. In addition, he was part owner of a charter airline, Overseas National Airways—a business that was growing by 22% annually, about double the rate of scheduled carriers. But it was actually the increase of his investments by Fred—rather than his business deals—that pulled him out of several jams and enabled him keep his airline aloft. "I couldn't have made the interest payments on the debt without Fred. I once told him, 'You only have to make one hundred percent a year so that I can carry my investment in ONA.'" Hickox recalled that Fred's performance was "anywhere from twenty-five to sometimes sixty percent."

Hickox paid him on a performance-fee basis, and Fred was consistently beating the market. "It worked out extremely well," said Fred. "He also brought in other business for us." One was the pension account of Baker Welfare Foundation, which Hickox later took back when he went into the investment-management business for himself.

In Hickox's time, ONA was a darling stock on Wall Street. Hickox bought in at $3.33, mostly with letter stock, and cashed out at $34 in 1969, two years after the airline went public. Within eight months ONA stock had fallen from the skies down to $4 a share.

With a bundle from the ONA transaction and the acclaim for having outsmarted Wall Street, Hickox made a move into the investment-advisory business, using Fred as his money manager. "First I gave all my business to Fred," he said. "Then I took on a partner, Parry Jones. We picked six managers and spread the assets around according to different styles and performance. Of course, everybody lied like crazy in those days, except Fred. There weren't any consultants, and no one was measuring anybody's lies."

There was a brief split between the two men when they couldn't see eye to eye about brokerage payments to Hickox on Fred's advisory accounts. So Hickox's newly formed Devin Management formed a pact with institutional broker Conan & Co., an arrangement which was dismantled by the termination of fixed-rate commission schedules, which led to the closing of Conan's business. Hickox then double backed to Fred, and Ashland Management was born at 26 Broadway as a guaranteed subsidiary of Fred Alger Management in order to obtain reimbursement for brokerage commissions.

In 1977 Hickox split completely from Fred and jumped whole-hog into money management by withdrawing $10 million from his own nest egg in Alger's care. In the process of interviewing money managers, Hickox contended that he had sufficiently figured out the business and could market his own investment approach, which might appeal to institutional accounts. He was joined by Joe Davis, from a previously failed advisory opportunity, and together they invented a proprietary investment model called Ashland Strategy, based on timing market entry and exit points.

The asymmetrical alliance between Fred and Chat had run its course. Hickox elaborated, "At certain point in the game, Fred got to a size where having us as a guaranteed subsidiary meant all kinds of reporting problems for him. At the same time commission rates declined to a point where it didn't make any sense for us either. Each of us had to start answering questions from our clients about the relationship. It was a marriage that no longer made any sense."

In September 1980, when Ashland was managing $60 million, the firm's model gave a signal to exit the market, and Hickox pulled out all the money until the indicator was reversed in August 1982. With that triumphant call Ashland went on a roll into the pension business. Its model has kept it in the market since then, and assets under management in its portfolio of growth stocks touched $1.5 billion in 1995. Even after Hickox broke off with Fred, he kept a portion of his personal portfolio with his company.

Though they were close friends, Fred and Hickox approached their businesses quite differently. "Fred liked the controversial, and he himself was controversial," said the burly, gruff-voiced Hickox. "Fred was on an ego trip, that's what I really thought. One of Fred's drawbacks in gathering accounts was that he was so aggressive that although his performance was great, he was frightening to a prudent investor. His intense drive could be off-putting. Fred always reserved the right to kinda go and do whatever he wanted to with your funds. And sometimes what he did was a little scary."

Another divergence was the way the two men marketed their respective companies. For example, Ashland bid for wrap-fee accounts which, until recently, was shunned by Fred Alger. In this type of investment relationship, large brokerage firms consign blocks of their client accounts to money managers and compensate them with a single fee which includes all administrative, management and brokerage commission charges.

In Ashland's conference room, still at 26 Broadway and decorated with hunting scenes and a patriotic picture of an American bald eagle, Hickox gave a strong impression that he admired Fred greatly even though they ended up as challengers for the same accounts. There was perceptible remorse over the lost association. He was quite looking forward to toasting Fred at the going-away cocktail party coming up at the Knickerbocker Club.

7 🜲

Partners

To create his company, Fred had gathered around him a nucleus of kindred spirits who might strengthen the enterprise in areas where he was wanting. Fred set the stage, and he welcomed players who could take his strong direction.

It's uncertain how William Scheerer II, Fred's first partner, parlayed his affection for a family-run dairy business into an enthusiasm for the stock market, but when Fred met him he was already a popular and well-respected figure in the Wall Street fraternity and vice president of research in the brokerage firm of Lawrence Douglas & Co. Previously he had been an executive in the institutional wing of McDonnell & Co., another NYSE member firm, where he started as a minority partner in 1957. Fred had used some of his investment ideas and assigned some commission business to his firm.

Reluctant for some time to sign on with Fred, Scheerer was finally lured into the firm by the prospect of potentially huge performance fees accruing from the IOS business. He recalled his excitement at the first flush of money from Bernie Cornfeld.

"In fall of 1965 Fred took me out to lunch. He had been promised five million dollars from the Fund of Funds, and the compensation would be five percent of the appreciation he generated. At the time Fred probably had no more than six million dollars under management with the Security Funds, which provided only a small management fee. This new arrangement looked promising from Fred's point of view, but it didn't seem like much to me, so I turned him down.

"Then at Christmas Fred called again and asked me to reconsider. Bernie was now talking ten million dollars. The market was on a roll. It seemed that the two of us could work quite well. Ten million dollars generating fifty percent appreciation would mean five million, and five percent of that is two hundred fifty thousand dollars. All of a sudden it began to make sense to me. Soon after I got together with Fred, Cornfeld called up and asked if we could handle twenty million dollars. It was electrifying."

Bill brought balance and respectability to the firm. Tall and with weathered good looks, Scheerer, a jazz pianist, was the firm's éminence grise and exerted a leavening influence on the audacious Fred Alger.

"He was very good for me," Fred said about Bill. "He cleaned up my act a little bit. Because I was so focused and so competitive, I think I rubbed a lot of people the wrong way. Whereas everybody was crazy about Bill. In many, many ways it was a perfect marriage. We were very complementary personalities in every respect."

While Fred focused on growth companies, Scheerer's accent was on undervalued companies, low price-to-earnings stocks, turnarounds and special situations. His métier was oil stocks, and in that his expertise was so substantial that even the Department of Energy would call for his advice.

During the Arab oil embargo, Bill got Fred into oil stocks, and they made a "ton of money" when it was rough sledding for most in the energy field. OPEC's oil embargo and the Watergate morass combined to throw the markets into a tailspin in 1973 and 1974. The Dow corrected about 50% and the rest of the market plummeted over 70%. These were the worst declines since the 1929 to 1933 period, and by some measures, even worse.

It was the spirit in which Fred and Bill worked as a team that bound their relationship. Day in and out, they were face to face in a closet of a room, grinding out their research and firing ideas at each other. It was a charged atmosphere that remained unaltered for nine months, until the next Alger employee came on board.

As analysts, they relied on sell-side brokers to provide most of the research and grew increasingly displeased with the quality of investment information released to them. As a small firm, Fred Alger was a low priority. When corporate news finally filtered down, it was likely dated or faulty. "We were always skeptical of the advice we got on the Street," said Bill, "and for the most part it was pretty bad. Ultimately we began to rely more and more on our own work by expanding the research staff." Meanwhile, although Fred and Bill weren't market technicians, they discovered charts from a California company that allowed them to spot trends early and predict the next big stock opportunity.

By disposition, Bill was described as genial, thoughtful, astute, even-handed and a good analyst. He was a major force in enhancing the firm's standing and bringing talented people into its fold. Moreover, he had a bedside manner which was appealing to both investors and the financial community. This was something Fred never possessed.

"If you were a little old lady whose husband had just died and left you some money, and you came to my office to interview me and didn't know much about the business, I would never get your account," said Fred. "There isn't that transference of trust that goes between me and people. I know that about myself. One on one, there's something about me that people basically don't believe."

"He was wildly popular among the other people in the firm, almost without exception," offered Bob Emerson, a former senior analyst and partner. "Bill is a very intelligent, sweet human being," said George Boggio, Fred's next partner after Bill. "He was an older guy, but more in tune with the times than the youngest of us."

"We went through some difficult times together," said Fred, "but we also had a lot of fun together. Bill's a great guy to work with. Very easygoing. Wonderful judgment. Extraordinary memory."

From Bill's viewpoint:

Bill Scheerer, Fred's first partner. They were complementary personalities in every respect.

"Fred gave us the philosophy that kept us on the leading edge of the stock market—to always seek out new and better stock ideas that would push out the laggards. At the same time he was very good with the stick and carrot in motivating people. He could also be very generous and complimentary."

Not everything was always peaches and cream between the two men, which was to be expected since they were in such close quarters. Here's how Bill described an unpleasantness when "Fred was jerking me around." Bill had bought shares in a firm that began to lose its value very soon after his purchase. "Fred kept after me to defend my decision," said Bill. "'What about this? What about that?' He kept hounding and hounding, asking me very tough questions about the company. In the end I said, 'Gee, Fred, you may be right. Perhaps we should sell it.' He had put me in the position of giving up on the stock—not for good reason, but because of his sheer pressure.

"Fred's response was, 'I don't want you to just give in. I want you to defend the stock.' In other words, he was playing me. Fred was such a demanding person," Bill added. "My tension would stem from feeling that one could never do well enough to please him. There's enough pressure in this business; you don't need additional pressure from your partner."

In the end Scheerer was a casualty of lightning changes in the investment industry and the ascendancy of computer technology in its research and decision-making process. By the early eighties the firm and the business had moved away from being spontaneous, informal and undisciplined. Competitive performance based on the individual intuition and personal insight that Bill had excelled at had lost its viability.

"The business became more systems-oriented, shifting away from the old school of the Lone Ranger analyst who kept notes on a pad or in his head," said Fred. "Bill's way didn't work for a company where you needed to put things on paper for others to see. Also, he had turned sixty and had had a heart attack. He didn't seem to want to do it anymore, be engaged in such a focused effort."

From 1972, the year he was stricken, until he left the firm ten years later, he was the only employee who normally left the office during lunch, often going for a swim at the Downtown Athletic Club.

Bill admitted, "Everybody else was running at one hundred twenty miles an hour, I was going eighty and wanted to do sixty. I was older than Fred by ten years. It cost me some money to leave, since according to the shareholder agreement with Fred, you had to stay twenty years to get full book value. By leaving early I got only half book value. But I'm satisfied. You get tired of doing the same thing all the time. Fred was the one who told me that we'd all burn out. And he was twenty-eight years old. I didn't believe it. But he was right."

What finally pushed Bill out the door may have been Fred's compulsion for creating a family dynasty. "I wanted to keep it a family firm and get the stock to David. I wanted Bill to cut back very sharply his interests and sell out to him. I really forced the issue."

At the start of their partnership, Scheerer owned 35% of the company through shares in Falcon Associates, the entity which held the Cornfeld account. David already had a stake in the firm, with 15,000 shares acquired in 1972 and 1,303 shares in lieu of a bonus in 1975. Of Scheerer's 10,858 shares in Fred Alger when he retired, 7,000 were returned to the firm and the balance was split evenly among David Alger, George Boggio and Irwin Schwartz.

"I had a hard time leaving," Scheerer confessed. "I hung around in the office for a couple of months. I just couldn't get used to the idea that I didn't belong there anymore."

After leaving Alger & Co., Bill remained in the business for another 10 years, at the brokerage firm of Legg Mason. Now retired, he splits his time between East Hampton and the Upper East Side and spends his leisure playing the piano and listening to jazz. In his seventies, he's still an avid tennis player and downhill skier.

George J. Boggio was Fred's and the firm's tax accountant at Lafranz, Walker, Jackley & Saville, several floors up at 56 Pine St. Because Fred Alger was such a small account they assigned him their youngest employee.

But Fred, taken by George's strong personality and professionalism, saw his potential and had an eye on him even as he was hiring Scheerer. With assets surging and the firm's accounting becoming more complex, Fred realized he needed someone in-house to keep the books. Fred was already managing Chat Hickox's money. IOS was on board with two funds, and even as an outsider, one of George's functions was pricing these portfolios. George, who was also Joe Reich's accountant and did Lester Colbert's taxes, knew the industry, understood Fred's finances, and was in sympathy with the Alger business philosophy. Also in common with Fred, he had twin children. But he got some resistance from Scheerer, who felt that Boggio was just too young for the responsibility.

Following Fred's standing order that fixed and variable expenses must be supported by corresponding income, George Boggio would have to wait his turn before joining the firm. The large account Fred was expecting didn't show until November 1966, and that's when George got his offer.

"I didn't have to think more than half a second," said George. He had the feeling that Fred Alger was going places and wanted on for the ride.

A bit old-fashioned like Fred, extra careful about propriety and doing the right steps in the prenuptial minuet, George sent Fred to ask for his hand from LaFranz's

Bridge was elemental for Fred. He played it every day at the Regency Club.

senior partner. The partner agreed, but asked George to stay until the end of the year. So George joined Fred Alger on January 1, 1967.

"It was terrific for the firm to have a person like George, with standards and a strong personality," Fred declared. This freed him to focus completely on picking stocks, running the portfolios and hitting the peaks of high performance. George saw Fred as "very dynamic and very bright, somewhat a genius who focused fully on the market." George knew his role, and he played it to perfection.

In those early days he was a one-man show for all administrative, accounting and tax matters. George priced the funds, kept track of performance and brought a higher level of fiscal control to Fred's operation. As the firm grew, he set up the brokerage business and the clearing operation, its telecommunications system and its computers for accounting. Basically he did everything but the research function.

"This firm ran like a Swiss watch," said Bill Scheerer. "There were no accounting or clerical screw-ups. We knew where every penny went. We never lost more than a couple of thousand dollars a year on fails-to-receive after we started clearing our business." (On Wall Street "fails" describe a firm's inability to complete a stock transaction, for whatever reason, within the required time.)

George's manner and methods enabled Fred to implement the distant management style he found so attractive in the Marines. For example, Fred had no appetite for confrontation. If there was a conflict, George dealt with it. "He left the nitty-gritty to George," said Irwin Schwartz. "He hated to fire people. Every time a female employee would cry, he would mutter, 'No more women. I swear, no more women.' Women analysts used to drive him crazy."

George implemented Fred's growth strategy down to the last detail. As Fred groped his way through a welter of new business ideas, George covered his every move. "Fred was a visionary and I was the detail guy," crowed George. "I prided myself on being able to implement anything, administratively, he wanted to do."

Lavaun Vawter confirmed, "Fred would have some very grand tax ideas and new ways of putting together corporations. George himself was not a very creative person, but he had a good style for carrying out Fred's instructions. He was able to coordinate and keep everything flowing. That was George's talent."

When Fred decided to buy his own building in 1982 as a check on spiraling rental costs and the unending distraction of locating additional rental space, it was George who made it happen. "When we moved into 75 Maiden Lane, he orchestrated the entire move," said Fred. "There was nothing out of place. It was as if we had been working there for ten years. Everything in order. There wasn't a hitch."

One of George's major contributions to the firm was in the management of customer accounts. In the mid-eighties he placed into service a number of complex procedures and systems, mostly enabled by computers, to ensure that the company wouldn't violate any client restrictions on their investments. For example, kicking out sin stocks or companies who did business in South Africa from accounts of clients with such prejudices, or blocking more than a specified percentage of a stock or an industry group from entering a portfolio.

"We had guidelines that you had to watch like a hawk," said John Raspitha, an accountant who worked under George. "It was the foresight of George Boggio that enabled our growth. When I joined, we had a couple hundred million under management, which peaked close to four billion dollars while I was there. The growth couldn't have taken place without his control."

Although George came on board as controller, he discovered he could make a special contribution in the client-services area. He enjoyed personal interaction with the clients so much that in the early days he would sometimes chip in and help Alger's high net-worth clients prepare their tax returns. For a nominal charge the company paid some clients' bills and balanced their checkbooks. "Our goal was to kill the clients with service," he said. At Alger the client came first. The firm came second. The client would take care of the firm so that the firm could take care of its employee. That's the Alger way.

George knew many of these individuals from the first day they became Alger clients. It's to his credit that many of them still keep their money with the firm. Especially vivid is his memory of two sisters, one of whom had become overwhelmed in balancing the economics of her life. She turned to George as a father figure and, for a time, relied on him for even minor financial decisions. With George's patient hand holding, Fred Alger became the stabilizing influence which enabled her to keep up her lifestyle. With delicious serendipity, George ran into this very lady on Madison Avenue as he was making his way to Fred Alger's thirtieth anniversary Christmas dinner.

When it was time for the firm to step up to self-clearing its stock trades, George saw to it and, in the process, opened a satellite office in Jersey City, New Jersey. Mike DiMeglio, one of George's recruits for that operation and now the firm's senior vice president of client services, recalled that in his job interview, George rolled up his sleeves and said, "This is the way we work." That's how George set it up.

George nursed the New Jersey operation to maturity. Eventually he turned it into his own sphere of influence separate from the New York headquarters. One of his personal touches, missed by the employees there today, was the inclusion of a personal letter of commendation with every bonus check.

George's strict personality determined the style of this Alger outpost and directed the high tone of its operation. Rosemary Kiernan insisted, "Nobody ever went out to lunch here. You never left the office . . . from Fred on down, either there or here. There was a time I even felt guilty about taking a vacation."

The ground rules were clearly conveyed to prospective employees, she added.

"No matter what you do, no matter what your job, nothing is considered trivial or unimportant. You're going to be asked to pitch in and help when there's a project to be done, which may be completely unrelated to your area. It should not be taken as being dumped on or something that is beneath you that others don't want to do. Everyone has to do here."

Though the place revolved around his demanding nature, it was less pressured than in New York. "It was always very busy here, but not as tense, because there was no Fred," Rosemary agreed. "George would rant and rave if something went wrong, but once he finished, it was over. Over there, things would hang."

A core tenet that took root in the operation was George's insistence on training employees in multiple business functions. "We were growing quite rapidly," George explained, "so we structured the firm in anticipation that what we could be doing the following year might be entirely different from what we were doing today." Aside from raising awareness of its business activities, cross training benefited the firm by decreasing the need and cost of temporary help while enabling the easy, lateral advancement of current employees. It turned out to be essential to the firm's smooth running, especially through several major transitions.

Another view from Irwin Schwartz: "All of us at the core were willing to take any job. One minute George would be treasurer, the next he was designing furniture. One minute I was signing the checks, the next minute I was emptying the dishwasher."

"No one is indispensable," George said. To remind himself of this, he kept a pointed maxim on his desk, which he paraphrased, "If you think you're the most important person in the room, get a bucket, fill it with water, put your hand in it and see the space it takes up. Then remove your hand and see how quickly the water fills back up.

"I proved this principle when I left the firm," he said. "As much as I did, people were able to fill the void. There wasn't one person who left the firm that ever left it lacking. There was always another person who could take his place. That started with the messengers and went all the way up to me."

George joined Fred Alger when he was 26 and retired a rich man at age 49. "I was there 23 years, and I woke up every morning enthusiastic about going to work. I really enjoyed the whole operation," said George. "And I conveyed that. The management styles of all five of us—Fred, David, Bill, Irwin and myself—blended so nicely. Any problem that occurred was not seen as a problem but a situation to be corrected."

This was the deal. When Fred invited you to become a partner, he sold you shares in the company for twice their book value. If you didn't have the money, he would finance the purchase at a nominal interest rate, but you were required to use the after-tax bonus money to pay off the loan. Except for Bill Scheerer, who bought his stock at par with his own capital and paid the money directly to Fred, this is how everybody else, including David Alger, got to be a partner.

The catch was, you couldn't retrieve your shares for book value unless you stayed in the firm for at least 20 years. If you left before that time, the agreement called for selling the stock back to the company at half the current book value; you would reach break-even only if the company's value quadrupled at the time of leaving. New partners were brought in through the redistribution of existing shares. In 1975, however, 13,027 shares were issued instead of bonuses. Half of these—6,513 went to Fred.

Even while they took it, some individuals who became partners viewed this agreement as a sleight-of-hand that would have made Machiavelli blush. "Fred, in effect, cooked up this amazingly bizarre, clever scheme to lock us in as long term investors in Fred Alger Management," said Bob Emerson. "In essence, it involved our lending him money, for which he charged us interest. It worked for him because it kept us earning just that much more money than we could earn anywhere else, and there was this huge haircut you were going to take if you left early."

Emerson purchased roughly $200,000 worth of stock for about $400,000. When he sold it back to the firm nine years later, it came to $800,000. Not a bad deal, but Emerson insisted that, except for the fact that the market had quadrupled during that period and there was an explosion of assets under management, he would have been better off investing in T-Bills.

Most of Alger's colleagues were like George Boggio, who gratefully accepted partnership as a gift from Fred. "My bonus was larger than I would have gotten anyway," he said. "I'm getting equity participation, and he's giving me money to pay for it. I saw it as Fred's money, which he was giving to me to give back to him."

Nonetheless, becoming Fred's partner required a leap of faith—faith in the investment-management business, faith in the firm and, most of all, faith in Fred. As the firm began to succeed, it became clear that the status of shareholder was something worth attaining.

For Fred this novel form of internal financing was not a machination built on intrigue but a strategic way of attracting talented people to the company, with compensation he could not otherwise afford. It fell under his overall scheme for accumulating and preserving capital, which was always the abiding principle of the firm.

"Instead of Sub S or partnership structure, we had a corporate structure," said Fred. "The accumulation of capital was essential for the company's long-term benefit. If you paid capital out to people or partners, there would be long-range problems recapturing it. That's why when you became a shareholder, you paid twice book value, and a large part of the bonuses had to go to paying off those loans, so that money was kept in the business."

"Fred gave us the philosophy that kept us on the leading edge of the stock market,"
said Bill Scheerer.

Today, partnership is no longer available in Fred Alger's company. It is firmly
in the family's hands, with Fred controlling roughly 80% of the shares and most
of the balance belonging to David. Ron Reel, Dr. Ron as he's affectionately called
because he's a medical stock analyst, is the only non-family shareholder left in
the firm.

"I don't think we'll ever sell stock again to anyone," said Fred. "That ended when we bought out George and Irwin. It doesn't mean anything to anyone. The lack of shares doesn't affect the way people perform. Money clearly does. That's why at the Christmas dinner I always report earnings before bonus and tax. A substantial part of those earnings gets paid out in bonuses. Ownership only reflects how much money you can make from the goddamn thing. Stability of capital is much more important. That the cow is healthy is more important for everybody than that they own a piece of the cow."

No one could figure out the rules for being offered ownership. It was arbitrary, at Fred's whim.

William A. W. Stewart III, one of Fred's earliest partners, is a perfect example. Stewart was an institutional salesman for the Chicago–based Bacon Whipple brokerage, who used to call on Fred for his business. Fred liked what he saw and took him on as an analyst in July 1967. In fact, he was so high on Will that he offered him 15% of the company right from the get-go, both he and Scheerer contributing a proportionate amount of their shares to make up Stewart's stake.

Even though Stewart was offered his shares at book, he wasn't able to come up with the financing. It was largely in response to Stewart's predicament that Fred contrived the twice-book-value scheme for financing participation in the firm as a shareholder.

Part of Will's eventual problem with Fred stemmed from his failure to appreciate that his ownership status was not an entitlement but purely an act of Fred's generosity. He never acknowledged that Fred had come up with a clever scheme that allowed him to become an owner of the company. He always regretted that he had to pay twice book value. He resented owing Fred the interest and felt that the bonus was his to spend as he pleased.

At some point he confronted Fred in order to negotiate a better deal for himself, thinking that Fred would back down and simply reduce his purchase price to par. Instead Fred stiffened and surprised him with a counteroffer: "If you find this arrangement too onerous," Fred said, "instead of fifteen percent, why don't we cut down your equity participation and reduce your liability?" Too late for Stewart. The decision was made. There was no backtracking. And there was no appeal.

During a quick succession of diminishing roles within the company, leading to a spot in marketing and client relations, Stewart withered under the strain of Fred's pressurized management style and ultimately left the firm in 1971. After Fred Alger, Stewart managed the considerable personal assets of CBS founder William S. Paley. Then he joined Morgan Stanley, and most recently he was a senior vice president of broker-dealer Dillon, Reed & Co. Inc.

Stewart's replacements were also early partners whose stay at the firm was relatively short, but who, unlike him, fared exceptionally well a analyst/managers in the company. Rufus G. Poole landed at Fred Alger in June 1971 from a vice presidency at Naess & Thomas Special Fund. Also joining the firm that summer was John E. Coughlin, whose prior experience was with Tarrytown, New York, mutual-fund manager E.W. Axe & Co.

"I just knew I had to get to Wall Street." Lavaun Vawter was bent on the financial capital, and she hooked up with Fred on the ground floor, perhaps the most exciting time in any company and certainly heady days at Fred Alger. It was the adventure of her life, all her dreams come true.

As a schoolgirl in St. Louis she preferred to read *The Wall Street Journal* over the fanzines and women's mags, and took delight in explaining the financial pages to her teachers and elders. When she was old enough to leave home, Lavaun boarded a plane for New York City, and her first stop on arriving was the New York Stock Exchange. She got the biggest thrill of her young life when the Exchange put her name up on the ticker and she saw the large letters crawling across the stock board from the facing tourist gallery.

Vawter's first job on the Street was as a secretary at Lehman Brothers. Soon she bounced to Fred Alger. "Fred Alger was young and vital; Lehman was old and stodgy," she said. "The prestige of a wood-paneled dining room, imported china and silverware was not what I was after." Fred offered her a job on the spot. She started in the summer of 1968 and stayed with him for nine years.

How this young girl of German extraction advanced from a secretary to vice president reveals more about Fred Alger and the way he ran his business in the early days than Lavaun's contribution to the company. "We had a very good rapport," said Lavaun. "I could always anticipate what he wanted and responded well to it. There was a lot of trust in the relationship." Lavaun believed she served Fred best by cooling tensions between Fred and the outside world of pension investors.

When women first started wearing pants in the office, Fred refused to tolerate such a trend in his company. "He just wouldn't allow it," said Lavaun. "It was the only time I became upset with him. Of course, he won." Despite this and other minor displays of chauvinism, Fred has actually been very open to empowering women in roles of authority and giving them prominent positions in his organization. The firm was a true meritocracy, and Fred was race-, color- and gender-blind. You hit the ceiling only because you weren't a member of the family.

Fred made Lavaun vice president of several companies which he was busy creating back then and made her an allied member of the NYSE for the firm. Later she asked for and was given the chance to administer the Castle Convertible and Spectra funds, two closed-end mutual funds which Fred acquired in 1975.

It was Lavaun's final challenge at the firm which ultimately ushered her out

Corporate leaders: Original partners George Boggio and Irwin Schwartz (standing), David and Fred Alger, with senior analyst Rob Lyon (seated near left).

of Fred Alger. The job of controller was apparently beyond her grasp. A telltale sign was the unusually long hours she spent at her desk. Then Lavaun took an unexplained absence that lasted a week. This gave John Raspitha his shot at the position. Lavaun eventually called and asked to return, but it was too late.

Today Lavaun Vawter sells real estate in southern California. She says it's a lot like the brokerage business. You make the money buying and selling, whether the market is rising or falling.

Irwin Schwartz was so anxious to ensure his place on Fred's team that he gave up his tickets to the epochal 1969 Super Bowl III, when the New York Jets under Joe Namath defeated the Baltimore Colts. His first day on the job was set for January 13, the day after the game, and Irwin was afraid he might miss his flight back from Miami.

Assets were swelling, and Fred needed another research person. Irwin was a broker at Reynolds & Co., later absorbed by Dean Witter, who wanted to stretch his skills as an analyst. Scheerer had a friend, another broker at Reynolds who, while calling on Fred Alger for commission business, would talk up this wizard at Reynolds who ran wonderful paper portfolios. He said of Irwin, "In his own quiet way, he has a good market feel and good head for stock ideas."

For Irwin, the most convincing of several interviews he had for the Alger job was the one when Fred was interrupted by a phone call. Irwin turned his thoughts away, feeling it inappropriate to eavesdrop on Fred's conversation. When Fred was done, he turned to Irwin and asked for his thought on the matter over the phone. Irwin replied, "To be honest with you, I don't know the first thing about what you're talking about." He added, "I think Fred liked that. At least I was honest."

When Irwin came on board, Fred Alger was a tight little company. "There I was, sitting in this little cubbyhole, facing the wall," he described. "The only place they could put me was near the only quote machine. People would always come from behind me to check the market. I always knew who it was without turning around by the noises they made. Rufus Poole's shoes always squeaked. Bill Scheerer had coins in his pocket that always jingled."

Although Irwin joined the firm as an analyst, he quickly made his mark in the trading pits of the New York Stock Exchange. For a man who loved to gamble, what better place to hit the jackpot than the ultimate auction market? Research and administration were in hand. Trading was the third area that needed management, and Irwin would take control.

Fred Alger's original seat on the New York Stock Exchange was contributed by Frank E. Pierce III, a sitting member of the Exchange who was hired by the company in July 1970. For the seat he was paid $99,000 in the form of 6% of the shares in Fred Alger.

Before Pierce left the firm in December 1971, and took his seat with him, Fred Alger acquired another seat for $200,000 from Fred A. Robinson on December 14 and placed it in Irwin's name, in keeping with what is called an ABC Agreement.

Only individuals, not companies, are permitted to be members of the NYSE, and so it is common for brokerage firms to buy their seat in the name of an employee. An ABC Agreement, sanctioned by the NYSE, defines the relationship between the individual named on the seat and the actual owner. The trader who owns the seat takes responsibility in the agreement. If a named employee leaves a firm, he has several options: He can keep his membership and purchase another seat for an individual designated by the firm, he can sell the seat and hand the proceeds to the firm, or he can transfer the seat to another employee in the firm.

Since Irwin was the only one on the Alger team who had ever been a stockbroker or who had even seen or entered an order to buy or sell a stock, the seat was put in his name.

As Fred Alger's registered floor trader—in those days an uncommon position with some cachet—Irwin could initiate and execute trades, both for clients and the company account, without prior approval. But, unusually, he was also the upstairs head trader and had the final authority over the settlement price of a trade. This dual role called for subterfuge, evasive action and even some physical exercise in a sport which Irwin was only too happy to play.

First he would decide which stocks to buy, write out the orders and send them down to the order clerk on the floor of the Exchange. Then he would quickly put on his coat and rush down to the floor to chase and execute those orders. Once completed and noted by the clerk, Irwin would race back upstairs with the reports and resume yet another role by distributing the shares into the clients' accounts after the market closed.

If anyone on the floor had known that Irwin had complete discretion over the orders, not only would he have lost his bargaining chip but a lot of friends on the Exchange. "At the post, the fellow would say, 'I can give you five thousand shares at three-quarters, check with your man upstairs.' I walked around a little bit and came back with the answer, 'No, he says one-half.'" It was Irwin's ability to sustain this bluff which first enabled the firm to provide superior stock trade executions for its clients.

Irwin called his five years on the floor "the best experience I ever had in the security business." He added, "I did almost every job and personally executed the orders, which gave me a tremendous advantage. To this day, when I visualize stocks, I see how they would move on the floor."

The benefit of better trades, the byproduct of Irwin's invention, turned into an enduring business model for Fred Alger & Co. The brokerage operation fortified the firm with high commissions, which Fred Alger was able to justify with its ability to capture better executions. This slammed the door on arguments that there was an apparent conflict of interest between the money-management goal of peak performance and the purpose of the brokerage business to make as high a commission from as many trades as possible.

The firm prepared monthly high-low evaluation reports, which favorably compared Alger executions against the daily mean of a stock's trade and established without a doubt that Fred Alger's brokerage activities were, in fact, saving the client money and therefore improving performance. In essence, they proved that he needed to keep the brokerage to ensure the lower cost of doing business.

When a change of rules in 1976 kept partners of brokerage firms from working on the trading floor, Irwin held on as head trader and developed and managed a network of $2 brokers to replicate his improved trading style. The firm continued to capture commissions from its trades, while all other money managers with brokerage divisions were frightened away from that secondary action and dropped out of the business.

As Fred Alger's trading system has evolved, it continues to use better executions to coax his customers into paying his higher commissions. If clients were unhappy in the abstract about the higher fees, the reports made them realize that the lower price paid for a stock actually reduced their net cost. "Once the client understood it, he became a believer," said Irwin. Moreover, Fred Alger runs its brokerage business only for clients and the firm's mutual funds. It doesn't handle outside trades. And that brokerage income was essential for financing the company's research division.

Brokerage commissions kick-started the company and kept it going during the distressing market collapse of the early to mid-seventies. In 1971 commission revenues exceeded management fees by 35%. By fiscal 1974 they provided 60% of the revenue, while management fees actually dropped 65% from the previous year. In 1975 commissions topped $1 million for the first time. That year management fees were just $235,000.

After Irwin left the floor of the Exchange, he was de facto the intra-day portfolio manager. He was never officially given this charge, and only rarely did he originate stock recommendations. Still he made sure the shares were fairly distributed over the client portfolios. "I saw myself as a conduit between the portfolios and the analysts," said Irwin.

True to his character, he often raised the ante. "I had the authority to reject ideas," said Irwin. "Sometimes I bought more than they wanted me to buy. Analysts don't want to go out too far on a limb. I remember once Emerson wanted me to buy one hundred thousand shares of a stock. There was this big piece for sale. I just bought the whole thing and then told him, 'By the way, we now own two hundred fifty thousand shares.' I always used to do things like that."

Irwin usually took his work home with him, to review the portfolios, improve the allocation and keep them, in his words, "sharp and fresh." He was instrumental in automating the process for allocating to customers their pro-rata share of an order, bought or sold, on the same day, at the exact price, down to the nearest odd lot.

Irwin claims he couldn't have done his job as well as he did without George's detailed reports and the "black box" computer system which stored historical data and other client information to help him manage the accounts and support his decisions. He would turn to George with his wish list. "If only I could do this or know this." And George would make it happen.

"Black box helped us as we grew," said George. "It gave Irwin all the information—immediate access to accounts and a system of reports linking brokerage to investment advisory—he needed to trade. On days when there was a lot of activity, I gave him extra reports so he wouldn't have to manually update his log." He added, "Irwin's time was valuable. By giving him current reports, Irwin was able to have better performance. Better performance gave us the ability to get new clients. New clients brought us more revenue."

"In doing the best for our clients, I was always aware of the ultimate return for the firm," said Irwin. "Let Fred and David worry about the clients. George would handle the expenses, and I would see to the profitability of the firm."

Apart from the "keen insight and superior market feel" which he took to the trading floor, roly-poly Irwin Schwartz exercised a calming influence on the company. A "laid-back, really sweet guy," his non-confrontational style worked wonders for the firm's morale.

"He was a great person to have around," said Tom Weil, who was brought into the firm in June 1980 to start up its back-office operations. "He loosened everybody up. Irwin was one of the funniest people on Wall Street. Nothing was sacred to him."

Because he was part court jester, part pop psychiatrist, most in the firm were uplifted by his cheery smile and serene control of his emotions. It was his attitude to life as much as his trading

"I owe my entire outlook on the stock market to Fred," said David Alger, who joined the firm in 1971 when it had fewer than ten employees.

skills that made him a favorite. "Nothing ever bothered Irwin," said David. "He used to call it 'throwing him the fuzz ball.' Anything that came up, Irwin would always find a way around it. He never let anything throw him off stride.

"One of Irwin's favorite expressions was 'Make money in the dark.' You should never bring your wealth to anyone's attention. Another one was, 'It's not my money and it's not my fault.' Every time the market would go down, I would be agonizing about it and getting upset that we wouldn't do well. Irwin was unfazed by any of it. "

Joe Maida, who took Irwin's place on the trading desk, recalled the only time he ever saw Irwin lose his composure. "Irwin had a younger cousin in the business who was very close to him. This man used to go running four times a week. One day, after completing his run, he relaxed against the stone wall of his neighbor's house, had a massive heart attack and died. When Irwin took the call and learned this, the first words out of his mouth were 'Son of a bitch.' He then got up from the trading desk and retired to his office for a while. When he came back, all he said to me was, 'My cousin died. I'm going to miss him.'"

David Alger is profuse in his praise of Irwin. "I was very close to Irwin on a personal level. He was, in a way, my alter ego. When he left I missed him tremendously. He had a wonderful sense of proportion about everything. Fred was a difficult guy to work for, and when he was younger, he'd come over and chew you out, not for any particularly good reason. Irwin was never upset by it. Irwin would ask, 'Is he still paying you your salary? Then why do you care what he says?' His was a very refreshing point of view. I didn't see him for many years until the anniversary Christmas dinner. Irwin gave me a big hug and a kiss on the cheek. It was wonderful to see him again."

Like George, Irwin treated the company as if it were his own. If he saw five checks being mailed to the same location, he would consolidate them in one envelope to save stationery and postage. Instead of calling Federal Express for a pickup, he took the package to a drop-off site to reduce expenses. That personal commitment and responsibility, that strong company feel, continued right to the end.

When Irwin's assistant, B. Anthony Weber, said he wanted to quit, Fred offered him shares in the company to change his mind. The firm was growing so rapidly that even paying twice book value, it wouldn't take that long to recoup your investment. Besides, Fred loaned you the money and gave you the bonus to pay him back.

Weber still had his doubts, so Irwin guaranteed that he wouldn't lose any money if he took the deal. When Weber left the firm in 1989, he took a $20,000 beating when he returned his shares. True to his word, Irwin sent him a personal check to cover his loss. "I felt a responsibility and he needed the money," said Irwin matter-of-factly.

Weber returned to his home state of Kentucky to be vice president of Shelby County Trust Bank's Security Management Co. and fund manager of its two tiny funds. Perhaps in part through his experience at Alger, those mutual funds ranked first and second in 1992 out of the 217 bank-pooled equity funds tracked by CDA Investment Technologies Inc., a leading firm that evaluates investment managers' performance.

"I enjoyed everything I did at Fred Alger," affirmed Irwin. "It was like a game: When you make a good trade, what you're doing is outfoxing the other side. You hold back for an extra quarter of a point and pretend you're not interested, and then the seller comes down."

In Fred's mind, Irwin's composure was his greatest attribute. "He always had good judgment," said Fred. "Uncertainty and insecurity drive everyone crazy, but he remained unruffled by this high-pressure, competitive business. It's very important to have stable elements, and he was very stable."

Since retiring from the firm, Irwin has been happily managing his investments from a baronial home in Warren County, New Jersey. He's especially pleased to be rid of the commute to Wall Street. Several times a year he takes trips to foreign lands. Italy is his favorite country, for the people and the food. He often visits the Orient, particularly China, Thailand and Indonesia. Irwin's theme parties are legendary. In 1994 it was Casablanca. He transformed his home into Rick's Cafe, with the added touch of belly dancers. With his looks Irwin naturally took the role of Señor Ferrari, the part played by Sydney Greenstreet.

Irwin's first big party in his Fred Alger days was his son's bar mitzvah. Fred was invited but never appeared. "I was actually relieved that Fred didn't come," said Irwin. "Not for my sake, but for the other employees, who might not feel very comfortable. They were always on edge when Fred was around. It would have diminished the experience, like the Christmas dinners."

While Irwin was casting the trading system and George was keeping the books, David Alger's role was bulking up the research department and pulling it forward through technology.

When David Alger joined Fred Alger & Co. in 1971, the firm had a net worth of $550,000, less than 5% of what it is today. There were fewer than 10 employees. Everyone worked in close quarters in a single room that seemed to be growing smaller day by day.

Fred's relationship with David was anything but fraternal. "Fred was trying to build a research department," David explained. "He said we would work well together and he would treat me as an equal. Fool that I am, I believed that. I signed on as an analyst, and he immediately started treating me like the local bootblack. He was incredibly distant the first years, so no one would say he was showing me any favoritism. For four years I couldn't do anything right. I was overworked, underpaid and abused."

Whether you regard Fred as a masterful administrator or a corporate despot, he put together a sturdy ecosystem in which all the elements were represented. George was the grounded earth; Fred, the riotous wind; David brought vital fire; Irwin was life-giving water; Bill, the ineffable ether. Their interdependent relationship worked because each one knew his place and everyone pitched in for the good of the firm.

"The nice thing about the firm as it developed with the five principals was that each of us carved out his own niche," said George. "We worked very well together. There wasn't any jealousy or ego. Most of the publicity went to Fred and some of it went to David. No one was ever envious of that."

"Fred was king," said David. "Fred was Louis XIV and we were minor barons. There was never any conflict with Fred on anything. Fred's word was law. This was unambiguous."

Good or bad, like it or not, it was *his* name on the door.

8

Head for Business

A DUN'S MAGAZINE feature about Fred in February 1970 was titled "No Way But Up." In it he offered President Nixon a prescription for economic recovery based on a budget reduction and retiring about $40 billion of the national debt.

That year, its penultimate year with Fred, the $18-million Security Investment Fund scored a 15.9% gain, which was superior to the Dow's rise of 9.2% and enough to make it the number-one growth and income fund in the country. Even after the loss of the Cornfeld business, in 1971 Fred Alger was left with $160 million in assets under management, had a net worth of a half million dollars and a head count of 10.

"Fred was absolutely right in his decisions about how the company should grow." Close friend and Alger Fund board member Arthur Dubow was unflinching in his endorsement of Fred Alger's progress through Wall Street and of the commercial instincts that propelled the expansion of his enterprise.

Who can quarrel with an unbroken financial record that has boosted the firm's net worth from a paltry $3,000 to over $100 million in just 30 years, from a small research firm to a fully integrated financial service network dedicated to the management of investment capital? Significantly, this increase occurred without any capital infusion and despite hefty payouts to departing partners. No Wall Street firm comes close to this sustained evolution.

Empowered by his insights into the economics of market psychology and the rhythms of stock movement and braced by a commitment to aggressive growth-stock investing, Fred advanced his company with a clear and original vision. In broad strokes: He positioned himself first as an investment adviser. To maintain strength in research and outpace the competition for investment ideas, he built a brokerage business to finance the company's independence. To deflect clients' worries about the seeming conflict of interest between intensive investment management and the generation of brokerage commissions, the company developed a trading system which reduced the ultimate cost of executions. Conservatively Fred retained the firm's capital, which enabled him to finance expansion and withstand the inevitable down drafts in the stock market. Fred filled his company with talented and well-paid professionals who were encouraged to participate in the firm's development. Over time he completed a grand design of vertical integration, which gave his company unrestrained control over its expenses and virtual autonomy from the Street.

Ultimately the history of the firm is a story of innovation and self-improvement by implementing new and creative solutions to business problems. Though many of Fred's strategies sounded odd or impractical at first, most proved right in the end.

In the life of Fred Alger the seminal events always centered on overcoming difficult conditions. He exemplifies the Latin maxim *Ad astra per aspera*—making good when the odds were against him. For instance, in one year, 1988, the firm lost a majority of its assets under management, down from $2.8 billion to just $1.2 billion. This alone would have been enough to turn out the lights at most other money-management firms. But instead of folding, Fred Alger was able to press on with the strength of its capital foundation even though it took six years to return to the previous asset level. And this steady retracement occurred despite a skittish investment climate following the 1987 crash, a public relations challenge from the SEC and a period of disfavor for investing in growth stocks. A little more than a year after hitting his old asset mark in 1994, the firm's investments bounded rapidly over $5 billion. Two years later, they had reached $7 billion. And in 1997, management assets were up to $9 billion.

The firm's history is about Fred's personal struggle to move beyond survival and toward the achievement of something outstanding despite obstacles, adversity, setbacks and disappointment. It might be said of Fred as it was said of his great-grandfather, "Step by step, steadily and wisely, he moved forward to the control of great commercial interests." Fred's assessment is less exalted. "Our business has changed several times over the years, taking us in new areas, new directions, which has ultimately been beneficial and right. Usually these were in response to difficult circumstances."

One of the first important periods of Fred Alger & Co. occurred when it switched gears from being an unregistered money manager to a Registered Investment Adviser and took the related step of becoming a member of the New York Stock Exchange.

Fred used his performance with the Security Management mutual funds to establish his reputation on Wall Street. This in turn attracted management contracts that yielded rich performance fees, primarily with the Fund of Funds, but also other investor groups. As described earlier, when Cornfeld sought to limit Fred's compensation to performance fees, Fred took a pass and opted out of the IOS business in March 1970. His timing was impeccable. A year later, when Cornfeld's house of cards suddenly collapsed, Fred was mostly untainted by the scandal.

"Fred was always a good businessman," said Joe Reich, who knew Fred best in those days. "A lot of people were associated with IOS. When it collapsed, they collapsed. Fred seemed to know that it wasn't going to last. He planned his future anticipating that it wasn't going to be around."

Giving up the IOS accounts at the same time as his links with Security Management was fraying, Fred was obliged to reengineer his business in order to secure continuing revenues.

First, he applied to be a Registered Investment Adviser. This was hardly a sure-fire solution. Taking on this designation carried some caveats which didn't support the firm's immediate revenue expectations. The Investment Advisers Act of 1940 required all money managers with 15 or more individual clients in a 12-month period to register with the Securities and Exchange Commission. It also prohibited registered advisers from accepting the type of high performance fees which Alger was used to assessing.

Therefore Fred was careful to keep his client base under that bar, limiting himself to 14 clients. Furthermore the rules were such that these had to be the same 15 clients in a 12-month period. Departing clients could not be replaced before the end of that time frame. Prior to 1970, Fred was unwilling to trade a certain steep revenue decline, due to the loss of performance income, for the potential escalation of his minimum guaranteed fee. Performance fees were the cash cow from which capital streamed into his coffers.

Avoiding the regulatory thumb of the SEC, Fred perhaps saw it getting in the way of his independence. That reluctance to surrender to SEC scrutiny would later be justified by the spurious charges it laid on Fred when he launched his mutual funds in 1986.

When Fred Alger registered with the SEC as an investment adviser, pursuant to section 203(c) of the Advisers Act, the firm took a hit on more than half its income. But there was a compelling reason to switch at that time. "The reason we became a brokerage firm wasn't for the dollars," Fred explained. "The quality of the research we were getting was very low. Research is the raw material of our business. We wanted to be responsible for our own fate.

"Previously we had used our brokerage to buy other companies' research, but we became disillusioned with this after the stock market break in 1969–70 when our own sources dried up or were bought away by more prosperous money-management firms.

"Say a Merrill Lynch analyst calls to recommend GM. If he turns negative on

Although many of Fred's strategies sounded odd or seemed impractical at first, most proved right in the end.

GM, would we be one of the first he would call or the last? A lot of times he might not even call at all, because he wouldn't want to be embarrassed by something he may have told us to buy a month earlier. Or if we see it doing poorly and call him, he might be responding to fifty other calls at the time. How could you become one of the major influences on that broker? You really couldn't."

Even though the move was fraught with uncertainty, circumstances militated that he take his company to the next level. At the same time Fred headed off the firm's dependence on inferior, secondhand research by cannily opening his own brokerage operation as a means of funding his own research facility. Then, as today, the fact that the company is a broker-dealer is coincidental to its activities as investment adviser and money manager. The brokerage firm only trades in shares of the firm's clients and the company's accounts.

But this solution raised another issue by vexing the Street with the firm's dual role of investment adviser and broker. There was an inherent conflict, it was assumed, between the two roles.

The firm justified the brokerage operation as a value-added resource for his clients by providing high/low evaluation reports, once a month for every client. "We would argue to our clients that their savings from stock-trade executions would more than offset the comparatively high brokerage commissions we charged," said Fred, "so that the net cost of execution on their behalf would run about zero over time."

"The decision to join the Exchange was incredible," said ex-partner Bill Scheerer. He reiterated that the firm's success was not just its great investment record but more clearly defined by Fred's excellent business decisions over the years.

With the brokerage business, Fred lengthened his shadow over Wall Street. While money-management revenues are usually steady and stable, the brokerage and securities underwriting businesses are cyclical and can often be explosive.

In his bullish projections for brokerage stocks, reported in November 1980 in *The New York Times*, Fred hailed brokerage firms as "the great vehicle of the recapitalization boom and the means of reindustrializing America." He defined brokerage as a "fixed-cost industry, for the most part, and this provides enormous operating leverage."

Fred knew this from experience. While he may never have intended the business as a secondary revenue source—"We went into it because we were not getting service from the Wall Street community"—Fred quickly recognized brokerage revenues as the major profit center for his firm, which turned out to be considerably larger than performance fees.

Fred Alger's revenues from management fees peaked at nearly $1 million in 1967, then declined steadily for a decade. It wasn't until 1979 that they again touched that figure. In contrast, commission revenues soared during the seventies, almost in a straight line, from about $400,000 in 1971 to over $10 million in 1982. Although he sold himself as an investment adviser, the bulk of the firm's money was actually made from brokerage commissions right through 1988. During the firm's sweet spot, from 1982 to 1988, brokerage commissions contributed even more significantly to the firm's capital structure and provided a vital boost for its operations.

The acceleration of brokerage income was taking place while the size of commissions in the brokerage business as a whole was in fact decreasing.

High, fixed stock-brokerage commissions ended on May 1, 1975, which became known grimly on Wall Street as Mayday. Mayday ushered in deregulated discount brokerages, negotiated commission rates and prompted diversification in the brokerage industry. Although deep-discounting had to wait for aggressive competition and the Internet in the mid-nineties, there was a lot for brokers to cry about following Mayday. Investors began switching their accounts to whoever would charge less. In its aftermath, revenues across Wall Street fell by about $600 million in 1976.

Mayday also closed the door on tacit reciprocal agreements which supported mutual-fund sales with a share of hefty brokerage commissions and created the opportunity for large firms to make upstairs markets with customers for the stocks they listed. The former, a once pervasive practice, took the shape of steering brokerage trades to specified dealers or splitting commissions as a reward for successfully marketing the investment company's products. The latter describes stock trades conducted within a broker-dealer's company without coursing the transaction through the intermediary of a stock exchange.

Fred Alger was able to hold his own in this newly competitive environment. The company's brokerage business catered to its own captive market, which was continually growing in relation to assets under management during most of the seventies and eighties.

Fred's firm was able to charge relatively high brokerage commissions—about 20% off Merrill Lynch's rates—right through 1987, when additional competition in the wake of the market crash forced a dramatic downward recalibration of its commission structure. The firm's subsequent diversification reduced its reliance on commission income, from a peak in 1987 of nearly two-thirds of the company's gross income, to just a fifth of its revenues in 1995, and continuing to drop.

After a down year in 1969 and smarting from a 20.3% loss in Security Equity Fund—his worst performance—Fred began in earnest to court the pension business. His rationale was simple enough. "Large pools of money were going into the hands of pension-fund managers with inferior equity records," said Fred in a 1981 *Forbes* interview about that period. "Our equity performance was superior, so we decided to move into that business."

Thus began the first of two distinct sales efforts to penetrate the pension arena, which coincided with purchasing a seat on the New York Stock Exchange and becoming a Registered Investment Adviser. In the main, this drive was a dud.

One attempt at soliciting new business was this straightforward pitch—the firm's first advertisement—in the April 21, 1970, issue of *The Wall Street Journal*:

> INVESTMENT ADVISERS
> Would you like to develop continuity and growth? We are a young, fast-growing registered investment advisor managing approximately $200,000,000. We have an interesting plan which will relieve you of the day to day management of your business without diminution of your income. Call William Stewart (212)425-0880.

Fred took on the unfamiliar role of salesman. Not surprisingly his approach was unique. First, there was cold calling, then direct mail, followed by more phone calls. For the final presentation, he brought along to the sales meetings a Super 8 infomercial about the company. Will Stewart, in charge of client relations, was given the backbreaking task of lugging the projector around.

Partner Bill Scheerer derided the latter marketing device as too "naive and obvious" for sophisticated pension people. "The movie never brought out the talent of the people we had," he admonished. "It was too scripted. We were too stiff."

In the film David Alger emphasized, "As a service to our clients, early in 1970 we acquired a seat on the New York Stock Exchange. We give net commission credit against the management fee which can wholly erase the fee. We wanted to get the best floor trader in the country, and we think we got him. Frank Pierce is one of 60 registered floor traders of 1,366 members. He also handles the largest trading account for Carlisle, one of the odd-lot houses."

Pierce followed David with remarks designed to blunt anticipated objections over Fred Alger's capture of brokerage commissions. "Fred has asked me to keep detailed records on our executions for our clients. We try to buy below and sell above the mean price of the day. The importance of this can be seen from a study we did recently on a fifteen-million-dollar conservatively managed fund. We found that if we saved an eighth of a point on all executions for a period of a year, it would have saved the fund over $300,000. We handle no commission business other than our own, and this leaves me free, if necessary, to spend all day executing orders for our clients."

Fred wrote a letter describing the Alger track record and sent it to the top 2,000 pension directors in the country. He also commissioned an expensive brochure for the firm. About this advertising Irwin Schwartz recalled, "When the proofs of the brochure came in, there was a picture of Fred posing at his desk and his galoshes were clearly visible. No one else had noticed it or thought that it looked bad." On his recommendation, they were airbrushed out.

Since Fred Alger had no track record among pension managers, getting the first account was a struggle. Fred's secretary Lavaun Vawter remembered, "At that time we primarily managed the money of high-net-worth individuals. So Fred got a list of corporate pension managers and started cold calling, over and over and over."

The fact that Fred assumed the salesman's role reveals the heart of his driven personality. "Cold calling is not Fred. He didn't like to do it, but he did it anyway because he felt he had to," Lavaun insisted, "because that was important to achieve his goal. Performance. Performance to him was everything." Years later Fred himself confirmed this in an offhand remark about his courting of an unsavory pension consultant. "Yeah, if that's the sort of thing I have to do to make it in this business, that's what I'll do."

His first home run was Stauffer Chemical. "Fred met this without jubilation," said Vawter, "more like relief. 'Now we've got one. We're finally on our way.'"

By 1971 several pension accounts had come Fred Alger's way, but there was still a lot of resistance to the company. Will Stewart remembered flying out with Fred to San Francisco to pitch the Crown-Zellerbach account. Alger eventually got some of its business. According to Will, "a lot of people scoffed at us because of our association with Cornfeld. Fred was the largest, most visible portfolio manager of one of the biggest swindles in the Western Hemisphere." Another major roadblock was the lack of a long-term performance record in that segment of the market.

Then came ERISA, which changed everything. The Employees Retirement Income Securities Act of 1974 established uniform funding regulations and incentives for pension and benefit plans, provided guidelines for their management and set up the watchdog Pension Benefit Guaranty Corporation, which had the authority to confiscate corporate assets if certain pension liabilities were insufficiently funded.

In David Alger's view, ERISA was the chief accelerant that fired up not only Fred's business but the entire investment community. "More than the pardon of Richard Nixon, Gerald Ford signed one really important law, and it created the modern stock market," said David.

"ERISA told companies, 'If you have a pension fund, you better be damned sure you can pay your employees in the future.' It created a pool of assets, funded over forty years, to ensure availability of retirement funds. Originally, most companies that paid pensions did so on a hand-to-mouth basis. With ERISA, companies had to put a lot of money in the market as a payroll cost. To control this expense, they sought higher rates. Billions and billions poured into the stock market to meet the terms of ERISA."

More important for Fred Alger, pension managers had their first real incentive to hire top-level money managers. This gave Fred the edge. His bullish reputation on the Street made him a leading contender.

Along with its promise of bright prospects, ERISA presented a stipulation which could have been calamitous for the company's revenues. A central, though ambiguous, feature of the law was that pension fund administrators could engage in either money management or the brokerage business, but not in both. It appeared that Fred was proscribed from making trades, even though he did so only for his own institutional clients.

In a "brilliant riposte" to the problem, the firm devised a trading system which utilized independent "two-dollar" brokers in 10 specific and strategic floor areas in the three rooms of the New York Stock Exchange to execute its trades. Two-dollar brokers, or "broker's brokers," got their name from their original compensation for executions, usually $1.50 to $2.50 for every round-lot or 100 shares.

"We picked outstanding floor brokers in each section and offered them the following three-part deal," Fred explained. "First, a monopoly on our business in each section, so that an order would not bounce from one stockbroker to another, day by day. Second, we wouldn't charge brokers with fails for their work. In those days five thousand dollars of fails could wipe out a floor broker's monthly profit. Finally, we would not negotiate floor-brokerage rates. We knew that these floor traders, working with the specialists, could reverse the normal auction bias of the floor and consequently buy below and sell above the mean price of the day."

Bill Scheerer praised this tactic. "Irwin set up this incredible trading system— a direct line with two-dollar brokers in every area of the floor," he said. "Alger was their best customer, and their main allegiance was to us."

A corollary to ERISA, SEC Rule 11A, enacted in 1976, also sought to keep investment managers from executing their own orders in order to avoid possible conflict. "Everybody in the businesses started sweating," explained Irwin Schwartz, who was the firm's registered floor broker at the time. "We said, 'Let's see what happens.'" While other investment firms, especially the larger ones, peeled off their brokerage operations and simply surrendered to the rule's strictest interpretation, thus avoiding the potential for censure, Fred was defiant. "I don't know how we had the guts to do this," recalled Irwin. The firm had relatively little money under management, and brokerage was seriously integral to his business. Until the ruling was clarified, he was determined to hold on to both operations.

"We waited it out," Irwin continued. "Then the SEC came to interpret the law in a very liberal way, where execution meant actually executing the orders on the floor. You could keep the commissions and put down the order, but a partner of the firm couldn't be on the floor." With his network of two-dollar brokers, Fred Alger had already left the floor, a strategy which might even have been enough to deflect objections from a conservative interpretation of the law.

Although 11A requirements have eased with the advent of computerized trading, and the firm can now freely send its own trader to the exchange floor and save on commissions, Fred Alger remains loyal to the trading system and the floor brokers that have served him so well. Fred wonders why none of his competitors has adopted such an obviously successful and lucrative trading program, which the firm has now had in place for over 20 years.

Although ERISA primed the pump, the firm's initial marketing efforts produced just a trickle of new pension accounts. By year-end 1977 Fred became impatient and once again took the offensive. He put in his crosshairs the pension fund managers of all U.S. corporations and he assaulted that target with tenacity. Fred took a shot at every one.

The way David described it, "Fred took a copy of the money-market directory into his office, shut the door, and started calling every major company in America. He did that for a year."

It was an incredibly disciplined and organized effort. Fred put the entire pension community on his Rolodex and systematically called each name at least once every quarter. "I made up to two hundred calls a day—day after day after day after day," Fred explained, "noting down how everyone responded to me; then followed up with letters on a regular basis, pointing out that if they achieved certain performance over time they could entirely fund their pension plans with portfolio appreciation."

Without question, the determination of Fred's post–ERISA marketing drive clinched the future of the company. "Fred did all the marketing. Fred devoted all his time to it," confirmed Irwin Schwartz. "We were told by the experts that it would take us eighteen months before we got our first account. That's exactly what it took, almost to the day."

Celanese Corp. was the first big institutional client, according to George Boggio. He quibbled with Irwin's recollection: "We got it after sixteen months."

"Although we weren't a very polished group then, what really did it was this pure energy and perseverance that Fred applied to the job," David Alger observed, "Really, the most important thing was the cumulative effect of one entire year of Fred marketing almost nonstop to the pension fund market.

"At that time I started taking over more and more the role of managing the analysts," he added.

Arthur Dubow offered this valuable insight: "One of the things that is not appreciated by a lot of people who don't know Fred very well is his toughness. He's relentless. When he goes after something, he's really, really focused and has

Promotional photo circa 1986. David led the firm forward by utilizing computers to improve stock analysis and selection.

a drive that is very, very, very intense and powerful. He wasn't just a genius in the market. He always worked very hard."

Fred's prodigious effort started paying off big-time. Pension money began flooding into the company. Assets under management in the tax-exempt area burst from just $28 million at the end of 1978 to $250 million by year-end 1979. That number swelled to $740 million at the close of 1980 and, for the first time, spilled over the $1 billion mark in 1981.

A trade paper in December 1980 publicized the achievements, placing Fred Alger at the top of the list of money managers signing up new pension clients. The figures that were published were even more impressive: Having started the year with $150 million in tax-exempt pension business, Fred Alger was said to be managing $850 million by October.

The numbers from this period vary according to the reporting period and the type of accounts which were included in the statistics, but their meaning was overwhelmingly positive.

Most of the pensions were underfunded, and their executives were eagerly searching for aggressive management to bulk up their portfolios. The Alger firm fit the bill, and its performance was extremely attractive from the late seventies into the early eighties.

In 1978 the SEC imposed a requirement for all managers of investments exceeding $100 million to file quarterly reports of their securities holdings and performance figures on its Form 13(f). This inadvertently threw a spotlight on performance just as Fred was hitting on all cylinders. The firm's growth-equity composite surged 50.7% in 1979 and climbed another 60.2% in 1980. Even after deductions for management fees, the performance was sterling: 49.6% in 1979 and 59% in 1980, versus 18.6% and 32.5% for the S&P 500 during the corresponding periods.

Fred Alger Management was named the best-performing investment-counseling firm in the third quarter of 1980, according to CDA Investment Technologies Inc., the Silver Springs, Maryland, research and advisory firm whose rankings of investment firms were widely followed by pension managers. Fred was up an enviable 33.4% for the quarter in his portfolios totaling $387 million.

When the money started rolling in, the firm began contemplating a buildup of corporate staff and hired, wholesale, an entire research group.

"We started getting much bigger clients," said David. "The business was growing extremely fast. Huge amounts of money were being poured into the pension fund area by American corporations. Many firms had underfunded pension funds, and they had to play catch-up with respect to ERISA. Plus there weren't that many people in the business, compared to today. ERISA was a field day for those of us who were trying to market to that area. And the amounts of money were gigantic, compared to what we were used to. The good performance in 1979 and our existing track record led to a tremendous buildup of assets."

Institutional Investor's annual listing of money managers who gained or lost pension accounts from the nation's 350 largest corporate funds between October 1, 1979, and September 30, 1980, ranked Fred Alger fourth. In the same survey for the following year, Fred Alger also came in fourth. His roster of clients included Aluminum Co. of America, Batus, Fruehauf Corp., Getty Oil Co., PepsiCo, General Signal Corp., BF Goodrich Co., Litton Industries, TRW, United Telecommunications, Warner-Lambert Co., and Owens-Corning Fiberglas.

Warner-Lambert deposited somewhere between $10 million to $15 million with Fred Alger, according to Joseph Joshi, manager of its pension investments, in a September 1982 *Institutional Investor* article. He subsequently enlarged that account based on Fred's performance and noted, "Alger even had a surprisingly good year in 1981, hardly a favorable time for coming up with hot-performing stocks." That year the S&P 500 lost 5%.

When Fred started the marketing push, he was acutely aware of his limitations as a salesman. In order to sharpen his performance, he put himself through a one-week Xerox sales training program. "The story goes that Fred wasn't very comfortable speaking to larger groups," said Rob Lyon, a senior analyst at the firm from 1981 to 1988. "While he was very confident in his abilities as an investor and analyst, he didn't feel he was good enough at selling himself. The training gave him certain ideas and the confidence to articulate his game plan."

"I went on a few marketing presentations. Fred always made very compelling arguments," described George Boggio. "Though he was not a born salesman, he put himself through the paces of becoming one—the correct way to carry and set down the briefcase, the proper way to pull out your paperwork. It was not beneath him. I was fascinated."

At one account meeting Fred was so self-absorbed, he nearly blew the account before he started the presentation. Pitching the Pepsi account, he absentmindedly asked the managers whether they would like "a Coke or a cup of coffee." Despite this incredible faux pas, Fred still won the account. "I didn't realize what I had done until a moment after I had done it," he said.

The sales techniques Fred learned gave a polish to his presentations but added little to the essential virtues of his business discipline or his already superior track record for managing money. The bottom line was that between 1976 and 1981, Fred Alger's composite pension portfolio posted a startling compound annual return of 34%, or more than double the S&P average. This led to his "discovery" by a set of pension consultants. One of these forged a curious alliance with Fred and was widely credited for boosting him into the pension business by obtaining many—one magazine article claimed as much as a third—of his accounts.

With the verve of a theatrical agent, Rogers, Casey & Barksdale, a Greenwich, Connecticut, pension consulting firm, hitched itself to Fred's strong record and started promoting him as its star find among money managers. However, like many of Fred's business connections outside his company, this relationship ended in disagreement, public controversy and separation. And eventually, as instrumental as it had been in opening doors for Fred Alger, Rogers, Casey was just as critical to closing them. It was reported that John Casey, one of the named partners in the firm, was "furious with Fred because Casey claims Alger had promised him he would shut his doors to new business when he reached five hundred million dollars."

"Rogers, Casey and Barksdale was one of the first consultants to pick us up," Fred specified. "They gave us a lot of business, then they took it all away from us. They wanted to keep us small, believing, with some justification, that small size and performance go hand in hand. They claimed that we promised we would never get larger than two hundred million dollars in assets under management. Our goal, however, was to get big so that we'd have more money to manage."

As vast as Fred Alger's client list and revenue stream were, they might have been wider and deeper. Despite the initial surge of accounts, the firm's pension business stalled in the mid-eighties. Some of the problems grew out of Fred's and the firm's character; others were a function of the pension business's perverse internal logic, which was accented by the timid approach of most corporate retirement managers.

First, the firm was quickly the victim of its own success. "The pension fund business had really grown tremendously in terms of assets," David explained. "In the mid-eighties it became obvious that most American corporations' pension accounts were becoming fully funded. If you're fully funded, there's no reason to shoot for the moon. You can just buy bonds and call it a day."

"The better we did," Fred explained, "the less they needed us."

"We lost accounts because we did too well," confirmed Irwin. With an apt metaphor he added, "We're like doctors. If you cured the patient you lost the business. If you killed the patient you lost the business. Celanese was the first one we lost after making them a lot of money."

Second, Fred's insistence on doing things his way sometimes had unfortunate consequences. "There was a story on the Street years ago," offered H. Bruce Levine, one of Fred Alger's two-dollar brokers. "I got it secondhand that Fred was in some resort out West, in Arizona or Denver, with one of his good pension clients. Apparently these people had a few drinks, and they grabbed Fred and threw him into the pool. The next day he had all their assets transferred away from the firm. He wasn't going to tolerate this kind of behavior. Business didn't matter. They insulted him as an individual. He wouldn't be doing any more business with this firm."

David gave a more colorful and detailed description of the episode: "One of our original clients, Gannett Inc., had a lot of oddities to it. They liked to have a lot of different meetings with their managers, and they had this bizarre structure where the managers themselves would set the asset allocation. We'd get together and just schmooze about it. They wanted four meetings a year, which was a tremendous amount, and these were multi-day meetings. As they were a hard-drinking and fun-loving lot, the meetings took the form of two-day drinking bashes at these resorts.

"This particular group would occasionally lapse into playing practical jokes, especially after a number of drinks. One day they decided that, since Fred is basically a stiff, as he was always into business and not much fun, they were going to throw him into the pool. They snatched him and attempted to dump him into the pool with his suit on. Fred became very upset. He screamed to me for help, so I grabbed him around the waist and was actually able to prevent them from throwing him into the pool. We would have kept the account longer if he had let them throw him in."

"Gannett fired us. We didn't fire them," Fred explained. "One year we were up fifty-eight percent; the next year, up seventy percent. We made them a huge amount of money, and they fired us because we had so fully funded their pension plan that they didn't need us anymore."

As discussed above, another factor which abridged the firm's ambitions in the tax-advantaged arena was fund managers' preference for passive investing once pension accounts attained their full funding.

In passive investing, fund managers replicate a market index, like the S&P 500, which ensures their performance to be no better or worse than the market as a whole. This modest approach, expressly antithetical to Fred's action of attacking and beating the market, was a safe haven from risk and instability for a whole crowd of consultants, the investment managers they endorsed and pension executives in corporations. It provisionally gave the appearance of limiting management fees and reducing brokerage commissions, which was a desirable goal for the pensions' corporate sponsors. Since most active managers were underperforming the market anyway, why pay for taking apparently superfluous risks?

In this cautious climate the investment weathervane swiveled away from growth stocks and pointed toward value investments. This also threw the Alger company out of contention in many quarters. Eventually the increasing domination of consultants over the pension business was the decisive blow to Alger's pension business. ERISA may have turned on the tap, but the consultants pulled the plug and gradually drained it of accounts.

Next, Fred Alger handled its own trades and insisted on keeping brokerage commissions. Pension fund managers saw this as a controversial practice and weren't disposed to put their jobs on the line to defend it. Fred was alert to this hazard from the start. If you recall, in the firm's 1971 promotional film, he used David to counter this with the strategic inducement of discounting management fees by a percentage of the brokerage commission.

"The commission thing was both good and bad," David qualified. "Good: When rates were higher, it made us a lot of money, which we put right in the bond market and is still sitting there in a big pool. Bad: It kept us from getting accounts that we might have otherwise gotten."

The larger conflict with respect to commissions, however, centered on compensating pension fund consultants, who proliferated in the mid-eighties and became the dominating influence in the selection of investment managers. As corporations faced the onslaught of management firms, their pension managers found it easier to consign the scrutiny of these emerging advisers to consultants. For providing research and performance data, consultants expected a say in where the brokerage business was directed. In exchange for a referral, a broker would pay out a portion of his commission to the consultant. Since, unlike other investment managers, Fred retained his brokerage commissions, he was automatically excluded. Why would a consultant ever recommend Alger if it meant the certainty of losing these soft-dollar revenues?

By many accounts, Fred Alger personally deserved much of the blame for underestimating or perhaps for refusing to fully acknowledge the consultants' increasing grip on the pension business during the mid-eighties. He knew enough to state that "the business is controlled by consultants and the consultants, in turn, can be controlled in several ways—most predominantly by money," but he somehow seemed unwilling to put that assumption into practice. It was clearly a failure of marketing to the consultants that eventually corroded the firm's account base and all but obliterated the company's hard-won gains in the pension marketplace.

"Our perception of the importance of consultants was very much less than it should have been," David admitted. "We have never been a strong firm in terms of marketing. We were, I think, very weak at that time.

"Fred missed the point that consultants were becoming the factor in getting the business. He always felt that consultants were a fifth wheel on a car," David charged, "and we made very little effort to court them. In fact, we got very many of them very pissed off at us. Fred has always been a great believer in doing things his own way. He was not good at adopting the same solutions that everyone else takes. So we've always had a different look to us than a lot of other managers.

"Fred's view of the business was that it is like being a doctor or a lawyer. You hang out your shingle. You get references. People come to you. They entrust all their money to you. You make the decisions for them. They leave you alone and pay you very well. How you go about managing their money is your business, not theirs.

"As the pension fund business evolved, marketing became at least as important, if not more so, than managing the money. Most firms spent a great deal of money on marketing. A lot of this was courting the consultants. Fred never accepted that idea."

David's assessment of why Alger was routinely squeezed out of the running for pension accounts exposes the overriding "play-it-safe," "don't-rock-the-boat" mind-set of consultants and corporate pension managers. "They look for reasons not to hire you," David explained. "The more excuses you give them, the less business you're going to get." Fred gave them lots of reasons to suspend his name from investment-manager searches.

They might exclude him because he retained brokerage commissions. There were his prior affiliations with Cornfeld and the baggage that stayed with him from the go-go sixties. His foray into mutual funds in 1986 threatened and alienated many of his existing pension clients. They could also knock Alger out because of his SEC troubles. David reiterated, "If the firm hits a two-year stretch of weak performance, as it has in the past, the client has reason to question the consultant, 'Why ever did you ever pick Fred Alger?'"

In the lately litigious business atmosphere, consultants are attracted to no-risk or low-risk situations in which sticking their neck out for an investment firm won't land them on the chopping block. Fred Alger never made them feel secure enough. In his case, even its superior performance worked against the company. It was too good. If it somehow failed to live up to advance billing, who would get the blame?

When Fred negotiated for accounts, his personality usually became the critical issue. He had too much attitude and a lot more intelligence than the traffic could bear.

The outside opinion was that Fred's recondite ways had a limited appeal among pension fund managers. "As a salesman, Fred tended to be a little too esoteric," according to Chat Hickox, Fred's friend, former client and eventual competitor for pension accounts. "That's his biggest problem. Fred was so gung-ho on his stock ideas that you'd get the feeling that he was not exactly rational."

"Fred would ramble on about some very arcane notion. Incisive as it was, it would be way over the head of the audience," explained Will Stewart. "Everyone was looking for simple answers, simple assurances, not the wild ramblings of wisdom."

Measuring his own performance, Fred admitted, "People would say, 'Jeezus, I never met a smarter guy in the stock market in my whole life.' But are they going to give me their money to manage? Probably not."

Fred was taken by the grandeur of his ideas. "As the market for pensions was growing, Fred became arrogant," volunteered a senior analyst at the firm. "Fred never liked marketing, and sometimes clients could perceive that," said George Boggio. "Still, when he lost the accounts, Fred felt terrible. He took it personally. That was his money. He worked as hard for them as we would for our own money." According to one colleague, "when consultants and potential clients rejected him, he became defensive, acting as if he didn't want or need them. 'Who needs to be kicked around by clients' was the impression he gave."

A few key individuals in the firm said there was a more obvious explanation for the lack of results in the pension fund area than prejudice against Fred Alger and pointed to the poor compensation of its pension sales force as the culprit. Alger suffered more, according to these sources, because the firm failed "to reasonably invest in senior marketing guys who could hand-hold investors, appease the consultants and calm chief investment officers."

"I always thought that we should have been able to bring in more clients," George Boggio said, mystified by the scant yield of their efforts. "Obviously we weren't doing something, but what that something was, I don't know. Other firms had poor performance and weren't as good as we were overall, and yet they were able to bring in accounts."

In Fred's words, "the biggest disappointment I've had in the business is that we aren't much bigger than we are, despite our tremendous performance. I would bet that our record of management is incomparable over any time period of any length. The way information flows, I would have expected that much more business would have come our way.

"A) I've been viewed as somewhat difficult. B) The industry has been taken over by consultants. I've not been working them. C) As a fully integrated firm, we're an island and don't have too many contacts. I'm not a part of the group. When I die, you won't see an overwhelming crowd at the funeral home."

In the final analysis, Fred deserves less criticism for the ebbing of pension accounts than credit for the initial inflow of this business. "Virtually every

The stockpicker's stockpicker

**THE
MONEY
MANAGERS**

By Robert Lenzner
Globe Staff

NEW YORK – Fred M. Alger must be the only money manager in America to set up his own private headhunting expedition for the best stockpickers.

Analysts Resources, Alger's wholly-owned subsidiary, has interviewed 1100 security analysts from coast to coast and produced three stars for one of the most spectacularly successful investment management operations anywhere.

The 46-year-old Alger is adamant and brash about his expensive quest for the smartest people in the investment business.

"We have a monopoly in locating the best people. We treat them like Reggie Jackson. We'll pay them anything to come to New York and work for us," says the man who was the No. 1 investment manager in the bull market of 1965 when his tiny Security Equity Fund was up a resounding 77.5 percent.

Alger and his group of "Reggie Jacksons" could not have kept up that torrid pace for the last 16 years. Still, the performance of his main company, Fred Alger Management Inc., has placed him at the very peak of the industry, a 21 percent rate of return, annually compounded, for the period 1965 to 1980 – more than three times better than the Standard & Poor's 500 market average.

Over the past five years, Alger's team has made corporate pension fund managers' mouths water with a 33.5 percent annual return compared to 13.6 percent for the S & P 500. No wonder the assets under management have grown from $75 million to $1 billion.

"Fred wants to beat everyone each day. That's what I like about him," says the pension overseer of a major oil company. The inveterate bridge player has been known to play cards the same way that he picks stock, a combination that many successful stock traders like because of the competi-

tion and knowledge that, win or lose, the results show up quickly.

Nevertheless, the Alger penchant for aggressive investing has resulted in a 1981 performance that is down and running slightly behind the broad market averages. Alger is fully invested because he thinks the market hit bottom on September 25th, and should end 1982 a good deal higher than the current 1000 book value for the Dow Jones Industrial Average. In fact, Alger

wrote the shareholders of Spectra Fund, which the firm manages, "The next time the Dow crosses 1000 could mark the last time it sells in the 900s. Your management company is very optimistic about the future."

Alger does not believe that huge federal budget deficits and inflation are linked. And he predicts the slower money supply growth of recent months will ease the un

MANAGER, Page 36

Fred Alger, described by one colleague as a "determined decision maker who builds loyally ... loves making money."
PHOTO BY SANDRA WEINER

The Boston Globe, December 21, 1981.

client we have was brought in by Fred or because of Fred," observed George.

Since Fred wouldn't condescend to account managers or "make nice" to consultants, he did the next best thing. He went into the mutual-fund business to cancel out his revenue dependence on pension accounts. His timing was bang-on. As the firm's pension revenues drained out in the late eighties, mutual-fund fees progressively poured in to replenish the loss.

That mutual-fund strategy, though muddled by a disastrous advertising campaign and a damaging SEC probe, preserved the firm and became its franchise. In March 1995, assets in the Alger mutual funds—including defined contribution accounts, insurance-company relationships for annuities and subadvisory management contracts—outstripped its holdings of tax-exempt accounts for the first time. In 1997 corporate pensions, public funds, religious and endowment accounts at Alger were only about 25% of total assets. So great was the growth of mutual-fund assets, both in terms of capital appreciation and new subscriptions, that money was rolling in at an average of $1 million a day.

The firm is not challenged for its capture of brokerage commissions by this market segment. In mutual-fund accounts, redemptions are relatively benign compared to the large void left by a departing pension account. With annuity contracts, there's the added certainty that funds will remain for an extended period.

Through its growth waves in the seventies, Fred Alger & Co. identified, reinforced and fulfilled several core business virtues which were integral to the company's progress. At the same time they are a guide for those who would embark on any successful financial enterprise.

A primary driving principle of the firm is a dedication to its clients' best interests. "The client's interest comes first, the company's interest comes second, and the individual's interest within the company comes last. That's the order of decision making," Fred explained. "In this way we recognize that the company is the cow from which we all feed."

The company scrupulously maintains high professional and ethical standards to reinforce that position. The firm has to be, first and foremost, trustworthy of its clients' investments.

The next value is operational and derives from the military model which Fred adopted as the framework for his management style. There was no mistaking that Fred ran this ship with quiet military efficiency.

Fred understood the objectives of military engagement to be analogous to goal setting in the business environment. The business was approached as a battlefield for daily struggles and victories. In the office, consider the positions around the trading desk as the front lines. The analysts are the back-room tacticians who determine where and how to attack the market. The portfolio managers take charge of deploying their stock picks for the victory of increasing performance.

The military paradigm translated well in an autocratic environment where Fred's unquestioned leadership drove performance. "A company is not a democracy. It's more like an army than a democracy," he said. "Even though we try to have everyone involved in the decision making, decisions are made largely by the one person who has to lead. You can't be fatherly and expect to get good performance. To get this outcome, you basically have to be feared a little bit."

Fred's terms of engagement might well have been lifted wholesale from articles II and III of the Marine Corps Code of Conduct:

Article II: I will never surrender of my own free will. If in command, I will never surrender my people while they still have the means to resist. While many Wall Street firms were falling around him after the crash of 1987, Fred kept his company going and triumphed over a stunning decline of assets under management.

Article III: If I am captured, I will continue to resist by all means available. I will make every effort to escape and aid others to escape. I will accept neither parole nor special favors from the enemy. This is how Fred fought back SEC objections to his right to advertise the firm's complete performance record.

While a business-as-warfare ethos permeates the firm, the military model is hardly evident in its chain-of-command structure. Decisions are made quickly, without onerous layers of management. With Fred's door open, one could easily take new ideas right to the top and get the green light for a project. The firm's small size kept all its key people accessible.

For Leszek James, president of Metro*soft,* the small software company which designs, programs and implements the firm's operations and customer-service information systems, this quick turnaround gave the firm a clear advantage in its relationships with its outside vendors.

"Something that distinguishes this company from others is the decision-making process," he said. "It is absolutely great. It enables us to get things done fast. When we're given an objective or propose a solution, a short exploration and explanation is all that's required. Even if it doesn't work out at first, we're already on the job and have the chance to quickly make changes and improvements."

Another important principle which empowered the firm was its refusal to assume overhead, especially the hiring of employees, without corresponding income to support it. This gave the firm an extra comfort zone during industry downturns and periods of transitional growth.

Industry veteran and Alger back-office manager James Barbi contrasted this axiom with many other brokerage operations. "Typically it was, 'We'll build a magnificent plant with all sorts of automation and somehow we'll get the business.' Not here!" he emphasized. "This is an income-driven business. Go get the business, then somehow we'll manage. That was Fred's approach, and it has served us in good stead."

The order was invariable: The first cry was for assets. Out of assets came revenues. From revenues, profits.

In the pursuit of excellence, Fred was unabashed, even adamant about charging a higher price for superior value in terms of performance and customer service. "I think one should charge whatever one can, considering the number of money-management decisions that will be made in the funds," he said in an interview after launching the Alger Fund in 1986. Years earlier, he defended performance fees of 10% of total appreciation and a minimum 1% of the client's portfolio this way: "We think it may be too low."

When it came to investments, Fred Alger sticks to what it knows, and among Wall Street firms, it knows growth stocks exceedingly well. Fred hung on to aggressive growth stocks even when they were seen as ugly by the Street. In fact, the firm is almost blind to any other investment assumption.

Critics carp that the firm might have done better by responding to stock market cycles and shifting to a value-driven approach during periods when it was in vogue, but this criticism ignores the firm's uneasiness with the value-investment formula. By remaining loyal to its investment character, Fred Alger & Co. established a forceful, consistent identity in the investment community.

Another decisive component in the firm's success was its application of the vertical integration of its business functions. "We try to control every element of production, of the process," Fred said, "the purpose being to make us the best at every level possible."

Highly integrated firms usually take it on the chin during down cycles because of the enormous strain on resources. In Alger's case, the firm actually benefited. Being totally integrated enabled the firm to ensure performance, control spending, manage growth and retain revenues. Additional revenue, though an unintended and welcome outcome, was hardly the first purpose of this observance.

The company acquired controlling interest in its own building on 75 Maiden Lane in 1982 to avoid high rents and relieve the stresses of dislocation. But it also made money on the investment when it refinanced the property in the late eighties and was netted rental income of $500,000 in 1995 when the building was fully occupied.

Fred Alger gave up the Bank of New York as its transfer agent in 1989 to assume more efficient and accurate control of customer-service issues. It turned out to be a fortuitous decision, because the bank exited from the transfer agency business shortly after it lost the Alger account. Though the move was not made for the money, the company's transfer-agency operation does contribute under a million dollars a year to the firm's gross revenues.

Integration also helped the company preserve its administrative talent in the wake of the 1987 crash, when most Wall Street firms were slashing staff to stay afloat. Fred Alger found another place for them within the organization, usually with the opportunity of upgrading their skill level. The only departures came through normal employee attrition.

Barely acknowledged and little known outside the firm, the human factor is perhaps the most valuable element in the firm's equation for success. Fred made a solid commitment to the people in his organization. The covenant between Fred and his employees reveals a soft core beneath the firm's hard edge. Though his expectations were high, Fred acted with great solicitude and took seriously the company's responsibility for the lives and livelihood of its people.

"Many of our senior, seasoned employees, who have been through a number of Wall Street firms in high positions, understand and appreciate this," observed Jim Barbi. "They feel it. They are aware that when assets under management went south and there was all this upheaval, they were always taken care of without really understanding how Fred managed it. If they looked at the numbers, they would understand the soundness of the foundation. Some of the new, younger people don't understand yet because they have no measure or way of knowing that it's not normal on Wall Street to be taken care of this way."

Irwin Schwartz provided anecdotal evidence of the Algers' benevolent attitude: "After the loss of the Security Management business, it came to a point where I actually had to take a salary cut of perhaps ten or twenty percent. What impressed me was that six months later, when we started getting accounts, my salary went right back up, which was very honorable. I hadn't expected that. Most employers would have stretched that time a little longer. As soon as the accounts came back, the salaries went right back up."

For Fred, care of the firm's employees is a basic tenet. "This company is successful because of its people, the desire to excel, and having the capital to survive times that are not so great."

The final commanding principle of the company is its dutiful allegiance to the process of capital retention. In Fred's eyes, nothing has been more meaningful for the company. "I think my people believe, and rightfully so, that I've not sucked money out of the company or paid myself an outrageous salary," Fred said. "The firm has grown; the book value has grown. As a company we've had our ups and downs, but nonetheless the firm has stayed solvent."

The Algers have kept their money in the company. Fred and David paid themselves relatively little compared to others with similar rank in the industry. "I make maybe thirty to forty percent more than our highest-paid analyst," Fred revealed. "David and I make more or less the same kind of money.

"Capital is important for the employees so that they know they won't lose their jobs," Fred affirmed. "We have about one million dollars in capital for every employee. When the whole world is crashing around you, you need to know that you have a job and what you're doing is important and valuable. Capital also gives management the confidence to take steps without feeling the enormous pressure of avoiding mistakes.

"The accumulation of capital was essential for the long-term benefit," he added. "We never spent the money we made, particularly the performance fees from IOS. This is unlike what most firms would have done."

The preeminence of capital for the firm was invoked most obviously in the financial obligation of its shareholder agreements. That's why the firm's shareholders had to pay twice book value for their stock, were required to use most of their bonuses to pay off their loans to the company, and were penalized if they left the firm sooner than 20 years.

Contrasting the firm's cautious investment policy with the vigorously aggressive investments for its clients' capital, he explained that until fiscal 1986–87 most of the firm's assets were invested in long-term treasury bonds. At that point, as a partial response to declining assets, the firm put some money in growth stocks. Today, about 40% of the firm's capital resides in portfolios of the Alger Fund.

"I think that all of us feel that if the market goes down sharply, we're going to have enough problems with our clients being unhappy that we don't also want to worry about the capital of the business having problems," noted David Alger. "Also, if you own a stock personally, it makes you less dispassionate about that stock. You're less able to do what you have to do, psychologically. You may not want to sell it for the accounts. Under the last in–last out rule, you're going to pummel your own portfolio. "

Last in–last out requires the investment manger who buys or sells a stock for the company account while at the same time owning it for a client to be the last to buy during accumulation and the last to sell when liquidating. In other words, clients' orders should receive precedence over the manager's transactions.

"Fred's greatest contribution was that he capitalized that company extremely well," David suggested. For his part, Fred seemed genuinely impressed by the company's growth and almost detached about its ability to retain and build its capital in an almost straight-line path.

The figures tell the company's story. One line in the ledger shows the firm's capital doubling to $10 million in one year, 1980 to 1981, and setting off a striking explosion of growth in advance of the first leg of the latest bull cycle. Another section proves that its capital base held firm, at $65 million, during the period between 1987 and 1990, despite searing changes in the company led by a disapproving investment climate, the agonizing entry into the mutual-fund arena and the departure of two of its main partners.

Irwin Schwartz said, "Fred believed that if we made money for the client, money would grow naturally under management and the firm would profit from the fees, so we don't have to risk the firm's capital. This viewpoint was changing as I left; he wanted to be more aggressive with the firm's money."

When advised that as much as 40% of the firm's capital is now in the market, he remarked, "It's probably too much. It would make me nervous. I'm glad I'm not there. I sure wouldn't want the responsibility of the firm's money."

The first time the firm made decisive use of its accumulated capital was in 1974, when Fred acquired the management contract of two closed-end mutual funds, C I Fund and Spectra Fund, and the Percy Friedlander Co. brokerage firm from City Investing Co. for $300,000.

"How important was capital to buying those funds!" Fred stressed. "That additional fee income saved us."

City Investing Co. was a seventies-style holding company for a conglomerate of disparate firms, including Rheem Manufacturing Co., World Color Press, Home Insurance Co., Motel Six and General Development Co., a Florida real estate operation. It had sales of around $6 billion and $1 billion on its balance sheet in 1974, according to Stephen E. O'Neil, its executive vice president when Fred Alger made his bid for its mutual funds.

Money management no longer served City Investing's business plan, and the funds' small size—$2 million in Spectra, a stock fund, and $12 million in C I, a convertible-bond fund—barely provided a reason to keep them going.

The funds were weak sisters to other corporate interests. For example, in 1975 World Color Press received a five-year $60 million contract from Peterson Publishing for printing all its magazines and another $22.5 million deal to print *Oui, Golf Digest* and *Tennis*. Its Hayes International subsidiary was awarded a $9.2 million agreement from the U.S. Air Force for depot maintenance and modification of C130 transport planes. In the same year, one of its units signed a production-sharing pact with Syria for offshore oil exploration in the Mediterranean.

The firm's net income in the year ending December 31, 1974, was $45.5 million, and it declared a quarterly dividend of 16.5 cents.

City Investing was looking to unload the funds at the same time Fred Alger needed something to offset a loss of roughly $150 million in assets and $175,000 in management fees from the departure of the Security Management and IOS contracts. With less than $50 million in managed accounts coincident with a dreadful 1973–74 bear market, Alger found itself in a difficult situation. Salaries were cut. Bonuses were nonexistent. "It was the only year the firm didn't make money," volunteered Irwin Schwartz. In its 1974 fiscal year, Fred Alger & Co. chalked up an after-tax loss of almost $116,000. It wasn't until after Irwin left the firm that it registered its second and last losing year in fiscal 1990.

For an idea of just how ugly things got on Wall Street during the seventies bear cycle, a seat on the New York Stock Exchange which sold for $515,000 in 1968 was available for $75,000 in 1973. In the same five-year span, the number of Big Board members dropped from 646 to 543; assets in mutual funds, which had ballooned to $60 billion by 1968, were deflated to $36 billion in 1974.

To dodge the landmark June 1971 U.S. Court of Appeals ruling by Judge Henry J. Friendly, which attributed profits from the sale of a mutual fund to its share-holders and not the management company, City Investing packaged the funds' sale with divestment of its flagging Friedlander Inc. brokerage unit in order to prosper from the transaction. In effect, Alger bought the funds for book value and paid the premium in the Percy Friedlander trade.

Fred Alger was one of several candidates—and certainly not City Investing's favorite—for obtaining the funds' management contract. "The board decided that Fred was an acceptable buyer, but there was a lot of skittishness about the transaction because of his reputation," said O'Neil. "One of the conditions of the sale was that I remain on the board to make sure, in their view, that everything would be done correctly." O'Neil has stayed on the board of those funds and was also installed on the board of the Alger Fund when it began in 1986.

"They took Fred over the coals," George Boggio recalled about their negotia-tions for the funds with City Investing's board. "We weren't so confident they would accept our offer; but they did." He principally credits O'Neil for their suc-cess in making the deal. "I knew about Fred's reputation, and I always felt it was undeserved," said O'Neil. "He got tarred with a broad brush, but that didn't bother me. Fred managed money very well.

"Besides, I like Fred. He is an interesting guy. He always had a different take on things, thoughtful and farsighted. He's not one of the boys, which allows him to be a little more independent. He's not a trend follower and doesn't run with the crowd. Plus he has this unusual ability to take macroeconomics and use it to make superior investment decisions."

Though initiated in 1974, the purchase was actually consummated in Janu-ary 1975, when the Percy Friedlander team hunkered down with Fred Alger & Co. on the fifth floor of 26 Broadway.

Percy Friedlander & Co. originated in the fifties as a retail brokerage partner-ship between Percy and his son, Robert J., who joined the firm in 1952 upon his return from the Korean War. The firm purchased its seat on the NYSE in 1955 for $88,000 plus a $4,000 initiation fee. Forty-two years later, the asking price would be 20 times that figure.

"We were wondering how we were going to survive; then Fred walked in one day and said, 'I'm interested in buying your firm,'" Robert remembered vividly. Friedlander was occupying 3,500 square feet at 140 Broadway—once a bustling hive of 30 employees but at that time seemingly vacant, with a body count of only 10.

"He needed the mutual funds, but was not averse to getting some retail business too," said Robert. At best, Friedlander brought about $400,000 in retail accounts to Alger. It also engaged in a trifling arbitrage between the Philadelphia and the American Stock exchanges. The Percy Friedlander Corp. was dissolved and reconstituted as the Friedlander Division of Fred Alger & Co. Although Percy didn't receive an equity stake in Alger, he and his partners retained 80% of the profits of the division.

The Percy Friedlander acquisition imposed a regenerative structural change on Fred Alger & Co., which included a stretching of its personality and opening it up to new faces, mostly senior in age and not cast in the Alger mold. Percy was in his seventies; Robert in his fifties. Overnight it doubled Fred Alger's size.

Fred's secretary, Lavaun Vawter, was dispatched to Boston, where the funds were domiciled, to wind down City Investing's ownership and bring them into the Alger fold. Desperate for a new challenge, she asked Fred for a permanent place as their administrator. Fred had already hired someone else for the job, but Lavaun was so insistent that he gave in to her.

Fred Alger's first order of business after absorbing the mutual funds was to rename C I, which stood for City Investing. After the withering market declines of 1969–70 and 1973–74, Fred thought its new name should convey strength and substance. He visualized a castle. So the fund was rechristened Castle Convertible Fund.

Castle Convertible, which trades on the American Stock Exchange with stock symbol CVF, was enormously successful from the start. Steered by David, whose prominence in the firm was enhanced, it was number one in its category in 1975 and held its impressive ranking the following year. As a convertible-bond fund, Castle invests in interest-bearing debentures and dividend-paying preferred shares that can be exchanged for common stock on a predetermined basis. A convertible fund is attractive to investors for its dividend yield, more so when its market price is bid at a discount to the underlying value of the common shares into which the bonds and preferreds will be converted. Castle has consistently sold at a price below its asset value, making it a tempting investment.

Spectra Fund came to Alger as a diversified investment company and was then trading on the over-the-counter "pink sheets," reserved for small capitalization, low-priced and thinly traded stocks. Like Castle Convertible, it was a closed-end fund, one which issues a fixed number of shares and is traded as a security, usually on a stock exchange. While keeping it a closed-end fund, Alger immediately transformed Spectra into a non-diversified investment company to provide extra leverage as an operating company or a vehicle for acquiring other operating companies.

During the year after Alger's takeover, Spectra Fund's price sank 26%. But apart from its shaky start, Spectra has been an inside success story. In fact, both funds have proven to be resilient performers over the last 20 plus years. Speculation that Fred kept Spectra just for sentimental reasons ended when it was converted to an open-end fund in February 1996. An open-end fund is the typical mutual fund that issues and redeems shares on a continuing basis, with the net asset value of each share determined by the securities and other financial instruments owned by the fund at the close of the trading day.

In the year prior to September 30, 1977, while the Dow Jones industrial average lost 132 points, or 13.6% of its value, Castle Convertible was up 16%. Its two-year performance was 62.7%, and three-year track a lofty 115.2%. The fund enjoyed the best one-, two-, and three-year performance in its category during those years versus the S&P's return of -4.3%, 24.7% and 72.2% respectively.

"One of the things that is not fully appreciated is Fred's toughness," said Arthur Dubow. "He's relentless. When he goes after something, he's really, really focused and has a drive that's very intense and powerful."

Its action was so impressive that it caught the eye of financier Carl Icahn, the notorious corporate raider, most recently attached to deals at RJR Nabisco, TWA and Marvel Entertainment. Fred fended off his attempts to control Castle Convertible for short-term gain by amending the fund's charter to make 50% of the vote of "those who vote" instead of the normal 50% of outstanding share holders the measure of a ballot victory. Fred knew that only about half of Castle Convertible shareholders ever voted, and with this modification he was able to block a takeover. Fred always felt that Castle was a great play for someone who wanted a convertible portfolio because of its 1.75% expense limitation.

Nineteen years later Castle Convertible was still beating the averages. Through April 30, 1994, Morningstar, the advisory which ranks mutual funds, rated it fourth in its class, with a yield of 4.9% and a three-year average annual return of 14.4%. Castle Convertible's assets stood at $57.6 million, and it was selling at a market discount of 8.7%.

The fund maintained its superior ranking through 1997 as it traded in a range of $23 to $28 a share for its roughly 2.25 million shares outstanding and typically at a 14% discount to the value of its underlying holdings. Its dividend yield has been between 5 - 6%.

Spectra Fund was no slouch either. It regularly found its way to the top rankings of closed-end stock funds. In the week ending February 4, 1995, when the Dow crossed 4,000 for the first time and fully 74% of all closed-end funds were either higher or unchanged, Spectra stood first based on the 9.1% increase in its market value for the year-to-date period.

Soon after it became an open-end fund in February 1966, Spectra's assets quadrupled, from $9 million to $36 million, in a little over a year. Investment writers have finally discovered the fund and begun recommending it for its superior three-, five-, ten- and twenty-year performance records which have consistently placed it at the top of U.S. equity mutual funds. Spectra is unlike other Alger Fund no-load portfolios in that it extracts no deferred, vanishing sales charge (from 5% down to 1% over five years) or 12b-1 sales and marketing fees. Sporting a five-star Morningstar rating, the fund is chartered to invest up to 20% of its assets in foreign securities and may engage in futures and options trading for non-hedging purposes. Its management fee, at 1.5%, is nearly double that of the other Alger Fund portfolios.

"By acquiring Castle and Spectra, Fred hoped to regain growth," said George Boggio. The bet paid off in spades. By 1976 the firm's assets under management had burst through $53 million, of which Castle represented 60%. Alger's income from management fees grew nearly 60% between 1975 and 1976, while its commission business almost doubled during the same period. The firm was once again on the move.

Unlike the mutual funds, which played into Alger's natural strengths in research and investment counsel, the Friedlander Division presented a novel challenge for the company. To offset its extra load of manpower and overhead, Fred began to look for ways to fortify its brokerage trade.

"Friedlander needed energy. Old man Percy was retiring. His son, Bob, was not the ball-of-fire salesman that the firm required," Fred said.

He didn't have long to wait. Enter Ray Dirks. April 1975.

Raymond L. Dirks, one of Wall Street's indomitable mavericks, received his notoriety as the stockbroker who ripped open the early seventies' Equity Funding swindle, to date the largest corporate fraud in America, and who was subsequently indicted for his role in the SEC's first prominent insider-trading case.

The story of the $2 billion Equity Funding conspiracy reads like a potboiler. It's an astounding tale in which investment professionals and insurance examiners were hoodwinked by 64,000 fictitious life insurance policies, phony death certificates, $25 million in counterfeit bonds and $100 million in missing assets. Eclipsed only by the Watergate affair, the scandal's magnitude was a body blow to a Wall Street already reeling from a declining dollar, waning investor confidence and a foul market.

Using Bernie Cornfeld as a role model, its founder Mike Riordan, in cahoots with IDS-trained sales whiz Gordon McCormick, built Equity Funding Corp. of America from a meager $10,000 investment in 1960 to the management of $1 billion in assets by 1973. It was reportedly the fastest-growing insurance and financial company in America prior to its plunge in stock price and trading suspension by the SEC.

Equity Funding's marketing scheme drew from the mostly discredited, popular and lucrative selling of mutual funds by contractual plans. Plying their wares door to door, its salesmen, like Fuller Brush men, pushed fixed, small-dollar periodic investments in mutual-fund shares over many years and profited mightily by extracting enormous commissions from the early installments.

Equity Funding's prize, conceived by Riordan and McCormick, was a tiered financial instrument which combined mutual-fund savings with the benefits of insurance protection. After placing consumers in its mutual-fund shares, Equity Funding simultaneously obtained a loan against their value and locked the buyers into purchasing a separate life insurance policy; its salesmen accruing huge commissions on both sales. The leveraged transaction was especially attractive to low-income buyers for its cheap entry point and interest deductibility.

Despite the appearance of a Ponzi scheme, the SEC qualified this amalgam of insurance and fund shares as a security and required its registration in 1962. In 1964 Equity Funding sold its stock to the public on the American Stock Exchange. Sources said the SEC first got wind of the scandal in 1968, when its regulators uncovered record-keeping anomalies while investigating the firm's reciprocal agreements. Still, the company was allowed to move its trades to the New York Stock Exchange on August 20, 1970.

Some insiders speculated that Equity Funding's transgressions were foisted by its auditors and grew out of the sloppy market in 1969. Others claimed its principals started as early as 1965 to build the company around the "wholesale creation of fictional insurance policies," later sold to reinsurance companies, with a total face value of $2 billion.

The problem with Ray Dirks was not that he was the whistle blower. Surely his actions were a public service. In its case against him, the SEC alleged that Dirks violated its rules by first informing his clients about the fiasco so they could bail out of Equity Funding before the inevitable fallout.

Actually Dirks was only the messenger. The first person to leak the news was Ronald Secrist, vice president at Equity Funding, who passed the information to Dirks in March 1973. The scandal hit the press as a front-page *Wall Street Journal* article on April 2, 1973. Three weeks later, Equity Funding's illusions vanished with its stock value. In November 1973, 22 individuals, including 20 executives at Equity Funding, were charged on 105 counts of fraud and conspiracy by a federal grand jury in Los Angeles.

Dirks's battle with the SEC lasted 10 years, and he was finally exonerated by the U.S. Supreme Court in 1983. His 1974 book, *The Great Wall Street Scandal: Inside Equity Funding,* written with Leonard Gross, is a detailed investigation of the corruption and venality that was the practice of that company.

A scandal-scarred legend, "the famous" Ray Dirks needed a place to hang his hat. Fred brought Dirks out of the cold and gave him a home at Fred Alger & Co. "I felt great sympathy for Ray. I believed he was unjustly being persecuted by the SEC," Fred confirmed. "He was really getting a bum rap on the Equity Funding case. He was just doing the job of an analyst. So what if one of his sources was an inside source?"

"*I* approached Fred," Dirks recalled. "I knew this girl who knew Bill Scheerer, whom I first met at Goldman when I was starting out. Fred was a bright, well-known, successful, and solid research-oriented money manager. It was my opportunity to build something in alliance with a good research company."

Welcome Ray Dirks.

Under the aegis of the Friedlander group, Dirks was offered the same deal as Percy—80% of the profits in his division. And so was born the Ray Dirks Research Division of Fred Alger & Co.

Dirks got a running start and was at once an impact player, bringing a wicked splash of high energy and enthusiasm to the firm. More than that, he brought heavyweight producers into the company. The brisk expansion forced Fred to lease additional office space one floor above, on the sixth story of 26 Broadway, right next door to Chat Hickox's Ashland Management.

"I was fairly aggressive in marketing securities," Dirks verified. "Fred let me do what I wanted to do, which was solicit business from institutions plus some retail accounts and bring in producers to do the same thing. I primarily stuck to my strength, which was insurance stocks."

The portly, puckish and pugnacious Ray Dirks had made his reputation as an insurance stock analyst at Bankers Trust from 1955 to 1963, when it managed the largest portfolio of stocks in the country. For the next few years he worked at several brokerage houses, including Goldman Sachs, before being named a senior vice president at Delafield Childs, Inc., from where he exposed the Equity Funding scandal.

Fred seemed smitten by Dirks. He recognized Ray's marquee value, the allure and mystique of a man who brought down Equity Funding. Sure enough, his aura initially had a heartening effect on the firm.

Certainly there was a likeness between the two men. Both mavericks, they operated by self-appointed rules. Dirks foreshadowed Fred as a victim of SEC character assassination. There was one clear difference, however. Ray skated close to the edge of the law. Fred never did. In the end, however, he proved a redoubtable foe, especially to George and David, and his sojourn at Fred Alger turned into a brief tenancy rather than a tenure.

Ray Dirks had an easygoing sales manner and a cherubic countenance which Fred saw as natural for the camera. So, "in order to create some excitement," Fred arrived at the idea of using him as his alter ego in a series of television ads promoting his retail brokerage business.

With a theatrical flourish to reinforce Dirks's guileless demeanor and play up his innocence against the railings of the SEC, Fred had Dirks dress in a white suit. As David deftly put it, Fred turned Dirks into a "a bizarre version of Colonel Sanders for the stock market." Quickly and unequivocally, Dirks attached himself to that affectation, maintaining the white costume long after his Fred Alger experience.

The theme of the three 30-second commercials was that regardless of the economic backdrop, and especially so when things look bleak, it's always a good time to buy stocks. To put that across, the visuals in one commercial showed a long line of disaffected customers, passbooks in hand, snaking around an imposing S&L during the Depression. A second ad raised the specter of jackbooted German troops trampling over Poland during World War II.

The historical stock footage was in stark black-and-white, hammered in by harsh, authentic period soundtracks. In contrast, the studio shots which followed were quiet, absent even of white noise, and in soothing color. Dirks, attired in his white suit, joined in one instance by Robert Friedlander and in another by Walter Untermeyer Jr., a broker on his team, in another, spoke sedately to the camera as it zoomed in closer.

First ad. *I'm Ray Dirks. The stock market was able to look beyond the bad days of 1932, and from its July low it tripled within eighteen months. As an experienced stockbroker, I have an eye for value and a sense of market timing. I can help you make money. Call Ray Dirks.*

Second spot. *I'm Ray Dirks. Sometimes the stock market overreacts to bad news and offers opportunities for substantial gains. Such was the case between March and November 1938, when the market went up sixty percent. An experienced broker like my associate Bob Friedlander understands market timing and can help you make money. Call Ray Dirks.*

Third version. *I'm Ray Dirks. Nineteen fifty-eight had serious problems. Unemployment up. Earnings down. But the stock market looked beyond the recession and advanced continuously throughout the year. An experienced broker like Walter Untermeyer understands market timing and can help you make money. Call Ray Dirks.*

A flash card with the Alger phone number popped up on the screen at the conclusion of the monologue.

This was the first of two fruitless Fred Alger ad campaigns. The series had a brief and limited airing on local stations in the evening-news time slot. A roomful of operators waited attentively by their telephones for the anticipated avalanche of calls. None came. "The ads were singular in their failure to attract new business," said Dirks.

The effort, however, did engage public attention, and Ray Dirks gained in celebrity. David's dentist-landlord, for one, was so incensed by the Nazi ad, he accosted David in the hallway outside his apartment and lambasted it as an attack against all Jews because it trivialized the Nazi experience. This ad was quickly pulled from the air.

The backlash from the Depression-era S&L ad actually saved the campaign, but not before the stations airing it were asked to chase it with a disclaimer stating that the run on the bank was not a current event.

"The U.S. Savings and Loan Association was outraged that we would show such a scene," Fred recalled about the incident. In its eyes the ad's frequency and placement alongside news segments was augmenting an already negative consumer sentiment against its members. The association eventually offered to buy the film to get it off the air. "What would it cost?" they asked Fred. "Fifty thousand dollars," he submitted hopefully. "Done."

"They paid us the entire cost of the campaign, which we were about to cancel anyway," Fred added.

This misguided ad campaign gave Fred his first taste of the value of brand identity. It also set the precedent for advertising as Fred Alger's electrified third rail. Touch it and you fry. The often repeated adage that "Fred Alger isn't very successful with advertising" turned out to be a gross understatement.

While indications were that the somnolent Friedlander division needed a shot in the arm, Ray Dirks as the cure brought on alarming side effects. The firm's attentive seneschal, George Boggio, admitted, "Ray Dirks drove me crazy." He felt that his carefully guarded systems of checks and balances were being violated. He could never be certain if or when Dirks was in compliance.

"I prided myself on being able to implement any internal control for any situation," George explained. "That's what I enjoy doing. Ray Dirks was a very aggressive salesman, a very good salesman who also did research, but he wouldn't think twice about all the regulations, and that was my responsibility. As much as I would stay up nights dreaming up ways of how to put up systems, he would stay up nights figuring out ways of getting around them.

"It wasn't a personality conflict. We were both after the same thing. For me things are black and white with some shades of gray. To Ray they were probably gray and black. Ray had a bad image with the stock exchange and the SEC, and I was always afraid that if we allowed him to do some of the things he wanted to do, it would come down on Alger.

"I always feared he would do something to bring down the company, and we were getting such a small percentage of his business that it wasn't worth the risk."

George found a sympathetic ally in David Alger. Most offensive to him, Dirks's pawky band of brokers didn't jibe with the character of Fred Alger. "Ray brought in incredible amounts of unusually profitable business," said David, "but we felt he was bending the rules and George couldn't handle it. He was doing more business than we were. It was like drug addiction; you enjoy it but worry about the consequences. I really disliked him. Fred liked the money that was coming in."

The other partners of the firm agreed with George and David.

"Ray Dirks was a compliance nightmare," said Irwin Schwartz, "a loose cannon. His questionable activities and transactions made George very nervous; but Fred didn't seem to care. Fred never had to sit in on an audit with the SEC, NASD or NYSE."

"He just got too big for us," said Bill Scheerer. "We were scared to death of him. David, George and I had a little trouble persuading Fred that he had to let Ray go. Thank God we got rid of him."

Remember, Fred Alger was set up primarily as a money manager, and Ray Dirks was luring it into his widening net of brokerage activities. Although Fred appreciated the income from Dirks's operation, he eventually heeded the hue and cry and returned brokerage to its originally intended role in the firm as an adjunct to the investment advisory.

In the end, Ray Dirks proved more irksome than dangerous, and he was whisked out as rapidly as he came in.

Exit Ray Dirks, September 1976.

What took so long for Fred to take out Ray Dirks? Was it the money? In his year at Alger, Dirks estimated that he generated a little over $1 million in commissions. Was it respect? Fred was especially proud of his "incredibly good salesman."

"I remember Fred crowing about Ray and how wonderful he was," said Chat Hickox, who observed the action firsthand. "When Fred got hot on something, there was no end to what was great about that particular guy. I guess Fred figured, in those days, if he had been Ray Dirks, he might have done what Ray had done. The problem was that Ray had a penchant for breaking the rules."

In his postmortem on the Dirks experience, Fred said, "We ended our relationship because George couldn't stay on top of him. Ray was always several steps, from a regulatory standpoint, ahead of us. It's a shame because he was a tremendous producer and had a way of inspiring other people around him to produce, and was a lot of fun to work for. The brokers really liked it."

"I'm sure there were some things I was doing that probably caused Fred to be concerned about whether it might impact his business," admitted Dirks. "If the SEC was successful in pursuing me or came up with something they could nail me on, Fred Alger would be drawn into it."

Dirks, however, couldn't contain his personal displeasure at being booted out of Alger. In a rant, he spilled his hurt. "I was disappointed that Fred didn't want me anymore. Fred could have built a substantial brokerage operation. We didn't even get to know each other or share lunch even once. That's typical. Stand in line. Fred keeps people at arm's length. He doesn't even socialize with his brother. He certainly has to have the last word about everything. He doesn't give much authority to people."

A month after Dirks left, Fred brought in East Hampton friend and institutional broker John Westergaard to tidy up Ray Dirks's division.

Dirks transplanted his frenetic operation to the brokerage firm John Muir & Co. Dirks lured Robert Friedlander, his costar in the Alger ads, to John Muir with a "a proverbial deal I could not refuse." With him gone, the Friedlander brokerage division dropped out of existence at Fred Alger.

9 🐎

Fearless Fred

I N THE MAKING of Fred Alger & Co., three attributes of Fred's intrepid nature stand out: first, his inventiveness as a businessman; second, his novel ways of attacking the stock market; and third, his predilection for defying convention and challenging authority.

Jerry Tsai, in whose footsteps Fred followed, made this observation: "I always thought that he was very smart and creative, very innovative. I would even use the word courageous. My definition of courageous—he would do things that an ordinary, conservative, old-fashioned manager might not do."

At heart, Fred Alger is not so much driven for financial reward as inspired by an implacable need to work out his ideas. The company was his proving ground in every domain: research and analysis, trading, back-office fulfillment, business development, management, technology. No area was spared Fred's urge to innovate. His readiness to back up bold theories with capital and energy and willingness to assume the risks they entailed kept the company on edge and gave it a certain élan. In its formative years the firm was a nervy work in progress. Everyone who labored with Fred had a chance to make his mark and get in on the action.

Sometimes he operated on blind courage. While many Wall Street brokerages, including the venerable Merrill Lynch and Donaldson, Lufkin & Jenrette, turned tail and spun off their money-management divisions at the onset of Rule 11A in the mid-seventies, Fred Alger held his ground and, by doing so, was able to retain both the brokerage and the money-management parts of the business. The final SEC interpretation proved he was wise to reject the conventional view.

"He questions everything, the basic premises that others take as givens," said Fred's lawyer Ray Merritt, who has carried the firm's standard in many of Fred's challenges to the system.

Sometimes it was stubborn courage, as when Fred wouldn't give in to the demand of an important prospect that the firm cede its brokerage commissions as a condition for getting the account. Moreover, even though Fred Alger was desperate for the business, he advised its pension managers that it wasn't the best time to be investing in stocks. That judgment turned out to be the correct, and that company today is the firm's biggest single account.

But it was never false courage. Especially when Fred took a stand on the market. Usually on a different track than Wall Street's herd and often ahead of it, Fred was, in the early years, fashionably up-front with his economic views. His pronouncements were widely noted by the press, as he was singled out as a fresh new voice in America's rising mutual-fund industry. With a few exceptions, Fred's uncommon, sometimes revolutionary insights were remarkably on target.

In a provocative interview which appeared in *The New York Times* on April 2, 1969, Fred Alger coolly forecast "the possibility of a major depression that could last ten or fifteen years." He showed the culprit for this negative environment to be a "parochial and pedestrian" political leadership that was "out of touch and out of tune with the vital and interesting aspects of our society." Specifically he railed against Nixon's hard stand against student protesters and Congress's moves to curb corporate takeovers. Scoring points, Fred illustrated the potential for bank insolvencies and expressed concern that mutual funds were being sold as stock equivalents and therefore prone to heavy liquidations, which would lead to lower prices. He used the rapid decline of the Mates Investment Fund as an example. It was a surprisingly bearish, anti-establishment stance for this diehard Republican, one-time Nixon supporter and typically bullish analyst.

For the photograph that accompanied the *Times* article, Fred adopted his customary pose for the media. He is shown to be absorbed in thought, leaning back on an invisible chair and balancing himself with one shoe propped on his desk. His eyes glance off a slide rule gripped with both hands and gaze remotely beyond the camera. Dressed in a white shirt, business tie and suspenders, he evinces relaxed self-confidence. His casual air is underscored by his tousled hair. On his desk is a plastic coffee container—the refillable kind that takes paper cones.

What was enticing about Fred's pessimistic take on the market was that he had just nailed down two banner years of stock market performance. In 1967 Security Equity Fund vaulted 67.8%, in contrast to the Dow's paltry gain of 19.2%; in 1968 the figures were 12.1% and 8% respectively. Security Investment Fund grew 27.5% in 1967 and another 26.2% in 1968. Fred reasoned that he was in cash at the top and fully invested at the bottom of the market. So when he turned his back on this market, it was news.

It was a bigger story when he reversed his position just 10 months later, forcing a puzzled investment community to take another look at him. For an article in the February 1970 issue of *Dun's Magazine,* Fred struck a similar pose to the photograph in the *Times* story. Leaning back on a chair, shoe on desk, coffee con-

Fred strikes his signature pose for the press during the sixties and seventies.

tainer in foreground. This time Fred is sans suspenders and slide rule. With head turned downward he rubs his chin and appears even more contemplative and remote.

Fred's about-face on the market might have appeared to be contradictory and inconsistent, but Fred was just telling it like he saw it. If the indicators changed, he was ready to take a new position. In July 1969, just three months after the *Times* feature, he did just that. At month's end Fred was once again fully invested. He surmised that while the Dow was hitting new lows, other indicators were turning positive, which laid the foundation for a bullish second half of 1969. Sensing this to be an opportune time to enter the market, Fred convinced Security Benefit to open up its $3 million closed-end investment trust, Ultra Fund. Under his management, from September 17, 1969, through the end of the year, it gained 9.2%, versus the Dow's loss of 11.8% for the entire year. Mostly by capital appreciation the fund grew to $15 million in 1971.

In the *Dun's* article, Fred asserted that "the market . . . is not likely to be any higher than 900 on the Dow." He compared the economic health of the nation to a man recovering from a stroke, bound for "years of convalescence and the slow rebuilding of liquidity for the American economy." The market must have liked what it heard, for it fell nicely in line with his projections. The Dow ended 1970 at 838.92, from a mid-year low of 631.16. But his mutual fund results were mixed. Security Investment bounded 15.9%, even as Security Equity declined 16.4%, and Security Ultra dropped 10% against the Dow's yearly advance of 9.2%.

Fred's favorites were "zippy" stocks like Milgo Electronics, Telex, TelePrompTer and Memorex. He was one of the first to recognize the cable TV industry as a true growth industry and placed early bets on a "breakthrough in the integrated circuit group" with investments in companies like Fairchild Camera, Texas Instruments and Motorola. As Fairchild Camera evolved into Fairchild Instruments, whose top three scientists left to form Intel Corp., it can be said that his first chip stocks are still the semiconductor leaders of today.

Fred had a knack for calling the lows in the market. "The most money is made in the first three months of any stock market recovery," Fred believes. He kept an eye out for market bottoms while combing the stock world for momentum growth companies. Purchasing these stocks when they were most unloved contributed greatly to the firm's superior long-term performance.

While no major depression actually occurred after Fred's 1969 pronouncement, his long-range prognosis was borne out by the market's subsequent action. Deep into the 1973–74 bear swoon, Fred correctly identified the stock market as "within a heart beat of a significant bottom." In his quarterly report to Spectra Fund shareholders on September 25, 1981, Fred was ahead by a year in forecasting that "the next time the Dow crosses 1000, it would be the last time it sells in the 900s." It took the entire decade of the seventies before the Dow Industrials could break the 1000 point barrier; when it finally did, in 1983, it never looked back.

"Fred was very much a controversial character in those days, as he has been throughout his career in the business. Nothing has changed," said John Cleland, chief investment officer of the Security Benefit Group of mutual funds. "'Fearless, Frenzied, Frantic Fred,' we teased him in Kansas. Fearless Fred was the moniker we laid on him."

Cleland recalled a time when Fred came out to Topeka to meet the local brokers and fire them up about selling Security Equity Fund. When Fred stood up to give his first presentation at Beecroft Cole & Co., he was perhaps inappropriate but unafraid to announce that "cash is the best investment now because the market is overvalued."

"Walter Cole chewed me out," Cleland remembered. "He said, 'I just sold one hundred shares of Security Equity to my best customer. Your star guru in New York is telling the world that cash is the best investment now! What are you trying to do to me? How can I possibly sell your fund?'"

"Fred has always been outspoken and says what he thinks," Cleland added. "Here, we were trying to sell the fund, and Fred was telling people to keep their money in cash.

"Fred had a very real knack for identifying stocks that, for whatever reason, were likely to be recognized with significant market performance. He was very self-confident, always had a strongly held opinion about the markets and the economy."

Right from the start, Fred was unabashed and confident about publicizing his unconventional, often esoteric views, which were usually in opposition to the conventional thinking of most money managers.

Fred's ideas frequently spiced up Robert Metz's Market Place column in *The New York Times*, which was daily fare in the investment community for most of the seventies. Metz, who had won acclaim for his 1965 book, *How to Shake the Money Tree*, served Fred's savory opinions to attract readers, and Fred used Metz to share his original thinking with a wide audience of potential investors.

On November 15, 1978, Fred gave an "encouraging prognosis" for stocks during a reported "period of deep gloom over the market's prospects in the light of competition from fixed-income securities."

Hailed by Metz as a solitary voice of optimism, Fred used his research to illustrate that previous recessionary periods were good for the stock market. In 1958, for example, he stated that when corporate profits were down 30% from the year earlier, the stock market zoomed from 420 to 600, its largest advance to that date in the postwar period. His analysis also revealed that it was uncommon for the Dow, certainly never in its history for a full year, to sell below its calculated book value. "Even assuming a thirty percent earnings decline in 1979, the book value of the combined Dow Jones stocks should be approximately 925 by the end of next year," Fred was quoted as saying. This equated to a Dow advance, with dividends, of more than 20% of its current level.

In Metz's March 30, 1979, column Fred coolly offered shale oil as a radical cure for a stock market that was slumped over from America's dependence on Middle Eastern oil. Fred's strong medicine was a 25-cents-per-gallon tax on pleasure driving, which was projected to realize $15 billion annually and provide an incremental drop in oil consumption. He said the government should then use this capital to construct shale oil–producing plants in Colorado. The government wouldn't run the plants but would lease them out to private companies. Fifty plants, Fred promised optimistically, would lead to self-sufficiency by the year 1985. He based this on a daily output of 100,000 barrels selling at a market rate of $18 a barrel and current imports of nine million barrels a day. Fred's plan also called for increased reliance on natural gas, coal, nuclear power and Alaskan oil, as well as renewed focus on conservation.

Fred was enthusiastic about this plan for a multitude of reasons: It insured against foreign domination. It fixed energy costs and controlled inflation. It improved the balance of trade. It would help America regain its self confidence. "I estimate that a trigger like this one quickly would send stock prices to levels double of those today, " he pledged.

In the realm of research, Fred had a consuming passion for the macroeconomic region. Despite the firm's primary reference to an individual stock's earnings and growth prospects, the reality is that share prices don't move in a vacuum but often rise and fall according to a broad backdrop of economic and cultural factors, like inflation, interest rates, economic activity, consumer sentiment, investor psychology and political leadership.

A seductive theory that Fred proclaimed as "one of his most interesting findings" was that psychological attitudes and not supply-demand factors were really responsible for the price movement of commodities. The important corollary of this idea was that real long-term interest rates have less to do with Federal Reserve policy and the realities of deficits and credit demand than with people's attitudes toward the economy and inflation.

Fred was led to this speculation by a *Newsweek* article in the early eighties where Nobel Prize–winning economist Milton Friedman fretted that interest rates should be lower than they were since inflation had abated.

It's interesting to observe how Fred concluded why a parallel downward move failed to materialize. First, he established the measure of "real" interest rates was the difference between ten-year government bonds and the consumer price index. Next, he noted that after the collapse of the Bretton Woods Accord in the early seventies, which established a system of fixed exchange rates among 44 countries, commodity prices doubled for the next couple of years *regardless* of supply and demand. Fred postulated that they were aroused by the psychological implications of the Accord's collapse as well as the real decline of the dollar. U.S. interest rates, however, did not rise correspondingly during this period. In fact, they turned negative.

"I theorized that interest rates were so ubiquitous in our society and culture that they would change only when attitudes changed about inflation," said Fred.

But how to measure attitudinal change in America? This is where Fred made one of his bold leaps of insight that often provoked skepticism.

Fred explored "two decisive cultural events" in order to gauge the rate of change in popular attitudes. The first was the time it took to alter America's feelings about Germans after World War II. The second was the speed of changing sexual mores as expressed by the acceptance of premarital sex following the widespread availability of oral contraception in 1960.

"In each instance it seemed eight years passed before a dramatic shift took place," Fred said. He elaborated that in both instances most of the change occurred in the eighth year. "It took nine and a half years for real interest rates to become strongly positive after Bretton Woods," Fred added. Consequently, he theorized that it would take at least eight years after Federal Reserve Chairman Paul Volcker's clamping down on money supply in 1979 and Ronald Reagan's 1982 tax cuts to "convince the markets that inflation was under control" and for real interest rates to return to the norm of around 3% above inflation. This is exactly what happened in 1990.

The point of all this, Fred explained, is that "the biggest obstacle to a long-term market boom is the high level of interest rates relative to inflation. With yields on thirty-year treasury bonds at about seven percentage points above the inflation rate, the bonds are favored over stocks in many investors' minds."

Fred predicted that ten years would pass before interest rates would return to their customary premium of 200 to 300 basis points above the underlying rate of inflation. Over that period, he said, stocks would become more and more attractive. If his prediction was wrong, if government rather than cultural attitudes was the primary influence, why hadn't real interest rates plunged after the Fed attack on the money supply in 1979?

Not surprisingly, *The Wall Street Journal*'s "Heard on the Street" column which presented Fred's thesis to the world on Valentines Day 1983 included the caveat that this was "a far-fetched theory."

The way Elizabeth M. Gregg, a vice president and senior analyst at Fred Alger, who was Fred's right hand in developing his economic theories, understood all this, "In the seventies, in the real world, we had rising inflation; but investors were very slow in adjusting their attitudes about what to expect as inflation. They were frequently counting on its severity. Conversely, starting in 1979 when Volcker embarked on a rather Draconian policy to rein in inflation, the markets were very slow to accept the idea that inflation was going to subside. We had a period of extremely high real rates. I think Fred's thinking was that inflation was not going to be the bugaboo that the markets were expecting it to be. It would take a while for the markets to adjust attitudes. That led him to go outside of the markets to get some feeling for how long it would take for attitudes to change.

"Basically after the first oil shock, the collapse of Bretton Woods and the ramp-up in commodity prices feeding into labor costs, inflation not only went up, it really got embedded. And we did have a period of negative real rates from early 1973 to '75 and again in 1978 and '79.

"If you stick to Fred's timetable, it appears that the market hasn't fully adjusted to what he has laid out. We have been in a fairly low inflationary environment for quite a while. If this holds true, everybody will get adjusted to it at about the time inflation will start rising again."

Fred ascribed the 1994 spike-up in real interest rates, recently at 4% above inflation, to the better returns in the market, increased demand for capital and lingering concerns about inflation.

To corroborate his conclusion, Fred offered a compelling set of charts: real interest rates from 1959 to 1995, the spot prices of four commodities from 1968 to 1978, the two attitudinal studies and a 10-year production-cost vs. price chart for margarine. The margarine data illustrated that prices quintupled without any relationship to supply or demand and without any change in the cost of its ingredients. Much of this research was assembled by Fred's daughter Alexandra during a summer job in 1981 at her father's company.

Margarine, sexual freedom, Nazis. Fred found a way to piece them together as a way of understanding interest rates.

Though much of Fred's thinking was for internal consumption only, he thought enough of his proposition, long after he developed it, to frame it in a letter dated September 1986 to James Tobin, Nobel Prize winner and Sterling Professor of Economics at Yale. Fred was prompted to exchange ideas with the esteemed professor after reading his article in the Sunday *New York Times*.

Fred asked Tobin to consider that the Fed is "relatively powerless to control the level of interest rates. Despite two cuts in the discount rate since July 10, 1986, long-term rates are higher than they were then. One could go further and suggest that overt steps to lower rates are counterproductive because they adversely affect attitudes about the long-term outlook for inflation."

Pressing his case further, Fred answered Tobin's response with the following: "Central to an attitudinal theory on interest rates is the observation that supply-demand for money has only a transient effect on the level of interest rates. For instance, the year-over-year demand for money from all sectors was 12.5% higher in the first half of 1986, well above the growth in the economy, and yet long-term interest rates declined nearly 200 basis points. An attitudinal theory explains more—doesn't it? Should it not have a higher weighting than supply-demand?"

In another exchange with Professor Tobin, two years later in February 1988, Fred promoted another one of his lofty theories which projected that the Social Security trust fund and the federal budget would be balanced by 1997. This was in reaction to another *New York Times* article which attributed to Tobin the "thought to immobilize capital by restricting stock trading through tax policy."

Fred sent Professor Tobin a table of statistics and forecasts from 1985 to 2020 which projected a rosy scenario of balanced budgets and sustained large surpluses for the coming decades. He wrote enthusiastically, "The table shows that if one extends the five-year trend of federal government revenues and spending (assuming a little relaxation on the spending side), and taking into account the rapid buildup of the Social Security trust fund surpluses, one should have a balance in the unified budget by 1997. Even more intriguing is the fact that if one extends this same trend for another decade, there will not be one penny of federal debt in public hands. Or stated another way, the entire federal debt could be retired in less than 20 years."

Lisa Gregg, who handled this research challenge, explained how they approached this discovery. "In 1983 Greenspan headed up a commission aimed at shoring up the Social Security trust funds, including modest reforms like extending the retirement age, phasing in higher payroll taxes and bringing more people into the program," she began.

"Some commentator got a hold of projections and showed these humungous surpluses well into the twenty-first century. When Fred saw this article, he became mesmerized by it because people were already lamenting the deficits and the burden of debt for future generations, which contradicted this assessment."

Working with actuarial figures straight from Social Security, they began calculating how Social Security revenues and outflows might somehow point to budget balance in 20 years. Fred recalled, "The Social Security Administration put forth four scenarios: two of these were optimistic and two were bearish. We used the more optimistic of the bearish scenario. The fifth scenario was positively affected by much larger than expected employment gains, much lower inflation—which affected payouts—and a much lower interest-rate assumption. On the negative side, wage gains were less than expected because inflation was lower."

"What we found, when we ran through it the first couple of times"—according to Lisa, the project lived on and the analysis evolved for several years with many variants—"was that if you didn't alter the growth path of federal taxes and federal spending, even with the projected growth in Social Security surpluses, you would never see a balanced budget. You had to make some, radical then, assumptions—faster-growing revenues, slower spending or both."

Lisa added, "It was fairly complex research. One difficulty was that the numbers we were given were quoted in nominal—unadjusted for inflation—dollars. But the deficits we were looking at that existed in the mid-eighties were in 1983 dollars and we were talking about year 2020 dollars. So we went through a process where we projected the federal government's inflation assumptions. Social Security may have eliminated the annual deficit, but it certainly wouldn't have eliminated federal debt outstanding in the hands of the general public."

Fred continued, "The only wrinkle was that non-military spending grew more quickly than GDP, because of new programs introduced by the Democratic Congress. The exquisite irony of this is that George Bush went back on his pledge, 'Read my lips. No new taxes,' and signed a bill which required that any new spending initiative had to be funded by specific and hard reductions in existing programs or by specific tax increases. Consequently, non-military spending slowed to the GDP rate, and we now see the kicking in of the Social Security surplus to balance the budget. Clinton is reaping the fruits of Bush's political suicide."

Lisa Gregg summarized why this analysis was important to Fred. "For many years it was a large part of his presentations to explain away the concerns about Social Security that might have worried our clients. He was able to show that it was not a problem. With a robust economy and just some remedial steps in spending, they could continue to have faith in America and therefore have faith in the stock market.

"Fred was correct, in the sense that what he laid out has indeed occurred, but not exactly the way he projected it. The budget did get balanced, and a good portion of the deficit reduction came from the discipline side, which he also projected. And it came when nobody at the time was talking like this."

You're always in the game with Fred Alger. "Fred always wants to be ten steps ahead of everybody, but the market is only three steps ahead. If you're ten steps ahead, everybody just looks at you and shakes their heads in bewilderment," David Alger observed with some ruefulness.

Fred certainly confounded the investment community with his ideas, but that was never his primary intention. He reconnoitered the fixed universe and, expanding its boundaries, searched for any way to gain a competitive advantage in picking stocks and managing investments.

"This is an intensely competitive business. And you have to really like competition. I do like it. More than that, I think I have an ability to assemble a diverse base of information in a different, possibly creative way to see value where others haven't seen it," Fred said.

His imaginative mind and restive energy also respond creatively to business challenges for achieving long-term financial goals. In most situations, he was trail-blazing, a quality perhaps inherited from his great-grandfather who tamed the virgin Michigan pine forests.

For example, in order to boost dealer sales of Security Equity Fund, Fred structured an intricate compensation plan which commingled management fees and commissions to create a virtual pension fund as an annuity benefit for its salesmen. "The idea was that, over time, a salesman could earn additional compensation with shares in our various funds," said Fred. This was even before the enactment of IRA retirement accounts.

It was "complex and imaginative, but it didn't work because it was not too practical," according to Bill Scheerer. Not so, recalled George Boggio. He said Fred couldn't get it past the SEC, despite the advocacy of his Washington lawyer Bobby Hoffman.

Another example: Like all expanding investment-management companies, Fred needed a supply of analysts to support his growing business. His solution: he formed the headhunting firm Analysts Resources, which gave him access to the best available research minds in the investment community.

Wall Street is not for the faint of heart. To win big in investing, you have to be bold and brave. Fred had an abundance of both qualities.

Fred's earliest dashing exploit was Southland Investors Ltd. It was his earliest institutional, fully discretionary account, and it gave the company its first taste of significant investment income.

Inspired by his hedging strategies for A. W. Jones, Fred walked into the office of John Jennings at Security Benefit in Topeka, Kansas, in 1965 and asked for his assistance in setting up his own limited partnership. Southland, as it came to be named, would serve two functions: one, provide an end-around to the restrictive cap on the number of investors he could serve as an unregistered adviser; and two, allow him to reap more than just management fees from his investment insight.

Jennings told Fred he knew of only one place where they might raise the money necessary for that kind of speculation, the cotton fields of Mississippi. They got on Jennings's private plane, flew down to Jacksonville and met up with Ellis Sylar, a "huge mutual-fund investor who was coincidentally a Baptist minister." Described as a "fat man with fallen arches," Sylar, with his well-heeled contacts, was the pivot of the partnership. Fred saw him as "one of these great Southern salesmen, the kind who could sell you snake oil."

The deal was a three-way, Alger-Jennings-Sylar split of 20% of the partnership's capital appreciation against a 1% minimum fee on assets under management. Their initial goal of raising $500,000 was exceeded, and all in all they finally attracted $2 million in seven or eight months from 10 individual investors. When Fred was trying to raise money, he rarely tempered his voice or character in order to get on the good side of his audience. Jennings recalled a time when he and Fred stayed at the house of one of his Southern contacts. "The guy wouldn't let you smoke at his house. But Fred did." The brashness of this clever New Yorker didn't appear to dampen his appeal among Southland's resolute investors. It may have even enlarged his image.

For Fred, Southland was a high-wire act, because he was unregistered and technically prohibited from publicly courting investors. The rules were such that he couldn't even use the word "investments" on his business card. Also, because he was unregistered, there was a ceiling on the number of clients he could have.

Even though they worked side by side, Fred employed his distant management style with David.

Would Southland be considered a single entity, or would its investors be counted separately? "The whole thing was tricky," Fred admitted. "The law wasn't sophisticated enough to know that you could have one hundred investors in a hedge fund and count it as one client."

The source of the funding was another concern. Southland's partners were an irregular, if not regionally colorful collection of individuals, and one man was known to the group only as "Blood."

Southland Investors was an instant hit and an easy home run. In three years, assets in the partnership flew higher than $10 million. Since Fred was able to extract one of the highest fees ever seen in money management, Southland was a real boon to the company. "It was easier to make the money than to raise it," Jennings admitted. "We just invested in rapidly growing companies, the same kind of companies we were buying for the Security funds and our other clients," Fred revealed. "It might have done better because we may have used some leverage."

After this bravura performance Fred took his share of the 20% and suddenly walked away from the lush deal. He renegotiated the Southland contract for the standard one-half of 1% for managing the fund. Southland had met its objectives, and his partnership ties could no longer be prudently maintained with the increasing odds that official scrutiny might damage the rest of his business.

Winning with Southland swelled Fred's sense of his own invincibility. "I was so self-confident that I always felt there was no challenge I couldn't solve. There was nothing I couldn't do. I believed that if I had been trained in physics, I might have invented tremendous things. Any problem that came my way, I'd either go under it, around it, over it or through it. I didn't even think of it as a problem. It was just a thing to be done."

Summing up this upbeat approach to life, he counseled, "It doesn't pay to be pessimistic—ever. You can always figure out a solution if you think about it hard enough. Since solutions are possible to come by, it pays to be optimistic. Generally things work out in the end. It may take some time, but they do work out."

Fred was popping with ideas which were often opportunistic and imaginative, even if they didn't provide optimum results. Case in point: DMA, a novel way to market mutual funds, which followed on the heels of Southland Investors.

"One of our crazy ideas in the late sixties was DMA, which stood for Divorced and Married Associates," Fred explained. "We had a notion about selling mutual funds—a convergence, really, of several ideas. How might divorced women with children make money? At a party I ran into a woman friend from business school at Michigan who was a lawyer and divorced and was looking for ways to make money part time—at home or while socializing. I then thought, getting registered and selling mutual funds would be a good profession for women like her." Because of their social and financial difficulties, divorced women were presumed to have the natural motivation to succeed, and those with social position had ready access to potential investors in congenial settings. "Fred felt strongly that mutual funds are sold and not bought," explained George Boggio.

DMA had two lead partners: Fred's lawyer friend, described by George as "a very attractive woman" who later married the son of a U.S. president, and another of Fred's friends from San Francisco, a tall, "imposing" woman who was a prominent feature in New York fund-raising circles. The plan was to fashion a sales force from the ranks of upscale women who had a lot of time on their hands and were likely to make the social rounds. "We would hire only women," George confirmed.

With convincing flourish, DMA set up shop at a condominium in Manhattan's east fifties, which the company bought and converted into a stylish cosmopolitan environment. That appeared to be the extent of its achievement. Despite Fred's bountiful support for the venture, this one never lifted off the ground. While revealing Fred to be fallible, it also demonstrated his propensity for radical means to turn on the jets in his business. David lumped DMA, which took place before his time, into the bag of Fred's "weird and wacky marketing theories."

After DMA petered out, the apartment was turned into a crash pad for late-working executives and out-of-town visitors. That's when it got interesting.

George tells this story about the time he walked into the DMA apartment and found a naked lady in the shower, which proves there were at least a few high jinks in the staid, conservative world of Fred Alger.

"Every week one of the secretaries would go into the apartment to clean up and dust. She came to me one day and said there were fresh flowers in the room and women's clothing in the closet. 'Are you having someone stay there?' she asked. Only partners should be staying there, I thought, let me ask Bill and Fred. They knew nothing about it.

"At lunchtime I decided to go up there. I ring the doorbell and hear some noise, but no answer. So I let myself in. The bathroom door is open and the shower running. 'Hello,' I call out. 'Hello,' I hear this charming French female voice call back. 'Who are you?' she asks. 'This is my apartment. Who are you?' Then she came out of the bathroom wearing nothing but a towel.

"For some reason a research associate straight out of Harvard wound up with a key to the place and had offered it to her. She had been staying there for months. Not only was she occupying the apartment rent-free, she had been drinking up all our liquor."

In the early seventies, investors opened *The Wall Street Journal* to full-page ads hawking a research report on TelePrompTer Corp., a leader in the nascent cable-television industry, for the serious price of $20,000 a piece. That was Fred Alger.

With TelePrompTer in tow, Fred unleashed CI Associates, described by him as "the greatest tax shelter of all time." He had the right idea, but his timing was early, and TelePrompTer's chairman was ultimately enmeshed in a bribery scandal. Though highly beneficial at first, the partnership ended in 1991 with most of the profits swallowed up by taxes.

Another bright idea in the late eighties was Fred's Charitable Giving Program, an inventive solution for rich men like himself to become large benefactors of their favorite institutions while receiving tax-exempt income that replaced the pledged capital. As a bonus it also provided the security of an insurance component. The program was so radical and complex, few people other than Fred could fully understand it. So far, only Fred has taken advantage of the program.

Fred once toyed with a construct for a derivative financial instrument called the Two-Way Option, exercisable within a short period of time, perhaps seven trading days—a tight option, 5% either way or one-way only. "You just concentrate on stocks that are really volatile," Fred explained. "The advantage is to the guy writing the option. He'll always have five percent to play with. With the five percent, how could you not make money?" Even so, Fred's conservative instincts kept him from realizing the plan. This one stayed in his head.

Fred was also first to come up with the notion of rewarding mutual-fund investors with frequent-flyer miles. In this incentive, the longer you kept your money in the Alger Fund, the more miles you earned. While the SEC told Fred this proposition was "absurd," it subsequently green-lighted three American AAdvantage "Mileage Class" money-market funds in 1991, which were administered by the San Diego–based discount broker Jack White & Company. Investors received one AAdvantage mile for every $10 deposited on an annualized basis. The SEC once again reversed its thinking in 1995 and grounded American from issuing frequent-flyer miles to its money-market investors.

With the approving backdrop of the Statue of Liberty, Wall Street, like no other place in America, provides exaggerated possibilities for roaming free in the land of the brave. Its best legends are made up of big strikes in glamorous stocks. That's where its role models are found. Fred Alger has played a part in a few of these tales.

In 1965 Fred was applauded for picking Gulf+Western "within a point of its low" and gaining an extra lift from his stake in miscast Paramount Pictures prior to its acquisition by the conglomerate. He turned heads with the brassy proclamation: "I didn't like it when I bought it at nineteen. But I knew it was going up." By the summer of 1966 it was selling for $120.

Twenty years later, the buzz was about how he made a killing in Genentech. What impressed the crowd was the size of his bet and his willingness to speculate in a biotech firm. It was Fred Alger's largest stock position during the second half of 1986, an investment of $26 million that showed a gain of $46 million by the end of the year.

Fred's Alger's escapade with Mary Carter Paint Company, which would eventually transform into the charismatic Resorts International gaming empire, stands out as an early example of his aptitude for placing bold investment bets that led to huge gains.

The overture to Mary Carter Paint originated with Sam Clapp, the canny Cornfeld cohort who engineered the clever IOS tax-avoidance and kick-back scheme which funneled brokerage commissions through his Bahamian wife, Martica. In February 1967 Fred and Eleanor were Sam and Martica's guests at their sprawling vacation home on exclusive Paradise Island in the Bahamas. Through the Fund of Funds, Fred had become a trusted friend and chairman of the investment policy committee for Clapp's Fiduciary Trust Company's Fiduciary Growth Fund, a modest, proprietary mutual fund which operated from the tax haven. Fred headed Fiduciary Growth's investment committee for about three years, before it was eventually closed. That had nothing to with Fred, who "wasn't managing it anyway," according to Clapp.

One morning after tennis, the conversation turned to the casino on Paradise Island and the new bridge under construction to reach it across 400 yards of narrows separating it from Nassau. Fred reacted to this development with wide-eyed interest. "It was clear that the casino would make a whole lot of money once the bridge was finished," he said. The gambling mecca had been accessible only by boat, and with the bridge nearing completion Mary Carter had the look of a winner—a striking model of the Alger vogue for companies on the verge of a life-

Developing his economic theories with Lisa Gregg, vice president and senior analyst. Chief trader Joe Maida is on the phone in front of them.

cycle change. Fiduciary Trust then owned $100,000 in Mary Carter promissory notes which could be converted to common at $5 a share.

Mostly Sam and Fred played tennis. "He was a reasonably good tennis player," remarked Clapp about Fred's tennis skills. "He wasn't very fit in the heat down here, though he may have been a good player in New York."

That June, as Egyptian forces surprised Israeli troops in the opening salvo of an abrupt Arab-Israeli war, a buoyant Sam Clapp walked into Fred's new office on 120 Broadway and offered him some letter stock in Mary Carter Paint for "five or six dollars a share."

"We said, 'Yeah!' and at once bought three or four million dollars for the Security Equity Fund. In the next twelve months the stock went up tenfold," Fred recalled. Clapp recollected the incident more vividly when he spoke by phone from London, where he now resides.

Clapp had with him James Crosby, the high-rolling, somewhat reclusive chairman of Resorts "who at that point was in need of financing," for a face-to-face with Fred. "It was very amusing meeting," observed Clapp. "He told Fred the Resorts International story, which wasn't well known, and said that they expected to get a license in Atlantic City. Crosby already had this casino operation in the Bahamas for a long time.

"They spoke for about half an hour. All of a sudden Fred pounced on the phone, called his broker and put in an order for 50,000 shares. It all happened so quickly and effortlessly, I was dumbfounded.

"Whereupon Crosby said we can sell you this investment letter stock at a discount. Whereupon Fred decided to buy a couple of million dollars' worth." Obviously he liked the fact that Crosby was aiming to turn Mary Carter Paint into a diversified leisure and travel company. And letter stock—a way for companies to raise money without increasing capitalization and for investment managers to jack up portfolio values—was win-win for both sides. After Resorts International moved into Atlantic City, its stock zoomed "from two to two hundred," said Clapp, who was based in New York at the time. "It was probably the best investment you could find in ten years," Clapp continued.

The papers reported in June 1967 about a private placement of two blocks of unregistered shares: 268,000 with the Fund of Funds and 100,000 with Security Equity Fund for $9.50 a share or about $3.5 million. Also indicated was a $70,000 fee to Sam Clapp's Fiduciary Trust and its earlier purchase of 56,000 unregistered shares for $7 each.

The swiftness of Fred's decisive action was typical of stock selection at the firm, especially during the early years, which largely revolved around Fred's freewheeling investment insight. "Resorts International was the first casino to be legalized in the Western Hemisphere," remarked Bill Scheerer. "The excitement was incredible. It enhanced the value of our portfolio tremendously."

Rosemary Kiernan offered this glimpse: "At the time we managed the Alger Fund for IOS, he had just six accounts. I used to price the fund out once a day using an old calculator. I remember Fred standing over me every day waiting for the stock price of Mary Carter Paint. He had a slide rule, and while I was adding up the value, he would say, 'No, that's not right.' He was faster with the slide rule than I was with the calculator."

The flap over Resorts International came when they tried to sell the letter stock. Sam Clapp made it clear:

"Investment Letter Stock—or large blocks of shares not offered publicly but sold privately, usually at a discount—were supposed to be held for investment purposes and not for trading," he explained. "There were very complicated provisions as to how long one needed to hold this stock before you could sell it. There's a holding period which the SEC enforces but which it never defined as a law. It was whatever their administrative interpretation made it out to be.

"We bought Resorts International debentures which were convertible into common stock. We held the debentures for a year. When it came time to sell the common stock, we took the position that it was one continuous investment and we could tack on the holding period of the debentures to the holding period of the stock. Therefore we believed we had held the security long enough to sell it.

"Some large New York law firm also gave the opinion that our transaction was valid; we could sell the stock. The SEC had a different idea. It said we had to buy it back. So we had to take the stock back, which then went down and hurt our performance. We had a choice, of course, but we didn't want to litigate with the government. It wasn't worth the hassle.

"Subsequently things were codified. Some years later the SEC reversed itself in the two points that involved us. We were vindicated, but it was all water over the dam."

Another Fred Alger play in the gaming industry was with Parvin-Dohrmann Co., a Los Angeles–based supplier of hospital equipment and services and owner of the Fremont and Aladdin hotels in Las Vegas.

The central figure in this investment was Delbert William Coleman, the Cleveland–born son of a bartender who made Harvard Law School, then abandoned a middling law practice for the life of an entrepreneur. Coleman had come to Parvin-Dohrmann through the introduction of millionaire Chicago lawyer Sidney R. Korshak, an alleged adviser to the Capone gang, who earned his notoriety by obtaining early parole for Charles "Cherry Nose" Gloe in 1947 in a high-profile motion-picture extortion case. The firm's 70-year-old president, Albert B. Parvin, was eyeing retirement, and Coleman, with plenty of cash from the sale of his stock in the Seeburg jukebox company, was promoted as a viable stand-in for playing the company's hand in the gambling business.

Fred met the debonair and perennially suntanned Coleman in 1968 at a party at the home of Bobby Freedman, where he had met Bernie Cornfeld. He was quickly taken by the smooth-talking, 43-year-old Coleman, whose forte was scaring up stock prices with stories of his intended takeover of a targeted company, B.F. Goodrich in one instance, then selling his shares for a quick profit instead of going ahead with the deal.

Fred pledged $5 million to buy 142,857 unregistered shares of Parvin-Dohrmann, in part to facilitate its planned acquisition of the Stardust Hotel-Casino for $15 million in cash. While he didn't have to put up any money, he had to sign a promissory note which kept him from selling the stock for a period of one year.

"They needed a bunch of money to control the Stardust, which would boost its earnings from one to three to four dollars a share," said Fred. "If we gave Coleman a commitment of five million dollars immediately, we wouldn't have to pay for it till December. I said, 'Great.' We had made all this money in Mary Carter Paint, and I felt we knew all about the casino business. The five million was split between IOS money and Security Equity."

Parvin-Dohrmann stock began to soar almost immediately. Rumors of large gaming profits rocketed the AMEX–traded shares from their mid-1968 low of $14.25 to a close of $141.50 on May 13, 1969. Fueling the rise was the appeal of its new management and a relatively thin supply of available shares. It was the stock story of the year. Fred's accounts were showing huge profits even before paying a dime for the shares.

"Fred owned a ton of this stock and felt the sun rose and set on this idea and Del Coleman," recalled his friend Joe Reich. But cracks were forming in the stock's speedy engine. Coleman's transactions, both secret and open, had sparked several regulatory probes which would shoot the firm back down to earth. But not before a few of its investors, Fred among them, made a great deal of money in a very short time.

On March 26, 1969, trading in Parvin-Dohrmann stock was suddenly halted, and the following day Coleman's private placement of shares came to public light for the first time, the details of which immediately raised the hackles of the Nevada Gaming Control Board. Parvin-Dohrman had been seeking to expand its Las Vegas gambling franchise by acquiring the Riviera Hotel. With that disclosure, the regulators had a reason to block the transaction since the Fund of Fund holdings of Parvin-Dohrmann, concurrent with its stake in an offshore Bahamas casino, were a violation of Nevada law. Fred was therefore ordered to liquidate his interest in the company tout de suite.

In compliance, the Fund of Funds reportedly sold its 81,800 shares on April 24, 1969, to an unidentified group of private and institutional investors for $90 a share. Not a bad profit for Fred. In fact, it was fantastic. "There was a big field trip with institutional buyers to Las Vegas for letter stock which I hadn't even bought or paid for yet," Fred said. But he was totally put off about having to trade his shares in the company. Under the gun, Fred eventually sold them at a huge discount. "It made me mad, because I was on a performance fee and I was taking a thirty-point hit. I was mad as a snake about this." Disagreeing with press reports, he recalled that the actual selling price was $110.

Fred might have been a little more gracious about this fateful intervention. The Nevada Gaming Control Board's "closed-door" investigation was just the tip of Parvin-Dohrmann's unraveling. A computer warning triggered SEC scrutiny of Coleman's stock transactions and his suspect cozy dealings with brokers and fund managers. There were telltale signs of stock manipulation, insider trading and the distinct appearance of impropriety. After Fred cashed out, Parvin-Dohrmann's shares completed a round trip back down to $12.50 by the spring of 1970.

Further afield in the early seventies, Fred took a shot at building a European merchant-banking operation in Paris called Lansdowne Ltd.

Fred saw the venture as a bet that the budding European securities industry would eventually need U.S.–style investment-banking services to fuel its growth. In Europe at that time such support was sparse and limited in availability from the big banks who maintained minuscule merchant-banking operations. A merchant bank is the Continental equivalent of an investment bank/venture capitalist, which "looks for new companies with good ideas that can be brought to prosperity." This may be accomplished with dollars, usually by taking debt and equity positions, and advice, typically in mergers and acquisitions, and then by arranging for the company's shares to be sold in a public underwriting, namely guaranteeing purchase of the issue in the absence of demand.

Fred had a second motive, which was to use Lansdowne as a means to market his company's investment-research capabilities in Europe, either in an advisory capacity or through mutual funds.

Both expectations, however, were ultimately unrealized.

Though Fred was a distant player in New York and only an occasional participant in the dealings of the company, his influence uncannily ruled the operation by pushing it to assume a more dynamic character than its European counterparts.

Lansdowne's founder was Francis O. Hunnewell, a mutual-fund operator in Paris whose wife was a college friend of the wives of Fred and Chat Hickox, and who had met Fred during his Winfield days in San Francisco. Hunnewell was suitably charmed and impressed by Fred's "enthusiasm, commitment and extraordinary focus," which would eventually lead them into business together.

The next Lansdowne player to come in was Jan Bailey, a London stockbroker who provided the details of Lansdowne's origins in a phone conversation from London. Hunnewell was a friend of a friend at Oxford who was managing a fund-of-fund type mutual fund in Paris called Olympic Capital Fund. Unfortunately it fell into the clutches of two majority shareholders, the Greek shipping tycoons Goulandris and Niarchos, who were attempting to use their large positions to gain control of the fund's management. The ensuing struggle capsized the fund, and with excessive redemptions it had to be liquidated.

"The question then was, what to do next? They had a good office there in Paris. Hunnewell's partner, Harvey Wachtel, decided he'd had enough and left France to get back to Boston. Frank and I decided to stay on and form a small investment-banking business, which was Lansdowne," said Bailey, who was called in by Hunnewell to help him close Olympic Capital.

Enter Richard Thompson, who had met Fred socially in the mid-sixties in New York through Hunnewell. If his memory is correct, they usually gathered at the home of flamboyant American businessman Charles Osborne. Thompson was living in Paris and was an on-site director of a "big division" of an unnamed American public company.

Finally completing the first tier of partners was Fred Alger, who invested $50,000 in the venture.

The next column of partners in the original company came in through Fred: Cornfeld's broker Arthur Lipper, Swiss banker Beat Notz and Chat Hickox. Fred introduced the first two to the idea in a sauna, which was significant because he passed out from the heat during the meeting. Notz and Hickox subsequently made larger investments in the firm to create Notz Bank, and Hickox finally wound up owning all of Lansdowne after it crashed..

Lansdowne Ltd. was actually an off-the shelf company of Bahamian registry which took a name that was intentionally pretentious and sounded vaguely aristocratic to mask its true identity and in order to appeal to Europeans. Said Thompson, "It was launched with a great deal of expectation and optimism. We really set out to become a buying department, in the old-fashioned sense of the word. We all had a lot of friends at Rothschild, Indosuez and Worms, and we got deals from them because they really didn't have the people to handle them."

The Paris offices were on rue de la Paix, near rue Vivienne and the Bibliotethèque Nationale. Hunnewell and Bailey manned the operation with the support of four assistants and secretaries.

The first potential blockbuster deal for Lansdowne was the popular European hotel chain Novotel, which was an embryonic enterprise when it was introduced for financing by Beat Notz. But Lansdowne didn't take advantage of its early lead and left a lot of money on the table. From Bailey's point of view, this was due to Fred's insistence on working the deal as it might have been done in the States.

"I remember after our first meeting I rang up Fred and said, just to get the ball rolling, send along a little money. Fred said no. 'You don't do that. Don't ask me for the money. Go out and raise it, like they do at Lehman.' Of course, it really doesn't work like that in France. If you give off a scent that you're not actually acting as a principal, that it's not your money and that you're going out and raising it—which is the normal way of doing things in the States—then they tend to shun you.

"That was an interesting lesson for us. It meant that we had to become a lot more entrepreneurial rather than act in a traditional way. I don't blame Fred for that. It's just the American way. That's how he expected things to be done. We made only a small amount off it. The point is, had we come up with the money as the principal, we would have been right in there from the start, and it could have been an investment banking client and a very good one for the rest of our time."

One place where Lansdowne succeeded better was in high-income U.S. real estate syndicates with businessman Stanford Triester, who "owned a piece" of boxer Smokin' Joe Frazier and sent him on a singing concert tour of Germany after his retirement from the ring. There were about three or four of these deals which "made some nice money and very good returns for the investors." The last one, however, Mustang Island, just off Corpus Christi, Texas, wasn't so productive. They entered the investment just as the "bottom started dropping on the financial world." Defaults left Lansdowne with most of the resort property, but also saddled it with most of the debt payments which were "large and painful."

Another project that "went quite well" was a syndication of large tracts of wine-producing acreage in France, Spain and Italy, which was prompted by depressed prices and turned on the selection of properties that qualified for *Appellation Contrôlée* designation. (*Appellation Contrôlée* is the French system for regulating wine production by providing assurances of geographical origin from a specific district. It dates back to 1935 and identifies over 200 different categories.) "Until 1970, Bordeaux wines were underpriced. Wine and land were cheap: twenty five thousand French francs for a hectare—which is about two and a half acres—or about two thousand dollars an acre," said Hunnewell, explaining the setup for these investments.

Lansdowne worked the financing deals through Société Viticole and, acquiring numerous properties with the Château Margaux family, became the largest grower of *Appellation Contrôlée* Bordeaux in France, in addition to owning 1,000 hectares in Spain and another 800 hectares in Italy, according to Hunnewell.

When wine prices began bubbling up in 1972, the group considered starting a wine fund, but then settled on a more traditional route, harvesting wine profits. "So we created a company that made wine. We bought some land, quite a substantial amount, in fact. We put together a large underwriting with various banks in Europe and England. That was reasonably well received because it had the backing of real estate. It didn't have the risk of a new company because one was buying land," Bailey said

One of Lansdowne's most fascinating adventures was an effort to sponsor and host the 1972 World Chess Championships in Paris. Although Bailey claimed credit for discovering the idea, Hunnewell believed that it was actually Fred who came up with it.

In any case, the prior year's world chess finals, in which Russia's Boris Spassky had been victorious, relinquished a purse, "extraordinarily low for the finest minds in the world," of only $2,500. " Fred became enamored with chess and its promotional value," said Hunnewell, and Lansdowne courted the French Chess Federation with an offer to underwrite the competition and provide $50,000 in prize money, which was an unseemly large sum at the time. As luck would have it, the federation's office was next to Lansdowne's.

Lansdowne hoped to gain not only by publicity but also by receipts from sponsoring the matches. The Paris venue was fixed for the Musée de l'Art Moderne, with a seating capacity of 3,000.

In the final bidding, which came down to three countries, France, Yugoslavia and Iceland, Reykjavik won by floating a 50-cent levy on its population to finance the event, which was one of the most heralded sporting competitions of the decade. That was the year when Robert James Fischer of Chicago became the first American chess player ever to win a world chess championship.

Lansdowne was probably spared considerable financial grief over footing the bill for a drawn-out series. "I was extremely relieved because Bobby Fischer didn't even turn up for the first match," added Bailey. "It would have been a total disaster if we put up all the money." It really didn't matter much to Fred, who had lost interest in the promotion by then. "When Fred loses his enthusiasm, he stops becoming a catalyst," said Hunnewell. But it demonstrated once again how Fred Alger is way ahead in his thinking, even about possibilities for this remote area of sports promotion.

Finally there was Lansdowne's stake in Notz Bank. When a Saudi sheikh was forced by Swiss banking authorities to give up his ownership of Intercredit Bank of Zurich, it became an important Lansdowne trophy. Hickox contributed new financing, which constituted Lansdowne's position, while Notz held 50% stake in the bank, which was renamed Notz Bank. Notz himself had to liquidate his minority position in another Swiss bank to comply with "one bank per person" statutes.

One of the benefits of a bank acquisition was an open funnel for Fred Alger's investment research into the European marketplace. As a small bank, Notz found it "heavy going," according to Bailey, especially with regard to the introduction of Fred's aggressive investments. "They were extremely cautious in the wrong way," he said. "They were perfectly happy losing money in an inflationary envi-

ronment instead of going into an Alger fund, when actually Fred was less speculative, because you had equities run by one of the great fund managers of the
world. It should've succeeded. It's a pity. It was exactly what was needed at the
time, but we were ahead of the curve."

Notz's banking activities, on the other hand, provided moderate success and
profits for the partnership. The reward came just two years later when they sold
out to Notz for "a lot of money." Not nearly enough, however, for Fred. He felt
his Paris partners never had the right commitment or long-term outlook for the
enterprise. "It floundered because they lost sight of the interests of their money
partners," he proposed, "and they had a very short-term perspective, which is a
shame. "

"We did some interesting deals, I must say," said Thompson about Lansdowne.
"We had a lot of fun in Paris during the early days. Fred and I certainly had enormous fun setting up the operation."

But the allure of Lansdowne for Fred was more than good times in Paris. He
had aspirations of becoming a "big player" in merchant banking. It was his
chance, according to Hunnewell, "to bring Lehman Brothers to its knees." When
it unfolded that Lansdowne couldn't deliver on that promise, that it couldn't
dazzle the European banking crowd as much as Fred had hoped, he turned sour
on the operation.

Lansdowne barreled along for several quarters, essentially from 1970 to 1973.
Then OPEC spoiled the party. As oil prices escalated after another Arab miscal-
culation of attacking Israel in 1973, the kind of investment deals available to
Lansdowne, even the "zanier" ones outside the mainstream, dried up.

"Nobody was interested in that type of deal at all," Bailey explained. "Paris
really became extremely difficult. In 1974, cash was the name of the game. That's
all anybody cared about. Therefore we started doing badly 'round about that time.
Our business ceased, which was rather entrepreneurial in any case." Oil had spiked
from $3 to $12 a barrel. Long-term money disappeared from Europe, reverberat-
ing from the muffled hysteria in a ravaged U.S. equity market.

At that point Lansdowne effectively ceased to exist as it was initially construed. With the doors slammed shut in Europe and at the instigation of new
associate Michael Pochna, Lansdowne picked up its caravanserai and followed
the cash to the deserts of Saudi Arabia. Essentially Bailey, Hunnewell and Pochna
spun off a separate operating company within Lansdowne Ltd. called Lansdowne
Financial Services, while Hickox took over the parent after fresh capital infusion
from Thompson.

Lansdowne Financial then became involved with Binladen Telecommunications and Bell Canada as a sales agent for a piece of the plum $3.5 billion Saudi
telecommunications-modernization contract in 1978, a deal which quickly soured
and wound up in litigation in the Canadian courts for more than a decade.

Although Fred was still a partner in the firm, he had suspended his participation. In fact, he turned silent on the group. Saudi Arabia wasn't in his vision for Lansdowne.

At worst, Lansdowne was an unproductive business caper that missed out on a number of opportunities, as it was unable to debunk the norms of the European financial community and its confident drive was stalled by the OPEC oil squeeze on the Western world. At best it was a playful *passe pied* of primary deals with a Swiss bank, a hotel chain, a resort development and French wine estates.

Fred downgraded the Lansdowne "misadventure," as he typically referred to failed entrepreneurial efforts, as just "a fun thing to do." Thompson, however, held both Fred and the effort with greater affection. "This was a very, very good idea," he said, "the right thing at the right time. Perhaps we had the wrong people. Even if it didn't work as well as it should have, Fred did more things than he realized."

Among Fred Alger's various wagers, perhaps none was as heady as handing over the reins of his company to David Alger in 1995. Typical of Fred, it was no ordinary retirement. He would also absent himself completely from New York and, in a move that many considered shocking, discard his American citizenship.

It was a solution that served a confluence of personal and business needs. For one, as he grew older, and by his own admission, Fred was tiring of the rigors of the business. In March 1995 he remarked, "The last couple of years I've gotten really tired. I'm looking forward to leaving and letting other people do it."

Second, in saying good-bye to America Fred traveled the final mile in securing a strong capital base to the future of his company. New citizenship was available in St. Kitts-Nevis, just beyond Puerto Rico and near Antigua, for an ownership of $150,000 in local property and fees of $50,000. Such a gambit might permit Fred to avoid estate taxes, currently a whopping 55% for those with assets over $3 million. The West Indies island nation levies no income or estate taxes.

Finally, by setting up residence in Geneva, Switzerland, he could distance himself from a rancorous divorce and be well situated to effect his designs of selling the Alger Fund in Europe. He would be returning to familiar and friendly turf. He speaks French fluently and spent many summers in Europe during his youth and when he owned a small château in the food-loving Perigord region of France.

To no one's surprise, many in the investment community looked askance at his plans. One question which was frequently asked was why Fred was taking such a drastic step for a benefit which would accrue only after his death.

"It's not a matter of greed to him. It's a matter of dynasty—making sure that the firm has capital that doesn't have to be taxed," said David Alger. "Also, it probably has something to do with beating the system. Fred doesn't go along in life the way everybody else does. It just doesn't challenge his intellect. He's got to do it differently."

It's not really that extraordinary these days for wealthy Americans to opt out of citizenship to escape excessive estate taxes. There's even strong precedent within the mutual-fund industry. The doyen of international mutual-fund investing, Sir John Templeton, a native Tennesseean, said good-bye to America and set up shop in the Bahamas in 1962. He reportedly sliced more than $100 million off capital gains taxes when he eventually sold his mutual-fund management company to Franklin Resources Inc. for $913 million in October 1992. His aide-de-camp at the Templeton Fund, J. Mark Mobius, also made tracks out of the country by adopting German citizenship and residing in Singapore and Hong Kong, where he is closer to the emerging markets which he covers as a fund manager.

Despite all the practical reasons, there was intense family debate over Fred's determination to give up America and leave the firm. One of his strongest critics was his daughter Hilary, who had spent five challenging years working for his company. "It bothers me that he's leaving the country," she said. "I have all kinds of opinions that he sees as irrelevant. The whole thing could have been handled differently. The rest of us don't care about the family fortune. It's his own dream, so unrelated to us. He thinks he's sacrificing himself for us. We don't want him to sacrifice himself for us. We'd rather he be in the country and pay his taxes."

In his willingness to take a bullet for the firm and ultimately his family, Fred showed how committed he is to the idea of capital retention. Not even the birth of a longed-for grandson, Davison Alger Chung, to his daughter Alexandra in February 1995, could stay his departure. He wasn't scared away by the tough decision, at age 60, to once again reinvent himself, as long as he felt it was necessary to achieve his goals.

David was more forgiving when he mused about Fred's departure. "I'm not sure if it's a bad decision or a good decision. It's his decision. I don't find it morally reprehensible. He may be leaving for all the wrong reasons, but I don't think there is necessarily a downside from his standpoint," he said. "What do you really lose by not being an American citizen in practical terms? Maybe a lot, maybe a little. If the world goes to war, will he become a man without a country?

"As I see my life now, I would much rather live in the U.S. than anywhere else on a permanent basis. I grew up in Europe too. I hate paying taxes too and wish they'd lower the taxes." Clearly Fred was more adamant about avoiding what he saw was an exorbitant and confiscatory levy.

Fred made his move even though, when he left, Congress was racing to redraw the rules to make it tougher for recent and prospective expatriates to avoid paying taxes.

This wasn't a bold venture just for Fred alone. The firm also would be taking

Fred's daughter Hilary joined the firm in 1987 and worked for five years as a
research associate and analyst.

off into uncharted territory—for the first time without him at the helm. While it surprised many intimates that he should depart after so many years of imprinting his personality on the firm, leaving the company to David posed less of a challenge, since for many years he had been in charge of the portfolios and was well versed in the firm's business affairs.

Still, there were feelings of frustration and displeasure at his leaving. "Ideas will percolate for a while. He won't check or seek the advice of others: lawyers, specialists, researchers. No. It's entirely in his own head," said his daughter Hilary. "Then, once he decides something, he'll just do it. 'Well, I think it sounds like a good idea, let's just do it.' Then he'll draw lessons from it when he doesn't necessarily know what the lessons are."

"He has incredibly strong opinions and really won't take other people's advice," she concluded. "He doesn't know when he doesn't know something. He doesn't know when he needs help or another point of view."

That may have been the case in the early years when Fred displayed an all-too-evident disregard, some say disrespect, for the Wall Street establishment that often sent Bill Scheerer reeling toward some act of damage control. Fred didn't seem to care that his bravery had consequences.

In public and through the media, for example, he would go out of his way to thumb his nose at those who were regarded as industry elders. In one instance Fred locked horns with no less than Howard Stein, the powerful chairman of the billion-dollar Dreyfus Corporation, who was promoting the elimination of the income tax on dividends and the raising of taxes on capital gains to be on par with earned income.

Fred openly rebuked him in Robert Metz's "Market Place" column in *The New York Times* on November 21, 1977, for a "serious ideological error which will reduce job-creating investment." Fred argued instead for the reduction of the 40% maximum capital-gains tax to "pre–Nixonian 25% levels" and the elimination of a holding period. Fred reasoned that with Stein's proposal, new and fast-growing companies which need access to the capital markets would be deprived of the "incentive represented by the tax differential between capital gains and wages." He swore by the supply-side credo of tax reduction as an instant panacea which would stimulate investment, boost trading and financial employment, and result in "positive changes in sentiment" about the economy.

"Fred has rubbed people the wrong way," said Bill Scheerer, who shared another revealing incident, in which Fred was at odds with Cy Lewis of Bear Stearns & Company. "We gave Cy Lewis a block of stock to sell. We were quite new in the business, in the late sixties. Fred didn't like the execution, and he really chewed out Cy. I said, 'Fred, maybe he did give us a bad execution, but you don't talk to a guy like Cy Lewis like that because he's a big man on the Street and we're newcomers and we have to watch our relationships.' I had a hard time convincing Fred that he was wrong."

John Cleland offered the story of a feud between Fred and Muriel Siebert, who in 1967 became the first woman to own a seat on the New York Stock Exchange. Originally an aviation specialist at Bache & Co., where she started on Wall Street in 1954, Muriel Siebert claims to have pioneered discount commissions since May Day. When Fred knew her, the bulk of her business was in "pick-up" orders, which meant that if she recommended a stock to an investment firm, it would normally ask her to buy it for them.

"Mickey Siebert was particularly close to Jim Ryder, the founder of Ryder Systems," explained Cleland, "and spent a good deal of effort cultivating Fred and getting him to take a fairly large position in Ryder. She felt that Fred never paid her commissions for that information, being the primary influence for getting him to buy Ryder for his accounts. Fred bought the stock from another brokerage firm.

"One might say that Fred was not above using sources of information when they were available to him, and was never worried about paying compensation to the people providing him with the information. Whether they deserved to be paid or not, they probably thought they did, and resented the fact that Fred used them."

In a sort of roundabout payback, and to her credit, Muriel Siebert, who today runs a well-publicized and thriving retail brokerage business, belatedly cadged Fred's brokerage strategy and made it the focal point of a short-lived promotional campaign in 1995. Her Siebert PowerTrade touted better executions as "an enhanced service enabling sophisticated individual investors to obtain a better price on their stock trades . . . for the advantages of institutional traders to get a price between prevailing bid and asked spread." Sound familiar?

When Fred was first starting out, many in the industry saw him as a precocious kid with a problem personality. Many of his contacts and clients assumed he was speaking down to them. And his self-confidence was seen as either intimidating or grating. But he was more misunderstood than actually errant in his ways.

The unfiltered take on Fred was that he was seldom immodest and usually sharp with his opinions. This, combined with the isolation and independence of his self-contained firm, and the fact that he was making a lot of money—which always brings out the buzzards—gave Wall Street an excuse to be less approving of Fred than he deserved.

"Fred has always been controversial and never been well liked as part of the Wall Street community," observed John Cleland about Fred's early exploits on the Street. "Fred played by his own rules. He never wanted to be a member of the club, never made much effort to play by the unspoken rules of the club. To some extent, I think he trampled on some fairly large egos over the years. Fred was always one to look down his nose on the poor mortals who were not as smart as he was, and he was not above telling them so."

He added, "Fred has made no shortage of enemies along the way and attracted a great deal of envy. He has also earned a lot of admiration and gratitude from the people who have worked with him. I am in that camp.

"The same things that make him so great are the same things that have caused him a lot of problems. He's his own worst enemy."

10 ⟨⟩

His Brother's Keeper

D AVID DEWEY ALGER was born in San Diego on December 15, 1943. An infant in wartime America, he did not see his parents' grand home in Grosse Pointe until his father finished active military duty in 1946.

David admits to a pampered childhood. Yet growing up, he viewed his parents distantly as "absentee landlords" and was essentially brought up by the family servants. Special among them was Mary McCrone, who started out as a housemaid but became his nanny after a year or so. "She raised me," he said. "I saw my parents as fantasy figures, deities who appeared occasionally; I really had very little interaction with them."

Like Fred, he was relatively solitary as a child. "I was put out to play like a cat and wandered around the property essentially by myself from morning till night," said David. What interested him most, and likely by genetic transfer, were things military. "Ninety percent of my pastime was consumed with playing games of war and combat, soldiers or cowboys and Indians."

David's first vivid childhood memories date from his ninth birthday when the family moved to Belgium for his father's diplomatic posting. The Algers arrived at Le Havre on the SS *United States,* the most elegant of the luxury transatlantic ships and the favorite of presidents, royalty and movie stars. It was the speediest too, making the journey in four days and nine hours, about half the time of other ships. The Algers were received by a "tremendous throng of press and dignitaries," with all the pomp and ceremony befitting the representative of the country that had saved Europe.

The imposing embassy compound on 27 avenue du Régent and the luxurious, formal ambassador's residence attached to it—newly constructed and whose first occupants were the Algers—turned out to be a fantastic playground for young David. Several incidents from this time have become family lore:

Once he hit the Spanish ambassador's wife on the head with a dart gun and got into "an amazing amount of trouble." Another one of his darts found a Belgian *gendarme* guarding the compound.

But the story that made it back to the *Detroit News* society pages described him as a proper little gentleman. "When the wife of the ranking German diplomat, named Pfeiffer, came to call, and they couldn't find a common language, Mrs. Alger summoned young son David to sing the Pfeiffer beer jingle. The lady 'ambassadress,' hearing her name over and over, was charmed, and the ice was broken. Mrs. Alger is proud of David for taking top class honors at his Belgian school. He's now bilingual, wants to be a nuclear physicist." Perhaps his academic prowess emerged after he was admonished to "curtail his childish tendencies."

David found it "exciting and odd to live my life as an American child in Europe." Instruction in Belgian schools was carried out in French, and David was kept back a grade to learn the language and catch up on other subjects when the curriculum was ahead of American standards. "I was daunted by extraordinary academic and disciplinary requirements," David elaborated. "No recess. No sports. I was totally lost for six months until I learned to speak French. I had to cross my sevens or be hit on the head with a ruler or for just about every infraction. I'm surprised I didn't sustain permanent brain damage."

In Europe David grew close to his mother. "She took an actual interest in me, treated me as a small adult rather than a child, with long lectures about seventeenth- and eighteenth-century furniture and how many mistresses the king had," which he later thought "quite inappropriate for a child of ten."

During two summers between the academic years, David boarded at the exclusive Institut le Rosey in Rolle, Switzerland, where Europe's upper-class children are still sent for their studies. "Originally I went there to improve my French, then to better my English," he said.

As the baby of the family, David was his mother's favorite. For her he could do no wrong. Their father doted on daughter Suzy, the firstborn. Fred was lost in the middle.

David spent his formative years in Europe apart from Fred, except when he visited during the American holidays. The nine-year age difference increased the geographical distance. "Fred was very wild, stayed out all night, partying and going to nightclubs. I never saw him," said David. "The last year we were abroad, mother was, as usual, irritated with Fred's wild behavior." So she punished him by giving him the task of teaching David American history and training him physically in order to turn him back into an American kid. "I was out of shape and never did any sports," David admitted. "By mutual agreement we canceled the history lesson, but Fred thought it was a good idea to make me run, even though I had no desire for it."

For his exercises Fred took David to a large rectangular park in front of a girlfriend's apartment and sent David racing with the caution that he was timing his laps from the overhead balcony. David figured out a way to trick Fred and save himself some exertion by resting behind some bushes at the far end of the field and progressively reducing his wait time to show Fred an improvement in his speed. Eventually David told Fred that he had been "cheating all this time, and if he had paid attention he would have noticed." Upon which Fred disclosed his own deception, which was that he always took a nap while David was out exerting himself. He could have cared less about David's performance. "Both of us were scamming each other from a very early age," David declared.

Back in America, David followed Fred into Milton Academy, starting in the seventh grade. "It was a nightmare of enormous proportions for the first couple of years," David admitted. "I was unprepared for an American life and unused to living in a boarding school instead of an embassy, where I had a butler to pull out my chair for me at dinner. I was totally unathletic and very European."

But David developed quickly at Milton. By the ninth grade he was six feet tall and weighed 180 pounds. Playing both offensive guard and defensive linebacker positions, David became a football hero. He could even have played running back, since he set school records for the 100-yard dash. Obviously his running regimen with Fred had not been completely wasted.

Coming easily by his intelligence, David succeeded in schoolwork without much effort. He was never driven; he never had to be. Like other adolescent boys he was mostly interested in playing sports, chasing girls and having a good time. "When David was brought up, Daddy was drinking very badly and Mummy was dying," said his sister, Suzy. "He could run and do whatever he wanted."

David took the path of his grandfather and father into Harvard College. Freed from the strict boarding school environment, David saw Harvard as a place for an education in college fun and parties. Backgammon was his favorite pastime, and he was an excellent student of the game.

Still David claimed that "the things I learned at Harvard really enabled me to succeed in business, but they weren't what you would advise your children to learn." The endless games of backgammon instructed him about odds and risk taking, while cramming math into his head. Since he was lax with his course-work, he did most of his studying in the last two weeks before exams. "This taught me how to work under a great deal of pressure," he said, "and since Harvard favors elegantly written essays and I didn't have too many facts, it taught me how to write well as a means of getting by." He graduated in 1966 with a major in American history.

After college David faced the options of working for a year or so before entering graduate school, which made him vulnerable to the military draft and the prospect of seeing action in Vietnam, or pursuing his MBA directly at the University of Michigan. The choice was obvious for many in his generation, who were looking to avoid the draft; for an Alger, given the influence of ancestors who

David Alger's yearbook photo at Milton Academy.

had vigorously pursued war as their contribution to the nation, the decision was considerably more complex. In opting to attend Michigan, where Fred likewise earned his business degree, David became the first of his line on both sides to shun the armed services. He would save his budding militaristic impulses for business.

David expected to breeze through business school just as he had at college, but Michigan was much tougher than Harvard. He did poorly in calculus and economics, which he had never taken at Harvard. Accounting and statistics were "unbelievably difficult." His remedial classes were attended mostly by undergraduates. David's deficiencies could have had serious consequences. "In those days at the Michigan Business School, if you flunked a course in the first term, you were out without any recourse. It got very scary," he admitted.

David finally shed his indifference to studies after convincing an accounting professor to let him by with a C minus. "Then I really got down to work, and terribly hard." The rest of his grades were high, and he graduated in 1968 near the top of his class.

"Business school was a wonderful experience. I am extremely indebted to the University of Michigan because they took a really lazy liberal arts major and converted him into a really sharp, hardworking businessman in two years," said David. "As a state resident, at that time the tuition was eight hundred or sixteen hundred dollars a year. I've subsequently tried to make it up by gifts to the university because I feel they really gave me so much for so little."

Since their mother died when David was just 18 and his father when he was 23, it was natural for Fred, nine years his senior, to stand in for their parents. As a father figure Fred held much sway over his brother, especially in the direction of his career.

It was Fred who inspired David to get involved in the stock market. During his junior year at Harvard, David had his mind set on becoming a criminal lawyer like TV icon Perry Mason. Though, like Fred during the summers, he apprenticed at First of Michigan, he had never considered investing as a career.

"The event that caused me to go into the business involved Fred," David explained. "By 1965, Fred had founded the company and become quite famous. I had a girlfriend and we wanted to visit New York together. Fred and Eleanor were going to be away, so I asked him if I could stay in their apartment. He said fine, as long as I slept on the couch in the living room."

The trouble was, David failed to mention his girlfriend, and instead of the living room they took up sleeping in Fred's bedroom. When Eleanor discovered this, she chewed him out. Embarrassed by his wife's upbraiding and unable to apologize for it, Fred "did the next best thing, which was to give me a stock tip, McLain Industries. He said it was going to triple."

David continued, "I didn't have much money, but my girlfriend had twenty thousand dollars, so we put it in McLain with the understanding that I would get half of the profits. The stock went up a lot, and I collected. I thought, 'Gee, this is so easy. Why would anyone want to be a lawyer?' I made more money in a month than most young lawyers at that time made in a year. So I immediately directed my plans toward the stock market."

Just as Fred had whetted David's appetite for stock market riches, he helped him along in the money-management business after Michigan.

For a young man out to conquer Wall Street, the hottest firm to join in 1968 was Donaldson, Lufkin & Jenrette. It had set up shop as an investment boutique with a half-million-dollar investment in 1959 and had grown to managing $600 million in discretionary accounts, primarily through the "growth of mutual funds and the tremendous roll-over into equity investments by the insurance companies and pension funds."

Although David was "dazzled and impressed" by DLJ, he took a job at Irving Trust Co. instead. It was Fred's advice which guided his decision. "'Don't work for DLJ because you don't know anything, and the first thing you'll do is screw up and you'll lose your job, and that will be the end of your career. Get a job at a bank, where you can learn at their expense,'" said David, summarizing Fred's instructions. "I was irritated by that advice because I wanted to be one of the big stars at DLJ," he added.

Irving Trust was just then getting involved in active money management and building a hive of new MBAs to form its research department. Although David called that entry experience "wonderful" because of the latitude it provided and the chance to follow leading stock sectors, like oil, retailing and special situations, he remained at the bank for only a year. With his discovery and recommendation of fast-growing Pro Golf, "the Callaway Golf of its day," which bounced up quickly following his call, David was snatched away by the house of Lombard, Vitalis, Pagannuci & Nelson, which was attempting to clone the success of DLJ, as were other research boutiques in that period of undiscounted commissions.

While DLJ had its roots in Harvard, LVPN's heritage was at Dartmouth, where Dick Lombard, Paul Pagannuci and Bill Vitalis had met as undergraduates. The firm was a high-rolling, fast-paced environment that celebrated the youth culture of its analysts. "The brokerage business was fabulously profitable, and the institutional market just taking off. It was a free-flowing, wild-frontier-town atmosphere," said David.

As a special situations analyst, David got lucky with Milgo Electronics Corp., one of the early leaders in electronics manufacturing and the hottest stock on the American Stock Exchange in 1969. As the analyst who discovered the company for Lombard, David received his first shimmering moment in the Wall Street limelight by way of a *Fortune* magazine feature.

Victories can be fleeting in the stock market, and in the summer of 1969 many of Wall Street's successes started unraveling during a vicious slump which sent growth stocks reeling. David missed the worst of it by serving for a handful of months in the Army Reserves so he could retain his civilian status. On his return the climate was still dampened by weak investor sentiment. "Lombard was beginning to have problems and became less lively and not much fun, so I started looking around," said David.

His timing was impeccable. A couple of years after he left LVPN, Pagannuci and Vitalis sold their stake in the company to Dick Lombard, Wally Nelson and several other shareholders, and the firm was renamed Lombard, Nelson and McKenna. The partnership didn't last and was absorbed in a merger with New York brokerage Dominick & Dominick Inc.

David's next offer looked like the opportunity of a lifetime.

On July 1, 1970, Glore Forgan Saats, Inc., a major old-line investment-banking institution merged with Francis I. duPont & Co., then third in size among the nation's brokerage firms, after Merrill Lynch and Bache & Co. Forgan's 20 branches and $19 million in capital combined with duPont's 95 offices and $62.5 million to make F.I. duPont Glore Forgan & Co. the largest brokerage partnership on Wall Street.

Just 26 years old at the time and on the strength of his single hit with Milgo, David was recruited to be the new entity's director of research. The job came with all the trappings of power, and to entice David to take it, he was guided through what would have been his spacious office on 100 Wall Street, with an adjacent private dining room that came with a personal chef. They were offering him a blank check to fashion a research department with analysts, just like himself, who were young, hip, aggressive and smart. It was more than he could have wished for.

David, however, refused the fat job that could have made his name on Wall Street based on the fact that "any company stupid enough to hire me and give me my own dining room because of Milgo" was surely capable of greater blunders.

As it turned out, he was quite perceptive. Had he taken the princely position, his tenure at the firm would have been brief. Glore Forgan saw duPont primarily as a financial backer that wouldn't interfere with its management—a perception that turned out to be incorrect. It didn't take long for the merger to disintegrate. By August the firm took in a $15 million capital infusion from a group of Texas investors headed by computer millionaire Henry Ross Perot. In 1971 Perot–controlled PHMFG Corp. had to cough up another $10 million to rescue the firm from collapse, and it eventually put up another $30 million for a greater than 80% stake in the firm. But no amount could stave off bankruptcy, the only one among Perot's numerous business ventures.

In January 1971, instead of a cushy top-level job at a leading brokerage firm, David Alger opted for a junior position at his brother's firm. The year earlier Fred Alger had signed up as a registered investment adviser and, with assets on the rise, was eager for fresh analysts to man the research desks.

"I very consciously didn't want to work for Fred," David revealed. "I don't think he very consciously wanted me to work for him either." But there were obvious and compelling synergies that attracted David to the firm, and for the first time, the brothers would get to know each other as adults in business together.

Though David was still green, he came on by asking for a shot at managing a planned hedge fund. "Fred became very angry with me," recalled David. "I remember his saying, 'This is real work. You don't just show up and automatically become good at the stock market. This is a trade you learn after many years of beating your head on the floor.' That stuck with me a long time."

Fred recalled the incident less forcefully. "I didn't take his idea seriously," he said. "In those days you couldn't be a member of the New York Stock Exchange and charge a fee based on performance. We had left that structure behind in 1970 when we became members in order to finance our own research."

Another early pronouncement from Fred also hit the mark. "'Marine sergeants are better at their job than you are at yours,' Fred admonished, 'and they work harder.' I found that very insulting at the time, but I've come to recognize that (a) it is probably true, at least when he said it, and (b) it is important to respect someone who does something very well by working hard at it."

One would think that Fred might go easy on his brother, but in fact, quite the opposite occurred. David's initiation in the firm was tougher than for the others. Analyst Bob Emerson recounted a time when "Fred brought David in to dress him down and had the whole research department come in and watch." Later Bob said to David, "He could criticize you in private. Why would he want an audience?" David replied partly in jest, "To protect himself. He knows I have a black belt in karate."

At times his experiences at Fred Alger reminded David of their boyhood relationship. "Once when we were children Fred wired me up to the transformer of his train set, told me it was a lie detector and said that if I didn't tell the truth he would electrocute me. His questions were macabre, like 'Do you really love Mother?' I was so scared that even if I said yes, I would get electrocuted. I remember that as a particularly terrifying afternoon.

"He used to find different ways to persecute me, and I remember getting angry and breaking one of his airplane models when he went off to boarding school."

Despite Fred's harsh handling, and in some way perhaps because of it, David made Fred his sole mentor. "I owe my entire outlook on the stock market to Fred," he declared emphatically, "from what makes stocks go up to how to deal with people. In some sense he's also a role model for me because he's worked really hard in his professional life.

"When I first joined the firm I thought the business was very flashy. I believed that great flashes of raw intelligence were all that was necessary in order to succeed. But basically this is a business where you have to conscientiously apply yourself to the process, day in and day out. And eventually you learn how to do it. The idea that you have to just keep plugging away is very much at the cornerstone of Fred's philosophy of life, and I've always tried to emulate that." As a disciple of Fred's theories on investing, David seized on his brother's ideas and built them up into his own principles.

When Lester Colbert, his old friend and board member of the Castle Convertible Fund, described Fred as a "visionary at getting the right people to work for him," he certainly had David on his mind. For David completed the circle of partners who carried the firm forward through its complex development in the seventies. It was David who fortified Fred Alger with his accent on technology stocks and, long before its impact in the eighties, began to compose and implement the Alger system of stock selection with the help of computers.

One of David's earliest contributions came from his knowledge of the cable television industry and his prior involvement in an Ann Arbor cable system. For two years before David entered the picture, Fred was actively promoting TelePrompTer, then the largest cable television franchise in America, and concurrently developing a pioneering tax shelter called CI Associates to feed off one of its operations.

"Even back in 1969 Fred saw that cable television would be the wave of the future," observed George Boggio. "Fred's genius was creating all these different schemes, and CI Associates was one of the best."

Fred unabashedly called it "the greatest tax shelter of all time." CI was a 20-man limited partnership with Fred as general partner, designed to extract the benefits of depreciation and tax credits for losses from the capital-intensive effort of constructing TelePrompTer's cable TV franchise in West Palm Beach, Florida.

Fred explained it like this: "Whereas it was readily known that by building a cable system or something similar one could deduct depreciation and interest, it was generally unappreciated that since such operations typically remained unprofitable for several years, one might also use the operating losses as a shelter." Fred's twist was finding a way to do this. It worked by TelePrompTer's loaning CI the money for building the system, paying the interest and covering operating losses as a way of manipulating earnings. "At no point did anyone have money in it," said Fred. "We were getting write-offs and investment tax credits; and in those days the marginal tax rate was fifty percent. Our write-offs and investment tax credits were greater than two to one. The tax savings were paying for the entire investment."

Bill Scheerer, one of the CI partners, said that "less than one million dollars was involved in the borrowed money supplied by TelePrompTer." He described it as "a most complex deal. The only one who must have understood it was the lawyer who drew up the document, and of course Fred. I just raised the money."

The race is on. David Alger, near left, emerged as a track star in prep school.

Fred continued, "The stock then was around thirty dollars. The workout at the end was that after six, seven or eight years, whatever was left in assets we'd balance with an offsetting amount of debt. Then we'd sell the corporation to TelePrompTer for shares and take a certain amount of shares to retire the debt, leaving us with a profit." The actual number of shares depended on a stock price ranging from $30 down to $15.

Said David, "Fred was extremely enamored of the cable-television industry and its potential, as was I. At that time the tax rules were such that cable television franchises threw off enormous amounts of non-cash write-offs in terms of depreciation and investment tax credits. You could have write-offs of eight to one or ten to one and leverage it up tremendously. Since there was no recapture, you could recover your investment from tax savings in a very short time. It was a great deal whether or not the cable system survived."

The plan went without a hitch for a couple of years—TelePrompTer secured the Manhattan cable franchise, moved into other media areas, and its stock was trading on the American Stock Exchange for $74 in November 1970—until TelePrompTer's chairman and president Irving B. Kahn was indicted in 1971 for bribing city officials to win the cable rights in Johnstown, Pennsylvania. Fred Alger was caught off guard by the event. "When the news came out, the stock dropped twenty percent in one week," he said. From that point on, the company and its stock price never completely made it back, and the promising CI shelter suffered in the aftermath.

Although Kahn surrendered his TelePrompTer titles in 1971 to battle the bribery and conspiracy charges, he held on to the voting rights of 500,000 shares and remained as a consultant in the firm until 1976. Months after his resignation, his compensation from the firm was unaltered: up to $225,000 annually depending on profits and the use of the company limousine and its corporate apartment in West Palm Beach.

David recalled, "We all went down to Irving Kahn's trial to watch him defend himself. In those days we didn't have very many stocks, so we paid a lot of attention to the few we had." That didn't keep Kahn from getting convicted or save TelePrompTer from going down the drain. A noisy shareholder revolt ensued, led by Washington Redskins' owner Jack Kent Cooke, who held 509,000 shares, the largest position in the company. Hughes Aircraft, which owned 168,000 shares, also sought to retrieve its voting rights.

When TelePrompTer tentatively survived the Kahn affair, Fred Alger implemented a novel promotion to drum up attention in the company, which David was responsible for producing. Having followed the company on a research basis and with his background in cable, David was charged with writing a comprehensive investment report on the industry, centered on TelePrompTer, which the firm could then advertise and market to the trade. His efforts took the shape of the TelePrompTer book, a slim, 60-page hardbound volume printed on newsprint that touted the upcoming glowing age of cable television and was available exclusively from Fred Alger & Co.

"Somewhere along the way we got this wacky idea of trying to sell research for hard dollars," said David. The company purchased a full-page ad in *The Wall Street Journal*, costing $30,000, to offer the book along with five years of updates on the cable industry for an astronomical $10,000 or $30,000 worth of commission business.

Five hundred books were printed in all, but no more than ten copies were eventually sold. The SEC wanted the book for free, but Fred insisted that it pay $10,000. "Fred always saw the SEC as obstructionist. They were a thorn in his side most of the time," explained George Boggio. "Our lawyers finally said we had to give it to them."

The TelePrompTer publication was barely worth the effort and just "another one of Fred's off-the-wall, very unusual, unique marketing ideas," David proposed. "The cable industry never got where it was supposed to go," Fred admitted. "Still it was a fun idea."

More than fun, the book contained a lot of valuable information and prescient insight on the cable industry, and included perhaps the first use of the word *superhighway* in reference to electronic communication.

"In those days cable TV was only conceived of as a way to get better off-the-air reception of community channels," David elucidated. "The FCC was still trying to decide whether it would be allowed to import distant signals from stations outside the normal market. The whole idea of pay TV was unheard of."

Despite Fred Alger's efforts, TelePrompTer stock and the company never caught on after Kahn. At its best, in fiscal 1972 the stock sold at $45, or 52 times earnings. Its worst level in 1974 was $1.50. A *Money* magazine feature on Fred, "Return of the Gunslinger" by Gretchen Morgenson in November 1986, called it an "ignominious strikeout."

Another sidelight of TelePrompTer involved Hubert J. Schlafly, its vice president of research and development after Kahn, who went on to become its president. "Fred was having a vigorous phone conversation with Schlafly," David recounted. "I don't remember what the conversation was about, but Fred was screaming that the guy said something or didn't do something. All of a sudden there was this clunk on the other end of the line. We thought he'd hung up on us, but he had fainted. Oh, my God, I thought, Fred gave this guy a heart attack!

"TelePrompTer was ultimately taken over by Westinghouse," said David. "The stock never fulfilled the promise which I portrayed for it when I wrote the book. However, I was right about the industry. It did work out to be this great glorious industry that we now know, and our predictions of penetration were well exceeded.

We just didn't have quite the right vehicle." Consequently this yielded inferior results for CI Associates.

"Then the 1974 stock market crash came along, leading the stock down to five dollars," Fred said about CI's conclusion. "At that point we wouldn't have enough stock to pay the debt according to the agreements. The whole deal had to be refigured, which it was, and which took a lot of time and effort. The partnership expired in 1991 and we got a whole bunch of cash, but most of the cash went to pay taxes. However, we received all the write-offs, and the partners made money on an after-tax basis."

Fred was in the right industry at the wrong time. "If Irving Kahn had been someone else and the stock went to fifty or a hundred dollars instead of five, we'd have made a fortune," Fred added. "The workout for cable TV was that way, except we were ahead of the game and took up with the wrong partner."

Bill Scheerer said that CI Associates was finally liquidated in 1993. "In the end it was no bonanza. Our equity position simply repaid investors enough to cover taxes on capital gains realized at a fifty percent tax rate ," he said.

Another CI partner Joe Reich recalled, "Fred was the first person I knew to verbalize the potential of cable television. The deal with CI Associates and

Alger East (New York) battled Alger West (New Jersey) in a softball match which was the highlight of the company's annual picnic during the early eighties.

TelePrompTer was not a success because he backed the wrong horse. Still it was a hell of an idea to be investing in cable twenty-five years ago."

In between his first and second years at Michigan's business school David Alger married Roxana Scoville. Their daughter, Roxana Scoville Alger, was born in New York on October 24, 1972. Two years after that they separated and subsequently divorced.

David met his current wife, Josefina Romañach, on Independence Day 1975. She was a high-powered executive at Chase Bank and the "brilliant" daughter of an influential Cuban architect. They were married in October the following year. "Josie's wise and smart and very good for David," said Alger board's Arthur Dubow. On February 20, 1980, Cristina Alger was born to them.

For those observant of historical conjunctions and karmic coincidences, Josie's Cuban heritage summons up David's great-grandfather's role in the Spanish-American War in that country.

David Alger inherited Russell Alger's verbal eloquence and command of speech making. He relishes standing behind a podium and is well regarded for his oratory. He has a way with words on paper as well. According to Bill Scheerer, "David writes beautifully." According to Bob Emerson, "David, in terms of verbal gymnastics, can sound like Tom Stoppard. He is capable of the wildest, most brilliant flights of verbal fancy of anyone I've known in my life."

David Alger looks rugged and strong even in a business suit, perhaps from his sports, tennis and squash and all that early training in tae kwon do. He's gregarious, quick-witted and positive in his outlook on life.

David's colleagues were unanimous in describing his volatile personality, especially when he was younger. He had a short fuse and could explode in a flash. "David is more mercurial than Fred," said Greg Duch. "He flies off the handle quicker. But when he realizes he's wrong, he is quick to apologize. I'm not sure that Fred would ever apologize."

Bob Emerson confessed, "David and I have a strange relationship, in that I didn't particularly enjoy working for him, but he's a very amusing, verbally gifted guy and a fascinating conversationalist, very smart. An erratic, volatile personality, but very colorful and pretty good fun. Like his brother, over time he's a good investor."

Irwin Schwartz testified, "David is very emotional. I used to hug him when he got out of hand. He needed a hug, that's what he needed. And he would calm right down or come into my office for a chat." By David's admission, Irwin provided a necessary calming influence for him at work.

When David asked his wife for her take on what drove him, she observed, "It certainly isn't money . . . it must be winning." David tried to put that a nicer way, but ended up agreeing that it was "pretty much true."

In business, "more than a trading game, it's war with him," said portfolio manager Ron Tartaro. "He likes to be proven right on everything that we do. He takes the wins and losses very seriously and personally. The idea of winning is what makes him tick."

One anecdote about David's competitiveness, involving his behavior during the short-lived Alger annual company picnic, is recalled with considerable relish within the firm. The first year, 1982, he was the pitcher for the analysts and traders of Alger East in the softball match against the back-office and administration crew at Alger West. David nearly got into a brawl with an entire fire department for usurping the field beyond its allotted time. "They looked at us as a bunch of four-eyed Wall Streeters and saw us as sort of wimpy," said David. On that basis, and stimulated by a "bit of beer," they refused to relinquish the field and laughed at the Alger protests.

David finally marched to the pitcher's mound and disrupted their game, "whereupon he was immediately surrounded by forty-five hefty firefighters who didn't know he was David Alger or couldn't have cared much," according to Rosemary Kiernan. There was no brawling—only a piercing exchange of words before the firemen abandoned the field. David explained, "I finally got a little angry and lost my temper. I guess I might have taken them on, but nothing happened. We got the field, so it was effective."

In the second picnic, 1983, it was real hot, a scorcher of a day. David was pitching, and Arthur Simon was at bat. His first pitch cracked off Artie's bat and popped David right in the kisser. "Artie was afraid he would get fired." said Rosemary.

In 1984, the third picnic, David didn't even get a chance to play. He twisted his ankle while stepping off a sidewalk curb, and both David and Fred left the scene in an ambulance.

Like Fred, David frequently applies battlefield analogies to running the business and to selecting stocks that perform well. "I think of the business in terms of military strategy," he said. "One of my great hobbies is medieval history, which is largely military in nature. My years of martial arts training have also given me a martial, if not a military bent."

David's pull toward warfare goes further back in time than his illustrious forebear in the Civil War. The War of the Roses in fifteenth century England is where it all began. For, if he's to be believed, he imagines himself to be the modern reincarnation of Edward IV, the first monarch from the House of York.

So who was this king whom David once was, and what might be their resemblance?

Edward IV, the great-grandson of Edward III and elder brother to Richard III, was born on April 28, 1442. He was crowned king after defeating in battle his rival from the House of Lancaster, Henry VI.

But Edward's secret marriage in 1464 to commoner Elizabeth Woodville won him the enmity of Woodville's cousin, the powerful Richard Neville, Earl of Warwick. Neville defected to the Lancastrian camp, which was exiled in France, and formed a military alliance with Henry's wife, Margaret of Anjou, to return Henry to England's throne. They were successful in this, and Edward was forced to flee to the Netherlands in October 1470.

The manner in which Edward reacted to this defeat, as well as his military cunning and courage in regaining his crown barely a year after he was deposed, is the basis of David's identification with him.

On the continent, against all odds, Edward managed to enlist the support of the powerful Duke of Burgundy. Barely six months later he defeated Warwick in the Battle of Barnett. A month after that, in May 1471, he routed Henry's forces at the Battle of Tewkesbury, killing his young son, Edward. Henry VI was assassinated on the day that Edward entered London to reclaim the kingdom.

David's impassioned retelling makes these distant events thrillingly alive. "To say that all hope was lost was an understatement. Yet Edward managed to convince the Duke of Burgundy that if he was supported in an invasion of England, this would head off an Anglo-French alliance against him.

"So the duke equipped him with maybe a thousand men and a few ships to sail back to England. Landing in the north, he proceeded south. He was so immensely charismatic that as he marched south, people rallied to his banner. He was one of the great generals of all time. He had the ability to move men quickly and was also tremendously lucky in battle.

"After defeating his former ally and cousin in the Battle of Barnett, he wielded his army around to cut off the fleeing Margaret of Anjou and only a month later— which was fast in medieval times—faced her off at the Battle of Tewkesbury. He eliminated all his enemies in one quick, emphatic stroke.

"The thing that was so impressive about it was that a lot of lesser men would have given up. Everybody around him was disillusioned, disheartened and unwilling to go on. Yet people just naturally gravitated to him, and he was able to accomplish this amazing comeback."

Edward's dark side manifested largely in his tyrannical second rule, which ended at his death on April 9, 1483, at the age of 40. In that 12-year reign he enriched himself by confiscating his enemies' estates and investing that money with London merchants.

The postscript to his story is well known through William Shakespeare's *Richard III*. Richard, Duke of Gloucester usurped the throne from Edward's son, Edward V, after imprisoning, then killing him and his brother in the Tower of London. Before ascending to the throne on July 6, 1483, Richard had coerced the Church and Parliament to declare Edward's marriage to Woodville invalid and their sons illegitimate.

"Edward was never at his best during any of the good times. He was always at his best with his back against the wall and could battle back," observed David knowingly. "The flaw in his character was that when things were going well, he tended to get a little too involved with the ladies and also make decisions of a personal nature that were not always the most well thought out. He also had his own brother, the Duke of Clarence, put to death by drowning him in a vat of malmsey." Malmsey is the darkest, sweetest type of Madeira.

David concluded, "The point of this is the thrill of pulling your troops, marching them forward, winning and conquering against the odds. The parallel here is inheriting this medium-sized money-management firm and building it up, in what is left of my productive lifetime, into a really big money-management firm, just on the force of will and personal charisma."

Addressing his wife's perceptions about his motives, David added, "Would I like to be the richest guy in the world? Yeah. But I kinda view money more as a way of keeping score."

If Alger clients are thrown off by the presence of a fire-breathing Edward IV as the head of the company that manages their investments, they should remember that performance is what counts, and David's record—like his hero's—is nothing short of spectacular.

Following a rough patch in the late eighties, the firm's comeback was sparked by David's direction of the Small Cap Fund to the number-one spot among mutual funds in 1989 with a gain of 64.54%. Once again the Alger name was up in lights. For the first time assets started flowing into the dormant mutual funds. Excitement returned to the company. David had the hot hand, and *Business Week* heralded him in its Christmas 1989 issue as the "Best Equity Fund Manager" in the country.

The Alger Small Cap portfolio had started 1989 strong. With only about $4.4 million in assets, it sprinted ahead of the mutual-fund pack in the first quarter with a burst of 20.21%. The fund had barely acquired enough shareholders, 1,000 investors, to merit inclusion in the newspaper fund listings. Kaufmann Fund, which had been the winner the previous year, and also small with $12.2 million in assets, hugged the number-two position. The relatively large, $290 million, 20th Century Ultra fund trailed in fourth place. The country's biggest fund, Fidelity's Magellan, with $9.67 billion in assets was up only 9.52%. The S&P 500 shuffled forward 7.13% and the average fund returned 6.6%. Restricting investments to companies with a market capitalization under $1 billion, the fund held just 35 positions, including the frozen-yogurt franchise TCBY Enterprises and Office Depot.

Small Cap slipped to number seven in the second quarter rankings but was still second overall for the first half of the year.

Up a whopping 69.64% at the end of the third quarter, it decisively reclaimed the lead and stayed there till the end of the year. In the third quarter Small Cap also sported the winning performance for the previous twelve months, ahead by 75.58%, and its assets swelled to $12.8 million. Close behind David's 12-month performance was former Alger analyst Tom Marsico's Janus Twenty Fund. David's winning proclamation—"The growth style is coming back into favor, and we're having a very good year for our clients"—found its way into numerous publications.

Despite its final-quarter slump of 2.69%, Small Cap marginally beat out second-place United Services Gold Shares, which was up 64.73% for the year. The fund took the award for top small-company growth fund as well as the overall number-one ranking. Among the mutual-fund winners that year, only Alger Small Cap was aggressively in growth equities; the rest were either invested in gold, natural-resource commodities, utilities or overseas stocks. Janus Twenty had dropped out of the winners' circle altogether. The S&P average moved up nearly 32%, and the average U.S. equity fund increased 23.81%. By year's end, Small Cap's assets had nudged up toward $14 million.

"A renaissance of capitalism is sweeping around the world," David proclaimed to his newly adoring investment public. He advised that corporate price-earnings ratios would expand, and that made him extremely bullish about the stock market in 1990. "Instead of looking for undervalued companies, I think the market will begin searching out really good companies that are showing earnings growth," he added. "There is a scarcity value in these companies, so we believe their values will be bid up." Despite his positive forecast, Small Cap sputtered during the year and gained only 6.7%, while the top fund, Phoenix Capital Appreciation, rose 20.5%.

The Street began to wonder if the Alger firm had a subgenius in David. Small Cap's victory had pushed him to the limelight, and for the first time he began grabbing the headlines away from Fred. By every account Fred was pleased with his brother's performance. As

Raging Bull

How to Invest in the Growth Stocks of the 90s

David Alger

David's market visibility began to crystallize, it appeared that he would emerge with his own power and might eventually take over the company.

On the strength of his 1989 ranking, David received a commission from publisher Business One Irwin to put down his investment ideas in a book. Published in December 1991, 100 years after his great-grandfather's personal account of the Spanish-American War, David Alger's *Raging Bull: How to Invest in the Growth Stocks of the '90s* is an incisive explication of the aggressive Alger investment style. Two hundred pages in length, it reveals David's way of defining and evaluating growth stocks during this decade and locates them in the principal sectors of health care, medical technology, semiconductors, data processing, software and communications.

David admitted that writing the book was a difficult process. "I got through Harvard by writing elegant prose, and I flattered myself that this would be nothing more that writing a long term paper that I could dash off over a couple of long weekends and a week or two—a no-brainer.

"I was so flattered about being asked to write a book, I even thought it might be lot of fun and, anyway, it would be good publicity for the firm. Almost all of that, except for the publicity, turned out to be totally wrong. The process turned out to be a nightmare."

Writing in the evenings after work, David completed the first draft in three months. But it was the chore of editing the book which tried his wits. The book was finally done after a year, and about 5,000 copies were printed and distributed, giving a nice public-relations boost to the company.

Writing *Raging Bull* at a time when the stock market was deeply disillusioned by the Gulf War and the Dow Jones was buried under 3,000, David had the temerity to predict that the Industrials would reach 6,000 by the millennium or sooner based on the following seven propositions: the end of the Cold War and reemergence of American confidence, high levels of employment, modest inflation, nominal interest rates, rapidly expanding exports, the elimination of the deficit and rapid technological change.

Alger Small Cap's glories were not left behind in 1989. After its brief drop in 1990, it returned to the top of its class. For the three years ending March 31, 1991, it was above all mutual funds with an average annual return of 33.2%. By May it had $43.7 million in assets in 44 stocks with a weighted average of $354 million in market capitalization. For the year the Small Cap Fund soared nearly 56% versus the S&P 500's gain of about 24%. Its asset size nearly doubled—to $80 million—and it led the load-fund list of small-cap funds with a load-adjusted five-year annual return of 29.5%, eclipsing the S&P's average of 15.4% for the same period. The following year, 1992, Small Cap's assets hit $200 million, and nearly $300 million in 1993.

In mid-year 1994, its assets were poised above $266 million even as its year-to-date performance slouched a bit at 17.6%. Still, David voiced optimism that signs of a slowing economy would trigger a significant bond rally and therefore a resurgence in the stock market. "We're optimistic, we're unconcerned," he said. Although it continued its slide for a loss of 23.7% into July, the fund closed down only 4.62% for the year.

In 1995 Small Cap was up 48.93%, far ahead of the dramatic 37.53% gain in the S&P index. By the second quarter of 1997 its assets had grown to $496 million, and despite a healthy average annual return of 21.11% over the preceding three years, it received a stingy two stars from the Morningstar mutual-fund–rating service.

But the fund received many accolades from other sources in the interim. *Your Money* magazine gave it play in its February/March 1993 issue in an article, "Funds That Can Double Your Money." *Personal Finance* listed it in "The Best Funds for Your Nest Egg" in January 27, 1993. Appearing high in its screening of 250 no-load stock funds, it listed Small Cap's six-year total return through December 31, 1992, at 206.7% versus the S&P 500's performance of 116.5% during the same period. Appropriately, Alger Small Cap has for many years been a part of *Investor's Business Daily*'s Mutual Fund Index.

David is superstitious when it comes to the market. Somewhere above us, he believes, is an arbitrary and unforgiving stock market god who won't tolerate arrogance and excessive jubilation over investment gains and who delights in damaging those who dare to challenge him. So even though David is a fanatic for cars, he has never rewarded himself with the Ferrari he desires for fear of offending that almighty deity. He was tempted after the Small Cap success in 1989, but turned cautious and bought himself a Lotus instead. Perhaps he remembered that three years earlier Dennis Levine, the Wall Street star who fell from grace due to insider trading in 54 deals worth $12.6 million, had just given himself a new bright red Ferrari before he was taken down by the SEC.

In contrast to David, the closest Fred has ever come to acknowledging the fates is the following extended epigram on luck and change. "We've been buyers of change. Rapid change for the better usually comes in rapidly growing companies. Buying change for the better is where money gets made. It produces surprisingly good results. Organizing to get lucky is the serendipitous factor, and you can only get lucky when things are changing rapidly for the better. If you can identify rapid change, chances are you will make a lot of money."

There is a nine-year age difference between Fred and David, and some of the cultural distance between them is generational. The year Fred was born, *It Happened One Night* with Clark Gable ran away with the Oscar derby. When David was born, *Casablanca* starring Humphrey Bogart picked up the Oscar for best picture. Fred went willingly into the Marine Corps. "I was of a generation that believed and still do believe that it's an honor to serve your country in the military," he said. David came from the class that avoided the Vietnam War. At the same time, the distinctions between the brothers are fundamental and apparent in a number of ways that have nothing to do with age.

In a Pythagorean universe, their differing personalities could be measured by numbers. David was born on Wednesday, which is associated with number 5, while Fred came in on Thursday, which is a number 3 day. According to noted numerologist Cheiro, number 3 people are "decidedly ambitious; they are never satisfied in subordinate positions; their aim is to rise in the world, to have control and authority over others. They are excellent in the execution of commands; they love order and discipline in all things; they readily obey orders themselves, but also insist on having their orders obeyed."

Number 5 personalities are "quick in thought and decisions, and impulsive in their actions. They detest any plodding kind of work and seem naturally to drift into all methods of making money quickly. They have a keen sense of making money by inventions and new ideas. They are born speculators, prone to Stock Exchange transactions, and generally are willing and ready to run risks in all they undertake. They have the most wonderful elasticity of character. They rebound quickly from the heaviest blow; nothing seems to affect them for very long."

Then there's the congruous transposition of the last two digits, 4 and 3, in their birth years. By the numbers of their birth dates, they are described by Cheiro as follows: 20 for Fred is "attributed to 'awakening' of new purpose, new plans, new ambitions, the call to action for some great purpose, cause or duty." David's 15, which is also the compound number for the alphabet of his name, is "peculiarly associated with 'good talkers,' often with eloquence, gifts of music and art, and a dramatic personality, combined with a certain voluptuous temperament and strong personal magnetism."

Because they grew up nine years apart, Fred always saw David as a kid. But also because he was nine years his junior, David gave the appearance of being much younger and people would always mistake him for Fred's son, which Fred found pretty annoying.

The most apparent correspondence between the two brothers was their route into the stock business via apprenticeships at First of Michigan and MBAs from the University of Michigan at Ann Arbor. Naturally there also are the physical resemblances, which are most conspicuous in their eyes and facial features. David is taller and more massive, and both wear glasses. On the home front, Fred and David are both earnest and devoted family men. Perhaps their greatest common strength in the investment business is their awareness of historical tendencies. Both men possess a tremendous sense of history about themselves, their company and the Wall Street community.

Even though Fred's personality loomed large over his professional life, David retained his independence from him in the office and at home. David ran on a separate, relatively autonomous track. Theirs was never a co-dependent relationship, and this is no buddy picture. Neither is there any resemblance to the inseparable attachment shared between their grandfather Frederick and his brother Rusty two generations earlier. Ultimately their competitiveness, which is as tradition-bound as the rivalry between their respective schools, Harvard and Yale, kept them from becoming true teammates. Analyst Ginger Risco disclosed that when David went on vacation, Fred would sometimes undercut his authority by rearranging a portfolio in his absence. "Fred was out to prove that he could call the shots."

Fred extended his distant management style even to David. "It's an interesting partnership," said Alger board's Dubow. "David, whom he sees every day, may not know things about Fred's personal life. They don't go out and socialize and have meals together or relax and have a few drinks." This distance was maintained even though they lived a few blocks from each other on Park Avenue.

Still their relationship, if not totally caring or socially conventional, was unusually intense and always grounded in their fraternal ties. "David was motivated by a tremendous desire to please Fred," observed Bill Scheerer about their early days in business. "David has always been in awe of Fred, with good reason."

If Fred applied pressure on David, the outcome was usually positive. If David was hell-bent on proving himself to Fred, Fred was happy to keep the pressure on by driving him to do better. "Fred, in a strange sort of way, could always push David around," remarked a former Alger intimate. "In the early days Fred had an unearthly control over him. David was highly excitable, yet Fred could put him at ease with just a few words."

On a baser, practical level, Fred liked to keep the temperature hot in the office, while David preferred a cooler environment. Fred's trusty tool is a slide rule, while David's instrument of choice is the computer. David participates religiously in the Episcopalian church and Fred, though God-fearing and perhaps perversely more spiritual, is not affiliated with any denomination.

It is no coincidence that their offices are at opposite ends of the twelfth floor at 75 Maiden Lane. Nor is it incidental that David's desk is at an angle while Fred keeps his square. David's office is cluttered with family pictures, which are absent from Fred's room. And while Fred likes his world tidy, David doesn't mind the clutter of computers, bric-a-brac, magazine stacks and trade show materials.

Neatness, for Fred, is a virtue, a sine qua non in business organization. He complained, "My brother gets upset when I insist that he keep his office neat. He just doesn't get it."

But as much as they were opposites, they were rarely in opposition. In many ways it was because their differences were complementary that they could balance each other in a way that was beneficial to the company. Like oil and vinegar, they didn't mix unconditionally but functioned well together. As they gave a great deal of confidence to each other, the combination of their personalities led to powerful business.

If one was deliberate and methodical, the other was meteoric and unpredictable. One brother was generally more patient, the other more pliable. Though Fred may have thought up the strategy, it was David who identified and implemented the technology-driven systems for growing the firm.

Of the two, David was harder to repress when working through stock disasters. Fred was always more composed. "David reacts. Fred is calm under fire," observed Alger Fund portfolio manager Seilai Khoo. "When things are going against him, he can calmly sit down, pick apart the situation and figure out what to do. David is very expressive. If he doesn't like it, he'll tell you. You can read from his face. If he's mad at you, he'll scream at you, and in an hour he'll forget and apologize. Fred is more difficult to read, and you can't tell if he bears a grudge."

Co-portfolio manager Ron Tartaro agreed. "David is enthusiastic, outgoing, knowledgeable and emotional," he said. "Fred is more reserved than David, more calculating and precise, not as excitable. He comes up with ways of looking at individual stocks, ways of solving problems that others would not."

"David might get more involved in the details than Fred," George Boggio said in sketching out the brothers. "He was also more emotional. Following every tick of an eighth of a point will make you very emotional. David is exceptionally bright. Whether he is as great a visionary as Fred, only time will tell."

David described the discrepancy between them with a curious melding of frustration and veneration. "Some days you walk into Fred's office and he'd be walking on the ceiling 'cause he's figured out that, for him, defying gravity is the best way to do things. Some of these leaps of understanding are startling and brilliant, and some of them lead us to directions which are . . ." he said without completing the thought, then added, "To him it is clearly important to find a new and unique solution to a problem. For me, it's not. For me, if someone's already figured out the best solution, I'll take it. I just want to get results. I'm not interested if we look different or whether we've done it a different way to get there.

"Fred always wants to do things different from everybody else. Sometimes that leads him to great insights, when we would jump ahead of the rest of the industry. Sometimes it's distracting because everything has to be built from the ground up. If we did things the same way as everyone else, we would have been better off.

"I'm sure if we set out to build a car, the car would have five wheels because Fred would feel that it was beneath him to submit and simply make mild improvements on the traditional design."

In business David prefers taking the bullet train straight to his destination.

Fred, he's learned to expect, will choose the road least traveled and perhaps make several detours simply to see what's available along the way. For Fred the journey may be as important as the destination.

"One of the things that's really interesting about Fred," concluded David, "is that his great unique asset and his one great flaw are the same thing."

As managers they also observed different styles. David explained, "Fred has certain theories about personnel management. He was very struck by the idea that lieutenants in the Marine Corps would hold themselves aloof from their troops. That style of management has never particularly appealed to me, nor does it suit my nature. My nature is more modern—management by walking around."

Former analyst Rob Lyon reiterated that point. "David's importance was that he brought a more human side to the equation. Fred is very intellectual, and so is David, but Fred is more on the intangible side. David would be very concerned about people, the things that could go wrong or right in someone's personal life. Fred might not be aware of it. David would be more concerned about people as individuals." Boggio affirmed; "Fred is more imaginative than David, but David has better interpersonal skills."

Former analyst Shelton Swei observed, "Fred is important because he presented a consistent strategy—'Own growth stocks. Don't worry about price-earnings multiples'—which he essentially sticks to tenaciously, and this has had an effect on the firm, the analysts and our performance.

"David is important because he was somewhat more responsible for stock selection, the process and the consequent records. David is less tenacious, more willing to adjust. He likes growth, likes technology, but he's not as rigid and inflexible as Fred."

Even before taking over Fred's company, David was becoming increasingly instrumental in keeping it on an even keel. This begs the question: Who was really looking after whom?

"That's what makes the firm more successful. The two brothers bring it together in just the right format," Alger board's Dr. Nathan E. Saint-Amand said, searching for the right words to describe their synergy.

"They make a really good team because they balance each other out. Now that Fred is leaving, the balance is gone," said Hilary Alger before her father departed for Europe.

Fred reflected, "David is going to miss me as I would miss him. It's nice to have someone around who's just there. Of course, I will be there in Geneva, but that's not quite the same."

Although they normally stood apart, on rare occasions they enjoyed some experiences together. In one good-natured episode the Alger brothers played stock angels to an unsuspecting young sun worshiper on a beach in La Jolla, California. One afternoon during a break from a marathon Gannett pension meeting, they decided to take a stroll near the water even though they looked uncomfortably out of place in their dark business suits and pale skin from the East Coast winter.

Spying an attractive woman sitting alone ahead of them, Fred threw David a dare. "Fred said to me, 'David, you've been married two years now, let's see how much you've lost. I'll bet you twenty dollars that you can't go over and start up a conversation with that girl.'" Accepting his challenge, David marched over to the young woman.

"The vision of this hulking guy in a dark suit striding across the sand to her must have flipped her out," David continued. "I got lucky, because I soon discovered this girl had a passion for the stock market. As soon as she figured out I knew something about stocks, we had this great chat; she told me all the stocks she owned. Fred, meanwhile, waited on the promenade, watching to see how I was doing."

Letting enough time pass to prove his success to Fred, David trudged back across the sand to rejoin Fred, collect his $20 and return to the Gannett parley. Halfway back, Fred suddenly asked David, "Did you tell her about Crown Central Petroleum?" which was a hot stock they owned. David said he hadn't. "Oh, you've got to tell her about Crown Central Petroleum," Fred insisted.

"So I trudged back across the sand, in shoes and a full business suit and said to her,'"You know that Kodak you've got, you ought to sell that and buy Crown Central Petroleum, CCK on the American Stock Exchange. It's going to go up a lot."

She thanked him for the stock tip, and David walked back to Fred.

The happy postscript was that two days later CCK reported spectacular earnings, and the stock, David believed, doubled over the next three weeks. "Fred and I have this fantasy that somewhere there's this woman who must think she's had an hallucination and returns to that same spot on the beach to wait for the man in black to reappear and give her another stock tip."

Dealing with both Fred and David in the same situation often called for strong political instincts and required one to execute a clever balancing act to satisfy both men while keeping things in line.

Said trader Joe Maida, "The most difficult part of my job was being a mediator . . . keeping the analyst happy and keeping Fred and David happy, as everyone comes down on one side or another of a trade. Even I have an opinion. For example, David would say we should be seven percent in cash. Fred would insist it should be ten percent. I'd privately set up a compromise target between the two levels and hope it would work out. Sometimes the market bailed me out by going up so that Fred didn't mind."

According to Alger's convertible-bond expert Lisa Gregg, "Sometimes if Fred liked an idea and David didn't, then some very funny things happened. Either too much was bought or nothing was purchased. They finally realized this type of war was unproductive, so they formalized it with Fred hearing a story and giving a nod and David also giving a nod."

"Fred and David form such strong opinions that they sometimes don't listen to what their people are telling them. While oftentimes they're right, sometimes if they listened it would work out better for them. Both are iron-willed and stubborn, and this could lead to conflict between us and them and them and them," portfolio manager Ron Tartaro indicated.

In many ways the star of Fred Alger & Company has shone more brightly because of David. His first year as head of the company was a tour de force. David's Capital Appreciation Fund brought home the prize for the best mutual fund in the country, and Alger's three other equity portfolios stood near the top of their investment categories. In 1995 *Mutual Fund* magazine named Alger its number-one fund family from a field of 67 mutual-fund companies.

In taking charge, David finally broke free of his orbit around Fred's fixed sun and began emitting his own light without taking heat from the brother who had always eclipsed him.

Some of the employees were apprehensive at first. "It was fear of the unknown, his completely different style," said Rosemary Kiernan. "We knew how Fred took care of us. Would David do the same? "

There was no such caution or hesitation within the Alger board, which registered broad conviction that David had the right stuff to carry on the company. "He may not quite have the same conceptual ability as Fred, but in terms of being focused on the stock market and his sensitivity to the market, he's every bit as good as Fred," said Arthur Dubow. "Fred didn't actually pay that much attention to the portfolios. He pretended to." David had a strong hand in running the portfolios, and that experience was considered more relevant than managing the company, which was not altogether foreign to him.

Those who had worked closely with David expressed their confidence. Bob Emerson said, "David brings a tremendous breadth of knowledge about a lot of industries. He's witnessed, as has Fred, the same patterns, how firms grow and stumble. He was good at bringing skepticism to all sides of the stories which came to him."

And surely some Alger investors must have been relieved at the hand over. For David's manner, more predictable and less intimidating than Fred's, was comforting and appealing to many. He would seek to win people over instead of rattling them with a take-it-or-leave-it attitude. Even with his tremendous performance, investors were often distracted by Fred's reputation. If they gave him their money, it was despite a sense of trepidation over his bellicose approach to the market.

David was mindful of his new authority. "I'll be dealing with a wide variety of issues, some of which I never had to think about very much before," he said. "I feel like the guy who leaves the house and must return thirty minutes later because he has this delusion that he left the iron on. I keep guessing that there's something in this business that I don't see and I don't know what it is. I keep looking at more numbers, delve into new areas, exert more control. I'm afraid something will jump up and bite me from some angle that I'm not familiar with, and I won't know what it is."

As expected, David's elevation was a tranquil process, seamless within the company and at first barely recognized by the financial community. He intended no seismic shift, just a gradual easing of the firm toward normalcy and incremental changes to its corporate culture and business direction.

Fred Alger is now David's firm. "David will be freer and better without Fred— not better than Fred, but better than under Fred," analyst Ginger Risco mused insightfully. The only catch for David is that, no matter how significant his additions to the firm, it will never be his name on the door.

11

Foundation of Research

H E WAS KNOWN by the code name *Angel of Death*. He claimed rank in the shadowy world of special forces and whispered hints of a clandestine past with the CIA. And, for an instant, he was a military adviser to Fred Alger Management.

The Soviet Union had just raised a heavy hand to quell Poland's first labor uprising. "There was a real question about what was going on," David Alger worried. Agent *Angel* was brought in by one of Alger's analysts, Richard B. Stewart. He seemed credible enough and well informed. He said that he was shipping out to Germany for a PX job, but *Angel* winked and everyone was supposed to know better.

"So we put this guy on the payroll, not for very much money, to advise us on military matters," David explained. "The idea was to receive advance warning if the Soviets were preparing to attack, or if there was a troop buildup anywhere of any sinister nature." Any Soviet action was certain to roil the financial markets.

Fred Alger's appointment of *Angel* sharply illustrates the company's affirmation of its devotion to independent research and unflinching readiness to make off-stride, pitched moves to reach its pinnacle. "He never reported anything to us," David admitted. "He collected his checks, then disappeared in the mist. And we never saw or heard from him again."

To be sure, *Angel* was no phantom. Tom Weil, who set up Fred Alger's back office in 1980, remembered seeing him show off hand-to-hand combat in the office. "One time he gave David a gun and dared him to fire at him; but not before warning, 'Before you shoot, I'll have you disarmed.'"

With this one capricious exception, giving rare meaning to the idea of original research, most of the firm's efforts to bolster its research apparatus were more traditional. A few, however, were outright brilliant in their ability to gather, distill and employ investment data.

To win at the money game, one has to bet with investment ideas. In the sixties, Fred Alger achieved tremendous results by relying on his original theories about the market and by personally selecting the growth stocks. As the investment community grew to share his aggressive approach, he was regularly squeezed out of the primary trove of information required to maintain his performance.

Since he couldn't count on Street research, Fred Alger knew the only way to hold a winning hand was to develop his own team of investment analysts. The mission, then, was to institute a disciplined, rational approach to picking stocks in a research-intensive environment dedicated to uncovering investment opportunities far better than the rest of the market. As his company entered the seventies, Fred Alger staked its future on that concept. Three decades later, the Alger commitment to independent fundamental research is undiminished and wholly integrated into its core. Fred Alger Management generates substantially all its own research, which is used exclusively for its clients and inaccessible to outside investors.

"What makes Fred Alger Management successful?" Alger Fund board member Dr. Saint-Amand offered this explanation: "In a word, they do their own research. They don't use other sources. They're not reading the same information everybody else has. They have the best or are willing to go out and bargain to get the best. The fact that they don't have to listen to what the Street hears enables them to be somewhat contrarian and to look at companies with a more intelligent, individualistic perspective."

The Research Associate program was an early and crucial implementation that fulfilled Fred Alger's craving for independent research. A fabulous feeder system for its analyst corps, it was rooted in the guild atmosphere which Fred found so appealing at North American Securities.

The first wave of RAs passed through the firm in a relatively informal way. Fred was juggling several balls at the time: a new brokerage business with a seat in the New York Stock Exchange, fresh demands as a result of becoming a registered investment adviser, and an aggressive marketing drive into the pension arena. When David came into the firm in January 1971, he quickly picked up the reins of the loosely structured RA program and began taking control.

It wasn't until the early eighties that a second wave of research associates experienced a more regimented form of the RA program, owing to David's development of sophisticated computer systems to refine and illuminate the research data. Even greater formalization was established in 1985, when large amounts of investment capital rushed into the firm. As moles for investment data, research associates were instrumental in the firm's progress. Fred would often take guests and prospective clients to the warren of offices that make up the research area and show off his RAs navigating the Alger database.

"Fred had several strokes of genius. This was one of them," said George Boggio. "It was a very good program."

Each novice associate was given over to a senior analyst for grooming—two RAs to an analyst. They learned by performing the prep work, which freed up the analyst for more important reflection and enlarged the number of covered companies.

The original view of research associates was that they had a two-year shelf life and were expected to leave the firm after that period. They were considered a disposable resource, low down in the food chain. So the first recruits tended to be "generally intelligent people, but not the type who would have any long-term interest in the stock market business."

"We ended up with some very odd characters," David disclosed, "including an aspiring soap opera actress. Some of the people we had, though very bright, really didn't want to be analysts, but were killing time before going on to grad school. It was quite a high-spirited group at that time."

As the program evolved, the company realized that it was giving up too quickly on a potentially precious resource. "Some years later we recognized that our RAs were smarter than most people's analysts, and we were foolish to send them away; that in fact we should put them through a more formal training program and keep them as analysts." The need to establish career-track continuity for researchers increased during the company's belt tightening after the 1987 market crash.

"We had a flawed policy," Fred admitted, "so we changed our hiring focus." Today Alger expects its research recruits to take a professional career path through the company.

The drill was the same then as it is today for all draftees into the Alger squad. Every research cadet is expected to attain Certified Financial Analyst (CFA) qualification, which is awarded by the Institute of Chartered Financial Analysts, for passing a series of three six-hour exams. Coursework involves economics, financial accounting, portfolio management, security analysis and standards of conduct.

In Alger's current training system, it takes from four to six years for a researcher to be promoted to junior analyst and then analyst. The Alger approach is different from the Street's in that the company shields its researchers and analysts from any sales and service responsibilities or administrative duties and places them in a rarefied environment where their goal is original, critical thinking about stocks and the financial markets. The research area has the quality of a laboratory rather than a busy office.

While the RA program was difficult, as both Fred and David were viewed as excessively demanding, it was able to attract squadrons of smart, aggressive young people. If Fred picked you for his team, it was a rare chance not be missed. "We have one of the few systematic training programs, and we've probably put three hundred people through our program here since its inception. Many of them have gone on to be some of the biggest names on Wall Street," David told *Investment Advisor* magazine in August 1995.

The inside track to Fred Alger Management ran, obviously enough, right through Yale and Harvard in addition to the other Ivy League and top-tier colleges. Where better to harvest individuals who are up to the discipline of investment research and capable of supplying the raw energy and intelligence for the firm?

For example, Ashley Leeds, hired straight out of Harvard in 1980, significantly helped the company perfect its early use of spreadsheets to document corporate data. David called her "an extremely brilliant young woman." After Alger, she attended the Stanford Business School and in 1995 held the position of senior vice president at investment banker Lehman Brothers.

Despite being the primary source for Alger talent over the years and a fortuitous link in numerous business affairs, the Yale factor is receding at Alger. David reported with odd glee and some fascination that not a single Yale graduate was employed in the firm at the end of 1995. Perhaps with Fred gone, that strong undercurrent with the university and its alumni was finally severed. David's a Harvard man, and since he's now at the helm, one can assume which tie will become more prominent.

While the Alger crowd comprises mostly conservative, button-down types, the company has hardly been predictable in its selection of its initiates. It might be instructive to see how the following two individuals found their way to the firm and made it through the research associate program. Both rose to be vice presidents and senior analysts within the company. One stayed and the other left.

Ginger Risco landed unconventionally at Fred Alger Management in 1981. A native of Brooklyn, she hit the road after high school for a six-month California adventure. After she came down to reality and returned to New York, her grandfather, a runner on the Street, helped her get a job as a typist at a money-management firm. She worked in administration, then research, and discovered she preferred the latter. Eventually Ginger dallied at night school before quitting her job to earn a college degree at Columbia University almost eight years after finishing high school.

The gravitational pull of Wall Street delivered her down from the Morningside Heights campus to Wall Street, where she got a job as assistant to a hedge-fund analyst at Drexel Burnham Lambert. She described the position as "a little trading, a little research, a little liaison." It didn't last, and anyway, she was pining to do research. She had had a fair amount of on-the-job training: compiling data for lists of recommendations and assisting in valuing and picking stocks. More important, all her friends were in research, and she wanted in.

One day she bumped into Bob Emerson, whom she knew from a stint at Salomon Brothers, who was working as an analyst for Fred Alger. Would she like to come aboard? he asked. After a brief interview David offered her a research job.

PENSION MANAGEMENT

The resurrection of Fred Alger

The star of the go-go era has been reborn as, of all things, a pension manager. And he's making a bundle.

by Anise Wallace

"**I**f you had asked me a year ago to make a list of the people who were going to be successful in this business, I would have put Fred Alger at the bottom," says one pension fund consultant, who today is frankly astonished at the turn in the money manager's fortunes. Fred Alger — preeminent mutual fund gunslinger of the 1960s, ill-fated money manager for Bernard Cornfeld's Fund of Funds and then for years a seeming has-been scrambling to survive — has made an amazing comeback. This year his firm is right near the top of the list of managers signing up the most new pension clients. Indeed, five years removed from ERISA, and apparently convinced there will be a place in the 1980s for the go-go era revisited, the people who sponsor pension plans have swarmed to a man promising them all-out performance.

In 1978, some ten years after his star began to eclipse, Alger had a mere $25 million under his roof. By the start of this year, things had picked up a bit, but the $150 million his firm had under management was still a relatively modest sum, equaled by a host of other firms characterized as boutiques. Yet today, Fred Alger Management Co. could hardly be called a boutique. And by October its assets under management had exploded to an amazing $850 million, according to trade sources who track this sort of thing, and these same sources predict that it won't be long until the firm crosses the billion-dollar mark. Alger is now running money for an impressive list of clients that include ABC, Burlington Northern, Litton Industries, TRW, CBS, B.F. Goodrich, Owens-Corning and New York University. And his success at attracting such new clients has paid off very handsomely indeed for Fred Alger himself (see box, page 95).

The flood of funds has come in such a rush, in fact, that few clients are even aware of what has happened. In early October, one assistant treasurer who had recently hired Alger said he did so because he wanted a small manager; he thought Alger managed only $200 million. Another long-standing client, who could be presumed to keep close tabs on the firm, guessed that Alger ran $400 million. "People think they've got a small money manager," chuckles one corporate official. "What they don't know is that they're all

After some very tough years, his new pension business is paying off handsomely for Fred Alger; 1981 profit estimates run as high as $7 million

INSTITUTIONAL INVESTOR 91

Fred is on top of the world. From Institutional Investor in December 1980.

"I didn't know about Fred's history during the go-go years," Ginger said. "Others advised me that it was a tough place to work, that he was hard on people, but it was a place for smart, aggressive people. All those things sounded good to someone starting out."

It's no cakewalk for a researcher at Fred Alger. You must get to work by eight-thirty in the morning and are pushed to the limit until six or seven every evening. Originally Ginger was assigned to David, but by her account, "it didn't work out personality-wise." She was then given to the care of Baruch Halpern, with whom she fell more comfortably into the rhythms of the research process. In 1985 Risco passed the third and final level of the day-long examinations administered annually by the Institute of Chartered Financial Analysts, leading to her CFA designation, and was promoted to analyst. Now as a senior analyst, she has her own research assistants.

Ginger spoke candidly about her experiences as a researcher with Fred Alger. "In the beginning I didn't have much contact with Fred. He was out marketing a lot, and I didn't have any direct responsibility for stocks.

"Fred likes being right—and he is right most of the time. You can never change his mind, no matter how air-tight the argument. Even if he can't win, he has to get in the last word. If you argue for or against a stock, he'll purposely take the other side. Fred doesn't massage egos or give credit even if it is due. You have to give yourself credit if you don't want to lose your confidence.

"In the company there's no place to take your grievance. Over time, the firm has lost lots of talented people because they had no place to go here—because of the dominant personality of the Algers."

She didn't let up.

"Fred could be mean, ruthless, cold—really unpleasant. There might be nothing wrong in his criticism, but the delivery of that criticism was often too harsh. He could somehow get to the core of whatever it was that made you fearful—and it was different for each person. On a professional level, he never cut you any slack. He decided that's the kind of relationship he wanted to have with his employees. When I joined the firm, he was harsher, more critical. He has mellowed over the years."

The RA class of 1984 produced several standouts. Among them, Helen Young Hayes and Warren B. Lammert III, both from Yale and also part of a defection from the firm in the late eighties to Denver–based Janus Capital Corp., where they are now high-profile portfolio managers.

The valedictorian, however, was Shelton Y. Swei, whose hedging strategies during most of 1995 were instrumental in keeping the Alger Capital Appreciation Fund in the running for top honors among mutual funds in the country, which it went on to win despite Swei's departure from the firm prior to the victory to start his own hedge-fund operation.

When Shelton Swei entered Harvard in 1980, he dreamed of an engineering degree leading to law school and a job as patent attorney. That all changed when he began making money in the stock market.

After his freshman year he invested his meager savings from a summer job as a computer programmer for Union Carbide in several long-term corporate bonds. "Within weeks I caught the bottom of the market and made a lot of money in a relative sense," said Shelton. He had tasted blood and liked it. A month into his sophomore year, he changed his major to economics.

The following summer he put his savings into Tandon, a now defunct floppy-disk drive maker. Again the market bottomed shortly after his investment. Tandon stock quadrupled in 12 months. He figured he was on to something, which pushed him further into the investment business.

The winter of his sophomore year, Shelton decided to take a stab at finding a job in the investment business. Using a directory of money-management firms, he issued a mass mailing to 200 of the largest companies. Fred Alger wasn't among them and Shelton didn't get a single response.

In his junior year Shelton posted another 200 letters. This time the investment advisory Value Line gave a nibble. It was in the process of expanding stock coverage and offered him a job for $5 an hour. IBM also wanted him—but for programming, not investing.

Undeterred, he sent out another 200 résumés during his senior year. This effort netted seven interviews. He knew his chances were poor without an MBA. But the interviewers from Fred Alger, two recent college graduates who were RAs, said the company was impressed by his letter and the high level of interest he expressed. Except for Fred Alger, his only other offer came from Prudential Insurance for a job in Newark, New Jersey, for "not very much money."

After receiving his A.B. in economics from Harvard in September 1984, Shelton moved to New York and Fred Alger Management.

Shelton was tight-lipped about an office anecdote involving David Alger, which seemed to be a source of personal pride for him and a potential embarrassment for David. The incident was a quick round of liar's poker that had David doubling his losses from a $1 bet to finally fumbling a bundle to Shelton. "I ended up losing a thousand dollars in less than an hour. Shelton just beat my brains out," David admitted. For his part, David took the event lightly, but the fact that Shelton was so circumspect about such a minor event illuminates the total power monopoly which the Alger brothers have over the firm.

David took Shelton's departure in stride. "He always wanted to go and start his own firm. Shelton loves making money, and he perceives being a hedge-fund manager as a way of making more money than even here. He was able to raise, my sources tell me, twenty million dollars to manage and form his own organization."

Because it is difficult to inculcate established analysts with the Alger investment style, it is rare for the firm to invite outside professionals to its senior analyst clique. There are exceptions, however, like Teresa McRoberts, who was a vice president and pharmaceutical analyst at J.P. Morgan Securities before joining Fred Alger in 1994. Lisa Gregg, a vice president and senior analyst at Fred

Alger, who started as Fred's assistant for economic research and then was put in charge of the firm's convertible-bond portfolio, is a good example of promotion from within.

Lisa is convinced that Fred gave her the job because, like him, she went to Yale and she speaks French. That's being too modest. Her credentials include a doctorate from Yale and an MBA from New York University. Before Lisa found Fred Alger, she was a food-industry analyst for scandal-tinged Drexel Burnham Lambert, and before that a financial-markets researcher at Citibank.

Lisa was unemployed in March 1983 when she sent out her résumé all over Wall Street. It surprised her that she received the call for an interview with Alger. Only then did she start reading up on the firm. All she knew was what she had heard about Fred during the sixties. "His reputation was still fresh."

The company had achieved a fair amount of success with the RA program, and Lisa offered the kind of character or experience the firm was seeking. "My letter showed up at just the right time," Lisa said. She must have made an extremely positive first impression, for Fred offered her a job as his assistant within 30 minutes.

One of Lisa's first assignments was to sniff out the considerable discrepancy between the growth rate in the monetary base published by the St. Louis Federal Reserve and the one computed by the board of governors of the Federal Reserve in Washington. It took a bit of sleuthing to figure out whose numbers were more appropriate for analysis.

"The monetary base is not a clean number, because it consists of two factors—currency and bank reserves—which change all the time," Lisa explained. "It's pretty arcane stuff—but something Fred was interested in." In the end, they stuck with the Washington calculations because they "gave a better outcome."

The Federal Reserve System, or Fed, comprises 12 regional Federal Reserve Banks, their 24 branches, and all national and state banks that are part of the system.

Lisa's big challenge every quarter was writing the Alger Economic Outlook, a précis of the market for Alger's pension, endowment and high-net-worth clients. "Fred is very meticulous about the stuff that goes out to clients," she said. "All your sources had to be identified."

She believes her elevation to portfolio manager of the firm's investments in convertible securities, including the Castle Convertible Fund in March 1989, can be attributed to Fred's hypothesis that any person who's intelligent and hardworking should be able to tackle anything; and he'll challenge you to prove it.

"The convertible thing is something that Fred came up with one day," said Lisa. "We had pretty much mastered so many issues on the economics front that he may have sensed I was running out of new, complex things to figure out." She added, "I was thrilled beyond belief. This was more operational, real-world than just watching the economy."

Lisa had never managed anything before, much less a portfolio of securities worth millions of dollars. David had been managing it previously, with his assistant doing most of the grunt work and three or four others helping with the analysis and security selection. When the last of them dropped off, Fred thought it extravagant to hire a new assistant solely for the convertible business. Cautious at first, Lisa worked in David's shadow, producing the spreadsheets. As her knowledge expanded and her comfort level increased, she was gradually forced into the decision-making role by David's regular unavailability to focus on this subordinate piece in the Alger investment universe. After about four years she was managing the whole thing on her own.

Fred is driven by intense intellectual curiosity and often demonstrates gravity-defying leaps of imagination.

Lisa is truly enamored with convertible securities. The best part for her is "executing a good trade and timing an exit well." But Lisa cautioned, "You can't pat yourself on the back for that. This is a very humbling business. The chapter is never over. The next morning the market opens again, and you have to do it all over again. And just because you did a good job on ABC doesn't mean it will go so well for DEF." One success she recalled was buying Ford preferreds, even though "Fred didn't think it was a good idea," which then went from $50 to $110 with an $8^3/_4$% coupon. "You have to buy them when they look like they're going out of business," she advised.

"I always take more comfort in owning something where we also own the underlying common. Not only is it monitored better, but we have a clear set of expectations for the company," she said. "If it meets them, we know you are on the right path. If it falls off, we have a better handle as to whether it's a temporary problem or a terrible departure and so should sell it immediately. It's always nice to own a convertible whose common goes up because you tend to make a lot of money."

Lisa Gregg works apart from the Alger stock-research process, but she draws from the rest of the firm's research. "I want to know enough about the market or a security so that I don't get blindsided because there's one little piece we missed," said Lisa Gregg in explaining the complex nature of Fred Alger's research. "The same is true for Fred. He expects very thorough research."

Here's a quick primer on the Alger way of making money.

The Alger investment doctrine revolves around the idea of growth-stock investing and buying stock in American companies that reflect high unit-volume growth and a positive life-cycle change. Fred Alger Management has strictly—and successfully—adhered to this core investment philosophy through all the business cycles of the last 30 years.

High unit-volume growth is attributed to a company that sells more and more products—not simply experiencing higher sales—in an expanding marketplace or new and improved products in an industry sector that is experiencing rising demand for its goods and services. This is likely to be a creative firm whose growth rate outstrips the market and, consequently, whose stock price is expected to grow faster than the stock averages as the expanding growth translates into higher bottom-line earnings. The company is attractive if the price-earnings multiple of its stock price rests below its potential or projected growth factor. A portent of such earnings momentum is the company's dominance of its industry with a proprietary product, service or technology. "It is with these companies that pleasant surprises can occur, called 'the serendipitous factor' by the firm, or being organized to get lucky," according to Fred.

A major, positive life-cycle change can be had in one of several areas: a corporate restructuring, the replacement of management, the introduction of a new or unique product or an industry or market shift that spurs demand for a company's goods or services. Here again, earnings growth is expected to translate to a rising stock price.

By and large, Fred Alger takes a bottom-up approach. A good growth company can be found in any industry, within any market capitalization and regardless of the macroeconomic factors. What's important is the intrinsic value of a company rather than the level of its stock price. In the opposing style of value investing, the assets and goodwill of the company place a ceiling on the stock price. For Fred Alger, high earnings expectations and rising growth rates establish a momentum that can propel stock values to the stratosphere. Fred Alger sticks to a fundamental rather than a valuation perspective.

Fred Alger made a strong case for his life-cycle theory in Robert Metz's "Market Place" column in *The New York Times* on November 3, 1980. He cited the oil industry as a no-growth business, which had nonetheless experienced a 10-fold increase in unit price. "As a consequence, earnings turned out to be surprisingly good, attracting heavy speculative interest. Investors made huge sums of money," Fred said in the article. At the time he had similar positive-cycle expectations for brokerage firms, as "great vehicles for the recapitalization boom," and for railroads, which could soon start competitive pricing as a result of deregulation. High-technology firms were his favorites in the high-unit-volume growth category.

Fred Alger Management employs an extensive set of productive filters in a unique risk-reward model for portfolio management. Its Portfolio Analysts Report, for example, draws out 25 separate indicators of a company's economic and stock market outlook. Twice daily, managers evaluate stock and portfolio performance on absolute terms and relative to the market on 5-, 10-, 15-, 20-day and year-to-date bases. There's also a 5-day relative-price action model, which identifies stocks in the early stages of an uptrend.

One of Fred Alger's unique tools is the P/V, or price-volume indicator, which identifies stocks that have been sold out completely and provides an early warning of their forthcoming rebound in price. The change principle is applied here on a stock's price as well as on the company itself. Its earnings have likely stabilized. All the bad news is out. Everybody who is going to sell the stock has already sold it. All that remains is a hard core of inert owners willing to serve as a base for the new uptrend.

The indicator is established by tracking average prices of stocks in 48-week, 32-week and 16-week periods to detect for issues that are drifting progressively lower on progressively lighter volume. If the price and trading volume have been decreasing progressively from the longer to the shorter duration, then the stock qualifies for Alger's P/V sheet.

"Every major move in a group during the sixties was preceded by a sold-out condition," according to Fred Alger. "The same was true for the market as a whole. When it was at an absolute bottom, the market was drifting lower on lighter volume. This is useful since popular mythology in the markets has you buying on large volume breakouts on the upside, when actually the reverse holds true. When a company turns up on the P/V sheet, analysts are encouraged to find out if management is working to turn it around. That initial bounce is usually significant."

Said former analyst Bob Rescoe, "We tried different ways of interpreting the P/V findings. Could you get a buy signal just on sold-out price and not volume, or on volume without the price? The one that seemed to have the most validity is when you had the P and the V corresponding." He called it "a neat little insight, a nice combination that seemed to work."

Another former analyst, Rob Lyon, added, "Once everybody was out of the stock, it would take little volume to cause the stock to go up. P/V was a pretty good indicator for spotting saucer bottoms and identifying improving situations. The concept was not necessarily unique, but Fred's way of defining and structuring the P/V was exceptional.

"Fred's point was that things go in cycles—good and then bad. When things are going bad, people sell the stock, but the natural human instinct is for people to improve their lot. Either the management will improve or sanctions would be applied in some form, which would show up in the stock price."

Though an important clue to stock performance, this indicator is understood in the larger context of other variables. Fred cautioned, "You can never make money with formula investing."

Fred has never been shy about calling market bottoms and has often been prescient about gauging market direction from a broad historical perspective. It was perhaps a sold-out condition that enabled him to spot the stock market's nadir prior to the start of the Reagan bull market in 1982. When very few professionals could see that far, he predicted that the Dow would rocket past 3,000 with this insight:

"The market tends to move in trading bands, which last a remarkably long period of time. When they break out of these bands, they tend to go up two or three times whatever the previous high was before establishing a new trading band. The market had been in a trading band between five hundred to one thousand for a terribly long time: 1960 to 1980. It's not atypical for these to be established. I must have theorized that it was time to break out of this trading band and that the breakout would be a substantial one."

One method Alger used was screening for companies that have outperformed the S&P 500 by at least 3.5% during the previous five days. The rationale was that a stock that will outperform over the long term must start by outperforming in the short term. This notion, however, has lost much of its relevance in the current explosive market environment when stocks, especially the technology stocks which Alger favors, frequently bounce up or down by at least that much in a single day. Once a salient point in the firm's promotional brochures, David Alger has removed its mention from recent marketing efforts.

Another proprietary Alger filter is ranking stocks from 20 to 0 using four elements that enable relative valuations across industries which are in different market modes. These are: prospective growth which can translate to earnings; consistency in improving or maintaining that growth rate; the strength of the company's balance sheet; and the ability of its products to achieve dominant market positions.

To illustrate, Fred mentioned Nucor, a rapidly growing steel company which is in an industry that's barely seen any appreciation in recent years. He contrasted that with Intel, in the booming semiconductor business, which sells at a fraction of the Nucor multiple, even though it is just as dominant in its own industry. Despite their contrasts, the Alger system correctly pegged both companies as top buys.

Growth stocks—securities whose price is mainly driven by corporate earnings—rule at Fred Alger. They have since the beginning. The Alger view is that the faster the growth rate—in absolute terms or relative to earlier results and the average of other firms in its sector—the better the company. Fred Alger has never been timid about paying a high price for a good growth company. He would sooner pay 20 times earnings for a growth company than buy a cheap cyclical with a 5X multiple. Cyclicals, for example, paper companies, which are sensitive to economic demand for their goods and services, have no intrinsic appeal in the Alger formula for investing.

The value proposition—looking at stocks primarily on the basis of low price-earnings multiples with the hope that their prices will eventually rise to more appropriate market valuations—is anathema at Alger. "Value is another way of buying cheap stocks," said Fred.

"Fred has been a great believer that you buy great companies. No multiple is ever too high for a great company. People are always restricting themselves by placing price limits based on these multiples," said David. "Fred is always recollecting markets in the past where these stocks sold at much higher multiples than they do now. If you get into a really good market, the stock should also sell much higher, so you shouldn't sell out of good acting companies or good stocks just because they reach a certain level."

Fred learned this during the go-go years when he saw stocks with "wild technological stories" being jacked up far higher than he imagined. For example, Mohawk Data didn't impress him at $25, but he bought it at $60. Victor Comptometer spurted from $30 to $90 while he resisted its move. Fred insisted on "guarding against getting fixed ideas." The company used this lesson superbly

David Alger researching stocks in the seventies. The firm's reputation for great performance was built on it's research.

in 1995, when the stocks of many technology companies kept zooming ahead, despite lofty prices and multiples, to stump the models of most investment managers.

"Don't think cheap. Don't think multiples. You make money by buying vital, creative companies," David has preached. But Fred said it first, in *Forbes* magazine in May 1981.

Alger's marketing chief Ray Pfeister recalled watching Fred give a stirring defense of growth stocks that made him as proud of his boss "as ever an employee could be." Evaluation Associates, a large consulting advisory firm for pension, foundation and endowment money, had invited Fred to debate the growth case versus the value ideal held by Michael Rose of the Philadelphia–based Delaware Group of mutual funds. It packed the seminar with its biggest and best clients, all billion-dollar mutual funds.

Pfeister saluted his commander in chief for a marvelous performance: "Rose was glib, relaxed, did some homework—but not too much. Fred, always being studious and detail-oriented, had done a monstrous amount of preparation—not only for his presentation but learning about his competition. Rose was throwing some light barbs at Fred and growth, and Fred eloquently and humorously laid waste to him. The people at Evaluation Associates and in that room remind me, even today, of that performance as the finest example of dueling titans in the industry, and Fred was clearly and unconditionally the victor."

But aren't growth stocks more volatile? Sure, their price swings tend to be wider, but if one picks the right companies, one can benefit from the fluctuation. Fast growers have proven to be more resilient in the roller coaster of market cycles and over time are likely to deliver superior performance for investors.

An early eighties tracking survey by Computer Directions Advisors of 131 firms with nearly $112 billion in holdings found that high beta stocks did significantly better than the S&P during the prior 2 $\frac{1}{4}$ year period. Beta is the coefficient of a stock's volatility relative to the Standard & Poor 500 stock index. A beta greater than 1 suggests that a stock is likely to move more sharply, up or down, than the market as a whole. CDA reported to *The Wall Street Journal* that the average beta of the 26 stocks in the $539 million Alger portfolio was 1.66, equivalent to 66% more volatility than the S&P, yet its gain of 72.7% was the second-best in the survey. The largest gainer was A.R. Schmeidler & Co., also of New York, whose $284 million portfolio with a beta of 1.80 had a gain of 88%.

And what happens when Wall Street pulls the plug on growth stocks, as it did for most of the span between 1983 and 1988? Did Fred Alger change its tune? Quite the opposite. The firm pounded the growth drum harder, even though it was out of step with the market. "There's not much we can do when growth is out of favor and replaced by other approaches, like cyclicals and value," said Fred. "The periods when this is the case are shorter and shorter because of the massive flow of information. If you have a company which is growing and making money and continuing to grow over a period of time, you will make money, and a competitive amount of money."

Lisa Gregg, Fred Alger's research maven, explained it this way: "We want growth stocks with rising earnings. When growth stocks were misbehaving, for a time we dabbled in non-growth. But it was really halfhearted." In other words: no matter what happens in the short term, don't hold your breath for Fred Alger Management to walk away from its growth-stock scenario.

Since the sixties Fred Alger has been hot-wired to technology as a critical instrument for research and the mother lode of rapidly appreciating stocks, as well as a fine medium for providing customer service, administration and trading.

But it was David Alger who is responsible for the company's technological transformation through information management. When he joined the firm in 1971, Fred Alger had no computers. "Analysts worked with slide rules. People did spreadsheets by hand." One of the prizes he brought along from Lombard was a "four-function calculator the size of briefcase," a Sony which he picked up for $800.

By the late seventies primitive personal computers started showing up in stores. One of these caught his eye, David said as he narrated how computers found their way into the company.

"Some time around 1977 or '78 I started reading about a company called Apple Computer, which made small personal computers. They had just come out with a product called Apple II, which came with a spreadsheet package called Visicalc.

"I had absolutely no idea if this would be useful for security analysts to do spreadsheets. Since I didn't want to invest the company's money in this computer too hastily, I decided I would buy one for myself. I lugged it back to the office over the weekend and tried to read the manuals, which I'm not very good at. I became so frustrated with this stupid machine that I took it back to the guy who sold it to me and said, 'It doesn't work.' He persuaded me that I was too intelligent not to know how to work a computer, which I thought was great salesmanship on his part.

"Anyway, I persevered and realized that it was indeed a terrific tool for doing spreadsheets." With that epiphany, personal computers started cropping up all over the company. David retooled the RA program, and RAs were charged with feeding the database and maintaining the computer records prefatory to analysis.

By the time the company moved to Maiden Lane in 1982, it had already cast away its Apples and graduated to Lotus 123. The unique way it used the spreadsheet brought Fred Alger to the forefront of financial-information systems.

"At that point it occurred to me, why wouldn't it be possible to load up all those worksheets into a bigger computer and have that bigger computer extract data from them to create a database which we could all share and use, to manipulate and search or whatever," said David.

This was likely the first thought of networking computers in such an ambitious way on Wall Street, or elsewhere, for that matter. It was a primitive client-server model which would barely pass for low-tech razzle-dazzle among today's highly evolved systems, but it was a pioneering effort and, for the self-taught David, an occasion to make a substantial contribution to the company.

What he proposed was "radically different from the way anyone operated at the time. The idea of a network for research was unheard of," said David. "No one had ever tied a bunch of PCs to a larger host computer. I had no idea how difficult it was at the time. I just assumed it could be done."

David initiated a thorough search for a computer company to be a partner in developing the system he had envisioned. Seven firms, all leaders in systems computing, were invited to bid for the project. The trouble was, these companies had barely any experience with personal computers.

Hewlett Packard couldn't supply the hardware. IBM was so consumed by its flourishing PC business it wouldn't give David the time of day. Data General "had some good technology but they were a little scatterbrained." That left DEC, which said yes.

As David designed the system structure, DEC's programmers wrote the software code and implemented the program. It was a very advanced system which took over a year to get working. While developing the network concept, which gave the firm's analysts simultaneous access to all parts of the research information, David also started figuring in new features and data-retrieval capabilities to advance the company's proprietary strategies for research and analysis. Software was custom-written to serve Alger's complex requirements.

DEC was so proud of the work it did for Alger that it gave David a starring role in an advertising campaign. The print ads featuring David ran with the headline, "Customized software that's right on the money for Fred Alger Management," and quoted him as praising DEC for "the expertise and enthusiasm to make it happen."

For its part, DEC lauded David for "his gutsy approach to go where no money manager has gone before" and hailed the company for its "real-time computer models to predict the performance of individual stocks and entire portfolios." Trumpeted David in the ads, "Our computer models are so sophisticated, we sometimes forecast a company's earnings almost as accurately as the company does."

Through the Alger Database Management System, the firm closely tracks some 1,400 companies; through research available from other Wall Street brokerage houses, it keeps tabs on an additional 5,000 U.S. corporations.

The difference at Alger, claimed David, is "the way we aggregate information, how we process it. A lot of it is unique." Other firms have similar systems, but they don't attack their data quite the same way.

"Our research is much more thorough," Lisa Gregg affirmed. "We have a much better knowledge of the companies that we own than any company our size, and

this is reflected in our stock performance through the years. Really big companies have much larger research staffs to attain the same information."

Beyond standard financial variables like revenue, profit margins, cash flow,
and earnings per share, Fred Alger's computer research contains a heavy arsenal
of uniquely phrased data components to identify winning stocks.

One of David's inventions was giving the computers the ability to segre-
gate earnings from a quarter which has ended but whose earnings are not yet
reported. How a stock moves is often dependent on quarterly-earnings estimates and revisions of forward earnings established by Wall Street analysts.
When expectations of a company's earnings are raised, it tends to lift the stock
price with it. For a company with rising earnings, the price-earnings multiple
applied by the Street will sometimes expand as well, which makes the stock
go up even more.

In the context of the market as a forward-looking entity, David explained it
is important to know which quarter's earnings are being reported. "For stock market purposes, the relevant quarter is either the one you are in or the one which
hasn't been reported," said David.

"Let's say it's July fourth and the relevant quarter ended on June thirtieth.
The reported earnings no longer belong to the current quarter, which is the September quarter. We named it the Lame Duck Quarter."

David tapped on his computer keyboard and sucked up some data on Intel.
It was June 15. "The current quarterly estimate is $2.07, compared to a $1.46 four
quarters ago for a year-to-year quarterly gain of 41.78 percent," he said in a flash.
"If it were October four, the system would automatically signal this data as Lame
Duck and correctly compare it with the preceding earnings periods. When the
system is updated with the current quarter's estimates, the Lame Duck identifier
goes away and the comparison data is also automatically revised."

Fixing earnings results as either Lame Duck or current is another way that
Fred Alger is able to attain a better appreciation of earnings growth. "This was
one of hardest things that we had to figure out and execute," David maintained.

Fred commended his brother. "One of David's greatest contributions is putting
the computer system in place," he said.

George Boggio affirmed, "The reason we could manage as much money as
we did with so few people is because the firm had a lot of technology. We had
ten ways from Sunday to analyze every stock. Just as Fred would come to me and
say, 'I wanna do this,' he did the same thing with David. He knew what he wanted.
'Can we do this? How about this?' He knew what was important. How David
delivered it was David's problem. He put in things that were important to Fred,
but also things that were important to him."

As financial information has swelled, the process of distilling financial data
and establishing systems for making the right investment decisions has become

paramount. One can no longer invest on instinct, as one could during the go-go sixties. Fred is emphatic about this.

"In the old days it would be more appropriate to describe the process as the 'art of investing,'" he said. "Today it's more in terms of systems, because information is swirling all around and you have to have a huge research staff to collect and evaluate the information that comes in and then develop it in into forecasting models. Today, one is managing billions of dollars. You just can't move that much money around on one insight or several right insights.

"So it's become more systems-oriented, where portfolios are much more diversified, with many more stocks. We're gathering and evaluating much more information. To stay on top of all the information that's generated, you really had to become highly computerized. And because the markets in individual securities have become so volatile, we've had to diversify our holdings. A portfolio may have a hundred stocks, not just twenty-five. If you're closely following a couple of hundred companies that you own for all your clients, you're also following several hundred-fold more that you might own at some point. All of this requires a lot of organization."

One example of the firm's more structured approach to market analysis is the Alger Economic Index, which was first developed in 1985 to receive advance warning of a recession. It's a monthly survey of business opinion from 150 companies in several industries and various geographic regions.

Companies are graded on a scale from 1 to 4. A 4 means that business is extremely good, better than the previous month by a lot. A 3 says that things have remained just about the same. A slight decline qualifies a company with a 2. If business is terrible, it gets a 1. Alger analysts and researchers were already speaking with these firms, so why not ask the additional question and codify the results in an index? "What we've gotten has basically fluctuated around three. But it has been a fairly accurate predictor of the economy," said David.

Fred Alger Management has the largest dedicated analyst and research team on Wall Street for a company its size. If the firm has a reputation for great performance, it was built by that research. Even without Fred the firm continues to be recognized as a market leading producer and distributor of original investment research in the financial community.

12 🐍

Analysts Game

I F IT'S MONDAY MORNING, there must be a research meeting at Fred Alger Management. Eight-thirty sharp. The hard core of six senior analysts, two portfolio managers and a dozen or so junior analysts gathered around David and Fred at the head of the long table in the cramped main conference room with a clipped view of the Wall Street skyline. It was unusual that Monday in 1994 for Fred to show up at the meeting. Since David had taken over as the firm's chief investment officer in 1992, he usually presided over the Monday affairs. Fred was involved only peripherally in investment decisions; the analysts presented their ideas to him separately. Was something afoot? Not really. By his presence Fred was just exercising a prerogative of ownership. He just wanted to mix it up again.

One by one the analysts took turns informing the group about meaningful conditions in the stocks and industries they covered. As each one spoke, Fred turned up the heat. Everyone got a grilling. Both he and David were deliberately contentious. They wanted to be certain that all the bases had been covered in the stock analyses. The proceedings were civil, sure enough, but they weren't particularly genial.

Some of the analysts were plainly suffering the post-weekend doldrums, which made it tricky fending off Fred's piercing questions. The typical load of an Alger analyst is close to 150 stocks. Taking into account months and years of accumulated data on each company, one has to be totally primed for Monday morning.

In the trading well outside the closed doors of the meeting, senior equity trader Morty Frankel was contemplating a break-in. A report had just crossed the wire that Harley-Davidson was going to miss its quarter. That's shorthand for failing to meet earnings expectations—usually a bad sign for the stock. The analysts should be alerted at once, in case they need to sell off some of the firm's holdings. But he hesitated from charging into the conference room. After all, this was not one of the daily, one-on-one analyst conferences for a quick review of the previous day's stock action, or one of the powwows about 3.5% or 7% moving stocks. This was the big weekly research meeting, when crucial decisions were made about attacking the market and deploying, at that time, nearly $4 billion in assets. Chief trader Joe Maida believed Morty's news could wait. He'd seen this type of action before, when a sharp down move on missed earnings is just a weak gut reaction and not driven by a fundamental change in a company's position.

"When we're in the midst of some stock disaster, that is, with a big position in a company reporting bad earnings and then the price drops, we have to decide whether this is really as bad as the Street is letting us know or a chance to double up," Joe explained. "Fred has a knack for reading between the lines," he added. "When everybody seems to be looking to sell, Fred will come away and do the opposite." In November 1994, the bad news for Intel was its buggy Pentium chip. The stock slumped 10% in one day. "'This sounds positive to me,' Fred said. He did buy a couple of thousand shares. Six months later the price had doubled. This happens time and again."

David Alger even had a name for this phenomenon of bad news becoming yesterday's news. He called it the "Ethiopia Principle" in *Investors Business Daily* on August 27, 1993. The article described how the scare over cellular phones causing brain cancer led to a steep sell-off in McCaw Cellular Communications, one of Alger's largest holdings. Several weeks later the stock made a smart about-face and resumed its spectacular ascent until the company was eventually sold to AT&T at a high premium. David advised the paper's readers that this underscored the need for independent research to rise above the noise. "Too much information is getting out too fast," he said in the story. "One analyst cuts his earnings estimate, which tends to prompt others to do the same, and suddenly the stock is squashed by sellers running for the exits. Investors often miss the forest for the trees this way."

Transfixed with uncertainty, Morty waited briefly outside the conference room. Finally the adage that Fred expects "No Surprises" overruled his hesitation. With a sigh he darted in and announced that Harley-Davidson stock was starting to tank and might require immediate action. It turned out to be a non-event. The portfolio managers agreed to stand pat on the stock, and the meeting broke up soon after he turned in the news. Having received their orders for the week, the analysts filed out to engage their companies and scour the media for the information edge in securities analysis.

The routine for Alger analysts to present their investment ideas has evolved nicely over thirty years. In the seventies, when the research corps was considerably smaller, each analyst or researcher had a solo turn with the fearsome Fred. Expectations were always high. Don Besser explained it best in the company's 1971 promotional video:

Once a week each analyst manager meets with Fred for several hours to discuss his research work. At each meeting he must present complete reports on at least six different companies. These reports represent ideas that have been developed from technical stock-price action, reading annual reports, talking to different members of an industry or occasional conversations with other brokers. A complete report for Fred means having checked competitors, suppliers, customers and having complete statistics. Fred rewards very highly the management methods affecting our companies. For example, one time I kept track of the shipments of a manufacturing company by talking to the state inspector who was required by law to examine each machine before shipment. The day before each analyst-manager meeting we often are in somewhat of a panic, and frankly sometimes we think too much is expected of us. Because we know that Fred will immediately sense if any of our research work on the companies that we are reporting on is at all missing. Moreover, Fred keeps track of every one of our recommendations, and he reviews these recommendations every six weeks.

Then, as now, the key element in the investment business is productivity—defined by the output of new and superior investment ideas from analysts. As Fred put it, "Performing better than the market requires a constant flow of new ideas attacking the market and replacing existing ideas in the portfolio, so that they are continually fresh." Irwin Schwartz told it this way: "All Fred wanted was good ideas. It didn't matter if it was a railroad or a chemical company," he said. "I could tell when he wasn't interested in an analyst's pitch within the first three minutes. If he asked, 'What's the balance sheet look like?' I knew it was over. He didn't have a story."

While the RA program was a fabulous feeder system providing analysts for the company, there was another fine analyst conduit into Fred Alger: Analysts Resources, the first Wall Street search firm which dealt exclusively with investment analysts. It could get you into Alger—and this was a secret on the Street—because it was created by Alger, owned by Alger and worked exclusively for Alger during its first two years.

The sole recruiter and administrator of Analysts Resources and keen-eyed gatekeeper for Fred Alger's analysts is Monica L. Smith.

It was the summer of 1979 when Fred first introduced the idea of forming Analysts Resources to the former pension executive at International Paper. Their association had begun the previous year when Fred had gone after a slice of IP's $650 million pension pie, and she was its Director of Trust Investments Employee Benefits Assets. "Fred had an ongoing need for professionals as his asset base expanded," said Monica. "I wanted to do something entrepreneurial. I knew the firms where the candidates could be found." After they discussed the idea for over a year, the firm formally got off the ground in October 1980.

A ringmaster in a one-woman show, Monica said she works independently of Fred Alger & Co. and claimed to have a "good relationship with Fred." Analysts Resources exemplifies Fred's hands-off posture toward his entrepreneurial ventures and administrative managers, which sharply contrasts with his in-your-face, confrontational relationship with analysts.

In the beginning Analysts Resources joined Alger at 26 Broadway. Then the firm moved to 230 Park Avenue "when it was advisable to be at arm's length" from the company. Following the stock market crash in 1987 and subsequent supply-demand imbalance for analysts in the industry, the firm came home to Alger headquarters. Today it operates at 75 Maiden Lane.

Before Fred thought up Analysts Resources, there was no comprehensive database of investment analysts in America. In order to build this human inventory and develop a comprehensive profile of each analyst, Monica Smith employed extensive taped interviews, which were ultimately transcribed. Her facile interrogations got to the heart of the prospective analyst's investing mind-set and gave Fred Alger access to the best thinking in the investment community. It also helped provide a potential pool of extremely talented research analysts for its growth in the eighties.

What was Monica looking for in an analyst for Alger? "A documentable record, the ability to think in a certain way, a raw intelligence to think logically, concisely and creatively." She described the latter as the sense-intuition to stay ahead of the curve. Fred Alger had special requirements, she said. "The team approach to managing funds and accounts is a very rigorous, stimulating process here. Everyone is highly motivated to come up with ideas and act on them with immediate impact. Stocks quickly get into the portfolio without a deliberate, consuming process. Fred hires very smart people who must be interested in moving ahead. This is different from other firms. Analysts here are the focal point."

One of the analysts drawn to Fred Alger from Analysts Resources' nearly 2,000 records was Robert H. Lyon, from Institutional Capital Corp. in Chicago. Lyon had heard about the firm when a colleague, Bob Emerson, informed him that he was leaving Salomon's Chicago office for Alger in New York. He had shelved their conversation until Monica called inquiring about another analyst who was a friend and reference, which led to his being considered for a job.

Lyon's interview with Monica took place in the Windy City's famous Pump Room in early spring 1981. "She came in with a big fur coat and promptly placed the tape recorder in the center of the table."

Lyon confessed that he was eager to join Alger. "I kept bugging her because the more I heard about the firm, the more I was really interested. I had just gotten married to a lady from the New York area, and we thought it would be advantageous for us to move there. I don't know if Fred had seen more than fifty analysts when I wanted to sign up. It was pretty difficult to get past her."

After talking to Monica, Lyon flew to New York to meet with Fred and David in "the crummy old office" at 26 Broadway and passed their initial screening. "Fred was always looking for somebody who is articulate, enthusiastic, had original insight and could really tell a good stock story—and not only tell it, but really back it up with documented evidence," said Lyon in summarizing his qualifications. "The more independently researched the evidence, the better."

Rob was informed that his next trial was to deliver a full-blown stock presentation to the group of Alger analysts. "When can you do that?" Fred asked. "Right now," Lyon replied without hesitation. Fred and David shot surprised looks at each other and then told Lyon he could return after lunch for his performance.

Lyon had done a lot of work on Holiday Inn, which was preparing to thrust itself into the gaming business, and felt he had the stock down cold. Little did he know that Fred, David and many of the Alger analysts were also well versed in the outlook for the company. "I thought it was sort of a new idea," said Lyon. That was his undoing.

"It didn't matter what I was going to say because it devolved almost immediately into a huge intellectual free-for-all, like the British parliament," Lyon added. "It quickly became a trial of fire. Fred asked me if I'd read *Rouge et Noir,* a periodical devoted to gaming. I had never even heard of it."

Lucky for Rob, he was given a second chance. He said Fred told him, "While some people were disappointed with your presentation, others thought that you could conceivably have something good going on. It hadn't really been a fair test, because you weren't really that well prepared."

Acknowledging the higher set of expectations at Alger, Lyon involved himself in careful research on Taft Broadcasting, which reflected his greatest area of expertise, in media companies. "I looked for a stock that was a big enough company that people would know what it was, but obscure enough that Fred's knowledge base would be relatively small and I wouldn't run into the same type of problem that I faced with Holiday Inn," he said. Having been burned once, Lyon made sure to read every industry publication. He even traveled down to the firm's base in Cincinnati, Ohio, for a lunch date with the firm's chairman, Dudley Taft, and other key company executives. He wasn't about to blow another chance at Fred Alger.

The outcome of his effort was a 40-page report on Taft Broadcasting, which he distributed at his next Alger appraisal. "I was as informed about the company as any of its directors by the time I went into the Alger meeting several weeks later," said Lyon. "I could answer all the questions this time."

"Fred and David form such strong opinions that they sometimes don't listen. Both are iron-willed and stubborn," said portfolio manager Ron Tartaro.

Later that day Fred called Lyon and offered him a job, which he accepted on the spot. Back in Chicago, he gave up his secure vice presidency at Institutional Capital, passed on a pending offer for more money from Dean Witter and packed his bags for New York. Lyon wound up being at the front end of the tremendous manpower surge at the firm, which began in 1980 and culminated in 1987.

In explaining Fred's success, Alger board's Arthur Dubow suggested that it relied as much on his business savvy as it did on his investment skill. "One of the most brilliant things he did was set up this employment agency to find good research people and cull the best for himself."

Not everyone was as enthusiastic about his starting a recruiting firm on Wall Street, for it gave him a direct pipeline to America's best analysts and their investment ideas. Naturally his rivals bridled when it was discovered that Analysts Resources was a plant for Fred Alger. They were irked by, and perhaps even jealous of, this extra source of stock ideas and Fred's leverage in hiring analysts. All that wailing ceased when Analysts Resources opened its personnel database to the rest of Wall Street and helped other investment firms reduce hiring costs and broaden their analyst searches outside the New York area. The benefits of an analyst-search firm for investment companies were obvious after Fred showed the way, but no one before him had the imagination to bind these businesses so cleverly.

Most of the interviewed analysts were unaware that Fred Alger was the figurehead behind Analysts Resources. Some reported to the business press that the tape-recorded interviews were "grueling." Others said they felt "raped" by the process. Only one, however, was enraged enough to ask for his interview tape back, which was ultimately returned and erased, though not without considerable argument from Monica Smith and the involvement of lawyers. She was seeking to detect how an analyst arrives at stock selection and not the discovery of a particular stock. "If they're confident about what they can do, they are not afraid to reveal anything," she said.

When the eighties rolled around, Fred Alger was short of analysts to support a swelling asset base that, for the first time, turned the corner on $500 million. In picking off the top talent that successfully passed through Analysts Resources to the Alger starting gate, Fred aimed at fashioning an elite corps, much like the Marines, of highly motivated professionals who would accept his leadership in the vigorous pursuit of winning stocks and market-beating performance. They were expected to be independent and imaginative, yet also conform to a disciplined Alger system, which would be instilled by training and management.

Lyon described Alger analysts as a mirror of Fred: "Virtually all were some form of Type A. Not that we were all homogenous, except for the fact that we were all very aggressive, very competitive and entrepreneurial and were very into the stock market. We had the whole spectrum, except I think the intensity level probably carried over into everybody's life."

For some the advance to Alger was a move from the bush leagues to the big league. Take Ronald M. Reel, for example. If one seeks evidence that meritocracy is the chief driver in the Alger corporate culture, Ron provides ample proof. In dramatic contrast to the button-downed Alger personality, Ron, with his short silver ponytail, cowboy boots and casual attire looks more like an aging hippie down from Woodstock for a Dead concert than a vice president and senior analyst in Alger's conservative lair. He is the only surviving member of the cream 1980 hires and the only non-family left with a small share of the company.

Like Fred and just a few others, Ron uses a slide rule to calculate stock values. In his early fifties and the same age as David Alger, which is positively ancient for a securities analyst these days, he's worked at the firm longer than anyone but David.

Ron has been a securities analyst since graduating from Texas A&M in 1965. For fifteen years he plied his trade at American General Capital Management in

Houston, where he watched over health care, drug, medical devices and hospital-management stocks, the same groups he covers today for Fred Alger.

In 1980 he was baited by an employment listing in the *Wall Street Journal* which promised he could "make $100,000," which was considerably more than he was earning at the time. The listing led to Monica Smith, and when recruited initially, Ron never knew he was headed for Fred Alger. In New York, it was David who conducted the interview. He never caught sight of Fred and believed he had no say in his hiring. "A lot of new money had come in. They were on a roll," said Ron, who met Fred only after he was offered the job.

"Fred was a legendary character in the investment business. From a distance I always followed his career because he seemed to have the same investment philosophy as I did: If you're going to make any big money in this business, you're going to have to take some risks. The book on Fred was that you must buttress that risk and back it up with innovative, in-depth research."

Bob Rescoe was another analyst coincidentally mined from American General, which managed ERISA accounts, individuals' assets and several mutual funds. Fresh with an MBA in finance from the University of Texas, Rescoe joined American General as an analyst in December 1978 and remained there for five years until he moved up to Alger.

Here's how he made it through the Analysts Resources channel. "Monica would contact me every four or five months, fishing for what I was recommending, what I liked in the market," he said. "This would include the mention of a possible job opportunity, but I didn't know at the time that she was controlled by Fred."

Rescoe went on, "The process took a year or two. I would always talk to her—she's really pleasant—until one day she offered to bring me up to New York for an interview. I knew American General was up for sale. In this business, if you are bought out by another money-management company, there's usually a lot of overhead left over called people."

Rescoe's Alger interview was vividly clear in his mind. It was a bitterly cold day in February 1983, and had just started to snow when he went in at ten A.M. By the time he was done at three-thirty in the afternoon, there was two feet of snow on the ground and his flight back to Houston was ice-locked at La Guardia Airport.

First he met with Fred, then David, then one of the senior analysts. It was lunchtime by the time he got around to presenting his stock idea, Reynolds and Reynolds Company, the diversified Dayton, Ohio, business-forms manufacturer, which was shifting away from its dependence on the auto industry.

"It was a turnaround story, with some growth to boot," said Rescoe. "I didn't know Fred was pure growth. Fred and David sat at one end of the table and me at the other end, with several of the analysts in between, all firing questions at me. If you could ever finish one sentence, you were doing pretty good. Fred was extremely friendly and cordial, and asked great questions. He's the kind of guy who could fly through all the bullshit and really hit the nail on the head with just a few questions.

"Then all the other analysts left, except for Fred, David and me. They asked a few more questions. Finally I was asked to step out of the room. A little while later David called me back. Fred had already left. He said, 'Well, we hated your idea, but we want to hire you.' Reynolds and Reynolds wasn't growthy enough. These guys really like growth. It was a great stock subsequently.

"It was an interesting process for me. I had done some research on Fred. Everything I heard was terrible. I was told, 'He's a really tough guy to work for.' 'He pays well, but you earn it.' Differential combat pay, I think, is an appropriate way of describing the situation there. It's a pressure shop. You're constantly under the gun."

The way Rescoe saw it, here was a chance for a large salary increase and a way to move back East. "I would be ahead of the game even if I lasted one year," he said. "They offered me a job right on the spot and wanted an immediate answer. 'You got me,' was my reply. I started three weeks later."

Rescoe survived ten uneasy years at Alger. Fred's purpose in hiring him was to beef up the firm's coverage of technology stocks, which had been routing the averages for several years. Unfortunately for Rescoe, his arrival coincided with the height of the technology fever, which dropped mightily during the subsequent five years.

Once an analyst has made it to Fred Alger, he or she quickly realizes that it is truly unlike any other money-management operation, and in very major ways.

For instance, the usual way of structuring investments on Wall Street is by fiat of a portfolio manager or an investment committee. Fred Alger's process of stock selection, which eliminated the manager position and delegated power and responsibility directly to the analysts, was unusual by most industry standards. In forsaking the traditional structure, Fred gambled on the strength of the analyst. If he was right in choosing his analysts, then their stocks would accordingly provide superior performance.

In the seventies, before the team concept came into being, here's how stock decisions were reached. "The buy selections were made by analysts who would sit around the table, and I would—I was considered head of research, but I followed stocks as well—we would all vote on other people's stock ideas," said David. "Then the stocks would be distributed to the portfolios by Irwin Schwartz, largely doing it by hand."

Even though the analysts considered a stock as a group, the analyst who proposed and covered a company was ultimately held responsible for its stock performance and had the primary authority of selling it when appropriate. However

David, Bill, Fred and Irwin could, as a council, react if the analyst failed to act soon enough. But they could never revoke an analyst's sell decision.

"What was unique about Fred Alger Management?" Bob Emerson mulled over the question. "There were no portfolio managers for a long time. That was pretty unusual. People still scratch their heads about that."

Many clients found the analyst system attractive, concluded a December 1980 *Institutional Investor* article. David Hammerstein, manager of benefit assets at B.F. Goodrich, took a shine to this approach, he said, because "there is less potential for slippage between the research and its implementation." Analysts likewise found it appealing. "It's a dream of a job for any analyst. You're given total responsibility," one gushed in the article.

"It was a system which was effective because we didn't have very many accounts and not a lot of money," David added. "And our base of analysts was fairly small. There weren't a lot of egos. This system by the late seventies was to grow very cumbersome, with lots of analysts, lots of research associates, and the analysts' egos were so great that very few new ideas were getting through. It was very contentious, and the mechanism of delivering all this research power into the portfolio was seriously eroded."

Fred Alger's team system was born in response to the increasing inefficiencies in stock selection due to the growing number of analysts. In this extension of the individual approach, analysts were pitted into two competing teams with leaders assigned by Fred. Each team made its stock selections independently at weekly meetings, with a rule that stocks had to receive unanimous assent by all team members.

Rob Lyon was one of the chosen few to head up these teams. Wiry and intense, Lyon, above all the analysts in the firm, resembled Fred in his strong devotion to the stock market.

"I was one of the last two or three people to come on board in the early Monica days," he explained. "Pretty much everything was covered. It would have been up to me to ferret out or steal stocks not covered by others. If you found a good stock, it was yours. If you found a stock in an industry someone else was covering, you might have the good manners to avoid it, but not always."

Lyon continued, "All the analysts were fairly aggressive. It was a free-for-all, and even I did my share of poaching. The good news for me was that Larry Haverty, the man I replaced, had a great group of stocks, including Waste Management, Toys R Us, Warner Communications and Apple Computer. All these companies were well positioned for the eighties. When I showed up the first day, David said, Why don't you take his stocks? Without knowing what they were, I answered, 'Well, it sounds good.'

"It turned out that this group of stocks was in an area which I had some experience and, more important, had an interest in—particularly media and that part of the technology that dealt with personal computers and personal communications." In this business and most situations, it's often better to be lucky than smart, and Lyon got lucky. He paid Haverty the ultimate compliment: "Larry is one of the great analysts in the business and a classic Alger guy, even though he didn't work for Fred for very long. He is well known and respected in the industry for being extremely independent and outspoken."

Lawrence J. Haverty, a senior vice president at State Street Research & Management in Boston, was part of the bumper 1980 crop that harvested Ron Reel, Baruch Halpern and Robert Emerson. To set the chronology straight, he joined Alger in October 1980 and left in July 1981, just as Lyon walked in the door.

Another other key team leader was Robert L. Emerson. Monica hit him up in August 1980. The lure to Alger was lucre. "The Algers were offering a pretty competitive salary for those days—one hundred fifty thousand dollars a year," Emerson allowed. "I was the second-best paid analyst at Salomon, and I wasn't quite making that."

When Emerson sought out advice before joining Alger, a senior colleague at another research-oriented Wall Street firm warned him, "You know, you're going to find that Alger's system works well in terms of producing good investment results, but the firm itself will never outlast him because he is so abusive to people that all the good ones leave. He'll just hire new ones. The stamp of his personality and methods will, on the one hand, produce good results, but it also will ensure that the firm cannot perpetuate itself."

Emerson's opening seasons at Alger went this way: "In 1981, the areas I knew a lot about—restaurants, beverages, tobacco—were very hot. It was a lousy year for the stock market, but those particular industries did very, very well. By February or March that year, there were two teams of four analysts. I headed one; David, the other. I stayed in that position for a couple of years. Then my stocks went out of favor, and as far as Fred was concerned, of course, because your stocks were out of favor, you became an idiot."

That was when he was benched as team leader, and Fred passed his baton to Baruch Halpern. It wasn't long before Halpern had his own fall from grace and Emerson was returned as team leader.

As originally constructed, the teams served the firm well for a time; but it was not without its perils, especially for a team leader, as Emerson was eager to illustrate. "This team leadership was a gigantic pain in the neck. There was no upside to it. You didn't get paid for it. Fred thought of it as an honorific, but it wasn't anything anybody particularly wanted to volunteer for. If a stock that one of the analysts recommended went down and that person wasn't around for Fred to beat on, he'd pick on the team leader.

"The team meetings were very unpredictable—often merely a rubber stamp for stock ideas, but at other times there were violent disagreements. The draw-back was, particularly after we started hiring lots of research assistants, these meetings would become enormous consumers of the analysts' hours. Four ana-lysts—each with two assistants—arguing for two hours. All these people were sitting around fighting for one story. Is this really the most effective use of your staff? Fred and David might argue that the only way to make junior ana-lysts and research assistants capable of making investment decisions is to let them to watch the process. Up to a limit. There was also a lot of snoozing and doodling."

Even so, Emerson readily admitted that Fred's analyst system and, by exten-sion, its team approach were imaginative solutions to a nagging problem in invest-ment management. "The analyst and the portfolio manager essentially don't like each other. There's a natural conflict between the two positions," he said. "Ana-lysts are resentful of the portfolio managers, who get all the hockey tickets, the big corner offices and make a lot more money. They get their name in the paper. If an analyst gives the portfolio manager a stock that works, the portfolio man-ager takes credit. If the thing goes down, then he blames the analyst. Why not just excise the portfolio manager's role and have analysts argue among them-selves whether they should buy a given stock, and let the allocation of that stock to individual accounts be done by a low-level statistician?"

Eventually the biggest job of Alger management was to rein in the large per-sonalities of the very intelligent, highly paid analysts in this fluid, pressure-packed dynamic. When the chemistry was right, the ideas were productive. When the mix was wrong, the scene was combustible. "The most difficult part of the job of research director was dealing with the egos of analysts trying to strike a happy medium between being an autocrat and being collegial and getting people to do what you want," said David.

"There was a time when I had a lot of highly paid analysts all working under the same roof and gave them a lot of latitude in which to operate and a lot of power and control over the process," he continued. "What I discovered was that it had a *Lord of the Flies* quality. What I thought would be a wonderful collegial experience turned into a real survival-of-the-fittest situation generating a great deal of personal enmity, where people would do outrageous things. I never could find the balance of getting these people motivated and working hard without wanting to throw each other out the window."

The Tuesday night meeting, when analysts defended their worst stocks of the previous week, became the main stage for this contest of wills. The usually riotous affairs began around five-thirty at Alger's 75 Maiden Lane penthouse executive conference room, adjacent to its modest corporate library. It came with catered meal, typically burgers and Cokes, and a trip home in a company paid limou-sine when it let out at eight.

No soiree this. The analysts hunkered down with their stocks and butted heads for supremacy. "The analyst who followed the stock had to mount its spirited defense. Initially this worked very effectively. Over time it degenerated into a great deal of animosity, grandstanding, name calling and occasionally sporadic outbreaks of book throwing," said David, who was the referee on most nights.

Fred explained that the team system addressed the following issues. "One, it mitigated the problem of manager burnout. Two, it solved the problem of which clients would get which manager if a client perceived one manager was better than another. Three, it prevented a manager from building up a relationship with a client and, if he moved, taking the client with him." Fred insisted that while the portfolio manager is important, success is a matter of stock selection, which is mainly accomplished by the research department. "Research is more important than the manager," Fred asserted.

The firm's analysts came down on both sides of the team approach.

"The team concept entailed too many meetings. It took longer to get ideas through these meetings because unanimous approval was required. And the meetings themselves kept the analysts from research," observed Ginger Risco. "In a perfect world it would be great because you get input from all the people and you cover all the bases. You know that your idea is attractive relative to all industries, all companies and your peers."

According to Lisa Gregg, Fred's strong opinions often presented a quandary in which Alger analysts usually took the course of least resistance. "If he didn't like a stock, it could still get into the portfolio over his objections; but most analysts weren't going to fight back hard if Fred didn't like it," she said. "They don't want to have to go back to him with a mea culpa. It was bad enough if the stock goes sour with Fred liking it."

"The advantage of the team was that analysts got more involved and were responsible for the performance of the entire firm. They were also exposed in greater depth to industries they don't normally cover," said Ron Tartaro, one of two portfolio managers in Alger's current modified team approach.

Whether Alger's teams, in fact, produced better results than the same research might have yielded with the control of a portfolio manager is hard to say. Irwin Schwartz, for one, was convinced it made no difference. But it was certainly a time waster for team leaders, who had to summarize the best stock ideas in a separate presentation to Fred.

The fact that Fred Alger began to rethink the team system beginning in 1987 and finally installed portfolio managers in 1994 was a big surprise to many older analysts and outsiders who follow the firm. The company had been such a booster of its unique analyst system, which was a key element in all its promotions and a highlight of its massive advertising campaign in 1986.

David explained what undid the team approach. "The problem was that you really needed someone to make the final decision and have final authority over the portfolios because the analysts were hopeless at selling stocks and frequently turned down each other's ideas purely out of ego," said David. "It became a very clumsy system with analysts stepping over each other's toes."

Fred put it in perspective: "We were constantly fiddling with ways to increase productivity and the flow of new ideas and make individual analysts aware of the entire market, not just their stocks. We tried a lot of things and abandoned some of them because they didn't yield anticipated results."

When performance was high and the company flourished, Fred generally kept his hands off the research mechanism. When he grew impatient with results, however, he would try to jump-start the action. In 1983, for example, after the move to 75 Maiden Lane, he took the step of formalizing the distribution of stocks for analyst coverage, which coincided with David's preoccupation with the computer integration of the Alger database.

Again in the mid to late eighties, Fred abandoned marketing and took the wheel when a serious swoon in growth stocks was having a drastic impact on the firm's performance versus the S&P. He became the official screener of all stock ideas, with David taking the job of portfolio manager. This was the harbinger of the eventual dissolution of the analyst system.

"It was clear that Fred was going to be very much a participant in the buy decision and I would make the sell decisions myself without regard to the analysts' feelings. So it was no longer germane to have a Tuesday night meeting where everyone had input in everyone else's ideas. By general conclusion, we had decided that the Tuesday night meetings had outlived their usefulness," David explained. The firm closed the door on the Tuesday night affairs as a cost-cutting measure after the Crash of 1987.

Prompted by a significant increase in the number of its analysts, the firm started inching toward a portfolio approach, and in 1989 the team concept and the analyst system was formally replaced by a pure portfolio system, with David solidifying his role as portfolio manager. In 1994 two senior analysts were promoted to portfolio managers. At that point David assumed the title of president and chief investment officer.

With the teams out of the way, Alger embarked on a more structured and typical Wall Street setup of analysts individually turning over their recommendations to the portfolio manager. Rescoe felt that the firm may have given up its edge by surrendering its old approach. "I thought it was a great way, a chance for a lot of discussion and rooting out a good story. We lost the value of being exposed to other ideas."

In his postmortem of the team system, David reflected, "We had assembled all this talent and great resources in computers, but I think our process wasn't controlled enough. It was too democratic." In hindsight, the basis for the performance lapse in the mid-eighties was not the analyst system but the general underappreciation of growth stocks.

Fred Alger's analysts games stand out as unique examples of the firm's energy in training and motivating the firm's analysts and researchers. The first of these games was developed in 1984 partly as a way to lick the malaise of market underperformance. It was made to advance competition, boost creative ferment, condition the analysts and give a certain praxis to the real-life warfare of the money management business.

For the game, each analyst ran a separate paper portfolio entirely at his or her discretion which was completely distinct from the team recommendations and the firm's holdings. At year end, the "manager" of the highest performing of these faux portfolios was named the year's star analyst; a consolation prize was given to the next two best performers. The game was big. Part of your bonus depended on it.

Every Monday morning the company handed out a report card of the analysts' standing in the game, with the quarterly performance breakdown as the benchmark. The game was bound by an extremely sophisticated scoring system that endeavored to mimic real-world trading conditions. A 3 to 5% charge was assessed to emulate concessions for liquidity and transaction costs. The analysts were further evaluated against the group of companies they were formally charged with following.

The best thing about the game was that it fired up the place. Perhaps paraphrasing Fred, George Boggio observed, "The key to successful money management is the high output of new investment ideas forcing their way into existing portfolios. The game was designed to keep productivity up. It allowed you to sell with confidence and keep attacking the market and to have bonuses related to the output of new ideas. It kept the analysts from just sitting around and watching their existing portfolios."

The worst thing about it was the intense competition, which was not only antithetical to a team approach but actually severed the lines of communication among the analysts. In the end, what was originally prescribed as a catalyst for new stock ideas devolved into puerile blood sport. The analysts' game performance became disconnected from their real investments. The game created a parallel, virtual realm that began taking precedence in the analysts' minds over the securities in their portfolios. Several times, for example, when Fred complained about an analyst's poor performance, they would point out that their game score was up.

David described the mood around the game: "Theoretically the thing should have duplicated the performance of their stocks. What we found was that the analysts game, though we never solely based compensation on it, became their reason for existence. They took it so seriously that they stopped thinking about the stocks as they actually existed in the portfolios. One example of that was clocking out—as we used to call it—which meant putting a stock up for sale. They would then wash their hands of it despite the fact that we could own the stock in the genuine portfolio.

"It became a tremendous diversion. There were various ways the analysts developed to, kind of, screw around with the numbers. I don't know what the techniques were, but they found a whole bunch of ways to improve the performance. The irrational thing was, if most of their compensation was tied to the results of the game, it would have made sense. But it wasn't."

In the end, this game was undone by its own success and the tremendous divisiveness which grew around it. "It didn't really accomplish much and forced the analysts to focus on the wrong things. I didn't think it was a particularly good tool," admitted David. Ironically, however, its time was the period of the greatest economic stability and personnel retention in the firm. Emerson offered cynically, "They disbanded the game in 1987 because David was doing so badly." David's rebuttal: "When we went to a full portfolio system, the analysts game became irrelevant because the portfolio manager assumed control over what got bought or sold and not the analysts."

"People pay us to put their money at risk" was Ron Reel's cogent phrasing of the social contract between the investor and his money manager and, by extension, the analyst. And pay well they do, directly through management fees to the firm. It's no secret, money is the main attraction for most people in the securities business.

After seeking out the best and the brightest analysts, Fred Alger was ready to pay top dollar for their talent. Just as he never hesitated paying a high multiple for rapidly growing companies, he was lavish with analysts who showed promise in expanding the value of the firm.

"When Fred wanted someone, he would go after that person and be very generous with whatever package he offered. I would not be surprised if we were usually the high, not the low offer," George Boggio said. "Where we invested our money was in analysts. We paid analysts very high compensation."

In addition to the high salary, financial remuneration arrives in a number of ways, including a pension, a profit-sharing retirement plan and medical benefits. Next there's an overall bonus based on a wide variety of subjective factors, not limited to the quantity of the analyst's accepted recommendations and his or her contribution to overall performance.

There's a second bonus, which is based on the results of a new analysts game started in 1994. This contest is for the largest number of net winning stocks recommended by an analyst during the quarter. First place takes $25,000, second gains $15,000 and third wins $10,000. The game starts fresh every quarter, so there's a potential windfall of $100,000 to the consistent top performer. Unlike the old game, this one is focused in the real world of the company's stocks. Its purpose is to pry analysts from a risk-averse reliance on their proven winners that have gone up in price and add vitality to their portfolios.

The final source of income—a personal contest—constitutes a shrewd training program for stock-picking and portfolio-management skills. At the start of the year the company lends its analysts a slice of the firm's trading account for them to manage. Any gain above the 10-year treasury-bond yield is theirs to keep. Losses, on the other hand, are borne by the firm. A junior analyst gets $100,000 to play with. A senior analyst's pot is $400,000. In between, an analyst's portfolio kicks off with $250,000. This sport ensures that all Alger analysts are firmly committed in the market and makes up for the fact that the firm has dispensed with offering partnerships to employees outside the family.

Robert Rescoe described a time in 1991 when he was indecisive about the market and therefore meekly positioned with 60% of his $400,000 in cash, then he heard Fred deliver a compelling case for being fully exposed in stocks. So impressed was Rescoe that he put all his money to work in the market that day, which turned out to be the bottom of the market after the Gulf War. "Stocks took off," Rescoe said happily. "I went from down in the hole to making a lot of money, even after the cost of capital."

For those intent on a career as a securities analyst, the following well-observed reports from the trenches captures the quality of an analyst's life and illustrates the vagaries of working with Fred.

From Rob Lyon: "Our view is that there are always some stocks that are going up, and your job is to find them. If it is a very bad environment, you might want to be more conservative. Even in down markets there are companies turning around, or offering new products or some story. Your job is to get rid of all the other stocks, filter them out and focus on those stocks where there is really something going on."

From Ginger Risco: "Fred was always positive about the stock market and investing. He was very clear in his thinking and message to us, and never waffled even if the market was down. He'd rather be invested in stocks. His path was clear. We may have disagreed with him, but we always lined up behind that."

From Robert Rescoe: "In this business you create pressure for yourself. It's inevitable you're going to make mistakes. Just pull yourself up and make a decision. If stock is down, hold or sell. You have to know how to say, 'I made a mistake.' You have to respond or you'll be out of a job. You can't get emotional in this business.

"A lot of people fall in love with their stock ideas and hate to sell them. But in this business we get judged quarterly, which is really too short. The average investor actually does better over time than the professional money manager. That's because he doesn't have to dance to a quarterly review."

From Ron Reel: "This job is a combination of poker and chess, with more emphasis on poker. But it is no different from a professional gambler— calculating the odds and putting money down. Anyone can do the research. There's no particular skill in that. The skill comes in determining how the market will respond to the research you uncover. That's the crap shoot. Just like a gambler, if you have more good days than bad days in any one year, you make a lot of money."

Research analysis involves more than due diligence over balance sheets, earnings momentum and management. There's a quantum of instinct and intuition that must be stirred into every decision. Can these qualities be learned and developed? Fred often instructed from experience or by personal example.

"I forget the stocks we made money on," he said. "But I remember the disasters. We dwell on them here. We talk about them over and over, trying to figure out why they failed, why they crossed up our ideas. Emotionally it is terribly draining." It was with this in mind that he instituted the Tuesday evening ritual when analysts faced off in defense of their worst-performing stocks.

What part, if any, does luck play in one's success? Fred belongs to the school which teaches that those who work hard are the ones who get lucky. "You have to organize your portfolio around the half-dozen stocks that might do better than anyone anticipates to maximize your chance of getting lucky," Fred said in a May 11, 1981, article in *Forbes* magazine.

David observed, "It's really just grinding it out and doing a good job every day. There's no magic. There's no genie in the closet whispering the names to buy. It's just very highly trained, well-qualified people doing hard work."

Several analysts reported that it was not uncommon for Fred to emerge from his office with a suggestion to buy several thousand shares of a particular stock. When, seemingly at his bidding, the stock would promptly rise, he would get a real kick out of it. Frequently he would play the role of headmaster, stopping by an analyst's office to administer a pop quiz, force an idea, or hector for better performance. Unfortunately Fred never graded on a curve. "Fred doesn't care if he's worked with you for twenty-five years. If your stocks aren't doing well, you're going to know about it and in no uncertain terms. You are going to get the same amount of heat whether you are his brother or his best friend or his child," observed a former employee. Resigned to his uncompromising nature, Fred pleaded, "I don't know how to do it any other way."

There's a story, perhaps apocryphal, that Fred once shunned Gillette as a stock idea because he didn't know its products, even though the company has been one of the most consistently rewarding growth stocks since the fifties. "True, I don't use shaving cream," Fred reasoned, "and it is very possible that I turned down Gillette as an investment for that reason. I don't remember doing that, but it's possible." His reaction may appear irrational, but it's faithful to the well-worn dictum to "invest in what you know."

Irwin Schwartz always trusted he knew the secret to winning the stock market game. "You focus on where a stock will be six months from now; what people are going to be thinking about this company by then.

"In stock picking, you either have it or you don't. I don't think you can teach people that," he continued. "When I used to interview people, I'd ask, 'Have you ever been to the racetrack?' If they said no, I didn't want to hire them.

"When a new analyst or RA came to work for us, Fred would urge him to keep a diary, as he had done when he started out in the business. Keeping a diary is valuable so that years from now you can look back and revisit your thinking. Or buy a *Wall Street Journal* and put it away for six months, then read it to realize that what was written had little bearing on what eventually took place."

David's recurrent warning to new analysts is to view the research information with a heavy dose of skepticism and guard against being conned by management about the company's financial results.

"The hardest chore for an analyst is to see things clearly, in a disinterested way," Fred declaimed. "Even if the stock is running hard, he should look at information dispassionately. All of our research tools are structured so that analysts can respond to information as it's coming in and respond properly—not with the emotion of the moment. It is very important for analysts not to get swept up by the movement of the stock or by what other people are saying. It's a tough job when the market is falling or rising rapidly. It's hard to keep your balance."

Paradoxically one of Fred's most peculiar tools for analysts to maintain an even keel, stay focused and clear and unmoved by emotion relied on the analyst's emotional assessment of a stock which he called the Psych Line. Invented by Fred in 1984, the psych line was a stock diary in chart form, which analysts were expected to maintain for every one of the 100 to 150 stocks they followed.

This assessment was primarily based on direct conversation with the firm's management. In a notebook, underneath the price chart for each stock, the analyst was required to describe in red ink his state of mind about the company. If his feelings were positive, he should assign it a plus sign, or even two plusses if he felt extremely optimistic. If his feelings were negative, he should give it a minus sign. One could only feel better or worse about a stock. A neutral position was not allowed.

Analysts had to explain their reasons for reacting as they did to the stock, either for better or worse. Was the competition getting tougher or falling off? Did the firm introduce a new product or receive a patent? How did the employees react to the recent turnover in management? The correspondence between the

trend of the stock price and the analyst's emotional view of the company provided the real payoff in this research tool, which created a distinct profile of a
stock's characteristics over a stretch of time.

Was the stock moving ahead of or in reverse of the analyst's opinion? The
psych line helped to demystify the market by showing that psychology plays as
much of a role in stock prices as do valuations. For example, when management
was sounding progressively more optimistic while the stock remained static or
was just beginning to budge, it was likely a great time to buy the company. After
all, the reason why a stock is sold is that someone else wants to buy it. The psych
line was special to Fred as a tactic for harnessing the energy and concentrating
the minds of his analysts—and woe to anyone who didn't take it seriously. Bob
Emerson related an incident between Fred and an analyst who wouldn't do them.

"As a team leader at this point, the analyst reported to me, and Fred advised
me that he was going to come around and audit the psych lines. I told him, 'If
you don't start doing these lines, I assure you that you're going to regret it. Fred
can be a very tough guy, and he's going to be very angry if he finds out that you
cavalierly disobeyed his instructions.' He replied with a heavy Boston accent,
'Bob, I'm a professional investor, with fourteen years' experience. Nobody is going
to tell me that I have to draw smiley faces next to charts of my stocks.'"

Sure enough, several days later Fred called the analyst into his office and asked
him to bring his notebook with the psych lines. "The guy grabbed his book, which
was empty, and strutted confidently into Fred's office," Emerson continued. "Several of us were waiting in the trading room to see what would happen. Several
minutes go by, then Fred closed the door. There was no sound. Forty-five minutes later, he came out, white as a ghost, and muttered under his breath, 'Bob it
was like a date with Dracula.' Next week he was drawing psych lines like the rest
of them."

The large and loquacious Emerson gave this brief on why Fred's psych line
deserved a high place in Alger's process for evaluating stocks. "I do believe in
whatever keeps you on top of a stock, particularly a stock you don't like or something you own where things have gone wrong. The human impulse is to just take
the thing off your screen and pretend that it has gone away. This was a good tool
for making sure that you didn't suppress your problem stocks, to the extent that
you were strictly required to have an updated opinion and keep thinking about
and constantly reviewing your stocks. It always seemed peculiar. But when you
looked at it after the fact, it wasn't as crazy as it sounded.

"The psych lines were probably effective; a lot of Fred's best ideas were. I
remember the summer of 1982, just before the market took off. It was a very
depressing time. Stocks just kept going down. Morale was lousy. Fred made an
interesting observation, which was quite accurate: It is exactly during times like
these when you have to follow disciplined routine. If you are preoccupied and

mesmerized by the action on the screen and feel shitty as the market keeps going down, that's totally unproductive."

With Fred leaving and David flying solo on the administrative and sales side, it was inevitable for the firm to soft-pedal its hard line on the analyst system and create a new hierarchy of portfolio managers to relieve organizational pressure and deal with the resurgent swing of assets into the company.

In grooming Seilai Khoo and Ronald Tartaro to be the company's first official non-Alger portfolio managers, Fred and David bypassed their most experienced and tenured senior analysts in favor of youth and dynamism. The energetic duo that navigates the company's new formation are miles apart in terms of culture and life experience. They are alike only insofar as both of them believe in the Alger growth-stock proposition. They are also similar in two fundamental traits coveted by the Algers: the ability to pick stocks that go up and the sense not to fight the market.

Why dual portfolio managers? Fred explained, "We didn't want to be dependent on one person. What happens if one of them leaves?" He insisted, "This is still an analyst-driven system."

Seilai, who hails from Sabah in Malaysia, received her degrees in economics and computer science from Columbia University in 1986. Her first job was in the pension-consulting division of Refco Group Ltd., a futures and options brokerage, where she helped to monitor the performance of its clients' money managers.

After two years she hooked up with RHO Management, a New York–based international money-management firm but soon crossed swords with its chief economist. Responding to a classified ad, she interviewed with David, whom she described as "very animated." Lively but prim, Seilai appeared to fit the Alger mold and was hired as a research assistant.

Seilai, who claimed Fred as her mentor, abruptly launched into a pellucid tutorial on the Alger investment creed to make sure you knew it was integral to her investment cosmology. "I've heard them so often that I find myself repeating a lot of the same things that Fred has said over the years to the analysts," she admitted. His knowledge seemed to burn inside her.

"Fred would say, 'The market is about change. You have to focus on change. Recognize change. Capitalize on change.' The problem with stocks is you can always find positives and negatives. If you let the potential negative event weigh you down, if you wait too long, the stock has already moved.

"Concentrate on the inflection point of change. That's where the greatest amount of money may be won or lost.

"The price-earnings multiple is only secondary to change. Something good is happening to keep that multiple at high levels. If that something good is sustainable, the multiple will always remain high; so if you wait for the multiple to come down, you will never buy the stock. The multiple will come down when there is another change for the worse; and that's not the time to buy."

Seilai threw out another nugget from Fred. "We're not business analysts. We're stock market analysts. You have to be in tune with the stock market. A company may be great and in a great business, but its stock may be a dog." She used Chrysler as an example. It was repurchasing its stock. Its Jeep and Neon lines were selling well. It had a great balance sheet. Its pension funds were close to being funded or overfunded. It was awash in cash flow and raising dividends. But it wasn't a great stock in 1994. Why? Because the Fed raised interest rates and the economy slowed down.

The ideal Alger stock, by contrast, is a company like Intel Corp., whose sales are growing even faster than expectations and whose profit margins are rising as a result of innovative new products and reduced manufacturing costs.

Singing his praises, Seilai explained, "Fred is very good at sharpening analysts' analytical skills, because he's so sharp. He has deep insights and he makes a point of it in a way that you remember. In a stock story, if there's a hole, he'll find it in no time and tear it apart. There's no way you can get around Fred. As he says, 'Picking stocks is like learning a language. It takes time, and you have to learn the vocabulary. After you learn the words, then you have to become fluent in it.'"

While Seilai seemed to hang on every one of his teachings, she was quick to slam his 3.5% filter—of stocks-that have outperformed the S&P average by 3.5% in the previous five trading days—as ridiculous. "It's just his way of keeping tabs on how analysts are spending their time. The analysts are working hard enough. Everyone is competitive. I paid attention to it only because I had to meet with him."

From the moment Ron Tartaro hit Alger, he has been on a fast track. After receiving a master of science in operations research from Columbia University's School of Engineering in 1986, he went to AT&T's Bell Laboratories as a quality consultant.

Ron began investing in the stock market and soon fell under its spell. "I fell in love with it because of the way it worked rather than the possibility of making or not making money," he said. "I knew I was more interested in the stock market than a career at AT&T." His fascination was further stimulated by the fact that his longtime sweetheart and fiancée, Karen Reilly, was a securities analyst at Marinevest, a subsidiary of Marine Midland Bank. Ron admitted, "Her career appeared to be more exciting than mine."

In 1989 Karen Reilly joined Fred Alger Management. As part of her professional progression, she needed to take the CFA exam, and Ron, at first, served as her study mate. Then he decided to sign up for the exam as well.

Ron's CFA exam was set for June 1990. Shortly before then, however, came his

lucky break into Fred Alger. One of the rating services had given the firm an inaccurate ranking, at least Fred thought so, and he was trying figure a way of correcting the situation. It was a complex matter involving statistics, which Karen
knew was Ron's forte. So she suggested he take a look at the numbers and offer a
solution.

"The way they were looking at it was totally wrong. I know it after only a couple of hours," said Ron. "They were grouping Alger with other types of fund managers, whereas we are specialized in the growth area. They were also using a very
limited sample and drawing conclusions which were inaccurate." Ron proved all
this in a detailed report to Fred, who appeared to be pleased with his analysis.

About that time an RA position opened up, and Ron scored an interview with
David. The rest, as they say, is history. Ron finally met Fred at the Monday morning meeting on his first day of work, July 2, 1990.

Starting out as a research associate, Ron's path was clearly laid out. First he
passed CFA 2 and moved up to associate analyst. When he completed CFA 3, he
was promoted to analyst. The next rung was senior analyst, then associate portfolio manager. Finally he became portfolio manager. Along the way, of course,
was a lot of work.

Ron credits his success as an analyst and exciting rise in the firm to "having
a phenomenal mind for numbers." He rattled off why that was important. "There
are so many different companies, so if you have an idea of what stock prices are
and what earnings are going to be without having to look it up all the time, you
can make relationships and correlations on the fly. If you're sitting at the trading desk and managing a couple billion dollars and all of a sudden a trader informs
you that fifty thousand shares of XYZ are for sale at sixteen and five-eighths, do
you want to buy it? You only have ten or twenty or thirty seconds to make a decision. If you have to look up what the growth rate is, what earnings are, what the
stock could go up to, and which portfolio it can go into—or if you spend a lot of
time trying to figure it out—you can lose the opportunity."

Ron maintains that the most difficult part of his job is selling a stock. "You
often wind up getting too close to companies and falling in love with them so
that even when there is a fundamental change, you overlook it or fail to recognize the change."

Barely completing their first year of tenure as portfolio managers, Ron and
Seilai clocked in superb returns in 1995 and began taking their bows with the
new generation of young, aggressive portfolio managers who were making their
reputations in the same way that the go-go money managers summoned media
attention thirty years earlier.

Barron's was so wowed by Alger's mid-year performance in 1995 that it cited
11 of its public portfolios as "The Red-Hot Alger Funds" in its June 26, 1995 issue.
At mid-year, Alger MidCap blossomed 31.20%, Alger Growth rose 27.93% and

Fred on CNBC. He was often controversial in the media.

Alger Small Cap surged 34.37%. Though David Alger, who keeps vigil as titular portfolio manager of all the company's pension accounts, mutual funds and managed portfolios, was given most of the credit, both Ron and Seilai played a big role in the performance of all the portfolios, especially the three mentioned above. Attractive as Alger's mid-year results were, they paled in comparison to the end-of-the-year performance.

It was evident Ron and Seilai had learned their lessons well and that, especially over the second half of 1995, they would begin to share the limelight with David or make their own star turns.

The September 1995 issue of *Mutual Funds* magazine named Alger the first family of mutual funds over 61 other fund complexes for the period from January to June 1995. Alger's return was 25.7% and climbing while the fund family average was up only 16%. Alger Capital Appreciation fund was said to be up 41% and, with just $5 million in the portfolio, was well on its way to becoming the year's best-performing mutual fund. The article featured a hard-jawed head shot of Ron Tartaro and quoted him liberally throughout. David was nowhere in sight, and there was barely a mention of his name in the story.

At the same time the magazine was hitting the newsstands, *Investor's Business*

Daily, on August 16, 1995, led off its story on Netscape Communication Corp.'s soaring initial public offering with the mention of how Seilai flipped Alger Growth fund's entire allocation of 15,000 shares for a giddy one-day profit of $667,500 before trading expenses. The offering price was $28. She got out at $72.50 and was quoted as saying, "Selling is the only thing you could do. You can hold it, but it's not a meaningful position." Again, no mention of David.

Money Magazine, in its January 1996 issue, called David and Seilai the "dynamic duo" that was responsible for the by then $42.5 million Alger Capital Appreciation fund's stunning rise of 86% for the year as of December 1, 1995. The two-page spread posed David, arms folded and standing with Seilai seated behind him, on the staircase to the Maiden Lane penthouse. The article led in with the Alger Bulls winning their fourth straight Staten Island Industrial Softball League championship and closed by offering this prescient, though contrarian, market call by David. "Every time the earnings yield has fallen to around fifty percent of the long-bond yield in the past fifteen years, the market has proved to be overpriced. And when the earnings yield has approached ninety percent, it has proved to be cheap. Today it is above ninety percent."

Once they moved up in rank, Ron and Seilai had to let go of the relative tranquillity of stock analysis and the general comfort of their peer relationships to take on the proactive, confrontational and fast-paced routines inherent in the job of portfolio manager. To be a good portfolio manager, you have to be a good analyst. But a good analyst doesn't necessarily make a good portfolio manager.

The contest between portfolio manager and analyst is a fundamental property of money management. Ron Reel put it nicely, "Confrontations about stocks are a normal feature of this business. The decision is where the money is made or lost, where the hard answers are. My job is to influence the portfolio managers where we put our money. My bottom line: to make the firm do what I want the managers to do."

Seilai observed, "I soon realized that this was as much about managing people as dealing with their stock recommendations. For example, Shelton is generally more conservative, so when he's worried about a stock, it doesn't mean that I should sell it, but if Ron Reel, who never likes to sell a stock, comes in and says this is a sale, it probably is."

Around the same time the firm was anointing its new portfolio managers, small changes took place on its research side. The Alger company began opening itself up to outside research in order to gain a place at the table for profitable initial public offerings, like the earlier mentioned Netscape issue. Another adjustment in 1993 was finally subscribing to First Call, a fee-based service which electronically broadcasts earnings estimates and revisions of earnings estimates by analysts in major brokerage houses on Wall Street. Never a substitute for its weighty independent research, First Call estimates nonetheless give Alger analysts equal access to the accepted thinking on the Street, serve as a safety net for missed information, and provide opportunities when those figures are at variance with their own.

With its assets surging and performance booming, there is a constant requirement for new stock ideas to satisfy Alger's diversification rules, especially for small-cap stocks. Alger has set its guidelines as follows: No more than 20% of its assets in any one industry. No more than 5% of its assets in any one stock. It will not own more than eight days' average trading volume of any stock across all its accounts. Normally it owns fewer than three days' average trading volume. The obligation for NASDAQ stock is an even steeper four days.

Despite the shift toward portfolio management, the Alger system remains analyst-driven at its core. The analyst's enthusiasm for a stock and vigilance over its course determines its place in the portfolio. The old pecking order for selling a stock still applies. Analyst first, then the portfolio manager, then David.

Analyst-driven, yes. Personality-driven, no. After all is said about analysts and despite the personality cult that attended Fred's success and the rise of others in the industry, Fred Alger meets the challenge of investing by a disciplined adherence to systems. There's no alchemy or superstition in good performance—just hard work knotted on the backbone of a focused attention and repetitive action. In Alger's offensive scheme the personalities are interchangeable, even expendable. Uber portfolio manager David Alger explained why this was so:

"The stocks that we buy are so volatile that a price fluctuation of ten percent in a day is not infrequent, and this radically alters the appreciation potential of a stock on any given day. Plus, one can never be hard and fast about what multiple a stock should sell for. It has to be constantly adjusted against the nature of the market where those kind of stocks are selling. Finally, analysts are always changing their earnings forecasts. Consequently all parts of that equation are in flux, the price most of all, in any given stock. What the computer does is take all the stocks, make all the changes and rerank them as to where you have your best potential for appreciation.

"The kind of tools we have now were not available when Fred was starting out. For the last ten years anyway, stocks have been in a fairly narrow trading range in terms of what kind of valuation the market will give them, and this is a function of the intense computerization and institutionalization that has taken place in the market. It's the development of these tools that has stood us in good stead. In a sense, a stock can be a good sale one day and a buy the next. There's a zero-based budgeting approach to our portfolios every day. As a stock approaches its target points, we sit down with the analyst and determine either to raise the earnings, increase the p/e multiple, sell it, or skim it back."

Senior analyst Ron Reel seemed to ratify this systems-dominated view. "Rapid transmission of electronic information, index and other computer-related programs can move the market at an instantaneous pace," he said. "Because of the speed of the information flow, you have to move faster than you ever did in the past. All this creates opportunity, which depends on how you're postured to deal with it."

Fred Alger deals with information systematically. It starts with detailed and substantial note taking on every covered stock, which is dictated and transcribed nightly. At the same time data is continually gathered, organized and uploaded to the Alger database management system. The numbers are crunched into forecasting models on a quarterly basis as well as one- and two-year projections. This vast storehouse of organized information is what gives Alger analysts the cutting edge. "Getting new ideas is the greatest single problem any firm has," said Fred. "This output of ideas is the key to success. Other firms are not nearly as organized as we are, and longer term their records probably aren't as good."

For its size, analyst turnover has actually been minimal at Alger. Departures had more to do with an earlier absence of upward mobility and the lack of starring roles within the Alger system rather than any objection to Fred's tough-as-nails, in-your-face demeanor. In the late eighties the collapse in the firm's assets under management paved the way for the only prolonged exodus from the firm.

It is normal for analysts to close out their careers early—no more or less at Fred Alger Management. "Analysts wear out," Fred said. "They can't maintain the intellectual energy to keep attacking the market. It's a function of the business. It's too intense. Everything is being measured all the time, and it's not enough just to make money. You have to make more money than the next guy."

If there is a glass ceiling in the firm, it's because you are not family. But Fred's son-in-law, Daniel Chung, went through the drill just like every other research associate. "We're hoping that after David, he will be in a position to run the firm," said Fred. In any case, Chung has impressive credentials for the job. A Phi Beta Kappa at Stanford, where his father was professor emeritus of mathematics, he earned a law degree from Harvard and was an associate at Simpson Thacher & Bartlett before joining Fred Alger.

"However, while it is a family firm, it is an absolute meritocracy," Fred added. "The best people, the best person will run the firm when David pulls out. Dan obviously will have an important input, but if he's not the best person, he won't run it."

This was something Fred understood even when he was new to the business. The BBC's *Money Programme* which aired April 12, 1968, was the forum where he first publicly voiced the view of analysts as a disposable commodity. "We feel that running these portfolios, with the day-to-day measurements of performance, is a tremendous strain," he said on camera. "And we tend to think of portfolio managers as athletes, that they do have a limited life." They may burn brightly, but like shooting stars or comets, they also burn out.

The 30-minute series introduced Fred this way: "Working from an office high above Wall Street, it is something more than brains that brought thirty-two-year-old Fred Alger his million-dollar income. Fred Alger is one of Wall Street's stars, a fund manager with two hundred million dollars of investors' money to play with." True to form, Fred gave his interview over sandwiches at lunch and was dressed in his trademark white shirt and suspenders.

Fred followed his own counsel on analysis as a young man's game. Once he built his organization and as soon as it was prudent to do so, he withdrew from the daily grind of investment analysis to concentrate on management and marketing. Still, he met a half hour or so at least once a week with each analyst and charted his or her performance. Facing his own flagging enthusiasm, at the apt moment he quit.

Prior to leaving the firm in 1995, Fred observed hopefully as he forecast the certain completion of David's stewardship: "David will give it a good five to six years of solid effort, and the company should be at least twice as large at the end of five years as it is now." His estimate proved too cheap, since David is well ahead of his schedule for meeting Fred's goal and is surpassing even his own more aggressive agenda for the firm.

13 🐉

"Call Me Fred"

I N THE SPRING of 1995, just weeks before Fred would take flight from the company, an electronic surprise made its way into his office. Those who watched it wheeling by were astounded. The firm's old-timers stopped in shock. Horrors! Had their computer-dodging boss truly made up with modern age? The unbelievers came to see for themselves and, spying the gleaming new Pentium PC waiting next to his desk, went away with more questions. What fate would befall his trusty slide rule? What finally caused him succumb to technology?

Fred's office has had its share of unusual guests and gear. An exercise cycle when he trained for the New York Marathon. The language tutor for an hour each morning when he went on a French kick. But never before something as image-shattering as this. James P. Connelly Jr., who worked his way up to become the firm's mutual-fund manager and had recently become dear to Fred as his point man for launching the Alger Fund in Europe, claimed some credit for the computer's oddly timed arrival. Behind closed doors, he hovered apprehensively when Fred first placed his hands on the system.

Once the program flashed on, Fred's eyes lit up like a little boy taking out his first bicycle. A few keystrokes and he was up and away. It wasn't a spreadsheet or a database he was maneuvering, but the shape of an aircraft in a crude flight simulator. Yes, a flight simulator, to practice hand-eye coordination for his new hobby of piloting radio-controlled airplanes—something to fill up his free time in Europe. That was his concession to the computer age.

Watching Fred in action, so rapt in attention as he toyed with the throttle of the joystick, gave a rare glimpse into his playful side. There flashed a memory of the young lad who built swept-back winged airplanes and sent them down the toboggan slide on his family property.

His body language and the gleam in his eye notwithstanding, Fred's commentary on his effort was all business. "This builds your perspective," he said while negotiating the computer plane for a landing. "To do that as easily as I did is extraordinarily difficult and takes a long time."

Next to the computer manuals on his desk were several horticulture books that Lisa Gregg had given him in anticipation of the leisure-time activities he would enjoy at his new home, a 12,000-square-foot, $9,000-a-month chalet outside Geneva, which was being completely refurbished to his taste. Along with bridge, which he plays every day, tennis, whenever he gets a chance, and golf, skiing and travel, the flight simulator might be one of the ways for Fred to occupy his time away from the business that had consumed him for 30 years.

If there was any question about his resolve to leave the United States, the two container loads of personal effects that sailed from a Newark pier for Europe ended any wishful speculation. Dousing another hope that technology might win him over, Fred assured everyone that the computer would stay behind. It was a brief fling, for a specific purpose. At best, a fax machine and voice mail would serve him in Geneva.

Friends of Fred surmised that he hatched the plot to leave America and surrender his U.S. citizenship in displeasure over Bill Clinton's victory in 1992. Paradoxically that was the same time he was seriously thinking of running for mayor of New York against the weak incumbent Democratic Mayor David Dinkins, who had no serious opposition from the right. This adds to the evidence that Fred Alger's decision to leave America was not motivated by disloyalty toward his country. Rather, he saw it as his best option for shielding the firm's hard-earned assets from government depredation and preserving its capital for the Alger progeny.

Given his family history, it is not surprising for Fred to have political inclinations. How else can one explain his compulsion to charge into the 1993 New York mayor's race, fully cognizant that he lacked most of the traits of a successful campaigner? Fred was a political amateur — even though at the age of 18 he was inside his father's campaign for governor of Michigan, posing with the family for a picture that covered election brochures, leaflets and ads which promised "Good Government, An Alger Tradition."

While Fred's efforts in the public sphere never led to the kind of prominence achieved by his father, grandfather and great-grandfather, he was never estranged from the patriotic instincts that run deep in the Alger bloodline or from the conviction that his conservative agenda might improve society.

Fred had initially supported former Manhattan Borough President Andrew Stein for the mayor's job. Stein appealed to him because he was wrapped up in the theories of the Manhattan Institute, a conservative think-tank which Fred saw as "attacking urban problems with thoughtful solutions."

"The city was going down the rathole," Fred said. "It was going to implode, and it seemed as though nobody was going to do anything about it. The city was so uneconomic. In order to save it, everything had to change. We needed a rev-olutionary."

But after Stein's disastrous outing in the primary—he mustered just 2% of the vote—Fred saw no candidate stepping forward to lead the change. So he became serious about the idea of running himself—in that election or the next one. But then he backpedaled. "I probably would not have run, when all was said and done, simply because I don't have a winning personality."

Despite the betterment of New York during the administration of Mayor Rudolph W. Giuliani, Fred griped that he hadn't done nearly enough to turn things around. "After all, I'm expatriating," he argued, "which says something."

Daughter Hilary called Fred's mayoral aspirations "totally ridiculous." She said, "He needs a reality check every once in a while. And it wouldn't have sur-prised me if he had gone ahead and run, even though it was patently absurd and notwithstanding all protestations. He doesn't have a political personality. He would have hated it." It was hard for anyone to imagine Fred on the stump. He can be very convincing, even charismatic—but only on a personal level and in intimate settings.

Foolish as his drive for public office may have seemed, Fred might have per-sisted for the sake of finally putting things right in the city, with a platform that was more radical and libertarian than conservative. It is doubtful, how-ever, that any of his major themes would have caught fire with New York's melt-ing-pot population. Fred's best idea for New York was to turn it into a Hong Kong–style free enterprise haven for business. An economy and police force greater than that of many countries argued for the feasibility of his plan. Fred's campaign would have urged the near dismantling of the city's existing orga-nizational structure by cutting spending and reducing taxes proportionately, privatizing all city-owned housing and demanding individual accountability for social welfare. His vision even included a remote island prison for the city's criminal element.

With remarkable understatement Fred's lawyer Ray Merritt said, "Not all of Fred's ideas are politically palatable. They were hard to digest. People would have misunderstood." Saying it more forthrightly, he added, "Fred's a rock-ribbed con-servative of the first order, slightly to the right of Attila the Hun."

In the pulpit of his undisguised conservatism, Fred is eloquent in his hero wor-ship of former president Ronald Reagan. "Liberals say that the eighties were a decade of greed and that no good came out of it, but it opened markets to Amer-ican goods worldwide and contributed to the globalization of the world economy.

"I would argue that Ronald Reagan will go down as the greatest president in our history. In the sense that he really was the first person to reverse the trend of increasing government in our lives. At the same time he altered the balance of power between labor and management by firing the air-traffic controllers, which was an incredibly large step. Of course, he faced down the Soviet Union by escalating the Cold War to such a degree that the Soviet Union ultimately collapsed.

"With the collapse of the Soviet Union, we've gone from one billion market-oriented consumers to four billion market-oriented consumers. Every region of the world has adopted the U.S. as its economic model. That's really Ronald Reagan's doing. He won the major battles of the twentieth century."

Citizen Fred's first adult brush with politics occurred in 1967 when he objected to a city plan to turn Riverside Drive into a one-way thoroughfare with no parking, from 6 to 9 A.M. southbound and 4 to 6 P.M. northbound. Like many residents of Manhattan's Upper West Side, Fred used to park on Riverside, and this would have meant a great inconvenience.

Taking political action on his own, Fred printed 4,000 handbills, each with room for five signatures, for petitioning Traffic Commissioner Henry Barnes to put a brake on the idea. Early one morning he roamed up and down his neighborhood and stuck these on the windshields of parked cars. Part of the way through this endeavor, a cop ordered him to stop, but he went on anyway.

To Fred Alger
with best wishes

On the campaign trail with New York gubernatorial candidate Lew Lehrman and Vice President George Bush in 1982.

In all, Fred got back 1,600 petitions, each with an average of four names. Emboldened by this success, he planned a community march and was finally permitted to speak directly with the assistant mayor about the problem. His grass-roots undertaking was so impressive that it earned him an unlikely invitation to run for Congress on the Democratic Party ticket.

Would you believe Fred Alger as the Democratic standard bearer for the ultra-liberal West Side of New York?

Riverside Drive was witness to the start of another political friendship, between Fred and Rite Aid drugstore magnate Lewis E. Lehrman, which stalled just short of reaching the New York state house.

The two had met before, at a Southampton party, but it was an accidental encounter on Riverside Drive which led to their bonding. Fred's car was buried in a snowdrift, and Lehrman, driving by, stopped to help and pushed Fred out. After that they were on each other's side. Their personalities matched. Both were conservative and in the process of boosting their incipient companies. Lehrman, who was quiet, slim and ascetic-looking, gave Fred a seat on the Rite Aid board from 1968 to 1983. In a swap, Lehrman served as a director of the Castle Convertible Fund until he resigned in 1982 to face Mario Cuomo in a failed bid to become the fifty-second governor of New York.

As Lehrman's campaign finance chairman, Fred Alger was one of 20 or so generals in an elite force to swing Albany to the right. In a product-branding approach reminiscent of Fred's early publicity seeking, Lehrman dressed himself in a white shirt and fire-engine red suspenders for every public appearance. Running on the Republican and Conservative tickets, Lehrman waged a costly anti-crime campaign that, despite his long odds as a political innocent, lost by only 165,000 votes. It was a low-turnout battle, with Cuomo taking all five New York boroughs.

The final ironic twist of the Lehrman involvement is that opponent Mario Cuomo wound up becoming a partner at Alger's law firm, Willkie Farr, after he finally lost New York's governorship in 1993.

"Fred has an unerring sense of backing the wrong political horse," said David Alger about his brother's fiddling with politics. "Fred has as bad a sense for politicians as he has a good sense for stocks. I don't know why that is. He just doesn't understand the political. He doesn't back winning candidates at all, or ever. His candidates just simply don't win." Fred also supported Bob Dole in 1992.

In sister Suzy's eyes, all his posturing in the political arena was Fred's bid to revive a missing constituent of the Alger legacy. She supposed he favored Dole in hopes of gaining an ambassadorship like their father. Of course, now that Fred has given up his citizenship, that's out of the question.

"Father once said, 'In the scheme of things, your country comes first, your family second, and your party third,'" said Suzy. "He firmly believed that. He was very civic minded." Perhaps in filial revolt, Fred has reordered his priorities to put family and company first and everything else after them.

Back at the office, Fred's secretary Dolores Costa interrupted Fred's computer game with the signal that his next appointment had arrived. Fred executed one last landing but overshot the runway. "Aah!" He turned to his audience of two and noted again how difficult it was to get the plane on the right path because the joystick controls were a mirror opposite of the aircraft's action. Fred then hastily shut down the computer and walked out of his office to meet his visitor.

Alger Fund's Jim Connelly observed privately that at least in this one way Fred hasn't changed over the years. He still greets all his visitors in the waiting area and personally escorts them back to his office. Everyone gets the same treatment when they leave. Even when Jim first met Fred as a neophyte in the securities business, he recalled that Fred brought him in personally. "Right off the bat he asked me to call him Fred, not Mr. Alger. This man was such a forbidding legend, but in person he was fatherly, calm and soft-spoken. He made you glad you were here."

Dolores, who came to the Alger firm from Revlon, confirmed that it is not part of company etiquette to call him Mr. Alger. "When you first meet him, he begins by saying, "Call me Fred."

"When Fred greets you at the door, you know at once that this is a different kind of captain of industry," said client Martica Clapp about her visits to Fred's office. She and Sam Clapp have maintained a relationship with Fred and the firm since the Cornfeld and Resorts International days.

Even ex-Alger analyst Bob Emerson, who is usually restrained in his praise of Fred, was effusive about his special way with people. "Fred had an almost courtly bearing about him, which was quite at variance with most Wall Street types. For a lot of people, the fact that he'd walk you to the elevator might be considered common politeness; but on Wall Street . . . ! My God, what a gentleman!"

While forsaking a formal name or a secretary's introduction, Fred is, however, an extremely ordered and formal person. That's just one of the many ostensible contradictions in his nature.

Piecing together the puzzle of Fred's personality is as difficult or easy as one chooses to make it. There's the appearance that he gives. There's the reputation he's been given. And there are the varied impressions from people in his life. Put together, these never seem to add up to a cohesive whole. Just as the case is made for one side or the other about Fred, along comes another piece of evidence that obliterates the earlier notion. While that might be expected from any man who leads a successful and adventurous life and while few important figures can be summed up in 25 words or less, Fred Alger is perceived as multifaceted and multidimensional beyond the ordinary.

The key to decoding Fred's complex psychology is understanding that everything about Fred is purposeful, from his brisk gait to his stubborn inquisitiveness. If Fred has a goal, he will attack it fiercely until it is attained. Think back to the scrawny kid, overcoming a trick knee and, by concentration, iron will and discipline, coming out as a marathon runner at the age of 45.

The leitmotif in this story, and it bears repeating, is the rebuilding of the family fortune and recovery of the family name. This was no inconsequential impulse. Fred's dynastic inclination was very large, and it was a major influence in all his public and private pursuits.

Fred's boyhood chum Henry Earl remembered that when they were teenagers cruising around Detroit in their cars, Fred often expressed the desire to return the Alger family to its earlier wealth and prestige. Driving past the Boyer compound in Grosse Pointe, Fred spoke enviously, though approvingly, of his uncle's side of the family for managing their inheritance while Fred's father had squandered his.

Pushing him just as powerfully to revive his family's greatness are the secondary forces of personal redemption and paternal approbation. Straight from Psych 101, Fred can be taken as that classic personality type who strives for perfection to compensate for lack of approval as a child. Success and achievement made up for the void of love and attention.

One day after the firm had passed an important financial milestone, Fred blurted out of the blue to his first partner Bill Scheerer: "Gee, I wish my father were still around to see how well I have done." "It was very touching," Bill said. "He would have liked to show his dad that everything is now okay." Fred's sister, Suzy, supports this interpretation. "Fred may not admit it, but in many ways he was trying to emulate things that Father did," she observed in her attempt at explaining his motives. "It's very strange to me, but I think Daddy's been the role model."

Certainly, despite his modest beginnings in business, Fred's is no Horatio Alger story. He was never disadvantaged and downtrodden like Horatio's castoff boys. Fred had all the advantages of education, social class and access, and all the gifts of heredity.

With the sense of self-worth that was evident from childhood, Fred had no desire or need to conform to society. It was always easier for the world to come to him. "Fred does what Fred wants to do," a former analyst put it succinctly.

A conservative who loved the postmodern and extremely violent film *Pulp Fiction*. A hypochondriac who seldom sees a doctor. A financial titan who, once a week, received his spending money in cash from his secretary. The best picture of Fred is one that he paints of himself. "I always felt an outsider my whole life," Fred said in a rare moment of introspection. "Clearly there is something different about me, which is not normal."

Suzy isn't surprised at the confusion over Fred's character. "Fred has very many real sides to his personality," she insisted. "It's very interesting to me that many people see him so differently." Impressions about Fred range widely and, barbell shaped, usually pile up at the opposite ends of the spectrum. There's no middle ground in defining Fred.

He's described as charming, polite and understanding, but also as rude and arrogant. He's praised for his generosity by some and damned for his parsimony by others. He's admired for his scrupulous business and personal honesty at the same time that he's suspected of duplicity. He's reviled just as much as he's respected. His long record of investment performance may be second to none, yet critics will dismiss his success as a fluke of timing. His business accomplishments are exceptional, but detractors charge that he fell short of expectations and should have done more with his potential. People who barely know him believe they have the pulse of the man, while those who have been close feel they can hardly comprehend him.

"Fred is an unusual guy, there's no question about it," endorsed board member Steve O' Neil, "and I suspect some people walk away scratching their heads wondering what he said or why he said it." The complex fortress of his personality is as well protected and difficult to penetrate as the firm that he built.

Furthermore Fred is regularly out of step with the materialism of the money world. "I don't think is Fred is driven at all by money. If he was, he would probably sell this business because he could get a lot more money for it," said David Alger. "Money is not a defining theme for Fred. He's certainly not driven by luxuries. He could care less about what he's got on his body or what his furniture is or what his surroundings are." Sure enough, while Fred made a ton of money investing in color television companies during the sixties, it was years before he bought one of his own.

Fred has done little to correct these disjointed views and likely even added to them. He is self-made, and his ability to reinvent himself whole every couple of years has continued to keep people guessing.

"Fred is the kind of guy who can meet you at a party and say, 'Oh, by the way, my lawyers will be in touch with you because I'm suing you for five hundred million dollars, and you're fired and, oh, by the way, what are you doing later for dinner?' all in the same sentence," observed Irwin Schwartz. "And then he'd be puzzled at why someone would be upset.'"

What is never challenged about his character are his intense focus and driving energy, the sharp intelligence and unyielding determination, his unconventional and inventive ways, the persistence of his work ethic and constant striving for success and excellence.

As Fred aged, he has mellowed, though some will dispute this. A slight paunch betrays his middle. His imperious style has toned down, but his standards never weakened. It's just that now he's a bit more accepting of the fact that very few can live up to his expectations. But that too is debatable.

According to Greg Duch, "When I told Fred last year that he looked like he had loosened up, he argued no. He said he believed he had actually become more crotchety. That's when he made the final decision to move to Europe. David and I were sitting together with him, and Fred said, 'Well, I'm getting older. Little things bother me more than they used to.' But I found the opposite. I didn't see things bothering him more.

"Fred was once much fiercer than he is now. There are things he would scream about before that now he doesn't seem to be interested in. Perhaps it's the distraction of his retirement. He seems more interested in landing his plane on the flight simulator. He even took me on a test flight."

Old associate John Cleland said, "Fred has changed, as we all do with age, but he has never lost his zest for the money-management game. He's every bit as sharp today as he ever has been." Board member John Sargent added, "If anything, Fred is more confident now—and he's tougher."

Calling Fred tough was putting it mildly, especially during the early years. On occasion he tended to show a hypercritical temperament that caused even normally strong men to cower in fear. Without care for bruised egos, his devastating words usually had a demoralizing impact. It was nearly impossible to defend against his inflammatory opinions.

"Although everybody is well compensated, Fred has a way . . . he's very smart and so he doesn't have very much trouble taking someone apart intellectually," observed David, "and he certainly has done it to many people. It has been an intense environment, sometimes less than more."

For some employees their time at Alger may have felt like a season in hell rather than a feast in the mecca of money management. Ron Reel put an exclamation point on the analyst's plight: "He's run through analysts like crap through a duck. If they're not like-minded, they tend not to be around after a while."

Lavaun Vawter, who was at his side during his earliest point on Wall Street, gave this forthright psychological assessment: "He doesn't exactly attract somebody with a weak personality. He would spot the weakness and go after it, just for sport, like an animal after prey. It was just a powerful instinct. If you had a vested interest and let your guard down or showed emotion, all the violence could erupt with great force because you suddenly didn't play by the rules. Fred sets the rules up. That's the way it was."

For the investment team, Fred was a force to contend with every day. Ron Reel, whose longevity in the firm indicates a peculiar tolerance for the Alger system, explained what happened if you screwed up. "You have to take the long walk into Fred's office and have to endure his laser eyes burning a hole into your chest for doing something stupid, which you probably needed to be berated for anyway," he said. "Even though he's not at the office, he's only a phone call away. And I sense if I make a major screw-up, I'll get a call. He doesn't necessarily have to be present to make his presence felt."

Many saw Fred as a combative boss who rode them hard, was rarely satisfied and persistently striving to improve performance. That effort was "perpetual and intense," according to Ron. "It is difficult to maintain that level of intensity on a continuing basis."

From a distance, board member Steve O'Neil saw it as a matter of discipline. "You can turn over the discipline coin and find inflexibility," he said. "I don't think Fred is inflexible. He's got a point of view that he sticks to. He's not a reactor. His value added is having a unique point of view and having it implemented."

To make his case that Fred was, at best, inconsiderate, Bob Emerson told a notorious story—now a part of Wall Street myth—that Fred kept him in the office until seven P.M. on Christmas Eve to discuss some failure in evaluating a trifling oil-services stock. Doubtless embellishing, Emerson claimed that even strangers, other money managers he had never met, were so incensed by Fred's behavior they came up to him at meetings to commiserate.

Was Fred capable of such Scrooge-like behavior? Emerson stood by the story. David was uncertain. "It does ring a bell. I think I remember something about Christmas Eve. It has an eight out of ten in the veracity index, and probably is not exaggerated." Fred's memory is more selective. "I don't have any memory of that whatsoever. That sounds so unlike me," he said.

Ranjit Shastri, who studied with Fred's twins at Yale and whose overseas venture was initially funded by Fred, suggested another aspect of Fred's personality —that he has the capacity for nurturing. "Fred embodies a great work ethic. He values the work and is interested in the process of creating value. He wants to build. He wants to see us succeed and make the most of what we've got," he said. "He's not a flashy person. He's very humble, a modest person. That's reflected in the upbringing of his daughters. He's a great motivator and a good coach. He asks us to look at him, which shows, 'I can do it. I did it. And you can do it too.' We couldn't have done it without him. We owe him a lot."

Arthur Dubow came up with this description: "Fred is a very tough guy, which is belied by his laid-back manner. I've seen him get mad only once or twice— over personal disloyalty or somebody's bad behavior. In a crisis he's extremely strong. He believes in himself and his methodology."

To those who worked with him closely, Fred could be transparent. "I could read his mind. I knew his moods," said Irwin Schwartz. "I could tell, just by looking at him, what he was thinking. If he walked with his head forward and his shoulders back, then he was mad as hell. Stay out of his way. If he was lying, he'd take off his glasses. He can't see without his glasses, and he can't look at you if he's lying." Dolores agreed that there were telltale signs when Fred got upset. "I can tell when something's not right. A look, the walk. He becomes anxious about everything and starts losing his patience. I can tell he's under pressure by his voice. Sometimes you have to tell him to calm down."

Fred's other outlet for his extreme competitiveness is playing both mental and physical sports. In sports, as in business, he excelled by intelligence and persistent practice.

Analyst Bob Emerson's "favorite Fred story" occurred in 1982 at 26 Broadway, just before the firm took over its building on 75 Maiden Lane. He offered as prologue the fact that at the time David Alger, an adept at backgammon, was beginning to try his hand at chess. "I'm a passably good chess player, and David would challenge me good-naturedly," he said. "'I'll beat you in ten moves,' I would threaten. David is also very smart and he picked the game up quickly, and in a few weeks it became tougher to beat him.

"He challenged me to a match where he and Fred would play against me. Fred is absolutely a world-class bridge player and he said that he'd never played chess before, but he knew the rules and would be glad to try his hand. The office gathered around and watched. I was confident that this was a mismatch in my favor.

"It became obvious, after six or seven moves, that Fred is full of shit. Clearly he has played before and is good. So I decided to pay more attention; then I made an out-and-out blunder. I was a bishop or a rook behind.

"Fred took command of the game, and it appeared that no way could I possibly win. But I continued. It was such a sloppy game anyway. I set a trap and it worked, and I beat him. Fred was livid. He said, 'You know, a gentleman always resigns when he's hopelessly behind.' I've played chess tournaments and know this is true; in any sort of serious match, you do resign."

"But I replied, 'Gee, Fred, I was taught never to give up.' 'No,' he argued, 'you've lost and that's the way it is going to be.' An embarrassed silence fell over the crowd. The following Tuesday at the research meeting, David said, 'I guess everybody remembers how badly Fred beat Bob at chess last week.'"

Poor Emerson. The brothers Alger had rudely ganged up on him.

But wait. Here's David Alger's account of the same event:

"Fred is driven by intellectual challenges and the desire to compete intellectually. As a wonderful example of this, Fred has an incredible mind when it comes to games: cards or chess, even games which he's played very little. Bob Emerson—who is a good guy but at times has an extraordinarily high opinion of himself and is just vain beyond belief—at one point went on a kick of becoming the world's greatest chess player. Bob is a very, very smart man. No one would deny that. And so Bob bought a chess computer and spent hours and hours playing against it.

"One day Fred was out of the office. I told Emerson that I had played only two or three times in my life, but I bet him that I could hold out against him for twenty moves. Emerson said, 'I'll take you in five moves.' We took Emerson's chess board into Fred's office, where we wouldn't be interrupted, and closed the door.

"After about five moves, I had lost my queen, a rook and half my major pieces, but I was gamely battling away with Emerson. Fred came back unexpectedly and saw where I was and said, 'David, I will take over your position from here.' Down a queen and a rook, Fred just beat the hell out of him. Emerson was incensed because after Fred had equalized the situation and then gone ahead of Emerson, he said, 'Okay, Bob, I don't have time to play this out. You resign.' Fred was insisting that he resign because he was so far ahead of him or enough ahead of him that any decent chess player would have known he couldn't win. And we all had work to do.

"Emerson was incensed because Fred was ordering him to resign and was humiliated because Fred had just beaten the shit out of him—and Fred doesn't even admit to playing chess."

From Emerson's perspective: "That story sums up a lot of what I thought made Fred so interesting and at the same time so hateful. On the one hand, he set himself up in a position where he psychologically had nothing to lose. He never played before. At the same time, the idea of losing to an employee roiled him. Someone once said, 'Fred always treated his employees like the personal servants he grew up with in Grosse Pointe,'" he added severely.

This incident shows the complexity of manifesting a simple, congruent view of Fred Alger. It also exposes the subjective biases in all histories. Without knowing his purpose, be wary of the author.

Beyond his passion for bridge, tennis was Fred's game. Hilary remembered when she was young, "he would play tennis obsessively on the weekends. He would have spent more time playing tennis if his wife would have let him."

One of his proudest victories was the Men's B Singles Tournament at the Maidstone Club in 1977. It was a hard-won prize, and Fred had spent the previous two winters training, practicing and taking lessons just for that goal. "I wanted to win, and I was pleased that indeed I did win it," he said. "It was the high point of my tennis career."

The consensus on Fred's approach to sports is that he tackles them in the same radical, awe-inspiring way as he works, which makes him a formidable opponent on any court. David deferred easily to his brother's superior physical and cerebral agility in this close character dissection:

"Fred is a consummate competitor. He likes to compete in athletics, where he's an extremely good tennis player. He likes to compete in bridge, where he's an extremely good bridge player. And he loves to compete intellectually. Fred just has a genius when it comes to that sort of thing. He plays me just about even in backgammon, and I've played a lot, a lot of backgammon in my day. He doesn't even play backgammon.

"The difference between Fred's and my mind—I will admit to being very smart, and I think most people will agree that I am very smart—is that I proceed in a fairly linear, logical way and try to find linear, logical solutions. If I have to get to D, I will go from A to B to C to D, and I can probably do that somewhat faster than most people. But Fred will go right from A to D. Boom! It's startling! Sometimes he solves the puzzle way ahead of anybody else, and sometimes he comes up with a nonsense answer. So it's not always clear that he's doing the right thing by thinking the way he thinks, but it's a totally different way of looking at things. It's a way that, when it comes down to a game of cards or chance or logic, is sometimes startling.

"When he wanted to win the B Tournament at Maidstone, he took a tennis lesson every day. Fred will work with more single-mindedness at a problem than anyone I know. If he wanted to learn nuclear physics, he would study around the clock until he knew it. If Fred had set himself out to be the American chess champion when he was a kid, I have no doubt that he would have become the champion of America. I'm convinced that Fred could have beaten Bobby Fischer."

Board member Dr. Saint-Amand thumbnailed Fred this way: "Anyone who is around Fred realizes from the start that he's dealing with a very, very smart man. He's someone who is not going to try and impress you with his intellect. It just comes out that he's intelligent. And he doesn't get caught up in minutiae or get confused by details of the near term. He's always looking at the long term. That's really Fred's most outstanding characteristic, outside of his intelligence. He does really focus on the long term. He's very Oriental in that regard."

In March 1982 Fred broke away from Long Island society to pursue a developing passion in France and most things French. The new adventure began when friend Dick Tupper, who had in previous years guided him to vacation near the Dordogne valley, sent him a picture of a magnificent for-sale château in the heart of Perigord. Fred received the photo on a Monday and by Wednesday was on a plane to Paris to make the purchase.

Fred picked up the property roughly for the equivalent of $320,000 with five-year, low-interest-rate financing paid with dollars during a period of gradually appreciating U.S. currency. The acquisition was more than an investment, according to Fred. It was for "a nice shared experience—someplace new to go in the summer." Having tired of the Hamptons crowd, Fred and Eleanor sold off their by then rarely used vacation home for the 50% down payment on the European vacation home.

From then on Fred spent the first two weeks in July and three weeks in August in Marnac, France, at the château, called Mirabel. Dubow described it as "the

Fred's Château Mirabel in France's Dordogne valley, where he and his family spent most of the summers in the eighties.

most terrific property in the whole region . . . perfect in every respect." It lay deep in a lush valley—about 300 miles from the English Channel—which, as Eleanor of Aquitaine's dowry to Henry II, had been ruled by the English for two centuries. Probably worth $1.5 million today, Fred surrendered the place to Eleanor in their divorce settlement.

With the château Fred plunged deliriously into a love affair with French language and history that lasted over a decade. Hilary reported that her father "studied French religiously." It was a major event in the home and office. "A tutor came in every morning from eight to nine, and he would study it on weekends," she added. "He would sit in his chair and pore over vocabulary words in this horrible accent. He never studied the grammar, but could speak it fairly decently and communicate it fairly well. He knew a lot of sophisticated words. He would say, 'I can understand 93.5 percent of what I hear, but I can only express about 80 percent of what I want to express.' He'll give you these odd percentages."

David, who spoke French as a schoolboy, watched Fred "basically beat his poor head to death" in an effort to learn the language. He said, "Fred doesn't have a natural ear for languages, but he worked harder than any man alive to conquer the problem. This was Fred at his best. Total involvement. That's how Fred took up all his activities."

Fred knew his own shortcomings. "I'd listen to Radio France International while coming to work in the morning. Every year I'd learn a thousand and forget a thousand words. It's surprising how long it took for my ear to hear French and understand it. I still have to concentrate. I'm not good at this. I've been doing this for a helluva long time—ten or eleven years. I really worked at it, and I'm not as far along as I thought I might be."

Fred accepted his fate about speaking French in about the same way he faced the truth as a boy that he would never become a golf champion. Though it took him awhile to get the message, no one can fault his persistence.

Fred's crush on France led to an affiliation with the French-American Foundation and appointments to its international and New York boards. The foundation is charged with encouraging cultural, economic and political links between the two countries. It fosters professional exchanges, study tours, public-policy symposia, like the recent one on comparative maternal and child health care, and special events like the Thomas Paine Film Project on participatory democracy. Fred named the French-American Foundation, along with the Museum of Modern Art, as his beneficiaries in the Charitable Giving Program, a complex investment scheme which he devised in the late eighties.

Another outcome of the French experience was an investment in Bistro du Nord, a compact, bilevel restaurant on the southwest corner of 93rd Street and Madison Avenue that serves French fare.

"When I was still going to France, I had a vague idea of doing things there, since it was the middle of nowhere," said Fred. He flirted with the idea of buying and operating a restaurant in the valley and even knew the chef he wanted to run it. Bistro du Nord's owner was Fred's consultant on the venture and joined Fred at Mirabel to search for the right spot. The plan came to naught, because the owners of their hoped-for location demanded too much. As a good-faith gesture Fred lent his chef consultant some money to expand the New York eatery.

The French restaurant was just one of Fred's more recent extramural business interests. Over the years he has backed a handful of entrepreneurial ventures, peculiarly in the areas of jewelry and publishing, which at best were experiments for his lighter side, which spread his outposts beyond the narrow, intense scope of money management. Whereas he was careful and deliberate in making stock investments, he appeared to be relaxed with his outside businesses, only moderately focusing on financial return.

When asked to explain his casual way of selecting and approaching these niche opportunities, Fred often repeated, "It seemed like a fun thing to do. You take little shots here and there and kinda hope they'll blossom into something," he added. "Usually they disappoint, though not for very much money."

An early blip on the outside-business screen was a private cattle-breeding investment called F & W, which stood for Fred and William Scheerer.

"There is always an effort being made to be doing something different," said David by way of affirming that the creative impulses behind these escapades held something in common with the core uniqueness of the firm.

Hilary Alger reinforced the fact that Fred took on these projects just for the thrill of capitalism and largely to exercise his adventurous spirit. As a privately held firm, Fred Alger is accountable only to his tastes and instincts. "There was no process," she said. "Just him. It was his little project. There was not much thinking, or the kind of thinking he would employ to buy stocks." And what did it matter? she added. "For example, the PSi India investment came out of the family's shares of the company."

PSi, Inc. or Precision Sourcing International, was one of Fred's recent—and perhaps most successful—business efforts outside money management. Started in 1990, when he supplied $100,000 in venture capital for a partnership to wring out commercial opportunities in India, PSi took three approaches to business.

The first avenue was to help U.S. manufacturers identify and develop out-sourcing vendors and suppliers in India. These companies included United Tele-com of Kansas City, which is now Sprint Corp., and Lionel Trains Inc.

In its second channel, PSi has provided consulting for major U.S. corpora-tions seeking the best route into the Indian market, helping them achieve their goals with the right financial structure and finding competent partners to shep-herd them through the country's regulatory and bureaucratic complexities. Farm-equipment maker Deere & Co., cosmetics company Maybelline, oil giant Amoco Corp., drug firm Warner-Lambert Company, and communications chip leader Rockwell International Corp. are some of the companies who signed up for this service.

PSi's third—and also its most adventurous and lucrative—course was setting up a major, state-of-the-art tool-manufacturing facility in the industrial belt of Gurgaon just outside New Delhi's border. Geared toward an estimated Indian market of $1 billion, the plant was opened with an additional $500,000 invest-ment from Fred in 1994.

Ranjit Shastri, who pitched the PSi business plan along with Yale business graduate and partner Manu Bammi, credits Fred with contributing more than money for the venture's success. He also developed business contacts, provided office space at 75 Maiden Lane and put Alger analysts to work identifying poten-tial clients. They were helped by his critical thinking, which redirected their busi-ness focus, as well as his patient cheerleading. "He believed in us when no one else did," said Shastri. "We believed in his believing in us."

He continued, "Fred has been extremely patient, extremely supportive, and has always known what would eventually happen. He recognized that this venture is different from the stock market."

Fred's bargain with Shastri and Bammi for funding the operation was extremely clever. "They have the right to buy us out of PSi at whatever we paid for it, at our investment, and thereafter we get twelve and a half percent of their gross income forever. So that we don't run into any problems about ownership, expenses or salaries," Fred said. He was bought out ahead of schedule at the start of 1996.

Unlike the experience of PSi, some of Fred's outside investments failed to thrive. "The best thing that one can say about most of these ventures is that we kept them small," said David. "They were not especially profitable, but Fred is a very cautious man, so he doesn't ever put these business deals on such a large scale that they would ever imperil the company."

An industry observer dismissed these extracurricular adventures as inconsequential sport by saying, "Fred can drop a couple of thousand here and a million there and it'll come back because he's so good at what he does at the core of his business. If he has fifty million dollars, you know in three years it will be ninety million. So if he loses three million dollars along the way, so what?"

One of Fred's early ventures had the name of Super Stuff and was supposed to fan out a direct sales force of women, à la Avon or Tupperware, to demonstrate and market costume jewelry across California. Fred's business model was a close replica of the one Gay Boyer, the wife of his cousin Alger, had successfully implemented in her firm called Traveling Trinkets.

The idea was hardly off-the-wall for Fred. "I have always been interested in harnessing the theoretical potential of the selling power of women, who are tied to and knowledgeable about their neighborhoods," he said. Fred's Divorced and Married Associates had earlier unsuccessfully tried to exploit this presumed selling advantage of women to market mutual funds.

Super Stuff came about like this. "I met a woman on a plane named who was going to Germany to sell cosmetics on Army bases for Revlon or another such firm," Fred explained. "Some years later she contacted me because I had discussed Traveling Trinkets with her. Anyway, she wanted to do something similar in California. We gave her some money, but it didn't work out."

Actually she took the money and ran. "The first thing this woman said was she needed a car," David said. "Then she immediately absconded with the car and that was the end of that." The books show that she drove off with $25,000 of the Algers' money and delivered nothing, not even a joyride, for it.

"There have been a number of areas where people have taken advantage of Fred's wealth and his blind side," said his sister, Suzy. "Fred, like all people, needs his ego stroked, and that's how you get him. Because he has a great deal of money, he's easy to deceive." About Fred's dawning interest in horse racing and partial stake in a racing steed in France, she whispered with a sigh, "I hope the French don't take advantage of him." Spoken like a cautious older sister.

The second stab at carving a niche in the jewelry trade, this one more rousing and glamorous, matched up separate friends of Fred and David to fashion and sell prehistoric woolly mammoth jewelry in New York. Fred's chum was Charlie McAlpine, who knew him from his law school days at the University of Michigan. An exhibitor of woolly mammoth sculpture, McAlpine was sitting on a hoard of rare and highly prized extinct woolly mammoth tusks in Alaska. David's buddy was Bill McTighe, once a jewelry designer for Avon, who was then head of purchasing at QVC, the home-shopping television network. McAlpine's ivory was colorful and attractive. McTighe knew how to design. What else was needed?

They launched the line in grand style at the popular party bar No. 1 Fifth Avenue, which sadly was its best outing. While the pieces were unique and artistic, the public response was tepid. At least rough-and-tumble McAlpine, who flew down from Alaska for the showcase, was a big hit with the women.

Through a friend, McTighe booked space at Bergdorf Goodman's jewelry counter to push the goods. Each of the pieces was presented in a gift box, including its history and production notes. McTighe was an excellent promoter, but without a dynamic marketing plan, there was no way to spur demand. So the artisan entrepreneurs closed shop and packed away their unsold inventory.

"We had a lot of fun," said Fred. "I had a good time with it." In the end, the firm lost about $25,000. It wasn't a big deal. Fred still owns a fair cache of the jewelry, which is stored in the firm's New Jersey office.

One person who proved that, despite their intelligence and discrimination, the Alger brothers were fallible in their business judgment, was Heather Cohane, publisher of *Quest* magazine, a lifestyle publication for Manhattan's rich and famous. Cohane knew them because she lived in the same Park Avenue apartment tower as David, and her daughter often baby-sat for his children. When she needed an infusion of capital for her publication, she naturally approached Fred Alger.

After a fair amount of due diligence, Fred plunked down $700,000 for convertible bonds issued by the magazine. But Cohane defaulted on the loan almost immediately. "It was a troubled investment for both sides," remarked Steve O'Neil, who did the legal work for *Quest*.

"*Quest* was my disaster," David admitted with some irritation. "I was the one who really created the *Quest* mess. Cohane's lawyer was one of the people on our board, so I thought she was pretty respectable. It seemed like a very good idea. Reluctantly we piled a lot of money into that magazine. It was a tremendous mistake, because we got hit by a slowdown in the New York real estate market."

The centerpiece of Fred's art collection, Yasumasa Morimura's Blinded by the Light *graced the Alger executive boardroom at 75 Maiden Lane.*

A second publishing idea never made it over the development hump. Fred conceived a magazine which would treat contemporary artists and their works like commodities, and list them in the same way that companies are valued in a stock table. As envisioned, each issue would feature six current artists, rating them both in artistic and investment terms, leading up to the comprehensive roundup of about a thousand living painters at the back of the magazine. In addition to being evaluated in terms of the current market, there would be speculation about future trends in their pricing.

For Fred, this would provide a simple, comprehensible research source for art investors and collectors as well as insurance companies, museums and galleries. Such a publication might raise interest in an artist's output, just as narrowly focused trade publications have resulted in an appreciation of their constituent industries.

Said Fred, "I believe that art has outpaced society's ability to understand it. A hundred years ago, a person could look at a painting and somehow relate to it; this was even true of the Impressionists. Today art has become somewhat incomprehensible to the average person. We lack a common language to describe it. What does it all mean? Someone should be able to tell me, in simple language, why a painting is good or not good, its present and likely future value in relation to the works of other painters in the same genre, and why it's different or if it is underpriced or overpriced. Art is about money. This would be the greatest thing for artists. They could suddenly see themselves making money."

Former Doubleday chief John Sargent, Fred's adviser in all things publishing, saw him through *Quest* and also tried to develop an art mag plan for him. But the project died in the search for an art-savvy editor to direct the magazine. Art critic and historian Barbara Rose, who wrote for *Vogue*, was one of the people in consideration.

Still disappointed that the project was never realized, Fred said, "I've never been able to persuade anyone who could write well and knew a lot about art that this was a good idea. It is still valid, but try to find someone who is recognized in the art world and has the energy to put it together!" Here too Fred was avant garde. In 1996 something resembling his original decades-old idea appeared in bookstores. Richard Polsky's *Art Market Guide: Contemporary American Art: 1995–96 Season* attempts to define trading—buy, sell or hold—positions on art.

The art-magazine idea turned out to be a bridge for building the Alger art collection. It brought Leslie Alexander, who guided Fred in his acquisitions and has effectively been the curator of his modest, roughly 100-piece portfolio of artwork. Not coincidentally, Alexander is married to Lawrence Luhring, owner of the chic Luhring Augustine Gallery in New York's Soho, from which many of his paintings have come.

The exhibition space for the Alger works is the picture-framed left wall of the long, narrow corridor at the entrance of 75 Maiden Lane. While Fred saw his art as a neat way of brightening his building's access area and treating visitors with small doses of creative diversion, it is more perplexing and provocative than attractive or entertaining. The works have virtually no appeal to traditional sensibilities but cater to a more eccentric, evolved tastes. The building's concierge scratches his head in wonderment whenever the pieces are changed, once every six weeks or so by Alexander. And he's not alone in his bewilderment.

Fred started the collection in 1984 by acquiring paintings, but since 1988 he has been buying photographs, which offered better value and greater price appreciation. Now "a first-rate collection of photographs" makes up about 80% of the pieces.

The better known artists in Fred's collection—Vito Acconci, John Baldessari, Ross Bleckner, Barbara Ess, David Hockney, Sherry Levine, Richard Prince, Lucas Samaras, Donald Sultan, William Wegman and Leslie Alexander herself—though still not household names, are respected and influential in art circles.

The centerpiece of Fred's eclectic and hip collection and also its largest, most expensive work is Yasumasa Morimura's *Blinded by the Light*. An art world rave, Morimura was born in 1951 in Osaka, Japan, where he still works. A sardonic send-up of Flemish landscape master Pieter Bruegel's *Blind Leading the Blind,* his 1991 color photograph mounted on canvas, one of an edition of three, grafts together Oriental and Occidental images in a fusion of techniques that comically portrays, among other things, modern man's conditioned blindness to materialism, violence and banal pleasure.

In this pastoral pastiche, which includes an English steepled church and Mayan pyramids, there's a chain gang of blinded oddities like a beret-wearing painter with paintbrushes piercing his glasses; a man in military garb with grenades crossing his eyes; a shopper outfitted with Tiffany–like shopping bags, only the label reads "Too Funny"; a socialite with fake roses pasted over her eyes; and a Bushido businessman with yen notes pasted over his body.

The 7 ½ x 13 foot triptych, which dominates the company's penthouse conference room, is strange but does not seem out of place in its business setting. To the extent that it drains the stuffiness out of meetings and is suggestive of the wild streak of its owner, *Blinded by the Light* is clearly representative of Fred Alger's peculiar character. "This painting has a vision that is completely unique," Fred said. "It's hard not to be interested in it, and it is in great demand by museums and shows. Because of the artist's interesting and unique approach, we believe it will have lasting value and go up in value."

In terms of art, David Alger has a different sensibility from his brother and has derided the collection with particular intensity. David sees Fred's self-styled art patronage as an inferior copy of Donald B. Marron's at PaineWebber. As president of the board of New York's Museum of Modern Art, Marron proposed Fred for the board, where he was a member from 1987 to 1992. David praised PaineWebber's art program for investing in more popular artists, displaying the art in the office and subsequently offering it for purchase to its employees. "We've bought the worst collection of junk mankind has ever seen," he said "Better take all that money and buy one nice painting instead of all that crap." He decried the collection—most of which was acquired at bargain prices in the name of Fred Alger Management, Inc., as "unsalable," and suggested, "I'm sure it's a write-off."

Despite David's strident view, Fred's collection is no fake. Obscure? Yes. Incomprehensible? Mostly. But certainly not worthless. Fred easily accepts the skeptical reaction to his art. "No one would say that any of that shit is beautiful," he said about the current exhibit in his lobby. Contradicting David, he said, "We've made money on almost all this stuff. To the extent we haven't, we can get high valuations, give the paintings away and receive a tax savings." In a sly way, Fred's collection has a reference to the family by recalling great-grandfather Russell Alger's renowned art pieces.

Just as Fred was driven to overcome the shortfall of his parents' financial legacy, he was adamant that his children should never suffer from the emotional poverty he experienced while growing up. Life with father, as daughter Hilary saw it, was very much a typical "all-American situation." Fred was very down-to-earth in her eyes. "Fred was not an absentee father," she said. "He was very much of a presence, an involved father and relatively normal dad.

"He would come home at seven, and we would have dinner together. He was always there on weekends to take us places—ice skating, to the park, bike riding. People assume that I grew up on stock market lore and that our life was hectic like it was in the office. If he was distracted or absorbed, I didn't pick up on it as a kid. He very much separated home and office. We'd ask, 'So, how did the market do today? Good or bad?' It went up or down, so he was in a good mood or a bad mood. But that was the extent of it."

Fred's friend Arthur Dubow beheld it as an idyllic home life. "Coming home, his gin and tonic was ready for him, the girls sitting around, probably playing piano. He didn't have to shift gears for that."

He always had time for his girls, recalled Fred's former secretary Rosemary Kiernan. "Fred's twins were five when I joined the firm," she said. "It could be such a difficult day, but as soon as they called, his voice switched. 'Hi, sweetheart,' he'd say sweetly, as if he were two different people."

"His children make him happy. He dotes on his girls," reinforced current secretary Dolores Costa. Fred agreed without a doubt. "I have absolutely fabulous children who adore me," he said.

At home Fred was often a taskmaster. "For instance," said Hilary, "once he bought a large blackboard and created an extended timeline to show us what events took place simultaneously in history. We didn't care for it. But he thought it was terrific and couldn't see why we weren't as excited as he was."

For one so single-minded about the stock market, it's remarkable how well Fred managed his family life. Handling home and hearth was Fred's wife Eleanor. "In the office Fred's the law. At home my mother ran the home. She's even more strong-minded than my dad," Hilary revealed. "At home he let her take over, and he would back her up when necessary."

"Eleanor was instrumental," claimed Dubow, "to a much greater degree than most wives, in that she freed Fred up entirely so that he could focus on his work. She did all the social work, all of the house chores, the shopping, buying his clothes, picking his ties. He didn't have to think about anything involving the house in East Hampton or the château. She used to drive Fred in and out, in the old blue station wagon, so that he could sit there and think."

Early partner Bill Scheerer gave this account of their relationship. "She could handle him," he said. "It's pretty hard to talk down to Fred, but he would grin and take it." However, except for replacing some furniture when the firm moved to 26 Broadway and her presence at the Christmas dinners, Eleanor never had an active role in Fred's firm.

The Alger twins followed Fred by matriculating at Yale. Hilary, who has a greater resemblance to her father, joined the firm in 1987, but was unable to find her place in the business and lasted less than five years. Alexandra went on to earn a master's degree in journalism from Northwestern University and is currently a staff writer for *Forbes* magazine.

And while Fred obviously adores both daughters, he was remarkably candid about his disappointment at not having a son to continue his line. When he spoke about how some theoretical parents might fancy a son just like him, it seemed a transparent hankering for a boy to be Fred Alger IV. "You don't have the same feelings about a grandchild as you do your own children," Fred said, referring to his infant grandson Davison.

"I think he is very sad that he doesn't have a son," mused sister Suzy. "None of the children have been smart or politic enough to name a child Fred." The reason perhaps is that the rest of the Alger clan considers him a distant figure. "My children see him as being very austere and judging them," she added.

Despite this regret about no male offspring, Fred is held up by his great optimism; he works with a certainty that all things, even this desire, will work itself out in the end.

As Fred prepared to leave New York, there was a swirl of celebrations to bid him adieu and toast the momentous transition. Fred's daughters threw him a sixtieth birthday bash at 21 Club, which was pretty much a family affair. And there was a farewell dinner for Fred given by the firm, also at 21. Board member Steve O'Neil threw a cocktail party at the Knickerbocker Club for current and former friends and associates. Former partners George Boggio and Irwin Schwartz, however, were not on the guest list.

In assessing Fred at this new stage in his life, Arthur Dubow said, "I think he has a sense that he didn't spend sufficient time on his friendships. He's not an introverted man; but he was focused very externally on goals and how you go after those things. Whereas he has a broad acquaintanceship, I don't think he has very many close friends of the type you can discuss things that are troubling you. It's common for a lot of men, particularly of Anglo-Saxon background, to never have examined their feelings much. Feelings are something you keep under control. He commented several times that he wished he had taken a little more time with his friendships."

As Fred was making a break for Europe, Vice President Al Gore joined a final attempt to separate him from his money. The U.S. Congress made a show of diddling with the tax code to squeeze shut all expatriate openings with new exit levies. Those efforts were not only ineffectual and ill conceived but lost political mileage after a concentrated spurt of media attention.

Americans are obliged to pay federal taxes on income earned anywhere in the world as well as estate taxes of up to 55%. In 1994, over 1,000 wealthy Americans elected to surrender their citizenship, including classical violinist Yehudi Menuhin, as a way of protecting themselves and their descendants. The government charges full inheritance taxes on expatriates for 10 years.

When Fred announced his departure, his ever present critics resumed their attack on him for walking away after taking his fill of the American dream. With the lingering aftertaste of negative press due to the SEC probe and associations with questionable financial personalities, it was to be expected that Fred's departure would generate some heat. "It rubs a lot of people the wrong way," said Greg Duch. "They tell me, 'I can't believe what he's doing giving up his citizenship.' Of course, they're not in his position. It's easy to say, 'I wouldn't do that,' but they have no pressing need, whereas Fred saw this as the only way out of a particular situation. To me, this is no different than an English rock star taking citizenship in Monaco to avoid British taxes or a writer setting up residence in Ireland. It's really the same thing as this company setting up an office in New Jersey for rent and tax reasons. It's merely a rational business decision."

It was never Fred's goal to get richer by this but to execute a wealth-preservation strategy for his firm. Typical of his long-range thinking, he was taking care of a tax problem which would kick in only after his death.

On April 24, 1995, Fred Alger unceremoniously slipped out of the country to his self-imposed retirement in Switzerland.

It was a departure without remorse. "I have no disappointments as a person," he said in reflection. "Everything I've focused on, I've tried to do as well as I can. I've given everything to it. I've worked at one hundred twenty to one hundred thirty percent over long periods of time, not just for a month or two but years. I've taken things as far as I can take them and have no regrets about shortchanging things." Considering the future of his company, he reemphasized, "My biggest worry is, Can the business keep growing without me? It's more or less out of my hands now, which is pretty much how it's going to have to be."

Even with this concern, the best guess is that a more relaxed Fred will be playing at life a little harder in his new world. And after a decent interval, if his past record is any indicator, Fred will renew himself again. This odyssey which takes him to the shores of Europe actually extends his walkabout in the financial world. He's finally gone global to support a larger business plan. John Sargent offered the only plausible way of seeing Fred's future. "While you or I might be content to have accomplished what Fred has, he is likely out there looking for new challenges."

14 ✍

Global Reach

IN MAY 1994, a year before relinquishing his American citizenship, Fred Alger set out to conquer the Old World by offering three Alger Fund portfolios to European investors.

Using Germany as its strike base, the firm launched its funds in a tepid financial environment, where investors were barely interested in the notion of equity investing and even less interested in the U.S. stock market.

Germans have typically kept most of their savings and investments, roughly 80%, in fixed-income instruments. This bond-loving streak has been conditioned by deep scars from past economic excesses, government-funded financial safety nets and the stranglehold of the national banking sector over investment options. Free to operate like brokerage firms and unlike their U.S. counterparts, who are held back by Glass-Steagall rules, German banks have presented more than a psychological barrier against equity investing. They have also kept foreign financial firms out of the country's teeming capital streams.

The banks' domination was finally spoiled when a unified Germany cracked open the gates to foreign funds in 1990, which was when Fred first entertained the thought of bringing his mutual funds to Europe. He would overcome their distrust of equities by teaching Germans the Alger mantra of aggressive growth-stock investing, which had succeeded so well for American investors.

Undaunted by puny prospects in the near term, Fred anticipated the German investment horizon to be lit up by the release of some two trillion Deutschmarks by the turn of the century. He perceived the opportunity in strongly positioning Alger investment products ahead of the asset migration toward stocks. The potential he visualized was enormous, as he boldly predicted that a third of all new investments in the company would be derived from Europe "in a short time."

Forced into restructuring after the toppling of the Berlin Wall and facing larger capital requirements as a result of reunification, Germany was heading inevitably away from sole reliance on its overburdened state-pension system toward development of a 401(k) plan equivalent that emphasized personal responsibility. If so, equities would become more appealing to savers, and aggressive investments would be in demand for fighting inflation and improving retirement prospects, just as they had in the U.S.

Fred projected a profile of a more demanding German investor, resulting from the transference of inherited wealth to a new generation, more needful of vigorous equity performance and open to the adventure of global investing.

A surge in global investment management, with an emphasis on U.S. stock investing and consolidation of the financial-services sector, is sweeping across the worldwide business horizon, especially the U.S. brokerage and mutual-fund industries. In 1995, for example, Zurich Insurance Group paid $2 billion in cash for Kemper Corp., which included a mutual fund and an asset-management firm. U.K.'s Barclays PLC's investment-banking unit acquired Wells Fargo Nikko Investment Advisors, at that time the country's largest institutional investor with $170 billion in assets, mostly in index funds. Govett & Co., also from Britain, agreed to merge with Chicago–based Duff & Phelps Corp. in a transaction valued at $250 million, which raised its international fund-management assets from $9 billion to $50 billion.

With heated competition and a maturing market for mutual funds in America, Europe represents for U.S. financial companies the next big battleground for acquiring investment assets. With socialism vanquished and discredited, Europe has been eager to learn and accept the equity culture of American capital institutions. As European economies expand their money pools, investors will grow eager for new growth investments, among which mutual funds offer the simplest, most efficient way to receive exposure in the equity market. By charging ahead, hitting early and making his reputation before others joined the fray, Fred Alger hoped to gain an important edge in this competition. Just as the world drinks Coke to quench its thirst, Alger wanted to be the dominant global brand name identified with American growth-stock investing.

"We have to take the position that it's a long-term effort to develop brand recognition in Europe," Fred said. "American funds aren't sold there very much, and they're hardly sold in Germany. This should be a huge market for us. It may not be profitable for years, but the German market is so dynamic and gigantic, and Germany will increasingly dominate Europe. We have the financial strength to undertake things other firms can't, like advertising and direct payments to brokers who sell our funds." After he secured Germany, the next countries he planned to blitz included Austria, then Switzerland, Italy and the rest of Europe.

In order to set up the proper distribution framework to achieve its goals in Europe, in 1992 the Alger company allied itself with Noramco (Deutschland), a brokerage firm in the sleepy town of Bollendorf on the German-Luxembourg border, which, as a wholesale distributor of investment products, controlled a network of 600 established financial advisers. Heading up Noramco, which for years had been representing Templeton's 20 offshore mutual funds in Germany, was Joseph Becker, whom Fred had met in the sixties when he was one of Bernie Cornfeld's top salesmen.

A family business involving Becker's sons Paul and Roger, Noramco started out in Frankfurt in 1982, when it began selling Templeton's U.S. funds and later Putnam's OTC Fund and Emerging Health Sciences Trust. When Putnam withdrew its OTC Fund from the German market in 1993, Becker was looking for a replacement product, and that led him to Fred Alger. The negotiations between the two men culminated in spring 1994 with the offering of the Alger MidCap, Growth and Small Cap portfolios to the German public through a German registration rather than the normal way of originating an offshore fund in neighboring Luxembourg.

Alger's German portfolios carry the same attractive features as the U.S. B shares they mirror, such as low investment requirements—DM10,000, which is small by that country's standards—and decreasing back-end sales charges. With Noramco's brokers, the Alger firm acquired an instant army of sales professionals to extend its reach to the farthest points of the country and deliver Fred's gospel of growth investing in the personal manner that financial transactions are conducted in Europe.

Alger's mutual-fund chief Jim Connelly was dispatched to Germany to initiate product training for Noramco's brokers and assist in developing the aggressive million-dollar marketing and promotional effort that had been contracted to advertising and public relations firm Charles Barker GmbH. "Fred made a big contribution," said Joseph Becker. "His was the first company of our partners who ever invested money in order to get into this market. With Templeton we had no investment. On the contrary, we had to pay for a lot of their expenses."

Fred's daring to penetrate the German market, however, was exceeded by Connelly's cleverness in figuring out the process for Alger funds to stand ahead of the established competition and appear more valuable to German investors. This was achieved by providing a higher user-friendly standard of customer service over the telephone—something that most American mutual-fund investors take for granted but that was new to the Germans, despite the fact that the U.S.–based Pioneer Group and Fidelity Management have been active in the German marketplace since the sixties.

Fred Alger offered 24-hour, seven-day toll-free phone service to relay automated account balances, fund pricing, transaction histories and confirmations and enable the purchase, exchange or redemption of shares by phone. Getting this going in Germany—an advanced and economically powerful Western nation— was more vexing than might be assumed. The national phone system, though technically proficient and fully ISDN-capable, relied on the arbitrary and incon-

Fred got a tremendous reception from Germany's financial press in 1995, much like the one he received in the U.S. at the onset of his Wall Street career.

sistent transmission of telephone signals. The majority of lines responded to pulse beats, and many reacted to neither pulse nor digital. At the same time, a good number of phones were still rotary, and there was no word in the language equivalent to the term *touch-tone*. The solution for ordering this chaos was an advanced voice-recognition system. Functioning equally well in tone, rotary and null situations, it was developed for Fred Alger by Metro*soft*, a small East Brunswick, New Jersey, provider. "They have done wonderful things for us," Fred said in acknowledging Metro*soft*'s contribution to the company.

So overwhelming was the acclaim for Alger's superior telephony within the German broker community that envious competitors Pioneer and Templeton, among others, tracked down Metro*soft* and begged it to build a similar system for them.

There are other ways that Alger has harnessed communications in Germany to provide operational efficiency and deliver investor benefits to power ahead of its competitors. Alger's reporting to brokers and their clients is in German. The account data on investments is in Deutschmarks rather than dollars. Even German-language recordings of David's *Market & Economic Review* are available on the system. And because the data are transferred to Germany by an ISDN uplink for local printing and fulfillment, the delivery of statements is considerably speeded up.

Fred's optimism that Germany would quickly deliver $100 million in assets proved to be exaggerated when Noramco came through with only $17 million ten months after the launch. Still, he claimed to be "very pleased" and professed to have "no upside target" in his plan. The firm's commitment was long-term, and he let this bet ride.

By September 1995 assets had bounced up to $25 million, mostly on the momentum of capital appreciation. Asset growth was afflicted by a falling dollar, which stifled appreciation of and for American securities. There was a promising sign, though, in the scarcity of redemptions, which confirmed the European predisposition to stick with investments for the long haul.

Despite the funds' relatively weak performance in 1996, asset flows started to spurt as the dollar began gaining ground on a beleaguered German currency. Two years after their entry in that country, in the spring of 1997, Alger Fund assets from Germany had ballooned to $123 million. Four months later they were up above $150 million.

To establish a household presence in Germany, Fred Alger had put on a huge show of advertising and publicity, and it was beginning to pay off. This was primarily a print campaign and, briefly at the start, there were radio spots over Radio Luxembourg with Alger's German translator as the announcer. Stressing the benefits of association with Alger, the ads focused on the service orientation of the firm through its customer communications and worked in the themes of investing in America's growth, Alger's long-term performance record and the ease and assurance of mutual-fund investing. As Fred had correctly anticipated, the service improvements through technology held the greatest appeal and delivered the hook for brokers to reel in investors toward the Alger investment story.

The publicity machine drove hard the image of Fred Alger as the sage of American investing, and his thoughtfulness and intelligence transferred well to an audience, who hold wisdom, even genius, in high esteem. Fred has always appealed to Europeans, dating back to the Cornfeld days of the Fund of Funds, which first brought his winning ways to the attention of investors on the Continent. Preaching his message of investing in America through the Alger Fund, Fred must have reminded some older Europeans of the time decades earlier when

Cornfeld first exalted the concept of U.S. mutual-fund investing as the vehicle for achieving wealth.

With his name and face in front of that message, Fred got a sensational reception in the financial press—much like the one he received at the onset of his Wall Street career.

"Fred is a great salesman, a natural salesman," explained Castle Convertible's Lisa Gregg. "He speaks about what he believes with conviction. He'll paint a picture and then throw in some numbers. Fred can be very enthusiastic, and does a very good job telling a story."

"My German friends tell me that Fred's already become a household name in Germany," indicated board member Arthur Dubow. "He's much better known there than Fidelity or Templeton, which have been around much longer."

Fred's best press was a cover story in the July 28, 1995, issue of a leading business publication, *das Wertpapier, Deutschlands älteste Geldanlage-Zeitschrift,* which, in its mid-year roundup of mutual-fund performance, acclaimed Fred Alger for beating the market with the top two funds in Germany for the previous year. Up 30.42%, Alger MidCap was number one, followed by Alger Small Cap rising 29.95%. The third fund, Alger Growth, was likewise feted for grabbing the sixth spot with a rise of 19.4%.

Had the dollar not weakened, the article recorded glowingly, the Alger funds might have appreciated as high as 50%. This gave Fred the opening to address concerns about a falling dollar, which had depressed investments in his funds. "The bad times for the dollar are over," Fred proclaimed in the article. "From an analytical point of view, it has been undervalued for quite some time."

In fact, he had been predicting that the U.S. dollar would strengthen to a value of two Deutschmarks on the basis of America's low inflation, low wage growth, the strength of its service sector, rising export growth, strong economic outlook and the collapse of the Eastern bloc. With its period of structural transformation behind it, America, he said, would enjoy a period of expansion in diverse, specialized industries through new technologies and a customer-first business philosophy. At that time the dollar was down to a low of DM1,36 and falling. Most pundits saw his proposition of an undervalued dollar as preposterous.

"I think 1.35 Deutschmarks is probably the bottom for the next period of one or two years. But from a purchasing-power parity basis, the dollar should be at 2.20 marks," he said. "I think it is very undervalued. I think that psychology changes very quickly, so the next move will probably be up."

He exhorted, "If Germans want to make money in the stock market and at the same time profit from a weaker dollar, they should buy American companies." The German currency quickly complied with his order. It climbed almost in a straight line after that for the next two years, reaching a multi-year high above DM1,85 by the middle of 1997.

Another unusual concept which Fred began proposing at the time was the view of America as an emerging market country. "Forty-two percent of our holdings are companies that have been started in the last fifteen years," Fred explained. Dun & Bradstreet in 1997 confirmed his assessment of a youthful, emerging corporate environment by publishing research showing that 73.9% of American companies were started within the last 25 years and that another 19.2% were between the ages of 26 and 50.

Moreover, America's productivity was rising on the strength of technology, which was bringing about rapid change. Not any change, but "intellectual change—new technologies which represent a higher level of change—profound change." And therefore, he proposed, America was being improperly viewed through an old pair of glasses which didn't allow the world to see the true value of its markets.

"You want to invest your money in a dynamic part of the world economy, which is liquid and truly dynamic and changing," he counseled. "There's no protection in old companies. Money is made in periods of change. The more rapid the change, the more money is made."

In order to expand operations throughout the European Community, Alger opened a new mutual fund and registered it in Luxembourg. Established in the middle of 1996, the Alger American Asset Growth Fund is also available through the Noramco dealer network. Because of its Luxembourg registration there are even tax benefits for Germans to invest in this fund. Of the Alger funds in America, it most closely resembles Spectra Fund, and its assets were in the neighborhood of $15 million one year after it started.

Fred did not touch down in Europe with his mutual funds as a way of occupying himself during his retirement. It was part of a larger blueprint for his personal reinvention and the company's ascendant role outside the U.S. Unlike his earlier offensive in Europe, which was a strikeout, this time his mutual funds have a good chance of hitting a home run.

It took eight years after they started in the U.S. for the Alger Fund to catch fire. Fred is clearly prepared to wait at least until the year 2002 to see similar results in Germany. And his prospects in the rest of Europe are even brighter, as more investors learn to accept his American emerging-growth thesis and realize that his investment company can achieve sizable stock market appreciation from that opportunity.

But the real potential for Fred Alger remains in the rest of the world, as the expansion of the global economy lifts more people toward wealth creation and capital savings. This is just an early period of international interest in U.S. investments. The big payoff, Fred has figured, is yet to come.

15 ✍

Keeping Good Company

THE DECISION TO CROSS the Hudson River and relocate Fred Alger's administrative and clerical operations in New Jersey in 1980 was propelled by the attraction of lower rents—about $5 a square foot—and an opportunity to escape crippling New York state and city taxes. Furthermore it offered an effective way to separate the company into distinct zones—revenue and expense, administration and accounting, research, brokerage back office, investment advisory and money management—and for each to be situated in the best physical location. Finally, building its own brokerage-clearing operation in New Jersey established another zone in the firm's vertical integration. The tax differential has since then gradually diminished, but the company retains the advantages of lower overhead and operating costs in New Jersey. In interest costs alone, the first-year savings were estimated between $250,000 and $500,000.

The prospects for establishing a garrison beyond Wall Street were not as certain then as they are today—certainly not in Jersey City, which, apart from its proximity to lower Manhattan, had no other appeal. What is now a thriving commercial enclave dedicated to financial services and occupied by a large number of major companies was, when Fred Alger arrived, a dark and desolate neighborhood which bore the scars of economic neglect and despair.

The modern Harborside Financial Center, a focal point of the community's rebirth, arose from the ruins of a dilapidated and empty cold-storage warehouse. The breezy promenade leading to a manicured riverbank and a panoramic spectacle of the city's towering financial district was reclaimed from a craggy and unkempt coastline. Where columns of office buildings now brace skyward in earnest imitation of the big-time landscape across the river, there was once only a motley arrangement of barren lots.

"There was nothing over here," said Rosemary Kiernan, George Boggio's right hand in effecting the migration, about the time they first came to investigate the area. "It was just parking lots, the building we moved into and the Colgate factory, where Merrill Lynch is now. The biggest concern when we moved here was our safety. I was so nervous in the beginning."

Just a short one-dollar PATH train ride away and one stop from New York's World Trade Center, Fred Alger's Jersey City home at 30 Montgomery Street is an ordinary, rectangular office building built in the mid-seventies. George Boggio deserves the credit for overseeing the construction of the firm's original office on the 13th floor and the move of Alger personnel from Manhattan. Beyond that, the success of the back-office operation in New Jersey resulted from the good fortune of netting Thomas L. Weil, a top Wall Street veteran, to manage the start-up.

For Weil, then aged 60, starting up a back-office operation from scratch so late in his professional life was more than an income opportunity; it represented a challenging way to close out his career and "put his stamp" on something valuable and lasting. Speaking by phone from his retirement home in Florida, he affirmed, "After spending forty years on the Street and being involved in the same area in other firms, this honestly and truly is the first brokerage end of the business where the partner did not come in and say, 'This is the way I want it done' even though he didn't know what the hell he was talking about." Weil's independence was projected throughout the office and translated as the model for the conduct of its personnel.

In all Weil needed eight people for the new operation: two cashiers or cage clerks, one margin clerk, a dividend and transfer clerk, a purchase and sales (P and S) clerk, an order-room clerk and two runners. Many of the hires had some prior connection with him, and each one conformed to the Alger corporate image in terms of pride in work, high aptitude, self-confidence and versatility to perform multiple functions. His team stands out as perhaps the best collective catch of employees in the company's history.

John Raspitha, an accountant who went with the move to New Jersey, commended the effort. "The company picked up excellent people—not greenies. They weren't coming off the street. Despite the fact that Fred Alger was small, the firm attracted the right kind of people who were tops in their fields."

Beating projections by three months, Fred Alger's Jersey back office was up and running by August 1980. "It was an extremely smooth transition, one of the smoothest I've ever seen," Weil said. "We closed down PaineWebber, which handled our brokerage clearing, on Friday, and picked right up on Monday. In the first days there were only a few problems balancing the accounts."

The back-office world lurks in the shadows of the dazzle and light that is reflected from stock analysis, portfolio management and stock trading. It revolves around a series of repetitive and routine clerical functions that effect the transfer, validation and settlement of securities transactions: the movement of securities between brokerage firms, the delivery of securities to the custodial bank, which secures the actual shares, and the balancing of the investment accounts in the firm resulting from stock purchases and sales. Everything is done according to standard industry practices and in compliance with securities' regulations. The entire operation is sometimes referred to as the Cage area, a designation carried over from the days when funds for stock transactions were received and disbursed from locked-up stations similar to old bank-teller windows with bars.

However invisible, this department serves as the backbone of a smoothly functioning brokerage operation and the basis of providing accurate customer accounting. As Fred Alger was increasingly reliant on brokerage commissions rather than investment-advisory fees for its income during the eighties, an efficient back office, which improved customer service, contributed to the net value of the firm.

The back-office process is straightforward, though not always without complication. The duties of each job can be explained by following the process of a normal trade.

Alger sends a buy or sell order to the floor of the New York Stock Exchange. If the trade is accepted, notice of this is immediately returned by phone. At the end of the trading day, the company receives a floor ticket indicating price, purchase or sale, and the brokerage firm involved. Matching up that documentation to the original trading order, the phone verification and the Exchange confirmation is the job of purchase and sales, which then affirms the transaction by computer entry.

The following day the cashier or cage clerk sorts through printouts of the company's trades from the Exchanges. The client's account is debited or credited with the security after a corresponding withdrawal or addition of funds. Three days after the trade—it used to be five days until 1995—Alger and the brokerage firm participating in the stock exchange must be "in balance" with respect to the transaction, which effectively completes the trade. Seeing that the shares have been delivered as promised is also the responsibility of the cashier.

Meanwhile the margin clerk's duty is to ensure that the client's account has sufficient funds for the transaction. The margin department also polices the correctness of the trade and ensures that securities' regulations have been observed, especially those pertaining to margin requirements.

The dividend-and-transfer clerk tracks the receipt of dividend payments to the company's account and then distributes that money to the client accounts. Correspondingly, if a client had shorted the dividend-paying security, he would receive a bill for the dividend from this department.

The day after the trade is completed, runners hand-deliver confirmations to responsible companies and institutions as an official notification of the required transaction's execution.

Prior to 1980, Fred Alger's brokerage clearing was handled through New York Securities and then Mitchell Hutchins until it was acquired by PaineWebber in

1977. The investment-advisory back-office functions and accounting were handled internally from day one.

Michael F. DiMeglio, now a senior vice president heading Fred Alger's account administration, started out in the Cage in 1980. He had worked for Weil at Loeb Rhoades & Co. until it was swallowed up by Shearson. Weil wanted him to come on board, but Mike took some convincing.

"I never heard of Fred Alger before," said Mike. "I never even heard of Jersey City or knew how to get here. I remember interviewing with George. He was in a disheveled office with sleeves rolled up, and he said, 'This is the way we work. We roll up our sleeves and get to work—everyone from the secretary on up to me.' That was fine by me. I was used to working that way.

"But the brokerage operation was brand-new, and no one could say where it was going. No one knew if it would expand to fifty people or if, ten years later, they would even still be clearing for themselves. Tom Weil was a friend of mine. He taught me a lot when we worked together. He said, 'It's worth taking a chance on this company.' I came here on the basis of Tom's recommendation. I didn't think he would steer me wrong."

Mike performed in dividends and stock transfer for nearly four years before the opportunity arrived to get out of the back office and move up to account administration. After proving himself, he was promoted to director of account administration, whose primary function is reconciling client accounts, and made vice president in the fall of 1994. Looking too young for his achievement and responsibilities, Mike appeared at ease controlling his department. He's a prime example of one who has prospered within Fred Alger's pressure cooker.

"Even from a distance, Fred has in mind what you should be doing or he knows what you're doing and he expects you to do it," offered Mike DiMeglio. "The big thing about Fred is that he lets you do your job."

In the same spirit, DiMeglio tells his workers, "At every level of supervision, we're not over your shoulder. We let you know what we expect. Just get the job done and get it done right. After you learn what it takes to do the job, I'm going to give you that leeway."

Isabella Coari was already familiar with Fred Alger when she joined the firm in January 1977. She had been handling the firm's account at Mitchell Hutchins' margin department for several years and found it to be a well-run company because "the people at the Fred Alger end always made sure the trades were good."

Isabella sounded out Barbara Glazier, her primary contact at Alger, about a job. Barbara took the matter up with George, who took it directly to Fred. Isabella was hired. To get her on board immediately, the firm made up the difference in benefits she would have lost from leaving her job early. Lucky for her. "The day I gave notice to Mitchell Hutchins was the day that PaineWebber took it over," she said. When New Jersey became operational, she shifted over there.

After Alger began self-clearing, margin work ceased to be a challenge for her. "I didn't feel needed. There were no more problems," Isabella said. That led to an attraction for the growing, more visible mutual-fund side of the business and a new job in its accounting area that includes pricing the funds at the end of the trading day. She and Rosemary are the two women still in the firm from the original Jersey City occupation.

John C. Messina, "third in charge" of clearing functions at Neuberger Berman, heard that Fred Alger was starting a clearing operation from Isabella Coari's brother, a childhood friend growing up in Hoboken, New Jersey. He saw greater potential in working for a smaller company with strong growth opportunities, and went up for one of the two cashier openings. Neuberger was reluctant to let him leave. It tried to match Fred Alger's generous salary offer and put the word out that Fred Alger was a terrible place. Doubting his own judgment, Messina turned to one of Neuberger's partners for an opinion. "Fred Alger? Fabulous. Fabulous," the man said.

What finally put him at ease about joining the company, however, was the personal interest that George took in his situation. "He called me up at home and even spoke to my wife. He told me about the pension plan and the profit sharing. It felt good to have someone talk to you with that kind of respect."

John has never regretted his decision. "It was an exciting time to be growing with this firm and seeing the money rolling in. The environment was very positive." John is anything but reserved in pitching his group's contribution to the firm. "The main thing is your back office. It runs the operation," he boasted. According to him, what is highly unusual at Fred Alger is that "we've never had a single error—a trading error or a clearing error—associated with the back office.

"When the stock exchange auditors come in, they can't believe how clean our records are. It's sort of the Alger way, as we used to say."

Ronald F. Curtis is another journeyman who made the first cut in Fred Alger's back office. He was brought in as the head margin clerk. Like the others who were drawn into Alger's back office, his previous jobs constituted surviving a minefield of brokerage mergers. Such is the transient nature of clearing positions on Wall Street. In the industry's boom-and-bust cycles, their ranks are rapidly swelled at the top and then just as quickly thinned during a decline.

Not so at Alger. Through its tough as well as its good times, Alger has hung on to its people. If anyone has had to take a financial hit, the managers and top brass have been first in order. The back-office people have never felt the pinch. If they could be advanced, they were given the chance. Alger has cared for them like no place they have been or are likely to see. Which explains their unusual longevity, which explains the personal loyalty and intense work ethic that characterizes their performance.

Fred and CFO Greg Duch observe head trader Joe Maida executing a stock trade.

As Curtis explained, "At Merrill, Prudential, Smith Barney, you're just a number. Here you are family. Your talents are recognized, but so are your failures. At other firms you can get away with it for years. Here, you couldn't do that. You wouldn't want to work for any other firm after being here."

Ron's career at Fred Alger has not kept him chained to the margin desk. "The challenging part was moving into different areas of responsibility and successively applying my abilities to handling whatever was required," he said. Primed for cross training and comfortable in a filler role, he had stints in cashiering, P and S, the trading desk and reorg, which requires client contact relating to merger and other tender offers, as well as account administration. Since 1989, when Fred Alger brought its mutual-fund transfer-agency functions in-house, he's been assigned to Alger Shareholder Services, where he executes the daily reconciliation of the shares in the various mutual-fund portfolios. His duties also include "moving money in and out of the funds to finance redemptions and subscriptions and maintaining the bank accounts that pertain to that area."

Ron is earnest about his job. "If you're not in balance daily, then you're in trouble," he said. "We maintain a tight quality control over the reconciliation of accounts. I won't go home until I'm in balance—to the penny. It's computerized, but still you have to put the numbers together and know where they belong."

Having come from that era where judgment and experience counted, he brings the benefit of that perspective to the job at Alger. "I came in to work the Monday following President Kennedy's assassination," he explained. "We had to refigure every margin account because the market had plummeted so much. Today a margin clerk wouldn't know where to start."

Summing up his experience at Alger, Curtis said, "Here's a job I can finally settle into without worrying if the firm will go out of business or disappear overnight, like so many Wall Street businesses have over the years. We have a solid capital foundation; Fred has seen to it. My only regret is that I didn't start here sooner."

About Fred himself he admits, "I'm in awe of the man: a self-made guy who has proven himself over the years with his generosity, kindness toward people, guidance and professionalism."

Fred returned the compliment in discussing Ron's management of the Alger Bulls softball team, which won four consecutive championships in the Staten Island slow-pitch tourney. "Ron Curtis is a very demanding guy," Fred said proudly about his employee's leadership on the field. "He smelled beer on the breath of two guys before the game and wouldn't let them play. That's why the team is so successful. It's disciplined. Everything is done seriously."

Fred adopted the Alger Bulls in 1992 and provides funding, about $1,500 annually, for team essentials like caps, uniforms and jackets that sport the company name and colors. Ron was one of the original members of the team, which had a strong contingent from Alger's Jersey City office. In the years from 1992 to 1995, when the Alger Bulls won three championships, the firm fielded Mike DiMeglio, Jim Connelly, Ron Curtis, Charles Burgdorf and Keith Carroll. "Fred was really delighted with the team," said Ron. "He came down and watched a few games with David and provided a real morale boost." Obviously its victories meant a great deal to Fred, enough for him to make off with the trophies and construct a prominent showcase for them in the New York office.

It was a fairly pragmatic idea for Joseph A. Pakenham to take up with Fred Alger's purchase and sales unit. "I was working for a New York discount broker but lived in Jersey and wanted to work in Jersey for a good outfit that paid a bonus and had a good retirement plan," he admitted.

Beyond the Jersey locale, another strong incentive was getting in on the ground floor. "It was exciting that we set the back office up from scratch and had a chance to do it our way—the right way. We put in the systems in place today and had a proprietary interest in the operation," he added.

"From the very beginning, what really got to me was how concerned they all were about getting it right," he said. "I can't tell you how many times Tom Weil or George would call me up at home, even before I started at the firm, to ask what to do about this or that. I thought these guys are crazy. I assured them, don't worry. We'll handle it when I get there. But they had never done this before, and the imperative was to get it right, to make sure all the bases were covered. Another thing I noticed was that everyone who was coming on board was either a manager or supervisor in the brokerage industry at a generally higher level."

One of Pakenham's classic improvements was beating the deadline for delivering shares in institutional trades to the custodial bank, thereby obviating the need to borrow stock against transactions and stamping out some 3% to 4% in costs associated with buying that insurance.

Another upgrade was a reduction in bookkeeping that actually improved the chances of identifying and solving canceled or wrong trades. "We set up systems where it is virtually impossible for a stock to wind up in the wrong account," he said proudly, "because we pay attention to detail. The Alger way is not to assume that it is or will be okay. You must ask questions. You must check again.

"I come from an era when six million shares a day were traded and the Exchange had to be closed because the back offices couldn't handle the volume." Today the NYSE's trading volume routinely exceeds 500 million shares a day.

Pakenham continued, "When the market is busy, they show the floor brokers running around as if their life depended on it. I wish I had that kind of pressure. It's easy compared to what we have. They only live with the trades for one day. We live with the problem for a week till it settles." One of the trading conditions he is charged with resolving is the DK or Don't Know, which describes a trade that, having gone through the transaction process, is disavowed upon delivery by the receiving brokerage firm.

Joe expressed considerable job satisfaction due to his independence. "The nice thing about coming to work at Alger is that no one is over my head. It's hard work. We put in the hours. But it's also very rewarding." That Fred Alger is a special place was also confirmed by him. "Whenever we attended industry functions, it impressed others that we worked at Fred Alger. 'Wow, what a good company!' It is well respected in our end of the business."

In deference to their gunslinger boss, Joe named this first team at Fred Alger's back office the Magnificent Seven: Joe Pakenham, John Messina, Ron Curtis, Mike DiMeglio, Walter F. Stevenson, Stephen J. Melanaski and Nancy Colabella Santimauro.

For the group this was more than a picturesque appellation. It reflected a heroic attitude toward their job and the responsibilities they carried.

"The Magnificent Seven decided we would never have a suspense account that carried over to the next day, and they simply did not allow it to happen, even if they had to stay until three in the morning," said Weil as an example of the group's dedication. A suspense account is created by the inability to come into balance with the exchanges and the DTC at cutoff time. "We never wavered from this goal. We are perhaps the only clearing operation never to have a suspense account. We had so many checks, it was almost impossible except for an outright error. The challenge was, Am I going to balance tonight and how long is it going to take?"

The Seven is the group that gave cross training its good name. There was never just one person for the job, but usually two or three prepared to back you up, according to John Messina. Not only was this a good strategy for holding the line on costs, it ensured an unbroken continuity of service, which was considered critical for retaining accounts and maintaining profitability.

Perfection was the goal, and there were no slackers in this quest. "Even when we weren't feeling well, we used to come to work," said Messina. "We had a special kind of esprit de corps. We were a team. It was us against the world." Added Joe Pakenham, "The Alger way is simply doing the job you have and doing whatever it takes to do it right. We maintain high standards. We don't bullshit each other. We depend heavily on one another. In our area, when one function is over, it doesn't end but flows into another clerical function for which we share responsibility. There are times we slept here, like during snowstorms, not because we were told to, but because we wanted to."

Mike DiMeglio offered several examples of that dedication to perfection. His proudest effort was recalculating the firm's composite portfolio in line with a 1989 SEC rule change which required performance to be restated net of fees. "It was a huge project, just combing through ten years worth of data in less than a month," said Mike, "and when it was audited, they found no mistakes."

At least twice his group in New Jersey picked up the ball which had been dropped by New York. In 1987 he took over the task of measuring the Alger composite performance against the market indices—perhaps a dozen different composites, including the S&P, Nasdaq, Wilshire Small Company and the Russell 2000, to name a few. Previously the job entailed ranking performance against just the S&P 500. The assignment is further complicated by the requirement of measuring some client accounts only against the specific index which conforms to the portfolio's investment style or goal.

Another function absorbed by his team, which has since reverted to its normal place in New York's client-service area, was the completion of quarterly reports to pension managers and consultants as required for the databases that typically drive the selection of a money manager. In a manpower crunch, client services had fallen behind on the job and left a stack of unfilled questionnaires begging for attention. From his group Mike DiMeglio assigned Jeanette Borras to the task without relieving her of her normal duties. That extra work paid off for her, as it became a stepping-stone toward a higher position in the firm.

She had been upgrading her skills to increase her chances for a promotion by studying for an MBA. She believed her plan was a secret, but Fred Alger knew of it and beat her to the punch by offering her a new job before she completed her studies. "It was encouraging from a morale point of view," said Borras, "that they recognized that I wanted to do more than I was doing, and brought me to New York."

"We realize there's a huge pool of assets out there, and we have to go out and fight for it. No one is going to hand you the money," she said. Borras is the one who gets handed the ball once it's in Alger's court. In 1993 she was invited from New Jersey into client services in New York to support marketing's Matt Gotwols because, as she put it, it was "desirable and helpful for the company to have a woman in this highly visible position." She was eventually asked to head up client services and promoted to vice president in October 1995.

"Customer service is very important nowadays," said Jeanette. "As average investors are getting more sophisticated, they're demanding more from their investment committees, and they in turn are demanding more from their money managers in the way of timely and informative communications. I don't see that as slowing down. I make sure we give them an elevated level of service. Fred and David are both big believers in that."

Of course, with the increase in personnel and the gradual fragmentation of responsibilities, "the complexion of the place," as Jim Barbi, who replaced Tom Weil in 1988, put it—the previously congenial, family atmosphere at 30 Montgomery—has changed somewhat. In many ways, ramping up with the rest of the Street has come at the price of looking less dissimilar from other financial institutions and admitting certain imperfections.

Perhaps overcome by stress over Fred's planned exit from the company, Rosemary Kiernan burst into Greg Duch's office crying that "things weren't being run the way they used to be."

"But they can't be," Duch mollified her.

Still, she wouldn't be assuaged. "That's how I lived for over twenty years. That's how I worked. No one ever told you to come in on Saturday. No one ever told you to bring work home. You did things even if it wasn't your job. We had a vested emotional interest in the company." The firm was built in such a way that it was all-consuming, and Rosemary was emotionally stuck in that stage.

She needn't have fretted. Enough of that early spirit still percolates through the firm to spill over to its new recruits. For Mike DiMeglio the past is sustained through the original back-office and administrative teams. "It's a tribute that the people here have lasted so long." Of that group only two have left. Steve Melanaski was lured by greener pastures and has wound up at Bank of New York. Nancy Santimauro left to raise a family.

Because Fred Alger is open to initiative, and offers its workers a wide berth of responsibilities, there is a high level of employment stability. "At companies like Merrill Lynch, there's a tremendous turnover," explained Joe Pakenham. "Here they take pains to move people up or around. It takes a lot for the Algers to let someone go. They feel they have the best in that area, so if there's a problem they try to resolve it first." Marketing chief Ray Pfeister likened Fred Alger to one of the tough Ivy League schools — difficult to get in, but once you're accepted, just as hard to leave or get booted out.

Fred Alger puts its people on a career track. If you come in as a receptionist, you don't need to stay there all your life. "It was George's idea," said Greg Duch. "When you hire a receptionist, think executive secretary. Pay them enough money for them to stay and do a job they're overqualified for. Promote from within. They already know the Alger way."

Beyond business, the Alger firm has shown itself to be extremely caring about its workers' personal lives. The bottom line and attention to human needs are not incompatible concepts. Ron Curtis experienced this when his wife had a long struggle with breast cancer before passing away in March 1985. Tom Weil said, "Fred called Ron personally to his office and told him to go home and stay with her until everything was settled. Don't worry about pay or job. It will be here when you get back. The rest in the office will pitch in. Very few firms would do that."

"They were so compassionate, Fred and George," Ron agreed. "That builds a lot of loyalty. Loyalty builds loyalty."

The firm has a keen recognition that it is nothing apart from the individuals within it. "We've got a lot of talented people working very hard," said David. "Fred has instilled a strong work ethic here which permeates everything. That's really what makes it work. And everybody really likes what he or she is doing."

While New York grabs all the glory, it is all guts in New Jersey. The analysts and the traders may do the heavy lifting, but it's the quiet work of the troops in the back office that keeps the machinery of the company humming. The distance between the two offices is greater than the physical divide of the Hudson River or the segregation of income and expense and research from administration. In the culture of the company, it is a separate landscape, and not necessarily a parallel one, with the denizens of the New Jersey taking a backseat to their elite New York brethren.

"The differences between New York and New Jersey are class differences," observed Greg Duch. "The people here are largely clerical. Over there, they're professionals with advanced degrees." As with other caste distinctions, the pay scales are tipped in favor of New York. The analysts and traders are in Fred Alger's upper echelon of financial remuneration.

The back office is too remote for any shining stars to be fully observed. In New York the analysts' work often produces immediate and verifiable results and receives corresponding ego gratification.

There is, however, nothing resembling disunity between the separate parts of the firm. Rather, the New York and New Jersey offices are like different territories belonging to the same country, each with features appropriate to its functioning and the distinguishing marks of its chieftains. Fred was canny enough to define the absolute stress in New York contra the pressure drop in New Jersey as a function of his presence. "Unfortunately I'm in New York," he said.

The New Jersey back office is low-maintenance for Fred Alger. The atmosphere is more casual and boisterous than New York. In New York one is constantly under the gun. New Jersey people work independently and are left pretty much on their own. With the high caliber of personnel, no exaggerated involvement on Fred's part was required. "He is interested enough to be aware of what's going on, but not intrusive," Jim Barbi indicated. "Fred expects results. If you create a problem, he's going to be very unhappy about it. No surprises. No problems."

He added. "You could farm out the work here if you wanted to. Though it would get rid of all the overhead, we would also lose control over all phases of the operation, and the brokerage business has added greatly to the capital of the firm."

A couple of months after it opened, Fred appeared at the New Jersey office for the first time and gave a speech to welcome and congratulate all the new employees. And for about a decade Fred dutifully made a mid-year and a year-end excursion to 30 Montgomery to personally present his economic outlook and market projections to the staff and to generally make his presence felt. That frequency tapered down to once a year, around Christmas time, coinciding with a catered luncheon in the Jersey boardroom, usually several days after a similar event in New York. In 1993 and 1994 he dispensed with the speeches.

For many in New Jersey, this was their only chance to see Fred. David was all but invisible. The joke was he didn't even know how to find the place on his own and was thought to be clueless about its operation. It was George Boggio who served in loco parentis. Consider him the proconsul of this region, taking his authority from Fred though sharing little power with him. George in fact had an office in both locations: one next to Fred in Maiden Lane and a corner room with an expansive view on the thirteenth floor of Montgomery.

By the end of 1986 the back office was running smoothly on its own, and Tom Weil was ready for retirement. True to his word that he would give the firm a year's notice, he stayed on past 1987. But replacing him proved to be difficult. Walter Stevenson was next in line, but he "got on George's bad side" and lost his place. So did John Raspitha, who had responsibility for the company's internal and external reporting. Interviews with people outside the firm seemed to be going nowhere. Weil delayed his retirement roughly three months past his projected departure and finally left in March 1988 after nearly eight years of duty at Alger. He then took to the road with his wife, cruising 13,000 miles around America during the next four months.

His replacement, James Barbi, got the job by a fluke. A headhunter, also a common friend of his and Weil's, was seeking out prospects for the vacant Alger position. Why not me? he thought, and threw his application into the pot. Barbi had a senior role at L.F. Rothschild & Co., a now defunct Chicago brokerage which was beginning to suffer both from the 1987 crash and fluctuations in management. He had seen the firm's mutual-fund advertising and concluded "it had grown tremendously and looked like a nice, secure situation." He didn't know Fred, but he had heard "generally positive" things about him on the Street.

Barbi's background and experience had the right pedigree: Six and half years as staff supervisor at Peat Marwick Mitchell, cashier manager at Bache & Co., eight years as a partner at the W.E. Hutton & Co. brokerage, then another partnership at Edwards & Hanly, a senior vice presidency at Loeb Rhoades and a managing directorship at A.G. Becker & Co. before Rothschild. One thing in his favor and in common with Fred was a two-year tour in the Marine Corps after majoring in accounting in college.

Jim came on board as Fred Alger's director of brokerage operations on February 1, 1988. Until 1993 his group also accounted for the shares that traded in and out of the Alger Fund portfolios.

All said and done, there's little to complain about in terms of a back office or administrative job at Fred Alger. Quite the opposite. There is mostly praise and gratitude.

"The most important thing Fred did was to establish a future for me," Joe Pakenham proposed. "Everything he got into, he gave to his employees. The way he invested the company's money was the same as for his own account, which is good to know. He made me feel he was working for me."

John Raspitha joined the appreciative chorus while recalling his fateful decision to join the firm in January 1978. "It was the wisest move I ever made in my life. I never had a clue how successful or how great the opportunities would be."

16

Sweet Spot

THE EIGHTIES STARTED OFF inauspiciously, or so it seemed, with an *Institutional Investor* article that was to announce Fred Alger's second coming to the financial community. But that smile on Fred's face, as he was pictured astride a huge globe which introduced the article, would quickly twist to a sour frown when the magazine hit the Street. Far from the ringing endorsement he expected from friend Gilbert Kaplan's publication, Fred received a review that was, at best, sharply divided. Parts of the article were uncharacteristically rude and far too personal for a business trade article. In certain matters author Anise Wallace simply got it wrong. Rather than highlighting the company's revival from a presumptive decline in the seventies following the glory days in the sixties, "The Resurrection of Fred Alger" was more like an attempt to bury it in dirt. And despite the subsequent corrections and refutations, Fred was never treated kindly by the media after that.

To begin with, the article stigmatized Fred Alger's involvement in TelePrompTer nearly a decade earlier by making a correlation between the stock's 21% swoon and the Alger company's advertisement for its research monograph on the company in *The Wall Street Journal*. In a throwaway sentence, the article described Fred's jewelry-making escapade as "a desperate act" of a man "scrambling to survive." It also disparaged him as a rehabilitated publicity hound. Later the article drew attention to Fred's ownership of the search firm Analysts Resources and his affiliation with Monica Smith, stirring up an ethical controversy about that symbiotic relationship.

Its main complaint, however, was accusing Fred of attempting to seduce pension officers by feigning charm and "amiable camaraderie" and masquerading mildness. As proof the article described Fred's habit of personally coming out to the reception area to greet his clients. Further down, the article charged him with inattention to some accounts. For example, it said that reducing the number of meetings with Gannett, a client since 1979, from four times a year to twice annually was a breach of agreement and evidence of his inability to manage the firm's swelling asset base, which had surged from $250 million in 1979 to $850 million by October 1980.

The effect of the article was to warn its readership of investment professionals that Fred Alger was no longer the small, personal money manager he once was and still claimed to be. With perverse logic it argued that because of "vigorous marketing," consisting entirely of 1,500 to 2,000 sales letters every quarter, Fred Alger no longer qualified for boutique status.

Devoting a two-thirds-page sidebar to a sensationalized account of the firm's growth, Wallace figured Fred Alger's investment management fees—at the top of the scale among money managers—to be $2.5 million for the year. The company was charging 1% for the first $5 million of managed assets and .5% for subsequent amounts. She saw its retention of brokerage commissions, incorrectly estimated at $8 million for 1981 as questionable (the actual total was $9.9 million), because that expense is typically viewed to run counter to the clients' interests. The article deemed that the firm's net profits from commissions, projected at $4.2 million, were too large relative to management revenues of $2.7 million and quoted one pension consultant describing this as "awfully close to sinful."

The piece, however, completely avoided explaining how Fred Alger actually favored his clients with this value-added service. First, the firm never handled outside trades; brokerage was a captive service for its clients. Second, the income was used to fund the research which provided the investment ideas that yielded spectacular returns. Third, its trading system actually saved the clients' money by consistently buying and selling stocks for them at better prices than the average market transaction. It also never mentioned how Fred Alger had mastered expenses with self-clearing, low overheads and a regimented force of floor brokers.

The article sounded a positive note, however, with an account of Fred Alger's investment performance. Between 1976 and 1980, the firm's portfolios chalked up a 33.4% compound annual return that was more than double the S&P 500. In 1979, for example, 13 tax-advantaged accounts returned 47.8% versus the S&P's gain of 18.6%. And for the first nine months of 1980, Alger was up 40.2%—the S&P only 20.5%—and closed the year with a hefty gain of 60%. Nonetheless the article speculated that Fred would be a "sitting duck when the market goes south."

The feature's upbeat finish was likewise marred. "For a long time, Fred was just a small-time operator, hustling around the Street," it quoted an unnamed friend as saying. "But he paid his dues and now looks like he's hit the big time." No wonder Fred was upset.

The article ended Fred's long friendship with Gilbert Kaplan. "Fred and especially Eleanor were enraged," revealed friend Arthur Dubow. "Eleanor would never speak to Gilbert again. She was tough and unforgiving. Fred takes these things personally up to a point. Eleanor took these things very personally."

"Gil tried to make amends," Fred added. "He wrote a couple of letters saying he was sorry. If I had been a little older, I might have forgiven him quickly and easily."

Dubow counseled Fred about the article this way: "You always pick out the worst thing and think your life is ruined. Don't worry about it as long as they spelled your name right. It won't hurt at all."

Though Fred couldn't avoid taking offense, Dubow was right in the end. The investing community took its cue from the article's headline—Fred Alger had revived his career, for better, not worse. What seemed so controversial at first reading was actually a catalyst for the most financially satisfying period in the firm's history. Instead of being scared off by questions about his tactics and his personality, the industry took heed of his investment record and hastened to his side. Fred Alger was born anew.

In 1982 Fred Alger turned an important corner in controlling its overhead and securing a permanent presence on Wall Street by acquiring a controlling interest in its own building in New York's financial district.

As it required more space to accommodate its growth, the firm was facing escalating rents of about $35 a square foot. Asset expansion had already forced it to move seven times in the preceding 10 years, and the prospect was looking like more of the same going forward.

Fred learned about the availability of 75 Maiden Lane from a real estate broker at a cocktail party. He visited the building the next day and made a bid for it, finally paying $1.6 million for 52% of Maidgold Associates, which owned the 12-story structure with 144,000 square feet of office space.

The firm moved into the top one-seventh of the building, the dilapidated twelfth floor and penthouse, which had been used as storage. The entire space was gutted for a complete makeover. In a departure from its past, when the company's furnishings were patched together for functional efficiency and with little regard for style, Fred Alger assigned Jim Wagnon, a decorator who had done some work on his apartment, to give Maiden Lane its new look. All the old furniture was junked. Wagnon started afresh.

One of the novelties of the design scheme was painting the office walls pink, with hints of mauve and gray—something that was, er, different on Wall Street and obviously a physical expression of the firm's uniqueness.

There were two explanations for the pink office color. One unproven justification was that Paul A. Volcker, chairman of the Federal Reserve Bank, had his offices painted in that color. During his tenure Volcker brought about an immense change in the American economy by fixing the money supply, which had previously fluctuated with the business cycle, and allowing interest rates to float. If it was suitable for him, why not Fred Alger?

Another reason for using light pink was a prison study that showed that the color reduced violence and promoted creativity among convicts. And so, for its calming effect, even the lightbulbs were fixed in that pale hue. It was a company rule.

Just as George Boggio had engineered the Jersey City office construction in 1980, he orchestrated the move into Maiden Lane. He was a virtual dervish, moving back and forth daily between Jersey City and the offices in Manhattan. It was a flawless execution and done in record time. Concurrently Fred Alger was paying for considerable improvements to the building's common spaces, including new elevators. Fred praised Boggio for the job. "It was as if we had worked there for ten years. Everything was in order. We closed down operations at 26 Broadway at five o'clock on a Friday and were ready to go in Maiden Lane at eight o'clock on Monday."

The acquisition of 75 Maiden Lane, on the brink of its coming-rich period, was a watershed event for the company and one of Fred's better business moves.

Fred Alger's sweet spot, until recent times its most fecund period for profits and managed assets, spanned 1982 to 1988 and was mainly enriched by a hail of commission revenue. Between 1984 and 1987 brokerage fees gushed at an average of $2 million a month, and net after tax income topped $10 million a year.

"The most exciting time for me was when I became a new account administrator in the early eighties," recalled client services chief Mike DiMeglio. "It seemed we were getting one or two new accounts a week, fifty-sixty-seventy-million-dollar accounts. George would come out of his office with the management agreement and other documents and hold them up saying, 'Here, we have another account. Who wants it?' and we would fight over handling the bigger accounts.

"Fred was actively promoting the business. We were hot. Performance was great. Money was coming from everywhere. We had corporate clients which were huge, with names that everyone would recognize."

In terms of performance, Fred mounted the Wall Street bull at its sleepiest, at market bottom in 1982, and rode it strongly to the top. In 1982 the firm was managing $1.5 billion in 46 tax-advantaged accounts. It was rated one of the best investment advisers of the year with a composite gain of 36.2% versus the S&P 500's rise of only 14.7%. By the end of 1986, the firm was managing $3.34 billion and, at the market peak in August 1987, $4.1 billion. Even though stocks collapsed in 1987, Fred Alger was one of the few firms which remained upright. In fact, that year it hit its best mark for commissions and management fees.

The company had been constructed in such a prudent fiscal manner that it was almost impervious to market gyrations. How else could it have tacked an additional $9.1 million to its net worth, even as assets were falling, for a grand total of $73.7 million in 1988? Putting this accomplishment in perspective, the firm's capital was only $2.8 million going into the eighties.

And even though it was saddled with exorbitant advertising and operational expenses in 1986 and 1987 for the launch of its mutual funds, the firm was able to increase its financial muscle because it acted conservatively and well with its assets. Even as the market was reversing on growth stocks and Alger's pension clients began pulling their money out of the company, Fred drove his firm forward in a full court press for business expansion.

It's Fred's dictum that "you've got to invest when money is coming in, because they can take it out just as easily. No matter what the condition of the market, you have to find places to put the money. That's why they're paying you, and you ultimately have to beat the indexes."

The numbers tell the best tale of the firm's flowering. In 1979 management fees were under one million dollars. By 1987 they hit $16.3 million. Correspondingly, commissions in 1979 were under $3 million. In 1987 they topped at $32.5 million. The gross revenue of the firm was just $4.3 million in 1979, but that figure zoomed to a record above $49 million each year in 1986 and 1987. The company's peak year for net, after-tax income was 1985, when it made $12.3 million, an amount never again reached until 1991—a dramatic reversal from 1990—its second only and last losing year—when the firm dropped $1.6 million.

Another way of following the fortunes of the firm is by calculating its head count. Considering Fred's rule of avoiding overhead without prior supporting income, the increase in staffing speaks for the firm's growing financial strength. In 1980, after Fred Alger opened its back office, the firm had 42 employees. By 1985 it had enlarged to 80 employees, 17 of them analysts. Two years later, the staff total was 103, with 30 analysts, including nine with senior status. There were 18 research associates in 1985, compared to only three in 1980. The marketing staff grew from four in 1985 to 24 in 1987.

From 1980 to 1987 Alger harvested and prepared a new crop of analysts who are among the best-known professionals in the money-management field. The people brought into administration, operations, accounting and, to a lesser extent, marketing were exceptionally talented, hardworking, ambitious; they were the cream that fattened the firm.

During that period money was revved up by leveraged buyouts, junk bonds, arbitrage investing, derivative instruments, merchant banking, margin purchases and real estate speculation. The stocks that did well partook of those manias, a terrain largely unfamiliar to Fred Alger.

The stocks which raised the firm in this robust cycle endorsed Fred's concept of life-cycle change. Gulf & Western absorbed Paramount. RCA was swallowed

Surrounding Fred, left to right: analyst Dan Chung, Greg Duch, David Alger, and senior marketing vice president Ray Pfeister.

by GE. Fannie Mae was a turnaround story. Commodore International benefited from the dawn of home computing, then went bust because its machines never evolved toward the IBM standard. Rob Lyon got Fred Alger into Commodore stock, which for years was one of the biggest strikes of the firm. But, Lyon admitted, "it was Fred who helped us get out of it. He was better at spotting the top than I was."

In 1984 the firm bagged the retirement accounts of Alaska's public employees and teachers.

In 1985 Rob dickered publicly with David over GE's acquisition of RCA. At the time Fred Alger was holding roughly one million shares of GE. GE had offered $6.28 billion, or $66.50 a share, for the company, and David, as director of research, told the press he was warm to the price. Analysts at other firms, meanwhile, believed RCA should fetch $75 to $80 a share. While they were working out the merger, Lyon lamented to the papers that, as an independent company, RCA deserved a 15 multiple or closer to $90 a share.

In 1986 Fred Alger was the second largest institutional holder of the Singer Co., which was reducing its debt, spinning off operations and seen as a likely takeover candidate. Also that year Fred Alger Management emerged on top of money-manager rankings for the greatest increase in equity accounts—50% for the year ending in March. The firm's best investment that year was Genentech, which nearly doubled and was showing a $46-million paper profit in November; thereupon Alger reduced its stake in the company from 1.9 million to one million shares.

When *Financial World* released its "One Hundred: The Highest Paid People on Wall Street" for 1985, both Fred and David made the cut. David was listed at the baseline of $3 million, and Fred, then 51, was pegged with earnings of $5 million. But they were nowhere near the top.

Number one was 49-year-old Ivan Boesky, who made $100 million from risk arbitrage investments. Number two was George Soros, who, through Netherlands Antilles-based Quantum Fund, garnered $93.5 million, including a $10 million bonus from the fund's clients, by betting on the weakening dollar. The number three earner was Michael Milken, senior vice president and head of underwriting and junk-bond trading at Drexel Burnham Lambert, who raked in $50 million. Jerome Kohlberg, Henry Kravis, and George Roberts—the general partners of Kohlberg Kravis Roberts & Co.—took fourth place through heavy participation in leveraged buyouts. Numbers one and three on the list were eventually discredited and sent to prison.

Few of the business tycoons on the roster attained their wealth by managing money or by investing in stocks. If they were in investments, most were corporate bigwigs like Robert Rubin, then a partner at Goldman, Sachs & Co., who made $9 million in 1985. One notable exception was Peter Lynch, senior vice president and managing director of Fidelity Investments Co. and portfolio manager of its Magellan Fund.

Emboldened by rising assets, the surge in brokerage commissions and backed by his name recognition and a now muscular talent pool, Fred Alger scrambled up to the groaning board a few times to get a hand in the raging private placements. Three at least, were explosive deals, which, had they come off, would surely have blasted the firm into an exalted stratosphere.

It is a little-known fact in the financial world that Fred Alger tried to crank up a leveraged buyout of Ford Motor Car Co. between 1985 and '86. The audacity of such a move showed the best of Fred Alger's entrepreneurial spirit during the decade.

Coming out of the 1981–82 recession, auto stocks were "really on the balls of their ass," according to David Alger. The market priced Ford especially at a steep discount to its cash and other assets, so that one might take a loan against that equity, use it to acquire the company, then spin out or sell off undesirable and valuable components to retire the debt and own the company for virtually nothing. This is the way of LBOs.

Bob Emerson took a lead-off position in the engagement and credited himself with the opinion of taking the company private. He recounted one of the early, informal meetings to pitch the idea to Ford, which was more marked by atmospherics than serious consideration of the deal.

"Fred knew the Fords a little bit," he said, "so we got in to see William Clay Ford and Henry Ford II. Henry Ford was wearing cowboy boots and a pink cowboy shirt, not what I expected. He was on his way to grouse hunting in Scotland. Our lawyers counseled us on the way to the meeting. 'These guys aren't at all interested in a lot of minutiae. They want lots of money in cash, for them, real soon. Stress that.' Halfway through it Henry turned to Fred—he obviously wasn't listening—and asked 'Hey, Fred, weren't you once married to Lesly Stockard?' It turned out that this was true. I didn't know about this. David later told me even Fred's kids didn't know about it. Fred was married to her for about a week. This was all Ford wanted to talk about."

One time in the sixties Fred ran into Henry Ford in the men's room of New York's Doubles Club. It was a scene reminiscent of a business negotiation in Harold Robbins' *The Carpetbaggers*. Ford was on Fred's left, at the urinal trough, and Stavros Niarchos, who, along with Onassis and Goulandris, ruled the Greek shipping world, flanked him on the right. Fred greeted Ford, "Hello, Mr. Ford, I'm Fred Alger." Then Ford leaned back slightly and yelled in the direction of Niarchos, "I want you to meet Fred Alger. They say he's the smartest guy on Wall Street."

Emerson believed that the Ford deal ultimately collapsed from inattention. "If we had been Goldman Sachs, Morgan Stanley, Allen & Co. or Lazard Freres, if we had been a force in investment banking, going in with printouts and a team of twelve guys in blue suits . . . But Fred, his analyst and his lawyer going in and saying, 'We have this idea . . .' It didn't have clout. In hindsight, Ford should have done it. They had the cash to do it. The stock was way down. Interest rates were low enough that they could have made a bundle."

David had another explanation for what happened. "It was way too adventurous. Henry Ford II was the supreme king of the company. Though his family owned just seven percent of the stock, it controlled forty percent of the vote. To go to Henry Ford and say we want you to borrow several billion dollars, buy the company back from the shareholders, then sell off pieces so you'll own the car company for free—it takes some balls to do it. Henry Ford had a lot of balls, but not that many balls. It would have worked, and I think if he was a younger man he might have done it, but he was in his last lap at that point."

From Fred's perspective, the only reason the Ford buyout never material-

ized was: "Henry Ford II died within six months of our making the presentation. The stock was at twenty dollars. We were saying fifty dollars. He was thinking one hundred. It turned out, in those days we could have afforded to pay a
hundred dollars. But then he got sick and died. And unfortunately he was the
big contact."

The proposal's failure didn't stop Fred Alger from making money on Ford
stock. Ford was selling for $50 in November 1985. By April 1986 it had climbed
to $80. By the end of April 1987, Ford was up to $91 a share, after a three for two
split in June 1986. At that time Fred Alger owned 1.2 million shares and was buying more.

Another of Fred's attempts at orchestrating a corporate takeover was its involvement with Jim Crosby, chairman of Resorts International, in a hostile raid on Pan
Am stock in 1985.

To stanch the bleeding from string of $200 million-a-year deficits and an 80%
debt load, Pan American World Airways chief executive C. Edward Acker had just
dealt its Pacific routes and 11 jets with $137 million in lease obligations to United
Airlines in exchange for a sorely needed cash infusion of $750 million.

Bob Emerson was close to the negotiations in the movement of Pan Am stock
to Crosby. "Ed Acker came up with a pretty interesting coup, when he sold Pan
Am's Pacific operations to United Airlines for more cash than Pan Am was valued at in the stock marketplace. Pan Am was valued at five dollars a share, and
it had just received a windfall of seven dollars a share in cash," said Emerson.
"My theory was, in effect, you could buy this company for the cash in its balance
sheet, take over the company and have this whole thing for free."

"If the Pacific routes sale goes through, the value of the fleet and the cash
would be substantially more than the stock sells for without attributing any
value to the remaining international routes," Emerson was quoted as saying
in a December 1985 *Forbes* article. "This is not an earnings play. This is an
asset play."

Emerson added privately ten years later, "The trouble with this was, the company had a huge pension liability, huge debt, pilot contracts that were escalating and a money-losing domestic operation. You may have been able to buy this
pig for nothing, but it was worth less than nothing.

"We bought a small stake in the firm, perhaps five percent. Then Fred said
that Jim Crosby, chairman of Resorts International, had always expressed an interest in being in the airline business. He may have even made a run at Pan Am once
before. Why don't we sell this thing to Crosby? He can buy the company for no
money and shrink the domestic operations, which were losing money. Acting as
brokers, we sold Crosby ten or fifteen percent of the company—a pretty good-
sized chunk."

Emerson remembered correctly. Crosby had once before, in 1969, made a play for Pan Am. Then, the airline ran to Washington and panicked its friends in Congress into rushing through a bill which specifically thwarted Resorts' designs on the airline. On March 10, 1969, trading was suspended in Resorts shares for three weeks when it proposed acquiring two large blocks and options to buy more. Fear was raised about a gambling company's ownership of a national institution. Considering its subsequent bankruptcy and demise, Congress might have done better by letting Crosby take over the airline.

This time, with Fred Alger, his takeover scheme actually faltered when the sick and dying Crosby balked at buying the rest of the company.

"At one point Pan Am had sufficient cash so the company could have been taken over and the airline liquidated, their routes sold off at a great profit," said David Alger. "Unfortunately, over the next few years the company spent up all its cash."

"Despite our pleading, Ed Acker wouldn't shrink the size of domestic operations. So the company continued to lose money," Emerson added. He recalled that Crosby, who was stricken with emphysema and spoke through a breathing device, would call Fred frequently, sounding frightfully like Darth Vadar on the speaker phone. "Fred, Fred, I'm starting to get pissed off. I don't know when the goddamn stock is going to go up. When are they going to close the domestic operations?"

"We got out of our position," Emerson said in conclusion. "We bought it at around five dollars. It went up briefly to nine and three-quarters. Eventually we sold it back at five dollars. I begged Fred to sell it. It was a round trip to nowhere."

Unlike the Ford buyout, a private negotiation, Fred Alger's proposed acquisition of Levitz Furniture Corp., based in Boca Raton, Florida, was a matter of public record and widely reported in the press. It represented a real incursion for the company into merchant banking.

In background notes Rob Lyon, the lead player in the negotiations, whose idea it was to go after the company in 1984, described Levitz, one of the biggest names in manufacturing and selling home furnishings, as "prototypically a non-Alger kind of stock."

"It was a great interest-rate play," he explained. "In late 1983 the Fed reversed field and raised interest rates, taking the long bond, the thirty-year U.S. Treasury, to fourteen percent. All the stocks related to housing went down, and Levitz was no exception. It went from forty dollars to twenty-five almost immediately. But rising interest rates didn't seem to have much of an impact; their business was getting better." Levitz was operating 89 warehouse showrooms nationwide. Its 1983 sales were $645 million and net income was $17.4 million.

"In the spring of 1984," Lyon continued, "we owned maybe eight percent of the company. The stock had snuck up, and it was clear that the temporary tightening period would come to an end and Levitz would be a very good stock. The same thought apparently occurred to the Pritzkers of Chicago, who owned nearly twenty-five percent of the company. Irwin Schwartz called me one afternoon and said, 'They stopped trading in Levitz Furniture, and they're going to announce that the Pritzkers are going to make a bid for the remaining shares at twenty-nine dollars.' The stock was then at twenty-seven. We probably paid that much for what we owned, and it had been at forty dollars a few months earlier."

Said David, "The Pritzker family put in a bid that was actually below the market value of the company. We were so outraged that they would try to steal Levitz that we decided to make a bid ourselves."

Lyon went to Fred with the details. "Fred asked, 'What do you think this thing is worth?' It was a dominant company. It had very little debt and owned the land underneath the stores in Florida, Texas and California. At that time the valuations were really low compared to what they are now. I thought it was very clearly

David and Fred are alike perhaps only in their competitive drive and fierce loyalty to one another.

worth over forty dollars a share. With eight million shares outstanding, that meant 320 million dollars.

"'Why don't we buy it?' Fred suggested. I was just stunned. That's the difference with a guy like Fred. He's very creative. I might have considered suing them, or getting some other institutional investors to hold out and jack up the price since the stock ownership was pretty concentrated. But buying it, that was a bizarre concept to me."

George Boggio confirmed that Levitz was Lyon's deal. "It was a combination of his idea and Fred's willingness to pursue it," George said. "We prided ourselves on being astute businessmen who could put together the people to run that operation. That is the thing we loved doing. Fred was a visionary, and I was the detail guy. We were going to buy it with its own balance sheet by issuing Levitz junk bonds. Rob and I flew down to Florida to make a bid, but we were topped by Pritzker."

Here's how the story was reported in the press.

When Fred Alger made its competing bid for Levitz, the offer by Dalfort Corp., a unit of Pritzker–owned Hyatt Corp., which already owned 22.5% of the outstanding shares, had already been approved by Levitz's board on June 29, 1984. But the $27 to $29 bid, $162 million of it in cash plus additional securities, for 100% of the shares was unanimously viewed as inadequate or cheap by institutional analysts.

Fred countered in August with $20 in cash and $40 face-value, subordinated 15-year debentures for each of the 8.15 million outstanding shares, which was estimated at $34 a share, or $279 million for the entire company. The debentures were stipulated to accrue and pay an interest of 16% starting the sixth year after their issue date, subordinated only to the indebtedness of the new company's borrowings and were callable at par after five years. Additionally, the Alger bid reserved 15% of the surviving company for its management against Dalfort's sparing set-aside of just 5%.

The story behind the news was more complex and went unreported.

First, there was a legal conflict of interest between Alger's bid and the 5% of Levitz shares it owned through its clients. "Our lawyers made us give back to our clients the shares in their accounts, so this caused us to lose around thirty million dollars in assets under management," said David, "and our clients were weirded out because they wondered what we were doing in the LBO business anyway. We tried to point out that it was in their best interest, but it went to the issue of normalcy. This is not what a money manager does."

Returning the shares to clients created a fictional, though factual, arm's-length condition that appeased the law. The clients could vote the shares for themselves, and Alger was cleared by its lawyers to pursue the bid.

The next obstacle was financing. "We were doing this on a shoestring," Lyon continued. "We were looking to put up about five or ten million dollars. I can't remember exactly where we ended up—there were so many iterations. I think we increased our bid once or twice along the way."

After being turned down for financing by Bankers Trust and PaineWebber, the Alger company worked out a deal with GE Credit "to make a real bid for the company," Lyon declared

"We were proposing to buy the stock for forty-five dollars a share, of which twenty dollars was in zeros, in essence buying the company with its future cash flow and the rest borrowed from GE," he added. "The money we were putting up would have been absorbed by legal fees and other expenses. The ownership of the underlying equity would be split something like forty or fifty percent for Alger and thirty to forty percent for GE. The other twenty percent was reserved for Levitz management, which would basically be free to them."

In September, Jeffries & Co. agreed to underwrite the zero-coupon offering. In exchange for its commitment, according to *The Wall Street Journal*, Jeffries would receive equity in the company.

Next, in a surprise press release, Alger sweetened the pot, increasing the offer by $3 a share. The new cash-and-debt offer was valued at $37 a share, or $303.4 million.

Jeffries agreed to purchase the bonds for cash during a 20-day period. Shareholders would have received $17 for each tendered Levitz share on top of the proposed $20 cash component. But Jeffries reserved the right to reduce the exchange price for the debentures if interest rates on government securities rose in the interim.

The Alger offer blew Pritzker out of the water. A leading furniture-industry analyst, Frank Williams of the Cantor, Fitzgerald & Co. brokerage advised, "It seems to me to be a price that Levitz investors could accept." Levitz stock was hovering between $32 and $34 a share. Dalfort was claiming that its own offer was worth $33.50 a share, even though analysts uniformly disagreed and gave it a lesser value.

Erik Giese of the evaluation committee chaired by Drexel Burnham Lambert, the investment banking firm retained by Levitz to assess the bids, said they were "surprised and taken aback by the unilateral press release by Alger. It's unusual."

Subsequently, Drexel's Fairness Opinion applied a high discount rate on the Alger debt, thereby reducing its perceived value below Dalfort's bid.

On October 16 Levitz's board rejected the buyout offers from both Alger Associates and Dalfort Corp., stating that its financial adviser couldn't support either of the bids. As reported in the Journal, Erik Giese said that Drexel Burnham "had advised the committee that they could not give an opinion that the offer by Alger Associates Inc. was fair to Levitz's shareholders from a financial point of view . . . and both Drexel Burnham and the committee had reservations about Jeffries' commitment to purchase the debentures."

Ronald Alghini, president of Jeffries & Co., protested that he was "surprised and disappointed" by the rejection. "Our commitment to purchase the bonds was firm, and we had substantial financial resources to support it."

The outcome suggests there might have been more to Drexel's work for Levitz. On November 7, the Levitz board approved the company's leveraged buyout by a group including members of management, the erstwhile adviser, Drexel Burnham Lambert Inc., and its partner, Citicorp Capital Investors Ltd., for $39 a share or $318 million.

"It was a very good deal, except we did it all wrong," David conceded. "We fell into the typical Alger pattern of trying to reinvent the wheel that had already existed. We didn't appreciate the growing clout of Drexel Burnham in the takeover business. What we should have done was hire Drexel Burnham to finance it with junk bonds which they would sell. We didn't fully get what was going on.

"Our deal was superbly structured and would have worked. We even tried to convince Pritzker to sell to us rather than take over the company. But Pritzker didn't believe it. He was scared there was going to be a recession, which never materialized. We were right. He was wrong. We would have all been immensely rich if it had gone through."

For this failure the knock went to Fred, because of his refusal to acknowledge the realpolitik of the situation. "He needed help from the experts on Wall Street, but Fred didn't seek it out," said Bill Scheerer. "Fred is not the type of guy who will ask for help if he can do it himself."

Irwin Schwartz chimed in, "The problem was Fred tried to do everything himself. He had done that several times before. For example, Levitz Furniture. Drexel outbid us by half a point and took the deal away from us. If we had brought in Drexel from the beginning, we would have shared the profits. If something has been done one way successfully for a hundred years and Fred goes to do it, he must figure out his own way, whether it is important or not, whether it is efficient or not."

Drexel Burnham eventually went down in flames over junk-bond scandals in the eighties and filed for bankruptcy protection in February 1990. Levitz Furniture Inc. was recently operating 68 showrooms and 66 satellite stores in 26 states and reported annual sales of $966.9 million for its fiscal 1997. Its stock stair-stepped down from $16 to $3 a share between 1994 and 1996 and had a trading range of 47 cents to $4.63 in 1997. Robert M. Elliott, chairman and CEO of the company during the buyout, stayed in that position until the latter part of 1995.

The necessary precondition for the Alger Fund was the feeble performance of growth stocks from 1983 onward. Takeover stocks ruled. Since Fred Alger was unwavering with its growth strategy, the firm was constantly struggling below the market.

"We weren't really demolishing the S&P in those days the way people expected us to," said David. "The absolute returns were excellent, but the comparative returns were not that great." In 1983 the Alger composite gained 19.9%, but the market rose 22.6%. In 1984 it was down 2.8%, while the market was up 6.3%. In 1985 it finally matched the market's return of 31.7%.

It was that year, which delivered banner profits to the company along with a robust market outlook, when serious consideration for launching its own funds finally became possible.

"Parenthetically," David confided early in 1995, as a premise for his bullishness that year as well as a decade earlier, "there has never been a year ending in the number five when the Dow hasn't been up." The year's record proved him to be right. In 1965 and 1995 Algers ran the best-performing fund in the country. In 1975 as well, the Dow grew over 38%. Mutual-fund investors are advised to remember this when the next five year rolls around.

He continued, "There was a sense of frustration about how difficult it was to beat the S&P, but on the other hand, there was a sense of great prosperity at the company."

Along with its questionable performance in `83 and `84, Alger failed to keep up its customer relations. "Though a lot of money came in, we failed to establish rapport with our clients," added David. "They hired us, but many of them never felt very comfortable with us. As soon as an excuse came about to leave us, they did. There's the kind of client who will hire you as long as your numbers are really good. When they're no longer good, they leave. These aren't the kind of clients you normally want. If you live by the numbers, you die by the numbers. Relationship-based clients are always better than performance-based clients.

"We had nobody here to maintain those relationships. The research department was well staffed with highly paid people. The marketing department was incredibly understaffed. No one knew how to run it. No one made any effort to run it. It was a mess."

The reasons for operating its own mutual funds were becoming increasingly compelling.

First of all, assets were fleeing the company, and new accounts were harder to locate and develop. The pension business was maturing. Many more money managers had jumped into a shrinking field. As corporations reached their pension-funding goals faster than expected with strong stock performance, they put the brakes on contributions. With the S&P outperforming most money managers, investor attention was turning to passive investing, or betting on the market indices rather than active management. And the consultants, most of whom were never favorably disposed toward Alger, had consolidated their power and were exercising an ever greater say over the direction of tax-advantaged assets. Alger's pension business had hit the ceiling.

Additionally, brokerage commissions, which were so integral to the firm's revenue stream, were being seriously discounted in the industry, and Alger had to ratchet down its rates to remain in tune with the market.

"With his unusually astute sixth sense, Fred perceived that we were in danger of becoming obsolete," David disclosed. "We rode the crest of the wave, but the wave was essentially broken. So he decided to go into the mutual-fund business."

"Watching the pension-account assets contract by a factor of three, we started the mutual funds out of desperation," said Fred.

There was a lot riding on the funds. Not only were they a means to replenish dwindling assets and recharge the firm's sputtering reputation, they became the vehicle for unleashing the firm from its dependence on pension accounts and their domineering consultants.

The mutual funds were conceived as the bulletproof solution for the erratic and unrestrained asset flows inherent in pension accounts. Because of a pension account's large size and small number, the firm was vulnerable when one left. A mutual-fund client is one among a multitude; when an individual investor decides to close his or her account, the impact on the company is considerably smaller. At the same time, it was expected that the mutual funds could provide a back door into pension accounts, serving as advertising for the tax-advantaged and high-net-worth business. With the Alger Fund performance in plain public view in newspapers every day, pension managers and investors might be moved to consider Fred Alger for managing their assets.

At best, the mutual funds gave Fred Alger new vehicles for distributing and reselling its great research. The shelf life of a mutual-fund family is far longer than any pension portfolio. As an investment product it could be used to penetrate other niches of the financial industry. The same mutual funds and their variants could be sold or repackaged for retirement accounts, insurance annuities, foreign distribution, and marketing by other financial institutions.

Alger board's Arthur Dubow said, "It was an extremely daring move at the time. No one else was starting a public mutual fund, and the idea was met with a great deal of skepticism." When Security Benefit's Cleland heard that Fred was launching the Alger Fund, his reaction was disbelief. "To tell you the truth, I thought he was nuts, and I told him so. The idea that he could hire a bunch of people to answer the telephones and place ads in the paper and start selling mutual funds, I thought was absurd. We tried that. I knew how difficult that was."

Jim Connelly, who now runs the Alger Fund, was among the dozen or so telemarketing clerks recruited by Monica Smith for the support team from competing firms like Dreyfus and Merrill Lynch. He's the only one left at the company from that starting group.

Jim had spent the previous four years at a Dreyfus phone desk and was looking for a new challenge to get ahead. In the large firm, he was clustered in a four-person group which was graded and promoted as a single unit. It nettled him to be ranked in a collective entity with others of varying strengths. He needed his individual abilities to be recognized. Jim's head was already brimming with success stories from other Wall Street startups, and the Alger mutual-fund launch looked to him like just one of those opportunities. Alger offered him more money plus a signing bonus. So at age 25, along with several other mates from his old firm, he swung over to Alger.

Two days before he started at the firm, he had an automobile accident. "On my first day at work I looked like somebody beat me up with a bat," he said. "Part of my head was shaved and bandaged. I kept ducking so I wouldn't be noticed."

If Jim didn't make a good first impression, he's certainly made up for it by his deft handling of the mutual-funds business during his watch.

Would the Alger Fund live up to such a strong advanced billing? In time the answer would be yes, but there was a lengthy gestation period to be weathered. "Starting the fund turned out to be an exceedingly good decision," said David, "because our pension-fund business began to fall apart in 1987 and very seriously in 1988, and it never came back. But the implementation of the whole move into mutual funds was very flawed." He was referring to the misbegotten advertising campaign that introduced the funds, which invited a heavy-handed response from the investing community and a sobering attack by the SEC.

Fred concurred, "What turned the company around was the mutual funds. Our funds now are bigger than other assets under management. The funds are more profitable, assets stay with us longer, and they give us a focus. We were lucky to start the funds when we did."

"Fred had the extraordinary foresight to anticipate the reemergence of mutual funds, the end of aggressive management for pension funds and the much more competitive and difficult atmosphere," David suggested.

Fred saw it coming: that stocks would be recognized as the best bet for long-term investing; the fresh focus on investing by a maturing population; and investors' need for the cheap and easy access to professional money management that mutual funds represent. In 1986, the first year of the Alger Fund, it accounted for a scant 4% of the firm's assets under management. Ten years later, mutual funds made up almost 70% of the Alger business. During the same period the number of American households owning mutual funds grew from 10% to 40%, and the number of mutual funds offered for investment more than tripled.

Fred saw his future in mutual funds just as they were a bridge to his past. He had started and prospered with mutual funds. They gave him his original reputation. By returning to the mutual industry, he followed his own prescription for growth. Instead of just investing in growth stocks, he opened a business in the fastest-growing sector of the financial industry.

Fully charged with relentless activity, the eighties were a stirring growth phase for the company. Fred Alger expanded, acquired, improved, added, built and grew wealthy.

It seemed as if the firm was unstoppable and that Fred had finally crossed the Rubicon of his personal quest to rebuild the family empire. "Everything is in place to build a major company that will, ten years from now, be a dominant, dominant financial firm," Fred announced with brimming optimism to the press. But even as the firm was hitting its stride, the scenario was being scripted for its ensuing downward trajectory.

The Ford and Levitz deals may have crumbled on personality issues—Fred's personality. That same mistake would not be repeated with the Alger Fund. Or would it?

17

The $13 Million Advertising Blunder

To launch the Alger Fund, Fred turned to religion, the religion of advertising. After years of avoiding media attention and wandering about in publicity wilderness, his devotion was mighty and his pockets were deep.

Fred identified correctly, and long before his competition, that mutual funds were a consumer product, just like soaps and soft drinks, and that they would benefit from the kind of brand advertising used to promote consumer items. "Advertising doesn't sell," said Fred knowingly. "It creates brand awareness over long periods of time." The goal was to achieve positive recognition of the Alger name by giving the firm a 'distinctive image.'"

The objective of the advertising campaign was threefold, according to David Alger. "First, to go around the consultants and make a direct appeal to chief executives in large American companies. Second, to develop a business in the low end of the high-net-worth individual market: a quarter million to two million dollars for individual accounts. Third, to prepare our brand name for the eventual launch of the mutual funds."

The SEC had just revised its long-standing rules against performance advertising, and "basically Fred felt that this was our opportunity to advertise our record in a broad forum for the first time, and that this would make us stand out," David added. "It did, indeed, accomplish that." The Alger record was extremely convincing: a compounded return of 21.2% a year over 21 years, "probably as good as anyone had done in the business up to that point."

In choosing to proclaim his success, Fred departed from his earlier conviction that if your performance is good the investors will automatically come, that there was no need to hype it up. His new thinking seemed to be, "You can't win the game unless people know the score," and through repetition and intensity he would bore his superiority into the marketplace subconscious.

This was no redux of the piddling television advertising of eleven years earlier. Fred envisioned a monster of a campaign. He earmarked nearly $17 million for the operation, hoping that such a massive sum might finally vanquish every demon that had tarnished his reputation, from gunslinger to con man to also-ran.

The heavy outlay was expensed as an appropriate price of admission into a large, new business opportunity. The mutual-fund industry had been recharged by declining interest rates, rising employment and a partial redirection of capital gains from real estate investments. Fred anticipated, correctly, that media coverage would eventually attract many more players to the business, just as his first *Institutional Investor* feature fattened the herd of money managers. The competition for financial assets, especially mutual funds, would be fierce, and it would take a bold and startling crusade to head off his rivals and instill a lasting impression of the Alger name.

Instead of a slam-dunk on the competition, Fred hit the boards too hard and the ball just bounced off the rim. No score. No points even for dramatic flair or ingenuity. The promotion which David called "without any doubt, the least successful advertising campaign in history" was broadly received as Fred's *folie de grandeur.*

The firm paid a steep price for this brief extravaganza, especially as it was forced out of a lead role in the coming decade's strong rise in mutual-fund investing. Rather than taking the firm to new heights, the advertising sent it careening toward an uncertain future.

Fred charged a young research associate just out of Yale, "our brightest," Christopher W. Schmeisser, with organizing the search for an ad agency to handle the campaign. The selection was limited to mid-sized firms—so that the Alger account would not be insignificant—and to agencies that had demonstrated good creative work.

The field was narrowed to 10 companies, which brought their proposals to Fred Alger in the firm's penthouse executive conference room. "Surprisingly, their presentations were uniformly bad," said Fred. "If they couldn't present their own selves very well, how would they represent Alger?" Fred was so exasperated, he was on the verge of terminating the project. At that point he ran into John Howard, an East Hampton acquaintance who was a senior vice president at Foote, Cone & Belding Communications, and began complaining about what he had seen from the agencies. Howard asked Fred to give his firm a shot, even though it was a large agency. "They made a terrific presentation," said Fred, "head and shoulders above the rest, and so they won the account."

Foote Cone was untested in retail financial services but had a long history in consumer accounts like Frito Lay, Lipton and Colgate. In April 1985, in order to bolster its presence in New York City, the agency had merged with Leber Katz Partners. It was the newly commingled firm, judged by some of its peers to be creatively unimpressive, that was handed the Alger account.

Fiscal restraint was not a condition imposed on Howard. "Fred came to us and said he wanted to spend a lot of money promoting his new mutual fund," said Howard. "He wanted to make a big splash, to stir up the industry."

Inside Fred Alger, Howard's day-to-day contact was Robert D. Birnbaum, a Wharton business-school graduate and former assistant vice president in marketing at The Vanguard Group, who was brought in specifically to supervise the telemarketing and customer-service functions needed to trail the advertising. He had rosily predicted that the firm would ring up over $1 billion in new asset flows as a result of the campaign. Despite Birnbaum's title, however, it was Fred who was firmly holding the reins of the advertising wagon train.

In keeping with the firm's maverick reputation and the creative nature of consumer advertising, the campaign's key concepts deliberately shunned the commonplace, traditional and uninspired "tombstone ads" that were the norm in financial advertising.

Huddled around Fred, the Foote Cone team found his presence so essential to the firm that they readily concluded he should also be central to the advertising campaign. "The challenge was solved around Fred Alger—the person incarnate," said Howard. "We were talking about Fred and his performance over twenty-one years, and in no uncertain terms. Our creative guys just equated it with a genius for making money. Fred seemed to like that because he was featured in the advertising, visually as well as talking about him, and that's what the campaign became. 'Fred Alger has a genius for making money.' But we went through an awful lot of work before getting to that point."

"We worried that Fred wouldn't like it," Howard later told a reporter for *Money* magazine, "but he faced up to it like a man."

The concepts for the campaign were evaluated both within and outside the company to make the final selection. Everyone at Maiden Lane and even some in New Jersey weighed in with opinions about the various ads. But nothing conclusive resulted from this kind of testing. Reactions were pretty much split evenly.

Fred was extremely reluctant at first about being positioned as the main feature of the advertising. It was all right to focus on the performance. But on himself? He had to be persuaded. What finally put the "genius" idea over the top was its endorsement by a short-time player at Alger named Bruce Anderson, who was hired by the firm as a marketer to pension accounts on the West Coast. Since he was closest in the group to the customer viewpoint and supposedly knew what might appeal to Alger's intended audience, Anderson's opinions were accorded a weight beyond their worth. He may have had a brief role in the firm, but since it was essentially his outspoken regard for the genius concept that shouted down all other creative concepts, Anderson has a distinct place in Alger history.

In the Alger boardroom arguments were muted over the choice of making Fred's genius the focus of the campaign. The board's concerns generally involved the high cost of the program. Even though the firm might eventually recover the expense through 12b-1 fees, it was an awful lot of money to put out. "He was going to front-end it and take that risk," said Arthur Dubow. "It's hard to second-guess that—a guy who had been so successful up to that time and who was willing to risk his own money on the concept and his ability to deliver it."

Fred told his board, "We chose the campaign only because everybody in New York was telling us they thought it was the best one." If it was for the good of the firm, then okay. Once he owned it, in typical Fred fashion, he remained loyal to the end.

Fred's wife, Eleanor, implored him to remove himself from the advertising and was unflinching in her objection to the genius concept. Had he forgotten his personal reasons for staying out of the firm's 1975 advertising? A year after the campaign ended, Fred told the Detroit Free Press, "The only one who gave me any hesitation at all was my wife. I should have listened to her. No one really said, 'You're leading with your chin,' except her."

Even if he didn't listen to his wife, he might have been smarter to recall that Bernie Cornfeld once described him as "a fine artist" with respect to money management. "The Art of Investing," one of the concepts originally placed in contention, had resonated well in many corners of the office. "That's the one I liked," said David. "Fred found it too boring."

"We want to be the Frank Perdue of the mutual-fund industry," analyst Bob Rescoe remembered Fred saying. And certainly this wasn't the first time that a financial-services firm tried to wrap its fingers around a branding concept. Fidelity tried it in 1980, with no success, when it introduced a frog named Fidit to speak for its products. Perhaps it was Alger's scale which offended? Or was it Fred's message? There were never any objections to the ubiquitous roaring Dreyfus lion. After all, this was the year when Charlie Chaplin's tramp character was hawking IBM personal computers. If only Fred Alger's spokesman had been just as mute.

Daughter Hilary, as yet outside the firm, summed up the difficulties inherent in the project from the start. "Here's a private person who doesn't know or like marketing, but he spent thirteen million dollars on an advertising campaign," she observed. "He spent all his time hiding his light under a bushel, then he turns everything upside down."

The budget reserved for the project, including the mutual-fund launch, was about $16.3 million. The creative production and media placement took up $13.3 million, with the balance allocated for tactical support, which was essentially Birnbaum's telemarketing team.

"Fred wanted to shoot out all the lights," explained Howard. "We went in with what would be considered a normal budget for introducing this kind of a product, in this kind of a market, in that time period. I think we had four or five million dollars, which was a helluva lot of money.

"Fred insisted, 'You're not listening to me,' so we ended up buying anything and everything, including Wimbledon tennis, for God's sake! Fred wanted to make sure he was heard."

The first ad salvos, pitched in June 1986, were aimed at high-net-worth individuals and institutional investors and meant to prefigure a succeeding campaign to launch the mutual funds in November. The main publication ads were single pages or spreads, in black printing, but several smaller teaser ads were also released. The ads' consumer orientation was totally novel—and against the grain of typical financial advertising, which was verbally and visually restrained. They drove home two interlocking themes: one, that Fred Alger applied itself uniquely in managing its investors' money, and two, that the firm's past performance was vastly superior to the S&P 500 average.

The headline in the lead-off ad, which hit its mark in *The New York Times*, *USA Today* and *The Wall Street Journal*, asked the question, "What Does It Take to Produce Annual Compound Growth of 21% for 21 Years?" Answer: "A Genius for Managing Money."

Four images were laid out to advance that idea. The first, Fred's thoughtful pose, with fist on chin, seated next to the ficus tree in his office and looking straight into the camera. Its caption, in capital letters, "Fred Alger, the man behind the legend." Next was a close-up of a secure padlock. The caption—all the captions are in caps—"Research available only to our managed accounts." The biggest picture was of three fanned-out oyster shells, with one half open to reveal a pearl. Caption: "Systems designed to find the rare oyster with the pearl." Finally, a chart illustrating Alger's performance versus the S&P 500, with the words underneath, "Outperforming the S&P 500 better than 10 to 1 since 1965." These pictures, shot by prominent commercial photographer Henry Wolf, as were all images in the campaign, were used and combined with others in the next ads and supporting collateral pieces.

The copy began, "Meet Fred Alger. The legendary money manager whose unique investment disciplines over 21 years have outperformed the market averages. We know of no other manager or diversified equity portfolios who can match that record." The next paragraph articulated the chief message of the entire campaign: "$10,000 invested with Fred Alger in 1965 would have grown to $679,395 today: a gain of better than 21% compounded annually and more than 10 times the gain of the S&P 500 over the same span." An asterisk after the sentence directs the reader to an accounting notice within the performance chart which states, "Through March 31, 1986. Results for Alger and the S&P 500, an unmanaged index of common stocks, reflect capital appreciation and dividend reinvestment, but not advisor's fees to Alger." Clearly, Alger believed that he was taking every reasonable step to ensure accuracy and avoid misleading the public.

The long copy, which wrapped around the visuals in three columns in the single-page version and four columns in the spread, detailed numerous reasons for this superior performance. One of these took a pot shot at the competition, stating, "Fred Alger's analysts follow 1,400 stocks—250 more than Merrill Lynch—continuously."

The two-page version said, "The legendary money manager whose unique investment disciplines over 21 years have consistently outperformed the market averages and, to the best of our knowledge, every manager of diversified portfolios on Wall Street." There was also a fifth picture, a dramatic boardroom group shot with a caption: "A genius for managing money: Fred Alger, Irwin Schwartz, David Alger, George Boggio and Robert Lyon."

Another ad in the series advised, "9 Ways to Find Out if You Have a Genius for Managing Money." The subhead invited the reader to "Compare Your Investment Advisor's Discipline to Fred Alger's." Also available in single-page and two-page versions, it advanced the following reference points for Alger's superiority:

1. *Do all your own research. Keep it for your clients only.*
2. *Abolish portfolio managers and "Decision by Committee."*
3. *Let none but the fittest stocks survive.*
4. *Use P/V sheets to identify market behavior patterns.*
5. *Follow 1,400 stocks continuously.*
6. *Maintain an interactive computer system with the timeliest research available.*
7. *Organize to get lucky.*
8. *Hold no huge, illiquid stock positions.*
9. *Create an in-house firm to recruit the brightest minds on Wall Street.*

Next to this was a yearbook-type group shot of all the Alger analysts, with the caption, "More genius for managing money. Fred Alger's research analyst team."

A third ad raised the question, "What Does It Take to Beat the 'Lone Rangers' at Their Own Game?" Answer, "A Genius for Managing Money." Illustrations included a Lone Ranger mask and a fishing net. Next to the mask, "'Lone Ranger' investing doesn't work anymore." Under the net, "Aggressive management redefined. It starts with casting a wider net."

A fourth iteration in the print campaign inquired, "What Does It Take to Draw a Bead on 1,400 Moving Targets?" The answer was obvious by then: "A Genius for Managing Money." For the main illustration, a row of bullet-riddled target

Fred was spending a lot of advertising dollars to give the Alger name a lasting, positive brand identity in the financial services industry.

ducks, as found in a carnival sideshow. Also a new photo, Fred leaning over David, next to the ficus, as they gaze into a computer terminal. The caption, "Fred Alger and David Alger: Architects of Investment Success."

The smaller print ads, in the question-response format, keyed off the television commercials and provided much less copy.

"What Does It Take to Earn More for Your Estate Than Real Estate?" Under the headline, a picture of a mansion. "A Genius for Managing Money." Below the answer, a picture of Fred gazing at the reader.

The copy was truly compelling: "To equal Fred Alger's annual compound growth over 21 years, a $200,000 real estate investment in 1965 would have to be worth $13,587,900 today. Want to know more about the investment disciplines that produced such remarkable results?"

"What Does It Take to Paint a Brighter Investment Picture Than Gauguin?" Same answer. Different picture, but still just Fred.

"What Does It Take to Produce Annual Compound Growth of 21% for 21 Years?" Still more of Fred.

And there were many other variations on the theme, both small and large, and seemingly everywhere you looked in the print media. Ads targeting the high-net-worth market ran in *The New Yorker, Connoisseur, Smithsonian, Architectural Digest, Forbes, Town & Country, Golf Digest, Gourmet, Harper's, House & Garden, The Atlantic Monthly, Architectural Digest, Scientific American, Travel and Leisure,* and *Natural History*, plus magazine affinity groups like the Leadership and Ivy League networks. The core placements for the pension market were in *Institutional Investor* and *Pensions and Investing.*

This first wave of print ads ran from June to October, and smartly included a toll-free phone listing, which was hardly standard or routine at the time.

But it was the television commercials that generated the greatest awareness for the company. In a wild flurry from June to mid-August, Fred Alger popped up all over the television spectrum. Prime-time shows like *Cagney and Lacey, Hill Street Blues, 60 Minutes, Nightline,* the evening news and weekend news programs. The spots were prominent in special events like the Liberty Weekend and the Virginia Slims Tennis Tournament.

One of the TV spots, called Mona Lisa, was likely designed to satisfy Fred's acute interest in art. The commercial, which runs for 30 seconds, opens with an artist's paintbrush making an unflattering effort to reproduce, by formula, Leonardo Da Vinci's masterpiece. An orchestral rendition of Bach's soaring religious chorus *Jesus bliebet meine Freude* can be heard behind a commanding but friendly male voice.

"Investing by the numbers is a little like painting by the numbers . . . everybody else's research produces everybody else's results. And that's less than inspired . . . that's ordinary."

That said, a chart of Alger's investment performance is superimposed over the crude painting.

"At Fred Alger, we create our own research for our clients. Ten thousand dollars invested in Fred Alger in 1965 would be worth 685,000 dollars today. That's more than inspired . . . that's genius. A genius for managing money." The chart properly includes the standard industry caveat, "Past results do not guarantee future performance."

To close, the screen fills with a picture of Fred and the name Fred Alger Management in capital letters.

A second TV spot, the Dragster, was perhaps a nod to David's affection for glitzy cars. This ad was delivered in 30-second and 15-second versions. It starts with an overhead shot of the nose of a red racing car that vrooms and screeches as it takes off, and leaves tracks that quickly dissolve into the rising line of the Alger performance chart versus the S&P 500. Within the progression of the two images is a quick intercut of the Fred Alger name in block gray letters on a black background.

The same male announcer posits the question, "In the high-performance world of investing, what does it take to turn ten thousand dollars [here's where FRED ALGER appears] into nearly 680,000 dollars in twenty-one years?"

This spot also signs off with a boxed photo of Fred. When the answer is given, "A genius for managing money," it's a head shot of Fred facing the camera over the caption, Fred Alger Management, New York, New York.

The second phase of the campaign—a direct call for investing in the Alger Fund—was switched on in late October, ahead of the fund's November 11, 1986, launch date, and lasted through April the following year. Newspaper insertions were given to *USA Today, The Los Angeles Times, The Chicago Tribune, The Washington Post, The Boston Globe, The Philadelphia Inquirer, The Houston Chronicle, The Atlanta Post Constitution, The Dallas Morning News and Times Herald, The St. Paul Dispatch,* and *The Minneapolis Star Tribune,* with the concentration of the spending in *The New York Times, The Wall Street Journal* and *Barron's.* After the funds were registered, financial magazines such as *Changing Times, Financial World, S&P Personal Finance, Money, Business Week, The Economist, Forbes, Fortune,* and *inc.* were added to the media buying list.

One spread led off with this headline: "The Past: Fred Alger Turns $10,000 into $651,228 Over 21 Years." Underneath it, the familiar Alger performance chart versus the S&P surrounded by lots of white space. The genius part was left out. What was added was the length and detail of explanatory copy, which said: "Through September 30, 1986. Results for Alger and the S&P 500, an unmanaged index of common stocks, reflect capital appreciation and reinvestment of dividends, but not payment of Alger's advisory fees. Alger's results are for fully discretionary, equity oriented accounts managed for an entire year (1986 accounts through 9/30). For 1965, results are for Alger's only account, an active advisory account. Results are for accounts having the same investment objective and strategies as the Alger Growth Portfolio, which differ from those of the other Portfolios. See the prospectus for more information about the results. Past results do not guarantee future performance."

On the opposite page, above the picture of Fred behind his desk in a thoughtful pose, runs the headline, "The Present: Fred Alger Introduces the Alger Fund." The copy lists the six Alger funds with a brief description of each. Next to it is a tear-off reply coupon for the reader to fill in and send off. The bottom of the page is the tagline, THE ALGER FUND, 1-800-99-ALGER in the same bold face and large-size type as the headline, and the promise of customer response "24 hours, 7 days a week."

In her *Money* magazine review of the campaign, Barbara Lippert, senior editor and critic for *Ad Week* described Fred Alger's print ads as "well designed, bold and poster-like . . . intelligent, with a satirical tweak that offsets the heavy-handed genius part."

She continued, "Fred Alger is threatening to become the Leona Helmsley of money management. Both the self-styled queen and the genius have gotten tremendous awareness for their names and styles of doing business as a result of nervy, controversial advertising." Later in the review, "Some of the print ads remind me of Salad Master ads—you know, it slices, it dices. It makes you ask, 'could this guy possibly be telling the truth.'" But her final opinion was unequivocal. "The ads are effective and successful. He's also brought a certain buoyancy and bluster to financial advertising."

Mutual-fund bond marketer Jim Lebenthal of Lebenthal & Co., who has appeared for years as a spokesman in his company's spots, had this reaction. "When I first saw the ads, I took off my hat and did a low bow. But in some ways Alger is like the boy who strapped on wax wings and flew to the sun. . . . The genius ads suffer from advertising hyperbole."

Many in the financial community viewed the campaign as a sideshow. The buzz contained a lot of speculation about Fred. One article even reported that the ads were merely a prelude to selling the company after stuffing it with new accounts. And the outrage only grew louder as the ads continued to appear.

"Everyone looked at the ads and said, 'Oh, my God!' It was so promotional," confirmed Ashland's Chat Hickox. "Every broker in the land turned on him. It seemed that he was trying to go direct and cut them out. Whatever interest he generated got killed. Nothing could compensate for the negative word of mouth."

The loudest boos were raised obviously by other investment managers, but many pension-fund executives, their consultants and prospective mutual-fund competitors were quick to join in the disapproving chorus.

"Fred has an enormous genius, but he has a great shortage of what people could call just plain common sense," said John Cleland of Security Management, Fred's first client and soon-to-be competitor in the mutual-fund game. "Fred probably really liked the idea of using the appellation *genius,* and everyone around him was afraid to challenge him, least of all the ad agency, which had likely already pitched him five different ways from Sunday to get his message across. They were happy to get one idea approved. You have to stop your clients from hurting themselves. And they had hurt Fred enormously. There's no question about it.

"I laughed when I saw the ads and said, 'That's Fred.' I knew him, but the others who didn't know him or disliked him took issue with that boast, which was seen as a boast rather than a statement of accepted fact. Fred didn't mean it that way. It never would have occurred to him that people would take umbrage at that phrase."

But that's exactly what they did. In fact, a high-profile article in the July 7, 1986, issue of *Pensions & Investments Age* was dedicated to the objections to the Alger advertising. Here's a sampling from that piece, "Alger Peers Take Umbrage at Ads."

The chairman of New York's Bear, Stearns Asset Management chided Fred Alger for "mass-merchandising, which is not consistent with our approach."

"I'm sort of speechless by the whole thing," offered the chairman of Capital Guardian Trust Co. on the West Coast.

A mouthpiece for pension competitor Forstmann-Leff Associates made this allusion to medieval history: "Before you go into battle you blow the horns and make a lot of noise and scare the enemy."

Fred should have been wearing a flak jacket, he was taking so many hits. Obviously he had violated some long-standing, unwritten and sacred rule, understood by everyone on the Street but himself. The fact was, since he had never run with the Street crowd, he never guessed they would take such offense.

Inside the firm, the response to the advertising was emotional though guarded. The event was so central to the firm, everyone had an opinion, obviously ordered by hindsight of what was generally regarded as a fiasco. "I thought these were the worst ads," offered analyst Ron Reel, "but I did like the idea of advertising. At the time we were among the first to do a fairly aggressive advertising campaign."

"Once again we were doing something which was unusual," said David in retrospect. "Not only were we doing our own brokerage, not only was Fred the world's greatest marketer; in addition, we did our own research, and now we were advertising on television, calling ourselves a genius—doing a lot of things others just didn't do. This is an industry which values conformity to a certain extent. You have to look normal, and we were really looking far from normal at that point."

"The cards were stacked against us because of the old boy network," said Ron Reel. "They believed Fred was turning this industry into a Wal-Mart, cheapening the industry. It went against the hoity-toity image of the three-piece-suited, handlebar-mustached guys. If it worked, they would have to shell out too. Somehow they found it beneath the industry to do this."

Why did Fred's claim of genius touch such a raw nerve among so many on Wall Street?

David concluded that the word was anathema to Americans. "You can call yourself anything," he said. "You can say that you're a child molester, an ax murderer, a serial killer, and there'll be somebody to say, 'Well, a child molester isn't all that bad or a heroin addict isn't all that bad. There'll be support groups for whatever you are.

"But there is one thing you cannot call yourself in American life without engendering the hatred of anyone who listens to you, and that is to call yourself a genius. It's a form of self-flattery that no one appreciates. Those who come out and say they're geniuses are saying they're smarter than everybody else, and people hate that. Even Albert Einstein probably couldn't come out and say that he's a genius without twenty other physicists becoming irate."

Because the ads were so prominent and pervasive, and because they were seen as being too insistent about Fred's genius, the message of the firm's performance was overlooked. Had Fred's exposure been reduced, perhaps the impression might have been less imposing. But that would have been contrary to plan.

As the ads began appearing, the company braced for a flood of incoming inquiries. As a greenhorn at the firm, here's how Jim Connelly experienced it. "The phones were ringing off the hook. At first there were just two of us. Eventually more and more people were hired. We took speech lessons. Fred built a new area for us downstairs. Part of the day we took in-bound calls. Part of the day was outbound telemarketing to those who had requested information. There was lots of anticipation about the funds going on sale. Lots of people were calling. It was good to know we could soon start selling. When the funds were finally launched in November, there was a big celebration. We even received singing telegrams.

"Fred gave a speech and promised to make us all rich. I will never forget it, and I still think about it a lot. There was something about him that didn't make it sound like a bunch of bull. It seemed like he was really honest and sincere about all this, and he did have an interest in making us all rich."

It was virgin territory for the company. Fred's remarks in the July 15, 1986, edition of *Financial Services Outlook,* expressed the wonder of it all. "The newness is interesting and exciting," he admitted, "but the flip side is we don't know what we're really unleashing."

The advertising successfully elicited 100,000 respondents who were entered in a company database. But when the SEC made its case against Alger for misleading performance claims, the firm purged the entire list and lost the names forever.

Said David, "I invented a whole portfolio-management system which integrates the client account reporting system with the research, which to this day is unbelievably advanced. It was set up to handle a thousand new accounts in the low-end of high-net-worth individuals. We never used it."

Where to point the finger for such a painful and costly folly? Not all the responsibility belonged to Fred. There was enough blame to go around and many fingers to do the pointing.

The expectation was that as an ingenue in financial advertising, Foote Cone would produce an ad campaign that was fresh and highly creative. That may have been so, but it also made FCB exceedingly dependent on secondhand informa-

372   THE $13 MILLION ADVERTISING BLUNDER

tion about the financial industry. Lacking a nuanced perspective as well as requisite discrimination, it failed to anticipate the impact of calling Fred a genius. In other words, given Fred's strong character and perhaps because of it, the agency should have known better than to expose Fred in such a way that drew all this criticism.

According to David, complacency was the real culprit. "We were tremendously profitable in those years," he rationalized. "Like any other organization that is extremely profitable, inevitably someone will find a way to piss away the money. And we found it."

An important question—and apparently one nobody asked—was why take this route in the first place. Did it make sense for a money manager to appeal to consumers when the indications were then, and even today, that up to three-quarters of all mutual-fund sales in the U.S. are made via brokers and other institutional-distribution pipelines? And couldn't high-net-worth individuals be reached more efficiently—on a one-to-one basis—by a direct sales force? The thinking at the time was you needed to spend $100 in advertising and promotion to acquire a single mutual-fund shareholder.

Certainly it would have made sense to question the extreme cost of the Alger program. Dreyfus' ad budget in 1986 was only one and a half times larger than Alger's, though its assets were ten times greater. Perhaps Fred took his cue from Lew Lehrman's marketing success four years earlier, when massive advertising raised him from a political unknown to a popular contender for New York's governor's office.

Fred's old pal and mutual-fund marketer Joe Reich wasn't complimentary about the advertising. "I remember Fred running all these ads on national television and wondering if he had taken leave of his senses," said Reich. "We certainly found advertising not to work in what we were trying to do. If someone puts ten thousand dollars in a mutual fund, you're only going to get a hundred in revenue, and you have some costs. How could anybody expect to get a return on this kind of advertising from mutual funds? The cost of acquiring a customer is so high, it would seem you could never make your money back. But that's Fred. It seemed like something that Fred would do."

He continued, "When I started in the mutual-fund business, I was also advertising until I met someone from Dreyfus who surprisingly urged us to keep running our ads. 'Why?' I asked. He said, 'You're sending one out of two customers to us. We get fifty percent of all the business that comes from the public. Anybody who spends money on advertising only helps us by educating the public about mutual funds."

Looking back, David said, "We were spending an enormous amount of money without knowing if it would work. No one knew if we were addressing the right market. Foote, Cone and Belding was just terrible. They didn't lead us right."

"Our computer models are so sophisticated, we sometimes forecast a company's earnings almost as accurately as the company does," said David.

Board member Dubow agreed with him. "The ad agency failed to do research or acknowledge certain research," he said. "It was very happy, though, to spend Fred's money."

"The ad agency either didn't do any research or act on it," suggested ex-Alger analyst Rescoe. "They basically took Fred's money and ran. I always thought Fred was really smart, but he got taken on that one."

Former partner Bill Scheerer speculated otherwise. "When the ads came out, I could tell that Fred had written the whole thing," he said. "The ad agency must have had nothing to do with it but the mechanics of placing it. It was the Alger story that I had heard a million times—just the spiel that Fred would give when we talked to clients."

Not only was the Alger firm investing a lot of money in advertising, it was doing so by fronting its own capital—a move that its competitors considered daring but also foolhardy. By contrast, at the same time Fred was financing his ad program internally, Atalanta/Sosnoff Capital, an investment boutique which also had $3 billion in assets and was occasionally likened to Fred Alger, raised $53 million in a public offering to pay for its own marketing push.

The company was especially blindsided by the impact of the advertising on the firm's existing and prospective clients in the pension arena. Here is David's extended take on the touchy theme of fractured alliances.

"It never occurred to us that the campaign would have a negative effect on our existing business. It brought in a lot of leads—a hundred thousand—which we couldn't use, but it also so alienated the investment world that our pension-fund business suffered dramatically from it, and is still affected to this day. Our pension-fund clients, the pension-fund industry and the consulting portion of the pension-fund industry got the impression that we were abandoning the pension-fund business to go into the mutual-fund industry, that we were changing our focus and orientation and were no longer interested. That created a whole lot of problems. I believe the advertising campaign actually cost us more business than it gained.

"It certainly created a lot of bad will of all kind, including all manner of people sidling up to me and snidely commenting about what a genius I was when the performance went south. We all bear responsibility for the campaign. I didn't like the genius ad, and I wish I had thrown myself in front of the onrushing car."

The final expense for the campaign was booked at $7.5 million for the firm's fiscal 1986, and $5.75 million for fiscal 1987. Media buys broke down as follows: $1.23 million for newspaper advertising, $1.12 million for the business and financial press, $3.16 million for television broadcast and $858,000 for consumer magazines.

One of the regrettable ramifications of making such a large and bungled commitment to advertising was that it left Fred disillusioned with the idea of publicity. And so the firm retreated back to the promotional wasteland whence it had so recently emerged. This denial of the value of marketing neutered the company and kept it out of public contention at a time when other firms, following Fred's lead, were staking their claim in the mutual-fund industry and raising their own brand profiles on Wall Street.

There was at least one big missed break as a result. "When they pulled out of marketing completely, it led to even slower growth," said board member Dr. Saint-Amand. "In 1989, when David had the best performing mutual fund in America, they never used it to market the way it could have. No PR people were hired or contacted. No capital was made of it from a marketing point of view.

"Fred was really gunshy about hiring somebody. And whenever the subject came up in a meeting, he said he wasn't willing to take that chance again with marketing people."

For the next six years the firm demonstrated unusual laxness even in the smallest of promotional areas. For example, a lack of uniformity in the logos on its stationery and signs. For a firm so conscious of corporate branding and identity, such lapses can only be attributed to the lingering effects of the 1986 campaign. Finally in 1995, and only when David took the helm, the company started stepping out again and reinstated marketing to its proper role in the firm. Fred Alger established a meaningful budget for such activities, upgraded its promotional materials, and actively began to court the financial media for positive coverage.

Having taken the firm through such an unpleasant patch, it's hard to imagine that Fred could announce, "I don't think I've had any failures in business," when asked to assess his legacy as he prepared to retire from the firm. Perhaps because the company has made it through every problem that followed in the advertising's wake, the genius campaign was—ultimately—not a failure. Financially the firm is stronger than ever, and its mutual-fund income today surpasses all other classes of revenue. In Fred's mind, at least, the event is not a blemish but a well-worn scar.

"We're not sorry that we made the effort," Fred said unapologetically. "We took a shot and it didn't work."

Of the six portfolios originally offered by the Alger Fund, only Small Cap, Growth and Money Market survive. The rest were shut down due to lack of investor interest. Fixed Income and High Yield went early; Income and Growth lasted until 1995. They were replaced by a Balanced Portfolio, which opened on June 1, 1992, a MidCap Growth Portfolio on May 24, 1993, and the Leveraged AllCap Portfolio, which started November 1, 1993. Leveraged AllCap was renamed Capital Appreciation in March 1995. And so the Alger Fund has the same number of portfolios as it started with.

Arthur Dubow stood with Fred. "I didn't really regard the promotion as a fiasco. It didn't net nothing, though it could have been done better," he explained. "The fact is that the funds were launched and are very successful. Fred wanted to be in this business, and he felt he had to get his name known outside a very small number in the investment community. The question is whether those mutual funds would have been able to succeed without that up-front expenditure to get his name out before the public."

FCB's Howard came to his own defense. "No matter what you said, nobody was going to be interested in a brand-new mutual fund. When the market tanked in November, it was easy for people to say, If you're such a genius, why are you tanking along with the rest of us? Anyway, it didn't do Fred any lasting damage, unless you want to consider spending a couple of million bucks he shouldn't have spent, which he'll recoup eventually from his funds anyway because of twelve b-one."

12b-1 fees enable mutual funds to pass through promotion and distribution expenses, especially for acquiring new accounts, through a small annual assessment of shareholder assets. By SEC rules the current upside limit is .75% of assets, with an additional .25% permitted for account services.

In rounding up the 1986-87 advertising experience, several points appear to be material.

One, the timing for introducing the fund may have been off by about a year and three months. When it was launched, the market was hostile toward Fred Alger's growth style of investing. Nine months later, stock prices began trending lower and hit bottom in the October 1987 crash.

Two, Fred Alger clearly overspent for the advertising, and also erred in its choice of creative concept.

Three, the reliance on advertising to enlist new accounts was excessive, especially with respect to mutual funds. Brokers held the hand in that market, and the practice was, and still is, to heed one-, three-, five- and ten-year performance rankings for making investment decisions. Although Fred Alger provided a superb overall track record, the performance wasn't specific to the funds being promoted. They had no record. They were brand-new. Try as the advertising did to overcome this, it is unlikely that anything but the test of time could have attracted accounts in significant numbers. Building the brand name was the right idea, but it shouldn't have been concentrated in such an intense time span and at such a furious pace. The strategy was also flawed in expecting that a single appeal could win over several diverse markets.

Four, the attacks on Fred were an unfair response to his creative bravery and originality. The ads provided an excuse for venting old grudges and nursing competitive jealousy.

Five, Fred was first again. By promoting the firm's performance in such an aggressive and lavish way, he paved the way for the kind of mutual-fund advertising which was dismissed as routine and harmless just a few years later. Today's mutual-fund ads are far more provocative, artistic and consumer-driven than seemed possible before MTV, the gross popularization of financial investing and the enormous flowering of media outlets. Despite all the noise about Fred's performance, if you look at the facts objectively, it was no more than that—just noise. The firm's reporting passed every test of legitimacy and is a model of rectitude when compared to the cunning and fine print used in some of today's performance-oriented ads.

In the end, there was no second-guessing the campaign. There was never any scientific effort to assess its damage or make plans for a continuing program. Fred Alger had shot its load and would soon be engrossed in clearing up its mess. "There were no postmortems about doing anything differently," said Foote Cone's Howard. "If Fred hadn't insisted on spending that kind of money all at once, we could have put in the bag for six months and tried again after we had a clearer feeling about the campaign. We were there reading the tea leaves together."

After all the thunder came the lightning.

The ad campaign which stumbled over Fred's personality was only a teaser to the regulatory muddle which would entangle the firm with the SEC. Despite the blessing of its attorneys, the firm was imperiled by a blind spot in the 21-year Alger performance record that was the main feature of the advertising. Provoked by the media and mysterious unnamed complainants, the SEC bore down on Fred Alger with a force that threatened to unmake the firm.

The article that set it off was printed in *The Wall Street Journal* on Wednesday, October 1, 1986. The slug: "Making Claims." Headline: "Fred Alger Regains Wall Street Spotlight, But His Ads Rile Some." Subhead: "Money Manager Exaggerates Portfolio Gains, They Say; He Defends His Record." Finally the teaser: "Key Issue: What to Include." All this above the copy.

One month later *Barron's*, which has the same publisher as the *Journal,* did a lengthy article that was mostly a hatchet job. Benjamin J. Stein's "Pro and Con: A Hard Look at Fred Alger's Performance" raised the suggestion of trouble to come.

From these two flash points, Fred Alger became the fall guy for the SEC to flex its muscle over an expanding financial-services industry.

It may have been Fred's misfortune to have put out his advertising in the same year, and so soon after, the media and regulators had finished burying white-collar felons like Dennis Levine and Ivan Boesky. Levine, for instance, was nailed for insider trading in 54 deals with investment banker Drexel Burnham Lambert, including 30 takeovers and elaborate schemes to funnel funds offshore. Getting off on such big deals, the SEC didn't possess the residual goodwill to soften its stand on any presumed infractions, even in a minor case like this where common sense and oral evidence vindicated Fred's position.

In early September 1986, auditors from the SEC's Washington office descended on Fred Alger to verify its accounting records. They soon left satisfied that its reporting was accurate. After the articles and the prompting of an unseen hand, the SEC returned to the firm in December to search for documentary evidence of supposed miscalculations. While it is typical for the SEC to review new mutual funds in their first year, this scrutiny was much earlier than normal, which made it puzzling.

Assisted by the media, the SEC raised such a tumult that, regardless of the final moderate ruling, Fred Alger was damaged in the public eye. The old guard of the financial industry was as pleased by this as they were perturbed by Fred's rise and his manner of debasing their hallowed industry through popular advertising. One can put a spin on it, but the cumulative effect of the advertising, negative press and the SEC challenge was to prevent Fred Alger from achieving the goal of financial dominance that he sought at the beginning of the mutual-fund drive.

As *Institutional Investor* reported in "The High Cost of Advertising" in its March 1987 issue, "If he had known the ads would be picked over by the Securities and Exchange Commission, vilified by other money managers and savaged by the press, Fred Alger says he would 'never have gotten into [the mutual-fund business] at all.'"

Whenever there was a problem for the firm, Fred Alger had been fairly adept at surmounting the issue with his outside-the-box thinking and forceful action. This time it was different. There was a dark and fated quality to the onslaught of events. Looking pale and gaunt with worry, one afternoon Fred pulled George Boggio aside and, in a desperate voice and perhaps his only expression of weakness in 30 years, said, "We're finished!"

18

SEC Troubles

F RED ALGER had good reason to be alarmed. Soon after the ads came out, at an industry cocktail party, the director of a leading mutual-fund company pulled David close and whispered, "We're gonna get you." With that warning Wall Street served notice of its displeasure at Alger's performance advertising and braced the firm for an imminent attack on its fortunes.

But who would do the industry's bidding? How would it vent its rancor toward Fred? The answer wasn't long in coming.

The Securities and Exchange Commission started getting "a lot of complaints from people in the industry, I guess what I would call other competitors in the industry" according to Fred Alger's antagonist at the regulatory body, Kathryn McGrath, then director of its Division of Investment Management, which oversees money managers. "They were calling in and saying that Fred was not the one responsible for this performance," she recalled in a recent interview.

The obvious question was, as outsiders of the firm, how could they possibly know? And shouldn't such laments from competitors have roused suspicion about their motives and the veracity of their charges? Even so, the SEC proceeded because there were also calls from unnamed parties who had "been associated with Alger" charging that Fred shouldn't claim credit for the advertised performance because "he was a relatively low-level employee" and actually working under the thumb of an investment committee. This was their indictment of Fred's 1965 performance, which the company included in the Alger record.

Whatever the instigation, the SEC felt compelled to investigate. "I can assure you," said McGrath, "that the SEC would not bring a case unless it independently felt it had a solid basis for it. And, in fact, in terms of inquiry and investigation, we would always take a complaint from a competitor with a grain of salt."

The SEC has held its own as the bête noir of brokers, investment managers and security dealers ever since it was formed by the Securities and Exchange Act of 1934 as the government's watchdog and enforcer against illegal trading practices. Born in the debris from the 1929 stock market disaster, the SEC also figured to be a line of defense against future crashes. President Roosevelt named Joseph P. Kennedy as its first captain on the principle that "it takes a thief to catch a thief." Over the years, it has worked diligently, if not completely, to safeguard the investing public.

It was late summer 1986 when the dreaded SEC investigators first pounced on Fred Alger. The ads, which had passed initial submissions to the SEC and the NYSE, had been airing for several months. After a brief and uneventful inquiry of ten years' worth of record keeping—much longer than the SEC's required five years—the agency's operatives left, apparently content with their findings. With their departure the company was reassured about its advertising claims.

It was a false encouragement. That first probe was just the first act of a Kafkaesque ordeal that would try the character of Fred Alger, the man and the company. Several days later reporters from *The Wall Street Journal* turned up to get the scoop on the firm's performance advertising.

Internal memos by George Boggio for company files, dated September 17 and 18, 1986, reveal the reporting process for the first damning article which appeared in *The Wall Street Journal* on October 1, 1986. "Anders already had an angle for the story, namely that the performance numbers were overstated," he said about the initial meeting on September 9, between Fred Alger and Robert Birnbaum and *Journal* reporters George Anders and Beatrice E. Garcia, who shared the byline for the piece.

"Their main contention was we should have used Security Equity Fund numbers throughout." In the Alger advertising, only the first-year performance of Security Equity was used in tallying up the 21.2% average gain over 21 years. Since that year, 1965, was also its best year, what was the justification, they wanted to know, for excluding the remaining years it advised the fund?

The explanation was simple and innocent, at least to Fred Alger. All the accounts used to generate the performance reported in the advertising had to meet strict qualifications. As the reporters were informed, "only fully discretionary equity accounts who were with us for the entire year could be included. Margin accounts and accounts with unexpected withdrawals were not . . . . Security Equity was used in 1965 because it was the firm's only client and because transmission of advice was by telephone, not written reports."

Moreover, the first goal of the advertising had always been to attract well-heeled individual investors, and including mutual-fund performance would compromise the results with extraneous factors—transfer and administration fees, custodial charges, portfolio insurance, reserves for redemptions, and specific legal and tax issues—which are beyond the normal experience of pension and individual account management. So representing fund performance beyond that first year would have been inappropriate for its target audience.

Although Fred Alger made all the decisions, technically Security Equity could not be designated as a fully discretionary account because a management company cannot legally give up its final authority over investment choices. Nonetheless, in the first years of their relationship, Alger made all the buy-and-sell decisions for the fund. Because of the Pomerantz Strike Suit in 1969, Security Management increased its involvement in the fund to justify its management fees. Because of this, the prohibition against certain stock transactions and a new requirement for written recommendations, Fred Alger gradually and effectively lost command of the fund, which was reflected in its deteriorating performance that led to his resignation. Therefore it would have been unfair to figure those results into the performance, which was also the SEC's earlier ruling on the matter. Regardless of the reporters' concern for full disclosure, even the SEC found the Security Equity performance to be irrelevant and inadmissible except for the first year. The chief reason for its inclusion was because it was Alger's only account. In performance calculations for the subsequent 20 years, Alger used only private accounts.

Another objection by the writing duo centered around the exclusion of Spectra Fund figures in the 1974 accounting. That, Fred explained, was mandated by the firm's guidelines, which nullified any account with less than a full year's experience with the firm. First, mid-year accounts are susceptible to the vagaries of the market over the short term and, second, developing a separate composite for partial-year and terminated accounts was cumbersome and not regarded as helpful. As Fred put it, "Performance should be a reflection of what a manager can do over a period of time, not in a six-month period. It takes awhile to work into accounts." The assets in Spectra at the time, roughly $2 million, were also too small to have swayed performance.

What about the absence of Castle Convertible from the composite? Again, following the criteria, it was disqualified because it's not an equity fund.

"Since individual accounts were the initial and primary target for the advertising, we wanted to be able to show what we could do in the specific way that we manage those accounts," Fred added.

George Boggio, who participated in the first meeting only by conference call, wrote in the memos that the reporters requested a second meeting on an "or else" basis. They wanted to see data on "the dollar value of assets under management and the value of assets included in the composite for the early years." When George notified them that it might take some time, perhaps a week, to retrieve and compile these numbers, he was warned that without the data they would put in the article that "a senior official said that they did not have this information and that it would take a week to obtain," notwithstanding the SEC requirement that account statements go back only five years. The implications of that published statement set George on his heels.

To head them off, he rounded up his accounting team of John Raspitha, Greg

Duch, Rick Blum and Fred Koczwara to prepare the requested information. On Friday, September 12, all the files were open to Anders, along with data requested earlier by the SEC.

The follow-up meeting between lead reporter Anders and Boggio took place on September 16, 1986, at George's office in New Jersey. Anders took a special interest in the construction of the 1968 composite. Of Alger's eight accounts that year, five were excluded: three that were newly opened that year, a Hickox account that was opened and shut within the period, and the Robinson portfolio that was ineligible because of high margins and excessive withdrawals. Of the remaining three, Southland struck an annual gain of 58.7%, Pioneer popped 10.4% and Tri-Dell jumped 18.3% for a weighted composite of 36.3% in 1968.

From George's memo, "Anders was trying to make two cases about 1968. One, that among the clients included in the [advertising] composite, there was a large deviation from the [firm's] composite. Secondly, that since we only had a few clients we should have also included clients who opened accounts during the year." The latter would have violated the selected criteria, and there was insufficient data to prove the former.

Over George's objections and against all reasoning, Anders insisted on configuring his story around the divergence between Alger's advertised record and the firm's expanded performance, which he calculated to include the Security Equity results from 1965 to 1973, the Spectra Fund figures from 1973 through 1978 and a rating of Alger performance from pension-industry consultant Wilshire Associates from 1979 onward. For the sake of accuracy, it should be noted that the company lost the Security Equity account in 1972 and assumed Spectra in 1974, and that Wilshire Associates kept track of only a partial list of the firm's pension clients.

"I fear that by impugning the integrity of our numbers, there could be significant damage done to the firm," wrote George in the closing of his September 17 memo.

True to his word, Anders' article criticized Fred Alger for the selective use of accounts to manufacture the composite growth rate of 21.2% for 21 years. It informed the *Journal*'s readers of the omission of Security Equity Fund for all but its first and best year, when the appreciation topped 77%. It pointed out that the fund lost 23.5% in 1973, but never mentioned that this was after Alger. In 1971, the last full year of Fred Alger's advisory of the account, it grew by 29.2% versus the Dow's gain of only 8.3%.

The article also scored points for the following facts: that Alger left out accounts that didn't stay a full year; that four in nine of the company's clients terminated accounts in 1970; that the difference between the performance of accounts that stayed with the firm and those that quit in 1976 was a mere 0.2%; that Spectra Fund was omitted in 1974, which was a losing year; that Castle Convertible Fund was also omitted; and finally that the firm never subtracted its management fees from the performance.

No mention was made of Alger's criteria in choosing accounts, or of the fact that it was clearly noted in all the print ads that the performance wasn't adjusted for management fees. In all of this, the most damaging objection—because it was the one on which the SEC ultimately hung its case against Alger—was that the firm failed to sufficiently disclose in its print ads prior to September 15 its true relationship to Security Equity, which was not a fully discretionary account.

On the positive side, the article calculated the performance of the omitted Alger accounts, with an average annual gain of 15.8%, to be far superior to the S&P's rise of 8.7%. It also contained this hearty accolade from Fred's Southland partner John Jennings, "Fred is one of the most original thinkers on Wall Street . . . I wish I'd been invested with him longer. He's a long-ball hitter and he's had some fantastic years."

At the same time, it reported a caveat from consultant Samuel DeKinder of Demarche Associates—"There are a lot of ways you can make your record seem better than it is"—and insinuated that Fred Alger was acting in the base manner of most money managers. "Everyone in the world claims they've outperformed the averages." The article also divulged that both the SEC and the NYSE were in the process of scouring the company's records and cautioned that Fred Alger's performance had been healthier in the past, when its assets were smaller.

Fred Alger was appalled by the article. He construed it as a miscarriage of journalism, for its inability to digest his explanations and to present them in a complete and evenhanded way. Was he naive to expect more from an adversarial press, or did the story bear out his suspicion of a conspiracy?

The performance figures were developed in accordance with the strict standards of the Bank Administration Institute. And wasn't there support for his integrity in the fact that only those accounts he said measured up to the established criteria were in fact figured into the performance?

Even with losing or sub-par years in 1969, 1970, 1973, 1974, 1981 and 1984, $100 invested with Fred Alger on January 1, 1965, would have grown to $6,512 by September 30, 1986, based on the greater than 21% annual gain of its composite of individual and pension accounts during that period. Shouldn't this have been the primary focus of the article? Wasn't this the issue of greatest importance to investors? In fact, during the ten-year period which had been audited, 1976–1985, Alger's performance exceeded its advertising claims. It was up an average of 23.5%, in contrast with the S&P's return of 14.1%. Only on a minor point— the fact that the firm's performance from 21 years earlier was insufficiently footnoted in the first print ads—could Alger be faulted.

To understand why Fred was so wounded by the *Journal*'s story, Security Benefit's John Cleland proffered this insight: "Fred is scrupulously honest," he said.

"It would never occur to him to try to cheat anybody or to break the law." Cleland should know. It was the use of his mutual fund's performance in 1965 that was being challenged. That he rushed immediately and single-mindedly to Fred's defense confirms Fred's innocence in this matter.

Right on the heels of the *Journal* article, *Money* magazine ran "Return of the Gunslinger" by Gretchen Morgenson, which covered over nine pages, critiqued the advertising and pretty much recapped the Alger business saga up to that point. While it provided a generally favorable appraisal, it couldn't resist harpooning Fred over his high fees and straying into the murky ground of questionable performance claims and the accuracy of its audited record. It also touched on the deteriorating relationship between Fred Alger and Security Equity, which was a justification for excluding the Security Equity performance after the first year.

"In my most paranoid moments, I believed the SEC put *The Wall Street Journal* up to doing the nasty stories," said Fred. Irwin Schwartz also believed the conspiracy angle. "It wasn't *what we were advertising,*" he said. "The real reason was, they didn't like *the way we were advertising.* So they sicced the SEC on us."

Not so, objected SEC's McGrath. She insisted that the agency had no hand in provoking the articles. All SEC cases are in a docket which is open to the public. The press picked up the story on its own initiative. However, she added, "I always thought, in the back of my head, that it was odd. But given the fact that in the first place the inquiry was precipitated by complaints, my surmise was that some of these same people must have gone out of their way to say to reporters, 'Hey, you ought to take a look at what the SEC just did.' But I don't know that, because nobody from the *Journal* confided in me as to why they were interested in the case."

Whoever put them up to it, the press was sniffing around the story, and the whole thing smelled like a setup. From Alger's end, it looked as if an unholy trinity of financial-establishment types, bureaucrats at the SEC and an overzealous business press, each for its own reasons, were in a sneaky alliance to destroy the firm. Competitors viewed it as a way to finally give Fred his comeuppance. The SEC used Fred Alger as an object lesson to make a statement about its policing powers. The media, as it always is, was on the prowl for anything remotely sensational.

Fred Alger was not alone in picking up on the conspiracy theme. In "The High Cost of Advertising," for the March 1987 issue of *Institutional Investor*, writer Julie Rohrer quoted a mutual-fund insider who supported this notion. "The graybeards in the mutual fund industry are not very high on what he's doing. . . . Alger has insulted the SEC with his ads."

If Fred thought the *Journal* article was mean-spirited, he would find it kid-glove treatment, a model of fairness and accuracy, compared to the attack-dog approach of Benjamin J. Stein's rambling inquest into Fred Alger's performance in *Barron's* in November. "It just said some outrageous things," said Fred. In fact, he found 19 factual errors. "I wish we could prove someone was out to get us," he said, still obviously disturbed by this attack, and he contends, "*Barron's* has never said anything good about us, ever."

From the opening accusatory caption under an attractive, smiling picture of Fred to its final scornful sentence five pages later, the Stein piece portrayed Fred as this shrewd mountebank out to dupe defenseless investors with his advertising claims. "The bare fact is that Alger's name has not been an inevitable talisman of good luck to investors," shouted the large caption which introduced the article. To describe Alger's performance, Stein, who was billed as a triple threat—lawyer, economist and writer—wrote, "In classic pitch-man fashion, Alger trumpets as fine gold a pot that is really quite ordinary tin." In another passage he dismissed the advertising as "slickly crafted claims and boasts."

Very little of the article actually focused on the specific issue of Alger's advertised performance. Most of it took notice of tangential and personal factors which were apparently driving the writer's disaffection for Fred. First he wrote a copious amount of copy to describe the TV spots and print ads. Following that, a meandering excursion through Fred's personal and business history, with huge emphasis on his relationship with Bernie Cornfeld. In between Stein revealed an inordinate distaste for Fred's overuse of the word "unique" to describe himself and his company. Beyond that, he railed against the proven wisdom of the long-term outperformance of equities over all other classes of investments. In stretches of the piece, Stein sounded like a man possessed with issues greater than Fred, who just happened to be an opportune target for demonization.

When Stein singled out the company's periods of underperformance, he failed to balance it with the truth that such rough patches are normal for all money managers. Those who were invested during the market declines in 1973 and 1974, one of the fallow Alger periods cited in the article, doubtless experienced severe losses regardless of who was managing their money. Lost to Stein was the value and importance of Fred Alger's long-term performance.

In a subsequent section Stein sneered at Alger for claiming to engage in original research. To support this accusation, Stein submitted as evidence a boilerplate list of research sources which the firm had filed with the SEC, including financial newspapers and magazines, inspections of company activities, annual reports, prospectuses and filings with the SEC and press releases. Because this material was widely available, Stein dismissed it. But this simply betrayed his ignorance of the research process. He allowed for no special insights or interpretations of the information, nor did he admit the potential of individual resourcefulness in the information gathering process. Anyone in the business could have advised him that investment analysis requires more than the standard sources listed in the filings. With his background, he should have known better.

Eventually he got around to challenging the authentication of the Alger record between 1976 and 1986 by Coopers & Lybrand. Then he ricocheted back to his obsessive concern with Fred's self-proclaimed uniqueness. "There is no question that he is above average," Spiro Kripotos of CDA Investment Technologies was quoted as saying about Fred, "but I would not call him 'unique,' if by 'unique' you mean a uniquely good stock picker."

Instead of pointing out the flaws in the advertising and thereby debunking Alger's purported track record, Stein's account was striking for doing everything but sticking it to the Alger performance. It cleverly danced around the numbers to promote his primary aim of besmirching Fred's character. A disappointed pension manager was introduced as a hostile witness. "[Fred] showed me all kinds of data to prove what a good record he had before we hired him, but then, after he came on board, his performance was not up to par, and I certainly would not recommend him or use him for my own savings," she said.

About the advertising Stein charged, "It's amazing that ads like Alger's were allowed to circulate without deep skepticism from day one."

He pulled no punches in his closing argument. "At the end of the day, is the answer to be found about Fred Alger in P.T. Barnum's comments about the kind of people who are born every day?" he wrote. "Had he advertised his real skills and claimed only what could be proved, he would still have been impressive. Instead, by claiming an impossible level of genius and 'uniqueness' and inevitably inviting comparison between truth and the claims about Fred Alger, he has shown himself not at his best, but at his worst."

Terrible as it was, the offspring of this piece, in the form of a wire story from the Dow Jones News Service, was even more damaging to the firm's reputation. In it Stein's piece was drained of any nuance and condensed as a litany of the negative points which had been made about the firm. While the *Barron's* story was seen mostly by the investing community, the news service distributed it far and wide across the land, to every small-town paper which subscribed to its dispatches.

In his defense, Fred immediately fired off a letter of complaint to Robert M. Bleiberg, *Barron's* editorial director and publisher. He reproached the Stein piece for containing "19 serious factual misstatements about me and my firm" and invited Bleiberg and members of his staff to "visit me in my offices to set the record straight" about his "unique information gathering, processing and decision making firm." Fred's invitation was declined. Neither was his letter printed by the paper.

Fred continued in the letter, "I admit that I'm bewildered by the press attacks. I see myself as a businessman trying to appeal to consumer markets through advertising (a significant percentage of which has been given to *Barron's*), competing against larger companies. Why am I being singled out?" So used to the role of aggressor, Fred had uncharacteristically assumed the pose of victim.

"Barron's Mailbag" two issues later included two letters which praised Stein's muckraking investigation of Fred, but failed to print a rebuttal which Harvey J. Bazaar of Coopers & Lybrand had sent to *Barron's* on November 7 as a refutation of Stein's allegations about his company's audit of the Alger performance.

On November 25, Fred alerted Bleiberg of that shortcoming.

Barron's printed the letter in its following edition, December 1, 1986. In attempting to "correct any misimpressions" left by Stein's remarks, Bazaar affirmed that Coopers & Lybrand's examination of Alger's investment record, in contradiction to what Stein had either alleged or implied, "was performed in Alger Management's offices, not in our offices and not simply by reviewing selected information provided by Alger Management." Furthermore he stated, "We have had access to any data or information we have requested. Without such access we would not have been in a position to complete our examination of the investment performance statistics, or render an unqualified opinion, and would not have done so."

The letter reiterated the criteria for selecting accounts that were included in the performance statistics, which Coopers & Lybrand had authenticated for the previous 10-year period, and verified that they had in fact met those stipulations. One, they had been under management for the entire year; two, they were equity oriented; and three, they were fully discretionary accounts. "We developed verification procedures that, consistent with applicable professional standards, provided sufficient assurance concerning management's criteria for selecting accounts to be included in and excluded from the statistics for us to express our opinion that the data were fairly presented," Bazaar stated. "This was not merely a review of compiled statistics prepared by Alger Management."

In the aftermath of the *Barron's* reporting, Fred considered litigation but was advised against such a course because it would have been too difficult to prove either damage or malicious intent. Besides, as a semi-public figure, the press was accorded extra freedom to comment on his firm's performance.

From this maelstrom of media scrutiny, Fred took away a sobering mistrust of the press which hasn't been erased to this day. He believed the biased reporting had sullied his firm's name, something of inestimable value which was so carefully nurtured over two decades. As he looked back on this experience, the best he could summon was a perspective that could be construed as either Zen or Stoical. "Maybe God in his infinite wisdom creates trials so that people can't think the road is too smooth," Fred said.

When the SEC muscled its way back into Alger's offices in December 1986, this time with officers from its local bureau, it sent the firm hustling for finan-

The firm's costly advertising campaign was misunderstood by the investment community.

cial records all the way back to its beginning. "We'd already had our records audited for ten years," said Greg Duch, "but they wanted more. It was difficult to go back further than that because in some years, even though we kept internal records, we didn't retain bank records. The rules were you had to keep outside bank records only for five years, then you could destroy them."

To appease the regulators, Greg, Joe Pakenham, John Raspitha and Mike DiMeglio were sent forth by George to rummage through the company's old records, first at a low-ceilinged storage unit at the old building at 26 Broadway, then at the firm's records warehouse in Kearny, New Jersey. "We were climbing in and out of warehouses and over and under boxes," Raspitha recalled. "It was winter and I remember how cold it was. Everything was stacked haphazardly, and it was difficult to find what we were looking for, or if it even existed." Still they threw themselves at the task and worked many hours with great diligence in an effort to reconstruct the necessary files. Although some of the statements from the sought-after 1967–68 period were obtained, the accounting was incomplete.

The investigators were still poring over the files after Christmas 1986, and they hung around Alger's office into February 1987. When the SEC finally made its case in 1988, the best it could do was to charge Fred with potentially misleading customers by failing to convincingly and emphatically disclose the true nature of its participation in the 1965 Security Equity performance: that Fred Alger was acting only as an adviser and never had full discretionary control of the fund. Never mind that the initial fund prospectus made this eminently clear. Without referring to the prospectus, readers of the advertising could not obtain this information and were therefore likely to miss or skip it; and so, in the SEC's eyes, they were misled.

Especially in this case, the distinction between research consultant and investment adviser was purely semantic. Fred Alger might not have had discretion over the account, but he exercised virtual control of the investment decisions which were, except in one instance, followed to the letter by Security Management.

A secondary finding was that the initial ads gave the appearance of "gun jumping" the mutual funds—that is, the illegal solicitation of orders to purchase an underwriting before its SEC registration is complete. Technically ads for the Alger Fund did appear a few days before the ink was dry on the SEC document—November 7, 1986—but it was hardly an egregious offense, since registration was a foregone conclusion and expected imminently.

As a salve for these infractions, the Alger company gave up using the list of roughly 100,000 people who had replied to the advertising. The firm destroyed all the names, even of those people who came in under the high-net-worth and pension categories.

Those who were near to Fred found it astonishing that the SEC had its knickers in a twist over such relatively minor matters.

Board member Steve O'Neil observed, "It was a silly issue. Fred's dilemma was that he had a wonderful record as a money manager, but because he was always a money manager of private funds or pension funds, his reputation among the general public was zero. He felt he had to get his name and his image out in the public before he could sell the funds . . . which got him into trouble with the SEC. The cart kinda got ahead of the horse. The SEC accused him of trying to pre-sell the fund, which it deemed was in technical violation of their rules."

Did Fred's infraction warrant such an aggressive response? Was this some kind of payback or was the SEC simply following standard procedure? Whatever the motive or instigation, it was evident that the SEC was gunning for the Wall Street maverick.

Fred's reaction was unyielding at first. For nearly four years he fought back furiously. It was, after all, in defense of his honor and a case of fairness, if not justice. He believed in a conspiracy. Firing back was the only position he could take.

But when the dust finally settled in 1990, the lengthy battle had probably done more damage to the firm than if he had moved on quietly after the SEC had brought its case. By shouting his innocence, Fred merely prolonged the public-relations pain for his company. From the outside looking in, Security Benefit's Cleland had no hesitation in explaining Fred's decision to do battle with the SEC. "Sometimes Fred's common sense doesn't keep pace with the brilliance of his intellect," he rationalized. "Almost any businessman, as a matter of good, sound, fundamental common sense would never have taken on the SEC in what turned out to be an enormously expensive and protracted legal fight over what really amounted to a pretty insignificant difference in the long-term performance records of his accounts. He could have forgotten about that one year, 1965."

He was referring to the fact that even after the 1965 figures were removed from the Alger composite, performance was still a healthy 18.9% average gain over the 21-year period. Not good enough for advertising alliteration, but extremely respectable nonetheless, and certainly sufficient to have pulled him out of the fire with the SEC.

Despite all the negative media exposure and salacious gossip swirling about Fred Alger, no one on the inside doubted the integrity of the firm's position. The firm was never gripped with fear. "We had an accountant's opinion of our performance," analyst Ron Reel explained. "That proved we weren't futzing with the numbers. It was right there in the accountant's statement."

Bob Emerson gave a stirring defense of Fred: "The way the SEC rapped him, you would have thought that he violated every tenet of basic human decency on Wall Street. They kept harping on what happened in '65.

"I felt bad for Fred. I felt that he got a very raw deal. It wasn't a big deal, but they beat it to death, and Alger became known as the guy who fudged the numbers. Memories are long on the Street. It crippled his ability to raise assets. It was a little embarrassing, sitting down with guys in the business who would turn and say, 'Oh, you're the guys who make up the numbers.' It was a real mean-spirited coverage of the press, without stepping back and ever giving the guy the credit for having built, genuinely, one of the best investment track records, with or without that one year. It didn't amount to much, but the SEC was intent on making an example of Fred. What's ironic is this kind of advertising is pretty routine now. Nobody says boo. The timing was just off. Fred had gone all out to attract attention. He certainly did it."

Fred's attorney, Ray Merritt, saw the show as a backlash against Fred for trying something new and an exaggerated response of an out-of-control bureaucracy. "Fred wanted to aggressively advertise the new mutual funds at a point in time when advertising for mutual funds was considered inappropriate, illegal and in bad taste," he amplified. "Today such notions would be laughable. I was confident then as I am now that we, Fred Alger Management and Foote, Cone & Belding, didn't violate any of the laws. The SEC objected to the use of the chart going up, seen as subliminally telling the viewer that their assets were going up.

The SEC became virtually apoplectic about it. I was dealing with a staff mentality that was concerned about whether the Dreyfus lion was walking up the stairs or down the stairs, so they had it walk along the sidewalk so the lion wouldn't seem to be moving up or down.

"Fred was fighting tenets that may have been well founded at some other point in time but really lost their logic in this particular era. He was right about that. The SEC was wrong. It took, unfortunately, a substantial amount of time and money to prove that."

Outside the firm, many in the financial community were basking in fits of schadenfreude as they watched Fred being cuffed by the SEC. Perhaps second only to Hollywood, Wall Street delights in seeing its idols take a fall. In the court of public opinion, any presumption of Fred's innocence was overwhelmed by the size and character of the coverage in the influential press. The Stein piece especially made it sound credible that the firm was trying to defraud the public. As Bob Emerson saw it, "There was this explosion of articles in *Barron's* and *The Wall Street Journal*—publications he was paying millions of dollars to run his ads. They all thought they were Woodward and Bernstein."

It is both ironic and intriguing that a man who had stayed clean through connections with financial adventurers like Bernie Cornfeld, Delbert Coleman, Ray Dirks and Irving Kahn could be condemned for a technicality that his rich experience should have guarded him from making. Or did his involvement with these jaded figures instead confer guilt by association and provide additional incentive for the SEC investigation and the media charges? To quote the seventeenth-century Jesuit scholar Baltasar Gracian, "It is very easy to acquire a bad reputation, for badness is easily believed and hard to erase . . . . The crowd usually seizes on some outstanding weakness or some ridiculous defect."

In his personal anguish over this persecution by the media and the SEC, there is a historical resemblance to another attack—on Fred's great grandfather, who was bedeviled by public accusations that he was responsible for shipping tainted meat to his fighting men during the Spanish-American War. Like Russell Alger before him, Fred Alger was forced into a personal transformation that made him wiser and richer for all his trials.

The SEC charges against Fred Alger centered around a tiny transgression, as former SEC watchdog McGrath admitted years later in a phone conversation about the Alger inquiry. "It wasn't considered a terribly awful or severe case at the time, and looking at cases that have been brought since then, it was peanuts." Still, this relatively slight issue, not even a defect in record keeping but a subjective impression that the fine print didn't adequately refer its audience to the prospectus, managed to escalate into an inquiry register that filled over two volumes, a large investigation file and several transcripts. By the time the fine print in Alger's ads was amended in September 1986, it was too late to satisfy the SEC.

Unlike its softer stance toward other financial firms in subsequent cases, the SEC gave Fred no wiggle room in his ownership of the 1965 Security Equity record. The Haven Fund provides a good recent example of how the SEC can be swayed to show greater flexibility about mutual-fund advertising. Haven was originally constituted with $2.8 million in the mid-eighties as an exclusive limited partnership for the private assets of partners in the Goldman, Sachs investment bank. To avoid capital-gains-tax liabilities—its assets had grown to $40 million by the mid-nineties—the conservative fund successfully petitioned to execute a tax-free rollover and conversion into a public fund. But when it failed to attract additional investors because its record was poor as a public fund, it petitioned the SEC and was allowed, in August 1995, to include its ten-year history as a limited partnership in its marketing campaigns. Didn't this also have some potential for misleading the public? How different was the SEC's response in this case from its uncompromising stance toward Fred Alger?

As McGrath sees it, "I suppose it was just one of the early ones that happened to hit the investment-management industry and so, from that perspective, it may have stood out more than perhaps should have been the case." She pooh-poohed the conspiracy angle and, while not at all apologetic, suggested that any misstep on the agency's part was the result of the SEC's overblown enthusiasm. "This was one of the first cases. They got overzealous and really pursued it." She added, "It hurts a lot more on the other fellow's end, the private party's end, most of the time. And I think that any money manager who was involved, in any way, in SEC enforcement cases early on suffered a lot more as a result of the fact that they were among the first. Now name a firm that hasn't had a big smack on the head with a two-by-four. They're much more commonplace."

An amusing irony in this case is that one-time nemesis McGrath is now an advocate for Fred Alger. Like so many employees of the SEC, who use their brief time in the agency as a stepping-stone to more lucrative careers in fat law firms that support the financial sector, snuggling up to the very same characters they once saw as nefarious and were sworn to pursue, Kathryn McGrath in 1995 was a senior partner in Morgan Lewis & Bockius, a Washington, D.C., and Miami legal outfit which specializes in SEC matters that is on Fred Alger's payroll.

As Fred's lawyer Merritt saw it, playing hardball with Fred was a good way for the SEC to telegraph its message to the financial industry about aggressive advertising. If you're going to tout your performance, make sure it passes our smell test. That was the best it could do, since its guidelines were uncertain before Fred's campaign forced it to make up a new set of requirements for performance advertising. In retrospect McGrath acknowledged, "I can see that the Alger case brought scrutiny to the industry as a whole."

"The SEC's practice is to select a situation to make an example, which might be egregious or not so awful, to demonstrate that even the slightest variation or hint of impropriety would be vigorously asserted," said Merritt. "They took issue at 'rather impressive' performance claims. The SEC has always been concerned that consumers would be lulled into a false sense of security based on past performance, no matter how many times you say 'past performance is not a barometer or guarantee of future results.'

"The advertising was not misleading or the performance record a lie. The only thing you could say was that we didn't have an audited figure for one year, and despite the caveats, they were saying you can't tell the truth even when you tell the truth because we don't think what you're telling is the truth. Plus the industry leaders don't like anybody who rocks the boat. Fred was rocking the boat with something that hadn't been done before."

Fred's former cohort Ray Dirks, who is no stranger to SEC prosecution, affirmed that hypothesis. "It was a minor question about the validity of including the performance of a period when Fred was managing money for another firm. Today most firms do worse than Fred's own advertising, and there's much less scrutiny of the results. The SEC used the case as a symbol, a warning to others," he said.

The company was regrettably an available patsy for its unwritten agenda. It fell on Alger's shoulders to serve as a warning beacon for faults as yet unconceived.

Greg Duch concurs with that assessment. "My own take is that the SEC wasn't necessarily trying to take down Alger," he said. "The SEC doesn't originate laws. They find a situation and they hit on it, then use that to develop regulation." He gave an example from the nineties of how the SEC held up money manager Mario Gabelli to signal that it wouldn't tolerate mutual-fund advisers serving as directors or executives of companies that were also in their investment portfolios. Michael Price of Mutual Fund Series, Lawrence Auriana of Kaufmann Fund, and Martin Whitman of the Third Avenue Value Fund were also similarly cited. Whether there was any impropriety or not, merely the hint of a conflict of interest was enough to set off its scanners. Here, just as with Fred's advertising, first a situation presents itself, then the SEC responds, and then finally it establishes a regulation.

To deal with the Fred Alger situation, which it had never anticipated or encountered, the SEC reframed its rules on performance advertising by money managers of individual and pension accounts in 1988. Mutual-fund reporting was never the issue, since that performance is published daily by management companies, printed in the newspapers and distributed over financial networks. The SEC realized, through Fred Alger, that its rule of retaining records for just five years was deficient when money managers chose to promote records going further back. So it made a new rule, enforced retroactively, that before any performance can be advertised, corresponding statements must be available to corroborate the record, and only that record which is fully documented can be legitimately held out as the firm's true performance. "As a result of Alger, if you want to advertise performance, back to 1902, you have to have documents to support it back to 1902," said McGrath. In Alger's case, even its audited record for ten years became insufficient, since the firm was advertising a 21-year history.

For his part in clarifying its thinking on the matter and provoking the SEC into establishing this guideline, this regulation is fondly known in some circles as the Alger Memorial Record Keeping Rule. Ironically, it is another of Fred Alger's contributions to the workings of Wall Street.

On February 26, 1990, the SEC delivered to Fred Alger an "Order Instituting Proceedings, Findings and Order Imposing Remedial Sanctions in accordance with the Offer of Settlement of Fred Alger Management, Inc. dated February 2, 1990 . . . which the Commission has determined to accept . . . and shall be effective immediately."

The verdict allowed both parties to move on without either side admitting wrongdoing. Fred Alger had made a settlement, analogous to a plea bargain, that offered a qualified admission of the facts as both sides had previously agreed to, and provided a basis for the SEC to discharge the case.

The firm essentially reiterated what was already known by all concerned: that Security Equity Fund was its only active advisory account in 1965; that Security Management Company retained final authority over its recommendations and the selection of the executing broker; that Security Equity Fund's 77.5% increase constituted its entire performance of equity-oriented accounts in 1965 and was used to calculated the average return of 21.2% over 21 years; that had it been excluded, the firm's 20-year return would have been 18.9%; that the Registration Statement failed to disclose that Security Equity Fund was a non-discretionary account; and that this failure was misleading with respect to the earlier media advertising campaign because it did not mention the foregoing facts about the account.

Its penalty amounted to little more than a light slap on the wrist—namely that Fred Alger Management would institute and maintain internal records, procedures and records to facilitate compliance with the Investment Company Act, that the firm should retain the services of an outside attorney approved by the SEC to serve as its compliance offer, and that Fred Alger was bound to submit all performance-related advertising of its managed accounts to independent counsel for review. That was the entire outcome. All that *Sturm und Drang* had faded to a fizzle.

On March 5, 1990, Dow Jones News Service Wall Street Journal Combined Stories spread the news of the settlement in a wire story with the headline, "SEC

Says Fred Alger Funds Made Misleading Disclosures." The copy provided this qual-ification, ". . . without admitting or denying charges, Fred Alger Management consented to a settlement under which it agreed to implement internal controls designed to promote compliance."

The following day *The Wall Street Journal* ran a story by Kevin J. Salwen called "SEC Charges Fred Alger Funds Padded Data in '86 Campaign." Despite their accord McGrath climbed on her pulpit to send a parting shot at Fred in the arti-cle. "We viewed it as misleading to display a track record that wasn't yours, par-ticularly when it improved your results so dramatically. People can't run misleading ads then say that doesn't matter because we had the real stuff buried in the prospec-tus," she proclaimed.

Neither piece contained any offsetting comments from Fred Alger.

In his final defense, Fred coaxed Security Management's Everett Gille out of retirement in Tucson, Arizona, to ratify his implicit control over Security Equity Fund with a letter to *The Wall Street Journal* which was published on March 22, 1990. In "Alger: He Could Really Pick 'Em," Gille affirmed that "substantially all the buy-and-sell decisions were recommended by Fred Alger. I can recall only one decision that was turned down: that was a stock that had been bought and sold earlier and Mr. Alger wished to repurchase it in too short a time frame, in my opinion. I felt it would give the appearance of trading," he said.

"While it retained the right to make independent decisions, it did not choose to do so. The performance success of the Security Equity Fund in 1965 was a prod-uct of Fred Alger's ability to buy and sell stocks."

Although the settlement was easy, the process of getting there took a heavy financial and emotional toll on the company. For one, it was forced to delete those 100,000 plum names who responded to the ads. Had even 10% of them been converted into clients, how much might they have brought in assets? $100 million? $500 million? There's no price that can be placed on the lost momen-tum. How much larger might the Alger Fund be today?

Far greater damage came from the attacks on the firm's reputation. The SEC and the financial press had turned the tide of public goodwill away from Fred, and the investing community and its consultants washed away as well. The ver-dict was in before the case was settled. "Fred Alger was cooking the books. Fred Alger was just a bunch of crooks." From all the media coverage, rumors, investi-gations and innuendo, one had to come away believing this. No arguments were ever made in Fred's favor.

Partly as a consequence of the negative publicity, two-thirds of Fred Alger's institutional and individual business vanished in this three-year span. "Our busi-ness went down the rathole after this," said Fred. "By 1990, we were managing one-third of the pension business we had in 1987. We were already losing the business for all the other reasons—more managers, the rise of consultants—that's why we were doing the advertising. Also, clients left because they believed they would be submerged by new business resulting from the ads." But there was no new business from the ads. More than 10 years after the fact, Fred Alger was still tarnished by the stigma of its advertising campaign, at least in the eyes of some pension managers and consultants. Fred claimed that, despite his firm's superior performance, it had not received "one dollar of institutional business from a major consultant since the public became aware of his troubles."

Fred Alger is still haunted by the specter of the SEC. About McGrath and the SEC, Fred charged, "She, in essence, has ruined our business for a long time and may still be ruining it, because memories linger. If you question the record of an investment-management firm, that's all you're left with. It's your reputation."

A recent example makes his point eloquently. On August 7, 1995 *Barron's* published an article, "A Call to Glory" by Leslie P. Norton, about David's assumption of Fred's position in the company. It charged, ". . . the money manager was accused by the Securities and Exchange Commission of misleading investors by overstating results for its mutual fund during a high-profile 1986 ad campaign."

In his response to this falsehood—the advertising never mentioned mutual funds—Fred advised, "Sometimes history becomes what people say it is, not what the facts are. Such is the case in your article about my firm." Unlike his earlier response to the Stein article, this letter was printed in the paper.

The years between the costly marketing nightmare and the settlement of the SEC probe were perhaps the toughest in the company's history. Alger was under siege on all fronts. The quicksand of vanishing institutional assets was intensified by a Wall Street crash. Analysts fled and partners walked. The firm's national expansion flopped. Mutual-fund investors were slow to come. Fred Alger was hurtling into a tailspin during that painful season.

That grim period, however, was lit up with a few bright spots. The obvious one was the 1989 winning performance by the Small Cap fund, which took first place among 1,683 mutual funds that year. In solid Alger fashion, its return of 64.54% was more than double the S&P 500 gain of 31.7% and far superior to the stock fund average of 24%. Of greater significance, though, was the acceleration of its back-office integration.

There must be some truth in the teaching that by overcoming challenges, one is led closer to power and success. For as poorly as things went, the firm came through this period in better shape than seemed possible—and with greater security and confidence than many competing firms.

19 ✒

Downturn

Black Monday, October 19, 1987. A day of stock market infamy that cut at the heart of the financial world. The worst ever single-day collapse of share prices, and the climax of the eighties bull market.

Its impact was horrifying. Like the Kennedy assassination and the *Challenger* explosion a year earlier, it was one of those rare, shared cathartic events that enters sharply into personal and collective memory and slows the country to a standstill. Which investor doesn't remember his or her reaction to the news that the Dow was plunging down a seemingly bottomless pit and dragging the rest of the market with it? The declines raced by so quickly, most investors never got a chance to save their assets. Many of those who could get through to their brokers learned that there were no buyers for their stocks. Trading was delayed in many issues. People everywhere were so stupefied, no one was sure just how to respond.

All over the country noses were pressed to the windows of brokerage storefronts. Like slowing motorists at the scene of an accident, investors were drawn to watching the ticker. There was no denying the tape: stocks had fallen, and were falling lower still. It was like a deathwatch for an ailing friend. With no cure, the best one could do was keep vigil, which many investors did, as financial assets were ground down to a fraction of their worth on the opening of that fateful day.

Frenzy and panic attacked stock-exchange floors all over the world. Mayhem visited investment houses and brokerage firms. It was no different at Fred Alger. The mood was surreal. Traders and analysts collected around the trading desk, in the way that people come together during times of crisis. In the face of the crash, laughter seemed to be the best medicine. The atmosphere became carnival-like. Some became slap-happy.

"People were walking around laughing. They couldn't believe what was going on," said David Alger. "Afternoonish, the market down about two hundred and ninety points, Emerson blurted, 'You know, I never thought I'd live to see the day when the market would be down three hundred points. And you know what, if these heart palpitations don't stop, I still might not.'" It was the first day on the job for Jerry DeVito, Fred's new chauffeur, who received his initiation by way of the bedlam in the office.

A similar, though quieter scene was shaping up in New Jersey. Everyone was huddled around the Quotron. "Anyone who had money in the market was

Company chauffeur Jerry DeVito enjoying sunnier times with Fred. His first day on the job was Black Monday, October 19, 1987.

in a bad mood. George was not a happy camper," observed Rosemary Kiernan.

Not everyone, however, took it so badly. Analyst Shelton Swei admitted that he bought puts on the market, or bets that the market would decline, a week prior to the crash. He was slyly smiling through the carnage.

Trader Morty Frankel missed "the big hurt." He was taking his son for a visit to Binghamton College, some 250 miles outside New York, that Monday. The radio station could barely pull in a signal, but he gasped at the numbers through the static. "My wife and kid were thinking about college, but I wasn't so sure I would have a job the next day," he said.

Analyst Bob Rescoe gave his perspective. "The Friday before, the market was down quite a bit. We were talking about what might happen on Monday. My bet was that it would go down two hundred points. That's crazy, they said. To see it unfold, actually happen! We had stocks that were down forty-five to fifty percent that day. Fred was actually laughing, because what else could you do? I can remember looking at him watching the Quotron. 'Look at that stock. It was ninety, now it's twenty.' Then it got kind of somber.

"His response the next day was, 'Start calling your companies to find out if this will affect their business. Will purchasing habits or business outlook change because the stock market crashed?' It was impossible to pick up any information at that early stage, because everyone was still in shock. The right thing to do was regroup and put your money in the best names—that were the best names before the crash and were still the best names. The good names were, in fact, the best coming out of the crash."

The crash was doubly vexing for Fred Alger because the company had seen it coming. The kind of precognition which allowed Fred to gauge the start of the bull market in 1982 also enabled him to anticipate the 1987 debacle. But he was premature in his call and suffered by raising cash positions for his clients a little too early. As the market continued to rise in defiance of Fred's prediction, clients were unsettled by this defensive allocation and bullied the firm back into its normally aggressive investment posture—just in time to catch the crash.

In David's analysis, the chain of events leading to the crash began in 1986, when the Saudi government jolted the spot price of crude oil up to $18 a barrel. The Iran-contra transactions had led the Saudis to detect a shift in the U.S. position toward its meddlesome neighbor Iran. In retaliation for the perceived attitude change, the Saudis upped the price of oil. This was a sharp reversal of a previously accommodative policy which had kept oil prices down as low as $10 a barrel during the first half of the decade. Keeping up with oil's move, the prices for precious metals and other industrial commodities surged higher as well.

"For the first time in a number of years, the word `inflation' started to be used by Fed Chairman Paul Volcker in front of Congress," David said.

"In late 1986, even though we beat the market, the smaller, more aggressive stocks had performed very poorly, and this caused us some concern. Moreover, we had some technical tools that were starting to signal that the market might be vulnerable. Putting this all together, we decided that the situation was very scary indeed.

"Volcker was talking aggressively about the prospect of raising interest rates. Not only that, but we had noticed some alarming trends on the floor of the NYSE, notably the effect of programmed trading. Irwin actually stated that he thought programmed trading made the stock market so unstable that he would be not surprised to see a time when it would go down in excess of a hundred points in a day."

Gene G. Marcial's widely followed *BusinessWeek*'s "Inside Wall Street" column headlined, on January 19, 1987, that, "Fred Alger Is High on the 'One-World' Economy" even as he was "turning bearish and raising cash for the next buying opportunity, which he expected mid-summer." In the article, Fred revealed that he was anticipating a 200-point pullback from Dow 2,000 and then a reacceleration of its climb to a peak of 3,000 within two years. His reasons included a favorable outlook for interest rates, inflation and the dollar, as well as the expansion of global trade, which tempered the cyclical nature of the U.S. economy. Fred's stock picks were in drugs, telecommunications and biotechnology. The firm was underweighted in high-tech stocks but had a large position in Digital Equipment, which made the computers Fred Alger uses for its analysis.

The article was mistimed and appeared just as Fred was backpedaling from his bearish stance. At the close of 1986, the firm had shifted its cash allocation to 20%, a move which was contradicted by the market's performance. In mid-January Fred said, "We reversed that decision when it became clear that the stock market had disconnected itself from the economy and the bond market." By the end of the month, the firm was 12% in cash, still above its normal cash position of 5%. That was the first instance of walking away from its bearish outlook for stock market.

As signals of a likely collapse in stock prices persisted in the firm's analysis, Fred Alger once again took a drastic step away from its normal course of being fully and aggressively invested. "We reached a momentous decision for us," said David. "We thought the market would really come down substantially. We're not market timers, but we do have market-timing tools, which we use every decade or so.

"Fred decided to take a big risk and write all our clients a letter stating that, in our opinion, the market looks vulnerable, and in order to preserve their assets, we would increase our cash levels, which we proceeded to do."

The problem with such a decisive strategy was not that it might turn out incorrect but that, regardless of the outcome, it was sure to rile Alger's pension clients, who weren't in the business of paying money managers a fee so that they could to put their investments in cash.

On March 19, 1987, seven months to the day before the crash, Fred Alger raised its cash position back up to 20%. The next day Fred penned a letter to his pension clients explaining his outlook. While it meant to provide reassurance, it was also alarming.

The letter announced boldly, "Both contra-cyclical forces, the Federal deficit and interest rates were working against an economic advance. The federal deficit is declining sharply; the dollar weakness will keep interest rates higher than domestic economic conditions would warrant. We feel that [the market] has moved too quickly, and is vulnerable to a correction."

There were four signals that made Fred fearful of a steep market correction, and he shared them with his clients:

1) The S&P 400 had advanced 24% in 1987. Since 1960, only half the years showed a yearly range greater than 24%. Only one in five greater than 35%. Each one of these wide ranges occurred during a year when the stock market sold off sharply.

2) More than half of our universe of followed companies has surpassed its maximum multiple relative to the market. Relative multiples have risen like a rock attached to a string on a stick. When the stick is twirled quickly, the rock rises at the end of the string. If the twirling

stops, the rock will fall quickly. Similarly, when the market stops its spin, relative multiples will drop as fast as they went up.

3) Hourly up/down volume has the widest gap in history. This usually signals a peak in market breadth.

4) Our sold out index has plunged. A small proportion of stocks are sold out.

Fred warned emphatically, "Program selling and fear of lost profits could cause a sharp correction." He surmised that the correction would likely be short-lived and, pegging the Dow's range between 1,500 and 3,000, he explained that his strategy would be to raise cash at the high end of this sweep.

He also explained that he was prepared to reverse tactics if the market moved into "an even higher valuation perspective." The market's ability to react, he noted, was benefited by the liquidity formulas of the firm's money-management routines. Fred hoped his clients would realize that only indicators so severe would provoke such an bold move, that this extreme measure was essential for the preservation of their capital and that he was acting with the full realization that the firm's function was to invest their capital in stocks and not keep it dormant in cash.

Fred knew he was leading the firm on a treacherous course, so the indicators had to be compelling, as they proved to be when his predictions came true. "You can't take views, like, well, the market looks high to me so I'll move into cash and sit around till it looks low again," he admitted. "That's not the way to keep clients. That's the way for letter writers. That's not the business."

The benefits of Fred's careful approach were lost on many of his clients, especially since the firm remained heavily in cash while stock prices kept rising well into the summer.

David continued, "Nineteen eighty-seven proceeded along, and it was a year when price increases in industrial commodities, like aluminum and paper, were moving those kinds of stocks up quite dramatically—especially in the second quarter. We found ourselves not only in the wrong stocks but also heavily in cash. We were up at mid-year, about twenty percent, but the market was up a good deal more than that."

One of the first casualties of the firm's strategy was the state of Pennsylvania, a fairly new and hard-won pension account which had entrusted Fred Alger with $100 million. At the firm's presentation to the client, all that its managers wanted to know was why Fred Alger had "lost them so much money." They were uninterested in his explanations and gave David five minutes instead of the customary fifteen to defend the firm's position. It felt like an inquisition. Although Fred Alger hadn't really lost the state any money—it was up, in fact, 20% for the year—when David had finished his commentary, "We were summarily fired." This scene was replayed with increasing frequency during the months preceding the crash and certainly after it, though not always with the same swift conclusion. Another defection that year was the state of Florida.

"A great many clients raised strong objections to our raising cash," David added. "One, they didn't hire us as market timers. They didn't want us to be market timers. Two, we were wrong so far. As the numbers rolled in, so many of our clients raised the objection that they didn't pay us to be in cash. Couldn't we see that the market was going up?"

Succumbing to client pressure, the firm grudgingly reentered the market as it approached its top. "We got our clients out of the market twice before the crash and received nothing but heartache for it," offered Irwin Schwartz. "You're damned if you do, damned if you don't."

"Faced with clients' resistance, we decided maybe we were wrong," explained David, "among other reasons, because Volcker never raised rates. He talked about it and never did anything about it. He was replaced at mid-year by Greenspan. Greenspan was thought to be a real dove in those days, at least compared to Volcker. When Greenspan was appointed, everyone breathed a real sigh of relief.

"We reluctantly, and basically with our clients' gun at our heads, reinvested all the money. We said we were wrong. Let's put it back in the market. It's just a sorry chapter in our life. Let's pretend this never happened. It was July or August. We're now fully invested again and still have performance problems.

"Greenspan started to raise rates, but not very aggressively, so no one paid much attention. Sometime during early or late fall 1987, the takeover boom was in full blast, and a lot of people were getting concerned about it. Mike Milken was in his heyday and Dan Rostenkowski, chairman of the House Ways and Means Committee, proposed that the tax deductibility on takeovers should be eliminated."

It was this bogeyman that ultimately spooked the market and tripped the final bell on the bull run. "This really destabilized the market and led to the Friday before October 19, when the market was down about one hundred points," said David in conclusion. "It was a very, very bad week for the market. I remember I was out in my country house, and it was a very surreal weekend because the market was acting really badly. I became very concerned. Just prior to that, Greenspan had also jacked up short term rates very dramatically. It was not good. I was nervous."

At the end of the trading day on October 19, the Dow had swooned a whopping 508 points to 1,738.74, dropping 22.6% of its value on an unprecedented trading volume of 604.3 million shares. The one-day tumble nearly matched the two-day plunge of 24% on October 28 and 29, 1929, and presented the climax of a nearly 1,000-point drubbing since the Dow's peak of 2,722.42 on August 25, 1987. It is estimated that more than $500 billion in stock equity was lost on Black Monday.

The aftershocks of the U.S. market's collapse were felt all over the world. Japan's Nikkei 225 average, for example, slumped 13.2% in one day. Gold climbed $15.50 to $486.50. Thirty-year T-Bonds stood at 10.14%, from 7.9% a year earlier.

It was a financial phenomenon so huge that it crowded out all other news stories. Even in the frenzied New York sports market, the news that George Steinbrenner had rehired Billy Martin as the Yankee's manager for a fifth time was consigned to the back pages of *The New York Times*. The story that IBM had introduced its breakthrough mid-range computer, System/36, received short shrift.

Just as Fred Alger was certain that the market was headed for a fall, he was equally confident that it would quickly resume its uptrend. And he conveyed those sentiments to his clients via a reflective four-page letter dated October 27, 1987.

"Pulling together my thoughts has renewed my optimism that we are on the threshold of a major, enduring advance in world trade and financial transactions—which will lead to higher equity values in the months and years ahead," he wrote.

Fred ascribed the market's steep decline to a temporary overvaluation relative to long-term interest rates. Presciently, he projected that the three problems of the federal deficit, the trade deficit and interest rates would "resolve themselves in favor of a steadily improving market." Furthermore, since the decline had extracted the froth from the rapidly expanding economy, it augured well for more sustainable, longer-term growth.

"The worst is behind," he proclaimed. With the "accelerating tempo of business," the outlook was favorable for the world economy. As for the markets, he pointed to the historically low valuations and projected that, after a brief period of volatility, it would show good gains extending into the coming year.

Though sounding incredible at the time, Fred was right once again. Severe as it was, the 1987 market decline ended abruptly and well short of the 1929 disaster that led to an economic depression. Many money managers were so shell-shocked they failed to realize that Black Monday had created the "buying opportunity of the decade." By the end of the year stock prices began trudging forward again. Except for a correction due to the 1990 Persian Gulf War and a breather in 1994, the U.S. stock market has been racing forward ever since. Characteristically and in line with its advance, Fred Alger and his investments have zoomed ahead with it.

If only Fred Alger had stuck to his guns, he might be enjoying the halo effect which still surrounds Elaine Garzirelli and Martin Zweig, the two investment analysts who were lionized by the media for warning off their clients from the crash. Nearly a decade later, both are still making a living off their timely calls.

"We had the right idea," observed David. "The timing was wrong for six months. We would have been heroes if we had stuck to our forty percent cash, but we let our clients talk us back into it, and those clients left us anyway. Their response: 'You had full discretion. If you wanted to keep it in cash, you should have kept it.'

"The crash rearranged everyone's performance data quite substantially," he continued. "The market went down and then bounced, so that the S and P was actually up by the end of the year. We were down five percent, and the S and P was up two percent."

"We were all up at least 50% by mid-year," recalled analyst Bob Emerson. "Fred, somewhat confused by the market, went to a heavy cash position early in the second quarter, lugging a lot of cash around which didn't look good . . . . Then he got back into the market nearer the top. All it did was bring us back to where we were at the start of the year."

The day after the crash, workers on Wall Street felt the hangover of job insecurity. "The next day everybody was very glum," Morty Frankel remembered. "We were all afraid to walk into work."

Most Wall Street firms suffered from the 1987 crash. Facing up to losses in this demoralized climate, securities firms pulled in their horns by cutting salaries and laying off workers. The harsh effect was felt the most by high-priced analysts, whose value plummeted along with the shaken confidence in stock investments. A number of companies were pushed to the exits. The pain spread throughout the economy, more deeply in New York.

Set off from other investment firms by its strong capital foundation and unique integrated business model, Fred Alger was relatively unscathed by the economic battering which afflicted most of its competitors. In fact, the firm was able to bulk up its net worth by over $10 million, or more than 18%, that year. It never resorted to firings and layoffs as a solution to managing expenses, thereby preserving its manpower assets for the next positive business cycle.

Diverging once again from the industry, Fred held on to his soldiers in the administrative and customer-support front, who were considered the most expendable by the Street. "There were no layoffs. They maintained bonuses," said Joe Pakenham from purchase and sales, repeating the refrain that kept the firm whole throughout the crisis. "George announced, 'I met with Fred and he believes we're above water, and at Christmas time you won't be disappointed.' Every time there was a problem or negative news hit the paper, George was quick to counter with a meeting. Like family, he always got it out on the table." Despite losing 40% of its assets from the previous year, in 1988 Fred Alger handed out bonuses totaling nearly $2.5 million. Even in 1990, when the firm lost money, over $1.6 million went into the bonus pool. Observed back-office head Jim Barbi, "Fred demonstrated a lot of loyalty to the people working for him."

Even though it was going through a difficult stretch, there was never any question of the company's survival. "Fred is incredibly calm under pressure. He was tense but he carried on," said Fred's daughter Hilary, who joined the firm around that time. "I was new. I didn't know how bad it was. The attitude was, we're okay. We're hurt, but we're okay. The firm was not going to go belly up because it has a lot of cash reserves."

Faith in Fred and his management style was strong all the way to the back office. Ron Curtis of Alger Shareholder Services expressed his mood back then. "There was no panic after 1987," he said. "We moved with a great deal of confidence. We were pretty strong financially because of the brokerage operation, which was not overexposed financially. We traded only for our own accounts. There were no stock loans or short selling, where we might jeopardize our capital. Fred was very conservative—more than one would imagine—in managing the firm's capital." At headquarters this confidence was enhanced when "nobody at Alger took pay cuts. I don't think the bonuses were even cut," Bob Emerson confirmed.

The following year, when pension assets started streaming out of the company, the bonuses for the rank-and-file even increased. The financial pain was

Smiles all around as another fast grower is found. Alger's investment brain trust: David flanked by portfolio managers Seilai Khoo and Ron Tartaro and senior analyst Shelton Swei (right).

absorbed by the firm's top earners and managers, who took a 20% shave in income.

"After the crash we lost quite a few accounts. What was in the back or front of everyone's minds was 'What's going to happen to my job?'" remembered account administration vice president Mike DiMeglio. "There was wholesale slaughter over on Wall Street. You could hear the shrill whine of analysts and back-room people. People were being laid off in droves. But here you had a job, with no salary cut and bonus intact. The best thing is, they didn't panic—or they didn't show that they panicked to the employees. George called us in and said, 'Don't worry, we're not looking to lay off people. It was easy, because the crash coincided with the end of our fiscal year. The money was already in the bank. The clerical staff didn't take a hit. They showed their loyalty and inspired the employees. They couldn't have handled it better."

DiMeglio continued, "After that time there was not much hiring. People who left weren't replaced. We had a very lean operation. Even with fewer accounts, we all had more duties."

Following the advertising debacle and the spin-out from the SEC investigations, the 1987 stock market crash put an exclamation point on Fred Alger's downturn, which actually had started several years earlier in the midst of the firm's sweet spot.

Belying the firm's impressive gains in revenue and income for most of the eighties, Fred Alger's growth-stock investment style had actually fallen out of grace from poor performance as early as 1983. The resulting string of weak investment returns put the firm's clients on edge and made them mistrustful of Fred, whose investment strategy was being left in the dust of index investing and leveraged-buyout stocks.

Celanese Corp., for one, which was the firm's first major pension account and a client since 1976, left in 1985. In time it was followed out the door by a majority of the pension clients. In an exodus that accelerated through the latter half of the decade, the firm's asset character was eviscerated by an outrageous 60%—from a peak of $3.2 billion in 1986 to around $1.5 billion in 1989. The firm's downturn ran its course through 1990, when it lost $1.67 million, culminating in only the second losing year in its history.

Fred recapped why his company had fared so badly during this period. First, he said, "Growth stocks simply didn't do well. We did quite poorly relative to the averages." This coincided with the "increase in the number of investment advisers, ten thousand to fifteen thousand, all of whom were hitting on the pension-fund community. Consultants could be paid through the brokerage of the pension plan, so their services appeared to cost nothing. The consultants developed their list of favorites, and of course they wanted to get paid on commissions." Since Alger retains its commissions, this locked it out of the preferred lists.

"Also, pension funds got fully funded, and they didn't need people like us anymore," Fred continued. "In fact, their inclination was becoming increasingly conservative. Why take a chance? There was no incentive to make money. They just needed an overall balance to stay ahead of their assumed rate of return, which is tied in to actuarial factors.

"They didn't need intense managers. Risk, for a pension fund, is for the pension-fund manager to lose his job." In such an environment, with the confluence of these factors, Alger just didn't cut it.

How bad was its performance really? Or was Fred Alger's underachievement simply a myth—triply created by very high self-expectations, a declining preference for growth stocks and a refusal to play ball with the consultants?

Though David believed that Fred Alger's performance "started hitting a snag in 1985 and '86," some of the data from that period indicate otherwise. During the first quarter of 1986, from a field of 335 investment advisers with full discretion over a combined $331 billion in stock holdings, Fred Alger was tenth in the leader board with a 22.6% return, versus the S&P 500's gain of 14%, according to a survey by the research group, CDA Investment Technologies, Inc.

Another money-manager survey, of over 1,000 portfolios through November 30, 1986, by Indata of Southport, Connecticut, rated Fred Alger as one of the 10 standout performers. The S&P index was up 21.6%; but Fred Alger's portfolio gain was 24.3% and beat out financial powerhouses Bankers Trust Co., J.P. Morgan and Alliance Capital.

After that last spurt in 1986, however, it was true that growth stocks lagged behind the indexes. According to David, three factors were involved: one, the takeover boom did not touch the growth stocks; two, the rise of passive investing pushed more money into the indices, which preordained their advance; and three, when the economy is strong, as it was then, even great growth stocks don't attract money as do established, well-capitalized firms like Alcoa and International Paper, which offer the prospect of dividends in addition to capital appreciation.

"Then came 1988," David fretted. "Business couldn't have been worse. In a two-year period our tax-exempt business fell by more than half."

He continued, "Fred decided that he wasn't going to meet with clients anymore and basically told me that I would henceforth be meeting with them, which I did. All that I remember about 1988 is that I spent most of my time talking to disgruntled or disillusioned clients who were quitting us.

"Some were angry because we raised cash. Some were angry because we didn't keep the cash. Some were angry because the market went down. Some were angry because our performance wasn't any good. Some were angry because of the whole mutual-fund issue, which they never articulated but was lurking beneath the surface. Some were angry because we called ourselves geniuses and lost them money. It went on and on and on. Some were just outright hostile. Some were more friendly but fired us anyway. At the end of that year we were very demoralized."

By 1987 Fred Alger's tax-exempt business had dwindled to $2.5 billion. After the great exodus of 1988, a little less than $1.5 billion remained, which is where the assets stabilized the following year.

Only after David's Small Cap fund hit the top of the charts in 1989 did assets start straggling back to the firm, but not in the pension-account group. The new inflows were attracted to Alger's mutual-fund portfolios by way of new distributor and insurance-company relationships, which broadened their investment appeal. Although the firm has stitched over much of the broken net that allowed its tax-advantaged clients to escape, a decade later it has been unable to capture new accounts and meaningfully lift up its pension business to the levels achieved in the mid-eighties.

If its stubborn loyalty to growth stocks was the main cause of investor unrest, could the firm have avoided or even reversed the asset outflows by abandoning that strategy? There was a lot of soul searching among Fred Alger's analysts over that prospect.

Here's how Bob Emerson explained the period of doubt. "From 1983 to mid-'89, growth stocks just didn't work," he said. "And if you're a growth-stock shop, after five and a half years of lagging the market, you begin to doubt the validity of what you're doing. You root around and question the fundamental basis on which you built your business.

"That is a misguided response to the fact that there are just periods of time when the stock market doesn't pay for growth stocks. You can argue endlessly why that would be true. But Fred never deviated from his original growth strategy. As far as he was concerned, 'We believe there is only one way to make money, and that's our way.' But the industry moved away from us."

Each departing client further diminished Fred Alger's capacity to climb out of the rut of poor performance. When assets move out, it weakens the flexibility and strength of a manager's investment position. "With no new money coming in, there was a constant reshuffling of the portfolio," explained Bob Rescoe. "When people are pulling their money out, you have to sell what's most liquid, and that might unfortunately be the best names. Unless you are willing to take big markdowns on the illiquid stocks, your portfolio got out of whack."

"As the money left," described Irwin Schwartz, "I had less to do. The less you have to do, the more errors you make. Efficiency started to suffer. I'd have to find things to work on." To keep his area profitable, as people left, Irwin unhappily went back to handling some of the mundane bookkeeping chores.

The media was quick to delight in Fred Alger's dramatic downturn. Some even gave him up for dead.

"Theme of This Alger's Story Isn't the Same as Horatio's" was the headline of a February 28, 1989, *Wall Street Journal* piece by James A. White and George Anders, which also went over the Dow Jones news wire as "Money Manager Fred Alger Suffers Exodus of Clients."

The article announced that Fred Alger's clients removed $1.1 billion, or 44%, of assets under management during the fiscal year ended October 31, 1988. Among the longtime clients Anders listed as lined up outside the exits were French oil giant Elf Acquitaine and United Telecommunications Corp., both with the firm since 1980. Next to them was the $120 million account of TRW Inc., a client since 1981; Owens-Corning Fiberglas Corp.; and the U.S. Presbyterian Church, which was quoted as saying that the firm's brokerage-fee schedule became a issue when Fred Alger started to underperform.

Fred Alger was paying the price for two back-to-back years of failing to beat the S&P index. In 1987 the Alger composite declined 1.3% while the S&P 500 rose 5.3%. In 1988 Alger's gain was 9.4% against the S&P's total return of 16.6%. In the previous 10 years, however, the firm's composite 19.4% average annual gain was better than the S&P's rise of 16.2%. But that wasn't good enough for his clients. "They move very quickly," he explained to the paper. "They hire you when you're hot and fire you when you're cold. It's an impermanent business."

The draining of assets was just one piece of the downturn. Like falling dominoes, disagreeable things kept piling on the company.

For obvious reasons, the mutual-fund bet took longer to pay off. During the first four years, inflows to the Alger Fund were meager. In the summer of 1988 there was barely $25 million in the Small Cap, Growth and Money Market funds combined. Accordingly there was little income from its management and fees.

Before the turn of the decade there was a new round of brokerage-commission discounting, which couldn't have arrived at a worse time. Forced to discount its rates in line with the industry, the firm took a double hit because it traded only in its clients' accounts, and that investment pool was rapidly evaporating. Furthermore, brokerage revenues, not management fees, had been the firm's bread and butter for a decade and gave it the financial wherewithal for its research.

There were also losing and unrealized efforts to expand the firm through acquisitions intended to create a nationwide presence while broadening its expertise and product line in other investment categories.

In one of these attempts, synchronized with launching the mutual funds in 1986, Fred marched back into San Francisco, his first proving ground in the securities business, to take a prize from his old employer, Wells Fargo.

Having completed its $1.7 billion acquisition of Crocker National Corp. on May 30, 1986, Wells Fargo & Co. promptly set out to divest itself of one of Crocker's divisions which didn't fit in its investment program. The bank was "devoutly in

*David Alger sparked the firm's comeback by propelling the Alger Small Cap fund
into first place in 1989.*

passive management," with the bulk of its $28 billion portfolio held in indexed
instruments. Crocker Investment Management Corp. (Cimco), on the other hand,
was an active money manager with some growth characteristics. It was attractive
to Fred for its bond and fixed-income expertise, which could be used to augment

the initiatives in the Alger Fund. As a western beachhead, Cimco's Japanese clients were also expected to provide the firm with fresh international exposure.

"With the mutual funds we intended to come out with a fixed-income fund and a junk-bond fund. The idea was to acquire the company and retain the assets it was managing in pension funds and at the same time have a ready-made, fixed-income staff," said Greg Duch, who along with Fred Alger, George Boggio and Lisa Gregg formed the convoy to California to evaluate the Cimco purchase.

Fred Alger's interest in Cimco made big financial news. George Anders, who had broken the story on the firm's advertising claims, was already on Fred's trail. The teaser for his June 17, 1986, *Wall Street Journal* article announced: "Famed Stock Picker of the 1960s May Regain Some of His Renown." Its headline: "Money Manager Fred Alger Is Negotiating to Acquire Crocker Investment Unit." Anders reported the disturbing facts that Cimco wasn't currently profitable and had been losing both assets and clients since the defection of manager Robert C. Wade, Jr., to BankAmerica Corp. in 1981. The positive news, reported elsewhere, was that Cimco's portfolios returned 16.9% in the three years ended December 31, 1985, which was higher than the median return of bond managers and the Shearson Lehman Bond Index. In contrast, Alger's growth-oriented portfolios were up 55% for the year ended March 31, easily outstripping the S&P 500's advance of 38%.

Even *USA Today* picked up the story. Its June 18 feature, with the awkward headline "This Alger's Story Is of Ride to Riches" and a stock photo of Fred, revealed that Cimco, with $1.3 billion under management, expected to be sold for a price tag under $10 million. Fetching less than 1% of its assets, against the industry norm of 4%, the article called the transaction a fire sale.

The *San Francisco Chronicle*'s piece on June 20, "Go-Go N.Y. Money Man Is on a Roll Again," pegged Cimco's assets at a considerably lower figure—$700 million—and estimated the purchase price to be $2 million. The discrepancy in the reporting was due to the fact that half of Cimco's portfolio, a $700 million "advisory" account for the Los Angeles Department of Water & Power Employees' Retirement Plan, had decided to bail out of Cimco prior to the closing. The article led off with the inexcusably dumb one-sentence paragraph, "Fred Alger is a chip off the old Horatio Alger Block," and showed a picture of Fred at the head of a long and empty boardroom table. In the article, Fred called Cimco's operation "marginal" but reassured reporter Lloyd Watson, "We'll make it profitable for us."

Reporting that the deal had been completed, trade publication *Pensions and Investment Age* on June 23 provided a more detailed and insightful, though still imprecise, view of the acquisition. The story, "Alger Buying Crocker for Fixed Income Skills," described Cimco as a "balanced" manager with 70% of its assets in balanced stocks and fixed-income investments. The withdrawal of L.A. Water & Power was revised down to $500 million, and it announced that two more accounts would not be going along with Alger: Times Mirror Co.'s $50 million and Contra Costa County Employee's Retirement Association's $28 million. Alger would also not receive, nor did it require, the services of equity manager Rodney L. McBride and Cimco's chief investment officer, Kennard Woodworth Jr. However, its fixed-income talent, Gilbert R. Cipolla, Arnold J. Midwood and Sally Harrington, had agreed to sign on with Fred.

Only Cipolla and Harrington would make it to Fred's roster. Midwood, who directed the fixed-income team, took off to become a senior vice president at Robert C. Brown & Co. in San Francisco.

None of the papers ever got the deal straight. The true numbers were revealed in the minutes of the Alger board meeting that year. Cimco cost the Fred Alger $2.25 million for approximately $557 million in assets under management, plus its office leases.

Cimco was a trophy that got tarnished almost as soon as it got into Fred's hands. The intent was to run Cimco as a regional sales operation, independent of New York, but that goal was never fully achieved. Although Fred Alger didn't lose any money in the acquisition, Cimco never lived up to its possibilities. "Most of the people left. Most of the assets left. We retain one account from that period," said Fred.

One might argue that Fred Alger's inability to succeed with Cimco was because its investments were out of character with the essential nature of the firm. At any rate, it turned into another squandered opportunity that fed the firm's downturn.

"Cimco showed us how acquisitions don't necessarily work in this business," explained Greg Duch. "Buying assets under management, research staff and a California presence doesn't mean you will automatically retain assets. The clients didn't choose you. Fred Alger became their manager by default. There was no relationship, no long-term attachment. A year later, the market crashed. And since you have no relationship with the manager, you have more reason to leave."

As the western front collapsed, it was allowed to perish by attrition. Harrington left in the fall of 1987, when her husband transferred out of San Francisco. She was replaced by Robin Kelley, who decided a year later that she wanted to get out and raise a family. "The old assets were leaving fast. They weren't bringing in any new assets, and as the staff left us in San Francisco, we never replaced them," Greg elaborated.

The interim manpower crisis nevertheless created an opportunity for Joe Maida, in the firm via Mitchell Hutchins since February 1980 and assistant to Irwin Schwartz, to upgrade his knowledge, which eventually earned him a senior vice presidency as the firm's head of trading. He was assigned by Fred to control the San Francisco office and salvage what he could of Cimco's fixed-income, bond and money-market transactions. Since all those activities were taking place in

San Francisco, the New York office was virtually in the dark about those programs. Because its staff was on the way out, the firm needed to retain that knowledge. Taking off with him was Hugh Cole, a young RA at the firm.

The San Francisco leases were dissolved in early 1988. Later that year Cimco turned moribund and was finally dismantled.

About the same time a second marketing flank was built in St. Louis around Richard P. McGahan, a former pension manager at an Alger client. But that relationship with the company turned sour when his performance failed to live up to expectations.

Fred Alger embarked in another West Coast acquisition which he hoped would kick-start the fixed-income business and dovetail with the bond expertise gained from the Cimco deal. His bid in 1988 for BankAmerica Corp.'s advisory unit, BA Investment Management, which included the management contract for a closed-end bond fund, Montgomery Street Income Securities Inc., and the unit's Springfield, Massachusetts–based affiliate, Monarch Capital Corp., was lost in the end.

With no brighter prospects on the bond horizon, the Alger Fund liquidated its $5 million High Yield portfolio in September 1989.

As the assets departed, demoralized analysts left the firm in self-defense, thereby depleting its bench strength. Most of them stood Alger's ground in 1986, but into 1987 and after the crash, the strong nucleus of its analyst corps began fading away with the assets. Some headed toward higher, if not safer, ground. Others took advantage of vacuums created by the crash. And then there was the wholesale defection to Denver–based Janus Group of mutual funds.

Of the 26 "intuitive, creative" analysts introduced in a class picture for the 1986 brochure to support the advertising for the Alger Fund, only Ginger Risco, Lisa Gregg, Ron Reel and David Alger remained into the nineties. By comparison, nearly all of the original crew assembled by Tom Weil for the back office in 1980 stayed in place.

While the peeling off of various analysts caused a strain, its strict research associate program gave it the internal bench strength to slot new people in lead positions. A brain drain never materialized. There was always enough research backbone to power the growth of assets. Somehow the right people showed up just as the old people moved on. "They were all talented people, but we replaced them all with equally talented people," David confirmed.

As nature has a way of getting into proper balance, it was actually better for the firm when it lost many of its top people, who were also its highest earners. The elimination of their bulging salaries enabled Fred Alger to survive. "It was a great blessing," David added.

He continued, "The turnover coincided with the decline of assets after 1986 and the poor stock performance relative to people's expectations. In their calculus, the upside didn't look too good. But I don't think that's the only reason we lost people. Most of the people who left us wanted to get out of this business entirely, or couldn't take the pressure of the overall business." Biotech analyst Kathryn Whelan, for example, left to be a farmer in Maryland. David concluded, "Or they went over to career opportunities which were extraordinary. Unless we were able to let all these people run the firm, they could never have had that opportunity here."

Rob Lyon, one of the firm's most influential analysts and next in line to David in the ladder of authority, put in seven years until March 1988 and then dropped out for personal reasons. Chicago beckoned, his family's needs began to change and former employer Institutional Capital was up for grabs. Eventually Lyon took over the firm with the backing of outside investors, and its assets under management in 1997 were roughly equal to Fred Alger's.

Bob Emerson left the firm in 1989 to start Stonehill Capital, a registered investment adviser for pension accounts, and manages a leveraged hedge fund called Granite.

Worse than losing Lyon, Emerson and some of its key analysts, the firm's downturn created a condition which climaxed in the biggest departures—those of longtime partners George Boggio and Irwin Schwartz.

To shore up the firm against the ebbing flow of pension assets, Fred explored a number of maneuvers. Some, like stretching out toward the West Coast, ultimately worked out poorly. Others, like beefing up its mutual-fund distributor relationships and pursuing greater integration of its operations, were long-term strategies that provided no immediate relief.

At one point the idea of selling the company appeared, for a brief time, to be an attractive solution for preserving personal assets while ensuring the firm's future.

Putting the idea in play, Fred Alger retained Bankers Trust and Mitsubishi Bank to search for buyers and initiate deals for either an outright sale or partial financial participation. Japanese financial institutions, which at that time were devouring U.S. companies with their excess trading profits, were presumed to be the most likely prospects. With several other feelers in the market, there were a few nibbles. Don Marron at PaineWebber had been approached, and nudging interest was expressed by the French Pallas Group, Remington, and Cowen & Co., among others.

The most promising offer—and one that was very nearly realized—was from British merchant banking and trading firm Dawnay, Day & Co. The proposal was brought in by Richard Gangel, a crusty acquaintance from the Cornfeld days, who brokered the deal with one eye on a small piece of the new business.

Negotiations for selling Fred Alger moved forward aggressively between January and March 1988. Dawnay Day's designs on Fred Alger Management centered on its desire to gain a toehold in the U.S. financial industry. It also intended to market the Alger Fund in Europe, where Fred was an "attractive, well-known personality." Although no specific employment terms were discussed, Dawnay Day wished to retain the services of George, Irwin and David, while expecting Fred to retire.

Acting for Dawnay Day, from England came Guy Naggar and Ian Stautzker, who, apart from the world of finance, had attained some renown as a concert violinist. Alger found the Englishmen attractive. "We liked them. They knew investment banking and were well connected in Europe." Later the firm discovered that Dawnay Day had been victimized by a few questionable investment deals and had been named in a seventies real estate scandal. As his moods swung over the deal, Fred began questioning their integrity. But then, Fred Alger was not without its own tainted baggage from the SEC investigation.

Initially the London–based firm wanted to acquire Alger for cash, according to George Boggio, who carried the ball for Alger in the bargaining. But abhorring the tax bite of such a transaction, Fred insisted on a payout of roughly $100 million in long-term zero-coupon instruments and $45 million in seven-year treasuries. According to George, Fred was drawn to the idea of installment payments in order to minimize taxes. He could then take his notes to a bank and borrow against them to invest in the market. To circumvent New York state taxes, Fred even contemplated changing his residence to a nearby state.

Dawnay Day balked at first. It had the cash and wasn't looking for a lengthy financial entanglement; nor was it interested in being burdened by its interest debt. "With the crash and losing assets under management, they were probably right," said George.

For George and Irwin, getting cashed out in notes, payable over the long term, was also unattractive since it tied up their capital in the firm. With liquidity as his goal and purportedly with Fred's consent, George undertook a separate negotiation that allowed some portion of his and Irwin's compensation—perhaps $2 million out of $6 million apiece—to be distributed in cash at the time of the sale.

As the negotiations proceeded, Fred showed signs of having second thoughts about giving up his firm. He seemed to be placing obstacles in the way of the sale, especially in terms of how the zero-coupons needed to be structured. Or was it just shrewd bargaining on his part? There were many meetings and several different iterations of the package. The battle was never over the price of his company but how he would get paid for it. Fred pushed the resolve of the English buyers, who for the most part acquiesced to his wishes.

At the deepest level, it was probably too much for Fred to give up on his dream to create a new Alger dynasty. That goal had guided every proposition in the company and fulfilled a promise made to prominent Algers past while preparing the way for future generations of his family. Personally, he was irked that Dawnay Day didn't expect him to stay with the firm, although the Englishmen were probably right in figuring that Fred needed to be the boss and "wouldn't be comfortable working as someone's super analyst."

At the last minute, Fred came to his senses and recoiled from the deal. Losing his company wouldn't be the solution for saving it. On the technical evidence, however, the deal breaker was an argument over the cash payout negotiated by George for Irwin and himself, which Fred insisted occurred without his knowledge.

Rather than resulting in a sale, the Dawnay Day process ruptured the relationship between Fred and George. The denouement once again has a *Rashomon* quality, with each party disagreeing about what exactly took place.

The way George tells it, Fred had a change of heart at the eleventh hour. He was intimately aware of the details of his separate deal for cash early on, and he used that as an excuse to renege. On the morning of the fateful, conclusive meeting with the suitors, as they were mapping out the strategy for the final negotiation, Fred stunned him by saying that he too should get some cash.

Fred sees it differently. He holds that George was looking out for himself at Fred's expense. He believed they were all going to receive zero-debt instruments and was shocked to discover that George and Irwin had worked out a cash portion for themselves.

At that point Fred walked away from the deal.

How the deal unraveled that day is symbolized by the fact that when they sat down in a semicircle at the meeting, George took the side opposite Fred.

When he finally got around to reading the term sheet, Fred became silent. He then put on his game face and challenged George with the question: "If I'm not getting any cash, why are you? I thought we were all going to get the same paper."

Said George, "I remember Fred saying if he wasn't going to get cash, there was no deal." George tried to remind Fred that it was he who insisted on getting only notes, but he was acting "as if we never discussed it." Flustered, George snapped back, "Fred, whatever you want to do!"

The two of them then withdrew briefly in the outside corridor to sort out their conflicting positions privately. Fred reasserted his principle that all of them were to get 15-year notes. At one point in the conversation Fred indicated he was prepared to call off the transaction. Not wanting to scuttle the deal on the basis of friendly fire, George offered a way out of the impasse by telling Fred, "Buy me out at book and I won't stand in your way." Buying George out before the deal, Fred would have gained from the appreciation of George's shares. But Fred unequivocally said no.

Back in the conference room, the discussions with the lawyers drifted without much resolution and ended quite unsatisfactorily.

After the uncomfortable meeting, Fred and George repaired to the 21 Club, the scene of so many Alger Christmas dinners, to talk over what had just transpired. But even after several drinks, their opposing views didn't move any closer. George said that Fred "came on strong and was raising his voice out loud. Fred accused Irwin and me of teaming up against him, negotiating for ourselves. He said I was not going to get a better deal than he."

"Never before did I stand up to him," George concluded. "I said, I think, this deal is not going to go through." Their discussions ended in a standoff.

In the subsequent stages of negotiation, the cash portion was excised from the term sheet. But that didn't change the outcome, which was set up for rejection by Dawnay Day by Fred's insistence on securing the purchase with long-term debt instruments. Finally put off by the demands of interest and forced guarantees, the would-be buyer backed away. Ready to do the deal with cash from the outset, it saw no advantage in accommodating Fred's tax needs. Their view was, if Fred wanted zeros, he could take the cash and buy them himself. Even though he would have ultimately received a bigger package by taking the money and reinvesting it himself, he just wasn't interested in the tax liability at the time.

Had Dawnay Day taken over Fred Alger, it would likely have pointed the firm toward the European capital markets, which is ironically where the Alger Fund is currently staking a long-term position.

Fred Alger's legal adviser, Ray Merritt, confirmed, "They got very close to an agreement to buy out Fred. Negotiations broke down really at the last moment. Even though the price was substantial, Fred decided he didn't want to do it. He realized that he didn't want to give it up."

A curious footnote of this episode is that Fred's plans to sell the company were never revealed to his daughter Hilary, even though she was employed by the firm at the time and was groomed for succession. "Dad didn't volunteer such information. I'm surprised, though, that David didn't tell me. I never asked about George and Irwin leaving, because I knew it was upsetting, so I stayed away from the whole topic."

Fred sticks to his belief that George and Irwin moved to nail down a separate deal behind his back. "I didn't sell out because I didn't like the terms. There was a bit of duplicity. George was working on the terms. He had, without my knowing it, worked out terms so that he and Irwin would have gotten all the cash from the deal, and David and I would have gotten the paper, which is not exactly what we had in mind. My unhappiness with that is part of the reason they left."

David shared the same conclusion. "Somewhere in the last bit of the negotiation, George Boggio and Irwin made a deal where they would get cash for their stocks but Fred would get notes. I didn't know whether I would get cash or notes. Fred became quite irate at that, quite justifiably, because it looked like George had tried to negotiate a better deal for himself than for Fred. Since we were all in the same boat, we should have the same deal. He became very angry with George, and that poisoned the relationship, ultimately leading to the retirement of George and Irwin."

Boggio bristled. He maintains it was preposterous to suspect him of planning an underhanded move. "If you know Fred Alger, you know that Fred structured it. I could never structure a deal to sell the firm, in my wildest imagination, without Fred's strong involvement and tacit approval. No one could cut a separate deal. No way in hell."

Irwin, who was implicated in the collusion with George, added sarcastically, "Right, like we could structure a deal around Fred! He used that as an excuse. He was the one who structured it. We didn't have the power to structure a deal. He okayed everything. What it was, he didn't want any cash. He wanted long-term bonds because he didn't want to pay any taxes. George and I needed the cash. We were willing to absorb the tax liability because all our money was held up in the firm, and we didn't have any control over it. Here was an opportunity to have some cash and double our book value."

The subtle truth is hidden somewhere inside these men. To coax it out, David Alger, perhaps the most independent of the players, was pressed for some nuanced insight.

"I wasn't there. I participated in some of the earlier discussions but not the ones on the fateful day when the whole thing fell apart," he said. "My understanding comes from listening to both sides.

"The context was that we were all under an incredible amount of pressure. The firm was having problems. These people had come along, and we were negotiating around the clock.

"One viewpoint was that since George and Irwin had much less stock, they were to be paid out in cash and that Fred and I were to be paid out in notes. I was supposed to receive the same economic package as Fred. Moreover, the acquiring company did not think that Fred would be overly disturbed by this arrangement because he had the lion's share of the deal. At that time, as Fred was a little bit less involved with the running of the company, they believed it was his wish to retire.

"Fred's impression, going into the negotiation the final day, was that all of us were going to receive the identical package. When the final strokes came about, Fred looked at the deal and realized, to his horror, that George and Irwin were not getting the notes, they were getting cash, sticking Fred with the notes."

Ed Kleinbard, from the legal firm which put together the huge Phibro Corp. merger with Salomon in 1981, was the tax attorney in charge of preparing the term sheet for the purchase. For some reason, however, that duty was handed over to an associate who, due to some oversight, left out any mention of cash payments in the document's first draft. George says that even though he told Fred about the error, it was a mistake to give him that incorrect version of the term sheet. The corrected proposal was delivered to Fred only at noon on March 4, the very day of the meeting, to review the transaction.

David continued, "George's position seemed to be that (a) he was justified because this represented a good piece of his net worth and he needed this money, and that (b) Fred knew all along that they were going to get cash.

"My recollection, when I last left the negotiating table, was that all of us were going to get the same securities. But it isn't inconsistent to me that this could have changed without my knowledge. George was given the mission of getting this deal done.

"I don't think George ever felt that he was deliberately trying to screw Fred or the company. I think he felt justified in getting a different mode of payment because the numbers were so vastly different. But Fred reacted to it like George was trying to pull a fast one and cut himself a better deal.

"After working in this firm awhile, you learn where the boundaries are with Fred. You want to make sure that you don't exceed them. You want to make sure

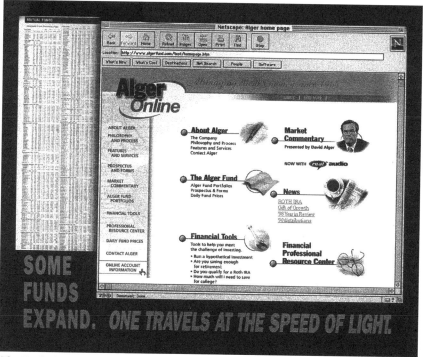

The Fred Alger Management Web site.

that Fred is informed about everything of substance you're doing. George should have known what would set Fred off.

"If George wanted to buy a house, he would need money to do it. Fred already had houses and things. He thought he was entitled to a little piece of paradise. I think George is absolutely as honest as the day is long, but I think he may have taken a calculated risk in not making sure that Fred understood correctly about the cash portion. He should have said it three times to Fred, 'I'm getting the cash. Fred, do you understand this?' A simple blink of the eyes is not sufficient. He wanted this deal to go through. We really wanted this deal to happen. And the climate at the time was, we all thought that the business was going down the tube and this was as good an offer as we were likely to get.

"The bottom line is that both Fred and George exaggerated what was going on."

Lamentably, that's how their relationship went forward, each believing that the other had turned the tables on him.

One might also conjecture that this was another grand maneuver on Fred's part—like the one that worked Bill Scheerer out of the company years earlier—to enlarge David's position in the firm. Though to say that he stage-managed this entire affair might be giving him credit for too much Machiavellian cunning.

In the end Fred may have reasoned that he still wanted his blood in the business, that without the firm, money wasn't enough. He had looked in the mirror, and, beholding the visage of his great-grandfather, he blinked.

The dustup over Dawnay Day irrevocably broke the faith between George and Fred. It's astonishing how the two men, who were so much in sync for 20 years, suddenly lost their connection.

By his own declaration George clearly understood his place in the organization. "I really felt that I was an integral part of that firm," he stressed. "If I could show him why something should be done, Fred was always willing to listen. I'd like to think that he respected my opinion. With Fred, until he made a decision, you could be as forceful in your disagreement as you wanted. He didn't want a yes man. But once a decision was made, even if it was a choice I didn't support, I pulled up my oars and acted as if it were my decision."

After March 1988 the perfect partnership of Fred, George and Irwin turned into a disjunctive mix, and the toxic atmosphere wove its way through the firm, pushing a few more restive employees out the door. With a trace of sadness, George and Irwin must have believed that Fred had drifted away from them. "Up until the last couple of years, it was 'We built this,'" observed Irwin, "but that 'we' changed to 'I.' It used to be 'us and us,' then it became 'Fred and us.' I began to wonder where I fit in." Fred saw their actions as a breach of loyalty, and that opened a fault line for them to drop out of the firm.

Both George and Irwin had given 20 years to the firm and were finally eli-gible to recoup their shares at book value—shares which were purchased for twice book and were worth only half book value until the twentieth year. The urgency to leave so soon after this milestone was reinforced by another clause in the partnership agreement which gave Fred Alger the option of paying them in notes due in ten years. "We put this into effect to forestall a liquidity crisis, not as a punitive measure," explained David. But George feared otherwise and pretty soon got Irwin to start believing with him. With the recent example of Fred's behavior with Dawnay Day deal, and especially in an environment of declining assets, slumping revenues and poor stock performance, it was easy for Irwin to succumb to George's anxious urgings. Their decision was to leave together, and as quickly as possible, in a countermeasure against the deferred payout clause.

It was eerie symmetry that the provision's tax implications for their families urged them forward, with the kind of liability-avoidance angle which dominated Fred's perspective in the Dawnay Day deal.

"I had a contract with the firm which gave Fred the option of not paying me my share for ten years after retirement, which set up a very awkward situation vis-à-vis my estate planning and personal finances," Irwin explained. "If he had held to that agreement, if I died, my estate would have a tax liability on the money coming from Fred Alger, even though I didn't have the money yet."

"That provision bothered me," George admitted. "If both my wife and I died during the ten-year period, then my sons would have to pay estate tax on a note receivable ten years hence. That was unacceptable to me. They would have to sell this house and everything we owned to raise money to pay the estate taxes. The chance of my living ten years from 1989 was greater then than if I left later. If I worked till I was sixty-five, I might get my money when I was seventy-five."

"George was always paranoid that Fred, if they ever decided to leave, would pay them with ten-year notes," David observed correctly. "It was never the intent of the rule that the company would withhold the cash if it could afford to pay it out."

That suspicion was not relieved when Fred resisted their appeals to modify the shareholders agreement and waive that option. Said Irwin, "He probably thought business is slow enough, and this would be a good way to get rid of us. Perhaps he thought we were bluffing. Even his lawyer asked him to change the agreement."

Despite appearances, it was hard for David to see how they imagined Fred would be vindictive toward them. "Fred has never ever done anything in my his-tory which is either unethical, dishonest or unfair when it comes to money," said David in Fred's defense. "When it comes to money, in the end Fred has always been a gentleman. In fact, when push comes to shove in really tough situations, Fred is frequently a lot nicer to people and a lot less vindictive than I would be . . . a lot less vindictive. He seems mean and very unfeeling and gives the appearance that he might screw you out of everything. You just have to look at the track record to see that isn't the case."

Fred never intended to delay their payments, which they found difficult to believe. As it worked out, Fred Alger never invoked the ten-year payout option. Rather than drag out the payments, George and Irwin received their cash within three years. All their bickering was unwarranted. But in the haste for their money, they took a slight trim on their severance—forfeiting certain provisions of the shareholders agreement relating to payment of ancillary sums of money to reflect the appreciation of certain assets.

"Then, it turned out, he paid me out very quickly. If he had formalized what he did anyway, I might still be with the firm," Irwin said. "I have nightmares about that because I sure like my life now." George added, "I can tell you that Irwin and I didn't want to leave, but, yes, it worked out very nicely."

In July 1989 George Boggio and Irwin Schwartz left Fred Alger Management for a rich life made possible by the appreciation of capital during their years with Fred and the skillful reinvestment of that wealth.

If Fred agonized over their departure, he did so privately. On the surface he defended its logic. "It was probably a good time for them to leave," he said. "The business changed dramatically after 1987. Not only did we lose assets under management, but we were forced to become more competitive on commissions. And people weren't buying our trading story anymore. They had both put in their twenty years, George more than Irwin. After you're with a company for twenty years, you become a little stale. They had their own interests, their own money, which they are investing."

Respected and loved as they were, it was only natural for morale to take a hit at the announcement of their departure. Nowhere was this felt more deeply than in the firm's New Jersey back-office enclave, where George Boggio held loyal dominion.

"It was like a big bombshell. We never expected it," said Isabella Coari. "Irwin and George leaving, that was very shocking," added Jim Barbi. "But George put a very positive spin on what was going on. He announced his leaving, and Fred came over to make a speech. It was extremely well orchestrated. Fred said, in effect, that he was sorry to see these guys going, but this made way for young blood and new vitality. George said he felt that the firm was in the strongest position it had been in years.

"I explained it to the people working for me like this. The critical thing in these situations is the guy who has money in the firm. The determination of that guy to stay in the business is the single most important fact."

"Any fear subsided when Fred came over to talk with us and assured us that

Fred Alger wasn't going to be taken over, and Fred Alger wasn't going to close the doors," confirmed John Messina. When he visited New Jersey, Fred reserved a private moment for Rosemary Kiernan, his oldest employee and George's secretary. He brought her into George's office, shut the door behind them and asked, "Ro, What about you? You're not thinking of leaving?" "No," she replied, "I'll work here forever."

The New York office was not without emotion over their departure. "George and Irwin's leaving was a morale sinker," according to Bob Rescoe. "They were the senior partners. Their leaving raised questions about what's really going on here. Are they bailing because they know something bad is coming down the pike? But Fred smoothed everything over and handled it well."

George and Irwin were so integral to the leadership and administration of the firm, but what might have been an event of seismic proportions barely registered a low rumble.

The strong upside of their departures is that it freed up fixed positions at the company's head which enabled movement through the ranks of the firm. Fred Alger was on a downturn, and many Wall Street firms were not faring any better after the crash. In such an environment their leaving created the only room for advancement and paradoxically kept the rest of the firm intact by making way for its smart, aggressive younger people.

George and Irwin's imprint gradually faded as a new crop of outstanding individuals rose up to lead the firm forward.

Greg Duch is the main reason that Fred Alger held up so well after the departure of George Boggio. Because of him, instead of coming up against a corrosive letdown of morale and administrative lapses, the staff could accept George's leaving as simply another turning page in the book of the firm.

Intelligent like Fred and with his mannerly way and a bookish appearance that belies his low-keyed management style, Greg Duch has improved the atmosphere at Fred Alger even while spurring it on to financial achievement and greater administrative competence.

He arrived on the scene when Fred Alger had started self-clearing and required professional support with its brokerage relationships. Greg's background—as senior manager in the banking and financial division of big-eight accounting firm Arthur Andersen—involved transacting with many broker-dealer firms, and he was needed to assist George Boggio, who was less involved in the brokerage area. A graduate of New York University in 1972, Duch joined Arthur Andersen straight from college and worked there for nine years before Alger. One of his clients, Mitchell Hutchins, had been clearing Alger trades, and another client, William S. Paley & Co., was being run by former Alger partner William Stewart. Serving large financial institutions like Prudential Bache and

Lazard Freres prepared Greg for his current Alger role as its chief financial officer and head of operations.

When it was his turn to take over the reins, he ran contrary to the authoritarian style that George had maintained. Said Greg, "My philosophy, especially as the firm was moving on, was to avoid doing things the same way as George and accomplish the work in my fashion . . . to do more delegation than George." For achieving that modern outlook, he was Alger's Man of the Year in 1990 and again in 1993.

Considering how obviously exemplary Greg has been at managing Fred Alger's operations, it was surprising to learn that he was not the firm's first choice for replacing George and "narrowly averted losing in a shoot-out for the second-banana position."

Duch was one of three executives in contention for Boggio's office. Accounting's John Raspitha was also vying for the job but came up short. Raspitha was the ex-Marine who had come to Fred Alger in December 1977 from Ernst & Ernst and Purcell Graham & Co. and was essentially responsible for internal and regulatory reporting.

"John was the epitome of the old-style accountant. He did everything manually—gigantic spreadsheets of green-bar paper and yellow accounting pads," said Duch. With his less-than-modern approach, it is understandable that he was passed over as the company's chief financial officer.

After missing out at taking over the back office from Tom Weil, Raspitha found a better opportunity elsewhere and left the firm. The company he joined eventually got folded into an affiliation with French bank Société Générale's SocGen Securities Corp. "I think John's leaving was a loss for the company," said Greg. "He was able to do so much work because of his old style, and it's almost impossible to find that kind of person anymore."

George's heir apparent and original choice was controller Frederick J. Koczwara, who was hired in 1986 with the hope that he would one day assume George's responsibilities. Koczwara had been a partner at the firm's auditor Cooper & Lybrand and, though lacking industry experience, possessed a great facility with numbers and solid management experience.

Though initially favored for his competence and penchant for slashing costs, as the firm was expanding, it became clear that Koczwara wasn't the one to lead it. He left the firm in 1989 with extremely generous terms, and the following year was working in finance and administration at the ADP Brokerage Information Services Group.

Only Greg was left standing, and Fred and David realized that they had probably overlooked some of the qualities that made him almost ideal from the start for the job. "In May or June Fred called me over and told me he was promoting me to take over for George, who would be leaving," said Greg.

He continued, "When I took over, we were in this whole downsizing mode. It is difficult to downsize and maintain a strong organization to do what we needed to do. A lot of times the people here didn't know how close we were to having to let them go. I was keeping everybody optimistic and upbeat while I knew disasters were taking place left and right."

David added, "George was an amazingly important component in building this firm, but Greg is also an extraordinarily talented man, and he has done a lot of things that George might not have done. He is as good as George but with a lot more youthful vigor. He has improved a lot of the systems and seems to do his work effortlessly."

When Greg took over, he confronted a "mishmash" of computers. David used the DEC VAX in New York for analysis. Also in New York was the costly DEC midrange purchased for the earlier, failed 401(k) record-keeping business. The mutual-fund accounting was handled on a Data General minicomputer with several dedicated terminals. The marketing of the funds and pensions was discretely attended by a McDonnell Douglas midrange. And finally, the transfer-agency work was turned out on a PC-based Novell network.

Software preferences had dictated the acquisition of such different hardware, but the company's productivity was suffering because all these applications and their data remained so unconnected. Greg changed all that quickly. Not only did he bring the firm up to speed with the latest technology for achieving operating efficiency, but he took it upon himself to consolidate the company's disparate computer systems and hinge all the company's hardware and software into a single, unified local-area, and then wide-area network.

In the fall of 1991 Duch managed another transition by converting from Automatic Data Processing Inc.'s PARS, or Portfolio Accounting Reporting Service, to an in-house-use system configured around Integrated Decision System Inc.'s Investment Manager II software.

PARS had handled the company's reporting since the mid-eighties. It provided overnight batch processing of customer portfolios, which was then delivered either electronically or as hard copy to investment managers from ADP's data center in Jersey City. But PARS lacked crucial intra-day portfolio updating and posed problems when extracting performance and accounting information. Apart from the higher outsourcing costs, another deficiency was its processing lag time.

The firm had been spending $9,000 a month for the services of ADP. By bringing its functions in-house, the cost was brought down to $2,000 a quarter after the initial capital outlay for hardware and software. Even with a high base price of $150,000, Greg found that Investment Manager II offered a better solution for managing customer data. It came with automated asset allocation, daily performance information and accruals which could be linked to a relational database to perform analytics. The software had already been tested and used by other fund managers and institutional clients.

Greg did even more to advance technology at the firm in a way that it served customers but also acted as a marketing tool. One of the suppliers that fostered Alger's New Jersey computerization was Metro*soft*, the firm responsible for the firm's groundbreaking use of telephony in Germany. In Metro*soft* Fred Alger lucked out with a vendor that was willing to work as a partner in developing information solutions for its highly specialized requirements. For Alger it is like having an in-house IS department without personnel demands or overhead.

"Alger is driven by ideas about how to do business," Metro*soft*'s Leszek James explained about developing technology for the company. "The firm is not interested in knowing the technical limitations." For one, the firm's data and voice lines have been integrated down a single path, making it easier for customer representatives to reach out and call out by pointing and clicking at a computer screen instead of dialing numbers. Additionally Alger's interactive voice-response system gives its broker-dealers automated access to up-to-date client-account information. "Very, very few firms have the capability of offering that kind of service," insisted James, "not even firms much larger than Alger."

Greg considers this as his greatest contribution. "Managing the whole transition and getting this side into the twentieth century, in terms of automation and leveraging the firm's manpower. Everything moved without skipping a beat . . . with the conversions and bringing all that activity in-house. It has been good for the company, as well as financially and personally satisfying. There's a higher level of technology and greater openness to technology here than you will find at competing firms."

Although Greg Duch was not the natural choice to assume George's chair, he fell very nicely into the position, thanks to the inestimable training given by George. Finding Irwin's replacement proved to be more tricky. Tony Weber, Irwin's backup who took over after him, decided to quit the firm two weeks into the job. David admitted that he promoted Joe Maida, who was next in line, with "serious reservations." Joe quickly proved him wrong. "I was absolutely flabbergasted about how wrong we all were about Joe," he said. "It was as though the man grew ten feet in stature as soon as he was promoted. He sat down at the desk and took over responsibility as though he had been born into the position. He is incredible. He is terrific."

John Messina seemed to have the right handle on why the outlook for the firm didn't change with George and Irwin's departure. "You have a chain of command, and you learned from the best. There's no reason for the future to be any different," he said.

"I was extremely close to Irwin," offered David, "but he had gotten a little older and was running out of gas. This is a young person's business. It takes a great deal of energy and drive. And that's as it should be. Once you get over fifty, you get a little slower, you don't want to put in the long hours. It's a very tiring and demanding business."

Another benefit, ironically, of George and Irwin's leaving was that it reduced the financial drain of their high salaries. "Their departure actually helped the company because assets under management were declining," affirmed Greg Duch. "It was a blessing in disguise."

David ratified his position. "When George and Irwin left—plus we lost a few of our big-deal analysts—we had a very substantial drop in our highly paid employee count. That was our salvation from an economic standpoint, even though we were tremendously sorry to see them go. That alone is what saved us from red ink. Suddenly we were in the black. We chopped our overhead enormously, and the cork bobbed back up to the surface."

Everyone prospered in the end. Irwin ended his dreaded commute. George controlled his own capital. Fred Alger, though cut to the bone, managed to stay healthy. With a changing of the guard, the firm was lifted by renewed energy. Its tax-exempt base soon stabilized, and the Alger Fund finally started growing.

The dismal act was reaching its finale. Happier scenes were about to be played out in the company.

20 🐾

Holding Firm

WITH THE BENEFIT OF HINDSIGHT it is clear that Fred Alger was right to withdraw from the Dawnay Day transaction and hold on to the firm. The wisdom of this decision was anything but obvious, however, in the last years of the eighties when it was hemorrhaging pension assets, the SEC was at its throat, and it was shunned by the investing community for its hyperbolic advertising. Between 1987 and 1990 management fees tailed off by 60% and commissions sank by nearly 90%. In 1990 the firm's net worth stood at $62.6 million—15% below the peak of $73.7 million two years earlier. By walking away from the company at that point, Fred could have comfortably cashed out with a small personal fortune.

If he held firm to the decision not to surrender the firm, one reason was that Fred Alger found a rainmaker in Ray Pfeister. Ray, who along with Greg Duch became an executive vice president after the departure of George and Irwin, showed the firm how, by expanding its distribution channels to include insurance companies, it could make up for its earlier failures in advertising and replenish its assets. In 1991 Fred Alger's net worth was back at $70.5 million and heading up. The swagger may have gone, but the firm was clearly on its way back.

Fred explained Ray Pfeister's role this way: "He opened our eyes to marketing. Without him I don't know where we'd be today." If proximity to Fred is a measure of stature, then by occupying George Boggio's old office next to Fred's at Maiden Lane, Ray Pfeister has found his place in the company.

Ironically Pfeister was able to convert the firm to the idea of service-oriented marketing and reverse its poor sales record because he was so out of character with everyone else. He had a swashbuckling, entrepreneurial style and was not about to be constrained by the Alger mode of doing things.

When Fred introduced Ray to his associates, it came with the warning: "He's as different from the rest of us as night and day."

It took awhile for Fred to get accustomed to the fact that Ray was a peripatetic fellow who is not averse to playing a round of golf or handing out cigars to make a deal, which he often said is what it takes to build a good business relationship. Pfeister defended his approach. "The most productive time is with someone eyeball to eyeball. I try to make sure I'm outside making it happen," he said. "There's no substitute to going out and buying lunches, shaking hands and making relationships. Early on, it was a little strange for them to see a real marketing guy in the company. 'Where the hell is Ray? Anybody seen Ray? You know where Ray is?' I knew Fred had expectations and needed to spend some time in the office, but if I wanted to make it happen, I had to be out. I'm not sure many in the company still understand that."

While board member Steve O'Neil deserves credit for bringing Ray Pfeister to Fred Alger, it was actually Steve's father, Ed, who provided his connection with the company. During his morning commute from Bronxville, New York, Ed regularly played bridge with a group that included Ray, and this led to an introduction to Steve. So when Fred Alger began searching for ways to rejuvenate its marketing department, Steve knew that Ray had all the qualities that were needed by Fred Alger and arranged a meeting in the firm.

It was a made-to-order fit. At that time Pfeister was a director at the accounting firm Coopers & Lybrand. He was a consultant for a large number of insurance companies and financial organizations, and his strengths were mainly in those areas where Fred Alger needed to develop.

Unlike many financial types who considered the word gunslinger as a pejorative, Ray instead found that handle to be intriguing. "The word on the Street was still that Fred Alger was as successful as any man in American history at picking growth stocks," he said. "To me, gunslinger was a glamorous, exciting and positive thing—a huge compliment, like Wyatt Earp. To me, being gunslinger was being a hero."

Pfeister's first impressions of Fred were that he was "a great listener, made good eye contact and bottom-lines conversations very quickly." During the job interview, Ray recalled, "I remember seeing George remove and then quickly replace his watch. That was how Fred and George communicated about the suitability of an applicant. In my case, it was good news."

Here is another instance of the right people finding their way to the company at the appropriate time in its history.

Soon after Ray entered the firm in the summer of 1987, he was faced with the fallout from Black Monday. "One of my darkest moments was experiencing the October crash," he said. "It had a numbing effect, after which there was a tremendous exodus of assets. A lot of people were on edge, and everybody was trying to keep a low profile in order to keep their jobs. But I never thought for a minute we weren't going to pull out of it. In fact, I wanted to be the guy that did it."

Ray knew exactly how to respond to the situation, and with the confidence and charm he typically radiates, he swung into action. He worked quickly to establish the type of marketing and distribution relationships that would launch the firm into new business zones. Ray's impact was almost immediate. His focused effort and virtuoso turn won him Man of the Year in 1988.

Beneath his cordiality Ray keeps a sharp edge. Like Fred, he moves fast and is always on point. Describing himself, Pfeister said, "I like being glib. I like telling Clinton jokes. I like standing ovations. I like closing sales." Perhaps after a round of golf or while relaxing with a good cigar.

Ray Pfeister's essential and enduring contribution has been to convince numerous insurance companies to offer the Alger American Fund, organized in April 1988, in their variable annuity and variable-life insurance policies. These insurance products provide a death benefit in combination with tax-advantaged mutual-fund asset appreciation. The variable or fluctuating return comes from linkage to the performance of the underlying portfolio selected by the purchaser of the policy.

A variable annuity is an investment contract to pay a changing amount, based on performance, to an annuitant at some future time, which is usually retirement. It may be offered as a single-premium or multiple-premium contract, and the insurance component is equal to the amount invested. Under current law, income from a variable annuity may be withdrawn at any time during the contract period and may take the form of periodic payments until age $59\frac{1}{2}$. The account, however, must be exhausted by age $70\frac{1}{2}$.

A variable life insurance policy also provides a floating rate of return, and, like an IRA, its earnings are tax-deferred until distributed. But only income which exceeds the premium paid is subject to taxation. The death benefit is assessed as estate and not individual income. Variable life policies are free from credit and claims and may be withdrawn at any time. With surrender charges and fees, however, one doesn't come into the money until five to ten years after starting the policy.

Among financial vehicles, Fred likened a mutual fund to an airplane, but he saw a variable annuity as a jet and variable-life policies as rockets. The appeal of the latter two is their capacity to lock in investment assets and management revenues for extended time.

Unlike the normal course of money-management firms that enter the insurance market as investment subadvisories, Alger's approach was to construct a separate pool of funds, known as Alger American, to be available on a wholesale basis by any number of insurers. Such external management and marketing arrangements were uncommon and barely considered at the time, even though they reduced legal, compliance and other expenses for insurers while enabling them to offer the convenience and selectivity of multiple investments. For Fred Alger,

Ray Pfeister (right) opened the firm's eyes to marketing and was responsible for establishing its variable annuity and variable life investment portfolios.

following such a strategy meant the potential for greater assets through a ready-made sales force while tying the insuring company to a long-term, co-branding relationship.

When Ray was hired to court the insurance business, he asked Fred and George to set meaningful targets for his efforts. "They were talking ten million dollars, maybe fifty million," said Pfeister. His aspirations were more modest, though equally unrealistic on the positive side. Holding up his end of the bargain, he "put up really big numbers." Ray explained, "I felt if we could generate one hundred million of this business over my career here, that would be fantastic."

Pfeister has far exceeded all those goals and expectations. Asset flows into Alger American have outstripped all other investments into Fred Alger during the nineties. By mid-1997, Alger American had over $3.1 billion in its accounts, making up almost 40% of the firm's total assets under management.

All this success with insurance-related assets didn't come quickly or easily. Ray had to overcome the firm's handicap of being an unknown quantity without any prior insurance-company relationships. After spending two years knocking on insurance doors, he got his first break from Mike Green at American Skandia, the U.S. arm of Sweden's Skandia Group, the leading Scandinavian insurance company. Founded in 1855, it manages over $30 billion in assets from 20 offices worldwide. "We owe our entry into this business and eventual success to Mike Green," Pfeister said solemnly, adding that Green, who has since passed away, was a "very polished, super, super guy."

It turned out that Green, one of only two people then running the Skandia operation, shared Pfeister's fondness for smoking cigars. Pfeister described how he cemented their relationship. "I always used to carry Macanudos in my briefcase. They were a nice way to establish friendship with a guy who likes smoking cigars. Mike had an excellent cigar cutter on his desk and a cigar ashtray, and guys don't have those if they aren't fond of good cigars. I offered him one of my Macanudos. They were big Macanudos. He shut the door to the office. We fired them up, and I knew we were good for at least an hour of conversation, because you can't enjoy a good cigar in less than an hour."

Initially American Skandia contracted with a third party, Planco Financial Services Inc. of Paoli, Pennsylvania, for sales and distribution of the annuities. But with the clear success of the Alger product, it decided to set up its own sales and marketing network. This worked out even better for Fred Alger, which expanded its partnership with Skandia in January 1992 by turning over the wholesaling of even its non-insurance Alger Fund portfolios exclusively to that organization.

"My strategy was to get the Alger name out quickly to as many places as possible," explained Pfeister. "Theoretically we could have created our own telemarketing unit to build relationships with broker dealers. But we didn't get to where we are because our marketers called up broker dealers and asked them to sign agreements. The business was driven to them by Skandia."

Fred provided the rationale for the unique partnership with Skandia. "It came about during a period when variable annuities weren't such a hot product," he said. "Skandia needed something for their people to market." The Alger-Skandia alliance was special because each company fed on the other's success and grew mutually from the partnership. Both started new in the business and in roughly the same cycle. The give-and-take went both ways. Skandia gave Alger more visibility. The Alger portfolios provided the fuel to develop and expand its marketing organization, which grew to a staff of over 400 in less than five years. "We have been a big part of their success in this country, as much as Skandia has helped drive this company to its level of success," said Pfeister. "We did it together."

On June 30, 1994, *Business Wire* reported that by May 1 of that year American Skandia, which had been marketing products in the U.S. only since 1987, had grown to be the seventh largest underwriter of variable annuities in terms of distribution by independent broker dealers. Its 1993 sales had jumped 300% over the prior year by offering 35 investment choices, not only from Alger but other firms like Eagle Asset Management, Alliance Capital Management, Janus Capital, Phoenix Investment and Scudder, Stevens & Clark.

Skandia's wholesaling relationship with the Alger firm continued until October 31, 1994. Explaining why it ended, Fred said, "As annuities became hot again, there was more money to be made selling annuities than wholesaling our mutual funds. Typically there is only time to show one product, and they couldn't do both properly. Annuities are more complex and unique and take more time to explain."

David added, "The money we gave to Skandia went directly to the wholesalers. Corporate management didn't get any of it, so they were never very enthusiastic about spending the time to give a full effort to it."

Jim Connelly's view was that the relationship fractured due to conditions leading to inadequate product support and service. And after all, wasn't the strategy of outsourcing its sales administration a gross violation of the basic Alger tenet of integration to control all business functions? Fortunately, the firm got its hands back into the sales effort to be ready for the advance of stock prices and the surge in mutual fund investing which began in 1995.

The second insurance firm to take on Fred Alger after Skandia was Ameritas Life Insurance Company of Westborough, Massachusetts. Next Pfeister brought in variable-insurance business from Aetna, based in Hartford, Connecticut, a major player in retirement benefits and life insurance, which has recently turned its attention to providing managed health care. This contract was won on the golf course with Aetna's Joe Thornton and Drew Lawton, who was once captain of the Yale golf team. Aetna had been the fastest-growing source of management assets among all Alger's insurance partners. Unfortunately, it pulled out of the relationship in 1998.

Fourth on board was Security Life of Denver.

With Pfeister's influence and effort, other types of relationships with insurance companies also materialized. In some cases Alger has acted as an investment

Jim Connelly emerged as one of the company's new leaders and now heads up the Alger Fund.

manager for funds run by insurance firms; it has also participated as a research subadvisor for insurance-company mutual funds.

An example of the former is the Netherlands' Aegon Insurance Group, one of the world's top ten insurance companies and the fifth firm which Pfeister corralled. Its Western Reserve Life subsidiary in Largo, Florida, offers Alger American annuities, and its mutual-fund distribution company, IDEX Group, also in Largo, uses Fred Alger Management to manage its Aggressive Growth portfolio.

The sixth and seventh insurance firms into the Alger camp, New York's Mutual of America and the Provident Mutual Life Insurance Company of Philadelphia, fell in by using Fred Alger in a commingled subadvisory capacity. One of America's top 25 mutual-life insurers, Provident Mutual offers trust, investment management and securities services through its Sigma America and Provident Mutual Investment Management subsidiaries.

The eighth and ninth insurance company contracts were also subadvisories: USAA, the San Antonio, Texas–based insurance company that primarily serves military personnel and their families, and Boston–based New England Life Insurance Co., which runs a family of mutual and variable-insurance funds.

Because performance drives assets into an investment product, Alger's insurance-related portfolios were powered by the appeal of tremendous appreciation. For instance, in performance calculations by Morningstar published in *Investment Advisor* for the years ending in April and again May of 1994, Fred Alger dominated the ratings. On April 30, 1994, Ameritas Overture III/Alger Growth, Ameritas Overture II/Alger Growth, American Skandia Advisors Plan/Alger Growth and American Skandia Lifevest/Alger Growth were on top of the heap. On May 31, 1994, the honors went to American Skandia Advisors Plan/MidCap Growth, American Skandia Lifevest/Alger MidCap Growth, Ameritas Overture III/Alger MidCap Growth, Ameritas Overture II/Alger MidCap Growth.

In February 1996 *Mutual Funds* magazine listed Alger portfolios with American Skandia as the top two picks among no-load variable annuities: America Skandia Choice/Alger Small Cap, with a one-year total return of 46% and annualized five-year performance of 25% in the aggressive-growth category, and America Skandia Choice/Alger Growth, with a one-year gain of 35% and an annualized five-year return of 23% in the growth category.

While the Alger Fund was established to shield the firm against the vagaries of the pension market, Alger American was responsible for enlarging assets to a breakthrough critical mass and extending its reach outside the boundaries of the Wall Street financial community.

Fred Alger's bet on insurance and faith in Ray Pfeister has paid off handsomely. By 1995 the firm received over $1 billion in investment assets—triple the amount two years earlier—from its insurance relationships. In 1997, primarily due to Ray's efforts, Alger American was carried by 27 insurance companies, and the firm has subadvisory relationships with another 13 insurance firms. In contrast, Fidelity, through its VIP Funds launched six years before Alger American, had 12 times as many assets but only six more insurance partnerships in 1995.

"We have penetrated the insurance business," Pfeister emphasized. "Our name awareness as far as outside managers, other than insurance companies which provide their own money management, is only behind Fidelity, Scudder, Neuberger Berman." Considering the size of Fred Alger, relative to the other companies and the brief time it has been in this market, that's impressive.

There's more growth ahead, according to Pfeister, who is actively tracking about 70 more companies that sell or plan to market annuity and variable-life insurance. "It takes a year from initial contact to get the thing going—and two years before we see any assets," he clarified.

Between 1987 and 1989, the same hectic period Ray was busy hatching the insurance business, it became apparent that attracting an appreciable sum of investments into the Alger Fund would take longer than expected. To bypass that process Fred began targeting other mutual-fund management companies for acquisition. Apart from bulking up the firm's asset base, the right acquisition would increase Alger's attractiveness to individual and institutional investors by complementing its existing mutual-fund fare with an expanded lineup of targeted investment options, perhaps fixed-income securities, international investments, mining companies or even an index fund.

Fred called on Ray Pfeister to spearhead the search for potential acquisitions. Ray accepted the challenge with customary enthusiasm. He saw his role as a bird dog, one who merely beat the bushes for prospects. Then it was up to George and Greg, and ultimately Fred, to crunch the numbers and work out the terms. "There weren't many firms that I didn't call," he said, "every one with assets over one hundred million dollars."

There were perhaps a dozen nibbles, and several real bites, but Fred Alger was unable to snag any of these deals. Buying a mutual fund this time around proved to be more complex than when Fred Alger picked up Castle Convertible and Spectra in the mid-seventies.

In 1988 Fred Alger considered purchasing Boston–based Ivy Funds, essentially for its expertise in international investing with portfolio manager Hakan Castegren. Another mark for acquisition was New York's Bull & Bear Group Inc. The big one that got away was United Services Advisers in San Antonio, Texas, right down the street from USAA, which Pfeister was pitching for Alger American. United Services might have increased Alger assets by $400 million, which was a large amount for the company back then.

After observing all the merger and acquisition activity in the industry during the nineties, David raised the possibility that the firm will once again rejoin the hunt for assets through strategic acquisitions. "There are a lot of little funds out there that want homes and are really inefficient. We've looked at them in the past and will continue to do so." Given the frenzied consolidation of businesses in the financial-services sector and the rising valuations of mutual-fund companies, Fred Alger will have to pay considerably more for a mutual-fund management contract than it may have intended to spend in the late eighties.

"You constantly have to market your brains out because you're going to lose assets," explained Ray Pfeister. "If we have a great performance year, investors send us money, when they should be doing it the other way around. For a long-term investor, the risk in investing in mutual funds reduces to zero over time."

A crowning outgrowth of Alger's insurance relationships was the invention of one of Fred's grandest investment ideas, the Program for Substantial Charitable Investors, a highly effective package of financial products that enables wealthy individuals to make a substantial charitable donation while holding on to their capital and enjoying the protection of life insurance.

Fred formulated the idea when he was invited on several charitable boards at a time when nonprofits were dealing with a change in tax laws that made charitable giving less appealing. The concept was then developed in partnership with Jerome S. Golden, chairman and director of the Golden American Life Insurance Company in New York, according to Ray Pfeister, "considered by most to be the father of variable insurance and creator of the first single-premium variable-life insurance policy."

The ideal participant, and the focus of Fred's projections, was a man like himself—rich, in his fifties, who likely had a substantial amount squirreled away in municipal bonds or bond funds and was eager to provide a large sum to charity—but felt constrained from doing so because of the loss of capital and the hindrance of taxation. If Fred could show him a way to trade in, let's say, a million dollars of those bonds for ten years without giving up any of the tax-exempt income thrown off by the bonds and without losing any of the principal or being forced to make additional investments, and also providing $100,000 to a charity during the first three years, wouldn't that be exciting?

The marketing targets for the plan were institutions which, it was assumed, would happily introduce the program to potential donors. Alger would make its money from management fees. The insurance company would earn its premiums. And so it seemed Charitable Giving was the ultimate win-win financial vehicle. Said Fred, "We thought we had the perfect solution for eleemosynary and charitable organizations to continue receiving money in an infertile tax environment and a way for them to open up a big market of givers."

Fred went on the road to promote this pet product. Pfeister recalled accompanying him on nearly 30 presentations to foundations and universities. Expecting Charitable Giving to be an instant hit, Fred was surprised by the unanimously negative results of the sales effort. The program was not at all unappealing. In fact, many rejected the plan simply because it was too good to be believed. Most prospects, however, were barreled over by the complexity of the scheme and all its arcane assumptions. Pfeister admitted, "It's a complex and convoluted instrument. If people ever took the time to understand it, it is a fabulous product."

Although Charitable Giving looked good on paper, there was no financial history to back up the investment. So Fred became the first to buy one of these programs, "just to make sure all our math was true," one of only two Charitable Giving contracts ever sold. "It worked perfectly," he said, "in fact, a little bit better than we had projected."

The results of his plan—from April 26, 1990, through June 18, 1993—were detailed in a second round of marketing. After exchanging roughly $1 million in municipal bonds and paying no sales charges for participation, he was able to contribute $111,740.06 to charity while deriving a tax-free income of $190,000, from an annual return of 6%, and receiving more that $3 million dollars of insurance coverage for two insureds on a "second-to-die" policy. Over the three years his capital actually increased from $1,007,442.79 to $1,052,633.44, and he received an additional distribution of $35,311.57 after the last insurance payment. The kicker was that the overall cost of the program, including investment management, life insurance and administration, was less than 2% a year.

An improved ten-year program was put on the table, which served up several new features as well as pegging the flexible premium variable-life policy to the Alger American portfolios. Doing so charged up the investment value of the program and added to its beauty as an investment beyond the charitable-gift component. As provided, the plan's assets were equally split between the Growth and Small Cap portfolios but allowed for portfolio switching with all dividends, interest and capital gains invested without tax liability.

The program showed projections assuming a 15% total annual return over 10 years that would have raised a million-dollar nest egg to $1,551,499 while giving $214,256 to charity. In point of fact, the returns would likely have been greater since Alger Growth and Small Cap averaged better than 15% during the same period.

David saw Charitable Giving as another one of Fred's brilliant but failed efforts at enlarging the business. He said, "The program may be very effective, but it is so complicated and so difficult to understand that I was fairly certain when I first saw it that no one would ever buy it. It didn't feel comfortable. It was too radical, too out in front, too leading-edge, too different."

As it turned out, Fred Alger didn't need to look so hard outside the firm for asset growth. Small Cap's victory in 1989 rekindled fervor in investing with Alger, and the subsequent inflow of money lifted the firm from its decline. After a long period of incubation, mutual-fund assets began to materialize.

It was a wild year for the fund and for David, who was responsible for the performance turnaround. "Nineteen eighty-nine started inauspiciously," he said. "Fred was furious at life in general and very angry with me, blaming our poor performance in 1988 on me. He was very abusive. He asked me to write a report outlining why the performance had been so bad. I was so close to quitting. I don't know why I even stayed. I was very upset.

"I wrote the report, and what I learned was that no stock which began the year with a price multiple greater than fifteen had beaten the market in 1988. There were no growth stocks that did well. It was just not our kind of market. After writing this report and really doing a lot of research, I presented that to him, and he, I think, grudgingly, accepted it.

"At that time the funds had virtually no money in them. We didn't know how to market the funds. We were running a sort of semi-analyst system. I was very much in control of it, but still we were kind of a hybrid. I think it was then that Fred decided to be re-involved in the stock market, to try and see if he could turn this around. And I took over direct management of the portfolios, especially the Small Cap fund, which wasn't a very big fund at all." Small Cap had started the year with barely $5 million.

David continued, "That year, a year delayed from the crash, growth stocks really came back from being badly hit. We were very lucky and very good in our stock picks. We had some amazing stocks in that Small Cap fund. The rest, as they say, is history. We had the number-one fund in America in 1989. We were up sixty-five percent. All of sudden we were set upon by the press, and I became an overnight folk hero, first on FNN, which is now CNBC, and all these talk shows.

"After that the funds began to ramp up on a lot of favorable publicity. The variable-annuity component came on after that. We had tremendously successful buildup of fund assets subsequent to that period."

In 1990 the Alger Fund portfolios continued to outpace the market averages. Small Cap had a total return of 6.69%, which was ahead of the S&P's 3.1% loss for the year and the Russell 2000 index of smaller companies' decline of 19.5%. Alger Growth meanwhile was ahead 2.19%, also beating the S&P. "A number of technicians are trying desperately to hold on to the fantasy that the market is going to go down. I think that's wrong," David advised a *Washington Post* reporter in an article which appeared on May 18, 1990.

There was more good news in 1991. Small Cap's total return for the year was a whopping 54.6%, ahead of the S&P by 24% and the Russell 2000 index by 8.5%. Growth returned 43.3%, which beat the S&P by 12.8%. Any way you sliced it, Alger was hot once again, and that was being translated into assets.

To bolster its presence among investment resellers, in 1991 Alger joined up with Fund/SERV, a service of the National Securities Clearing Corp. and a clearinghouse for mutual-fund purchases and redemptions and settlement and account registration by broker dealers and other financial professionals. The broker's work is simplified through a single repository for all transactions, which are then processed and delivered to the appropriate mutual-fund company. Fred Alger also signed up for Networking, another service from NSCC, which gathers account information from separate mutual-fund companies and consolidates the different parts in a customer's statement for broker distribution.

NSCC, which is jointly owned by the New York and American stock exchanges and the National Association of Securities Dealers, clears about 99% of all stock and bond trades and most of the mutual-fund transactions.

In 1992 David took over most of the investment decisions from Fred as he became the sole portfolio manager for all accounts. Very quickly he was recognized as the spokesperson for the firm. He was on the road a great deal to talk up the fund, "about twenty to thirty speeches to very large audiences around the country," he said. These were financial planners rounded up by American Skandia to get to know the Alger product.

On June 1, 1992, Alger rolled out a Balanced portfolio, comprising an initial weighting of 75% in equities and 25% in bonds. Money-market analyst and trader Steven Thumm handled the fixed-income component of the assets. Designed as an income-producing vehicle rather than a rocket for capital appreciation, the Balanced fund was somewhat of a stretch for Alger but necessary to enlarge its fund categories. It didn't raise any flags with its early performance and was up only 2.1% through September 1994.

Alger MidCap Growth started on May 25, 1993, and the Leveraged All Cap portfolio, now called Capital Appreciation, made its entry on November 1, 1993, fully seven years after the first Alger fund was launched. Leveraged All Cap also had a rocky start, returning only 2.5% through September 1994. Up 16.4%, MidCap Growth fared much better at first.

In terms of both assets and performance, Small Cap became the flagship of the Alger Fund. In February 1992 Lipper Analytical Services of Summit, New Jersey, conferred its top rank on Small Cap, as well as on Spectra and the Alger Money Market funds. Media praise was heaped on Small Cap with great frequency. In its November 2, 1992, issue *Investors Business Daily* named it second in its list of Top 25 Growth Funds for the years 1989 to 1991. In a mutual-fund survey to kick off 1993, *Money* magazine rated it first among "14 gems" in "The Only Load Funds You Need to Know About." Its five-year and three-year average return was listed at 29.5% and 16.7% respectively, despite a loss of 6.5% through November 30, 1992. In comparison, the average five-year return of no-load growth funds was 17%. By then Small Cap had $207 million in assets invested in 48 stocks, with a 39% weighting in technology. Small Cap was down as much as 20% in the middle of the year before rebounding briskly to just minus 4% at the close of 1992. That was weaker than the S&P by 3.2% and the Russell 2000 by almost 14.5%.

Small stocks and growth companies were severely out of favor during 1993 and 1994, and Fred Alger's performance reflected that reality.

While the acquisition of pension assets continued to elude the company, it was burning rubber with its investment performance—a fact that couldn't or shouldn't have gone unnoticed by the pension-consulting community.

In the March 1990 issue of *Corporate Finance*, CDA Investment Technologies ranked Fred Alger Management in sixth place, with a 10-year performance of 536% on its $908 million portfolio of pension assets.

In April 1991 CDA gave Fred Alger Asset Management, with an estimated return of 47.9%, the number-one spot among 540 professional money managers during the previous 12 months. Fred Alger Asset Management, it should be

Fred in front of his hand-crafted, custom-made, titanium gold Talbo, a sports car with French design pedigree.

recalled, is the separate entity that manages the firm's California clients. Fred Alger Management was in seventh place with a 37.5% advance for the year. Asset Management also ranked fifth in three-year performance with a total gain of 105.9%, which was not far behind the 111.2% return of leader Willoughby Holin & Renter of Plantation, Florida.

In the March 17, 1992, issue of *Financial World,* Fred Alger Asset Management made its "Best 25" list of investment advisers among institutional money managers. With its 72.1% return in 1991, it placed number 17, and its three-year gain of 152.9% raised it to the number six position.

By 1993 pension assets at Fred Alger had bulked up to $2 billion. That was leaps ahead of the $50 million mark, where it stood in 1977, but still just about half its pension jackpot in the eighties. That year CDA ranked Fred Alger Management fourth among 182 equity-investment advisers for its performance during the previous three years.

Fred Alger took a final, major step in its long drive toward total vertical integration in 1989 by establishing an in-house transfer agency for its own mutual funds. Transfer agency, normally performed by a commercial bank, is simply the maintenance of transactions in shareholder accounts and involves the electronic movement of securities between company ledgers. It represents the tail end of integration, since Alger is held back by law from physically holding the securities in the accounts, which is the responsibility of the custodial bank.

Fred Alger always intended to go the full integration route, but the opportunity to climb this last rung didn't materialize until after 1987. Next to reducing expenses, an important purpose of starting the transfer agency was to productively occupy those loyal employees who became surplus due to diminished brokerage activity ensuing from the crash and the reduction of pension assets. But neither of these was the main reason.

The company was literally pushed into doing the work for itself because its transfer agent, the Bank of New York, had fallen down on the job in terms of customer service. Improved technology, lower computer costs and the discipline of cross training made it possible for the firm to bring this activity in-house.

It was George Boggio and Robert Birnbaum, originally brought in as vice president of the Alger Fund, who kicked off the project. Setting it up in New Jersey was essential, since one needed to be a bank or a trust company as a transfer agent in New York. Once Fred gave it the green light, consultant Andy Shrever was brought in to initialize the transfer-agency process and see it through completion. This involved software evaluation, hardware acquisition, system maintenance, operation and control, technical support and troubleshooting. Shrever spent nine months with Fred Alger to finish the task and settled on Atlanta–based Phoenix Systems as the primary software supplier.

In the course of setting up the operation, Jim Connelly emerged as one of the firm's new leaders, in much the same way that retrofitting the company with the Cimco acquisition served to upgrade Joe Maida's skill set and prepared him for a much bigger role in the firm's trading business. Having been promoted to supervisor in 1988, Connelly—one of only two remaining Alger Fund telemarketers from 1986—was already moving up in the firm.

It was bad enough that George and Irwin were scheduled to leave the company in July. In the thick of organizing the transfer agency, Birnbaum decided to walk out in June. With the transfer-agency operation scheduled to go live in October, a huge management vacuum was created, with very little time left to complete the assignment. Seizing the opportunity, Connelly charged in.

"No one else had any transfer-agent background," said the genial and boyish Connelly. Jim himself was only slightly familiar with the process, having been the liaison between his former employer, Dreyfus, and its transfer agent, also the Bank of New York. Flying solo and by the seat of his pants, Jim took on the prodigious task of completing the necessary work by the October deadline. When things got tight, he asked Fred for an extra month's grace period. Fred said no. "He must have known better," Connelly reflected, "because we got it done. It was the hardest I've ever worked in my life. I worked for seventy-two days in a row, almost around the clock. A lot of nights I slept on the couch in New Jersey." Right on schedule, on October 31, 1989, Fred Alger closed out the Bank of New York as its transfer agent and brought all those transactions in-house.

Having proved himself through the experience, Connelly gained the confidence to tackle bigger roles in the company and, as senior vice president, heads the Alger Fund and launched the firm's marketing effort in Germany.

Meanwhile in August 1989, in conjunction with starting the transfer agency, the marketing of the mutual fund was moved out entirely from New York and shifted to New Jersey. The following month, the Alger High Yield Bond portfolio was closed for lack of interest. Frederick A. (Rick) Blum then took over finance and accounting, and Mike DiMeglio began running account administration. Both have since been promoted to senior vice presidents of the company.

Bringing the transfer agency in-house turned out to be one of Alger's shrewdest moves in terms of controlling the quality of its service to mutual-fund customers. It was also perfect timing. Shortly after the conversion the Bank of New York announced its intention to close down its transfer-agency business for open-end mutual funds.

Fred Alger has regularly received high marks for its transfer agency in the Satisfaction Survey of External Transfer Agents by *Dalbar*, a mutual-fund trade publication. In 1991–92 the magazine also rated it the lowest-cost transfer agency for mutual funds. Fred Alger became so adept at the work that it started receiving inquiries from other mutual-fund companies about using its transfer services.

With no outside transfer-agent charges, usually on a per-account basis regardless of the transaction size, Fred Alger can afford to waive high initial investment requirements. Just one dollar will get you into the Alger Fund, while the industry norm is between $1,000 and $3,000. Offering true dollar-cost averaging is unique among mutual-fund firms and provides a distinct marketing advantage for the company. In the April 1995 issue of *Mutual Funds* magazine Jim Connelly was featured wearing an Alger Bulls uniform and waving a fistful of dollar bills at the camera for the article, "No-Minimum Funds Let You Start With $1."

When Small Cap became number one and asset growth started picking up, Fred Alger was firmly in control of its costs and prepared for the clients and their money. Having the transfer agency paid dividends again when Fred Alger decided to extend the share classes in its mutual-fund portfolios in 1996 and 1997.

With the transfer agency under its belt, Fred Alger tightly commanded every aspect of the investment process: research, portfolio management, sales and distribution, administration, customer service, fund pricing, trading and clearing. While many firms find vertical integration to be an added burden after losing revenue, this was never the case at Fred Alger. The nucleus of integration kept the firm together while assets were eroding. It also ensures performance and profitability when its asset base is appreciating.

Fred Alger's transfer agency, Alger Shareholder Services, contributes a relatively small amount, about $1 million annually to its gross revenues. A good deal of that, however, is eaten up by expenses. Although it's not a big money maker, Greg said, "We always know who our shareholders are when they call with a question or problem."

In the bid to tamp down expenses subsequent to the erosion of assets after the 1987 crash, Fred Alger began converting its employees from a defined benefit to a defined contribution retirement plan. In doing so, it acted in accord with many U.S. corporations that were moving away from offering traditional pensions as a way of reining in employee costs. The configuration of the Alger employee offering served as a prototype of its product offering for this emerging sector of investing.

To satisfy its own account and, more important, augment its suite of products with yet another way of attracting institutional accounts, Fred Alger launched Alger Defined Contribution Trust in April 1993, a unique family of funds for 401(k) investing configured with the Growth, Small Cap, MidCap Growth and Leveraged All Cap portfolios. Diverging from the Alger Fund, DCT funds carry no sales charges, deferred or otherwise, no 12b-1 fees and low management fees.

Unlike a pension benefit plan, which promises workers a fixed income, usually a percentage of salary, during retirement and which is paid for solely by the employer, a defined contribution instrument, such as the popular 401(k) plan, allows employees to regularly contribute a percentage of their salaries toward investments, which then appreciate tax-free until retirement. An employee's fixed contribution may be matched completely or in part by the employer, and the retirement benefit is at-risk and wholly dependent on the return of the chosen investment.

Interest in 401(k) plans has grown because they allow higher contributions than pensions, offer greater appreciation, usually through a choice of mutual funds, and provide ultimate control of the assets to the participant. 401(k) plans are also portable and easily tracked in the financial pages. This nationwide shift towards 401(k) investing has been the primary trigger for the dramatic rise in mutual-fund assets during the nineties.

Also in 1993 Fred Alger teamed up with several firms which provided record-keeping services for companies offering 401(k) plans in addition to promoting the Alger DCT portfolios. *Pensions & Investments* reported such an agreement with First Trust Corporation of Denver, Colorado, on September 19, 1994. The article described First Trust's Daily Valuation 401(k) to be suited for employers with 100 to 2,000 employees. "Selection of the Alger Defined Contribution Trust will result in a trustee and record-keeping fee reduction of up to 50% of what the two firms would normally charge for their service," it said. First Trust was no stranger to Alger. One of the country's largest independent trustees of self-directed plans, it had been a longtime provider of trustee services for Alger's IRA and Keogh products. First Trust also offers a number of no-load mutual funds through Datalynx, its mutual-fund trading system.

Alger DCT also had similar relationships with William M. Mercer and Hewitt Associates.

The early nineties were a transitional time for the company. Fred Alger made it through this period by creative management and intelligent application of manpower and resources. As Fred was leaving the company, the end was in sight for nearly all of the company's pressing problems. Happily on the horizon was a surging influx of assets propelled by its improved distribution and an enhanced product line. The tide was turning in Fred's favor.

Heading into 1994 and for all that year, Fred's last full year at the helm of the company, the stock market weakened as interest rates rose to stifle and compress growth-company multiples. With shortsighted analysis, financial pundits were once again eschewing growth stocks for value and index-linked investing. But Fred Alger never wavered from its conviction in a slowing economy and multi-year declines in bond rates. Fred and David kept pounding the table that, soon to be released from artificial pressures, stocks would bolt mightily out of repressed price patterns during the coming years. No one could have guessed the total accuracy of their market prognosis. When stocks blasted off in 1995, Fred Alger was already strapped in and ready for the ride.

21 ✍

Power Shift

B Y THE CLOSING DAYS of 1995, some seven months after Fred had slipped away to Europe, the company had been almost completely recast in the style and personality of David Alger and manifestly revitalized by his leadership. Moving swiftly and effectively, David realigned the organization and refocused it toward new goals. The spectacular investment performance in his first year served as the vigorous pump for a broad set of initiatives that enlarged the firm's assets.

As a result of its transition, the firm acquired those characteristics that identify it, like an ideal Alger stock, as a company in the early stages of a positive life-cycle change—with creative management, a good product strategy and a favorable situation in a rapidly growing industry. Occupying a lead position in its niche category of growth-stock investment, it held the promise of expanding its earnings faster than the industry average.

In a mischievous twist of fate, it took Fred's departure to lead the company toward the fulfillment of Fred's vision. The second half of the nineties turned out to be the most fecund period in its history. Fred Alger sustained an expansion that challenged or surpassed the dazzling performance of Fred's early years.

The most obvious signal of the displacement of Fred's rule and the imprinting of David's style was the remodeling of the Maiden Lane offices.

The pink paint had always peeved him. "Why do we have a pink office?" he asked. "No one else I've ever known has ever had a pink office. Fred dotes on having eccentricities or idiosyncrasies of one sort or another in everything that we do. I think there's nothing wrong in having a normal-looking office like everybody else does, so that when your clients walk in, they don't say, 'I wonder why these guys have a pink office. What's this pink office supposed to be telling me?' Just a nice, attractive, conventional work space is fine." Besides, furnishings were already worn and didn't impart the rich image of a money firm.

So in September 1995 the pink walls were painted over, and a major renovation of the entry and common areas gave the company a swank new look. In the same effort to spruce up its corporate identity in accord with David's higher aesthetic standards, the firm also rebuilt its patio and garden atop the building.

Fred's portrait, which has hung on the twelfth floor of 75 Maiden Lane since 1993, survived the wholesale decorative changes. The painting faces the elevator, so that it's the first image that hits you when you step off the elevator and into the world of Fred Alger Management.

Wearing an open shirt and a blue blazer, Fred is isolated from the painting's darkly soft blue-green background and thoughtfully gazes at some point in the distance. Bespectacled, he has a concentrated look on his face and a hint of an emerging smile. A sheaf of documents is held tightly in his hands. Neither threatening nor inviting, the painting is like a mood ring for one entering the firm's doors. Angry for the analyst who has been derelict in his duties. Hopeful for an executive promoting his company to the firm as an investment.

The painting is the work of Fred's younger daughter, Nicole—a piece which she started in 1991 after returning from years of studying art in Italy. Fred sat for the painting for several months, and at first he was doubtful, even negative, about it. "For a while I didn't put it up," he said. "Some people didn't like it, and you wondered what sort of a statement it made." Sure, at first glance the likeness is not very strong. But it's an impressionistic work that grows on you. "The more I look at it, the more I like it," Fred added.

Though Fred's physical presence is less and less important to the firm's daily functioning, the portrait acts as a protective talisman, and a reminder, if one were needed, that the firm remains grounded in his energy.

The first Christmas dinner without Fred, at the Lotos Club on December 8, 1995, provided some evidence that a new era was under way at the firm—and this was despite the fact that Fred still choreographed the seating arrangements in absentia from Geneva. For the first time attendance was optional. This was not by design, but dictated by a lack of room in the dining hall to accommodate the enlarged head count of 145 guests. There was space for just 120. So employees were given a choice to pass on the event, an opportunity which many of the old-timers took. Those who were new to the firm never got to realize how strict a tradition attendance used to be.

As David and Josie, Greg and Eileen greeted the dinner guests at the staircase landing, Fred's presence was recalled but not so missed. Without him the event had a more relaxed quality, though as always a schedule was kept. Cocktails from seven to eight. Dinner at eight-fifteen, with sliced steak as the entree.

In years past there were usually several speakers—the Alger brothers and perhaps one or two of the partners. This time only David spoke. After the obligatory opening joke, he went religious. "When I was given my new job as CEO on January first, I asked God to give me a lot of wisdom and, if he could spare it, a little bit of luck. Somehow the Almighty seems to know more about what we need than we do, and so he gave me a tiny bit of wisdom and a whole lot of luck."

The market in 1995 had indeed been extremely kind to Fred Alger. Its mutual funds were all top performers, and Capital Appreciation was on the verge of concluding the year as the best mutual fund in the country. Assets under management were closing in on $5 billion—nearly double where they stood the year earlier and four times what they were just 10 years earlier. While the tax-exempt business remained under its 1985 mark, the firm's variable-annuity and mutual-fund segments had grown from $80 million to $3 billion. The company's net worth had, for the first time, closed the fiscal year comfortably above $100 million.

After describing all that he had to be thankful for, David began to commend the individuals involved in the company's achievements.

"The firm has never been as strong organizationally. Few executives have ever had as easy a transition of management as I have had. Greg has continued to run the administrative side of this business so flawlessly that there has quite literally been not one crisis, only the wonderful whir of a well-oiled machine running perfectly.

"Marketing is the heart of any business. Ray, of course, has done wonders in the variable-annuity area. We have greatly multiplied the number of insurance companies selling Alger products, and each one has become a center for asset gathering.

"The firm is blasting forward with a coherent new identity. All of the symbols which say to the outside world, 'We are capable, we are powerful and we are here to stay,' have been systematically revamped. Liz Murray worked very hard, and we enter 1996 with a new logo, new and improved marketing materials, and a consistency of corporate image throughout the company."

Several individuals were singled out for praise:

"Lisa Gregg for shooting the lights out in the convertible-bond management area while simultaneously doing a whole lot of economic research.

"Jim Connelly's entire organization for fielding an unprecedented level of calls—now up to one thousand one hundred a day—throughout the year.

"Jeanette Borras for taking over client services in an efficient and capable manner.

"The old-timers in the cage and other administrative areas: Mike DiMeglio, John Messina, Joe Pakenham, Walter Stevenson, Ron Curtis, Rosemary Kiernan and Isabella Coari, who have been a devoted and capable part of this organization since back in the days of the famous East-West softball games.

"We have two extraordinarily loyal and capable analysts, Ginger Risco and Ron Reel, who have been so much a part of our success in good and bad years. The same can be said for our older traders, Joe Maida, Artie Simon and Mort Frankel."

The last company honors were reserved for Dolores Costa, absent that evening, "who keeps the office running smoothly and was a saint and a rock during the construction phase in New York," and David's secretary, Louise Ulitto, "without whom quite literally I would never have begun to function in my new job."

About the remodeling of the firm's office on Maiden Lane, David said, "Our office in New York has been remodeled and given the professional and polished look that we deserve. Symbols are important. We are an impressive firm, and now we look like one."

Nothing beats being first in your class.

Alger ranked #1 mutual fund family for 1995*

Mutual Funds Magazine, March 1996

Alger Fund statement stuffer.

The final congratulation was personal. "I would also like to thank my wife, Josie, without whom I couldn't function, period!"

The next business was the introduction of new employees. In New York there were five new faces in research, including second cousin Alger Boyer, five additions to marketing and one in trading. Over in New Jersey eleven new people had joined in mutual-fund marketing, transfer services and corporate administration. Rosemary Kiernan's daughter, Karyn, was within that group. As their names were called, each one stood up to be recognized, which was another departure from tradition.

The last order was conferring the Man of the Year honors, modified first by David's remarks that "this is not a very politically correct term, as probably half of our ninety-four employees are women," and more important, then by distributing the award for the first time within separate areas of corporate responsibility.

Drawing from the symbolism of medieval battles when armies marched in three flanks, David had restructured the company into three wings with marketing and client services as the vanguard; portfolio management, research and trading as the center; and administration as the rear guard. Each group had its own Employee of the Year.

In the vanguard the prize went to Ray Pfeister, who "single-handedly created our marketing effort." The center winners were Seilai Khoo, Ron Tartaro and David Hyun. In the rear Greg Duch was called "indispensable" and the man "saddled with the hardest job of all, keeping the firm running smoothly despite having to deal with a new CEO and a variety of new requirements from the SEC, expanding technologies, new offices in New Jersey, renegotiation of our lease in New York, the reconstruction of our office in New York, the starting up of an offshore fund in Luxembourg, dealing with Fred's expatriation and more."

Lastly David asked the entire company to join him in a toast to Fred, whose "wisdom and decisions he made in the past, like getting into mutual funds, are the very fibers of all we do."

With the majority of stocks rising in price, 1995 was a grand year for most indices and many investors, but nowhere was it better than at Fred Alger. The year capped off with a victorious Capital Appreciation portfolio being named as the best mutual fund in the land.

In a nice bit of framing, this happened exactly 30 years after Fred captured the same crown and, coincidentally, also in his first year of running the company. David's success looks even sweeter when one factors in the competition. In 1965 the mutual-fund field had only 300 entries; by 1995 the number of equity funds alone had exploded to 2,221.

It may have been a name change that finally turned Cap App's performance around. Since its inception in November 1993 through September 1994, when it was called Leveraged All Cap—because, uniquely among Alger funds, it was constituted with the higher-risk strategy that allowed it to leverage up to 50% of its equity and to buy and sell options against the fund's owned securities—it registered a meager appreciation of 2.5%, and a decline of 2.2% in 1994. On March 27, 1995, the fund was reborn as Capital Appreciation.

The fund jumped off to a great start from the beginning, helped by its lean asset size of just under $3 million. On May 12, 1995, *USA Today* prefigured its ultimate triumph by trumpeting Alger's "three-bagger" with the best records since the Dow Jones average started its rise on November 23 of the previous year. Capital Appreciation was up 30%, Defined Contribution All Cap advanced 29.8%, and Defined Contribution Small Cap was boosted by a gain of 27%. David was quoted as predicting the Dow to rise soon above 5,000 based on cheap price-earnings ratios relative to strong earnings, falling long-term interest rates and a strong economy. The paper's only warning about Capital Appreciation was its high turnover rate of 232%.

By mid-year Alger Fund's Capital Appreciation stood first among 155 funds in its category with a gain of 45.4% versus the average appreciation in the group of just 16.6%. It was also tops among diversified stock funds, according to *Investors*

Business Daily. Key in its advance were large and correct bets on technology, specifically semiconductor and semiconductor capital-equipment companies, which constituted two-thirds of its portfolio. For example, Intel Corp. had zoomed 98%, and database company Informix had swelled 58%. Assets in the fund were varyingly reported at between $5.9 million and $7 million. David raised his target on the Dow to 5,600 and the Nasdaq index to 1,200.

Despite a summer rout in stocks, Capital Appreciation hardly slowed its pace. "We've been through sell-offs a lot worse than this in tech stocks," David said to reporter Doug Rogers in the July 20, 1995, issue of *Investor's Business Daily.* "It's never nice to lose money, but I don't think this is of long duration. These stocks are up a tremendous amount, and people have been waiting for an opportunity to take some profits. The correction was entirely predictable," he said. David was right. By the end of August, Capital Appreciation was ahead by 73% for the year.

After another brief market slump in September, Capital Appreciation fell back to a gain of 62%. Yet it was still the best growth fund and second overall only to Fidelity Select Electronics, a narrowly focused portfolio.

By the end of the third quarter, Capital Appreciation, then with $31.8 million in assets, a year-to-date advance of 78.3% and a one-year gain of 91.3%, resumed its leadership and was the number one in Morningstar's growth category. Alger Small Cap fund's 57.8% advance was good enough for fifth place in its aggressive growth list. Alger MidCap Growth, up 54.2%, was third in the capital growth group. The Alger Balanced fund, with a total return of 32.6%, was number three in Morningstar's equity division.

Capital Appreciation ended Alger's fiscal year on October 31 up 67.6% for 1995 against the S&P 500's rise of 26.4%. In ten months it had purchased 65 companies, sold 55 firms and held 21 for the duration.

Nearing the finish line in 1995, *Smart Money* magazine sent Robert Saffian to cover the race that was shaping up between Alger Capital Appreciation, Govett Smaller Companies and Perkins Opportunity to be number one in the country. Two weeks before the end of the year, tech stocks got winded and Capital Appreciation stumbled out of the lead—dropping back about 15 percentage points from its high on December 4—before another smart turnabout. Even as a first-place finish again seemed likely, David was not without anxiety. "I'm not counting anything until the last day," he said. "The stock market god is very vindictive. I don't want to jinx it." With five days left, he was confident enough to slip away for a short holiday in Jamaica. He was back in the office, however, for the last day of trading, on December 29, to savor the fund's victorious crossing of the finish line with a total return of 78.6%.

Perkins Opportunity at $68 million was second with 70.3%, and Govett Smaller Companies followed with 69%. Saffian's article, "Count Down," which chroni-

The Alger Growth Fund has consistently received Morningstar's top, five-star ranking.

cled the critical last month and the furious jockeying by the three fund managers en route to the finish line, appeared in the February 1996 issue of *Smart Money* magazine.

Respectful of David's punitive stock market god, the firm was restrained in its celebration. Of course, it spread the word of its victory. But success passes quickly on Wall Street, where the game begins anew on the first trading day of every year, and smaller battles are fought for prizes every quarter, month, week, day and even hour.

Qualifying his success in the August 1995 issue of *Investment Advisor,* in an article titled, "They Don't Call It Alger Growth Fund for Nothing," David revealed, "I'd like to tell you that it's because I'm really the smartest person that ever managed money, but I don't really think that's the case. There are really three reasons. One is, we're well organized. We have a specific system and we have our analysts. Two, we're very focused. We're not trying to be investment bankers or doing anything else. And we're not playing the options market or foreign securities. We're only interested in American domestic growth stocks. And three, we work very hard, with good research and a lot of analysts following a lot of companies.

"I just heard a quote from Thomas Edison, something to the effect of, 'Opportunity comes all the time. Unfortunately, it's usually dressed in overalls and looks like work.'"

Capital Appreciation was not alone in its success. Nineteen ninety-five was a breakthrough year for Fred Alger in nearly all respects. David had a hunch it would be a good year, based on the decennial cycle, which favors the stock market in years ending with the number five. That assumption was sustained by the revaluation and resurgence, throughout the year, of growth stocks—Fred Alger's forte. As Fred and David had predicted, once liberated from their tightly compressed multiples, stocks vaulted upward with a momentum that continued for several years. In line with this, Alger had "one halacious year" in its overall performance.

Among the Alger funds, the Growth portfolio is perhaps the best and most enduring proxy for the firm's long-term outperformance of the stock averages. In a fall survey by *Institutional Investor* magazine, Don Phillips, president of Morningstar, said, "There is nothing about this fund that is not spectacular. David Alger is an extreme, die-hard growth investor, and that's extremely rare."

Based on cumulative total returns through September 30, 1995, Lipper Analytical Services ranked Alger Growth as follows:

Number seven out of 585 growth funds, with a 46.1% gain for the year-to-date period. Number five among 549 growth funds, advancing 48.9% for the one-year period. Number 10 out of 320 growth funds, gaining 25.7% for the three-year period. Number 15 among 232 growth funds, advancing 25.3% for the five-year period.

"When it comes to old-fashioned growth investing, Alger Growth Fund delivers the goods—and then some," remarked *Investment Advisor* in August 1995.

Kiplinger's Personal Finance Magazine reported a clean sweep for the Alger Fund in its 1995 tally through August 21. In its aggressive growth list, Capital Appreciation was number one with a one-year gain of 98.9% and a year-to-date rise of 76.3%. Small Cap, ahead 69% in one year and with a 57.7% jump for the year-to-date, was in sixth place. In the long-term growth category, MidCap Growth grabbed second place with a one-year return of 62.2% and a year-to-date advance of 50%. Growth finished tenth with a 45.7% yearly rise and a 48.2% increase during the year. The Balanced portfolio came in third in the magazine's growth and income group by bouncing up 29.9% in one year and 28.6% year-to-date.

The funds ended 1995 not far from behind those positions and ahead of the averages in their respective categories. Small Cap closed up 48.9%. MidCap Growth advanced 46.5%. Growth was ahead by 38.4%, and the Balanced fund rose 31.3%.

The stock averages provide some insight on this gonzo performance. Between 1900 and 1995 the average annual return in stock investments was 9.78%. From 1950 to 1995 it was 12.42%. Even during the strong advances between 1990 and 1995 the average return was only 13%. And while the stock averages were up nicely from 1995 to 1997, most equity model portfolios and investment gurus failed to top the performance of the indexes.

Alger's sizzling returns caught the eyes of investors, and assets began pouring into the funds as well as other Alger investment products and accounts. Overall fund sales were about $1 million a day. In the 1995 fiscal year Alger Fund assets jumped from $558 million to $898 million. Insurance-related accounts rocketed from $640 million to $1.62 billion. The pension business grew from $1.4 billion to $1.8 billion. Even the Alger Money Market Fund saw cash rising to $186 million from $163 million the previous year. Finally, the German funds also started shaking the money tree.

After a couple of unremarkable years when its growth stocks were languishing, Fred Alger had the look of a player in the zone. Sure, the entire market was also up stunningly for the year, and mutual-fund inflows, breaking all records, provided the boost beneath those stocks. But no fund family racked up such an outstanding scorecard.

In the October 1995 issue of *Smart Money,* in an article entitled, "The Hot Hand at Alger," reporter Nelson Wang wrote, "Alger likens his funds to a football team that falls behind by 20 points after three quarters, then scores 50 in the fourth quarter to trounce the opposition." Wang continued, "David Alger accounts for four of the ten best-performing funds this year. No other fund family or manager even comes close."

As president, CEO and chief investment officer, David saw his way clear when he took over the company. His were worthy, aggressive goals, if only too ambitious, and he was not timid about articulating them. In its flashy promotional CD-ROM that was distributed to Alger's financial consultants and prospective investors, he committed the firm to the mission of reaching $10 billion in assets by the year 2000 and to $20 billion quickly after that, and performing as "the best money manager in America over a hundred-year period."

While the gospel according to David Alger, when it comes to stocks and investments, is pretty much taken from his brother—after all, he studied at the feet of the master—his views about running the company went a different way. Specifically, he sought to reposition the company to be more in line with Wall Street. Among other things, this meant changing the way in which the mainstream investment community viewed the firm—from a reflection of Fred Alger's personal record and dominant role—and reshaping it in his own, more conservative image. "I would like to do things a little more conventionally than in the past," David affirmed as he took charge. "I don't have Fred's need to be innovating at every turn. I believe there is a lot of virtue to doing things in a way that is generally accepted to the world. This firm may look a lot more like a conventional money-management firm, albeit a bigger money-management firm."

It was not a radical reconstruction or deconstruction David was attempting; rather he endeavored to add some refinement and stability to a system that was already running quite well. The $64,000 question was whether he could do this without canceling out some of the qualities that had made the firm so remarkable.

"When I first came in," David explained, "I had my list of all the things that weren't functioning right. You bitch and moan secretly about what Fred is not doing right, what you would do if Fred turned it over to you. I immediately put those things into effect.

"For example, I have put in place a completely different structure. It may not be apparent yet how different it is. But it is very different. It is based on my view that this company has three distinct parts: investing, client service, and marketing and administration.

"I have in my mind a medieval army, which always had three battles in a combat formation. These are the three battles of my army. Each battle had a leader, and frequently the king himself would lead one of the battles. By the same token I am the king, and I also lead one of the battles, the investing one.

"This is a much more formal management structure than we ever have in the past. Prior to this we've had the touch-football style of management, which is 'everybody go out and I'll throw a pass.' Fred was the quarterback and receiver and two or three of the linemen. If we're going to build this into a bigger business, I think we need a real structure. I put one in place. I'm more comfortable with it."

Another important aspect of David's leadership was setting the tone for the firm's office culture. Unlike Fred who managed from a distance, David makes his presence known. "In the Middle Ages it was incredibly important for a king to be seen at the head of his troops," he explained. "It was expected that he would be out front leading the way. I believe in a high level of interaction in terms of walking around and seeing what people are doing and encouraging them."

In practical terms, David spends about 50% of his time in the investing side, 30% on marketing and 20% devoted to running the business.

When David assumed control, he considered marketing to be the unstable third leg of the company and vowed to fix it. "We have been hobbling along on two and a quarter legs for years," said David. "We've had a stool that's basically been tipping over. We have a strong investment side and a strong administrative side, but no marketing at all, and this was because Fred wasn't too interested in that area. My main mission in life is to get us into the twentieth century as far as marketing is concerned."

That marks a big change for a company that once operated on the assumption that its strong record would automatically make it attractive to investors. In the increasingly competitive environment for investment assets, such an attitude did not work.

First on the list and requiring the most initiatives was the effort to increase Fred Alger's share of pension investing. "The pension assets have been unbelievably undernourished. We haven't bounced back at all since we got flattened in 1988," said David.

This was achieved by doubling the firm's manpower dedicated to that sector by hiring two sales specialists as vice presidents of marketing. With their addition to Matthew A. Gotwols, the firm finally had a respectable strike force to fight for the pension business. To enhance their enterprise, the firm configured a separate office on the tenth floor of Maiden Lane when New York City's Department of Housing Preservation and Development vacated the space in 1996.

The game plan was to attack the largest strongholds of money in America, which number around 700 corporate pensions, endowments and foundations with over a billion in assets. Marketing chief Ray Pfeister saw the struggle in terms of building rapport with the consultants who make up the list of recommended money managers while maintaining relationships with the individuals and committees who have the authority to act on those recommendations. It means knocking on doors and putting the firm out there at every opportunity.

As president of the company in 1995, David had to face several new roles and responsibilities which had previously been left to Fred. One of these was developing the firm's independent forecast, or big picture, of the economy. Unlike Fred's market opinions, which were shared mostly with its institutional clients and only sporadically among its distributors, David implemented regular distribution of his views in a newsletter format that served as a forum for his investment ideas. The "Alger Market & Economic Review" serves as an effective marketing tool to reinforce David's presence and credibility, and keep him in close touch with mutual-fund resellers. This pipeline to its independent thinking is also quick to reassure investment dealers during times of market slowdowns and crisis.

The "Review" goes out by fax to the firm's brokers, financial planners and media contacts about once every six weeks. It is also available on the Alger web site and as a recorded message on a toll-free phone line. Written in a conversational style, it provides a comprehensive and reasoned exposition of the myriad factors affecting market movements, like fluctuating interest rates, foreign turmoil, political change, earnings estimates and Federal Reserve action. Frequently the report includes David's market predictions—often boldly articulated and controversial. So far he's been more right than wrong.

In his February 28, 1995, message David made a strong case for an ebullient stock market. The factors behind this, he explained, were: rising adjustable-rate mortgages, a positively sloping yield curve, housing-sector weakness, falling auto demand, problems in Mexico and the budget imbalance. "We expect as the year progresses our stocks will do very well, absolutely and relatively to the market," he said, "Nor do we expect recession will be evident either late this year or in 1996." When he wrote this, the Dow had just crossed 4,000. It ultimately ended the year 25% higher. The Nasdaq's move was even more impressive as it passed 1,000 for the first time.

Three days after the 1995 Christmas dinner, David forecast in the "Alger Review," "The market is at an unprecedently low level given where interest rates are trading . . . . If good earnings levels can be maintained, the stock market should see record highs next year: 6,000 seems to be a nice round, attainable number." The January 10, 1996, issue of the "Alger Review" reaffirmed that prediction. "The stock market will have a good year, reaching 6,000 at some point during the year," David said emphatically. On October 14, 1996, the Dow Jones finally lived up to his promise, and by the end of the year it had exceeded 6,500.

Starting 1996, David was at the top of his game. His fund was number one. He was bullish as far as the eye could see. Bolstered by his outlook, he floated a Valentine greeting which departed from the "Review" format and went out as a special message from David D. Alger, President, Chief Executive Officer and Chief Investment Officer of Fred Alger Management, Inc. It was called "Ten Reasons to Be Extremely Bullish about the Stock Market." In brief:

1. The economy will grow at a slow but positive rate.
2. Inflation is still low.
3. The market is undervalued compared to both long and short interest rates.
4. The market is cheap within its own historical range.
5. Fund flows are incredibly strong.
6. Politics are favorable.
7. Good market years come in bunches.
8. Lagging growth stocks suggest the market has a long way to go.
9. Demographics favor financial markets.
10. Foreign investors are moving into the U.S. market.

In the September 17, 1996, edition of the "Review," David went further out with a calculation that the Dow average would hit 10,000 by the end of the decade. David explained:

> I believe that earnings per share of the Dow will be approximately $365 in 1996. If the economy is able to grow at a 3% rate in GDP, I believe the Dow can grow its earnings at a 10% rate. This should bring earnings in the year 2000 to about $535 per share. The median relationship between the earnings yield on the averages and the long bond has been 75% over the fifteen years. Based on this number, given a 7% long bond (which would presume a 3% inflation rate and 3% real rate of return), the market should have a multiple of 19x. This, multiplied by its earnings, gives the Dow a value of 10,190.

In his Christmas 1996 message David proposed that he "was comfortable with the Dow crossing at least 7,000." The Dow average made it past 7,000 on February 13, 1997. David was proving that his market prognostications were at least as good as Fred's.

With the Dow and other averages climbing beyond all expectations, on June 18, 1997, he offered a new target of 8,000. When that was fulfilled exactly a month later, on July 22, 1997, he wrote, "We believe the market could still go higher this year. I am not willing to forecast that the market will definitely go to 8,500, but I do think that this is not an impossibility." The Dow hit 8,340 on August 6 before deflating almost 10% due to violent cross-currents from Asia during the following two months.

Even then David was constructive on the market and exhorted investors to be patient. He reasoned:

> Presently the S&P 500 has an earnings yield of 73% of the long bond. This is very slightly below its fifteen-year average of 77%, which suggests that the market is a bit more expensive than average. Based on our analysis, the model shows that the market could appreciate 46.2% or decline 26.9%. Therefore the stock market is favorably valued in relation to the bond market . . . . I believe that there is a better than even chance that the long bond will close the year with a yield below 6%. Should this occur, the possibility exists that the stock market will increase 5% from here, which means that the Dow could close above 8,400.

Saying that David "has proved stunningly right on the market," Leslie Norton included these "Alger Review" comments verbatim in her "Fund of Information" column in the October 27, 1997, issue of *Barron's*. While his hope for stocks failed to materialize during the year—though it did come about in 1998—his projection for bond yields was amply realized.

Among institutional clients, though Fred Alger has always shown up well in terms of performance, marketing the firm has always been an uphill climb because of its retention of brokerage commissions. While that is not about to change, there is now an opportunity for the firm to seem more accommodative with David at its head, since he's always been more appealing to the investing community.

With the Alger Fund, unlike in 1986 when it tried to drive sales by consumer demand, in 1995 the company focused on its distribution to investment consultants and financial planners. Also unlike the past, when the firm counted too much on its performance to carry the Alger message of investing, this time it made sure that the brokers and their customers heard the Alger story loud and clear through an attractive and contemporary marketing presence.

Slick, oversized, glossy color brochures and folders were mailed to 5,000 brokers who had some history of soliciting Alger products. The hope was to bolster the existing 400 broker agreements with a larger sales force. As in the best marketing, Alger was putting the sizzle ahead of the steak, which was quite different from the way it had previously handled its corporate messages. The firm had learned the lesson that performance alone isn't enough. As Fred put it, "If buyers of money management bought substance, we'd have every penny in the world under management."

With the brochure, word went out of the firm's service-oriented measures, such as the Alger Fund-Fax, which provided the "Alger Market & Economic Review," a Fund-at-a-Glance monthly snapshot of portfolio performance and holdings, and Alger in the News, a clipping service of Alger mentions in the media. The Alger Access System, its vaunted toll-free phone service, which enables access to a panoply of information including a transaction review and account balance of their clients' accounts, was also touted in the mailing.

Alger had prepared an equivalent sleek package for the reps' customers and offered them these client kits free for their distribution. It was through the broker and representative network that the firm saw its best chances for increasing clients in the Alger Fund, which then numbered around 75,000.

Next the firm commissioned a beautiful new Alger Fund booth for industry trade shows and distributor-sponsored vendor fairs. The firm cranked up its publicity machine in these events by sponsoring lunches, participating in special presentations and handing out promotional items like clocks to raise its brand awareness. Previously limiting itself to fewer than ten such conferences annually, Alger now pushes itself to dozens more of these affairs.

Another marketing coup for Alger is its impressive CD-ROM presentation.

First issued in 1996, it fully explains the company's investing philosophy and process and describes its mutual-fund portfolios and their performance. The colorful show is designed around a sailing metaphor, with a mariner's global compass guiding the viewer through the menu and video messages from David seen through a mariner's spyglass.

In March 1997 Alger moved its digital front another step forward with a new web address at www.algerfund.com. Constructed by the same team that produced the CD-ROM, Multimedia Solutions of Englewood Cliffs, New Jersey, and Olga Lorenc Design Group in Harrington Park, New Jersey, the site carries over many of the design conceits, features and images of the CD-ROM and the corporate brochures. The web design employs the latest Java tools and multimedia utilities to provide a dazzling array of company data and offers an opportunity to request information and communicate with the firm directly via e-mail. Even more information on the company is accessible on the Web than the CD, including daily updating of the funds' net-asset values and a detailed view of the portfolios' current holdings.

A second phase of this ambitious project began in the summer of 1997. This gave users a chance to graphically compare the results of a hypothetical investment in any of the Alger funds against the performance of appropriate benchmark indices. Alger Online was already preparing for a third phase, enabling brokers to conduct secured transactions, engage in interactive chat sessions, view client accounts and their overall positions at Alger.

Alger's product support for the fund uses service and information rather than raw marketing to promote the Alger cause. David frequently presides over a national teleconference for brokers which is accessible toll-free. Tapes of his television appearances are likewise distributed at no cost, and transcripts of his market opinions are available both on-line and by phone.

Only rarely does Alger send sales material directly to its account holders, and these are usually stuffed with the quarterly statements. To advise them that Capital Appreciation was first in the class in 1995, it sent a pamphlet with a picture of a geeky-looking kid, with heavy glasses and a shirt-pocket protector, offering an apple in his outstretched hand. Later in 1996, when the company rechristened Alger Defined Contribution Trust as Alger Retirement, it carried over this theme by using a graphic representation of an apple as its logo. In contrast, after Small Cap's success in 1989, the statement stuffer was printed on a die-cut paper insert in the shape of a number one. "#1 in Total Return for the Past Three Years," the headline announced.

After a lengthy absence from advertising, Alger tested the waters in 1995 with a few full-page insertions in supportive financial trade publications like *Financial Planning, Investment Advisor* and *Registered Rep.* It also made the scene in *Mutual Funds* magazine with ads for Spectra Fund after it had been converted into an

open-ended instrument in 1996 and became available through superstore brokerages like Schwab OneSource and Fidelity FundsNetwork. This effort was nowhere
near the scale of the 1986 advertising but nonetheless provided respectable results.

Now the firm is drawing strength from the realization that the best advertising is by word of mouth, and the best word of mouth comes through its brokers
as well as getting good press coverage for its performance.

The advertising had some positive effect. When Spectra became an open-
ended fund in February 1996, it held $3.2 million in investment assets. By the
summer of 1997 that figure had grown to $54.5 million and was climbing rapidly.
At that time it was reported that Alger Associates had a 36% stake in Spectra and
that David Alger controlled 21% of Alger Associates.

Fred Alger's new vibrancy is best reflected in the way the firm has started using
media outlets to present itself to the world. After its bruising from the press
between 1986 and 1990, Alger retreated from publicity for most of the early
nineties. To illustrate, the only Alger mentions in *The New York Times's* 1993 index
of articles were the engagement and wedding announcements for Fred's daughter Alexandra.

David changed all that. With him running the show, the firm very quickly
turned from feeling media shy to acting media savvy. The Alger name started
turning up everywhere. In *USA Today, Barron's, Fortune, The Wall Street Journal,
Kiplinger's Personal Finance Magazine,* to name a few. As he told reporter Jack Egan
when he was featured in *Worth* magazine's cover story, "The Five Most Aggressive Fund Managers and Why You Want One in Your Corner," "I talk to everyone
in the press because it's good for business."

Most useful in promoting the firm's record were his numerous appearances
as a guest commentator and analyst on financial news network CNBC's segments
and shows like *Squawk Box, Taking Stock, Power Portfolio, Hot Hand* and *The Money
Club.* His normal way of being introduced, as "famous Fred's brother," has gradually tapered off. The television medium is extremely generous to David. He has
a great delivery and comes across as smart and prescient. Alger stocks have jumped
a point or more on his recommendation.

As the public face of Fred Alger, David has done much in three years to obliterate past media failures and end the firm's disenchantment with the press. Today
Alger easily tolerates negative mentions in the press. For instance, after naming
Alger the best fund family in 1995, *Mutual Funds* magazine ranked it as next to
worst in 1996. With an average gain of 10.1%, the Alger portfolios edged the last-
place finisher by just 1/10 of a percentage point, while the median fund family
gain was 17.8% and the best complex, Portico Funds, advanced an average of
25.8%.

"Our analysts made a few very bad calls," David said unapologetically. He promised a turnaround in 1997. "We have enhanced our research staff, and created a separate team to bolster analysis of small-cap growth companies." At another point he explained, "Our history has been one of having two mediocre years followed by a spectacular year, and it tends to work for us. Last year was awful. I'm not shrinking from it. But values are there for a spectacular growth-stock market within the next two years."

For 1996 all Alger funds registered gains, but these were below the stock averages. Balanced fund was up 6.63%, Growth ahead by 12.3%, MidCap Growth increased 12% and Small Cap popped 4.17%. Partly due to its cautious avoidance of leverage in 1996, Capital Appreciation gained only 13.8%

Furthermore, when the magazine revised its ranking system in 1997, by awarding stars to fund families on several measures of merit—five stars for the best—instead of just calling out yearly performance, the six funds in the Alger family received five stars.

The great value of Alger is ultimately and conclusively found in its long-term performance. For the three years to July 1, 1997, Kiplinger rated Alger Capital Appreciation, with an average gain of 40.6% and assets of $183.3 million, its number-one fund. In mid-1997, according to Morningstar, Alger Growth, with $321 million in assets, averaged a 25% gain for the preceding three years; MidCap Growth returned an average of 27% and had $161 million in assets, and Small Cap's average return was 21%, as the fund stood at $508 million.

Spectra Fund's average return of 32.5% in the same time frame earned it twelfth place. Comparatively, the average stock fund gained 23.4% annually over the three years and 12.9% over ten. The S&P was up an average of 28.8% in the previous three years and 14.6% in ten.

The company's latest advance didn't occur in a vacuum. Fred Alger was a beneficiary of the recent wave of American prosperity and the consequent rapidly accelerating and dynamic climate in mutual funds and other financial-services industries. In 1997, for example, more than 40% of American households—about 37 million—owned at least one mutual fund, and the mutual-fund industry, mostly through tax-advantaged retirement programs like the 401(k) and other defined contribution accounts, is the vehicle of choice for savings and retirement. Holding about a third of all outstanding shares in the market, mutual funds are the second largest segment of the financial marketplace. In 1996 and 1997 net inflows into mutual funds averaged $19 billion a month, and mutual fund assets ended the period at $4.2 trillion.

But it was not only the number of mutual funds—nearly 7,000 in 1997—that accounted for the industry's upsurge. The frantic pace of mergers and acquisitions involving mutual funds raised the profile of the entire financial-services sector as much as it increased the premiums paid for management assets. Spurred by fears of rising costs associated with winning and keeping accounts in an increasingly competitive environment, mutual-fund companies began seeing consolidation as their only chance of maintaining service levels and profit margins. At the same time large banks started picking off funds for their own portfolios in the drift toward creating one-stop financial-services supermarkets.

The binging commenced in 1993, when Mellon Bank Corp. gobbled $80 billion of assets in Dreyfus Fund, and the feeding hasn't stopped since.

Boston–based Cerulli Associates Inc. tallied up 22 such transactions in 1995 for $160.74 billion in assets. In 1996 Ivesco PLC acquired AIM Management Group for $1.6 billion in a stock-and-cash deal whose $150 billion in combined assets made it the world's twelfth largest fund. The value of industry consolidation grew and extended to brokerage firms in 1997, with the pairings either through mergers or acquisitions of Morgan Stanley and Dean Witter, Bankers Trust and Alex Brown, SBC Warburg and Dillon Reed, BankAmerica and Robertson Stephens, Nations Bank and Montgomery Securities, and CIBC Wood Gundy and Oppenheimer.

The message from this swelling of mergers and acquisitions was that the economies of scale made such consolidation essential for profitability and survival.

Running counter to trend, however, Fred Alger became even more adamant about its independent future. Its strong capital structure, full integration and diversified revenue streams kept it fairly immune from the evolving conditions in the marketplace that were impinging on other mutual-fund complexes.

In closing her August 7, 1995, Barron's article "A Call to Glory, David Alger Takes Over Fred's Firm," Leslie Norton suggested that, with roughly $4 billion in assets, David's best option might be to sell the firm out for a prospective price of $80 million. Two years later, when Fred Alger's assets were approaching $9 billion, applying her 2% multiple to the company showed its buyout value to be $180 million. Not bad for two years' work, which partly explains why the Algers are so bullish about keeping their own company.

The way things are shaping up in the financial services industry, Fred Alger's assets and value are likely to grow.

America's pension assets are expected to reach $7.4 trillion in 1998. 401(k) accounts are set to cross $1 trillion by 1999. There is nearly twice as much money in stock funds as there is in insured savings accounts. From this vantage point and with the virtue of hindsight, it appears that Fred Alger has made a lot of smart moves to arrive at its current lead position in the mutual-fund industry.

David expressed this optimism. "In a dollar-based world economy the U.S. is more supremely powerful than ever in its history. From an economic standpoint we've successfully colonized the world. Foreigners will over time invest more and more in the U.S. through mutual funds. The industry has a beautiful future ahead of it."

As a glut of new funds pushed its way into the market, one might suppose it to be unproductive for Alger to raise the number of its portfolios. Not so. Without any additional research activity and equipped with in-house transaction processing, the company expanded its distribution channel with the complementary extension of its existing product line. Five Alger funds were made available in two new classes aimed at satisfying the diverse commission and distribution models of brokers, financial planners and other resellers in the investment community.

With the exception of the Money Market portfolio, in the fall of 1996 the existing funds were designated as Class B shares and retained their original expense profile, with 12b-1 fees and vanishing deferred redemption charges, and commission structure.

Then in December of that year Alger Fund introduced a new A Class of shares for the same portfolios, which is sold with a front-end charge of 4.75%, instead of the deferred sales load. These shares do not apply 12b-1 fees and therefore obtain lower expense ratios. Class A shares were geared specifically for fee-based planners and wrap, or flat-fee, accounts marketed by large brokerage institutions for whom the sales charges are waived. Additionally the 4.75% fee accrues only to fund purchases up to $100,000. The percentage decreases for fund purchases above that amount until $1 million, when it is completely eliminated.

Alger's Class A shares effectively discount the sales charge and are appropriate for less patient investors. Paying a 4.75% fee at point of purchase can be cheaper than exiting with a 12b-1 charge and a rear-end load. Alger also benefits from this vehicle because it doesn't need to advance commissions to resellers and then wait to recoup the amount over time, as it does with B shares.

Another variant, called Class C shares, was added in 1997. It differs from A and B in its no-load structure and in the way that brokers are compensated for fund sales, by a smaller 1% commission at inception and a .75% trailing commission. This class was developed for the broker market beyond fee-based planners. Many fund resellers who had previously cleared trades through broker-dealers were moving their account management to institutional investment warehouses in firms like Linsco Private Ledger, Waterhouse Securities, Raymond James Financial, Walnut Street Securities and Jack White & Co. In order to get on their menus, a fund had to be without any front or back sales load. Additionally, these shares appeal to brokers who have faith in their ability to retain clients and the inevitability of capital appreciation. With Class C, Alger opened up an entirely new market.

Parsing the funds this way also gave Alger Funds distribution through mega-consumer retail outlets like Citicorp Investment Services, Chase Bank, Charles Schwab and Fidelity.

Once it had broadened its product options, Fred Alger filled in the gaps with a direct marketing campaign to independent brokers in organizations like the

Institute of Certified Financial Planners and the International Association of Financial Planning.

Additionally, the Alger Fund instituted a three-for-one split in the net asset value of its B class Growth and Small Cap portfolios in September 1995 to make their lower price more attractive to the average fund buyer. While raising the potential for asset inflows, increasing the number of shares also reduces the expense ratio—operating costs and management fees—of fund ownership.

For the most part, except for the low minimum $1 initial investment option, the Alger Fund provides investors with service and support features that are now considered standard in the industry, including: automatic investment-plan deductions; toll-free telephone access for account balance, transaction history and price-yield information; free check writing in the Money Market portfolio, with a minimum of $500; the purchase and selling of funds by phone; reinvestment of dividend and capital gains distributions, including cross investment to another Alger portfolio; and free portfolio exchanges.

For the Christmas dinner on December 13, 1996, Fred Alger was not about to repeat its mistake of the previous year by leaving out some of its employees—now over 100—due to lack of space. Obviously the firm had outgrown the Lotos Club. So it moved the event to the Pratt Mansion, one of three in a Beaux Arts compound on Fifth Avenue and 84th Street owned by the Marymount School.

Attendance was large and boisterous, packing two open, ground-level rooms where cocktails were served. It was apparent that familiarity would one day become a casualty of the firm's rapid and substantial growth. The way it was so informal, one might have mistaken it for a Wall Street Christmas party rather than one of Fred Alger's dinners. Even the meal started well behind schedule. The cliques of office friends worked their way to the upstairs dining hall to settle at their assigned tables. The huge room became congested quickly.

Toward the end of dinner David gathered himself at the podium to deliver his annual address. Perhaps mindful that 1996 was subpar performance year, he assumed the rousing tone of a cheerleader and rallied the firm around its achievements, notably its healthy 78% top-line growth and the increase of assets to $7 billion. David also repeated that his aim was to make the firm the best money manager in America over a hundred years.

Providing a link to the firm's heritage, he showed the 30-second Dragster commercial that had been produced for the ill-fated advertising campaign of a decade earlier. But that moment from the past seemed oddly out of context in his forward-looking presentation. After recognizing the usual suspects who regularly contribute to the firm's success, he announced the Man of the Year in the three divisions. So many new people had joined the firm, this year he dispensed with singling out each one for attention.

David closed his remarks optimistically with an illustration he often makes to prove the tremendous potential of stock and mutual-fund investing and therefore his confident faith in the future of the company. The same thesis found its way into the December 26, 1996, issue of *USA Today* in an article called "Aggressive Alger fund undaunted by off year."

"In 1972 I bought a brownstone in the Village for eighty thousand dollars," David said, "Today that town house would be worth at least one point six million. The house appreciated more than twenty times. The same is true for other hard assets. What you pay for a shirt today would have bought you a suit in 1972. What you pay for a suit you could have gotten a car."

In 1972 the Dow Jones industrial average was creeping around 1,000. By 1996 it was only six times as high. "Stocks are just starting to catch up," he added. "Some valuations might be on the high side, but they're not extreme. . . . Growth stocks tend to do their best in periods of relative slack earnings and can generate earnings gains independent of the economy. We believe we may have a trampoline effect next year."

The party disbanded abruptly after David finished his talk with thanks and congratulations all around, and good wishes for the new year. It was close to midnight when the building finally emptied.

As the stock market peaked during the summer of 1997, David received word that the firm's assets had crossed $8 billion. Just ten months into the company's accounting year, revenues had already surpassed the previous record year in 1995, and signs were pointing toward the most profitable year in the firm's history.

David's promised turnaround in the firm's investment performance did materialize, especially in 1998 when all the Alger funds, except for Small Cap, trounced the S&P average of 28.56%. Growth was up 44.07%, Capital Appreciation rose 37.38%, Mid Cap jumped 31.09%, and even the Balanced fund advanced 32.49%. Small Cap Fund's relatively meager spurt of 9.91% far exceeded its peer-group benchmark, the Russell 2000 Growth's rise of just 1.23%. Spectra Fund ended the year with a gain of 47.94%, while its asset size swelled to nearly $300 million. In the first quarter of 1999, investments began to pour into Spectra when its 10-year performance earned for David Morningstar's title as the best mutual manager for the previous decade, both at the close of 1998 and after the first quarter in 1999. Meanwhile Spectra and Capital Appreciation joined the Growth portfolio in receiving Morningstar's prized five-star ranking.

In December 1998, the firm took a major step forward into the David Alger era and toward the Wall Street mainstream by moving Fred Alger Management to gleaming new offices—36,000 square feet on the 93rd floor of One World Trade Center.

In 1999, the firm's identification with David's image was solidified when he broke into the elite money shows on television: CNN's *Moneyline* with Lou Dobbs and public television's *Nightly Business Report* and *Wall Street Week* with Louis Rukeyser. As in his regular appearances on CNBC, David was delivering an optimistic outlook for investing in America and projecting a confident, successful picture of the company.

David had long been playing the role of a super bull among analysts and commentators by predicting that the Dow Jones average would reach 10,000 before the end of the decade. He staked that position more aggressively and with even greater clarity in the "Alger Market & Economic Review" throughout 1998. "As the long bond approaches 5%, I believe the Dow will move towards 20x our estimate of $500 per share in earnings for 1999, giving a price of 10,000. This could happen as early as the fourth quarter of this year or the first half of next year," he wrote in the April 17, 1998 issue. And he never backed off this assertion despite the fierce market sell-off to the 7,500 level in the fall, which unnerved a number of previously bullish analysts into reversing or tempering their market stance. By the end of the year the Dow was back up to 9,181.43 and seemed to be moving agreeably toward confirming his prediction.

Even as the Dow was encountering resistance at the 10,000 mark in mid-March, 1999, he was arguing loudly that the Dow would double to 20,000 by the end of the first quarter in 2004. In making his case for the Dow's continued rise, David cited the following ingredients: the growing force of the Internet—"the most important thing to happen to the world economy since the advent of the computer"; the increase in technology-led manufacturing productivity; slowing international growth; and depressed commodity prices.

David has asserted that the U.S. economy can continue its healthy growth without inflationary pressure and that its disappearance—surprising the U.S. economy—would press the long-bond yield down to 4% by 2002. With average earnings growth of 8% and the market's level tied historically to its earnings' relationship with the long bond, it is inevitable in his view, and not at all exaggerated, to conclude that the Dow would reach 20,000 in five years.

When the market advanced powerfully through the spring of 1999, the Dow not only met but exceeded David's 10,000 projection and zoomed upward, well on its way to reaching his target for the year and, ultimately, his longer projection. David then increased his 1999 year-end objective for the Dow to 11,500. In concert with the market's rise and with an excellent mix of growth stocks, the Alger portfolios maintained their lead over comparable indexes in the first quarter of 1999. And the firm's asset base, which had vaulted $10 billion at the end of 1998, was already nearing $12 billion in April 1999, both as a result of asset inflows and market-beating investment performance.

Since he took over from Fred, David has increased the value and raised the profile of the company to such an extent that it is now recognized as much more than a strong niche player in the aggressive growth and small-stock categories, but for what it has always been—an A-list money manager that can provide its clients with a broad and diversified range of financial products and services.

As the firm closes in on its future goals, the next thrilling chapters of Fred Alger are still under construction. All the factors—population demographics, social climate, investment trends, low inflation, bond-rate scenarios, and the surging global economies—are extremely supportive of a continued boom in financial assets well into the next century.

Under David's leadership the company moves inexorably towards fulfilling his brother Fred's vision. Restoring the fortune and good name of the Alger family, David has been ahead of schedule in satisfying his own designs. Having surpassed his initial target of $10 billion in assets so quickly, his ambition for reaching $20 billion doesn't seem so transcendent.

Alger Company Historical Highlights
Important Dates and Events

1964, Oct.   Fred Alger starts Fred Alger & Co. at 56 Pine Street with $3,000 and a subadvisory management agreement for two mutual funds, Security Equity Fund and Security Investment Fund.

1965, Feb.   The firm's prospects are improved by running a dummy portfolio for hedge fund A. W. Jones and Company.

1965   Southland Investors Ltd., a partnership with Mississippi investors, is the firm's first discretionary account, earning it performance fees.

1965   Fred Alger leads Security Equity Fund to a 77.5% gain and first place among mutual funds.

1965, Dec.   Fred is tapped by Bernie Cornfeld to manage the Alger Fund within IOS's proprietary Fund of Funds.

1966, Feb.   William Scheerer joins Fred as the firm's first full-time employee.

1966, Nov.   Chat Hickox becomes the firm's first high-net-worth individual account.

1966   Security Equity Fund is the number-two fund in the country.

1967, Jan. 1   George Boggio becomes the firm's second employee.

1967, Apr.   Rosemary Kiernan joins the firm.
1967   Fred Alger moves to the old Equitable Building at 120 Broadway.

1967   An aggressive stake in Resorts International boosts firm's profile.

1968, Feb.   A cover story on Fred Alger in *Institutional Investor* launches his Wall Street identity.

1968   Letter-stock investment in Parvin-Dohrmann.

1968   Fred gets known as a hot-shot, go-go money manager when David Babson announces that there are "too many Freds" in the industry.

1968, end   Canadian Venture Fund started by IOS and given to Fred to manage.

Late '60s   Fred attempts a novel way to market mutual funds called Divorced and Married Associates.

1969, Jan. 13   Irwin Schwartz joins the firm.

1969   Abraham Pomerantz strike suit against Security Management forces a break in its advisory relationship with Fred Alger.

1969   Informal start of the firm's Research Associates program.

1969, Sep.   Fred Alger becomes investment adviser to Security Ultra Fund.

1969   Start of CI Associates, pioneering cable-industry tax shelter and promotion of TelePrompTer Corp.

1970, Mar.   Fred Alger parts company with IOS.

1970   Firm moves to the old Standard Oil Building on 26 Broadway.

1970, July 15   Fred Alger registers with the SEC as an investment adviser, pursuant to section 203(c) of the Advisers Act.

1970, July   Fred Alger's first seat on the New York Stock Exchange is contributed by Frank Pierce.

1971, Jan.   David Alger joins the firm.

1971   Fred Alger is attacked as a "gunslinger" by Adam Smith during an *Institutional Investor* meeting, solidifying his reputation as an aggressive money manager.

1971	Fred Alger starts courting institutional accounts using an "infomercial" movie in its presentations.
1971, Dec.	Firm's second seat on the NYSE is purchased in Irwin's name.
1972	Fred Alger is released from its advisory duties by Security Management Co.
1972, Dec.	The firm's first Christmas dinner is held at the 21 Club.
Early '70s	Start of Lansdowne Ltd., Fred Alger's European investment banking venture.
1974, Feb.	Acquisition of closed-end funds, C I Fund and Spectra Fund, and the Percy Friedlander brokerage from City Investing Co. C I is renamed Castle Convertible Fund.
1974	Chat Hickox's Ashland Management becomes a guaranteed subsidiary of Fred Alger Management.
1974	ERISA opens the door to pension accounts, and the firm redoubles its efforts in that market.
1975, Apr.	Ray Dirks Research Division begins at Percy Friedlander.
1975, May 1	"May Day" deregulation of commissions forces the firm to meet the competition.
1976	Celanese becomes Fred Alger's first big institutional client.
1976, Sep.	Ray Dirks is out of the firm. Robert Friedlander leaves with him and the Percy Friedlander brokerage disappears from the company.
1976-77	Fred Alger challenges Rule 11A, which sought to keep investment managers from executing their own orders on the floor of the Exchange. Devises unique trading system using $2 brokers.
1977	Ashland Management separates from Fred Alger.

1978, July   The NYSE seat in Walter Untermeyer's name that came with the Percy Friedlander brokerage is sold to Pittsburgh broker Parker Hunter, Inc.

1979, Aug.   Firm acquires another seat on the NYSE in Irwin Schwartz's name from Daniel J. Hanley.

1979   Excellent performance lifts the firm's aspect for an asset surge in the '80s.

1980, Oct.   Monica Smith starts Analysts Resources, a search firm for analysts.

1980, June   Tom Weil is brought into the company to build its back-office operations at 130 Montgomery Street in Jersey City.

1980, Aug.   Brokerage clearing operation begins in New Jersey

1980, Nov.   Trade settlement capabilities added to the back-room functions.

1981, Mar.   Greg Duch joins the firm. Advances to become the firm's chief financial officer.

1981   Firm purchases a 52% stake in 75 Maiden Lane.

1982, Apr.   Bill Scheerer retires from the firm. A third of his shares are divided among David Alger, Irwin Schwartz and George Boggio.

1982–86   Alger company picnics.
1982   Firm moves into 75 Maiden Lane.

1984   Company bids to acquire Levitz Furniture Corp.

1985   Firm backs Jim Crosby's hostile raid on Pan Am stock.

1985–86   Company attempts leveraged buyout of Ford Motor Car Co.

1986 $13 million "A Genius for Managing Money" advertising campaign is launched.

1986	Fred Alger buys Crocker Investment Management Corp. from Wells Fargo & Co.
1986, Nov. 11	Launch date for the Alger Fund of six mutual fund portfolios.
1987, Summer	Ray Pfeister joins the firm. Grows the firm's asset base by developing insurance company relationships.
1987, Oct.	SEC charges Fred Alger with deceptive advertising in its 1986 campaign.
1987, Oct. 19	"Black Monday" stock market crash.
1988, Jan.–Mar.	Acquisition of the firm by Britain's Dawnay Day comes to naught.
1988, Mar.	Back office's Tom Weil leaves the firm and is replaced by Jim Barbi.
1988, Apr.	Alger American Fund of mutual fund portfolios is organized for insurance companies to sell in variable annuity and life products.
1989	Mutual fund wholesaling agreement terminated with Rutland Associates.
1989, June	American Skandia signs on as the first insurance company to offer Alger funds in its insurance and annuity packages.
1989, July	George Boggio, Irwin Schwartz and Tony Weber resign from the firm.
1989, Aug.	The Alger Fund and its marketing operations move to the New Jersey office.
1989, Sep.	Alger Hi Yield Bond Fund is closed.
1989, Oct.	The firm begins acting as its own transfer agent.
1989	Fred Alger's first investment in Precision Sourcing International.

1989	David Alger's Small Cap Fund, with a gain of 65.08%, is the top mutual fund in the country.
1990, Mar.	Settlement of the SEC suit against Fred Alger.
1990, Apr.	Fred Alger markets a unique Program for Substantial Charitable Investors.
1991	David Alger's book "Raging Bull" is published.
1992, Jan.	Wholesaling agreement with American Skandia to market the Alger Fund.
1992, June 1	Alger Balanced Portfolio is rolled out.
1993, Apr.	Alger Defined Contribution Trust Portfolios are offered.
1993, May	Fred Alger starts selling three mutual fund portfolios in Germany through Noramco Deutschland.
1994, Sep. 20	First edition of the *Fred Alger Management Market & Economic Review* newsletter.
1994, Oct. 31	Alger Funds' wholesale marketing agreement with American Skandia is terminated.
1995, Jan. 1	David Alger becomes chief investment officer and president of the firm.
1995, Mar. 27	Leveraged All Cap is reborn as Capital Appreciation fund.
1995, Apr. 24	Fred Alger leaves for Geneva.
1995, May	Income and Growth portfolio is closed.
1995	Firm's net worth tops $100 million for the first time.
1995	David Alger is the top mutual-fund manager in the country. His Capital Appreciation fund is up 78.6%.
1996, Apr.	Alger Defined Contribution Trust renamed The Alger Retirement Fund.

1996, Feb.	Spectra Fund becomes an open-end mutual fund.
1996, July 15	Company switches to State Street Bank & Trust Co. as custodian.
1996, July	Alger American Asset Growth Fund is registered in Luxembourg for sale in Europe.
1996, Sep.	Firm sells its position in 75 Maiden Lane.
1996, Dec.	Class A of five Alger portfolios is offered.
1997, Aug.	Class C of five Alger portfolios is offered.
1997, Mar.	Fred Alger launches new, expanded Internet offering.
1997, Summer	Firm's asset base touches $8 billion.
1997, Sep.	Firm plans its move to New York's World Trade Center in December 1998.
1998, Dec.	Assets under management cross the $10 billion mark.

Investment Performance Statistics

YEAR	ANNUAL RETURN		
	Before deductions for management fees	After deductions for management fees [1]	S&P 500 [5]
1965 [2]	77.5%	77.5%	12.8%
1966	19.3	18.0	(9.5)
1967	52.5	49.0	24.3
1968	36.3	33.6	11.1
1969	(3.0)	(4.5)	(8.4)
1970	(6.6)	(8.0)	4.4
1971	43.7	41.6	14.4
1972	37.1	35.7	18.7
1973	(17.0)	(17.9)	(15.0)
1974	(15.3)	(16.0)	(26.6)
1975	23.2	22.4	37.3
1976	29.2	28.0	23.9
1977	10.1	9.1	(7.2)
1978	23.2	22.1	6.6
1979	50.7	49.6	18.6
1980	60.2	59.0	32.5
1981	(7.1)	(7.4)	(4.9)
1982	36.2	35.4	21.6
1983	19.9	19.3	22.6
1984	(2.8)	(3.3)	6.3
1985	32.7	32.0	31.7
1986	20.7	20.1	18.7
1987	(1.3)	(1.8)	5.3
1988	9.4	8.8	16.6
1989	39.6	38.9	31.7
1990	1.6	1.1	(3.1)
1991	58.8	58.0	30.5
1992	2.1	1.6	7.6
1993	15.5	14.9	10.1
1994	(0.6)	(1.1)	1.3
1995	41.3	40.8	37.6
1996	15.2	14.7	23.0
1997	24.2	23.7	33.4
1998	52.3	51.7	28.6

ANNUALIZED RETURNS

34 Years	20.7%	19.8%	12.2%
10 Years	23.3%	22.8%	19.2%

PERFORMANCE NOTES

1 Performance statistics after deductions for management fees include:
    • the effect of management fees charged directly to the accounts by Fred Alger Management, Inc., or
    • deductions for the imputed effect of management fees paid separately by clients.

2 Performance statistics for 1965 represent the performance of Fred Alger Management's only equity-oriented account, a mutual fund, for which the company served as a sub-advisor. For this account the investment advisor retained discretionary authority. See chapter 8 for further exposition.

3 Performance statistics for the period 1966-1987 are in accordance with Bank Administration Institute Standards and were constructed by the following criteria:
    • Composite results were calculated on a time-weighted rate-of-return basis using the all fully discretionary, equity-oriented accounts with a market value greater than $100,000 managed for the entire year.
    • Spectra Fund, a mutual fund under management since 1976, was excluded due to its small asset size.
    • Performance statistics from 1976-1987 were verified by Coopers & Lybrand, independent public accountants.

4 Results for the period 1988-1998 are in accordance with AIMR Presentation Standards which became the industry rule on January 1, 1993. Although not required by AIMR, performance statistics for the years 1988 through 1992 were voluntarily restated to comply with AIMR standards.

    An account is excluded from the performance statistics for a quarter if:
    • a capital contribution was received which is greater than 20% of the account's total market value at the time the contribution was made, or
    • a capital withdrawal was made which is greater than 10% of the account's total market value at the time of withdrawal.

    Performance statistics for 1988-1998 have been verified by BDO Seidman, independent public accountants.

5 Adjusted for reinvestment of dividends.

Text of 1971 Alger Promotional Film

Fred Alger: As a way of letting all of you know a little about us at Fred Alger & Co., let me begin by telling you that our offices are all the way downtown in the Wall Street district at 26 Broadway, in the old Standard Oil Building on the seventh floor.

I started the firm in 1964 on $3,000 in capital, running two small funds with $7 million in assets. Today we manage $160 million and the firm's capital is over $1 million. But the real purpose of this film is to introduce you to the people—some of whom could not be here today—the people who will be managing your money and to try to catch the spirit of the firm.

"Thirty thousand were sold . . ." Because of the closeness of the working environment, all our analyst-managers are totally immersed in the research process. This stretches their awareness of the market and increases their productivity. **Bill Scheerer** is one of my partners. He was the first person to join me. Certainly one of the best things that ever happened. Before joining me he was the managing partner of a New York Stock Exchange firm, and he is well qualified to talk about our investment philosophy.

BS: We try to pick out companies like ourselves, and we're continually seeking out superior companies that we think will give us excellent investment performance over long periods of time. Generally speaking, these companies have demonstrated an ability to think creatively in their own industry, and this almost inevitably results in a rising trend of not only sales but earnings per share. Occasionally, we feel that market timing can be of overriding importance, and at the same time we are always conscious of the fact that superior companies do not always make excellent investments, and very often some of the lesser companies provide us with really first-rate market opportunities.

FA: **Irwin Schwartz**, one of our senior analyst-managers, helps carry out this investment philosophy. Irwin has superb market feel, an important intangible of any research system.

IS: Our research system is somewhat different in that it does not include a portfolio manager. The classic pyramidal structure has been proven cumbersome. All the analysts have access to their stocks in every portfolio. Fred keeps track of portfolio diversification, makes the cash or no cash decision at the top or bottom of each market.

FA: To make the system work, we stress productivity in our research effort. We believe that we are more productive than any other firm. Some firms say they concentrate on a limited number of stocks. We say their research isn't productive enough. **Don Besser** is one of our analyst-managers. He typifies the intensive spirit of the firm, a key to high productivity.

DB: Once a week each analyst manager meets with Fred for several hours to discuss his research work. At each meeting he must present complete reports on at least six different companies. These reports represent ideas that have been developed from technical stock-price action, reading annual reports, talking to different members of an industry or occasional conversations with other brokers. A complete report for Fred means having checked competitors, suppliers, customers and having complete statistics. Fred rewards very highly the management methods affecting our companies. For example, one time I kept track of the shipments of a manufacturing company by talking to the state inspector who was required by law to examine each machine before shipment.

The day before each analyst-manager meeting we often are in somewhat of a panic and, frankly, sometimes we think too much is expected of us. Because we know that Fred will immediately sense if any of our research work on the companies that we are reporting on is missing. Moreover, Fred keeps track of every one of our recommendations, and he reviews these recommendations, every six weeks. That's what a research meeting is like at Fred Alger and Co.

FA: Another of the younger members of the team is my brother **David Alger**. He and I have talked about being in business together since we were children. When people started referring to me as David's brother, it was time for us to join forces.

DA: It was easy to join forces, largely because our thinking about the research process was so similar. We emphasize decision making. For example, we immediately classify all stocks as Buy, Sell, No Interest with appropriate reasons, Look at It at a future day, or Working. All decisions are posted into a master ledger, and those decisions which are deferred are posted on a bulletin board for easy reference.

FA: As a service to our clients, early in 1970 we acquired a seat in the New York Stock Exchange. We give net commission credit against the management fee which can wholly erase the fee. We wanted to get the best floor trader in the country, and we think we got him. **Frank Pierce** is one of 60 registered floor traders of 1,366 members. He also handles the largest trading account for Carlyle, one of the odd lot houses.

FP: Fred has asked me to keep detailed records on our executions for our clients. We try to buy below and sell above the mean price of the day. The importance of this can be seen from a study we did recently on a $15 million conservatively managed fund. We found that if we saved a eighth of a point on all executions for a period of a year, it would have saved the fund over $300,000. We handle no commission business other than our own, and this leaves me free, if necessary, to spend all day executing orders for our clients.

FA: To keep track of these various operations, **George Boggio**, our treasurer, has instituted a control system more comprehensive than any we have seen.

GB: Through the use of computers we have developed many valuable reports. The basic report that we provide our clients is a portfolio evaluation. This report is a lot-by-lot listing of the securities in the portfolio, showing the date purchased, cost, market value, unrealized capital gains, both long-term and short-term, the allocation of the securities, date the item goes long-term, the cash available for additional investment and the total value of the portfolio. We also have a schedule of realized gains and losses, which many clients use in the preparation of their income-tax returns. Another category of reports is our manager's reports, which are utilized by management to evaluate the investment decisions of each analyst-manager. We also have a performance report, which basically is measuring the performance of each client relative to the Dow Jones Industrial Average and the Standard and Poor's average. We also have commission analysis, which is a means by which we compute the commission credits applied to our clients' management fee. We also have a stock report. This report is a listing by security, showing each client and his relative holding of that security. This report is extremely valuable in block trading.

FA: Will Stewart, one of my partners, is in charge of client relations. Will was a portfolio manager, but as our business grew, he volunteered to take charge of this important area. The big change that has taken place in the past 10 years in the investment business has been a willingness to adjust portfolio mix. We feel the greatest speculation is inadequate attention and a reluctance to make decisions.

INDEX

Moulton, Freeborn, 64
Moulton, Robert, 64
Multimedia Solutions, 460
Munkácsy, Mihaly, 80
Murphy, Fred Towsley, 107
Murphy, Mary Eldridge Swift Alger, 107
Museum of Modern Art, 312, 318
Mutual Funds, 249, 293, 443
Mutual fund strategies, 26-33, 38-41
Mutual of America, 434

Naess & Thomas Special Fund, 153
Naggar, Guy, 415
NASDAQ, 35, 295
National Association of Securities Dealers (NASD), 128, 439
National Securities Clearing Corp. (NSCC), 439
Naval Reserves, 51
Nelson, Wally, 230
Netscape Communication Corp., 294
Nevada Gaming Control Board, 213-14
Neville, Richard Earl of Warwick, 239
Newberry, John S., 79, 80
Newberry, Truman, 97, 102, 104
New Breed On Wall Street, 31
New England Life Insurance Co., 434
Newsweek, 200
New York City Marathon, 33-34
New York *Post,* 15
New York Stock Exchange, 130, 155, 169
New York Sun, 85, 88, 89
New York Times, The, 196, 199, 202, 222, 261
Niarchos, Stavros, 215
Nightly Business Report, 467
Nixon, Richard, 54-55, 57, 161
Noramco (Deutschland), 323-24

North American Securities Co., 113-14, 252
Norton, Leslie P., 396, 458
Notz Bank, 215-18
Notz, Beat, 215-18
Notz, Clarina, 13
Novell, 425
Nucor, 263

Office Depot, 240
Ohio Automobile Co., 103
Ohio Society, 89
Olympic Capital Fund, 215
O'Neil, Ed, 429
O'Neil, Stephen E., 32, 184, 185, 315, 320, 429
OPEC, 143, 218-19
Osborne, Charles, 215
Otis, Coffinberry & Wyman, 67
Overseas National Airways, 117, 139-40
Owens-Corning Fiberglas, 172, 409

Packard, James Ward, 103
Packard Motor Car Co., 16, 63, 79, 103-4
Packard, Warren, 103
Packenham, Joseph A., 43, 335-37, 339, 341
Pagannuci, Paul, 230
PaineWebber Inc., 318, 332, 414
Paley, William S., 152
Pan American World Airways, 350-51
Papovich, Milan, 116
Partridge, Charles Jr., 116
Parvin, Albert B., 212-14
Parvin-Dohrmann Co., 212-14
Peat Marwick Mitchell, 341
Peninsula Car Works, 79
Penn Central Railroad, 28
Pension Benefit Guaranty Corp., 168
Pensions & Investment Age, 369-70
PepsiCo, 172, 173
Percy Friedlander Co., 184, 185-86

Perkins Opportunity, 451
Personal Finance, 243
Perot, Henry Ross, 231
Pfeister, Ray, 37, 264-65, 347, 428-37
Phibro Corp., 418
Phillips Academy, 48, 100
Phillips, Don, 453
PHMFG Corp., 231
Phoenix Investment, 433
Phoenix Systems, 442
Pierce, Frank E. III, 155, 167
Pike, Charles B., 99
Pingree, Hazen S., 94-95
Pioneer Press, 90
Pochna, Michael, 218
Polaroid, 28, 32
Polsky, Richard, 317
Pomerantz, Abraham L., 118-19
Pomerantz Strike Suit, 118, 381
Pomerantz, Levy, Hoodek and Block, 118
Poole, Rufus G., 153, 155
Portfolio Accounting Reporting Service (PARS), 425
Primerica Corp., 31-32
Prince, Richard, 317
Princeton Club, 122
Prismatic Club, 74
Pritzker family, 352-55
Program for Substantial Charitable Investors, 436-38
Provident Mutual Life Insurance Company, 434
Provident Mutual Investment Management, 434
Prudent Man rule, 26, 27
Prudential Bache, 423
PSi, Inc., 313-14
Psych line, 288-90
Putney Swope, 136

Quantum Fund, 348
Quarterly Distribution Shares, 116
Quest, 315-17

Bibliography

Alger, Alexandra. "Bringing An Ancestor to Life." *Forbes,* 9 Sep. 1996.

Alger, David. *Raging Bull—How to Invest in the Growth Stocks of the 90s.* Homewood, IL: Business One Irwin, 1992.

Alger, Russell A. "Final Official Statement." Washington, D.C.: 31 July 1899.

———. Interview. "How I Got My Start in Business."

———. *The Spanish-American War.* New York: Harper & Brothers, 1901.

Anders, George. "Abreast of the Market, An Appraisal: Strategy of Buying Market Leaders Returns to Favor." *Wall Street Journal,* 14 April 1986.

———. "Famed Stock Picker of 1960s May Regain Some of His Renown." , 17 June 1986.

———. "Managers Fail to Equal Rise of Benchmarks in Stocks and Bonds." *Wall Street Journal,* 2 Jan. 1987.

Anders, George and Beatrice E. Garcia. "Making Claims: Fred Alger Regains Wall Street Spotlight, but His Ads Rile Some." *Wall Street Journal,* 1 Oct. 1986.

Andresky Fraser, Jill. "These Seven Soloists Are Playing Sweet Music." *New York Times,* 1 Dec. 1996.

Baker, Molly. "Analysts See Boon for Dozens of Firms in High-Tech Area." *Wall Street Journal,* 19 June 1995.

Bell, Rodney Ellis. "A Life of Russell Alexander Alger, 1836–1907." Dissertation, U. of Michigan, 1975.

———. "Russell Alexander Alger 1836–1907." *Michigan History,* Feb.–March 1968.

Belsky, Gary. "A Dynamic Duo, Up 86% in a Year, Name Four Stocks to Gain 29% in '96." *Money,* Jan. 1996.

———. "Load Funds Worth the Price." *Money,* Jan. 1993.

Berger, Joseph. "Trying to Donate a School: Generosity vs. Regulations." *New York Times,* 20 Dec. 1990.

Bianco, Anthony. "Jerry Tsai: The Comeback Kid." *BusinessWeek,* 18 Aug. 1986.

Biller, Allan D. "Soft Dollars' Harm to Pension Funds, Markets." *Pensions & Investments,* 11 Nov. 1991.

Birmingham, Stephen. "Our Right People: The Pointe Seen from Afar." *Detroit Free Press,* 24 Nov. 1968.

Boynton, Walter. "And Surely You Have Met–Col. Fred M. Alger."

Brennan, Peter. "Jockeying for German Investors." *Wall Street & Technology,* vol. 12, no. 5. Nov. 1994.

Bright, F.E.W. "Alger Brothers Separated for First Time–by Death." *Detroit News,* 28 Jan. 1930.

Brooks, John. *The Go-Go Years.* New York: Weybright and Talley, 1973.

Burkins, Glenn. "Thinking Small Pays Off for Funds." *Dallas Morning News,* 16 April 1989.

Burton, Jonathan. "Raging Bull." *Dow Jones Investment Advisor,* March 1997.

Campbell, Robert. "An Inspiration Talk with Col. Fred M. Alger." *Detroit Sunday Times,* 4 Feb. 1923.

Cantor, Bert. *The Bernie Cornfeld Story.* New York: Lyle Stuart, 1970.

Cheiro. *Cheiro's Book of Numbers.* New York: Arco 1964.

Chipello, Christopher J. "Quarterly Review of Mutual Funds: Japanese Issues Help Top Mutual Funds Soar." *Wall Street Journal,* 5 Oct. 1989.

Citrano, Virginia. "N.Y. Heads Race to Invest in India." *Crain's New York Business,* 14 Feb. 1994.

Clifford, Mark. "Perils of Pan Am." Forbes, 16 Dec. 1985.

Cohn, Gary. "Levitz Furniture Rejects Offers from Two Firms." *Wall Street Journal,* 17 Oct. 1984.

Cohn, Gary and Clifford Krauss. "Levitz Furniture Receives Offer for All Its Stock." *Wall Street Journal*, 16 Aug. 1986.

Courage, Ray. "Alger Back in Politics With Fire in His Eye." *Detroit Free Press*, 25 May 1958.

Cousins, Fred W. "City Newsboys Mourn Loss of Their Best Friend." *Detroit News*, 3 Jan. 1934.

Crosson, Cynthia. "Variable Annuities Are Becoming User-Friendly." *National Underwriter—Life & Health*, 9 Dec. 1991.

Cuff, Daniel F. and Thomas C. Hayes. "Eight New Mutual Funds Set by Money Manager." *New York Times*, 2 Nov. 1986.

Del Prete, Dom. "Need a Money Manager to Watch Over Your Portfolio?" *Medical Economics*, 18 May 1992.

DeVoe Talley, Madelon. *The Passionate Investors—Secrets of Winning on Wall Street from Bernard Baruch to John Templeton*. New York: Crown, 1987.

Dewey, Charles S. *As I Recall It*. Washington, D.C.: Self-published, 1957.

Dirks, Raymond L. and Leonard Gross. *The Great Wall Street Scandal: Inside Equity Funding*. New York: McGraw-Hill, 1974.

Dorfman, Dan. "Heard on the Street." *Wall Street Journal*, 8 April 1969.

———. "No Clear Favorite in Crowded Field." *USA Today*, 14 Dec. 1992.

Dorfman, John. "Small Shares' Revival Helps Managers of Stock Portfolios Beat the Benchmark." *Wall Street Journal*, 5 April 1991.

Downes, John, and Jordan Elliot Goodman. *Barron's Finance & Investment Handbook*. Hauppauge, NY: Barron's Educational Series, 1995.

Eaton, Leslie. "Swinging Funds Race Ahead of the Pack." *Barron's*, 10 April 1989.

Egan, Jack. "The Five Most Aggressive Fund Managers: Why You Want One in Your Corner." *Worth*, April 1997.

Elia, Charles J. "Heard on the Street: Independent Advisers' Stock Picks Fared Better..." *Wall Street Journal*, 22 April 1981.

———. "Top Officer's Trading in Parvin-Dohrmann Shares Draw Scrutiny." *Wall Street Journal*, 9 June 1969.

Franzini, Kristin. "Small Companies, Big Gains." *Financial World*, 28 May 1991.

Freeman, Lisa Lee. "Top Manager Alger Goes Against Grain." *Investor's Business Daily*, 27 Aug. 1993.

Galluccio, Nick. "Concepts Revisited." *Forbes*, 11 May 1981.

Gille, Everett. "Alger: He Could Really Pick 'Em." Letter to the Editor. *Wall Street Journal*, 22 Mar. 1990.

Givant Star, Marlene. "Firms Taking Different Variable Annuity Route." *Pensions & Investments*, 12 June 1995.

Goldberg, Steven T. "A Fund Family for Some Seasons." *Kiplinger's Personal Finance*, Nov. 1995.

Goldberg, Steven T. "From Out of Nowhere? No, This Hot 'New' Fund is 28 Years Old." *Kiplinger's Personal Finance*, Jan. 1997.

Gottschalk, Earl C. Jr. "Parvin Chairman May Quit Post in Settlement." *Wall Street Journal*, 7 Jan. 1970.

Gould, Carol. "Mutual Funds: What Top Performers Bet On." *New York Times*, 14 Jan. 1990.

Graham, Bill. "Grand Marais Sings In." *Minnegazette*, July/Aug. 1987.

Greenwood, Tom. "Grosse Pointe War Memorial Is Monument to Culture." *Detroit News*, 15 June 1995.

Hagstrom, Robert G. Jr. *The Warren Buffett Way—Investment Strategies of the World's Greatest Investor*. New York: John Wiley, 1994.

Hamilton, Walter. "Funds Flip IPO Netscape for Quick Gains." *Investor's Business Daily*, 16 Aug. 1995.

Hart, William. *The Art of Living: Vipassana Meditation*. San Francisco: Harper Collins, 1987.

Hemmerick, Steve. "Alger Buying Crocker for Fixed-Income Skills." *Pensions & Investment Age*, 23 June 1986.

———. "Alger Losing Clients From CIMCO List." *Pensions & Investment Age*, 15 Sep. 1986.

Henriques, Diana B. *Fidelity's World: The Secret Life and Public Power of the Mutual Fund Giant*. New York: Scribner's, 1995.

———. "Bernard Cornfeld, 67, Dies; Led Flamboyant Mutual Fund." *New York Times*, 2 Mar. 1995.

Hershey, Robert D. Jr. "Closing Tax Loophole and Opening Another." *New York Times*, 10 July 1995.

Hershey , Robert D. Jr. "Youthful Fund Manager Voices Pessimism." *New York Times*, 2 April 1969.

Hershman, Arlene. "No Way But Up." *Dun's*, Feb. 1970.

Heuser, Hans. "Im Aufwind—30 Prozent Plus mit

Fonds." *das Wertpapier: Deutschlands älteste Geldanlage-Zeitschrift,* 28 July 1995.

Hill, G. Christian. "BankAmerica Unit Faces Competition as Montgomery Street's Fund Manager." *Wall Street Journal,* 4 Nov. 1987.

Hinden, Stan. "Tech Tack Dough: A Winning Fund Formula . . ." *Washington Post,* 9 July 1995.

Hurst, Ruth. "On-the-job Training at Warner-Lambert." *Institutional Investor,* Sep. 1982.

Johnson, Richard. "Wall Street Big Eyes Swiss Bliss." *New York Post,* 30 Sep. 1994.

Kaufman, Steven B. "Rich to Riches." *Individual Investor,* Sep. 1995.

Koflowitz, Lewis. "The New Kings of Wall Street." *Investment Dealers' Digest,* 23 Oct. 1984.

Krimes, Beverly Rae, ed. *Packard: A History of the Motor Car and the Company.* Princeton, N.J.: Princeton Pub, 1978.

Kristof, Kathy M. "Mutual Funds Had Big Gains During Year." *Los Angeles Times,* 5 Jan. 1990.

Kuhn, Susan E. "A Closer Look at Mutual Funds: Which Ones Really Deliver." *Fortune,* 7 Oct. 1991.

Laderman, Jeff M. "Big Returns in Small Packages." *BusinessWeek,* 17 April 1989.

Laderman, Jeffrey M. "Where Some Shoot-'em-up Managers Are Now." *BusinessWeek,* 18 Aug. 1986.

Lawrence, Ruth, ed. *Colonial Families in America,* Vols. 6, 12, and 13. New York: National Americana Society, 1928.

Lee, Jeanne C. "If It Moves, Get on It." *Fortune,* 18 Aug. 1997.

Leeb, Stephen, ed. "Small Dogs: Out of the Doghouse." *Personal Finance,* 27 Feb. 1991.

Lenzner, Robert. "The Stockpicker's Stockpicker." *Boston Globe,* 22 Dec. 1981.

Lenzner, Robert and Philippe Mao. "The New Refugees." *Forbes,* 21 Nov. 1994.

Levin, Doron P. "Heard on the Street: Big Three Auto Stocks Are Expected to Jump . . ." *Wall Street Journal,* 9 Sep. 1984.

Lewis, Michael. *Liar's Poker: Rising Through the Wreckage on Wall Street.* New York: Norton, 1989.

Lilly, Doris. *Those Fabulous Greeks: Onassis, Niarchos and Livanos.* New York: Cowles Book Co., 1970.

Lipman, Joane. "Ad Agencies Feverishly Ride a Merger Wave." *Wall Street Journal,* 9 May 1986.

Lippert, Barbara. "Alger's Dangerously Sexy Ad Campaign." *Money,* Nov. 1986.

Lorant, Stefan. *The Presidency.* New York: Macmillan, 1951.

Lowe, Janet Celesta. *Benjamin Graham on Value Investing: Lessons from the Dean of Wall Street.* Chicago: Dearborn Financial Publishing, 1994.

Lowry, Tom. "Aggressive Alger Fund Undaunted by Off Year." *USA Today,* 26 Dec. 1996.

Machan, Dyan. "The Financial World One Hundred: The Highest Paid People on Wall Street." *Financial World,* 22 July 1986.

Marcial, Gene G. "Fred Alger Is High on the 'One-World' Economy." *BusinessWeek,* 19 Jan. 1987.

Marvin, Robert B. D.P.A. *Packard: A Chronology of the Company, the Cars and the People.* Jasper, FL: R-Mac Publications.

Mayer, Martin. *New Breed on Wall Street.* New York: Macmillan, 1969.

McCartney, Robert J. "Dow Leads a Charge Alone; Other Indexes Aren't Keeping Up With Bullish Blue-Chip Stocks." *Washington Post,* 18 May 1990.

McElroy, Martin C.P., ed. *The Buildings of Detroit,* Detroit: Wayne State Univ. Press, 1971.

Metz, Robert. "Market Place: Convertible Funds' Gains." *New York Times,* 14 May 1979.

———."Market Place: Equity Funds Strategy Today." *New York Times,* 3 Nov. 1980.

———. "Market Place: Optimistic View on Stock Prices." *New York Times,* 15 Nov. 1978.

———. "Market Place: Reduced Taxes on Capital Gains?" *New York Times,* 21 Nov. 1977.

———. "Market Place: Self-Sufficiency Via Shale Oil?" *New York Times,* 30 March 1979.

———. "Market Place: TelePrompTer: Fight Widens." *New York Times,* 21 Nov. 1971.

Metzner, Douglas E. "Alger Leads 1995 Advance." *Mutual Funds,* Sep. 1995.

Mitchell, Constance. "Quarterly Review of Equity Mutual Funds: Small Firms Fueled Top 1st-Quarter Funds." *Wall Street Journal,* 6 April 1989.

Morgenson, Gretchen. "A Tale of Two Freds." *Forbes,* 2 April 1990.

———. "Return of the Gunslinger." *Money,* Nov. 1986.

———. "You Ain't Seen Nothing Yet—Money Manager Fred Alger Predicts an Expanding Stock Market." *Forbes,* 9 Dec. 1991.

Morris, Frank. "Alger's Back Where He Started–But With a Different Doctrine." *Detroit Times,* 23 July 1958.

Norris, Floyd. "Market Watch: Are Stocks Cheap? Sure, Just As in 1972." *New York Times,* 15 Nov. 1995

Norton, Leslie P. "A Call to Glory–David Alger Takes Over Fred's Firm." *Barron's,* 7 Aug. 1995.

Oliver, Susan. "I Can Get It for You Wholesale." *Forbes,* 20 June 1994.

Perrin, Robert. "Alger Happy in Brussels–But Thinks of Michigan." *Detroit Free Press,* 10 May 1954.

Peters, Ralph L. "Detroit Revives the Military Ball." *Detroit News,* 25 Feb. 1934.

Petre, Peter. "How to Pick and Use a Money Manager." *Fortune 1987 Investor's Guide.*

Philip, Christine. "Alger, First Trust Venture." *Pensions & Investments,* 19 Sep. 1994.

Pooler, James S. "Detroit Just about Decides It Will Go Back to Horses." *Detroit Free Press,* 25 Feb. 1935.

Putka, Gary. "'Life-Cycle Stocks Are on the Leading Edge As Perceptions Change, Fred Alger Believes." *Wall Street Journal,* 14 Feb. 1983.

Randall, Carter, and William J. Gianopulos. *Up on the Market.* Chicago: Probus Publishing, 1992.

Raw, Charles, Bruce Page, and Godfrey Hodgson. *Do You Sincerely Want to Be Rich? Bernard Cornfeld and IOS . . .* London: Andre Deutsch, 1971.

Robards, Terry. "F.I. DuPont Sets a Major Merger." *New York Times,* 4 June 1970.

Roberts, Johnnie L. "Heard on the Street: GE's Takeover Offer Is Criticized as Too Low . . ." *Wall Street Journal,* 17 Dec. 1985.

Rogers, Doug. "Aggressive Growth Funds Are Low on Cash." *Investor's Business Daily,* 13 May 1994.

———. "Alger Sits Tight Through Ugly Correction." *Investor's Business Daily,* 20 July 1995.

———. "Alger, Up 14%, Maintains Bullish Outlook." *Investor's Business Daily,* 11 May 1995.

———. "Buy Stocks With Rates Down, Alger Says." *Investor's Business Daily,* 14 Nov. 1991.

———. "Tech Stocks Lead Funds Higher in Quarter." *Investor's Business Daily,* 10 July 1995.

Rohrer, Julie. "So You Want to Start a Mutual Fund?" *Institutional Investor,* March 1987.

———. "The Winner: Here's How 1970's Best Performing Fund Did It." *Institutional Investor,* Feb. 1971.

Ross-Skinner, Jean. "The Many Woes of Bernie Cornfeld." *Dun's,* Jan. 1970.

Rothbart, Dean. "Heard on the Street: Advertis-

ing Agency Stocks Make Big Gains and Savvy Analysts Are Getting the Message." *Wall Street Journal,* 25 Apr. 1985.

Rudin, Brad. "Alger Peers Take Umbrage at Ads." *Pensions & Investment Age,* 7 July 1986.

Safian, Robert. "Count Down." *Smart Money,* Feb. 1996.

Salwen, Kevin G. "SEC Charges Fred Alger Funds Padded Data in '86 Ad Campaign." *Wall Street Journal,* 6 March 1990.

Sandler, Linda. "Heard on the Street: Ford and GM May Soon Create Separate Issues . . ." *Wall Street Journal,* 2 April 1986.

Schermerhorn, Jane. "Suzette Alger: A Woman of Courage." *Detroit News,* 11 March 1963.

Scherer, Johannes. "In 18 Months Over 5000 Points." *Börse Online,* Nov. 1994.

Schrager, Jeff. "Alger's Riches Are No Fable." *Individual Investor,* Aug. 1991.

Schwimmer, Anne. "Wall Street Stocks Capturing Hearts of Investors." *Pensions & Investments,* 26 July 1993.

Scott, Michael G.H. *Packard: The Complete Story.* Blue Ridge Summit, PA: Tab Books, 1985.

Shoenfield, Allen. "Alger Papers Tell Inside Story of the Strange Case of Gen. Miles." *Detroit News,* 12 May 1935.

———. "His Private Papers Reveal Inside Story of Alger's Feud With T.R." *Detroit News,* 5 May 1935.

———. "Russell A. Alger's Private Papers at Last Reveal Story of Betrayal." *Detroit News,* 28 April 1935.

Siconolfi, Michael, and Christopher J. Chipello. "Quarterly Review of Mutual Funds: Fidelity's Lynch Aims at Real-Estate Stocks." *Wall Street Journal,* 5 Jan. 1990.

Siedell, Tom. "The Best Low-Cost Mutual Funds." *Your Money,* Oct./Nov. 1994.

Smith, Adam. *The Money Game.* New York: Random House, 1968.

Smith, Randall. "Heard on the Street: Ford's Robust First-Quarter Earnings." *Wall Street Journal,* 1 May 1987.

———. "Heard on the Street: Genentech's Buyout of 2 Partnerships." *Wall Street Journal,* 5 Nov. 1986.

Sobel, Robert. *The Last Bull Market: Wall Street in the 1960s.* New York: Norton, 1980.

Sonenclar, Robert. "Bobbin' Along. The Singer Co.'s Move into Defense Electronics." *Financial World,* 27 May 1986.

Stark, George W. "Town Talk: Salutes the Memory of Gen. Russell A. Alger."

Stein, Benjamin J. "Pro and Con: A Hard Look at Fred Alger's Performance." *Barron's,* 3 Nov. 1986.

Stone, Andrea. "This Alger's Story Is of Ride to Riches." *USA Today,* 18 June 1986.

Stovall, Robert S. "A Mighty Merger: RCA Corp. and General Electric Co." *Financial World,* 21 Jan. 1986.

Surtees, Lawrence. *Pa Bell. A Jean de Grandpré and the Meteoric Rise of Bell Canada Enterprises.* Toronto: Random House, 1992.

Truell, Peter. "Journalism's Latest Odd Couple." *New York Times,* 6 Sep. 1997.

Tranquist, Robert E. *The Packard Story: The Car and the Company.* New York: A.S. Barnes, 1965.

United States Congressional House. "Eulogies of the Late Senator Alger." Washington, D.C.: *Congressional Record,* 24 Feb. 1907.

Van Lopik, Carter. "Descendants of First Families Continue to Build Michigan." *Detroit Free Press,* 15 Nov. 1959.

Waggoner, John. "Alger's Mutual Fund Success Story." *USA Today,* 12 May 1995.

Wagner, Michael G. "Native Son's Fiscal Gains Net Scrutiny." *Detroit Free Press,* 2 Nov. 1987.

Wallace, Anise. "The Resurrection of Fred Alger." *Institutional Investor,* Dec. 1980.

Wang, Nelson. "The Hot Hand at Alger." *Smart Money,* Oct. 1995.

Watson, Lloyd. "Go-Go N.Y. Money Man Is on a Roll Again." *San Francisco Chronicle,* 20 June 1986.

Welles, Chris. "Fred Alger: Portrait of a Star." *Institutional Investor,* Feb. 1968.

White, James A., and George Anders. "Theme of This Alger's Story Isn't the Same as Horatio's." *Wall Street Journal,* 28 Feb. 1989.

White, Tom. "They Don't Call It Alger Growth Fund for Nothing." *Investment Advisor,* Aug. 1995.

Whitehead, Jean. "Mrs. Frederick M. Alger Jr." *Detroit Times,* 1 Sep. 1957.

Williamson, Gordon K. *The 100 Best Mutual Funds You Can Buy.* Holbrook, MA: Bob Adams, 1994, 1995.

Zipser, Andy. "Patriot's Day: Fund Boss David Alger Scores Big With His Bets on U.S. Growth Stocks." *Barron's,* 15 April 1996.

———. "The Top Picks for '93 of Four Mutual-Fund Aces." *Barron's,* 4 Jan. 1993.

"100 Individuals Who Shaped the Decade." *Institutional Investor,* March 1977.

"Alger Associates Improves Offer for Levitz Furniture." Dow Jones News Service, 10 Sep 1984.

"Alger Associates Sweetens Its Offer for Levitz Furniture." *Wall Street Journal,* 11 Sep. 1984.

"Alger Funds & Growth Stocks Suffer." Dow Jones News Service, 27 June 1994.

"Alger, Hamilton Allen Set to Quit ADP Pars Bureau." *Investment Management Technology,* 2 Sep. 1991.

"Alger Is a Proven Vote Getter." *Michigan Tradesman,* 16 July 1952.

"Alger Is Best; Up 33.2% for Third Quarter." *Pensions & Investments,* 24 Nov. 1980.

"Alger Rolls Out Balanced Portfolio Offering." *Investor's Business Daily,* 2 June 1992.

"Alger's Optimism Could Be the Driving Force Behind the Fund He Founded." *Baltimore Sun,* 23 July 1995.

"All in the Family: Alger Leads 1995 Advance." *Mutual Funds,* Sep. 1995.

"All in the Family: Portico Tops Family Rankings in a Year of Reversals." *Mutual Funds,* March 1997.

"All Michigan Welcomes Alger." *Leslie's Weekly.*

"American Board Bans Trading Again in Stock of Parvin-Dohrmann." *Wall Street Journal,* 25 April 1969.

"Amerika Bietet Beste Chancen." *Cash,* Feb. 1995.

"An Offer for Levitz Is Made by Alger." *New York Times,* 16 Aug. 1984.

"Boom on for Fred M. Alger for Governor." *Detroit News,* 15 May 1912.

"Cable TV Franchises Voted for 2 Concerns by a New York City Utility." *Wall Street Journal,* 29 July 1970.

"City Investing Unit's Merger Faces Doubts at American Exchange." *Wall Street Journal,* 22 Feb. 1971.

"Col. Alger Dead; Served in 2 Wars." *New York Times,* 31 Dec. 1933.

"Col. Frederick M. Alger Is Taken by Death at 57." *Detroit Free Press,* 31 Dec. 1933.

Compton's Interactive Encyclopedia. 1995. Compton's New Media, Inc.

"Cornfeld and Another Former IOS Officer Barred from Brokerage Business in U.S." *Wall Street Journal,* 4 March 1971.

"David Alger of Alger Small Cap." "Ladenburg, Thalmann & Co. Inc. Monthly Newsletter," Feb. 1990.

Dictionary of American Biography. New York: Charles Scribner's Sons, 1928.

"Final Official Statement." Detroit Journal, 1 Aug. 1899.

"Foote Cone Sets Pact to Buy Leber Katz Through Stock Swap." *Wall Street Journal,* 18 April 1986.

"Fred Alger Readies First Family of Mutual Funds." *Securities Week,* 29 Sep. 1986.

"Fred Alger to Wed Ex-Wife of Topping." *Detroit News,* 7 Aug. 1963.

"Frederick Alger Jr. Dies at 59; Former Ambassador to Belgium." *New York Times,* 7 Jan. 1967.

"Funding Retirement: The Best No-Load Variable Annuities." *Mutual Funds,* Feb. 1996.

"Fundwatch: The Hot Hand at Alger." *Smart Money,* Oct. 1995.

"G.O.P Loser in Michigan Named Envoy to Belgium." *New York Times,* 15 May 1953.

"GOP Offers Bill to Close Ex-citizens' Tax Loophole." *Boston Globe,* 10 June 1995.

"Gen. Alger's Homecoming." *Detroit Journal,* 5 Aug. 1899.

"Gen. Alger's Washington Residence." *Detroit Free Press,* 24 April 1898.

"General Alger Vindicated, The Official Record Sustains Him."

"Going for Growth." *Mutual Funds,* Nov. 1995.

"He Suffered Agonies but Asked No Man's Pity." *Detroit News Tribune,* 30 July 1899.

"Honor Where Honor Is Due; The People of This City and State Paid a Glorious Tribute to Ex-Secretary of War Alger." *Detroit Journal.*

"How the Best Funds Got That Way." *USA Today,* 5 Jan. 1990.

"In Bitter Cold 27,000 People Wait in Street to Get a Last Glimpse of Face of Senator Alger." *Detroit News,* 28 Jan. 1907.

"IOS Considers Plan to Recapitalize as Part of Its Restructuring." *Wall Street Journal,* 27 Jan. 1971.

"IOS' Cornfeld, Vesco Said to Be Near Accord." *Wall Street Journal,* 12 Jan. 1971.

"IOS Funds Receive Late Yule Present From Polar Regions." *Wall Street Journal,* 30 Dec. 1969.

"IOS Issue in Europe Sells Out; Price Rises to $18.50 Bid From $10." *Wall Street Journal,* 25 Sep. 1969.

"IOS Sues John King, Who Files Own Action Naming Vesco, Others." *Wall Street Journal,* 28 May 1971.

"Is Germany the New Frontier for Funds?" *Fund World,* 5 July 1994.

"It Was Spontaneous, The Welcome Extended to Gen. Alger on His Return." *Saginaw News,* 2 Aug. 1899.

"Levitz Bid by Alger Gets Financial Backing of a Securities Concern." *Wall Street Journal,* 26 Sep. 1984.

"Marketing New Mutual Funds." *Financial Services Outlook,* 15 July 1986.

"Masterly Reply to Those Who Mocked the Conduct of the Late War." *Detroit Journal,* 5 Oct. 1901.

"Michigan Needs Alger Integrity Against McKay." *Michigan Tradesman,* 16 July 1952.

Microsoft Encarta. 1994. Microsoft Corporation.

"Military Funeral for Col. Alger." *Legion News,* 5 Jan. 1934.

"Miss Lesly Stockard Is Married Here." *New York Times,* 12 Oct. 1958.

"Money Manager Fred Alger Seeks to Buy Crocker Unit." Dow Jones News Service, 17 June 1986.

"Money Manager Fred Alger Stirs Controversy With His Ads." Dow Jones News Service, 1 Oct. 1986.

"Money Manager Fred Alger Suffers Exodus of Clients." Dow Jones News Service, 28 Feb. 1989.

"Mrs. Fred Alger Dies in Florida." *Detroit Free Press,* 8 March 1963.

Mutual Fund Directory. Investment Dealers' Digest.

Mutual Fund Fact Book. Washington D.C.: Investment Company Institute, 1995, 1996, 1997.

National Cyclopedia of American Biography, Vols. 5, 24 New York: James T. White, 1907.

Nelson's Directory of Investment Managers. Port Chester, NY: Nelson Publications, 1996, 1997.

"No-Minimum Funds Let You Start With $1." *Mutual Funds,* April 1995.

"Ontario Board Bans Cornfeld From Trading, Pending IOS Disclosure." *Wall Street Journal,* 10 Aug. 1971.

"Painting Gen. Alger Under Difficulties." *Detroit Journal,* 25 July 1899.

"Parvin-Dohrmann Co. Isn't Hiding a Thing, Its Chairman Says . . ." *Wall Street Journal,* 26 May 1969.

"Parvin-Dohrmann Says Officer's Common Sold, Buyer Named Chairman." *Wall Street Journal,* 13 Jan. 1969.

"Percy Friedlander's Proposed Acquisition Stirs Broker Concern." *Wall Street Journal,* 6 Jan. 1971.

"Professional Money Management. What It Is and Where It's Going." *Stock Market,* July 1970.

"Purchase of Crocker Unit OKd." *San Francisco Chronicle,* 17 June 1986.

Recruit Training for Men. Washington D.C.: United States Marine Corps.

"Scenes at the Funeral of Senator Alger." *Detroit News,* 29 Jan. 1907.

"SEC Cites Alger after 4-Year Delay." *USA Today,* 8 March 1990.

"SEC Says Fred Alger Funds Made Misleading Disclosures." Dow Jones News Service, 5 March 1990.

"Senator Alger Dead; End Came Suddenly." *New York Times,* 25 Jan. 1907.

"Senator Alger Is Laid to Rest With Simple Ceremony." *Detroit News,* 28 Jan. 1907.

"Senator Russell A. Alger Dies Suddenly in Washington." *Detroit News,* 24 Jan. 1907.

"Sheridan and Alger; Fighting Against Heavy Odds at Booneville." *Illustrated Buffalo Express.*

"Some Investors Find Fred Alger's Name Bad Luck." Dow Jones News Service, 3 Nov. 1986.

"Start der Alger Fonds in Deutschland: Absatz überstigt Erwartungen." *Wirtschaftskurier,* Feb. 1995.

"TelePrompTer Is Set to Acquire 8 Cable TV Units for $19.3 Million." *Wall Street Journal,* 2 Nov. 1970.

"The Alger Club of Detroit." *National Tribune,* 26 April 1888.

"The Desert Is Blooming." *Forbes Germany,* Nov. 1994.

"The Favorite Son; Michigan's Candidate for Consideration at Chicago." *Detroit Sunday News,* 27 May 1888.

The Money Programme. British Broadcasting Corp., London. 12 April 1968.

"The Red-Hot Alger Funds." *Barron's,* 26 June 1995.

"The Wall Street Transcript." 21 Dec. 1992.

"The Young Millionaires of Finance." *Business-Week,* 30 Dec. 1987.

"U.S. Settlement for Fred Alger." *New York Times,* 10 March 1990.

"USA Today All-Star Mutual Funds." *USA Today,* 27 Feb. 1995.

"Vesco and IOS' President Are Arrested, Jailed in Geneva on Dissident's Complaint." *Wall Street Journal,* 1 Dec. 1961.

"Where Are the Virtuosi of Yesteryear?" *Fortune,* 25 July, 1983.

"Who Did Best and Worst in the Eighties." *Corporate Finance,* March 1990.